Target: Israel
THE BOOK OF REVELATION
The Ultimate Survival Handbook

Revised Edition

Clay Houseman

TARGET: ISRAEL
The Book of Revelation
The Ultimate Survival Handbook

Revised Edition

Copyright © 2006, 2012 Clay Houseman
Cover Design Copyright © Laura Shinn
Formatting by Laura Shinn

ISBN-13: 978-1466405493
ISBN-10: 146640549X

Target: Israel is a work of fiction. Though the names of actual locations may be mentioned, they are used in a fictitious manner and the events and occurrences were invented in the mind and imagination of the author except where historically accurate facts are included. Similarities of characters used within to any person, past, present, or future, are coincidental except where actual historical figures are named.

Previously published 2006, iUniverse.

To view more writing and information regarding Clay's work and this book, visit: *www.clayhouseman.com.*

Dedication

This book is dedicated to my wonderful wife, Jenny, and to my four loving children, Shane, Starr, Skye, and Heath.

I am especially grateful to Skye and Heath for assisting so faithfully in bringing the book to its completion.

And, lastly, deep thanks and appreciation goes to Heath and Nonie, editors.

Clay Houseman

AFTER THIS: THE SEASON OF THE BEAST
Excerpt from Chapter 13

The Season of the Beast: Daniel 7:7 tells us: "After this (it's important to note the first two words stated in this verse, as they are very meaningful, for they refer to the sequence of events—Britain, Russia, the Arab Nations—*after this* comes the Antichrist) I saw in the night visions, and behold, a fourth beast, dreadful and terrible, exceedingly strong. It had huge iron teeth; it was devouring, breaking in pieces, and trampling the residue with its feet. It was different from all the beasts (or Seasons and their kingdoms) that were before it, that is Britain, Russia, the Arab Nations, and it had ten horns (referring to the Antichrist's control of his kingdom of ten nations)... . And there was another horn, a little one, coming up among them ... And there, in this horn, were eyes like the eyes of a man, and a mouth speaking pompous words (the *little horn* reference here is signifying the False Prophet)."

The Season of the fourth beast follows the Season of the third beast, the Leopard *(the Arab Nations)*, the Season that we are now in! The fanatical branches of the Arab Nations and radical Islam have engaged in acts of terrorism for decades, for the *Season of the Leopard* is upon us and it is rushing toward its climax with the hostile nations Gog and Magog and their siege on Israel. (Remember, the Gog and Magog siege on Israel is not to be confused with the war of Armageddon at the end of the Tribulation.) The first war with Iraq (1991), the war in Afghanistan against the Taliban/Al-Qaeda (2001), the second war with Iraq (2003), global acts of terrorism, Islamic terrorists bent on hostile jihad intending to bring down Israel and the might of America and western civilization with deeds of destruction against innocent civilians—all are forerunners to this mighty pre-Tribulation invasion against Israel by the Arab Nations who will join forces with Russia and her allies (*the hostile nations*). The invasion will be a clear indicator that the period of the fourth beast is about to arrive, the *Season of the Beast.*

The Season of the Leopard ends when this great army is totally destroyed by the hand of God! After this the fourth beast appears and the final Season in our dispensation begins, a period of seven years: the Great Tribulation. The words *after this* should ring in our ears, reminding us that we are now living through the Season of the Leopard!

* * * * *

NOTE FROM THE AUTHOR

It is not my intention to *in any way* add to or take away from the Scriptures in the Book of Revelation. I only desire to share with you the things that God has shown me through years of study and communion with him in regard to the meaning of this manual, in the hopes that it will bring you to a clearer understanding of future events and bring you face to face with two questions:

(1) What will you do with Jesus?
(2) How will you survive?

Table of Contents

Directory of Maps

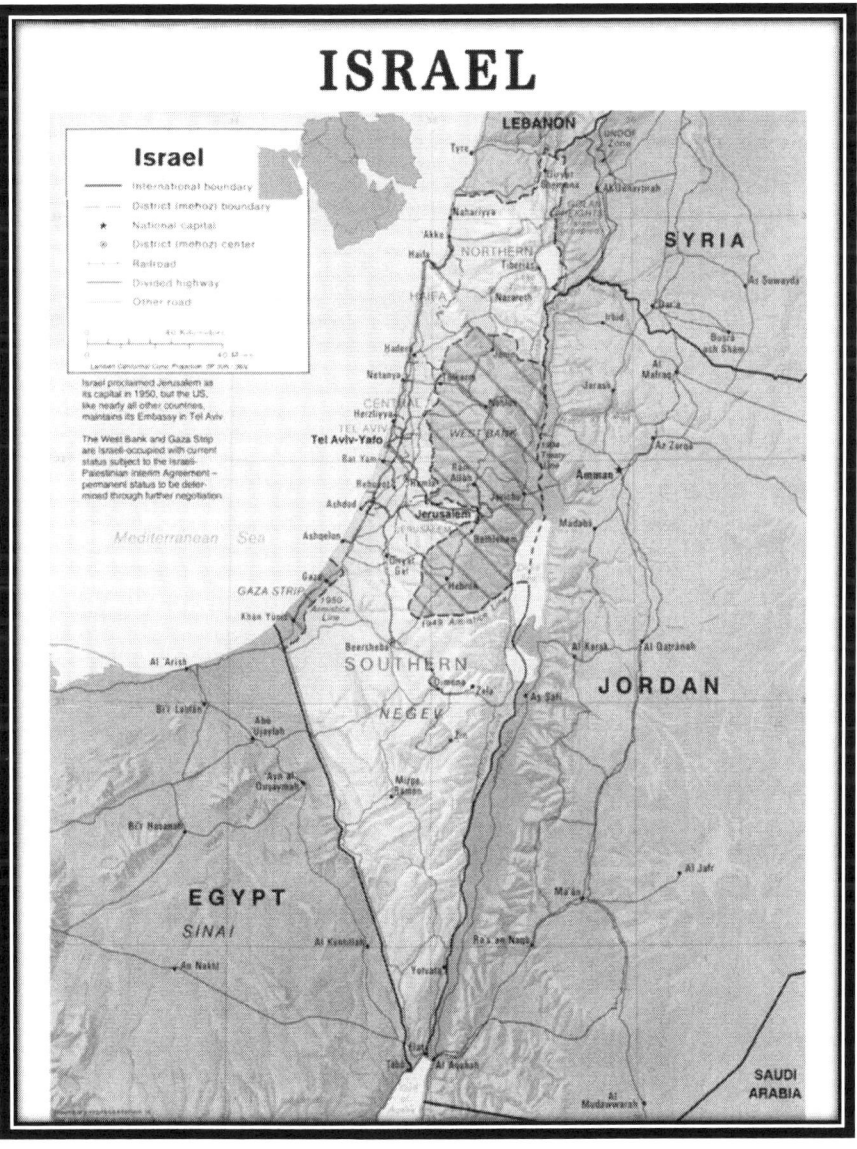

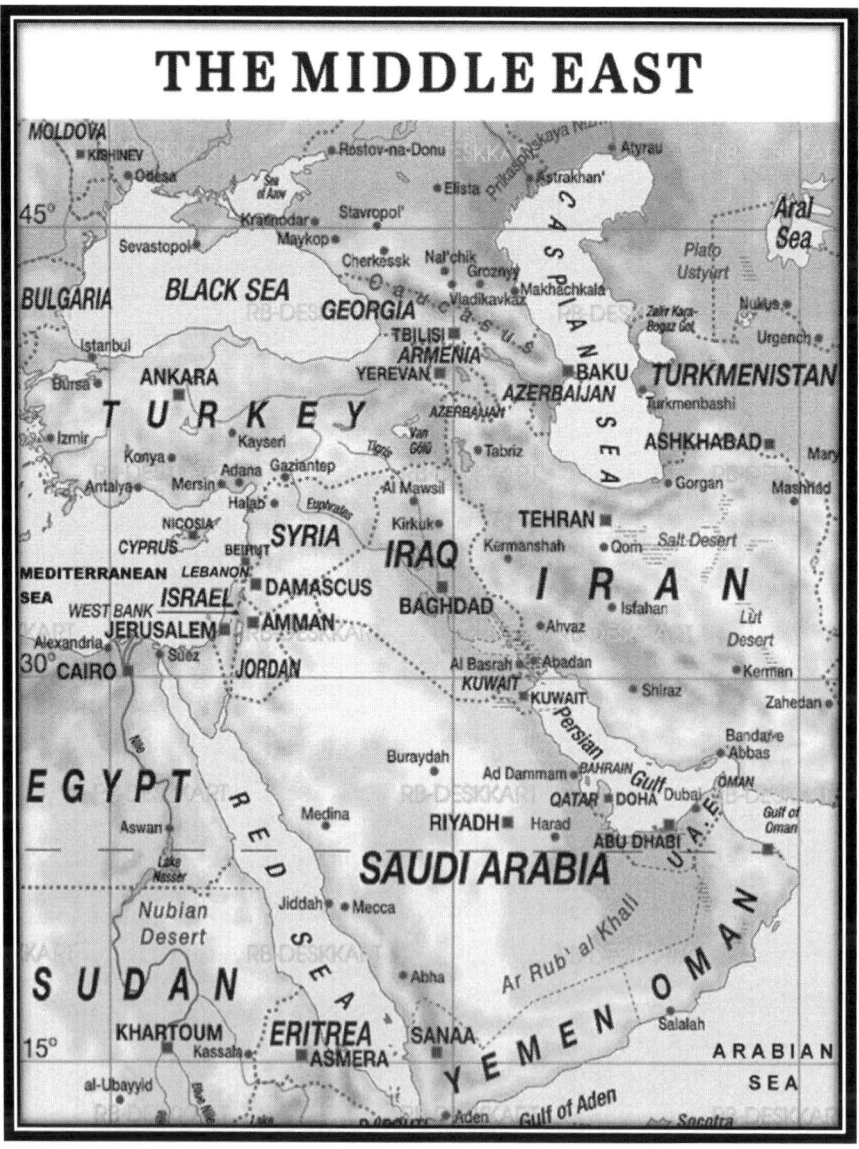

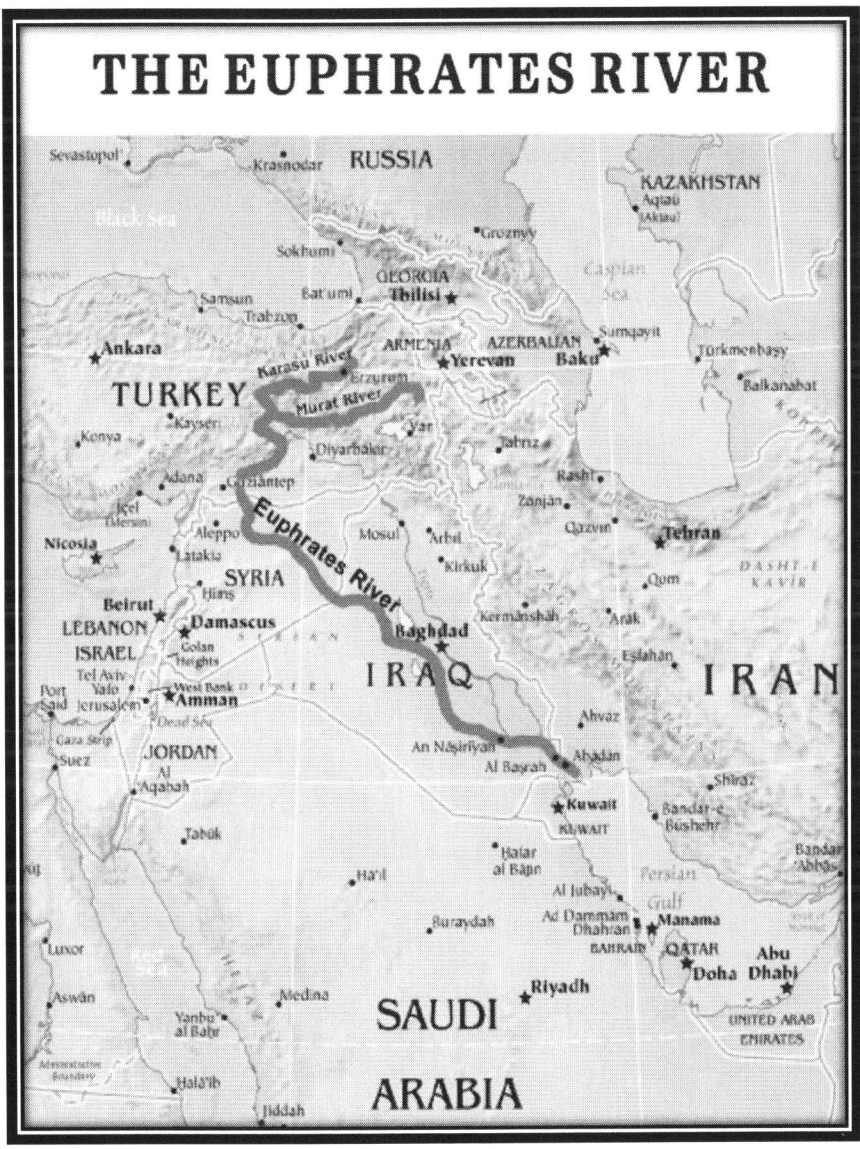

THE EUPHRATES RIVER

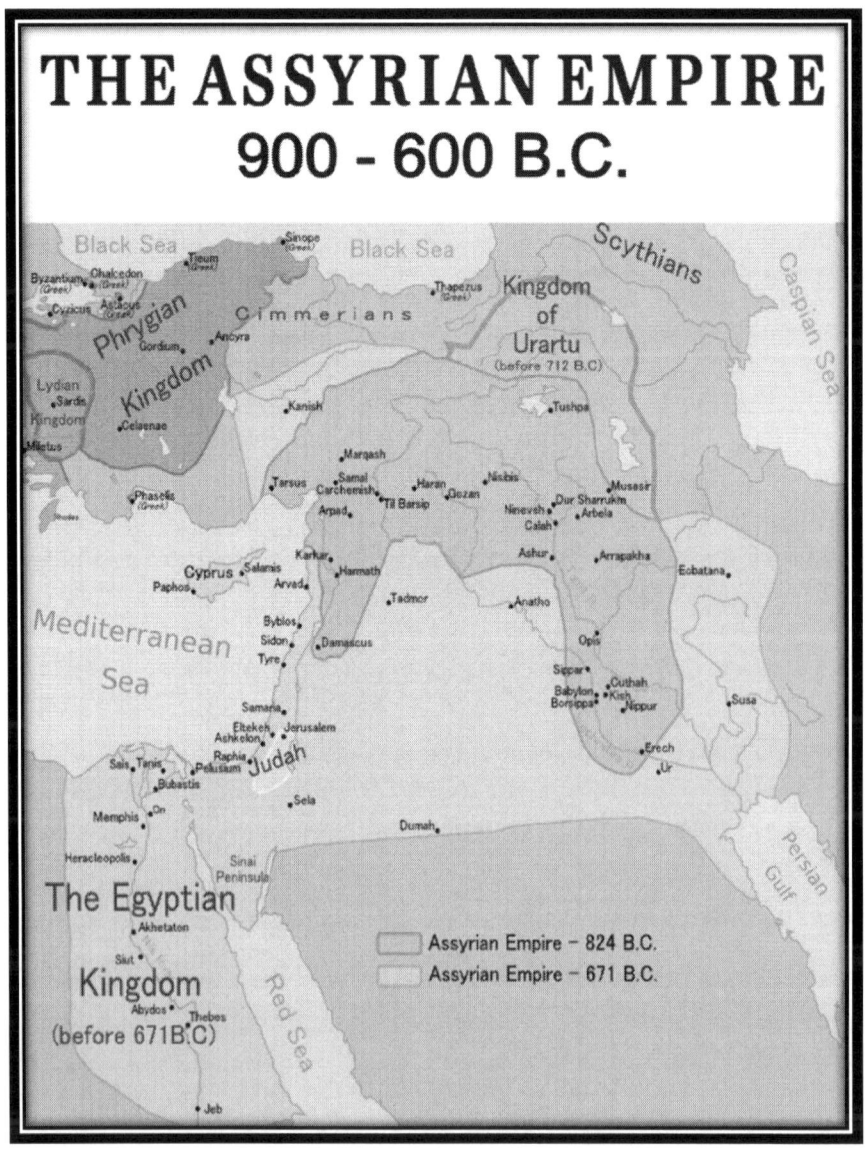

THE ASSYRIAN EMPIRE
900 - 600 B.C.

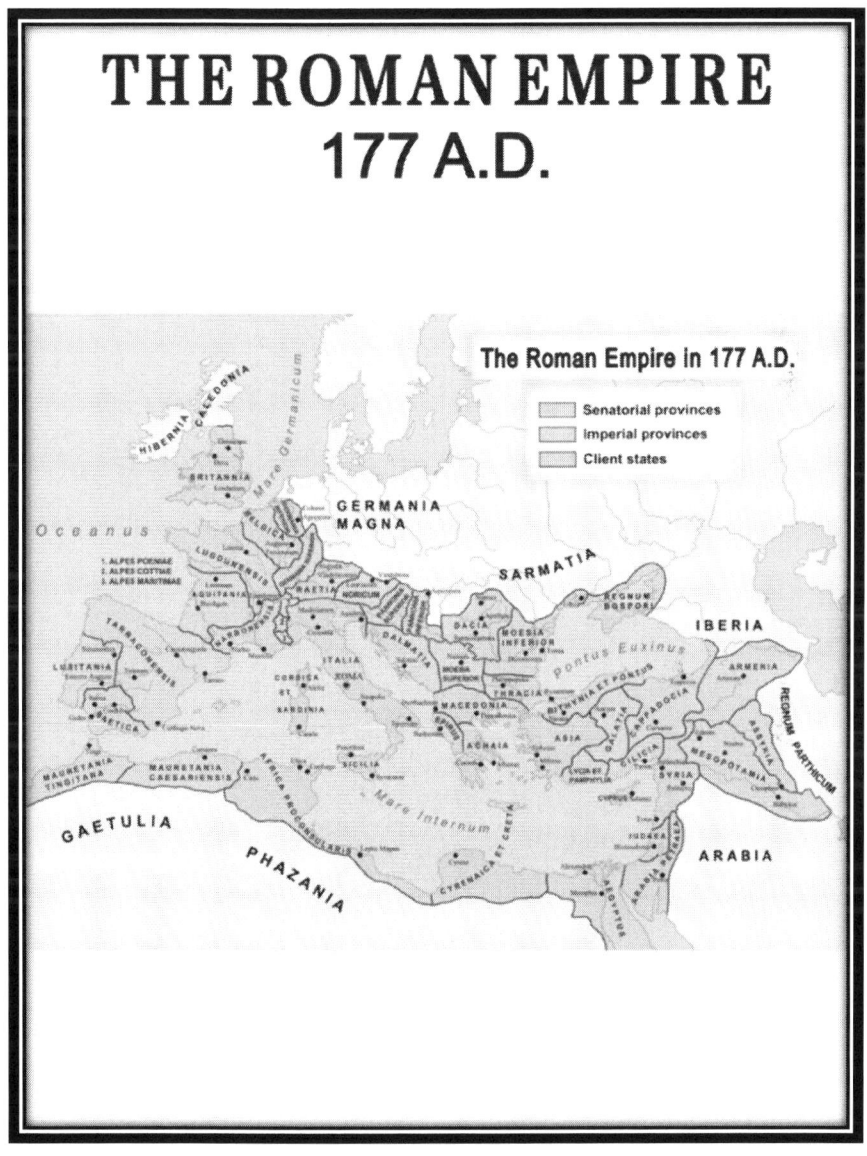

THE ROMAN EMPIRE
177 A.D.

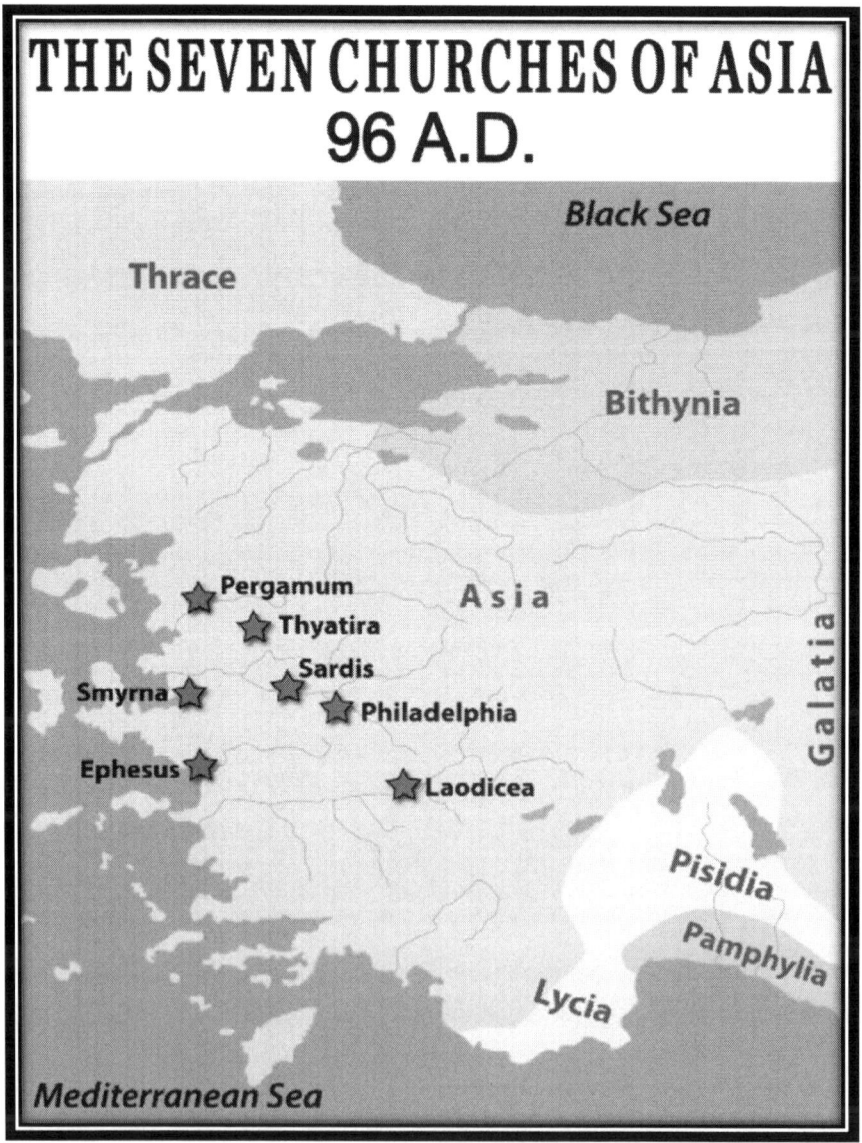

THE GARDEN OF EDEN BEFORE THE FALL

The White Nile and the Blue Nile link together near Khartoum in Sudan. The Blue Nile starts at Lake Tana in Ethiopia.

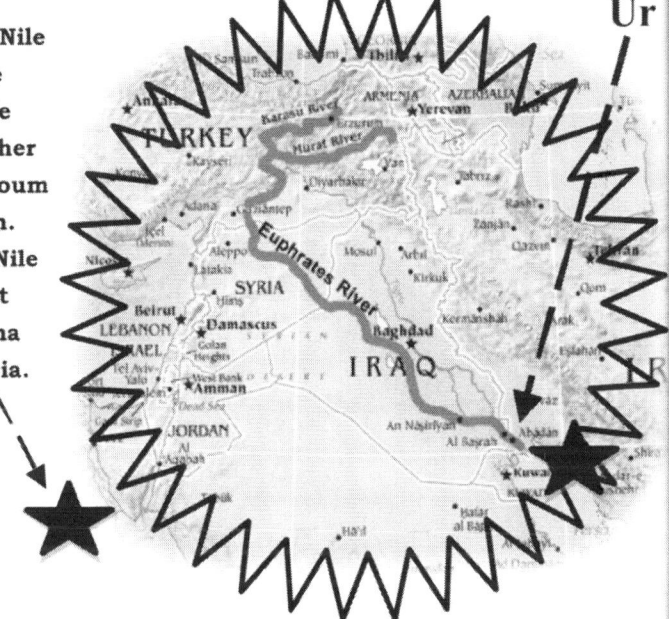

 The Tigris River and the Euphrates River flow through Iran and Iraq, so the location must be in this region. The large translucent star-polygon suggests that the Garden of Eden once covered the entire area. Traditionally, however, Eden is thought to be in southern Iraq, close to the city of Ur. Others argue the actual location of Eden is between the Blue and White Nile Rivers in Sudan and Ethiopia.

List of Diagrams

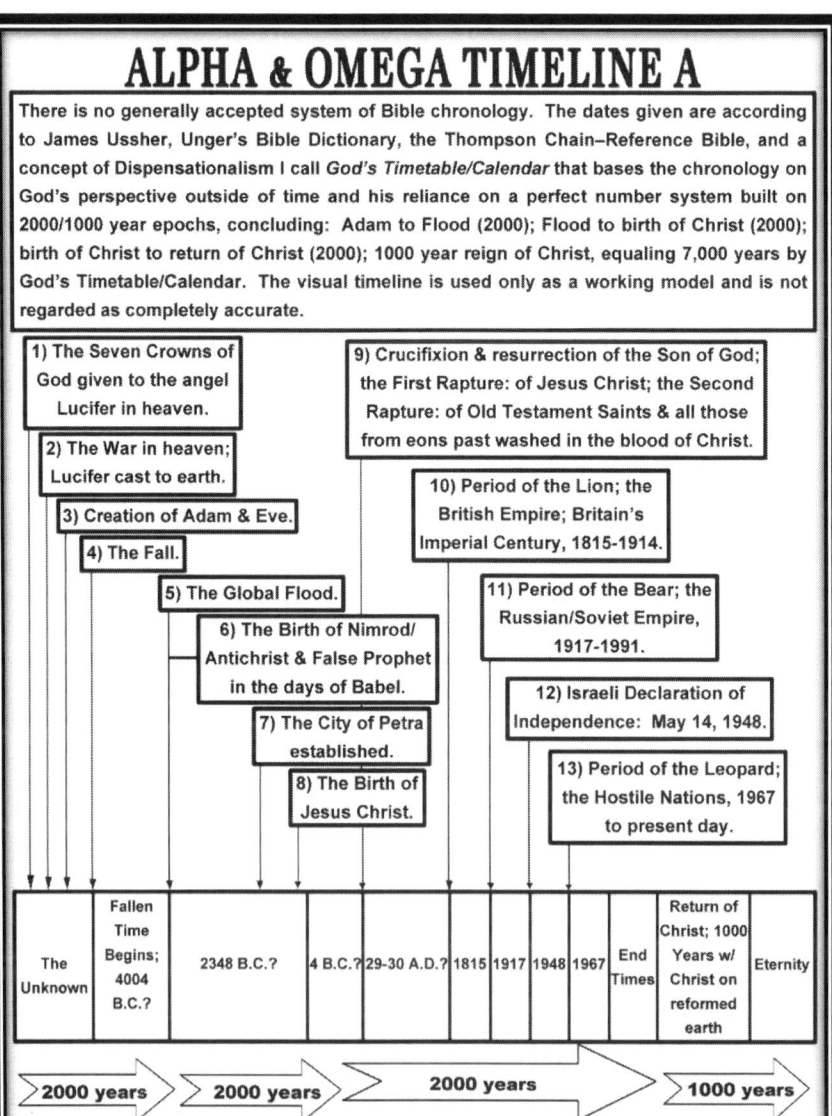

ALPHA & OMEGA TIMELINE A

There is no generally accepted system of Bible chronology. The dates given are according to James Ussher, Unger's Bible Dictionary, the Thompson Chain–Reference Bible, and a concept of Dispensationalism I call *God's Timetable/Calendar* that bases the chronology on God's perspective outside of time and his reliance on a perfect number system built on 2000/1000 year epochs, concluding: Adam to Flood (2000); Flood to birth of Christ (2000); birth of Christ to return of Christ (2000); 1000 year reign of Christ, equaling 7,000 years by God's Timetable/Calendar. The visual timeline is used only as a working model and is not regarded as completely accurate.

1) The Seven Crowns of God given to the angel Lucifer in heaven.

2) The War in heaven; Lucifer cast to earth.

3) Creation of Adam & Eve.

4) The Fall.

5) The Global Flood.

6) The Birth of Nimrod/ Antichrist & False Prophet in the days of Babel.

7) The City of Petra established.

8) The Birth of Jesus Christ.

9) Crucifixion & resurrection of the Son of God; the First Rapture: of Jesus Christ; the Second Rapture: of Old Testament Saints & all those from eons past washed in the blood of Christ.

10) Period of the Lion; the British Empire; Britain's Imperial Century, 1815-1914.

11) Period of the Bear; the Russian/Soviet Empire, 1917-1991.

12) Israeli Declaration of Independence: May 14, 1948.

13) Period of the Leopard; the Hostile Nations, 1967 to present day.

The Unknown	Fallen Time Begins; 4004 B.C.?	2348 B.C.?	4 B.C.?	29-30 A.D.?	1815	1917	1948	1967	End Times	Return of Christ; 1000 Years w/ Christ on reformed earth	Eternity

2000 years   2000 years   2000 years   1000 years

ALPHA & OMEGA TIMELINE B

There is no generally accepted system of Bible chronology. The dates given are according to James Ussher, Unger's Bible Dictionary, the Thompson Chain–Reference Bible, and a concept of Dispensationalism I call *God's Timetable/Calendar* that bases the chronology on God's perspective outside of time and his reliance on a perfect number system built on 2000/1000 year epochs, concluding: Adam to Flood (2000); Flood to birth of Christ (2000); birth of Christ to return of Christ (2000); 1000 year reign of Christ, equaling 7,000 years by God's Timetable/Calendar. The visual timeline is used only as a working model and is not regarded as completely accurate.

14) Siege of Israel by the Hostile Nations; the destruction of the Hostile Nations; Islam's Great Fall as a global power.

15) Seal One: White Horse Period: the return of the Antichrist & False Prophet; New World Order & One World Religious Organization (OWOR) established; Tribulation begins.

16) Temple sacrifice reinstated at the rebuilt & fully functional Jewish Temple; 3 ½ years of peace.

17) Antichrist received deadly wound.

18) Destruction of New Babylon/ Rome.

19) Third Rapture of the dead in Christ; Forth Rapture of the living in Christ.

20) Seal Two (Red Horse Period) Antichrist sets himself up as god.

21) Sealing of the 144,000 Jews.

22) Image of Antichrist erected.

23) False Prophet/Mark of Beast.

24) Seal Three (Black Horse Period).

25) 144,000 Jews flee to wilderness.

26) Return of the Two Witnesses.

27) Plagues of the Trumpets.

28) Seal Four (Period of Martyrs); Seal Five (Period of White Horse).

29) Fifth Rapture of the Martyrs; Sixth Rapture of the 144,000 Jews.

30) 7 Plagues of the Thunders.

31) 7 Plagues of the Bowls.

32) Angels (stars) fall from heaven.

33) Return of Christ (year 2000 A.D. by God's timetable/calendar).

34) Armegaddon.

35) Seal Six (Antichrist & False Prophet sealed in Lake of Fire forever within the earth; Lucifer thrown into Bottomless Pit.

36) Jesus reforms the earth/end of fallen mankind by earthquake, fire.

37) Saints transformed into the Second Phase of Body, the glorified body, reigning with Christ 1000 years.

38) Seventh Rapture: of the lost; Lucifer released from the Bottomless Pit for the final battle with the armies of the lost; all are consumed by fire.

39) The earth is transformed into its final phase: the eternal prison-place known as the Lake of Fire & Lucifer is cast into it forever; the Great White Throne Judgment commences.

40) Saints transformed into the Third Phase of Body, the super glorified body & transferred to the New Earth forever, a new planet that exists outside of time.

Tribulation (End Times) First 3 ½ Years	Tribulation (End Times) Second 3 ½ Years; totaling 7 years	The Return of Christ	The Kingdom Age: 1000 Years	Eternity: The Holy Age

→ The Human Age Ends

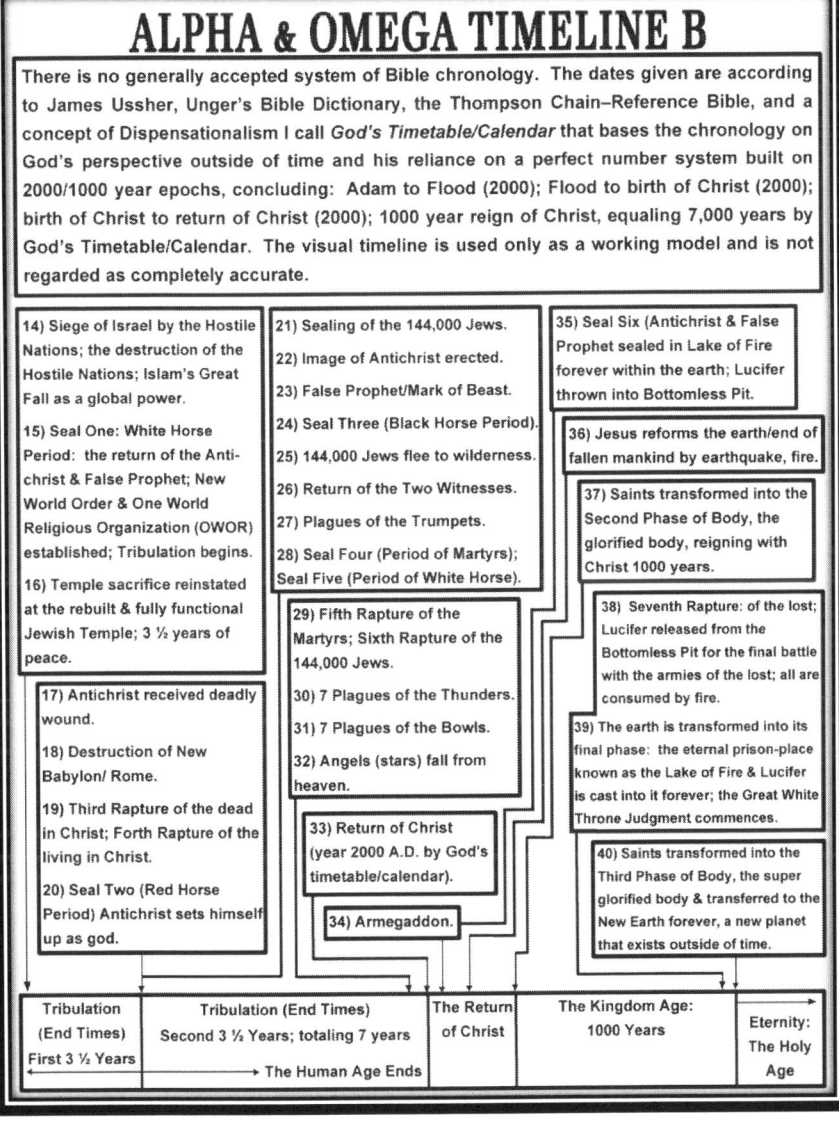

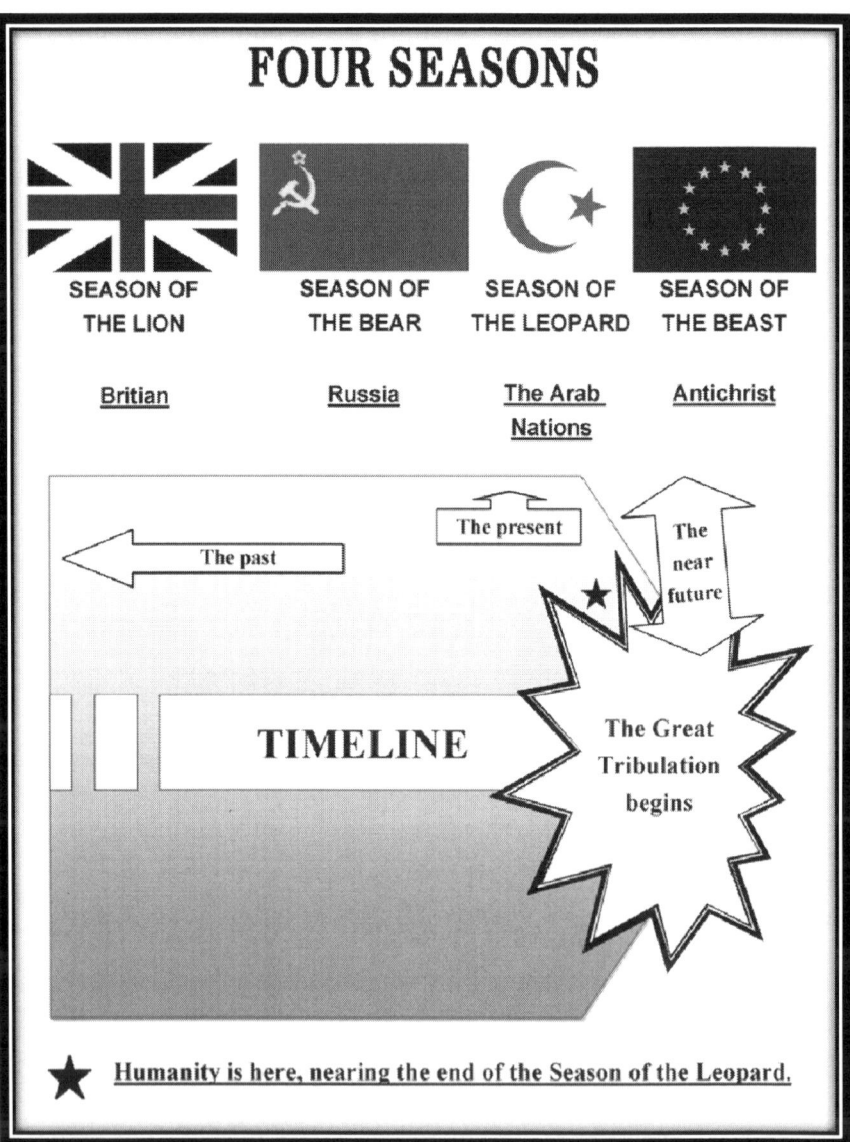

PHASE OF BODY

 1 Existing entropic/fallen state body

The physical body and spiritual state all humanity is born into now, being physically and spiritually separated from God and therefore reflecting an entropic nature, that is, a nature that reflects the degradation of all matter and energy in the universe to the ultimate state of inert uniformity, what could be termed *death through sin*, that which entered the world through disobedience.

 2 Glorified non-entropic body

The physical body and spiritual state all the saved in Christ will be raptured or translated into at the return of Jesus Christ at the end of the Great Tribulation. The unrepentant will be translated into this state as well, but at the end of the 1000 years; for the saved in Christ, the spiritual connection to the Holy Father is established through the grace of the Son and that connection will be reflected in the human body itself, which will be perfect in every way, uncorrupted, youthful, immortal, existing in a perfect reality within (perfect) time during the 1000 years (the Kingdom Age) with Christ on the reformed earth.

 **3** Superglorified non-entropic body

The cross-pollination of physical and spiritual in one body that all the saved in Christ will be raptured or translated into at the end of the 1000 years, existing with Christ into eternity on the New Earth and New Heaven, the third and final phase in the Phase of Body and thus made complete. The lost will remain in the Second Phase of Body for eternity and will in body forever remain incomplete.

THE PHASES OF THE EARTH

Pre-Fall Earth

PHASE 1

The present Earth in its fallen/entropic state, corrupted by sin, existing within an entropic universe where all matter & energy is degrading, or in other words, it exists within a dying universe.

PHASE 2

The reformed Earth, recreated by Christ after his return—the Earth and universe entire transformed into original pre-Fall perfection, existing in this state of perfection for 1000 years.

PHASE 3

The final phase for this old Earth: the eternal prison-place, the bottomless pit, the lake of fire, otherwise known as hell.

THREE HEAVENS

The Holy Father's reality

The original planet Earth that exists within the spiritual domain/reality of God, that is, the First Heaven, a reality intended only for the Holy Father and his angels.

THE FIRST EARTH
The First Heaven

The reality to come after the Kingdom Age (the 1000 years), the Holy Age of eternity with Christ.

Our present reality in its entropic state.

The Second Heaven

The Third Heaven

THE SECOND EARTH

The New or Second Earth, that is, the duplicate of the Father's original Earth in the First Heaven (the second copy), made specifically for the reality of the eternal Holy Age, intended for Christ and all the saved in Christ.

THE THIRD EARTH

The first copy of the original Earth, its perfect nature altered by the Fall of humanity into sin, giving it an imperfect, entropic nature; although the *first* Earth *copied*, called *third* because it is in the realm of the Holy Spirit; will be reformed into its original perfection for the 1000 years and reformed again as the bottomless prison-place, the lake of eternal fire for the lost.

SEQUENCE OF THE RAPTURES

The First Rapture
Resurrection of Jesus Christ.

The Second Rapture
Resurrection of the Old Testament Saints & all those from eons past washed in the blood of Christ, the saved dead who believed in God/called by God prior to his death & resurrection—the blood of Christ covers sin for all time in both directions, the future as well as the past.

The Third Rapture
Resurrection of the dead saved in Christ since his death & resurrection.

The Fourth Rapture
Resurrection of the living saved in Christ—occurring in the middle of the Great Tribulation.

Raptures 3 & 4 happen simultaneously

The Fifth Rapture
Resurrection of the Christian martyrs who died during the Great Tribulation.

The Sixth Rapture
Resurrection of the living 144,000 Jews who lived through the Great Tribulation.

Raptures 5 & 6 happen simultaneously

The Seventh Rapture
Resurrection of the dead unrepentant/lost after the return of Christ & the 1000 years on the reformed earth, but prior to their final battle with Lucifer against the Most Holy God & the subsequent Great White Throne Judgment.

INTRODUCTION
Israel Targeted and Under Attack

The assault has been going on for decades. It's difficult to pinpoint exactly when the attack upon the State of Israel began, and of course the dates are arguable, but the formation of Fatah (Movement for the National Liberation of Palestine) by co-founder Yasser Arafat in the late 1950s and the bloody birth of the PLO (Palestine Liberation Organization) in 1964 are adequate.

1965–67: Fatah bomb attacks, spearheaded by Yasser Arafat, destroyed water pipes, railroads, and villages, killing Israelis.

1968: the Palestinian National Charter officially called for the elimination of Zionism through armed struggle and commando action. Fatah joined the PLO and became the dominate power the same year.

1970: PLO terrorists attacked an Israeli school bus with a bazooka, killing nine schoolchildren and three teachers.

1974: 11 people in the northern Israeli town of Kiryat Shmona were killed by Palestinian terrorists—and so it began.[1]

The attacks have continued over the years, relentless and unabated, the number of bombings and victims swelling to the point of the indefinite: buses filled with innocent people in Tel Aviv have been blown apart; restaurants in Jerusalem have been reduced to rubble by members of Palestinian suicide brigades; individual suicide bombers have murdered countless innocent men, women, and children with the click of a button and self-detonation. Even now, fanatical splinter groups of the Muslim faith plan future attacks on Israel in spite of ongoing peace talks.

ALLIED WITH ISRAEL?

Allied with Israel, the United States and Great Britain have also been targeted with deadly effect: governmental embassies, military compounds, the World Trade Center in New York City, the Pentagon in Washington, D.C., United Airlines Flight 93, the London Underground, et al.

Historically, the relationship between Israel and the West has been challenging, but Great Britain and the U.S. have always been traditional allies. Now, that delicate relationship is being put to the test more than ever before as the Middle East and North Africa experiences revolution in the form of demonstrations and protests that may press the Arab Nations toward, not Jeffersonian democracy (as many hope), but instead an Islamic Caliphate, a Muslim political-religious state with enormous authority and power—indeed, this revolutionary "Arab Spring" may have profound biblical significance; and under the current administration, the United States appears to be strategically removing itself from its traditional position as a staunch ally. This dramatic political shift may be a herald to the End Times, for the Book of Revelation predicts that Great Britain and its allies, including the United States and the rest of the Western World, will stand back and abandon Israel completely.

THE INCEPTION OF GLOBAL TERROR

Even though the inception of global terror is debatable—where and who started it all—you can point to Lebanon and the initial suicide bombings in the early 1980s as the historical launching pad for the world in which we live today: global terrorists who use suicide bombers as their main form of terror. Hezbollah, the Lebanese Shiite terror organization, got so good at it and found it so successful that other terrorist groups, whether motivated by religion or politics, adopted it. By 1983 terrorist organizations began to adapt and perfect what Hezbollah started.[2]

THE PRESSURE IS MOUNTING

Suicide bombings continue to plague not only Israel, but the Middle East, Europe, Asia, and the United States. Homegrown terrorists bent on violent jihad are springing up in Canada and the U.S. War between Israel and Iran appears to be imminent. The whole planet is now experiencing what the Israelis' have experienced, and experienced intimately, for 30 years or more, and the world gasps at what is transpiring. The truth is, the twenty first century has hardly begun and the body toll is rising. The pressure is mounting. The world is about to come apart. For all intents and purposes, you could say this looks a lot like the beginning of the end of the world—and you wouldn't be far from the truth. In fact, you would be right. This *is* the beginning of the end of the world.

Two questions arise:
(1) Can you survive it?
Answer: yes, you can survive the end of the world.
(2) How?
Answer: we've been given the ultimate worst-case scenario survival handbook, the Book of Revelation.

THE ULTIMATE SURVIVAL HANDBOOK

It is imperative for you to realize that the Book of Revelation is your handbook to survival. It is your handbook for surviving the very end of the world. It is a worst-case scenario survival handbook with the best-case scenario outcome, illustrating step by step what is coming for humanity and how to survive what will essentially amount to the end of the world as we know it!

Other questions naturally follow: What is in store for you? Why have Israel, Great Britain, and America been targeted and attacked? Where is all this violence leading? How can we survive? What is the fate of America, Great Britain, Israel, Europe, China, Russia, Germany, and the Arab Nations?

If you desire to know the future and would like to understand, with clarity and certainty, future events of gigantic proportion that must come to pass while you yet live, events that are deeply connected to the Israel of yesterday, today, and tomorrow—you need to keep on reading, if not simply for your own revelation and insight into our future, then for your very survival.

These writings disclose great prophetic revelations, making known and bringing to view a manifestation of divine truth found deeply imbedded within the pages of the Book of Revelation. You will find the truth both remarkable and challenging.

Like all survival handbooks, there are two Golden Rules to Survival:

(1) You must be prepared.

(2) You must have a survival plan.

The Book of Revelation gives you detailed information on how to be prepared for and clearly lays out how to survive the end of the world as we know it, and not only that, but how to survive into the world to come—essentially, it teaches you how to continue to exist in peace forever.

Nevertheless, it is a complex survival handbook filled with complicated symbols of prophecy, formidable mathematics and provocative concepts. Indeed, it is hard to follow and it is difficult to understand. All the same, it is a book that is meant to be studied so that its *sealed* contents can be *unsealed*—we are meant to know and comprehend the nature of it (Rev. 22:10; Dan. 12:9).

Because all the prophetic veins and capillaries in the Bible lead to the Book of Revelation most eschatologists conclude it can only be truly understood through divine revelation and intense study of all biblical prophecy. (Eschatologists are those who seek to understand biblical prophecy, most of which deals with the end of the world and humanity. Formally, eschatology means *the study of last things*. The main eschatological artery in the Bible is the Book of Revelation.) You've got to seek the answers through prayer as well as research, trusting God to reveal the truth.

Now, in regard to this book, used with the disciplines I just mentioned, *Target: Israel* is the manual to that complex survival handbook known as the Book of Revelation. Practical, theoretical, and spiritual models will guide you on your path to eternal survival, clarifying the complex information within the Book of Revelation. You are encouraged to keep a Bible, the indispensable and required companion study-source to this manual, close at hand so that you can refer to it constantly, for that is exactly what you will have to do. It should be clear that in light of the End Times this manual is an essential survival tool, but because there is much within *Target: Israel* that you can apply to daily life and events, it can also aid you in your immediate and ongoing spiritual journey.

A RUNDOWN ON THE BASICS

What does *revelation* mean? If these prophecies are about to happen, when and how will they be accomplished? How can we be sure they will happen soon? Who is God? Who is Jesus? Who or what is the devil? Who or what is the Beast? What is the significance of the number 666?

These questions and more will be answered as you read *Target: Israel*, but do not be surprised if some of the contents within this manual come across as politically incorrect, for even though his writing was tempered with love, John, the author of the Book of Revelation, was straightforward and bluntly expressed his opinions—there is subject matter in this book that you will find difficult. Some of it will challenge your beliefs and lifestyle. (I, as the author of this manual, am not exempt from this admission.) You may even find some of it offensive. Even so, you are encouraged to tough it out and continue reading, and remember that the intention of this book is mutual enlightenment under the guiding and loving *Spirit of Glory and of God* through his Holy and unerring Word. In effect, God loves you, but he is not afraid to step on your toes!

Since the Book of Revelation is about *your* future (and very possibly your *immediate* future), it is essential that you understand this writing of John and how it affects you. For that reason, before we delve deeply into the prophecy, let us start with a clear description of the persons and some of the concepts described in the book, a rundown on the basics, if you will, so that we may have common frame of reference.

* * * * *

The Book of Revelation

Predictions of things to come, written by the Apostle John in A.D. 96 (according to traditional opinion) while exiled to the island of Patmos "because of the Word of God and the testimony of Jesus Christ" (Rev. 1:2), are found in the last pages of the New Testament of the Holy Scriptures in the book called the Book of Revelation. It is considered the sum total of all biblical prophecy where all biblical prophecy is made complete, disclosing the future of the Jew, the Gentile, and the Church of Christ and all humanity. The prophecies in the book focus mainly on the events preceding the Second Coming of Christ, the establishment of the millennial kingdom and, lastly, the eternal state for and of humankind.[3] The name of the book comes from Latin, *revelatio*,[4] meaning *an unveiling*; Greek *apokalypsis*,[5] meaning *the removing of a veil*. The book is often incorrectly called *The Revelation of the Apostle John*. A more accurate title would be *The Revelation of Jesus Christ* (Rev 1:1).[6] It is also known as *The Apocalypse*,[7] meaning *a prophetic disclosure*. As mentioned earlier, the purpose of *Target: Israel* is to deeply explore the predictions and images within the Book of Revelation, remove the veil a little bit more, to prepare you for the mightiest happenings to ever take place in the history of the world so that you might survive the end of the world!

* * * * *

Who is God?

As revealed through the Holy Scriptures, God is the One infinite and eternal Being, purely spiritual, the Supreme Personal Intelligence, the Creator and Preserver of all things, the Moral Ruler of the universe and all creation, the only proper object of worship, the tri-personal God, the Father, the Son, and the Holy Spirit (Gen. 1:1; Ex. 34:14; Ps. 90:1–2; 139:7–12; Job 26; Matt. 3:16–17; 28:19; John 4:24; I John 4:16).[8]

"In the beginning was the Word, and the Word was with God, and the Word was God. He was in the beginning with God (speaking of God's Son, Jesus). All things were made through him, and without him nothing was made that was made" (John 1:1–3).

He is the *Living Holy God* and the Creator of all things that exist! He spread the blanket of the universe with his fingertips! He has divinc authority of everyone and everything! *He is our Father, for he is the Creator of all life*—and that means *you!*

Interestingly, in Rev. 3:1 Jesus refers to himself as holding, or having, the *Seven Spirits of God*. I believe, as the author of this manual, that the Seven Spirits of God is an allusion to the very nature of God, a peek into the *internal workings* of the Father, if you will, and although it is not known exactly *what* the Seven Spirits of God *are*, it seems clear that they are intensely powerful, suggesting in a literal sense that the Power Source of God *is* the Seven Spirits of God. (This concept is explored in more detail in the following paragraphs, as well as Chapter 4:5, under the heading *The Seven Spirits of God*.) They are the very heart of God. The Seven Spirits of God are *the Life, the Light*, or simply put, *God himself!*

* * * * *

Who is Jesus?

Christian faith is founded on the scriptural teaching of who Jesus Christ is:

(1) Entirely God while being entirely human, unique, and perfect/sinless in regard to humanity and the fallen nature.

(2) All messianic (meaning *relating to the messiah*) Old Testament predictions were realized in Christ.

(3) The resurrection of Jesus from the dead is an absolute historical fact, the transformation/salvation of the individual believer secure in Christ because of his sacrificial act, holy grace, and the literal transforming work of the Holy Spirit upon the individual believer.[9]

"And the Word became flesh (when Jesus Christ was born as man) and dwelt among us, and we beheld his (God's) *glory* (in him), the glory of the only begotten (one and only sired Son, Jesus) of the Father, full of grace and truth" (John 1:14).

Jesus the Christ is the divine manifestation of God, his Father, and the Holy Spirit is the divine manifestation of Jesus Christ, the Son. They are all three One and yet separate, and together they make up the Holy Trinity. Together they are *the I Am:* 'I am who I am.' And he said (speaking to Moses), 'Thus you shall say to the children of Israel, 'I AM has sent me to you'" (Ex. 3:14).

Jesus, God's beloved Son, came to earth in the form of a man to show us *God's glory*. He is the true Light and he gives light (transforming salvation) to everyone who comes into the world. As many who receive Jesus, to them he gives the right to become the adopted children of God.

Jesus suffered death, but his great sacrificial act had deep purpose: to rid us of our sins so that we might gain eternal life with him in heaven. His death stretched through time and space, covering humanity in his grace from the beginning of time unto its end. Jesus is called *the Messiah* (Hebrew, *mashiach)* and *Christ* (Greek, *Christos*, a common word that means *anointed*, having the same meaning as *messiah* in Hebrew). He is the Messiah, the Anointed , the Christ, our Deliverer, as foretold by the prophets of the Old Testament. Hence, we call the Son of God, Jesus Christ, the Messiah.[10]

* * * * *

The Seven Spirits of God

Like his Father and the Holy Spirit, Jesus has the Seven Spirits of God (Rev. 3:1). The seven attributes of God—*the same seven pertaining to the I Am*—are the Seven Spirits of God: the Word, the Life, the Light, Love, Holiness and Righteousness, the Beginning and the End (John 1:1; 1:4–5; 8:1; 9:51; 1 John 4:8, 16; Rom. 1:4; Eph. 4:24; Rev. 1:8; 21:6; Prov. 1:7; 9:10; Rev. 1:8; 21:6; 22:13; Rom. 10:4). "All things were made through him (Jesus), and without him (Jesus) nothing was made that was made. In him (Jesus) was life, and the life was the light of men (and, of course, women). And the light shines in the darkness, and the darkness did not comprehend it" (John 1:3–5). "I am the light of the world. He who follows me shall not walk in darkness, but have the light of life" (John 8:12).

The Seven Spirits of God represent life and light. They also represent the seven attributes of God. It's reasonable to conclude that the Seven Spirits of God are the very nature of God. They're his heartbeat; his Power Source. The Father, the Holy Spirit, and Jesus *are* the Seven Spirits of God (the life) and the Seven Spirits of Life (the light), because each one *is* the Life and the Light, the I Am. All references to the Seven Spirits of Life in the following pages take this point of view. The term the Seven Spirits of God is a direct allusion to the awesome power and the glory that is God. (For more information on this subject refer to Chapter 4:5, under the heading *The Seven Spirits of God.)*

* * * * *

What is heaven?

It is the abode of God, his Son, and his angels. It is the place where the souls of those who are granted salvation go. It is a place of supreme and eternal happiness! (We will investigate the subject of heaven in more detail in Chapters 1:19, under the heading

Heaven & Earth, and 3:21, under the heading *Three Heavens Explored.*)

* * * * *

Who is the devil?

Lucifer, who was once God's *right hand* creation in *the First Heaven,* is spoken of as Satan and the devil. The Bible tells us there was war between God and the devil. After the battle, Lucifer was cast out of heaven and sent to earth. He remains God's greatest enemy. (The Great War and Satan are explored in more detail in Chapters 3:1, under the heading *The Destructive Path;* 5:3, under the heading *What is Under the Earth;* 9:14, under the heading *The Four Angels Euphrates;* 12:3, under the heading *A Secret Revelation;* and 12:17, under the heading *The Great War Revisited.*)

* * * * *

What is the meaning of the word *sin?*

Simply put, sin is disobedience and the breaking of God's law. The Lawgiver is God. Sin is everything in the nature, purpose, or behavior of God's creatures that opposes or is contrary to the will of God (Rom. 3:20; 4:15; 7:7; James 4:12; 17). All humanity is born into sin. Jesus Christ, the Son of God, came to deliver us from our fallen, broken nature.[11] (No matter how hard we try or want it, we cannot save ourselves because of our fallen, broken nature. Like broken machines we cannot repair/save ourselves—a more detailed discussion of sin can be found in Chapter 1:4, under the heading *Welcoming the Seven.*)

* * * * *

What is a revelation?

In this case, it is an act of revealing predictions, bringing about an understanding of something not previously known or realized. The prophecies with the Book of Revelation are the inspired words of a prophet (John) and are viewed as a declaration of divine will. As the predictions come to pass, you and all the living will experience the drama of these events, the most astonishing wonders in history. It is a privilege to be alive to witness them!

* * * * *

The End Times

If the prophecies within the world's greatest worst-case scenario survival handbook are, in fact, now taking shape, when will they be fully realized? Some believed the completion of the prophetic forecasts would be achieved by the end of the twentieth century! Others say the prophetic time clock will start ticking during the early part of the twenty first century. Some believe the clock won't start for 20 or 30 years, or even longer. (It should be pointed out here that some also argue—and this is put very simply—a number of, if not all, End Time prophecies, including the return of Christ, were fulfilled in the first century destruction of Jerusalem [AD 70]. They believe Christ's Kingdom is here now and that paradise has been restored, but only in the spiritual sense. This is called the *Preterist view*, and although I find Preterist arguments interesting and open to discussion and debate, as the author of *Target: Israel* I hold to what is called the *Dispensational Premillennial Futurist view*, the most accepted contemporary perspective on biblical End Time prophecy, which means that most of my eschatological contemporaries and I believe the majority of End Time prophecy has yet to be fulfilled.) Still others believe they know the very day and hour the End Times began: September 11th, 2001, the beginning of the end of the world.

* * * * *

No one knows

What's clear is that, Preterist viewpoints aside, no one *truly knows* the exact day and hour of the end of the world other than God himself. The Bible makes this clear in Mathew 24:36, saying, "But of that day and hour no one knows, not even the angels of heaven, nor the Son, but the Father alone"—and that would include Preterists and anyone else who claims to know the day and hour. Thus, the question remains: How can we be sure these prophetic events will occur *soon?* I argue the End Times and the prophecies associated with it are described so clearly in the Book of Revelation that they will be recognizable for those who have studied prophecy and for those who are paying attention. What is taking place in Israel and the world today, the ever increasing number of suicide bombings, the rise of fanatical splinter-groups within Islam, global terrorism, to name but a few, strongly suggests that the biblical prophecies in question are drawing nigh! If this is indeed the case, all who are living now will participate in what could easily and truly be called the end of the world! Reading and understanding the prophecies described in these writings will assist you in being ready and steadfast so that you can survive whatever worst-case scenario the End Times throws your way.

We begin with the first verse in Chapter 1 of the Book of Revelation, your ultimate worst-case scenario survival handbook.

* * * * *

SOURCES:

1. *Yasser Arafat's Timeline of Terror*, November 13, 2004, CAMERA, Committee for Accuracy in Middle East Reporting in America, <http://www.camera.org>.
2. *Suicide Terrorism: Historical Background and Risks for the Future* by Yoram Schweitzer, June 18, 2004; Yoram Schweitzer is the co-author—with Shaul Shay—of *The Globalization of Terror: The Al Qaeda Challenge and the Response of the International Community,* Transaction, July 2003, PBS online, Wide angle, Yoram Schweitzer, 2005 Educational Broadcasting Corporation, all rights reserved, <http://www.pbs.org>.
3. *Apocalypse,* C. Van Den Biesen, transcribed by Michael C. Tinkler, The Catholic Encyclopedia, Vol. 1, Online Edition, Kevin Knight (2002), <http://www.newadvent.org>.
   Revelation, the book of, pg. 1077, The New Unger's Bible Dictionary, Moody Press (1988).
   Revelation, Gray's Home Bible Commentary; *Revelation,* Henry's Concise Commentary, The Bible Library Delux, version 5.0. suite, CD-ROM, Ellis Enterprises, Inc. (2,000).
4. *Revelation, the book of; Revelatio,* pg. 1077, The New Unger's Bible Dictionary, Moody Press (1988).
5. *Revelation—Apokalypsis,* #602, pg. 14, Greek Dictionary of the New Testament, Strong's Exhaustive Concordance of the Bible/Dictionary of the Hebrew and Greek Words, Hendrickson Publishers.
6. *Apocalypse,* C. Van Den Biesen, transcribed by Michael C. Tinkler, The Catholic Encyclopedia, Vol. 1, Online Edition, Kevin Knight (2002), <http://www.newadvent.org>.
   Revelation, the book of, pg. 1077, The New Unger's Bible Dictionary, Moody Press (1988).
7. *Apocalypse,* C. Van Den Biesen, transcribed by Michael C. Tinkler, The Catholic Encyclopedia, Vol. 1, Online Edition, Kevin Knight (2002), <http://www.newadvent.org>.
   Revelation, the book of, pg. 1077, The New Unger's Bible Dictionary, Moody Press (1988).
   Revelation, Gray's Home Bible Commentary; *Revelation,* Henry's Concise Commentary, The Bible Library Delux, version 5.0. suite, CD-ROM, Ellis Enterprises, Inc. (2,000).
8. *Exposition of the Orthodox Faith (Book I)*, St. John of Damascus, Orthodox Christian Information Center, <http://www.orthodoxinfo.com>; from John of Damascus, *Exposition of the Orthodox Faith,* Post Nicene Fathers, Schaff Edition, Volume IX, Series II, translated by The Rev. S. D. F. Salmond, D.D., F.e.I.s., Principal of the Free Church College, Aberdeen. (1898).
   God, pg. 480, The New Unger's Bible Dictionary, Moody Press (1988).

9. *Jesus Christ,* pg. 682-687, The New Unger's Bible Dictionary, Moody Press (1988).
Exposition of the Orthodox Faith (Book I), St. John of Damascus, Orthodox Christian Information Center, <http://www.orthodoxinfo.com>; from John of Damascus, *Exposition of the Orthodox Faith,* Post Nicene Fathers, Schaff Edition, Volume IX, Series II, translated by The Rev. S. D. F. Salmond, D.D., F.e.I.s., Principal of the Free Church College, Aberdeen. (1898).
Jesus Christ 2, James Orr, The International Bible Standard Encyclopedia, Online Edition (2003), <http://www.studylight.org>.
10. *Messiah—mashiach,* and *Christ—Christos; Y'shua, Why That Name?* Stuart Dauermann, Jews for Jesus Online (2003), <http://www.jfjonline.org>.
Exposition of the Orthodox Faith (Book I), St. John of Damascus, Orthodox Christian Information Center, <http://www.orthodoxinfo.com>; from John of Damascus, *Exposition of the Orthodox Faith, Post* Nicene Fathers, Schaff Edition, Volume IX, Series II, translated by The Rev. S. D. F. Salmond, D.D., F.e.I.s., Principal of the Free Church College, Aberdeen. (1898).
Jesus Christ 2, James Orr, International Bible Standard Encyclopedia, Online Edition (2003), <http://www.studylight.org>.
Jesus Christ, pg. 682-687, The New Unger's Bible Dictionary, Moody Press (1988).
11. *Sin 1*, Francis J. McConnell; Sin 2, M. G. Kyle, International Bible Standard Encyclopedia, Online Edition (2003), <http://www.studylight.org>.
Sin, pg. 1198-1200, The New Unger's Bible Dictionary, Moody Press (1988).

Great Predictions About To Unfold

Jesus answered: "Watch out that no one deceives you. For many will come in my name, claiming, 'I am the Messiah,' and will deceive many. You will hear of wars and rumors of wars, but see to it that you are not alarmed. Such things must happen, but the end is still to come. Nation will rise against nation, and kingdom against kingdom. There will be famines and earthquakes in various places. All these are the beginning of birth pains.

"Then you will be handed over to be persecuted and put to death, and you will be hated by all nations because of me. At that time many will turn away from the faith and will betray and hate each other, and many false prophets will appear and deceive many people. Because of the increase of wickedness, the love of most will grow cold, but the one who stands firm to the end will be saved. And this gospel of the kingdom will be preached in the whole world as a testimony to all nations, and then the end will come.

See, I have told you ahead of time."

Mathew 24: 4–14; 25.

PART I
Chapters One, Two & Three

THE ALPHA & OMEGA
THE SEVEN CHURCHES

Chapters 1 through 3 can be considered something of a prologue to the prophecy in the Book of Revelation. There are prophetic events mentioned, but for the most part these early chapters focus on the initial remarks of John, the author of the book, and wise counsel to the early Christian Church, which can be directly applied to the ancient and modern reader, Christian or non-Christian alike.

This manual is a verse by verse study of the Book of Revelation. Following that guideline, the first three chapters will focus on the initial remarks of John, the description of Jesus as the Alpha and Omega, the seven letters to the seven ancient Churches, their place in history and how the letters apply to the ancient and modern reader, as well as deal with some of the prophecy and concepts associated with them, including exploration into other concepts of interest (not listed in any specific order): the Seven Spirits of God; the holy mathematics/geometry of God; three earths; three heavens; the order of the Raptures; the Phase of Body; God's timetable/calendar; dispensational time and the three Ages in time; God's perspective beyond or outside of time; pre-corrupted earth time or *perfect time*; creation; evolution; classical and quantum physics and the potential digital nature of the universe; hyperdimensional beings, i.e., angels; fallen angels and Satan; the Great Tribulation; the Trinity; salvation and how it works; plus additional related information.

Part II explores Chapters 4 and 5, the bridge to the prophecy.

Part III explores Chapters 6 through 22, the main body of prophecy.

Part I, Part II, and Part III are essential pieces of the whole—the three parts are deeply interconnected and together they make the prophecy complete. I have broken it into three distinct parts for organizational clarity.

CHAPTER 1
Vision Like The Son Of Man

Revelation 1:1

The Revelation of Jesus Christ, which God gave him to show his servants—things which must shortly take place. And he sent and signified it by his angel to his servant John...

PREDICTIONS THAT MUST TAKE PLACE

The Revelation of Jesus Christ: in these writings Christ has revealed a detailed record to all people throughout history—including you!—about amazing predictions that will (shortly) take place just before his Second Great Coming, as well as the events that happen after his return. The term Second Coming is not allegorical in nature here, but literal: Jesus Christ, the Son of the living and Holy God, will come back to earth in person. Even though he is now outside of time, from our perspective he has been with his Father in heaven for a period of almost two thousand years! The Word of Jesus is bathed in heaven—his power and his word reign supreme in all Creation, ie., whatever he says goes. He indeed will return at the appointed time!

Specifically, the revelation of Jesus Christ (the Book of Revelation) is an unveiling of his future plan for the earth and for all humanity, the saved and unsaved, both in time and beyond time, into eternity itself!

THE FUTURE & THE PAST

The first sentence of the first verse of *The Revelation of Jesus Christ* ends with the phrase "...things which must shortly take place." It conveys two simultaneous perspectives in time, that of the historic past and the prophetic future (what I think is our *immediate* future), or put more simply, God is going to show John two futures, his immediate future and the far flung future of humanity (our immediate future) at the same time. The historical past centers on John and events that shortly took place in and around his lifetime; and the prophetic focuses on events that will take place during what is commonly referred to in Christian circles as the End Times, the times I believe we are now in—those things that must shortly take place *now.*

THREE AGES

To make sure that it's clear, let's take a look at what is meant by the word *Age*. For the purposes of this book an Age is the divine order of worldly events covering the period of time during which human beings exist, from the time of the first person until the last. There arc three Ages:

(1) The Human Age.
(2) The Kingdom Age.
(3) The Holy Age.

The Human Age is calculated from the time of Adam until the last person alive on earth, approximately 6,000 years by God's timetable/calendar. (The concept of God's timetable/calendar will be explored in more detail in the following paragraphs.)

The Kingdom Age is the final one thousand years in (potentially) perfect time with Christ.

The Holy Age is eternity beyond or outside of time.

We are still in the Human Age, but if events unfolding in the world today are a good indicator the Human Age may be coming to an end sooner than later!

DISPENSATIONS

I adhere to the point of view of a dispensationalist, that is, I believe there are various dispensations within the first two Ages, the Human Age and the Kingdom Age.

Dispensations are long periods of time in human history. I believe there are seven dispensations in the first two Ages.

(1) The Dispensation of Innocence.

Adam and Eve in the Garden of Eden. They were innocent, naked, knew no shame, and had free will, but in order to have genuine free will the possibility to sin *had to* exist. Thus, they were in a state called *probation.* Humanity had to be tested by falling under God's divine law: he or she could eat from every tree within the Garden of Eden except the tree of the knowledge of good and evil. The earth and all reality were in a perfect state of existence, knowing no entropy or sin or death.

(2) The Dispensation of Conscience.

Tempted by Satan, Adam and Eve make the choice to fail, eating of the tree of the knowledge of good and evil. This causes the nature of Man and the universe to fall which brings sin, corruption, and death to them and all the world. This dispensation came to an end with the Flood.

(3) The Dispensation of Human Government.

After the Flood, humanity is given the authority to implement laws and carry out judgment. It fails because humanity is incapable of governing itself. This dispensation came to an end with the Tower of Babel and the confusion of languages.

(4) The Dispensation of Promise.

Because humanity has failed to govern itself, God chooses Abraham and his descendents and calls them his chosen people. The Israelites are required to trust that God will keep his promises. This dispensation came to an end with the bondage of the Israelites in Egypt.

(5) The Dispensation of Law.

The Israelites fail to trust God, so the Law is established. This dispensation came to an end with the birth of Jesus.

(6) The Dispensation of the Church.

The Israelites are unable to keep the Law, which ushers in the birth, life, death, and resurrection of Jesus Christ as the Messiah and the fulfillment of Old Testament Law, establishing a New Covenant of grace for all humanity because we're incapable of governing and/or saving ourselves. This dispensation comes to an end with the return of Jesus Christ.

(7) The Dispensation of the Kingdom.

The 1,000 years of rest after the Great Tribulation and the return of Christ, otherwise known as the seventh millennium or the Kingdom Age. When this dispensation ends, Judgment will come to pass, ushering in the Holy Age eternal.

The amount of dispensations within the two Ages is debatable, however. Some biblical scholars recognize less than seven, while others do not believe God uses dispensations to measure human history/experience at all. I'm convinced there are seven dispensations and that each one represents a test of some kind for humanity. Six fill the Human Age and the seventh is fulfilled within the Kingdom Age, the 1,000 years with Christ.

It should be clear that the dispensations in question, be they 3 or 4 or 7, and the three Ages are totally separate in definition and yet are interrelated in purpose. All of them fall into and under God's timetable/calendar.

GOD'S TIMETABLE/CALENDAR

Now, I'd like to clarify what I mean when I use the term *God's timetable/calendar:* we depend entirely on the time clock of God, not man and the calculations of man! What is meant by this is, simply, God's definition, and most certainly his perspective of time has got to be very different from ours! As an example of what I mean, one thousand years from God's perspective and one thousand years from our perspective don't necessarily have to agree because God is infinite and outside of time and we are finite and stuck in time, and even if they do agree humanity doesn't know when the clock started ticking (going on the assumption that imperfect time began with the Fall). Humanity is, therefore, unable to accurately measure and therefore know the exact timetable of existence and human events, especially those concerning the End Times and the return of Christ.

Nevertheless, we do have the Word of God, and because of that we can make educated guesses based on study of the Word that comply with the Book of Genesis (the beginning), recognizable biblical prophecy, and the prophetic events mentioned in Revelation (the end).

Lastly, I am sure God has his own timetable/calendar and that it is highly complex and mathematical in nature with consistent references to the numbers 3, 6, 7, and 40 (among many others), and thus, from our dimly lit corner of knowledge regarding the timetable/calendar and his holy perspective, combined with study of the Holy Scriptures and the guiding hand of the Spirit, we can calculate:

6,000 years from the Fall of Man and a final 1,000 years (the seventh millennium) make a total of 7,000 years by God's timetable/calendar.

Again, our human measurements of this span of time are not entirely accurate, but I believe they're reasonably close, based on those well studied educated guesses. Since that is the case, for the rest of the book we will stick to the model of God's timetable/calendar:

6,000 years + 1,000 = 7,000.

HIS CHOSEN ANGEL

John states that Christ sent the revelation to John through his chosen angel.

This particular holy angel is a created being that lives with God in heaven. He was especially appointed by God to show John things that must shortly come to pass.

Don't let the word *shortly* throw you here. Even though this sentence was written nearly 2,000 years ago you have to remember that we're dealing with things of a spiritual nature that are, particularly in regard to John's experience, simultaneously inside and outside of time—we'll study the concepts of time in more detail in 1:19, and angels in Chapters 4:8, under the heading *Creatures of the Spirit*, and 5:11, under the heading *Angels*.

THE APOSTLE JOHN

The verse ends with a reference to the author of Revelation. I'd like to stop here for a moment and give a quick recap on John:

He was one of the twelve apostles of Jesus, the son of Zebedee, a fisherman on the Sea of Galilee (Mark 1:19–20; Luke 5:10). He was probably the younger brother of James (Matt. 1:20). He is traditionally known as *the disciple whom Jesus loved.* With his brother, James, as well as with Andrew and Simon, John and his fellow disciples were called to be fishers of men, apostles of Jesus Christ (Mark 1:17–20; Luke 5:10). He was one of the first men to reach the empty tomb of (the risen) Jesus (John 20:2) and look inside (John 20:4–8). He was a witness to the ascension of Christ. He is the author of the Gospel of John, the three epistles of John, and the Book of Revelation.

CONFIRMATION

John confirms that he was given the job to show the servants of the Lord "...things which must shortly take place." Specifically, the prophecy of Christ.

We shall discover that much of the prophecy turns out to be more than mere metaphor and real in every sense of the word, as Jesus' own mouth commands them to take place!

Revelation 1:2

...who bore witness to the Word of God, and to the testimony of Jesus Christ, to all things that he saw.

TESTIMONY OF JESUS CHRIST

In a broad as well as literal sense, the Book of Revelation describes a meeting between the Son of God and John. Their dialogue, both verbal and visual, transcends time and space and reality as we understand it: on the island of Patmos in 96 A.D. two realities converged—the reality of our world and its laws as well as the reality of the spiritual and its laws, whatever they may be. John is thrust forward and backward in our time and reality and even, on occasion, pulled out of our time and our reality altogether and taken into the spirit! God is bending time and space—and when that sort of thing is going on you realize that *we're not in Kansas anymore.*

MIND-BOGGLING

The idea that John is experiencing visions from the sideline, that he's experiencing this from within the confines of his own head in the form of hallucination as some scholars like to argue, is incorrect. This view diminishes the prophecies and the supernatural nature of God, putting him in a limiting box. For that reason, we must think outside the box because as far as God is concerned there is no box. Anything is possible. Undoubtedly, this is no hallucination. This is a literal and real experience in and out of time. We're dealing with mind-boggling stuff here. It challenges everything we think we understand. It's important to keep that in mind as John takes us on his journey.

THE BENDER OF TIME & SPACE

John then makes a declaration of truth and writes down everything shown to him by the heavenly angel, making a dependable, thorough record of the testimony of Jesus Christ. John is the listener and Christ is the narrator, the Bender of Time and Space.

In Chapter 1, Jesus reveals to John that he is returning to this earth. He tells John that he is the First and the Last, signifying that he has always existed and always will exist.

Just to make it clear, because he is beyond or outside of time statements like *always existed* really have no meaning, other than helping our finite minds understand the concept. Outside of time God simply is *now*.

He tells John to write down everything shown to him and declares that he is of the seven churches (a clear representation of the Seven Spirits of God) that were active in John's time. When he says *churches,* he's not referring to mere buildings, but to the groups of people who make up *the* Church entire, past and present.

John is then told to send out this message to all the companies (churches) believing in Christ at the time—and that message has been sent to every believer throughout the world to this very day. One of the purposes of this, of course, was so that people who believe in Christ can spread the word about the predictions that will take place just before his second great coming, which focus on the last seven years of our present Age! "But of this coming, no one knows; no, not even the angels of heaven, but only my Father" (Matt. 25:36). Watch, therefore, for we do not know what day he comes; be ready for the Son of Man!

Revelation 1:3

Blessed is he who reads and those who hear the words of this prophecy, and keep those things which are written in it; for the time is near.

BLESSED BY THESE WORDS

One of the first important matters John learns from Jesus through the angel: whoever *reads* the words of this prophesy is blessed; whoever *hears* the words of this prophecy is blessed; whoever *understands through study and prayer* is blessed.

This is the only book in the Bible that contains a special promise to obedient readers (Rev. 1:3) and at the same time curses those who alter its contents (Rev. 22:18–19). To fully understand this we have to look at both sides of the issue, blessing and curse.

What does *blessed* mean? The common definition of the word relates to veneration or honor in worship, as well as consecration. Merriam-Webster's Online Dictionary defines it as: "1a: held in reverence: venerated; b: honored in worship: hallowed."[1] Specifically relating to this verse, *to be blessed* means *you will be blessed by Christ* if you read, hear, and study Revelation text. You will be venerated/honored through the sanctification of Christ, receiving happiness/bliss because you read, heard, and studied the Book of Revelation in obedience to the will of Christ. Notice that there's no doubt here. Indeed, *you will be blessed* if you follow in obedience. It's a promise, and one thing we know for certain is that Jesus keeps his promises.

That's clear enough, but now the question must be asked, what of the curse? John gives a very specific warning to everyone who hears the words of the prophecy of the Book of Revelation: "If anyone dares to add or corrupt or change anything to this book, the Word of God, either by adding to it or taking from it, God will add to them the plagues that are written in this book!" (Rev 22:18).

The common meaning of the word *curse* usually relates to misfortune, often linked to someone *that is* or *becomes* cursed because of a choice made, and the choice is usually a selfish and disobedient one. A curse is essentially punishment. In regard to this verse that's exactly what it signifies.

The reference to *adding to them the plagues* seems to be in the literal and not the figurative, although, clearly it cannot apply to the literal plagues of the Great Tribulation unless those whom God curses/punishes (because of their disobedience) will be living at that time. For those who alter the book and exist prior to the literal plagues of the Great Tribulation it seems that God will respond *in* kind, plaguing/cursing them either in their lives or perhaps after death in the life to come.

The whole answer to the curse is, nonetheless, unknowable at this time because it's veiled, other than the fact that we know there will indeed be some kind of literal consequence for those who add to or alter the contents of the Book of Revelation.

That being the case, the answer to what the curse/plagues will be or what God meant by using the word *plagues* is really beside the point. What should be crystal clear here is that a person will be liable: whoever adds to or alters the contents of the book will be held accountable by God for his or her disobedience. For those who do add to or alter the book there will be some kind of punishment that is similar to a curse—plainly, negative and literal, as opposed to merely negative in the sense of metaphor. Because of the literal consequence for adding to or altering the Book of Revelation the answer to the question of the curse/plagues can indeed be solved, even while the whole answer remains veiled: don't add to or alter the contents of the book!

Simple enough.

FALSE CHRISTS & REAL BEASTS

Those living in the times of the early Christian Church two thousand years ago hoped that the return of Christ was at hand, but it was not, as the appointed time had not yet been reached. I argue that this generation knows the time is surely at hand, for predictions that Christ revealed, very clearly described in the Book of Matthew, are presently happening! This evidence supports the idea that the end of the Human Age is near.

Let's take a look at that evidence now, measuring it up with some of Christ's major prophecies of the Last Days:

WARS & RUMORS OF WARS

(1) Matthew 24:6–8 says, "And (just before my return) you will hear of wars and rumors of wars. See that you are not troubled...for nation will rise against nation and kingdom against kingdom." Today, the world yearns for peace, for there are many rumors of wars. Indeed, there are many ongoing wars. Two world wars have come and gone—in a single century! Some say the Third World War is well on its way or that it has already begun because of terrorist bombings and the fundamentalist radical Islamic agenda. The world has seen much devastation through the recent rise of global terrorist attacks in the name of religion or politics, much of it aimed at the nation of Israel. Fact: there are more wars taking place right now on planet earth than at any other time in

humanity's long and bloody history, 40–100 at any given time today: revolutions, rebellions, internal problems, flashpoints, and trouble/hot spots.[2]

War, war and more war.

FAMINE

(2) Jesus also forewarns in the same passage, "And there will be famines, pestilences, and earthquakes in various places. All these are the beginning of sorrows (prior to my coming)."

Fact: daily news accounts are filled with reports of famines and uncontrollable disease.

Famines are often incorrectly looked upon as simple natural disasters where climate and environment failed, but the truth is much more complicated than that, for political and economic relations are often included in the cause. The Irish-potato famine (1846–1851) and the ongoing famine in Iraq (1990 to present day) are two examples of how interconnected climate, environment, politics, and economics are in the development of famine.

The point to be taken here, in relation to Mathew 24:6–8, famine, and the End Times, or as Jesus coined it, the Beginning of Sorrows, is just how complex famine is and how completely Jesus understood it. He not only predicted climate and environmental causes for famine, but political and economic as well—the world in which we live today. Jesus prophesied that before his return the world would be a complex place riddled with famine caused by climate, environment, political, and economic disasters. Or, as he simply, but so eloquently put it, there will be famine in various places, and clearly that is the case today.

PESTILENCE

When we think of what Christ meant by pestilences, the Avian Influenza (Bird Flu) as an Influenza pandemic threat comes to mind, as well as its lethal global potential, but the AIDS pandemic in Africa will do: 29.4 million men, women, and children are infected with the HIV virus, 70% of the total infected people worldwide. As of 2001, an estimated 21.5 million Africans had died of AIDS, and recent data suggests that a further 89 million people in Africa could be infected with the HIV virus by 2025.[3] HIV has become the leading cause for death in Africa, spread primarily by heterosexual contact and drug use. 58% of those infected are women.[4]

Fact: we also know of pestilences in the form of biological weapons manufacturing and use on innocent civilians.

The Iraqi regime dropped biological and chemical weapons on its own people before the Gulf War and as a result those victims and their families continue to live with the biological horrors and genetic mutations.[5] Indeed, numerous governments around the world manufacture illegal biological and chemical weaponry and weapon systems. Clearly, these *pestilences* exist.

EARTHQUAKES

Fact: state-of-the-art scientific evidence against an increase in global earthquakes is most compelling and yet the stance of many contemporary eschatologists is in direct opposition to those facts, arguing earthquakes around the globe are increasing, a clear sign the End Times are at hand. During my lifetime the world has witnessed many great earthquakes and because of this I could easily reach this conclusion. Which is it? Increasing or decreasing? What we have here is a scientific and eschatological divide, and what it makes most clear is that Christ's reference to an increase in earthquake activity as a sign of his imminent return remains mostly veiled in mystery. It is a topic open to debate, and of course there are controversial opinions and conclusions on either side of the argument. Because of this, I encourage you to research the data both scientifically and scripturally on your own so that you can make an informed decision as to whether or not globally earthquakes are increasing or decreasing and whether or not they point to the imminent return of Jesus Christ.

Above and beyond the debate over the scientific evidence, it's clear that Christ's reference to earthquakes here is layered in meaning (similar to his reference to famine), from the metaphorical (birth pains) to the literal, which could apply to a literal increase in quakes before his return, which if correct will happen at its appointed time, or to the many earthquakes that will occur during the Great Tribulation.

Arguments for and against aside, the most important thing to take from Christ's reference to earthquakes in Mathew 25: 7 is not the earthquakes themselves, whether or not they are increasing or decreasing, but what they tell us: if you are paying attention, you will be prepared and thus you will survive. Once again, it's a matter of survival and preparation, the Book of Revelation as *survival handbook*.

NATURAL DISASTERS

Fact: today natural disasters continue to slam the earth and humanity with an unrelenting and unsettling consistency that appears to be intensifying.

In 2004, hurricanes had a record breaking year for size and destruction; the Sumatra-Andaman Earthquake caused a tsunami that killed 240,000; deadly winter weather, floods, tornadoes, wildfires, etc.[6]

REBIRTH OF ISRAEL

(3) "Now learn this parable (lesson) from the fig tree..." (Matt. 24:32). Traditionally, the fig tree portrays the State of Israel, which was reborn in the year 1948. The dispersed Jews had originally lost their nation in the year 70 A.D. There hadn't been a nation of Israel for almost two thousand years, but Christ prophesied in that same verse, "When its branch has already become tender and puts forth leaves (when Israel flourishes), you know that summer is near."

Jesus is referring to the nearness of his coming.

Fact: the rebirth of the Israel State, whose *branch has now become tender and puts forth leaves,* occurred decades ago!

Christ predicted that this would happen close to his return. Is it possible that the autumn of the End Times has already slipped by and we are now in the winter, nearing its conclusion? In the next verse, Matthew 24:33, Christ predicted, "So you also, when you see all these things, know that it (my Second Coming) is near—at the door!"

WICKEDNESS PREVAILS

(4) "Assuredly, I say to you, this generation (the generation that witnesses these happenings) will by no means pass away till all these things take place. Heaven and earth will pass away, but my words will by no means pass away" (Matt. 24:34–35). Is the evidence mounting, suggesting that our generation is the one about which Jesus is speaking?

He also announced that he will return when wickedness prevails on the earth. It's a fact that the lawlessness of the people before the world flood as disclosed in the Old Testament, approximately two thousand years before the birth of Christ, came up before the Lord, and he destroyed most of humanity and much of the earth with it. It's a fact that the wickedness of Sodom and Gomorrah (Gen. 19) came up before the Lord and he wiped out both cities. It's a fact that today wickedness prevails throughout the earth like never before—and rest assured it comes up before the Lord.

It is true that the United States of America is a country founded on certain *unalienable rights* and we must never forget them—it is what makes this country great and unique. Following our Constitutional guidelines we must continue to love and encourage our brothers and sisters toward the path of Christ, be they gay, lesbian, bisexual, transgendered, straight, drug addicted, alcoholic, racist, skin head neo-Nazi, Democrat, Republican or Independent, and we must do this without hate or prejudice. But even so, it can be argued our society has become so liberal that it has lost sight of what it means to be obedient to the will of God. Truly, the days of Gomorrah have returned. Jesus will fight against this wickedness with outstretched hands and a strong arm. Because he is holy he can have nothing less, and within that holiness he will return, even in anger, fury, and great wrath! The unrepentant will not escape the wrath of God. He sets before us the way of life. And, truly, the way of death!

When men and women corrupt the body, sexually or otherwise, they do so (knowingly or unknowingly) as acts of worship to the evil one. Paul described our day particularly well when he said, "And even as they did not like to retain God in their knowledge, God gave them over to a debased (or corrupt) mind, to do those things which are not fitting; being filled with all unrighteousness, sexual immorality, wickedness, covetousness, maliciousness; full of envy, murder, strife, deceit, evil-mindedness; they are whisperers, backbiters, haters of God, violent; proud, boasters, inventers of evil things, disobedient to parents, undiscerning, untrustworthy, unloving, unforgiving" (Rom. 1:28–31).

Sounds like a normal day in the United States of America.

FALSE CHRISTS

(5) "Now as he (Jesus) sat on the Mount of Olives (in Jerusalem), the disciples came to him privately, saying, 'Tell us, when will these things be? And what will be the sign of your coming, and of the end of the (this) age?' And Jesus answered and said to them: 'Take heed that no one deceives you. For many will come in my name, saying, 'I am the Christ,' and will deceive many...and then the end will come (when this occurs, know that my coming is soon)'" (Matt. 24:3–5; 14).

Fact: today we hear of people claiming to be the Christ in many different places on the planet. They're everywhere!

Jim Jones of the Peoples Temple in Guyana (1978), the man behind the Jonestown suicide and massacre, labeled himself the Christ. In 1982, Benjamin Crème published in newspapers across the globe that "Christ was now here!" in the form of the New Age Christ, Maitreya. In 1992, Reverend Sung Myung Moon declared himself Lord of the Second Advent, the Messiah. David Koresh, founder of the Branch Davidians, who burned to death April 19,

1993 in Waco, Texas, called himself the Christ—and a handful of his followers continue to wait for their messiah to return from the ashes. At the turn of the Millennium there were 40,000+ reported cases of Jerusalem Syndrome in Israel, a (usually) short-term condition that convinces people they are Christ or some other biblical character. The UFO cult in France, the Raelians/the Raelian Revolution, refer to their leader *Rael* as the true face of God. In Siberia, a Christ is rising, known locally as Jesus of Siberia (Sergei Torop, a policeman who announced that he was the Son of God in 1989).

The Christian Church is not exempt.

FALSE CHRISTIANS

Fact: there are leaders within the Church (preachers, ministers, priests, celebrity televangelists, et al) that not only teach obvious heresies such as Jesus was not the Son of God, Jesus never rose from the grave, Jesus was not Jewish, there is no salvation or afterlife, and on and on (and, at that point, you have to wonder why these people call themselves Christians), but some actually suggest that they are as infallible as Christ, they have the absolute universal power of Christ, or simply forgoing any subtlety at all, they equate themselves to Christ by announcing that they are little Christ's or even Christ himself. There are so many examples it's more than disturbing, it's telling: "...for many will come in my name, saying, 'I am the Christ...'" Clearly, the evidence is mounting.[7]

The student of prophecy realizes that these Christs, whether secular or so-called Christian, are merely men and women more aptly named gods of darkness. They're charlatans selling snake oil to an emotionally needy and spiritually vulnerable population.

Many of these Christs have come and gone, it is true, and there will be more to follow, but there are two men in particular who will rise up in Europe and they will call themselves the Christ of Heaven—and they may already be well established in the political arena today. These men (the Antichrist and the False Prophet/False Pope) will fit perfectly into the puzzle of Revelation prophecies!

EURO BEASTS

(6) Two *Beasts* will take over the leadership of Europe. One of these Beasts is described as being the Antichrist, who works against the true Christ during the latter days of our age.

In spiritual terms, the Antichrist is the son of the devil, a literal spiritual being who, of course, hates God, his Son, and his believers, not to mention the rest of humanity. Jesus predicts that this Antichrist will rise from somewhere within the old Roman Empire and rule much of the world. Most scholars of Revelation prophecy assume that the Roman Empire reference suggests that he will come out of Western Europe, but there is always the possibility that he may rise up from the East, from within the Byzantine Empire, the Middle East, which was once part of the Roman Empire. Whatever the case may be, his power source will be hell and the devil himself!

Is this first Beast waiting now to take over the European Union and thus become a prominent political figure in the eyes of the world?

UNITED EUROPE

Fact: during the 1990s the countries of Europe hoped to become united—a United Europe.

A single Euro currency was introduced and they started to pull together. The unification continues, and even though it's going through what could be called difficult birthing pains, struggling to design an E.U Constitution, the European Union will be wholly born and complete and in line with Revelation prophecy sooner than you think. When this happens—and it will, make no mistake—those in the New Age Movement and similar movements or religions (including some branches within the Christian Church, as well as those in the Jewish faith) will believe in this man, the Euro Beast, and will be actively involved with him. He will lead the nations. But he will be a false leader and, like his dark father, a liar.

It is possible, perhaps even likely, that the first Beast waits as of this writing to set himself up as messiah and god?

A strong indicator that these events are steadily falling into place today is a warning in Scripture: watch out for those who call themselves the Christ! Beware of those who claim, "I am the Christ!"

THE SECOND BEAST

Could the second Beast be waiting for his cue to lead the world into a one-world/one-faith religious movement? Could he be the expected False Prophet? Revelation reveals one called by that name. He is associated with the first Beast and with the Dragon. He will be a miracle worker, powered by evil. He will command the people of the Tribulation period to make an *image to the Beast* in order to worship it and he will give that image life. He will demand that all who will not worship it be put to death. (Refer to Chapter

13:14-15 for related information.) He is an aide to the Antichrist, associated with the mystical number 666. He is not a true prophet of the Living God, but the exact opposite, and thus he was aptly named: the False Prophet.

THE BEASTS CONTROL EUROPE

After certain *Hostile Nations* war against the state of Israel and are overcome by the mighty hand of God, clearly prophesied in Ezekiel 38 in the Old Testament—refer to Chapter 12:1, under the heading *Ezekiel 38 & 39*—we are told that these two powerful men, the Antichrist and the False Prophet, will take control of a newly formed nation at a time when this new nation earnestly requires peace. It is revealed in Revelation that this newly formed nation will indeed be Europe United, and it is forming today. Strengthened by unification it will become the kingdom of Lucifer, ruled by the two Beasts.

FROM BELOW

As a side-note, Revelation reveals that both Beasts come up from beneath the earth's surface. They rise from a mighty prison-place located in the center of our planet. (Is this merely metaphor or is this where hell really is? Turn to Chapter 5:3, below the heading *Under the Earth*, for more information.)

John writes about the first Beast in Revelation 13:1, saying, "Then I stood on the sand of the sea. And I saw a Beast (called the Antichrist) rising up out of the sea," indicating that he ascended from hell, the bottomless pit (we'll get to the physics of hell in Chapter 5:3), where he was locked up and is released just before the return of Christ, shortly before the False Prophet is freed. In Revelation 17:8, John says, "The Beast that you saw (being the Antichrist) once was..."—the *once was* strongly suggests that he was flesh on this earth as a living man in days gone by. Perhaps he was the notorious Nimrod who defied God by building the Tower of Babel found in the Scriptures. (Refer to Chapter 13:1, under the heading *Nimrod, the Antichrist*.) Then John continues in that same verse, saying, "... (the Beast) now is not (for if he once was a living man, he faced death and died), and will ascend (or rise again, in direct and unholy imitation of Christ's resurrection—we know that the unholy trinity imitates the Holy Trinity in regard to number systems, but there is also unholy imitation in regard to design), yes he will ascend out of the bottomless pit (to live again as an immortal man and an earthly ruler) and go to perdition."

If we follow a linear timeline it would go something like this: long ago the Beast lived as a man and died as a man. After his death he was imprisoned in the bottomless pit. He later rises once again during the End Times as an immortal being bent on the destruction of humankind, freed from his spiritual prison just before Jesus' Second Coming.

John writes about the second Beast in Revelation 13:11, by saying, "Then I saw another beast (called the False Prophet) coming up out of the earth, suggesting that he ascends from the bottomless pit like the Antichrist, released just before the return of Christ—and he too, is disguised as a human being, but is immortal. He had two horns like a lamb (for he will be Christ-like in appearance) but spoke like a dragon (as his father is the devil)." Are we being informed that the earth is to be visited by these two immortal souls from hell? The answer: an unequivocal yes!

THEY WAIT

We will learn much more about these two men, the Antichrist and the False Prophet/False Pope, the Beasts who are released from their spiritual prison, awaiting their final confrontation with the true God! A decisive war, known as the Battle of Armageddon, between Jesus Christ and these Beasts will take place in the land of Israel at Jesus' arrival. An account of the mighty battle is recorded in detail in Chapter 19 of the Book of Revelation. Expect to witness earth's final war of the Age! They have Israel in their crosshairs. Is it not already the target? Of course it is, for we are not blind.

THE ONGOING & GREAT WAR

Here is wisdom! It is clear from Scripture that there has been an ongoing and Great War between God and his Son and Lucifer and his son, and that it all began in heaven (before or outside of time) and continues on earth (in time—where the war and time itself will eventually end). The human race has been drawn into the great battle. (Refer to Chapter 12:17, under the heading *The Great War Revisited* for more information on this subject.) Those on the side of the heavenly Father have been attacked by this enemy of God, but what if you are not on the side of the Great Creator? Whose side would you be on? Satan's of course! Know this well: if we are not with God, then we are with the Evil One! (Matt. 12:30). This is alarming, but true, for there is no in-between!

APOSTATE DOMINATE CHURCH

(7) Christ says, "Because lawlessness will abound (the way the world has now become), the love of many will grow cold" (Matt. 24:12).

The heart of humanity has been cooling, for the love of many has indeed grown cold and it is getting colder by the minute—this seems to be the case, but of course, coolness-of-heart is also a common, natural, and constant reflection of the fallen human condition.

Fact: the love within the Body of Christ has been cooling or, more specifically, changing. The heart of the Church is transforming, having a nature that has rejected, renounced, or abandoned its original religious faith and loyalty. It is becoming apostate in nature. (For related information on the prophetic apostate nature of the Church, refer to Chapters 3:15, under the heading, *Neither Hot or Cold*, 14:8, under the heading *The Fall of Modern Babylon* and 17:3, under the heading *Modern Babylon*.)

INTER-FAITH ECUMENICISM

In regard to global inter-faith ecumenicism: this specifically applies to *acceptance* of other world religions, practices, and doctrines within the Christian faith, as opposed to a healthy respect and vital communication shared within the Catholic, Orthodox, and collective Christian Church, what could be called a *productive internal ecumenicism*.

Inter-faith ecumenicsm is changing the internal structure of Christianity. It is having a profound impact upon the Body of Christ worldwide, quickly and steadily transforming it into the prophesized nature of the global Church before the return of Christ: a state of cool and indifferent apostasy.[8]

It should be pointed out here that the apostasy existing within the modern Church, the cool and indifferent nature of the Church today that will completely dominate in the near future, has taken some time to root, growing within the Christian Church for well on two centuries or more. Most scholars point to the Age of Enlightenment, when reason and logic replaced what the intellectual elites of the time called superstition or mysticism, what amounts to Christian faith, as the jumping off point for this change within Christian thought. (This radical change in thought applies mostly to the western Church.) The self-proclaimed *courageous elite* of the Enlightenment felt compelled to lead humanity out of dark, foolish ways of thinking, and in so doing reason and logic began to dominate not only secular thought but Christian thought as well.[9]

Tellingly, as the modern Church embraces inter-faith ecumenicism it is severing itself from its ancient past, abandoning its ancient teachings and traditions and replacing them with questionable, emotionally centered, and sensational doctrine/theology that is often times inaccurate, arrogant, and even heretical. Inter-faith ecumenicism has even led some who wield power within the Body of Christ to reject the heart of Christianity: biblical truth and the divinity of Jesus Christ. They are altering the heart of the Church through subtle, clever rhetoric and relentless revisionist teaching, encouraging the acceptance of other religions and religious practices and doctrines and highly suspect personal supernatural experiences. In fact, supernatural experience within the global Church is on the rise, and many of the experiences are either emotionally out of control, a state of being that is in direct contrast to the nurturing spirit of the Holy Spirit, or are so far removed from ancient Christian tradition as to be nearly unrecognizable.[10]

AFTER THE FACTS, THE CONCLUSION

At this point, it seems reasonable to conclude from the mountain of evidence that has been compiled here, fact after fact after fact, that this generation is indeed living in the times of the end just before Christ's Second Great Coming to earth, his Second Advent. There is more evidence to come, make no mistake. The facts continue to mount every day. Time, it seems, is literally running out.

But do not be discouraged. The Book of Revelation was written by John primarily for the last generation of this Age—our generation—so that you may know what is taking place and so that you can survive. Being well prepared will help you not to be afraid. It will aid in your survival. This is the greatest period of despair for the wicked; the greatest period of hope for the believer!

Christ delivers you from the hand of the evil one. He redeems you from the grip of the terrible, for his eyes are on all the ways of the people! You are not hidden from his face. Remember: "Blessed is he who reads and those who hear the words of this prophecy, and keep those things which are written in it; for the time is near" (Rev. 1:2).

The evidence suggests that the end of this Human Age is upon us. The great predictions of Revelation, which will greatly affect your life, are about to unfold. They are revealed in much more detail from Chapter 6 to Chapter 22. Read on, and discover what happens in the very near future. Put yourself in readiness, for you are going to be astonished!

Revelation 1:4

John, to the seven churches which are in Asia: Grace to you and peace from him [Jesus] who is and who was and who is to come, and from the Seven Spirits who are before his throne...

WELCOMING THE SEVEN

God's faithful servant is eager to deliver Jesus' disclosure of worldly events to the seven assembled churches in Asia. He announces, "Grace to you and peace from him..." which can be loosely paraphrased, "Good will and peace be given freely to mankind. Divine love and honor to everyone."

John reveals that God's Son is the One who *is* (he exists now) and who *was* (he came as the Savior, born as man on this earth, and died on the cross) and who *is to come* (he will return).

The good news is that he was raised from the dead by his Father and lives forevermore! He became the first to be resurrected and is now with God in heaven, and yet he is with us on earth through the Holy Spirit, for the Father, Son, and Holy Spirit are One, forming the Holy Trinity!) *Who is to come* is a clear reference to Jesus' Great Second Coming to the earth at the conclusion of the Human Age! This message comes from the Seven Spirits before the throne, which is just another term for Jesus Christ. (John is informing us that these words come from God's Son.)

JESUS SAVES US FROM SIN

To have a clearer understanding of why Christ came to save humankind and what sin is, let's do a little backtracking for a moment: God came to this earth in the human form of his Son, called the Christ, to conquer death for his fallen children who are facing punishment because of sin—*broken, separated, sinful*, all of these words are valid descriptors for the word *fallen* as it's used in this sentence.

Here's the underlying idea of sin: sin is everything in the nature, purpose, and behavior of God's creatures that is in direct opposition to the nature, purpose and will of God (Rom. 3:20; 4:15; 7:7; James 4:12; 17). Simply put, the sinfulness in sin lies in disobedience (Gen. 39:9; Ps. 51:4; Mat. 23:23)!

THE MORAL CONDITION

Now, the connection between the sin of Adam and the moral condition of all humanity—why we have such hearts of darkness in the first place—is a matter of great debate in Christian circles, and because of that it should be briefly discussed here.

There's the *Calvinist* point of view, *Arminian*, and *Pelagianistic*, but because the Pelagianistic point of view dismisses the need for the saving grace of Christ, I dismiss this view as entirely invalid and will not pursue an explanation of it here.

The Calvinists believe that the sin of Adam immediately went into the whole human family, the end result being that the entire human race is depraved, sinful, guilty, fallen, broken, separated from God.

The Arminian view believes that Adam's sin and moral state is connected to the natural law of heredity, or perhaps another way of saying it would be that the human race inherited the capability for sin at the genetic level.[11]

I tend to lean toward the Calvinist point of view, although, it's possible that both views are simultaneously correct in varying degrees, that it's a little bit of both—for the most part, this is a complex spiritual matter that reaches far beyond human comprehension, existing well within the miraculous nature and design of God and there it will remain. For Christians, this matter falls almost completely within the defining parameters of faith.

HEARTS OF DARKNESS

The most important thing here is to realize that our natures do not reflect the nature of God. We are all fallen and broken and at the center of our nature we have dark hearts that would much rather be disobedient than anything else, prone toward evil instead of good, disobedience instead of obedience: bad comes easy to us; good is much harder for us to do. In basic terms we call this sin. That being the case, we cannot hope to repair, or perhaps more accurately, save ourselves. A broken machine cannot repair itself, no matter how much it wants to, no matter how hard it tries. Only the Designer of the machine can repair what has been broken and make it work properly. It's very clear that we need repairing. The only One who can do that is Jesus Christ.

Whatever the case may be (I'm not going to debate the issue of Adam and the connection of all humanity and sin here), in the *Book of the Beginning*, relating to the origin and the Fall of humankind (*Genesis*), we learn what God has to say in relation to humanity and the nature and product of sin.

- 53 -

God said to Adam and Eve, the first created human beings who fell into sin/the Fallen Nature, who having been tempted by the lies of the Evil One were led into the state of sin by choice, "(because of your sin) In the sweat of your face you shall eat bread till you return to the ground (Adam will have to work and then eventually die—death was a new concept on earth, the entropic nature of the universe an entirely new reality), for out of it (the ground) you were taken; for dust you are, and to dust you shall return" (Gen. 3:19). Adam's body was made to live forever, but when he fell into the fallen state (the state that all humanity is in now), he was informed that his body had changed. Now it would surely grow old and die, and as a direct result the human soul would face eternal separation from the Creator, and hell for humanity was born.

Speaking of hell, I'd like to point out here that many people say they believe in a God of heaven and dismiss the reality of a dark god of the abyss. The fact of the matter is all of the living belongs to either one or the other after passing on, the Father in Heaven or the devil in hell, for eternity! Beware of treating the evil one as a joke, for he is as real as you are. You will meet the dark god of the abyss if you do not believe in Jesus Christ.

THE DARK GOD OF THE ABYSS

This mighty angel (Lucifer) was cast out of heaven before the first human was created on earth. The hostility between God and Lucifer since the fall of humankind has pulled humanity into the conflict, an ongoing battle between the Holy Spirit and his helping angels and the unholy spirit and his helping demons. We are, quite frankly, caught right in the middle, and we cannot join the family of God or the fight because we are born sinners (born into the fallen state of existence). The only way we can join the fight is to accept him through his most holy and redeeming Son. Once done, we become something like priest/prayer warriors who engage in the battle on a second by second basis, whether we like it and whether we know it and whether we admit it or not.

THE LIGHT GOD OF HEAVEN

This is the reason why God sent his only beloved Son into the world as a man. He came in the flesh to our earth to take on all the sins of the people of the world so that we would be free under his grace. He came to this world to die as man, making his life a sacrifice to save us from our punishment so that we might live. He said to his disciples, "But after I have been raised (from the dead), I will go before you to Galilee" (Matt. 26:32). Life does not end after our earthly bodies die! In a very real sense, we follow the same pattern as God's Son! Jesus came to this earth to conquer death to save humanity. If we accept him as our Savior, believe in his death and resurrection, and trust that our sins are washed clean by the blood of the Lamb, we are then to God the fragrance of Christ. In return for accepting him, God gives us eternal life with Jesus in heaven forever, even forever and ever! We, the unrighteous, made righteous by his blood become an aroma of life!

Jesus died a cruel, humiliating physical death and then endured an incomprehensible spiritual death (in the sense that he spiritually went to hell in your place) to save his creation from the fallen nature and fallen prince of this world. He gave so much for us! In return, he requires that we believe in him. It is as simple as that! We don't have to belong to a particular church organization or cult. We don't have to meditate ourselves into the Mysterious Awareness through trance-inducing, mind expanding chants. We don't have to be good and nice enough because the fact is we can never *be* good or nice enough. Being Mr. or Ms. Nice will never save you. You could give all your money away and live a selfless life helping the needy, but without Christ that goodness amounts to nothing, for the Lord says, "They did not know me on earth, I do not know them in heaven" (Matt. 25:1-12; 31-46). We don't have to go through certain rituals or religious ceremonies that demand of us to do such and such or speak this or that or flip upside down and inside out or handle snakes or run around the sanctuary and bark like dogs. We don't have to speak in mystical tongues or believe we must be one of the 144,000 mentioned in Revelation. We don't have to be vegetarians, go to church on Saturday or follow the canon, dogma, system of belief of anyone else other than Christ, no need to follow addendums to the Scriptures, so-called *holy and divinely inspired* books written by Jones', Smiths, or Popes. We don't even have to be baptized, although it is wise to take this step to show faithfulness. Simply, there is nothing we can do to save ourselves, not a single, solitary thing. The saving must be done by the Savior—and that's the simplicity of Christ and his salvation. All we need to do is believe in him! The rest; how to and what to do will naturally follow; because your very nature will have been altered and you will be guided and heavily influenced by the loving hand of the Holy Spirit. Surely, then, goodness and mercy shall follow us all the days of our lives!

People need the Lord, and when we accept him the Spirit of Glory comes in! Let no one who waits on him be ashamed! Let him lead us in his truth and teach us. The humble he teaches his way! He loves whom he makes. He is the Creator of all life and longs to share his glorious kingdom with everyone. He wants to save—to repair—every broken living soul!

Revelation 1:5

...And from Jesus Christ, the faithful witness, the firstborn from the dead, and the ruler over the kings of the earth. To him who loves us and freed us from our sins in his own blood...

THESE WORDS COME FROM JESUS THE CHRIST

These sayings come from Jesus Christ and were revealed to John through the angel. The Lord is the faithful witness and the first and only one to return to life after death! (An explanation is forthcoming!) John explains that Jesus is ruler of all people on the earth, small and great. He loves them and frees them from their sins by washing them in his own blood that he shed on the cross.

Now, at this point, we know that each living person is born a sinner. We know what is meant by the terms *sin* and *fallen*. We know that our sins are forgiven by Jesus when we believe in him, believing that he rose from the dead and washed away our sins in his sacrificial blood. And we know as Jesus is the firstborn of the dead, we shall be resurrected in like manner.

In regard to resurrection Scripture says, "But now Christ is raised from the dead, and has become the first fruits of those who have fallen asleep. For since by man (Adam) came death, by man (Jesus) also came the resurrection of the dead. For as in Adam all die, even so in Christ all shall be made alive" (1Cor. 15:20–22). "But each one in his own order: Christ the first fruits, afterward those who are Christ's (his believers) at his coming" (1Cor. 15:23).

THE ORDER OF RAPTURES

I'd like us to look at the sequence of the seven raptures (or resurrections) as revealed in Scripture:

(1) The resurrection of Jesus.

(2) The resurrection of the Old Testament Saints and all the dead that were saved by God prior to the death and resurrection of Christ, immediately after the resurrection of Christ.

(3) 2,000 years pass (by God's timetable/calendar) and then the rapture of the dead in Christ takes place—this happens approximately in the middle of the Great Tribulation, the first part of his threefold Second Coming.

(4) The rapture of the living in Christ occurs immediately following the rapture of the dead in Christ, also the first part of his threefold Second Coming.

(5) Three-and-a-half years pass, and at the end of the seven year Tribulation the rapture of the Tribulation martyrs occurs, the second part of his threefold Second Coming.

(6) The rapture of the living 144,000 Jews occurs immediately following the rapture of the martyrs—also the second part of his threefold Second Coming.

(7) The rapture of the unsaved into the Second Phase of Body, the glorified body, at the end of the 1,000 years.

WHAT RAPTURE IS

Before I delve into more detail about the raptures, I should briefly explain what *rapture* is and where the word comes from, so that we have a common frame of reference as we read: the word *rapture* refers to resurrection of the soul/spirit after death into what I call glorified bodily form. In the case of the Fourth and Sixth Raptures, those living are ruptured into the glorified body, the Second Phase of Body, without facing physical death. But on the whole, most of humanity, whether lost or saved, will experience rapture after death into the Second Phase of Body, the glorified body. The saved in Christ will also experience a Third Phase of Body, the superglorified body, reserved only for the saved in Christ and therefore the body cycle made complete. The lost will never experience the Third Phase of Body and so will therefore forever remain incomplete.

The word rapture *is* in the New Testament (I Thessalonians 4:17). It can be found in the Latin translation: *rapiemur* meaning *to take away by force*. The word is found in one of the oldest Bibles in existence, the Latin Vulgate.[12]

THE FIRST RAPTURE

(1) The First Rapture.

The resurrection of Jesus Christ from the dead; Jesus was the first person to be resurrected from the dead and, clearly, the power of God raised him from the dead. John 3:13 says, "No one has ascended to heaven but he who came down from heaven, that is, the Son of Man who is in heaven."

There is no inherent conflict between the First Rapture and the rapture of the Old Testament prophets Elijah and Enoch because the First Rapture involves resurrection from the dead. Elijah and Enoch are the only anomalies that we know of who experienced a rare miraculous event called *living rapture* or *living translation*. They did not experience physical death. This was an act of God that will ever be veiled in mystery. But because they are tied to the time from whence they came, pre-Christ, they must face death.

The Lord will return them to the earth during the Great Tribulation as the Two Witnesses so that they can experience death and resurrection. (For related information on this subject, refer to Chapter 11:3, under the heading *They Must Face Death.*)

THE SECOND RAPTURE

(2) The Second Rapture.

The resurrection of all the dead that were saved by God prior to the death and resurrection of Christ, what would amount to millions and millions of people.

THE PLACES OF WAITING

The souls of those who died prior to the death and resurrection of Christ went to *the first place of waiting* for the dead, what most biblical scholars call *Abraham's Bosom/Sheol.* They waited there in spirit/soul for the atoning work of Christ and the Second Rapture.

A company of Old Testament Saints, prophets, and holy people experienced resurrection into the Second Phase of Body, the glorified body, immediately after Jesus rose from the dead, including such people as Abraham, Joseph, David, Solomon, Moses, and many others who loved the Lord. "And the graves were opened, and many bodies of the saints who had fallen asleep (died in the Lord) were raised; and coming out of the graves after his (Jesus') resurrection, they went into the holy city and appeared to many" (Matt. 27:52-53). Once again they were of body, soul, and spirit!

Some of those who were resurrected into the Second Phase of Body in the Second Rapture were seen in Jerusalem after the death and resurrection of Jesus. These Saints were permitted to return to the earth and be seen in their glorified body as a witness to the glory and power of Christ. Those who were raptured out of the spirit and into phase two of the Phase of Body, the glorified body, during the Second Rapture did not remain on the planet, but were either supernaturally taken to *the second place of waiting,* otherwise known as *Paradise,* soon thereafter or with Christ 40 days later at the Ascension. They reside in Paradise now in physical form.

In the Old Testament, the Hebrew word for the place where human souls reside after death is *Sheol, the world of the dead.* Sheol isn't entirely a place of torment, however, because the Scriptures suggest that the place is split in two. Half of it houses *Abraham's Bosom* and the other half houses *Sheol.* In the New Testament the Greek word is *Hades* and it is used in much the same way. The words describe the intermediate place and state of being of the dead for the good and the wicked, the lost and the saved still in spirit form: the first place of waiting houses the paradisiacal Abraham's Bosom and its hellish anti-equivalent, Sheol, the antiparadise.

Acts 2:34: "For David did not ascend into the heavens..." David instead went to the first waiting place, Abraham's Bosom/Sheol, remaining in spirit with the promise that he would someday be resurrected into the Second Phase of Body, the glorified body (Hosea 13:14). All people, the saved and the unsaved, were believed to go to Abraham's Bosom/Sheol, the first place of waiting when they died (Psalms 89:48).[13] And of course this is ongoing.

There are, in fact, three places of waiting:

(1) A *waiting place* for the spirit after death.

(2) A *waiting place* for the glorified body after the raptures!

(3) A third and final *waiting place for all the saved*: the reformed earth of the seventh millennium, the 1,000 years with Jesus. (For more information on Abraham's Bosom/Sheol and Paradise and the waiting places, refer to Chapter 6:9-10, under the headings *The Three Waiting Places* and *The Call for Justice*.)

THE THIRD RAPTURE

The next resurrection will occur two thousand years later (by God's timetable/calendar). This is known in modern Christian circles as *the Rapture*. The Third and Fourth Rapture happen simultaneously. They are the first component of the threefold Second Coming of Christ.

(3) The Third Rapture.

The resurrection of the dead saved in Christ. In the middle of the Great Tribulation all the saved in Christ who had died prior to or during that period of time (the two thousand years since Christ's birth) will be resurrected.

THE FOURTH RAPTURE

(4) The Fourth Rapture.

The resurrection of the living saved in Christ—Christians who are alive today eagerly anticipate this event because it is similar to what Elijah and Enoch experienced, a rare *living rapture* or *living translation*. Blessed are they that take part in the Fourth Rapture, for they will never experience physical death. They will transform from the first body to the second glorified body and God will forever keep the sting of physical death from them. If you are ready and prepared for the return of the Lord you will experience this living translation, as this is indeed the generation that will face the Great Tribulation. The Fourth Rapture will take place in the middle of the

Great Tribulation, just before the time when the Antichrist proclaims himself to be god.

It is a more than a little provocative to note here that we have nearly reached the two thousand year mark since Jesus was on the earth! The question then arises, are we approaching the period of the Antichrist, the Great Tribulation, the return of the Lord, and the end of our present Age? Surely so, but time will tell. (For an in-depth look at the timing of these events in light of the different dispensations, see the text following Revelation 1:19.)

Paul describes the Third and Fourth Rapture by saying, "I do not want you to be ignorant, brethren, concerning those who have fallen asleep, lest you sorrow as others who have no hope. For if we believe that Jesus died and rose again, even so God will bring with him those who sleep (died believing) in Jesus. For this we say to you by the word of the Lord, that we who are alive and remain until the coming of the Lord, by no means precede those who are dead. For the Lord himself will descend from heaven with a shout, with the voice of an archangel (Jesus), and with the trumpet of God (the voice of Jesus Christ)" (I Thes. 4:13-16a).

THE FIFTH RAPTURE

The Fifth and Sixth Raptures happen simultaneously. They are the second component of the threefold Second Coming of Christ.

(5) The Fifth Rapture.

The rapture of the martyred Christians who were slain by the Antichrist during the Great Tribulation. This rapture happens approximately three-and-a-half years after the Fourth Rapture, near the end of the Great Tribulation.

THE SIXTH RAPTURE

(6) The Sixth Rapture.

The rapture of the living 144,000—another rare *living rapture* or *living translation.* As with the Fourth Rapture, those who partake of the Sixth Rapture will never experience physical death. In the twinkling of an eye the rapture of the living denomination in Christ, the 144,000 servants of God, the supernaturally protected and sealed Jews, occurs!

The Fifth and Sixth Raptures will occur near the end of the seven years of the Great Tribulation, probably a few weeks before the return of Christ, prior to the bowl plagues and the removal of the Holy Spirit from the earth. We are told that, "...the dead in Christ will rise first (those who die knowing Jesus—in this instance, the martyrs). Then we (believers) who are alive and remain (the 144,000 chosen of God) shall be caught up together with them (the martyrs) in the clouds to meet the Lord in the air (the Sixth Rapture). And thus we shall always be with the Lord. Therefore comfort one another with these words" (1Thes. 4:16b-18). These verses apply to both raptures!

The third and final component of the threefold Second Coming of Christ is the literal return of Jesus Christ.

THE SEVENTH RAPTURE

(7) The Seventh Rapture.

One thousand years pass before the next and final resurrection/rapture, the rapture of the lost. This rapture will include everyone from the beginning of time who rejected God. They are resurrected into the Second Phase of Body, the glorified body. They will remain in the Second Phase of Body for eternity, forever incomplete. In regard to God's holy mathematics/geometry, the seventh rapture makes the sequences of raptures complete!

RAPTURE DEBATED

It should be pointed out here that the order of the raptures has been debated about for centuries within the Christian community, especially in regard to the rapture of the living Christians, the Fourth Rapture. There are those who argue the Fourth Rapture will be a *pre-Tribulation rapture*—it will take place before the Great Tribulation begins; *a mid-Tribulation rapture*—it will take place in the middle of the Great Tribulation (argued here); and finally a *post-Tribulation rapture*—it will occur at the end of the Great Tribulation (presumably before raptures Five and Six or perhaps simultaneously).

The reasons for each argument are varied, complex, and certainly compelling, but I'm convinced Scripture supports pre-Tribulation or mid-Tribulation rapture. They are both the most scripturally accurate. I am most convinced that the Fourth Rapture will take place in the middle of Tribulation because of the *Doctrine of Imminency*, which teaches us to expect him at any moment (Phil. 3:20; Titus 2:13; Hebrews 9:28; 1Thes. 1:10; 4:18; 5:6; Rev. 22:20), and because the Bible paints a clear picture that one of the driving purposes of the Fourth Rapture will be to remove all living Christians (those expecting his return) from the earth so that they will not have to face the horrors of the last three-and-a-half years of the Great Tribulation. You are encouraged to study it further on your own so that you can make an informed decision.

BE READY

Be ready for the coming of the Fourth Rapture before the Antichrist is in full control of the earth! Blessed are those who are taken at that time, when the world is given to the Beast. Lukewarm believers in Jesus who are not prepared for his coming will not partake of this Fourth Rapture. They will be left behind to face certain death by the wrath of the Antichrist. He knows that he will only have a very short time: three-and-one-half years. This is the time when the Antichrist makes war with the believers that will be left behind. We are informed that "...The dragon (the evil one) was enraged with the woman (the Church of Jesus Christ, particularly the 144,000 Jews who believe in Jesus, supernaturally protected by the Holy Spirit) ..." (Rev. 12:17). Satan will be prevented from harming this great company, as we shall learn, and therefore goes all out to "make war with the rest of her offspring (the martyrs of Jesus Christ who do not partake of the Fourth Rapture), who keep the commandments of God and have the testimony of Jesus Christ" (Rev. 12:17).

The parable of the ten virgins (Matt. 25) reveals that only half of all who believe in/and are saved by Christ are ready for the Lord's return, making them worthy to be raptured. They are taken (the Fourth Rapture) from the earth by Jesus solely to spare them from the fury of the Antichrist. They will meet the Lord in the air!

Believers who are not ready for the coming of the Lord will be left behind to face the hateful Antichrist's rage and the horrors of the last three-and-one-half-years of the Human Age. They will remain on the earth and they will meet the Beast head on. No believing Christians will survive, not one!

"Then the kingdom of heaven shall be likened to ten virgins (representing all living believers in Jesus) who took their lamps and went out to meet the Bridegroom (Jesus). Now five of them were wise (half of all living believers are living their lives in the Spirit of the Lord, anticipating the coming of the Lord, are clean and open vessels through which Christ can flow), and five were foolish (half of all living believers are asleep in Christ, living carnal lives, caught up in themselves, not paying attention to the movement of the Spirit). Those who were foolish went with their lamps and took no oil with them, but the wise took oil in their vessels with their lamps.

"But while the Bridegroom (Jesus) was delayed, they all slumbered and slept (for many believers are not expecting his return to happen so soon). And at midnight a cry was heard: 'Behold, the bridegroom (Jesus) is coming; go out to meet him!' Then all those virgins rose and trimmed their lamps. And the foolish said to the wise, 'Give us some of your oil, for our lamps are going out' (their spiritual lights were fading, as they were spiritually lukewarm; they desired strength from the believers whose light was burning brightly for the Lord). But the wise answered, saying, 'No, lest there should not be enough for us and you, but go rather to those who sell, and buy for yourselves.' And while they went to buy (sought spiritual help among themselves), the Bridegroom came, and those who were ready went in with him to the wedding (the Fourth Rapture), and the door was shut. Afterward, the other (lukewarm or apostate natured) virgins came also, saying, 'Lord, Lord, open to us!' But he answered and said, 'Assuredly, I say to you, I do not know you. Watch therefore, for you know neither the day nor the hour" (Matt. 25:1–13).

He comes like a thief, unannounced!

The faithful wait for you, Son of Man. The desire of their souls is for your name, and for the remembrance of you. They long for you day and night. With the Spirit within them, they seek you earnestly, for when your judgments are on the earth, they want to be under your wing!

THE ORDER OF BODY

Now, we understand better the order of the raptures, but I'd like to clarify the difference between spirit/soul and body, in reference to the raptures and the three Phases of Body.

Scripture makes it clear that there's a difference between spirit/soul and body. When a human being dies on this earth the soul/spirit goes to the waiting place, and it doesn't go there in bodily form—for the body stays behind and turns into dust. What goes there is pure spirit/soul. For example, when the Third Rapture occurs the spirits/souls that have been waiting since their deaths (waiting in spirit/soul form) will be raptured into their glorified body, phase two of the three Phases of Body, by Jesus Christ.

Here is a word of wisdom! Every believer will experience three bodies. This should not come as a surprise, as three bodies represent the Trinity, which is completion! Sadly, every nonbeliever, those not saved by Christ, will experience only two.

THE PHASE OF BODY
PHASE I
The Fallen Entropic Body

(1) The First Body.

Our present fleshly and fallen natured bodies that last roughly 75 years on this earth.

PHASE II
The Glorified Non-entropic Body

(2) The Second Body.
The glorified body that is eternal in nature, both physical and spiritual, but not fully divine.

PHASE III
The Superglorified Non-entropic Body

(3) The Third Body.
The superglorified body, phase three of the Phase of Body, fully body, fully spirit, fully divine! We will experience the Third Body at the end of the Kingdom Age, the very moment we are transferred to the New Earth within the Second Heaven. Once again, we find we have a very consistent God, for his wonders always fall into the category of threes and sevens. (For related information on the holy mathematics /geometry of God refer to 1:19.)

THE INCOMPLETE BODY OF THE LOST

The lost will receive their second and only glorified bodies after their resurrection/rapture (the Seventh Rapture) at the conclusion of the seventh millennium. The lost will be in the first place of waiting or Abraham's Bosom/Sheol in soul/spirit form until the end of the thousand years, wherein they will be raptured into their Second (and only or final) Phase of Body, join Lucifer in his attempt to sway the Saints and corrupt the nature of humanity one last and final time, and then proceed to Judgment and eternal damnation in the lake of fire, which is Satan's kingdom in the bowels of this very earth. (For additional information on the lake of fire and the bottomless pit, refer to Chapter 5:3, under the heading *Under the Earth*.)

Again, the unsaved will only receive two bodies—their present fleshly bodies that last roughly 75 years and the Second Phase of Body, the glorified body, given to them at their rapture, lasting an eternity. Because they reject Jesus, they will not be rewarded with the superglorified transfiguration, the third glorified body; therefore, they will never be complete while suffering in the abyss, and this is part of the reason why it is called their second death. (For additional information on this subject matter refer to Chapters 6:14, under the heading *Great Cosmic Disturbances*, 7:16, under the heading *A New Reality*, 8:1, under the heading *A Controversial Subject* and *Kingdom Age Reproduction*.)

Revelation 1:6

...and [Jesus] has made us a kingdom and priests to his God and Father, to him be glory and dominion forever and ever. Amen.

KINGS & PRIESTS

The Spirit of the Lord continues to speak and his words are on John's lips! The writer declares that in the splendor and bliss of the kingdom of God, Christ makes his believers kings and priests. His dominion is glorified and his believers serve him and his Father forevermore.

These kings and priests will serve Christ during the one thousand years on this reformed earth, where he will rule his kingdom and control his government from the world's capital city of Jerusalem! This amazing new life begins at the conclusion of this present Age and the beginning of the seventh millennium.

When the Kingdom Age (the one thousand years on the reformed earth, the seventh millennium) is over, Jesus tells us that these kings and priests (all of his faithful) will then be transferred from this planet to a stupendous New Earth that exists in a new reality beyond or outside of time, what I call the Second Heaven where we will live in glorious harmony with Jesus for eternity, even forever and ever. (See the text following Revelation 1:19 for further explanation of the seventh millennium.)

HEAVENS

Just so it's clear, there are three heavens. (We'll get into this in more detail in Chapter 3.)

(1) The First Heaven.

This is the Father's Heaven where only the Father and his heavenly angels reside on the First Earth.

(2) The Second Heaven.

This is the Son's Heaven where the Saints will live with Jesus on the New Earth for eternity.

(3) The Third Heaven.

This is the Holy Spirit's Heaven where we exist in now, living on this earth, the Third Earth.

In many ways we have yet to understand the three heavens are One, just like the Father, Son, and Holy Spirit are One. Living in the Son's Heaven is living in the Father's Heaven! Jesus tells us if we have seen the Son, we have seen the Father. Likewise, if we have seen the Second Heaven we have seen the First. (For further information on the three heavens refer to Chapter 3:21, under the heading, *Three Heavens Explored!*)

Revelation 1:7

Behold, he is coming with clouds, and every eye will see him, and they also who pierced him. And all the tribes [nations] of the earth will mourn because of him. Even so, amen.

PREDICTION IN THE CLOUDS

John is summoned by the angel of Jesus. The words the angel says to the writer are these: "Look ahead, for Christ returns with the clouds!"

He informs John that every eye shall see Jesus' second great coming, on earth and otherwise, even the eyes of those who originally nailed him to the cross—how can that be? We will touch only briefly the possibility: those who are now outside of time, i.e. the dead and the ruptured, will be able to see his coming too. Essentially, it's the combination of literal sight (the living remaining on earth) and a spiritual sight that allows every human, living or dead, to see the return of Christ! In addition, the holy angels will witness the return, making themselves present exclusively to witness his great Second Coming. (See Chapter Six, in the text following Rev. 6:13.)

This hope awaits those who are ready and who love the Lord, for he is high above all, and his glory is above the heavens! The horn of his trumpet is exalted with honor from this time forth and forever!

THE EARTH WILL MOURN

Jesus not only confirms that every eye will see him when he returns, but that those on the earth, the remaining unrepentant, will mourn: "Then the sign of the son of man will appear in heaven, and then all the tribes (people) of the earth will mourn, and they will see the son of man coming on the clouds of heaven with power and great glory" (Matt. 24:30). The people that remain on earth will be spiritually dead toward Christ, and they will mourn because they have chosen not to know him. At the roaring of the Lion, the hair on their bodies will stand! Fear and trembling will come upon them, making all their bones shake! By the blast of Jesus, they will perish, and by the breath of his anger, they will be consumed!

When the Son returns he will reform the old earth and utterly destroy the unrepentant by global fire, earthquake, and hail; there will be no survivors. (This will be revealed in Chapter Six of these writings!) You might say this is very harsh. But you must understand that the Holy and Perfect God cannot accept any form of wickedness—all sin, no matter its depth of disobedience, is equal in the eyes of the Father. Therefore, he consumes the last of the unrepentant on earth. Pray that you escape this devastation, that you receive a new body and partake of the new life on the reformed earth! Be glorified by accepting Jesus Christ as your Lord and Savior. Your consideration in doing this is much encouraged, as it is a matter of eternal life or eternal death!

THE MOUNT

Jesus returns from above! His precious feet, marked by the nails that pierced him while hanging on the cross, will touch the Mount of Olives, the ridge of hills east of Jerusalem—and the very ground will split in two! I am absolutely convinced that this will occur at precisely the place where Christ was at the time he ascended into heaven two thousand years ago (Acts 1:11), the area known as the Mount of Ascension where the Church of the Ascension is built! The Mount of Olives is the holy location where the Lord Jesus Christ will proclaim his world government and rule his faithful followers!

THE NEW CITY OF JERUSALEM

Under his most holy and loving shadow they will walk through the new gates of Jerusalem (a new city which has appeared, not out of the debris of the old world, but completely out of nothing) into the seventh millennium, the Kingdom Age. It is Jerusalem proper that is the location that Christ requires! The State of Israel today is part of that land promised to Abraham by the Lord—it belongs to Israel and to the Lord. It is a place of holiness, in spite of the turmoil there.

FATHER ABRAHAM

The site of the city was chosen by the Lord long ago, during the time of Abraham. Let's nutshell Abraham here: he was the first father and leader of the Hebrew people, the father of Isaac. A native of Chaldea, a ninth generation descendant of Shem, the son of Noah, he was born in 2161 B.C. (Gen. 11.27). Abraham means *the father of a multitude*. He was told by God to leave his homeland and cross to the land that God would show him and give him, which is now Israel (Gen 12:1; Acts 7:2–3).

HISTORIC JERUSALEM

Now, I'd like to pause at this point and look back upon the historic city of Jerusalem: the city of Jerusalem stands on the same place/location where it was built thousands of years ago. The earliest record of Jerusalem is found in the description of the boundaries of Judah and Benjamin in the Old Testament (Josh. 5, 18). The history of the city from the time of Joshua to its destruction by Titus is a period of fifteen centuries. (It has existed for 38 centuries and is considered the oldest continuously inhabited city in the world!) It is a city historically littered with revolutions, sieges, surrenders, famines and on and on! It is believed that Jerusalem was founded by Amorites and Hittites (Ezek. 16:3, 45). As for the name of the city, over time the second part of the name became associated with the Hebrew word *shalom* (meaning *peace*), and so the name/word *Jerusalem* came to mean *city of peace*. (As it turns out, there is a certain amount of irony in this fact, as the city of peace is the most unstable and *peaceless* city that has ever existed.) It was the first city of Palestine, and today it is the holy city for three of the world's great religions: Judaism, Christianity, and Islam.[14]

Jerusalem will continue its importance in history and become the capital of the world during Christ's thousand year reign on earth during the Kingdom Age (the final human age in time). After the seventh millennium, the new and most holy city that comes down from God's First Heaven, resting on the heavenly New Earth as a great and impressive shrine forevermore (clearly, outside of time at this point), will be called Jerusalem! (A detailed account of this wonder is found in Chapter 21.)

THREE CITIES OF JERUSALEM!

Following this line of thought, the New Jerusalem, the one that will exist outside of time in eternal perfection after the Kingdom Age, will be a replica of God's illustrious holy shrine in heaven where he dwells (in the First Heaven). This holy shrine must and certainly will be called Jerusalem, for they are one. (We are to honor old Jerusalem on earth and always pray for its safety and the safety of his people there, for this is sacred ground.)

We learn of three cities of Jerusalem! One is in God's First Heaven, glorifying the Father; one is in God's Second Heaven, known as the New Earth, glorifying the Son; and the other is on God's present earth, glorifying the Holy Spirit—always three, depicting the Holy Trinity to satisfy the Godhead! The present city of Jerusalem will be reformed along with the earth when Christ returns, but it will still be a continuation of the present city, for Jesus will establish it on the same site and, in fact, on the same world!

THREE GARDENS OF EDEN!

Most bible scholars agree that the existing city of Jerusalem and the land of Israel are situated where the Garden of Eden once flourished on earth, made specifically for the children of God (a reproduction of God's Garden of Eden that exists in the First Heaven). In Ezekiel 28:12–13, we are informed that, "...you...the king of Tyre (Lucifer) ...were in Eden, the Garden of God (in heaven, before the earth was even created) ..." Since Jesus' domain is one with the Father's domain, then assuredly Jesus' New Earth also has a Garden of Eden, like the one found in God's heaven. Another amazing discovery! Three Eden's in one!

(1) The First Eden glorifies the Father in the First Heaven.

(2) The Second Eden glorifies the Son on the New Earth in the Second Heaven.

(3) The Third Eden glorifies the Holy Spirit on this earth in the Third Heaven! The garden (reformed) on the reformed earth is a continuation of the Eden that was on earth in the beginning! Always three, depicting the Trinity! God is outstandingly consistent!

The reformed earth, which will last a thousand years (the Kingdom Age), will have Jerusalem as its sacred world capital, Eden as the Son's sacred garden, and Jesus as the people's sacred living temple! Blessed are those who believe in the Lord Jesus Christ and those who read the words, understand them, and take to heart that which is written in this book. The mind of the Lord is beyond comprehension. You will find that the Holy Trinity and the Seven Spirits of God are found to dominate the very pattern of our existence!

Revelation 1:8

"I am the Alpha and the Omega, the Beginning and the End," says the Lord, "who is and who was and who is to come, the Almighty."

JESUS, THE BEGINNING & THE END

Christ speaks to John out of a whirlwind (the Holy Spirit). He causes his powerful voice to be heard saying, "(Listen to me and hear my speech :) I am the ALPHA AND THE OMEGA (the first and last letters of the Greek alphabet, used here to signify the eternity of God; see also Rev. 21:6; 22:13; and Isa. 44:6), THE BEGINNING

AND THE END (the Lord is called the Beginning by Paul and John in Clo. 1:18 and Rev 1:8; 3:14)"

Again, it's important to remember that the Father, Son, and Holy Spirit exist outside of time and that they have always existed forever there in something like a perpetual state of *now*—these words, Alpha, Omega, Beginning, End, are merely symbols to help us (finite creatures existing in time) try to grasp the concept of timelessness and the infinite.

He repeats this important fact by saying he is the One *who is from the beginning, who was* when crucified, and *who is to come* when his mighty return takes place at the end of this Age. Then he sets his glory among his nations of believers by proclaiming that he is the Almighty. Blessed is the one whom Jesus instructs! He is the great Teacher, and we who spend eternity with him will never know him completely, even though our knowledge of him will be complete—in a way, God is like an onion: you can peel away layer after layer in eternity and never get to the core because there is no core. There is only layer after layer after layer. In a very real sense we will know God deeply, but we will always be learning who God is too.

Revelation 1:9

I, John, your brother and companion in tribulation and in the kingdom and patience of Jesus Christ, was on the island that is called Patmos for the word of God and for the testimony of Jesus Christ.

PRISONER OF THE ISLAND PATMOS

Jesus' angel is about to present John with an awesome picture of God's Son. Before revealing this wonder, John explains that he is our brother in Christ Jesus and our companion in tribulation. He says he joins us in spreading the kingdom and patience of Jesus Christ. He suffered for preaching the truth.

John seems to have been a circuit minister at the seven churches of Asia, Ephesus, Pergamum, Smyrna, Thyatira, Sardis, Philadelphia, and Laodicea. He was confined as a prisoner on the lonely Patmos Isle in the Aegean Sea, one of the Dodecanese Islands (13 square miles in area) in the 15th year of Emperor Domitian, according to the historian Eusebius. (The date of the writing of the book has already been mentioned—96 A.D.—but I should point out that some scholars date it at around 68 A.D. I find their arguments for choosing the date unconvincing, especially in light of the fact that Eusebius, Irenaeus, and Clement agree historically that John's banishment to Patmos happened during the reign of Domitian, 81–96 A.D.)[15]

John was placed on Patmos by God purposefully: to be alone to receive this divine vision, giving him the time required to write the Word of God and the Testimony of Jesus Christ. It seems that John may have completed the work in a cave that still exists today.

Revelation 1:10

I was in the Spirit on the Lord's Day, and I heard behind me a loud voice, as of a trumpet...

IN THE SPIRIT ON THE LORD'S DAY

Behold, on the Lord's Day John is taken to see things that must come to pass. The meaning of Lord's Day here refers to the day Christ is predicted to return to earth. It is not necessarily a literal reference to the Sabbath—throughout the Book of Revelation John is being pulled from his time to a future time, even to places beyond or outside of time, by the Bender of Time and Space, Christ himself. John is being yanked in and out of the spiritual realm, into alternate realities and dimensions, and the only way that this could be humanly possible and survivable, of course, is complete and total immersion *in* the Spirit of God!

Behind him he hears a loud voice sounding like a trumpet—it is the voice of Jesus.

Revelation 1:11

...Saying "I am the Alpha and the Omega, the First and the Last," and "What you see, write in a book and send it to the seven churches which are in Asia: to Ephesus, to Smyrna, to Pergamos, to Thyatira, to Sardis, to Philadelphia, and to Laodicea."

JOHN IS TOLD TO WRITE

Jesus, the Alpha, the Omega, the First, the Last, tells John to write a book about the things revealed to him, and to let the book be known throughout the seven congregations that worship Jesus in the Asian cities of Ephesus, Smyrna, Pergamos, Thyatira, Sardis, Philadelphia, and Laodicea. The Son, who has the Seven Spirits of God, heads the seven churches, and it should be pointed out here that these seven churches are the representational model for every possible type of Christian (there are many variations to the themes, of course) throughout the ages to our present day.

Revelation 1:12

Then I turned to see the voice that spoke with me. And having turned I saw seven golden lamp stands...

THE SEVEN GOLDEN LAMP STANDS

John turned to see the Person who spoke to him and saw seven golden lamp stands. The meaning of the lamp stands is layered:

(1) They represent the Seven Spirits of Life or Jesus Christ himself—remember, the Book of Revelation is the *Book of Jesus*, the Christ, the only Savior of all humanity!

(2) This is a direct reference to the Golden Lamp Stand that stood within the Tabernacle of Israel, the place where man met God. Thus, it suggests that Christ has now become the Golden Lamp Stand or that he stands in its place.

(3) Jesus is the light of the world and like a burning lamp stand, he shines upon us the awesome radiance of his divine life and love!

Interestingly, there was no natural light within the Tabernacle, which when applied here seems to suggest that we human beings exist in a lightless world. You could say that we live within the darkened walls of the Tabernacle and Christ, our Golden Lamp Stand and only light source, illuminates our way. (1 Cor. 2:14-15).[16]

Revelation 1:13

...and in the midst of the seven lamp stands One like the Son of Man, clothed with a garment down to the feet and girded about the chest with a golden band.

THE BURNING LAMP STAND OF CHRIST

In the middle of the seven lamp stands, John sees Jesus, the Son of Man, dressed with a garment down to his feet, circled with a golden band across his chest. Glorious things are spoken of him. His foundation is the holy mountain (New Earth)! Righteousness looks down from heaven, and the Most High himself establishes his government on earth for all mankind!

Revelation 1:14

His head and his hair were white like wool, as white as snow, and his eyes like a flame of fire.

THE BRIGHTNESS OF CHRIST

John is permitted to see the Glory of Jesus!

His head and his hair are white like the brightness of wool, as white as snow—simply, the power within Christ is blinding, and the only way John can explain it is through beautiful, nature-inspiring metaphor: the brightness of glittering snow on a cloudless day at the rising of the morning sun!

His eyes are like a flame of fire. In Daniel 7:9 his garments are described as white as snow, his throne as a fiery flame, and its wheels—all representational of Christ and his power—as a burning fire. The disciples James, Peter, and John also witnessed Christ's glory while he lived on earth. Matthew explains in the seventeenth chapter of his book, verse two, that, "...He [Jesus] was transfigured before them. His face shone like the sun, and his clothes became as white as the light!" John is witness to the exuberant glory of the Lord Jesus Christ! No wonder he illuminates the new city of Jerusalem by his mere presence alone. (Refer to Chapter 21:1 for more detailed information on the subject of the New Jerusalem.) No wonder Paul was blinded by the presence of the Lord, for he tells us in Acts 26:13, "...at midday...along the road I saw a light from heaven, brighter than the sun (the presence of Jesus), shining around me and those who journeyed with me." From the brightness before him, he lights our lamps! The Lord our God lightens our darkness!

SPIRITUAL LIGHTS & INSIGHTS

Now hear this, for I am convinced that there are some who have the God-given gift of seeing this spiritual *light* shining from human beings while existing on this old, fallen earth. This is the light of the Spirit of God within each living soul. The more open the person is through which Christ can flow, the greater and more radiant the brightness becomes! "...And his (Jesus') countenance was like the sun shining in its strength" (Rev. 1:16b).

It should be pointed out here that this reference to spiritual light is not the same as the contemporary concept of *human auras*, which suggests that all human bodies naturally emit a glowing light, a concept that is often associated with the New Age movement. It's very clear that human bodies do not have auras. There is no energy field found around or emitting from human bodies—this is the conclusion reached and held by the contemporary scientific and medical communities.[17]

The light I'm discussing here is purely spiritual, having a connection with the Creator and the Spirit, the cause and effect of the light of the Spirit, not the physical fallen human body.

Allow me to explain further: those who are deep within the Spirit, those precious few who are saved and seek a much deeper path of experience and understanding with God, are blessed with a radiant spiritual countenance. Indeed, they do have a special *shine* about them that most of us sense indirectly—especially in their eyes, for the eyes are the windows to the soul! You can feel it when you confront them, for this is the love of the Holy Spirit, the indwelling Christ, shining and moving through them.

There are a few people who God has blessed with the gift of seeing or sensing this spiritual light surrounding humans, and they tell us that some deeply spiritual people are found to have this spiritual light radiance projecting six to eight inches from the body. The average for most of us, it seems, is somewhere along the lines of an inch or less! This spiritual shine appears like rising heat from the desert floor and is released around the body, sometimes in glowing white, sometimes in soft tones of color such as a pastel-mauve, turquoise, gold or purple! The Spirit is not invisible, but full of amazing color! Imagine the immense blinding light and color flowing from the Lord Jesus Christ, the Son of the Living God, he who has the Seven Living Spirits of the Almighty!

Let it be known, "The (new) city (of Jerusalem on the New Earth) had no need of the sun or of the moon to shine, for the very glory of God illuminated it. The Lamb (Jesus) is its light" (Rev. 21:23). "...I (Jesus, the Bright Morning star, the Light) will give him (the believer) the morning star" (Rev. 2:28). Become like Christ. Receive his light so that you can be blameless in a crooked and perverse generation among whom you can shine as radiant spiritual lights in the bleak and darkened world!

Revelation 1:15

His feet were like fine brass, as if refined in a furnace, and his voice as the sound of many waters.

REFINED BRASS & MANY WATERS

The Lord's angel shows John even more, for he sees Jesus' feet glowing, again connecting Jesus with the quality of radiant light. He turns to his voice: having the capacity to exercise all authority, it sounds like the roaring of the seven seas and it is as forceful as the sound of seven rushing rivers. John connects the Almighty Son of God with extreme brightness marked by extraordinary command!

Revelation 1:16

He had in his right hand seven stars, out of his mouth went a sharp two-edged sword, and his countenance was like the sun shining in its strength.

HIS HOLY COUNTENANCE

Jesus holds seven stars in his right hand.

Right hand is used here as a strong graphic image, not necessarily suggesting the literal right hand of Christ. In other words, because the original meaning in Greek is subtle enough not to fully translate into English very well when the word *hand* is added to *left* or *right* it only relates to a literal hand some of the time—that being the case, and since the right hand is considered in many cultures as a traditional symbol of goodness or truth as well, it's clear that its use here is as a graphic image intended to show the power of Christ.[18]

The seven stars represent the seven angels of the seven companies (churches), which in turn represent the Seven Spirits of God—all equaling Jesus! The fact that the Son of God holds seven stars tells us that he is in complete control of everything, including the universe entire, and that would include the body of Christ—he is in fact its head. He is saying, in essence, "I AM THE SEVEN STARS. I AM THE CHURCH. I AM THE SEVEN SPIRITS OF GOD."

A sharp two-edged sword projects from his mouth, informing us of the utter strength of the Word of God and the fact that it cuts both ways, for those who hear the Word as well as for those who speak it.

The Son of God is a shining wonder! He is as blinding as the brightest star! His garments are as white as the brightness of snow! The hair on his head glows like white wool on the brightest day! He is God, all power and all strength! The scene that John is witness to is extremely holy—after being in the presence of the Holy Lord is it any wonder that he is called John, the divine?

Revelation 1:17

And when I [John] saw him, I fell at his feet as dead. But he [Jesus] laid his right hand on me, saying, "Do not be afraid; I am the First and the Last."

JOHN FALLS AS IF DEAD

Finally, after witnessing the splendor, glory and might of Jesus, John is given the privilege of seeing through the blinding light of the Savior's brilliant brightness. To John, it must have been like suddenly being able to look directly at the sun without it hurting his eyes! He views Christ—and appropriately enough falls at the Lord's feet as if dead. Instead of burning John up into a bit of well-done mortal steak, this fiery, blinding, blazing God, Jesus, the Christ, does the most loving of things: he gently touches John with his right hand and says, "Do not be afraid; *I am* the First and the Last (forevermore, even forever and ever, amen)!"

Revelation 1:18

"I am he who lives, and was dead, and behold, I am alive forevermore. Amen. And I have the keys of Hades and of Death."

JESUS HAS THE KEYS TO LIFE & DEATH

Jesus is Life, that's what he's telling John here. As flesh, he came to earth. He conquered death after dying on the cross. Then, on the third day, he rose from the grave, alive for eternity. He confirms that, ultimately, he is in control of Satan, for he has the keys to the gates of Hades (the abyss) and Death. Satan portrays only death, for he and his followers are dead toward Christ.

Revelation 1:19

"Therefore, write the things which you have seen, and the things which are, and the things which will take place after this."

BEFORE GOING ON

From here on out, in regard to this particular verse and the rest of this manual, some of the material that will be discussed will include terminology and ideas that deal with quantum physics. Although I won't delve deeply into this complex area of science, I will brush the surface. You are encouraged to pursue the science in depth on your own.

When discussing high concepts in regard to the reality of God (outside time/beyond time, angels, demons, spiritual reality, heaven, hell, et al), I will often use the word *hyperdimensional* to describe the reality. This term alludes to realities beyond our experience and comprehension (for the most part) and for the purposes of this manual it should be understood that it is used as a *very broad defining label*. Now, let's explore classic and quantum physics together so that we have a common frame of reference as we read.

CLASSICAL & QUANTUM PHYSICS

Quantum theory not only specifies new rules for describing this universe, it introduces new ways of thinking about matter and energy, explaining the nature and behavior of matter and energy on the atomic and subatomic level.[19] Objects described by classical physics always have definite locations, speeds, paths, etc. But quantum theory describes extremely small bits of subatomic particles that do not have definite locations, speeds, paths. Because of this classical physics cannot be applied at the subatomic level—it just doesn't work. A new form of physics had to be created to, essentially, try to explain the bizarre behavior of the universe at the atomic and subatomic level: that answer was quantum physics.

On the subatomic level particles seem to do all sorts of truly bizarre things. For example, they don't move from point A to point B in an uninterrupted manner, as you might imagine they would or think they should, like a ball rolling from point A to point B— well, they just don't do that. What do they do? The particles *quantum jump* instead, that is to say, light-emitting electrons inside atoms instantaneously *jump* or *quantum leap* from one place to another. This has been verified mathematically and experimentally field tested. Experiments with subatomic particles have even confirmed that certain fields seem to have, for lack of a better word, intelligence.[20] For example, at the atomic and subatomic levels an atomic particle or photon of light can be a wave, but once we observe it the wave collapses and the same wave we were observing becomes a particle. Why? The answer seems to be *because of our observation of it.*

Further down the rabbit hole: when matter is broken down into smaller and smaller bits—electrons, protons, neurons—it eventually reaches the point where none of those bits posses the character or behavior of the original bit. They can behave like the particles in question, but they're effectively *dimensionless*, and that's in a literal sense all over the universe, what quantum physicists call *non-locality.*

Non-locality helps us grasp, in the most limited way, how Jesus can be everywhere at once and how he can be intimately connected to everyone everywhere at exactly the same time, all over and through the universe—omnipresent or non-locality. Take your pick. Both words define it.

Going even further, if a particle moves from one quantum state to another when it jumps or leaps it's like switching a computer bit from one state (1) to another (0).[21] This means, simply put, that quantum systems can exist in two incompatible states at once, a condition known as superposition.[22] This seems to support the concept of multidimensional reality and the crosspollination of realities—much of what the Book of Revelation is, in fact, revealing. It's likely that our earth/universe/time/reality is only part of a much larger and probably multidimensional reality or whole.[23] That of all Creation. The spiritual world, as well as our own reality, may simply exist within it, or more specifically, in the order of the reality of the First Heaven, the reality of the Second

Heaven, and the reality of the Third Heaven, our reality, and of course the multidimensional potential is infinite. In regard to the holy mathematics/geometry of God and his adherence to patterns and systems, it seems reasonable to conclude that there may indeed only be three realities/dimensions, but of course this is arguable.

To complicate matters, because of the bizarre behavior of these *dimensionless elements* which make up the universe entire, as well as additional evidence involving quantum physics and the nature of the universe, eschatological scholar Dr. Chuck Missler, a vocal and enthusiastic proponent of this theory, claims the data hints at the possibility that the universe may be digital in nature, or at least similar in concept, arguing that we may exist within something very much like a giant hologram, a computer simulation or program, a *Star Trek* holodeck.[24] Of course, if this were true it could lend support to Designer/Creator/Creation and the potential for multiple planes of existence (spiritual dimension). In light of the supernatural nature of God and all the amazing possibilities, as well as provocative verses in the Bible relating to the universe/reality and God, and the strong endorsement from the field of quantum physics this claim doesn't seem at all far-fetched.

Chapter 20:11, under the heading *Earth & Heaven Flee*, discusses the removal of this earth and universe after the final judgment, and in light of the so-called digital discoveries concerning the potential digital nature of our universe, coupled with Chuck Missler's digital theory—and as he often points out—it is not at all difficult to imagine how an entire universe could flee from the face of God if it is digital or something like digital in nature. In a simplified sense, it would be like removing or moving a digital data file within a computer: point on the universe and click.

Finally, the official view of quantum mechanics, called the Copenhagen Interpretation, states that nothing is there until we observe it. There is also the Many Worlds Interpretation (or universes) theory of Hugh Everett which suggests that every time you make a decision you jump into a new universe. Another view is that of David Bohm and Basil Hailey called the Quantum Potential Theory, which suggests that the universe is interconnected in a deep and dimly perceived way, on a level where time and space don't count.[25] That's the one I tend to lean toward.

WHAT YOU DO MATTERS

Ultimately, this information does not affect our individual experiential reality in any way, for clearly, even if we exist in a digital universe, our choices, actions, and the consequences of those choices/actions remain very real. Digital or not, what you do in this life matters.

What should be clear from the information provided above is that quantum physics studies the very boundaries of physical reality and those studies can take us to some pretty mind bending places. Similarly, like the behavior of the universe, quantum physics can help us understand the behavior of the Book of Revelation, a book which itself not only studies the very boundaries of physical reality in relation to humanity and the universe, but the infinite mysteries and complex behavior of God, who by his very nature takes us to some *pretty mind bending places.*

Before going further, I think it's important and fair-minded to point out here that there are some within the Christian scientific community who disapprove of the pursuit of trying to explain the physics of God and creation, the Fall, the spiritual world, angels and demons, believing the pursuit well intended but ultimately pointless and perhaps even destructive, for they argue it reduces an unexplainable, faith-centered phenomena to more human and therefore mundane terms.[26] By using these physical explanations we're putting God in an easily defined, understood and limiting box (from the human perspective), when clearly God is far beyond the box—when, in fact, he made the box. What this information should do for Christians, the argument continues, is remind each and every one of us of the enormous difference between humanity and God, as well as define the power and purpose of faith.[27]

THE PREDICTIONS

That which will take place before the coming of the Lord's Day.

Now, moving on, I'd like to explain further what *the Day of the Lord* really means: it is the greatest event of all time, for it is the day when Christ returns to this planet, spoken of as the Second Great Coming of the Lord Jesus Christ. He returns to establish his kingdom on earth, the final Age in time, the Kingdom Age of one thousand years. The Holy Age follows, for at the end of the Kingdom Age time ceases to exist! On the Lord's Day he will sit on his throne and usher in the seventh millennium, the New Age of Rest for his people—a wonderful thousand years (in perfect time) when his faithful prepare for the coming of the New Earth which will exist beyond or outside of time.

There is a number pattern here:

6,000 years of sin and death.

1,000 years of sinless life and rest.

6,000 + 1,000 = 7,000.

The pattern fits beautifully with the six days of creation/seventh day of rest blueprint.

Additionally, the Kingdom Age is the beginning of the new millennium, the third millennium since the birth of Jesus; the seventh millennium since the Fall of humanity (by God's true timetable/calendar).

3 and 7.

3 represents the Holy Trinity; 7 is the sacred number of the Lord.

Are we seeing a consistent God here?

HEAVEN & EARTH

Let's change gears for a moment: we're gaining an understanding of the importance of the perception and understanding of time and of the Day of the Lord, but where does heaven and earth fit in? We hear repeatedly in the Scriptures that the Lord made *heaven and earth*—that's clear enough, but why are they so important to him? The answer sounds simple, but it is actually very complex: they are the focal points of God's plan and universe.

The Father's heaven (the original earth, the First Heaven), the Son's New Earth (the Second Heaven), and our present earth are, in a very literal and true sense, the center of the universe. Or perhaps another, more accurate way of saying it would be they are *the center of God's heart and purpose.* This earth we're living on now is a stepping stone to the New Earth and heaven. How very significant this present earth is to the Lord, for all life and, more importantly, life altering salvation begins here! "The earth (all three earths) is the Lord's and all its fullness" (Ps. 24:1). Heaven and earth are the focal points of God's mighty plan and purpose, and since earthlings are clearly created to live on earth forever the question arises: Does Christ woo you to his New Earth or does Lucifer woo you to stay within the old?

EARTH, MAN, TIME & EVOLUTION

Returning to time and the Day of the Lord—the event that initiates the thousand years of the Kingdom Age—we should have a clearer understanding of where God is coming from in relation to the creation of earth, man, time, and how it relates to the theory of evolution.

CREATION OF THE EARTH

Earth: God confirms six times in the first chapter of Genesis that he created the earth and everything in it in six literal days, for he says, "And the evening and the morning were the first day (and the second, and the third, and the fourth, and the fifth, and the sixth!)." In Chapter 2, Verses 1 through 3, we read, "Thus the heavens and the earth, and all the host of them, were finished. And on the seventh day God ended his work which he had done, and he rested on the seventh day from all his work which he had done. Then God blessed the seventh day and sanctified it, because in it he rested from all his work which God had created and made (incidentally, out of nothing, over six literal days!)."

Some argue that each of the six days mentioned could be a thousand years, a million years, even a billion years. Not so, because the Lord distinctly repeats that each day is the length of an evening and a morning, evening covering nighttime and morning covering daytime, equaling one full twenty-four hour day.

Still, I'd like to point out here that one of the reasons some argue the *billions of years to a day concept of creation* is because of the standard contemporary models of science in regard to the age of the universe and evolution (requiring the universe to be billions of years old) and Genesis 1:1–2, which says, "In the beginning God created the heaven and the earth. Now the earth was formless and empty, darkness was over the surface of the deep…" This could suggest a couple of things:

(1) The word *beginning* is abstract and therefore we have no way of measuring where the beginning *was* or when it *began.*

(2) Because the verse says "…the earth was formless and empty…," the theory arises that the earth itself was already in existence, suggesting that it could have been billions of years old before God formed it.[28] His six days of creation would then be, in effect, six days of *re-creation* of an already existing but totally unformed thing which we now call the earth. But even if that were the case, the Scriptures clearly state that the earth was made (or re-made) in six literal twenty-four hour days.[29] The billions-of-years-to-a-day creationists have an argument against that, which I'll get to in a moment.

CREATION OF MAN

Man: Genesis explains in Chapter 1, Verse 26, "Then God said, 'Let us make man in our image, according to our likeness." The words *us* and *our* refer to the Holy Trinity, the Father, the Son, and the Holy Spirit. Verse 27 goes on, "So God created man (meaning, men and women) in his own image; in the image of God he created him; male and female he created them." Verse 31 continues, "Then God saw everything that he had made, and indeed it was very good. So the evening and the morning were the sixth day."

It is unambiguous here, as far as the Holy Scriptures are concerned, that humanity was created within a literal twenty-four hour period. There is nothing in the Scriptures to suggest that it was a process of evolutionary creation that took millions, perhaps even billions, of years, unless you agree with the argument that the verses are entirely metaphorical, the position the billions-of-years-to-a-day creationists tend to make against a literal twenty-four/six day creation process. Most Christian biblical scholars do not take the Scripture-as-metaphor point of view, but rather lean toward a more literal interpretation, as do I.

CREATION OF TIME

Time: this will be a light brushstroke of a very complex concept. It's the idea that time itself, or *time as we now know it,* began after the Fall of Man. I have called it *imperfect time.* There are two traditional points of view here:

(1) Time did not exist before the Fall.
(2) Time did exist before the Fall.

Whatever the case may be, it seems most agree that before the Fall the earth and all the creatures who lived upon it were in a state of perfection where time (or time as we know it) did not exist. But once sin entered the world and filled the universe, once the universe became entropic in nature, reality altered in a big way, and that alteration would have included time, had it existed. Entropy entered the universe—death was inevitable, becoming a part of the natural order of things. What's clear here is that the time we understand now is a result of sin. Time in a universe that is imperfect and broken and disconnected from its Creator reflects the nature of that shattered universe, in direct contrast to: if time existed before the Fall it would have been a time that reflected the perfect nature of the universe and would be, more than likely, entirely alien to the time we now experience, understand, and exist in. (For more information about this topic, including the death of Man and animals in relation to time and geology, refer to Chapter 6:8, under the heading *Death.*)

There are those who disagree with me, of course, arguing that because the Scriptures do not say animal life other than Man *did not* die before the Fall proves their point. This *conspicuous biblical silence*, this absence of evidence (which I argue is not evidence of absence), can only mean one of two things: in perfect time death existed for animals and perhaps even the planets and the universe entire or time and the universe were never in a perfect state to begin with. Only humanity was in a perfected state of being and existence. If that were the case, the Scriptures and geology would get along just fine, for the most part, suggesting that the universe and all life, other than Man, has been in its entropic death-state for billions of years. Of course, I do not accept the theory because it is not scripturally supported.

There is also a problem with their logic, at least, from the Christian perspective, as both physicist Lambert Dolphin and Dr. Bolton Davidheiser make startlingly clear: if the universe, earth, and all animal life already existed in something of an imperfect or cursed state of existence before the Fall does that mean the curse/Fall simply made things worse for the earth, animal life, and the universe, that entropy became more entropic, predatory behavior became more predatory, and death became, for lack of a better word, *deathier?* Their conclusion: if any death or entropy existed before the Fall then death was obviously not a penalty for sin, which at that point would make the Christian doctrines of sin and salvation moot, the salvation of Christ through his death utterly powerless, pointless, even ridiculous.[30]

Now, interestingly enough, the seventh millennium, the Kingdom Age, is the last 1,000 years in time for humanity, and during that time the earth and the universe will be in a state of perfection. Humanity will still be in time for 1,000 more years as well as being in a perfected state of existence. This suggests that for the final 1,000 years in time, time itself will be altered to reflect the perfect nature of the universe (or altered again to its original perfect state, if it indeed existed before the Fall). But when the Holy Age begins, time will finally cease altogether.

THE ORIGIN OF MAN

There are three major points of view within Christianity today about the Creation or the origin of Man:

(1) Recent/Literal Creation or Young-earth Creation.

(2) Progressive Creation.

(3) Theistic Evolution. To be precise, Theistic Evolution is for those who believe the Bible is mostly, if not entirely, metaphor and completely religious in nature. They embrace the theory of evolution as proven scientific fact.

Progressive Creation and Theistic Evolution Christians run into the same problems with entropy, death, sin, the curse/Fall, and the death and sacrifice of Christ pointed out by Lambert Dolphin and Bolton Davidheiser, as well as plenty of other theological problems, simply *because* they are professing Christians. What's more, Progressive Creation and Theistic Evolution Christians, as well as secular evolutionists, continue to face a vast amount of anomalies within the evolutionary paradigm.

Clearly, these concepts are complex and the debate is heated, and even though I am convinced in a young-earth and universe, taking the Creation account literally, I encourage you to pursue the truth of it yourself by studying the Holy Word of God and other credible source materials so that you can make an informed decision.

THE THEORY OF EVOLUTION

The theory of Evolution: I'm not going to get into a deep discussion of the theory here, other than to say that I believe the theory has enough consistent anomalies, or plot holes if you like, to place its validity and integrity in question.[31] That it opposes the majority of contemporary and ancient Christian thought and theology in regard to the creation of Man is obvious and so the conclusion is: it remains one hundred percent theoretical. I firmly disbelieve the theory and discard it as mostly speculation disguised as science wrapped in something like religious fervor, and I am convinced its dates concerning the age of the earth and the universe are invalid, or perhaps more precisely, incorrect.

The broad Christian view, of course, is that God brought into existence the universe entire, including both the material and the spiritual worlds, which would include, of course, the earth and the system to which it belongs.

According to Christian doctrine, God alone is eternal! Everything else, i.e. the material universe, matter itself and reality, as well as spiritual beings and the spiritual universe and reality, had a beginning and were made out of nothing—all, that is, except for God. All theories and interpretations aside, the most important thing to remember is that God gets the credit for bringing into existence, by the free exercise of his will and creative power, the universe, the world, and all the beings that live in it (Ps. 33:6; Isa. 45: 18; Jer. 10:12). We owe our origin to him.

THE THOUSAND YEARS OF REST

Genesis tells us that God worked for six days and rested on the seventh. As we have now labored for six thousand years our rest *day* is coming! In fact, it is likely that the beginning of our thousand years of rest is upon us! Our incorrect human timetable/calendar tells us we're entering the seventh millennium, bringing us to the seventh thousand year since the Fall of Adam and Eve, and so of course some ask, "Where is Jesus?" He did not appear in the year 2,000, as some thought he might! The reason is like the mind of physicist Lambert Dolphin, elegant and spectacularly complex: God's true timetable/calendar. Thus, we wait for the seventh millennium and the return of the Son of God! His Word is spoken and bathed in heaven! It must be so! Even the angels in heaven do not know the year of this great event! Only the Father, who has authority over every one and every *thing* in the universe and all creation, knows the very day!

SIX WORKING DAYS DONE

Even so, I argue that it's becoming more and more clear, more and more convincing, that the human race's six working *days* are almost done! On the 7th *day*, we earthlings will rest. God blesses our 7th day of one thousand years and sanctifies it because in it we rest from all our work that we have done. Indeed, the seventh millennium may be upon us, right at the door! Know that it is consecrated by God, just as our Sabbath is consecrated by God, for he says, "...Nor carry a burden out of your houses on the Sabbath day, nor do any work (nor buy or sell, for it is a day of rest), but hallow the day, as I commanded your fathers" (Jer. 17:22). Imagine, for a thousand years a restful, blessed earth that is completely reformed, without curse or sin or death! There will only be love and peace worldwide! This is the promise of God. "For the mountains shall depart and the hills be removed, but my (Jesus') kindness shall not depart from you, nor shall my covenant of peace be removed,' says the Lord, who has mercy on you" (Isaiah 54:10).

We will have peace through our rest period! With peace comes love, and we will be like the Lord, for the knowledge of the Lord will be upon the earth. During this period, "The wolf also shall dwell with the lamb, the leopard shall lie down with the young goat, the calf and the young lion and the fatling together; and a little child shall lead them. The cow and the bear shall graze; their young ones shall lie down together; and the lion shall eat straw like the ox. The nursing child shall play by the cobra's hole, and the weaned child shall put his hand in the viper's den. They shall not hurt nor destroy in all my holy mountain (the reformed earth), for the earth shall be full of the knowledge of the Lord (because he lives in it) as the waters cover the sea" (Isaiah 11:6–9).

FATES ETERNALLY SEALED

It must be pointed out here that our rest period cannot be shared with Satan, his army of fallen angels, or the unrepentant.

This is why they will be locked up like prisoners in the bottomless pit during the thousand years, with no parole or pardon considered—at that point their fates will have been eternally sealed.

A CONSISTENT GOD

God, our Holy Father, is the Great Designer, and as a Designer he consistently relies on blueprints, from DNA and the coded information within it, the blueprint of information for humanity (coded information cannot form by chance), to the complex patterns involving 3, 3 ½, 6, 7, 40, 6,000, 7,000 and his Holy mathematics/geometry, to order within the chaos of the Fallen universe and the staggering efficiency of random behavior—complex, clever, each one following a pattern based on a clearly designed blueprint.

NUMBERS & PATTERNS

Following this line of thought, there's a pattern in the number 2,000 I'd like to point out: First we have the Fall.

(1) 2,000 years later the World Flood occurred (by God's timetable/calendar).

(2) 2,000 years later Christ was born (by God's timetable/calendar).

(3) 2,000 years later we have the return of Christ (by God's timetable/calendar).

The pattern here is an obvious one, but it's also important. Why? Answer: about every 2,000 years something awesome happens.

Since 2,000 years have passed since the last event, surely another significant event must materialize soon! What will it be? The Book of Revelation points to the most dramatic, awesome, significant happening ever to hit the fact of the earth: the return of the Son of God 2,000 years after his birth.

Three periods of 2,000 years = 6,000 years.

One more period of 1,000 years = 7,000 years, which makes it complete.

Now, of course, this pattern fits into God's timetable/calendar perfectly, but since our human timetable/calendar is inaccurate, is *off* by who-knows-how-many-years, we can't say for certain exactly when the events happened or when the latest event is going to happen. For example, let us take the birth of Jesus. We are not sure whether his birth was shortly before year 1 A.D. or shortly after. (Biblical scholars suggest between 4 and 7 BCE.) This means we are not certain of where we are within that pattern—but based on deep study of God's Holy Word, as well as human history, archeology, geology, we can land well placed educated guesses, as well as accumulate accurate and reliable dates.

THE NUMBER 3 ½

The number 3 ½ is important within God's holy mathematics /geometry. It is referred to considerably in the Book of Revelation. 3 ½ is deeply entwined within the number 2,000 and the number 7,000. 7,000 years are made up of three 2,000 year periods and one 1,000 year period (the seventh millennium). It should be clear here that this pattern also covers the length of time that humankind dwells on this earth: 7,000 years (by God's timetable/calendar). Also, the first 2,000 years signifies the Father, the second 2,000 years signifies the Son, and the third 2,000 years signifies the Holy Spirit.

Knowing that we have a consistent God who cannot and will not break his own laws, who consistently adheres to his blueprints, patterns, numbers (his sacred mathematics, his mystical geometry!), could the fact that some 2,000 years have indeed passed since the birth of Jesus (in the human timetable/calendar) suggesting another significant event is due in human history, the return of the King? Our last remaining years are potentially just around the corner! You might say this is absurd, that life as we know it will carry on for another thousand years, on and on and on into the future for millions and millions of years, but this argument is flawed, for no matter how wonderful and clever humanity is—and humanity is wonderful and clever, don't get me wrong—it is doubtful humanity would be able to last. No, it's much more likely that before long humanity would blow itself into smithereens or poison itself with biological weapons or simply suicide-bomb itself into extinction, wiping itself out of existence forever, for clearly that is the path we are on, and if truth be told, it's the path we've been on since the Fall. Thank the heavens the real year 2,000 in God's timetable/calendar is coming (time and years are measured by God alone!) so that he will intervene before we destroy ourselves and end our existence.

Pray always that you are worthy to escape the predictions that must take place before this great Day of the Lord. "Therefore we also pray always for you that our God would count you worthy of this calling, and fulfill all the good pleasure of his goodness and the work of faith with power" (2 Thes. 1:11). "For what is our hope, or joy, or crown of rejoicing? Is it not even you in the presence of our Lord Jesus Christ at his coming?" (I Thes. 2:19).

Revelation 1:20

"The mystery of the seven stars which you saw in my right hand, and the seven golden lamp stands: the seven stars are the angels of the seven churches, and the seven lamp stands which you saw are the seven churches."

THE MYSTERY DEEPENS!
THE MYSTERY UNFOLDS!

Jesus explains the secrets of the seven stars held in his right hand: they are the seven angels, who identify the seven Christian companies (or churches), representing the Seven Spirits of God. He tells John that the seven golden lamp stands are the Seven Spirits of Life, being in essence the Seven Spirits of God. The seven stars represent the Seven Spirits of God! The seven angels represent the Seven Spirits of God! The seven companies represent the Seven Spirits of God! The seven golden lamp stands represent the Seven Spirits of God! And Jesus has the Seven Spirits, so we can conclude: "I AM THE SEVEN STARS! I AM THE SEVEN ANGELS! I AM THE SEVEN COMPANIES! I AM THE SEVEN LAMP STANDS!" Revelation *is* Jesus the Christ!

* * * * *

SOURCES:
1. *Blessed*, MERIAM-WEBSTER ONLINE, copyright 2005 by Merriam-Webster, Incorporated, <http://www.Merriam-Webster.com>.
2. *Ongoing World Conflicts,* <http://www.faculty.ncwc.edu>.
   World Conflicts; conflicts rage on most continents, CNNfyi.com, <http://www.cnn.com>.
   Wars Rage In One-third of the World's Nations, Washington Post (1999), 666 Watch, <http://www.av1611.org>.
   New and Recent Conflicts of the World; The History Guy, Roger A. Lee, <http://www.historyguy.com>.
   ICG, International Crisis Group, <http://www.crisisweb.com>.
   STRATFOR; Predictive, Insightful Global Intelligence, <http://www.stratfor.com>.
3. *Up to 89 mln more AIDS victims in Africa by 2025—UN*" March 4th, 2005. Tadesse, Tsegaye. MSNBC Wire Services, Reuters, <http://www.msnbc.msn.com>.
4. *Annan Calls On World to Help Africa Battle Aids And Ensure Peace,* United Nations, distributed by All Africa Global Media, allAfrica.com (2003), <http://www.allAfrica.com>.
   Aids Pandemic Killing Africa's Teachers, Sunday Times, "South Africa's best selling newspaper," Online Edition, Sundaytimes.co.za (2002), <http://www.Sundaytimes.co.za>.

Dirty Needles "Spread Africa AIDS," Nick Adcock, BBC News, Accra Mail (Accra), Distributed by All Africa Global Media, allAfrica.com (2003), <http://www.allAfrica.com>.

Aids in Africa; Issue Brief for Congress (received through the CRS Web), Ronald W. Copson, Foreign Affairs, Defense and Trade Division, Congressional Research Service, Library of Congress (2003), U.S. Department of State, International Information Programs, Global Issues/HIV/Aids, <http://www.usinfo.state.gov>; *International Aid Helping Combat AIDS Pandemic In Africa*—for more information, call 1-800-968-7490 or to make a donation to International Aid's ministry of compassion call the 24-hour hot line at 1-800-251-2502.

HIV/Aids pandemic in Africa, statement of congressman Sanders, May 15th, 2001, <http://www.bernie.house.gov>.

5. *The Enduring Pain of Halabja: Chemical Weapons,* Guy Dinmore, The Financial Times Limited, Financial Times (2002); U.S Department of State, International Information Program, <http://www.usinfo.state.gov>.

Unclassified CIA File: 970613 092596 ui txt 0001.tx, Iraqi Chemical Warfare (2002), <http://www.mprofaca.cro.net>, Profaca Mario's Cyberspace Station, the Global Intelligence News Portal.

Chemical Warfare in the Iraqi-Iran War, Stockholm International Peace Research Institute, (1984), Julian P. Robinson and Josef Goldblat, <http://www.sipri.org>.

6. *2004 Hurricanes Lead Record Disaster for FEMA.* FEMA News. January 5th, 2005. Release Number: HQ-05-001, FEMA web site, <http://www.fema.gov>; *Sumatra Earthquake Three Times Larger Than Originally Thought,* ScienceDaily. February. 12, 2005, <http://www.sciencedaily.com>; the story is reprinted, with editorial adaptations by ScienceDaily staff, from materials provided by Northwestern University.

7. *The Christ's Are Coming!* (2002), <http://www.letusreason.org>.

Millennium Chaos Feared in Holy City, Tony Thompson, The Observer (1999), Guardian Unlimited, "The UKs most popular newspaper website," <http://www.guardian.co.uk>.

Jesus of Siberia, The Guardian (2002), Guardian Unlimited, "The UKs most popular newspaper website," <http://www.guardian.co.uk>.

False Christ's/False Prophets, Prophecy Central, (2002), <http://www.bibleprophecy.com>.

The Raelian Revolution, <http://www.rael.org>.

8. *Ecumenicism; where do you draw the line?* Deception in the Church (1998), <http://www.deceptioninthechurch.com>.

The United Religions: Globalist and New Age Plans, Lee Pen, SCP Journal VOL. 23:2-23:3 (1999) *The United Religions: Globalist and New Age Plans,* Lee Pen, SCP Journal VOL. 23:2-23:3 (1999); "An earlier version of this story appeared in 'The United Religions Initiative - A Bridge Back to Gnosticism', published in December 1998 by the New Oxford Review. You may order the complete story from the Review, or subscribe to the Review, by calling (510) 526-5374, or by writing to the New Oxford Review, 1069 Kains Ave., Berkeley, CA 94706. Additionally, it also has been published as part of 'The United Religions Initiative: Foundations for a World Religion' (Part 1), published in May 1999 by the Journal of the Spiritual Counterfeits Project, Vol. 22:4-23:1. The information in this extract is a small portion of the information printed in the SCP Journal. You may order the complete story from the Journal, or subscribe to the Journal, by calling

(510) 540-0300, or by writing to the Spiritual Counterfeits Project, Post Office Box 4308, Berkeley, CA 94704, or by visiting the SCP web site, <http://www.scp-inc.org>."
Ecumenicism, Southwest Institute for Orthodox Studies, an Orthodox Apologetics Ministry; Orthodox Christian Information Center, <http://www.orthodoxinfo.com>.
9. *How the West Lost Mysticism—when did Western Christians stop expecting mystical union with God through Christ?, Spiritual Road Rules—six steps to becoming a Christian mystic,* Frederica Mathews-Green, Ancient Faith, Modern Life, Belief net Columnist, Beliefnet.com, <http://www.beliefnet.com/author/author_32.html>.
10. *Charismatic Revival as a Sign of the Times,* Fr. Seraphim Rose of Platina (1934-1982), written in the 1970s, Orthodox Christian Information Center, <http://www.orthodoxinfo.com>.
11. *The Five Points of Calvinism* by Herman Hanko, Homer Hoeksema, and Gise J. Van Baren, Reformed Free Publishing Association (1975), all rights reserved, the Protestant Reformed Churches in America (unofficial home page web site), <http://www.prca.org/index.html>.
Fall of Man, pg. 398-399, The New Unger's Bible Dictionary, Moody Press (1988).
Chronology of Biblical Christianity; Calvinistic, Armenian, The Bible Library Deluxe, version 5.0. suite, CD-ROM, Ellis Enterprises, Inc. (2,000).
12. *Rapio,* Latin. Internet Dictionary Project, translating dictionaries (2002), <http://www.ilovelanguages.com/www.June29.com>.
rapiemur; "...deinde nos qui vivimus qui relinquimur simul rapiemur cum illis in nubibus obviam Domino in aera et sic simper cum Domino erimus..."
1Thes. 4:17, the Latin Vulgate Bible, translated from the Hebrew and Aramaic by St. Jerome in 382-405 A.D., the Online Book Initiative, the University of Pennsylvania Center for the Computer Analysis of Texts, <http://www.music.princton.edu> & The Internet Sacred Texts Archive, <http://www.sacred-texts.com>.
Our Blessed Hope, Personal Update News Journal, Chuck Missler, Ph.D., Koinonia House (2002), <http://www.khouse.com>.
Resurrection of Christ, A. J. Mass, transcribed by Donald J. Boon, the Catholic Encyclopedia, Volume XII, Online Edition, Kevin Knight (2002), <http://www.newadvent.org>.
13. *Sheol,* pg. 1178-1179; *Hades,* pg. 512-513; *Hell,* pg. 550-551; *Gehenna,* pg. 462, The New Unger's Bible Dictionary, Moody Press (1988).
Gehenna, Geerhardus Vos, International Bible Standard Encyclopedia, Online Edition, <http://www.studylight.org>.
14. *Jerusalem,* pg. 675-680, The New Unger's Bible Dictionary, Moody Press (1988).
Arch 343: Cities in History; Lecture: 2 Jerusalem: The City and Memory, Dr. Richard Ingersoll, Rice University, <http://www.owlnet.rice.edu>.
15. *St. John, the Evangelist,* Leopold Fonk, transcribed by Michael Little, The Catholic Encyclopedia, Volume VIII, Online Edition, Kevin Knight (2002), <http://www.newadvent.org>.
Eusebius of Caesarea, Church History: Book III, St. John the Apostle, Narrative Concerning the Apostle John, <http://www.CBN.com>.
St. John the Apostle, Patron Saints Index, <http://www.catholic-forum.com>.
John, the Apostle, pg. 698-700, The New Unger's Bible Dictionary, Moody Press (1988)

16. *The True Tabernacle; See The Bible Through Jewish Eyes,* Dr. Daniel Goldberg, Chosen People Ministries (2002), <http://www.chosen-people.com>.
The Temples at Jerusalem, W. B. Don Falconer (1998), <http://www.geocities.com>.
Temple, pg. 1259-1264, The New Unger's Bible Dictionary, Moody Press (1988).

17. *Human Auras and Energy Fields,* David Lindsay (1998), <http://www.Don-lindsay-archive.org>.
Auras, The Skeptic's Dictionary, Robert Todd Carroll (2002), <http://www.skepDic.com>.

18. *Hand,* pg. 522-523, The New Unger's Bible Dictionary, Moody Press (1988).

19. *Quantum Theory,* Whatis?com, <http://www.whatis.techtarget.com>
About Physics Dictionary: Definition of Quantum Theory, <http://www.physics.about.com>.
Physics; Quantum Theory, Microsoft Encarta Encyclopedia (2002).
Classical and Quantum Physics, <http://www.kheper.auz.com>.

20. *The Soul and Quantum Physics,* Chapter 28, Eliot Rosen; *Experiencing the Soul: Before Birth, During Life, And After Death,* Fred Alan Wolf, PhD, Carlsbad, CA: Hay House (1998), GrizzleGrits.com, <http://www.grizzlegrits.com>; "Dr. Fred Alan Wolf is a theoretical physicist and international lecturer on consciousness and the new physics. He is an award-winning author of ten books on this subject."

21. *Physics; technical-articles,* Chuck Missler, Koinonia House, <http://www.khouse.com>.
Physics; Quantum Theory, Microsoft Encarta Encyclopedia (2002).

22. *Understanding Quantum Physics,* Y. C. Leung, University of Massachusetts Dartmouth, <http://www.umassd.edu>.
Quantum Physics: The Boundaries of Reality, article, Chuck Missler, Koinonia House, <http://www.khouse.com>.
Our Digital Universe? Quantum Teleporting: Part 1, article, Chuck Missler, Koinonia House, <http://www.khouse.com>.
Physics; Quantum Theory, Microsoft Encarta Encyclopedia (2002).

23. *Quantum Teleporting, part 2: Our Holographic Universe,* article, Chuck Missler, Koinonia House, <http://www.khouse.com>.
The Aether, Yes or No, Ken Seto, Physicist, Lambert Dolphin's Resources, <http://www.ldolphin.com> & <http://www.kenseto@erinet.com>.
Stretching the Heavens and the Dilation of Time, article, Chuck Missler, Koinonia House, <http://www.khouse.com>.
Physics; technical-articles, article, Chuck Missler, Koinonia House, <http://www.khouse.com>.
Ross Tessien: Aether Theory and Related Papers, Ross Tessien (1996), Lambert Dolphin's Resources, <http://www.ldolphin.com>.
Quantum Theory, <http://www.thebigview.com>.

24. *Cosmic Codes—Hidden Messages From The Edge Of Eternity,* pg. 333-346, Chuck Missler, Koinonia House (1999), <http://www.khouse.com>.
Quantum Physics, <http://www.kheper.auz.com>.
Identity and Individuality in Quantum Theory, Stanford Encyclopedia of Philosophy, Steve French (2,000), <http://www.plato.stanford.edu>.
Our Digital Universe? Quantum Teleporting: Part 1, article, Chuck Missler, Koinonia House, <http://www.khouse.com>.
Quantum Teleporting, part 2: Our Holographic Universe, article, Chuck Missler, Koinonia House, <http://www.khouse.com>.

Quantum Physics: The Boundaries of Reality, article, Chuck Missler, Koinonia House, <http://www.khouse.com>.
Physics; technical-articles, article, Chuck Missler, Koinonia House, <http://www.khouse.com>.
Stretching the Heavens and the Dilation of Time, Chuck Misled, Koinonia House, audio cassette, (1999), <http://www.khouse.com>.
The Creator Beyond Time And Space Audio Series; includes *The Creator Beyond Time and Space, The Bible: An Extraterrestrial Message, Immanuel: The Deity of Messiah,* and *The Divine Watchmaker,* Chuck Missler and Dr. Mark Eastman, Koinonia House, audio cassette (1996), <http://www.khouse.com>.
Physics; Quantum Theory, Microsoft Encarta Encyclopedia (2002).

25. *American Institute of Physics, History of Physics and Allied Sciences; resources of the Niels Bohr Library,* <http://www.bodley.ox.ac.uk>.
Identity and Individuality in Quantum Theory, Stanford Encyclopedia of Philosophy, Steve French (2,000), <http://www.plato.stanford.edu>.
New Scientist's Guide to the Quantum World, NewScientist.com, <http://www.newscientist.com>.
Sixty Years of Quantum Physics, Edward U. Condon, Washington University (1960), <http://www.philsoc.org>.
Physics; Quantum Theory, Microsoft Encarta Encyclopedia (2002).

26. *Theological Reflections on Chaos Theory,* The American Scientific Affiliation, from *Perspectives on Science and Christian Faith,* John Jefferson Davis (1997), <http://www.asa3.org>.

27. *Theological Reflections on Chaos Theory,* The American Scientific Affiliation, from *Perspectives on Science and Christian Faith,* John Jefferson Davis (1997), <http://www.asa3.org>.

28. *Evolutionists Battle New Theory on Creation,* James Glanz, Free Republic.com, "A conservative News Forum" (2001), <http://www.freerepublic.com>.
Science and Scripture; Geology and Genesis, Christian Geology Ministry, <http://www.kjvbible.org>.
Is the Young-Earth Interpretation Biblically Sound? Rich Deem, Young Earth Creationism, God And Science.org, <http://www.godandscience.org>.
Christian Science Evangelism: FAQ on Hugh Ross, Bolton Davidheiser, Logos Publishers (1993); *An Open Letter to Hugh Ross,* Lambert Dolphin (1989), Lambert Dolphin, Lambert Dolphin's Resources, <http://www.ldolphin.com>.

29. *The Ruin of Creation,* Lambert Dolphin (1996), Lambert Dolphin's Resources, <http://www.ldolphin.org>.
The "Days" of Creation in Genesis 1: Literal "Days" or Figurative "Periods/Epochs" of Time? Gerhard F. Hasel , John Nevins Andrews Professor of Old Testament and Biblical Theology Andrews University (1994), Lambert Dolphin's Resources, <http://www.ldolphin.org>.
Earth Age, Young or Old? Creation Science Resource, <http://www.nwcreation.net>.
Creation and Catastrophe Chronology, Barry Setterfield, Lambert Dolphin's Resources, <http://www.dolphin.org>.
The Young Earth, Henry M. Morris Ph.D., Institute for Creation Research (1974), <http://www.icr.org>.
The Earth's Magnetic field: Evidence That the Earth Is Young, Jonathan Sarfati, First published in: Creation Ex Nihilo 20(2):15–17 (1998), Answers in Genesis Ministries, <http://www.answeringenesis.org>.

30. *Creation Science Evangelism: FAQ on Hugh Ross; A Statement Concerning the Ministry of Dr. Hugh Ross,* Bolton Davidheiser, Logos Publishers, 1993; Lambert Dolphin's Resources, <http://www.ldolphin.org>; *An Open Letter to Dr. Hugh Ross,* Lambert Dolphin's Resources, 1989, <http://www.ldolphin.org>.
    Christian Views of Science and Earth History, Rich Milne & Ray Bohlin, Probe Ministries International (1998), <http://www.probe.org>.
31. *Birds, Beetles and Life*, short essays and studies, Barry Setterfield (2002), <http://www.setterfield.org>.
    Molecular Biology and Evolution: The Crisis and the Challenge, Thomas B. Fowler, SC. D., Article taken from the summer 1993 issue of *Faith & Reason.* Subscriptions available from Christendom Press, 2101 Shenandoah Shores Road, Ft. Royal, VA 22630, 703-636-2900, Fax 703-636-1655, published quarterly at $20.00 per year (Online Edition, 996 EWTN); Global Catholic Network, <http://www.ewtn.com>.
    The American Scientific Affiliation, *creation/evolution page* (2002), <http://www.sas3.org>.
    The Biochemical Challenge to Evolution: Exploring the Elegance and Irreducible Complexity of Biological Systems at the Molecular Level, Nancy Pearcey, Access Research Network, The Nancy Pearcey Files, Christianity Today, Inc./*Books & Culture* (1996), file date 1999, <http://www.arn.org>.

Further Reading:

Tomorrow's Soldier: The Warriors Weapons and Tactics That Will Win America's War in the 21st Century, David Alexander, Avon Books (1999).
Terrorism Today, Christopher C. Harmon, Frank Cass & Co. Publisher (2,000).
Planet Earth—2,000 A.D., Hal Lindsey, Western Front Publishing Co. (1994).
Age of Enlightenment (Great Ages of Man), Peter Gay, Time Life Publisher (1966).
After Modernity... What?: Agenda for Theology, Thomas C. Oden, Zondervan Publishing House (1992).
An Encyclopedia of Claims, Frauds, and Hoaxes of the Occult and Supernatural, James Randi, St. Martin's Press (1995).
God and the New Physics, Paul Davies, Simon and Schuster (1983).
The Theory of Creation, Jim Schicatano, iUniverse Publisher (2002).
Darwin's Black Box, Michael Behe, Touchstone Books (1998).
Creation and Time, Hugh Ross Ph.D., NavPress Publishing Group (1994).
Creation and Change, Douglass Kelly, Christian Focus Publications (1997).
The Young Earth, Dr. John D. Morris, Master Books (2,000).
Genesis, James Montgomery Boice, Zondervan Publishing House (1982); Baker Books (1998).
The Biblical Bases of Modern Science, Henry M. Morris Ph.D., Baker Book House Publisher (1984).
Evolution: A Theory in Crisis, Michael Denton, Adler & Adler (1986).
Did Darwin Get It Right? Catholics and the Theory of Evolution, George Sim Johnston, Our Sunday Visitor Publisher (1998).

CHAPTER 2
Loveless, Persecuted, Compromising, Corrupted

Revelation 2:1

"To the angel of the church of Ephesus write, 'These things says he who holds the seven stars in his right hand, who walks in the midst of the seven golden lamp stands:'"

LOVELESS

Even though John gives a detailed and historic account of the seven companies (churches), I said in Chapter 1 that they also represent every possible type of Christian throughout the ages to our present day. Thus, if you're a follower of Christ, as you read about these churches keep in mind that they also apply directly to you. They apply to those who do not follow the teachings of Christ as well.

As you read, ask yourself what church you belong to.

The seven churches will be discussed through Chapters 2 and 3. The Book or Revelation was written especially for these seven churches of Asia, as well as other churches in Asia Minor, and including, of course, the future Church.

The first letter is written to the angel of the congregation in Ephesus, the loveless church. Before diving deeply in to this subject, let's skim the angelic surface of the angels of the seven churches of Chapters Two and Three.

These angels have a meaning that is twofold:

(1) Each angel represents the literal human and angelic ministers of each church.

(2) Each angel represents one of the Seven Spirits of God. Jesus is showing John and the world how deeply involved and a part of his church he is—human ministers, angelic ministers, even personally as an angel/minister to each church, ministering to each individual member himself; he is also showing us that he is the Seven Spirits of God, the I Am. Keep that in mind as we examine each church in detail, especially when you come across the reference to the angel of each church.

EPHESUS

Now, let's backtrack for a moment and walk the streets of the historic city called Ephesus: a Greek city in Ionia near the Aegean Sea, in legend said to be founded by female warriors known as *the Amazons.* It was one of the most prosperous cities in western Asia

Minor at the time, important to Rome because of its political and economical status and its major trade routes. Ephesus was considered the religious center of the world. The temple for the goddess Diana (or Artemis) resided there, one of the seven wonders of the ancient world, an amazing, breathtaking work of art with columns standing sixty feet high. The temple was destroyed in 356 B.C. Alexander the Great rebuilt it. During the first and second centuries the city had a population of about half a million. In regard to early Church history: the Apostle Paul conducted his ministry there for three years. The Third Ecumenical Council was held there in A.D. 431. Today, a small Turkish settlement called *Selçuk* rests on part of the original city site.[1]

THE ONE

John confirms the identity of the One who is confronting him. The speaker is unambiguous: it is Jesus, for the One giving the message to John holds seven magical stars in his right hand. (Refer to the previous chapter, 1:16, under the heading *His Holy Countenance*, for related information on the word *hand* and *left* or *right* as it relates to the original Greek and English translation.) We are also informed that the One who confronts John walks in the middle of the seven golden lamp stands—again, another clear indication that the speaker is Jesus who has the Seven Spirits of Life before the sacred throne. Christ speaks to John!

Revelation 2:2

"I [Jesus] know your works, your labor, your patience, and that you cannot bear those who are evil. And you have tested those who say they are apostles and are not, and have found them liars...'"

TRYING HARD

Jesus announces that he knows his believers were laboring and trying hard in the days of John—part of the reason he knows this is simply because he sees the fruits of their faith and labor. He is pleased with their patience and hard work in spreading the Truth. He understands they are dealing with the internal pressures of some who say they are followers of Christ but are not.

Revelation 2:3

"'...and you have persevered and have patience, and have labored for my name's sake and have not become weary.'"

BEARING PATIENCE

John is informed that his Master is aware that his believers are bearing much for his most holy name. They not only stand up well to the strain, they remain patient throughout the ordeal.

You have to remember the church was, after all, based in the religious center of the world. The external pressures of living in a major modern city like Ephesus (comparable to living in a major modern city today), and the added pressures from the Roman government breathing down your neck, the dominant religious institutions and cults, and the customary immoral behavior of many locals would have been enormous for an early Christian. Undoubtedly, this kind of pressure is familiar to us because we can apply it to our modern times when so many have turned their backs on God; when the Christian Church, unlike the church of Ephesus, seems to be buckling under the internal and external pressures of modern day living, its love noticeably cooling.

Revelation 2:4

"'Nevertheless I have this against you, that you have left your first love.'"

NEVERTHELESS!

As satisfied as Jesus is with this company, he sees a fault that greatly displeases him (and obviously hurts him). He speaks to his faithful in Ephesus (and those living beyond, through the millennia, but most especially to the believers living at the End Times) by explaining that he understands that they're living as Christians under enormous societal pressures and doing a pretty good job. Even so, they have forgotten their First Love: Christ Jesus, the Lord.

How did this happen, you may ask? How could this be possible when they were so focused on Christ? Answer: when people first accept Jesus as their Lord and Savior they tend to be extremely devoted, dedicated, loyal. They love the Lord with all their hearts and with all their souls and with all their minds and with all their might, but after a little while, sometimes their priorities get mixed up and their First Love gets left behind, sometimes even forgotten. They place other things before Christ, things like careers, romantic love, relationships, power, wealth, sex, drugs, adultery, value— what the Ephesians did was place themselves first and Jesus last.

This is the case today. People are depending more and more upon themselves, our intellect, science, and technology, relegating God to the so-called inferior wastelands of the weak-minded, but their needs, their desires, their lusts, everything about themselves, comes first, and depending on and living for God—even the thought of leading a selfless life for God—is considered something of a modern joke. Today, celebrity is king. Celebrity is worshiped. Celebrity is god. People sell their souls to get on TV so that, for half a millionth of a second, they can be more than just human. They can be a star.[2]

Revelation 2:5

"'Remember therefore from where you have fallen; repent and do the first works, or else I will come to you quickly and remove your lamp stand from its place—unless you repent.'"

FIRST IN EVERYTHING WE DO

Jesus instructs his believers who have forgotten their First Love to be wise and repent. When they fall, he warns them to look to God for help. His faithful must set an example to others and stand out as different, for they are shining lights to the world. They should not only put Jesus first in Christian matters, but should have him in mind constantly. They should ask God to change their mind and the desires of their hearts.

Through John, Jesus warns his people that when they become weak in spirit and do not place him first in their lives, he will not put them first in his life—the Father is always loving and forgiving, but disobedient behavior always has consequences. The choices and actions we make and take matter. Disobedience is always costly.

Revelation 2:6

"'But this you have, that you dislike the deeds of the Nicolaitans, which I also hate.'"

CULT-FAITHS

The Lord acknowledges that these believers show displeasure with the ways of the Nicolaitans, whose ways he dislikes intensely.

Historically, the Nicolaitans were a pagan sect that had fastened itself to the early Christian Church. No one seems to know much about them, other than they, apparently, worshiped and followed the teachings of Balaam, ate food sacrificed to idols, mixed idolatrous worship with Christian worship (inter-faith ecumenicism), denied the existence of God, and were sex centered to such a degree that the word *loose* doesn't come close to defining their obsession and addiction properly. Where the sect came from and what it came out of is unknown.[3]

For those of us living today, the Nicolaitan sect is clearly alive and well! The Christian Church finds itself in bed with world religions and even cults that support similar Nicolaitan doctrine![4] Jesus says that he finds these deeds distasteful. They were as bad in John's time as they are today, and far too many of the Lord's faithful are caught in these webs of iniquity, becoming his loveless company of believers.

Revelation 2:7

"'He who has an ear, let him hear what the Spirit says to the churches. To him who overcomes I will give to eat from the tree of life, which is in the midst of the Paradise of God.'"

THE HOLY TEMPLE, THE HUMAN BODY

The Lord urges everyone to hear what the Spirit says to his faithful. He beseeches those who overcome to continue to always place the Lord first. People who believe in him are living temples themselves in which Christ's Holy Spirit resides! Our earthly bodies house the Spirit of the Lord, for he lives within us.

Scripture clearly entreats us: "...know that your body is the temple of the Holy Spirit who is in you, whom you have from God, and you are not your own" (1Cor. 6:19).

We humans defame our inward temples with such things as impure thoughts, sexual sins, unhealthy habits, and so on. We often denigrate our temples outwardly as well. This is what Paul had in mind when he said, "Don't you know that you yourselves are God's temple and that God's Spirit lives in you?" (1Cor. 3:16). We should respect God's temple. I argue that we should not dishonor it, and so I encourage you to try your best to avoid tattoos, body-scarring, piercings, and things of that nature. Do not blemish that which is holy (Lev. 19:28).

THE TREE OF LIFE FORETOLD

The Revelation of Jesus Christ to his servant John lists several glorious and wonderful rewards for those who remain his faithful. To all who overcome and put Jesus first in their lives he will give them the right to eat from the tree of life, which is found in the middle of the New Jerusalem on the New Earth (in the Holy Age, beyond time).

In Chapter 22, Verse 2, Revelation says, "In the middle of its street (of the city), and on either side of the river (of the Water of Life), was the Tree of Life which bore twelve fruits, each tree yielding its (own) fruit every month..." Of course, the Tree of Life also stood in the midst of the Garden of Eden (Gen. 2:9; 3:22).

There were actually three trees in the original Garden—and you can count on it that there will be three trees in the New Jerusalem: *the tree that was pleasant to the sight and good for food*, *the tree of life*, and *the tree of the knowledge of good and evil* (Gen. 2:9). Most biblical scholars believe the tree of life existed in the Garden of Eden in the first place because it showed us that life came, not from within humanity, not from within our selves, but from without. Life came from God (John 1:4; 14:6). In Scripture, the tree of life is often equated to finding wisdom or being wise (Prov. 3:18). In the Book of Revelation it is also considered a symbol of eternal life with Christ and the joy that life will bring.[5]

THE TREE OF THE KNOWLEDGE OF GOOD & EVIL

The tree of the knowledge of good and evil is always identified with the Fall of humanity and the reason why it existed should be explained in more detail here: humanity was in a state of moral purity or perfection in the beginning. Adam and Eve reflected that purity and perfection, having a nature similar to the pure, perfect, non-entropic universe and its Creator. But to have genuine free will the possibility to sin *had to* exist—if the possibility didn't exist you end up with something like human beings as mindless robots. This possibility is often called *a state of probation*. To have genuine free will humanity had to be tested by falling under God's divine law: he or she could eat from every tree within the Garden of Eden except the tree of the knowledge of good and evil.[6]

THE TREE OF LIFE IN THE NEW JERUSALEM

Now, leaping forward to the New Earth and the New Jerusalem, the tree of life will once again flourish, illustrating the lesson of the pre-Fall tree of life: humanity's life comes from without, not from within. It will also represent Christ and his restoring grace and the Holy Trinity, and as said in the paragraphs above, like the original Garden of Eden there will be three trees in the New Jerusalem. (Refer to Chapter 22:2, under the heading *The Tree of Life* for more information on this subject.)

Reward Number 1
TO EAT FROM THE TREE OF LIFE—
God's gift of eternal life!

Revelation 2:8

"And to the angel of the church in Smyrna write, 'These things says the First and the Last, who was dead, and came to life...'"

PERSECUTED

John writes to the second angel of the company in Smyrna, the persecuted church; this also applies to the persecuted throughout the ages.

SMYRNA

The city of Smyrna was prosperous, about 40 miles to the north of Ephesus at the mouth of a river. It was called *the lovely, the crown of Ionia, the ornament of Asia,* so it's clear people thought that it was one of the finest cities of Asia. It was home to the Roman army and plenty of pagan temples. Today, it's the biggest city in southwest Turkey, with a population of more than one and a half million.[7]

John confirms again that Jesus is the speaker by saying that these things are mentioned by the First and the Last, who was dead and came back to life. Only Jesus is this One, for the Son confirms in Revelation 1:18, "I am he who lives, and was dead, and behold, I am alive forever."

Revelation 2:9

"'I know your works, tribulation, and poverty (but you are rich); and I know the blasphemy of those who say they are Jews and are not, but are a synagogue of Satan.'"

RICH IN CHRIST

Jesus firmly states that he knows the works of his people in Smyrna. He knows the trials and persecution they face, just as he knows his persecuted company of believers and what they face today! He is aware that they are fiscally poor, but knows that they are spiritually rich in the Lord Jesus Christ. He is aware that they deal with many leaders within many houses of worship, both Jew and Gentile, who say they're servants of God but who actually worship Satan, perhaps literally (for those involved in actual satanic/pagan worship), as well as figuratively (for those who have strayed from the path and unintentionally honor Satan).

The company faces difficult times, but even so, they remain faithful—this is the only church out of the seven that Jesus does not give a stern warning to. Clearly, these were a faithful group of believers facing intense persecution. A good example of the intensity of their situation and their faithfulness is the martyrdom of Polycarp, put to death around 155-169 A.D.(?), a Christian who ministered in and around the area.[8] It's likely his example is one of too many to count. Persecution and martyrdom was common in

John's time. Christian martyrdom still happens today, all over the world, of course, but modern followers of Christ will face the most intense period of persecution and martyrdom in the history of Christianity and Judaism during the coming Great and Terrible Tribulation.

Revelation 2:10

"'Do not fear any of these things which you are about to suffer. Indeed, the devil is about to throw some of you into prison, that you may be tested, and you will have tribulation ten days. Be faithful until death, and I will give you the crown of life.'"

TEN DAYS OF TRIBULATION

John explains here that Jesus does not want his believers to be afraid, but regardless, they must expect to suffer for him. He knows they are trying to be faithful. He knows some are going to die for his name. They know it too—a remarkable faith indeed.

In modern times, his supporters suffer martyrdom still: the number of martyrs for the year 2,000, which included Catholics, Orthodox, Protestants, and Evangelicals, numbered some 165,000 Christians, according to Protestant scholars.[9] In the future (the *near* future!), during the final three-and-a-half years of the Antichrist's reign (the last three-and-a-half years of the world/reality/time as we know it), the slaughter of believers in God will be most intense.

Now, there's something very interesting in this verse. Even though it is in direct reference to the Smyrna believers and the persecution of their times what Jesus says concerning their period of persecution may apply prophetically to those living in the End Times in this regard: the devil causes people to be held in jail for ten days as a test, the almost certain outcome, death.

There doesn't seem to be any direct evidence historically that followers of Christ during the time of the Smyrna church were held for a ten day period before being martyred or that ten days in prison was a customary part of the Roman judicial system, so this suggests two things:

(1) Christ was speaking figuratively in reference to his followers being held ten days.

(2) He was speaking *prophetically.*

If it was purely figurative, then the ten days reflect any period of trial and tribulation that any believer will go through, no matter the length of time, suggesting that we are all going to be tested by the devil in one form or another and we are all going to suffer for Christ.

Specifically for the Smyrna church, it meant some of them were going to be tested and suffer intensely—the historical record tells us that this is exactly what happened.

If it was also a prophetic reference, and I believe it was, it means that there will be a time when followers of Christ will be held for ten literal days in prison. I believe Christ was referring to the End times—and, again, historically, there is no direct evidence *anywhere in any society or in any judicial system* of a ten day stay for Christians facing death. This tells us that it was a figurative *as well as* prophetic reference, applying directly to the Smyrna church and the future Church simultaneously.

In these violent and increasingly bizarre and violent modern times, it doesn't seem at all unlikely that something like this could happen: Christians not killed *out in the field* will be thrown into prison for a total of ten days (of torture, coercion, brainwashing, you name it), and if they fail to denounce Jesus by the end of the ten days they are put to death.

How can we survive this worst-case scenario? Through dedicated preparation by studying the survival handbook, the Book of Revelation!

THE CROWN OF LIFE FORETOLD

Here comes the good part: after the martyrs have been put to death they will receive *the crown of life* from the Lord! The phrase *crown of life* means *one Spirit in us*, which is the blessing of eternal life. The original Greek word, *stephanos*, can be translated *twine* or *wreath*, a symbol of honor and royalty, and literally or figuratively *crown*. It can also be associated with the Greek word *diadema*, which means *diadem* or *crown*, a clear indication of kingly and queenly authority and royalty.[10]

Reward Number 2
TO RECEIVE THE CROWN OF LIFE

Revelation 2:11

"'He who has an ear, let him hear what the Spirit says to the churches. He who overcomes shall not be hurt by the second death.'"

THE SECOND DEATH!

For the second time, Jesus tells his loved ones to listen and understand the Spirit. He promises those who overcome— specifically, *those who overcome persecution*, but in general, those who overcome the tribulations of life and retain their faith in Christ—they shall never be hurt by the second death.

To understand what is meant by the second death we're going to need to examine the concept of salvation in more detail, get down to the nuts-and-bolts of it.

SALVATION: HOW IT WORKS

We are told by Jesus that all have sinned and fall short of the glory of God (Rom. 3:23), but we are *born again* when we believe in him.

The term *born again* is no mere metaphor here. When we accept him as our Lord and Savior, believing that he rose from the dead and is alive forevermore, the human being's soul is literally transformed—it is not a physical change, but a literal spiritual change of heart, or rather, change of nature, from fallen nature cocooned in Christ's death to holy butterfly. To be born again is to place the *old self* (the fallen nature) aside and step back and watch the *New Self* replace it (the nature of God, as referenced in 2Cor. 5:17). But how does this happen?

How it works, essentially: it's specifically the job of the Holy Spirit, he who comes into your heart/soul and, in a way we do not understand, performs an *operation from within* (in a hyperdimensional sense). He does this because in faith you've asked Jesus Christ to be your Lord and Savior, a faith which he has, in fact, given you through Christ, or perhaps another way of saying it is, he first reached out to you in faith and then you responded in faith. (Faith is a gift given to us by God, part of his most excellent grace.) As a result, the Holy Spirit is kind of like an Emergency Medical Technician. He provides emergency services the instant you ask him to rescue you, and once you've been healed by the Great Physician, the healing lasts forever (John 3: 5–8; 14–16; Gal. 3:24).

The most amazing thing in the universe, the most unexplainable and mind altering and life changing experience anywhere, more intriguing than the mystery of black holes and bigger than the blast of supernovas and infinitely more complex than the human brain—and it happens at the speed of faith. Truly amazing indeed.

Now, as I said, how this is done is a complete and total mystery. My granddaughter recently said in reference to this topic, "It's a God thing." She's correct. That's all the answer we're going to get and it's probably all the answer we need.

The operation changes us in a deeply profound way. The change is hyperdimensional, existing in this reality as well as the reality of God. It not only fixes what once was broken, it brings what was once removed from God into God, and you can't get any closer than that. At that point, we are able to be directed or guided by the Holy Spirit, and the reason for this is because of the emergency operation and the fact that the Physician, the Holy Spirit, now resides within you. This is known as the *Indwelling Spirit.*

Good works appear in our lives, as well as the fruit of the Spirit: love, joy, peace, patience, kindness, goodness, faithfulness, gentleness, and self control. At the point of the Holy Spirit's operation, the human soul is then "...dead in...trespasses and sins..." (Eph. 2:1) because it is washed in the ever-cleansing blood of Christ, the Redeemer.

Then a most amazing thing happens: the saved human soul becomes a participant of and within the divine nature of Christ himself (Gal. 2:20; Eph. 2:10; Col. 1:27; 1Pet. 2:23–25; 2Pet. 1:4). We live out our lives on earth in the still physical and fallen body/nature, and, yes, we continue to battle with our fallen nature and the fallen world we exist in, but we battle it out with a changed, or more precisely, *regenerated* heart/soul.

It should be pretty clear that being born again or saved—being a Christian—whether Catholic, Orthodox, or within the collective Christian Protestant Church, is essentially the reception of an entirely new and alien nature, the divine and holy nature of God, which is a staggering thought![11]

SALVATION: HOW DEATH HAS PHASES

The first death is the physical death with which we are familiar, our first and only experience of death through and because of sin. Most of humanity will experience the first death.

The second death is the final transformation of humanity at the end of the seventh millennium. The saved and the unsaved will experience it.

The unsaved will be transformed into the Second Phase of Body, the glorified body, and will remain in the second body to face judgment and eternity, their body cycle forever incomplete.

The saved in Christ will face the *second death* knowing full well that Jesus promises that it shall not be painful. For them, it will be the last and final transfiguration within the Phase of Body. They will receive a special body like they have never before experienced, a new and utterly perfect physical and spiritual body. This is the really exciting final transfiguration that happens at the end of the Kingdom Age, when time itself ceases—this is the second death for the saved. We will be given *superglorified bodies* that will be totally spiritual, totally physical, totally eternal and divine and, clearly, incomprehensible.

Remember, repentant humanity will pass through three transfigurations; three different body-phases:

(1) The fallen.

(2) The first transfiguration.

(3) The final and complete transfiguration, and as usual it's tied into God's holy mathematics/geometry, a beautiful representation of the most Holy Trinity! Always three!

Our new and exciting bodies will be transferred from this world to the New Earth that comes from God (from his heaven, the First Heaven), when the Holy and eternal Age of mankind begins. Remember, the third and final Age of mankind is complete perfection, such as we cannot imagine! If you think the present world is glorious now, you haven't seen anything yet! The beauty of the reformed earth during the Kingdom Age will be breathtaking and awe inspiring as well, but the New and final Earth's beauty is going to be unimaginable.

At the close of the seventh millennium—this is when the new, shining city of Jerusalem will come down from God's heaven and rest on the New Earth, our place to live forevermore! Yes, even forever and ever! This New Earth is heaven itself to the saved, with Jesus as their God for eternity!

Reward Number 3
NOT TO BE HURT BY THE SECOND DEATH!

Revelation 2:12

"And to the angel of the church in Pergamos write, 'These things says he who has the sharp two-edged sword...'"

COMPROMISING

John writes to the third angel: the Lord, who has the sharp, double-edged sword, announces, "These are my words." He is urging John to narrate the third message to the company of Christians in Pergamos, who, like the two previous churches and their congregations, portray all believers in Jesus Christ from John's time until today—specifically, he's speaking to those who are yielding in their faith.

PERGAMOS

But first, a little history: Pergamos was a Greek city in western Asia, about 60 miles north of Smyrna and about 20 miles from the sea, beautiful and wealthy and often called *the first city in Asia*. It was also known for its idolatry. That's why it was also called *the city of Satan*. It was famous for an architectural wonder, a religious grove filled with all kinds of statues and alters. Undoubtedly, the city was a violent place, as Antipas was martyred there (Rev. 2:13). It had an enormous library containing 200,000 books, a university, a royal residence, and just like all the other cities in its neck of the Asian woods, it was considered something of a pagan religious center. As an interesting historical side-note, in the late 1800s, Carl Human, a German engineer, discovered the great altar of Zeus there, which some believe to be *Satan's seat*, the throne of Satan mentioned in Revelation 2:13. The altar is now located in Berlin.[12]

Revelation 2:13

"'I know your works, and where you dwell, where Satan's throne is. And you hold fast to my name, and did not deny my faith even in the days in which Antipas was my faithful martyr, who was killed among you, where Satan dwells.'"

HOLD FAST TO HIS NAME

The Son of Man knows the deeds of his believers in this congregation. He is aware that they live in a city that viciously ridicules Christianity. The people of Pergamos have great hostility toward the sovereign God, the very One who created them.

Leaping to the present, even though thousands of years have passed things have not changed very much, for the same kind of hostility from the wicked against those believing in the Lord is experienced today in many countries around the globe, including America where people favor removing any reference to God from schools; prefer that their children not know the Lord—and so their children become violent, abusive, destructive, self-destructive, and lost because that is the natural outcome of the lack of the knowledge of God and the absence of prayers to assist them through the day; favor choice over the innocent, voiceless, and helpless cries of unborn babies; embrace every form of sexual immorality and the so-called liberating freedom of hedonism, i.e., self-worship and self-indulgence; celebrate dishonest Presidents and corporate-puppet politicians. In a word, they have forgotten their God.

For all intents and purposes, it appears as if the prince of darkness may be winning the battle, for his throne, Satan's seat, is the earth entire—it's not *only* in Berlin! This is a powerful motivator for Jesus to return, as he will come to destroy the Evil One and those who follow his wicked ways.

"Do not be deceived, God is not mocked; for whatever a man sows, that will he also reap. For he who sows to his flesh (to please his or her own destructive and dangerously self-absorbed desires) will of the flesh reap corruption (he or she will be planting seeds of evil and will surely reap a harvest of spiritual decay and death), but he who sows to the Spirit, will of the Spirit reap everlasting life. And let us not grow weary while doing good, for in due season we shall reap (we will be blessed) if we do not lose heart. Therefore, as we have opportunity, let us do good to all, especially to those who are of the household of faith (those who belong to the family of God)" (Gal. 6:7-10).

Revelation 2:14

"'But I have a few things against you, because you have those who hold the doctrine of Balaam, who taught Balak to put a stumbling block before the children of Israel, to eat things sacrificed to idols, and to commit sexual immorality.'"

ON THE CONTRARY

Jesus respects this company of believers, but affirms that he does have some things against them: they are mixing with the heathen who believe in idols, and of course this is harmful to them, influencing them to leave the Path, causing them to sin all the more.

It's clear that this passage applies to contemporary believers. It's telling us that we need to separate ourselves from a debasing lifestyle. Christians need to love the world but not its ways and follow Christ in obedience, and fittingly, their lives should reflect this. Otherwise, they will be and probably *are* caught up in its immoral ways, just like the company of Pergamos.

Many people today believe in the Lord, but again, their lives hardly reflect the relationship they have with their Creator, the relationship they *could* have—there is so much potential lost here! They say they honor God but visit *dens of iniquity*, like, for example, strip clubs, pornography web sites on the Internet, and on and on. They flock to see immoral movies that are filled with graphic violence and explicit sex. They do drugs and over-indulge in alcohol. Their tongues are tainted with vulgarity and they don't think twice about it. They constantly use the Lord's name in vain, displaying clearly that they are no better than the lost, when in fact they are worse because they should know better! They have indiscriminate sexual relations, as if the sacred and beautiful act of sexual intercourse were something as banal and unimportant as turning the TV set on and off or microwaving some popcorn.

They're hateful and practice racial/religious prejudice or physical/verbal/emotional/sexual abuse—and these are practicing Christians!

This destructive double life can be seen in less obvious (but no less extreme and destructive) ways: dishonesty; lack of integrity; gossip; apathy; lust; lack of respect for others exemplified by explosive temper; constant strife and bickering; henpecking; unrealistic, self-centered expectations placed on others; lack of control of the imagination in regard to sexual fantasy or mental adultery—the whole ball of secret bad habits and emotional wax.

The Christian is called to be honorable in public, reflecting the nature of his/her Creator publicly, and honorable *in secret*, reflecting the nature of his/her Creator in private. The Christian is called to be honorable inside the individual home/family as well as *inside the individual mind*—this may sound nearly impossible to accomplish, that kind of mental control, but through the grace and power of Christ it is indeed not only possible, it's doable and useful!

"So I tell you this in the Lord, and insist on it in the Lord, that you (believers) must no longer live (mix with) as the Gentiles (unbelievers) do, in the futility of their thinking. They are darkened in their understanding and separated from the life of God because of the ignorance that is in them due to the hardening of their hearts. Having lost all sensitivity, they have given themselves over to sensuality so as to indulge in every kind of impurity, with a continual lust for more" (Eph. 4:17–19). Turn away from following the examples of the lost, for our children pick up their habits and fall right into the grasp of the ruler of the kingdom of the air, that wicked spirit who is now at work on those who are disobedient.

CHILDREN:
LOVE THEM & LOVE THEM

When departing from this earth who can take their worldly riches with them? No one can! The only thing eternal in this world is the human soul. Therefore, look upon your children as your most precious possessions: of all the things you have on this earth, your children are more precious than diamonds, than moon rocks, than anything in the universe entire. They are the only ones you can take to heaven! Nothing else from this earth can follow you there. Love them and then love them more, and more, and more— you can never love too much in this world! You can never forgive enough in this world!

Love them and forgive them and teach your children to fear and honor the Lord your God and to keep all his commandments to the best of their ability—to love the Lord with all their hearts, with all their souls, with all their minds, and with all their might. Teach your children diligently to know the God of heaven through Christ Jesus. Talk of the Godhead when you sit in your home, when you are out walking, when you go to bed, and when you arise in the morning. Build for them the foundation upon which they will stand for the rest of their earthly lives, so that when the storms come and they are blown away and beaten, battered, and perhaps even broken, falling away, they will regardless fall onto their solid and unmovable Foundation that is Christ Jesus—and so they will be rebuilt by his love and stand firm once again. They will follow Christ instead of Satan. They will live in heaven with you and Christ, instead of in the lake of fire with the lost and the devil. They will be blessed by knowing the knowledge of God.

SONS & DAUGHTERS & STANDARDS

Teach your sons, your daughters, and your grandchildren to know the Lord, that your days may be prolonged (1Ki. 3:14; Ps. 91:16; Pr. 10:27; Ecc. 12:1). Restrain from using bad language at all, but especially in the presence of your spouse and children, for the standard you reflect is the standard they follow. Never allow your children to use the Lord's name in vain. If you refrain from it so will your children.

Because of sin, life is a cruel and difficult road, it is true, but it's a beautiful and hopeful road too, filled with so much promise— your children are part of that hope and promise. Never forget that. Life is wonderful in countless ways; always remember that it is a privilege to be alive and thank God for the life he has given you, but remember that children are a precious part of that life. Even when life is hard and unrewarding; even when life is cruel and filled with tragedy and it seems to make no sense at all, be thankful for your life and the children in it! For God created you and them out of his Complete and Total Love—if your life reflects this standard, it will reflect in your children.

Revelation 2:15

"'Thus you also have those who hold the doctrine of the Nicolaitans, which thing I hate.'"

THE END OF THE HUMAN AGE

God's Son says his followers believe in him, but some members of the Pergamos church were following the ways of the Nicolaitans. You remember them. Christ detested this sect enormously, and he makes that clear enough. Verse 14 begins with "But I have a few things against you…" Verse 15 continues with "…who hold the doctrine of the Nicolaitans…" It finally ends with a rather powerful word to explain just how he feels about this sect: *hate*. This is very clear indeed.

Since the practices of the Nicolaitan sect seems to be alive and well today, in one form or another, imagine his enormous disapproval of our behavior! Add to that the fact that our contemporary behavior is indicative of the times that Jesus told us to look for that show the end of the Human Age and you could argue, and pretty strongly too, that those End Times are here!

Jesus informs us that, "Because lawlessness will abound, the love of many will grow cold…and then the end will come" (Mat. 24:12–13). He also says, "…scoffers will come in the last days, walking according to their own lusts, and saying, 'Where is the promise of his (Jesus') coming?'" (2 Pet. 3:3–4a). He says in Matthew 24:37, "As the days of Noah were, so also will the coming of the Son of Man be!" It's pretty clear that our days are, if nothing else, strikingly similar to the days when Noah was on earth. The world has become as depraved and lost as it was before the world flood, and if you think that's overstatement, I argue: the world has learned how to wear its sin better so that it doesn't appear as sinful. It doesn't appear as sinful because of science, technology, education, and a shrinking global community.

Specifically, of course, fallen human nature hasn't changed a jot since day one. All the sin that was going on in Noah's day has been going on since Noah's day, right on into our present day, but today it's just not as noticeable in some corners of the world where it may appear toned-down, politically correct, or controlled, or even overcome, but of course that's not the truth. It's still here, alive and well in every human heart. Read your local paper or watch the evening news or get on the Internet and you will see it. The world is still the same as it was in the days of Noah, it's just better dressed. But I believe the world is about to lose its well mannered, well bred, well educated, tolerant Tuxedo, for the sinful truth is about to come out, and comparably, the days of Noah will be looked upon as the Good Old Days of Decent Behavior.

AFTER THE TUXEDO

Only during the Kingdom Age will humankind finally be sinless, for sin will be removed from the hearts of men and women. Then they shall be like him, for they shall be washed clean by the blood of the Lamb.

By equating the End Times to the period of Noah and its uninhibited wickedness, Jesus is indicating that an immensely wicked period of time is coming upon humanity—our time, when the tolerant Tuxedo will come off! In the past, humans were destroyed for being exceedingly sinful. Because of their great wickedness God caused the earth to be completely flooded, and you know the rest: except for Noah and his family the entire world population perished! The sign of the rainbow that followed the global flood was a promise that he shall never again destroy humanity (or *all flesh*) by floodwaters. But the Scriptures do not suggest that he would never again move to destroy all fallen-natured flesh. Clearly, at his return the unrepentant (fallen-natured flesh) will be totally obliterated, not by floodwaters but by fire, which in turn will cleanse the earth, for God's moral law surpasses all aspects of his creation.

Revelation 2:16

"'Repent, or else I will come to you quickly and will fight against them with the sword of my mouth.'"

TIME TO REPENT

There is still time and the time is now. Let us overcome sin by repentance and make Jesus our first love. Jesus says, "He who overcomes... I will not blot out his name from the Book of Life..." (Rev. 3:5). The Lord quickly comes with the sword of his mouth. The believers who insist on living as their *old selves* are encouraged to repent. Put off the kingdom of darkness and let the *new self* be filled with his light, in you. Be renewed day by day by his unfailing love. There is no creature hidden from his sight. All things are naked and open to the eyes of him to whom we must give account!

Revelation 2:17

"'He, who has an ear, let him hear what the Spirit says to the churches. To him who overcomes I will give some of the hidden manna to eat. And I will give him a white stone, and on the stone a new name written which no one knows except him who receives it.'"

HIDDEN MANNA

For the third time we are informed by Christ to listen and understand what the Spirit says to his believers throughout the ages. Those who overcome are first rewarded by receiving *hidden manna.*

In regard to manna, we're not entirely sure what the exact nature of hidden manna is, at least, in a literal sense. In a figurative sense, it's clear that the word is used here as a symbol of immortality.

We do know that it is a direct reference to the manna spoken of in the Old Testament, the food God gave the Israelites while they wandered through the desert. Manna was a gift from God and not a true product of nature—it came from beyond our world and universe. It had a supernatural, perhaps even multidimensional nature. When the Israelites saw it they said, "What is it?' For they did not know what it was" (Ex. 16:15). It appeared every morning, except on the Sabbath, small, round seed-looking things. It may have looked like an early morning frost. It had to be gathered in the morning because the sun, it seems, would melt it, and apparently it had to be gathered every day. If it wasn't gathered every day it decomposed. The Israelites ground it down and baked it, and as far as we can tell it tasted something like olive oil and wafers made with honey. The entire nation of Israel existed on it for 40 years. It stopped appearing when they got new grain from the land of Canaan (Ex. 16: 14–36; Num. 11:7–9; Deut. 8:3; 16; Josh. 5:12; Ps. 78:24–25).

Now, it seems that hidden manna is, first and foremost, used in this verse as a symbol of immortality, but some eschatological scholars tend to think it might apply to something literal, *a spiritual nutritional supplement* perhaps. As intriguing as this concept sounds it seems highly unlikely to me that humanity will need a spiritual nutritional supplement because we will be perfect in nature and body and clearly immortal through the grace and power of Christ, and that being the case we will not rely on anything other than Christ to sustain or even promote life.

Whatever the case may be, the most important thing to remember here is that this manna was of God and whatever it refers to, be it literal or figurative, or both, we can be sure that it is a wonderful blessing![13]

NEW NAMES

The second gift is a pure white gemstone. Jesus gives a pure white gemstone to those who are faithful! On the stones are written their new names, chosen by the Son. No one knows this very special name except the one who receives it!

No one else bears this new name, for it is his or hers alone. No more will people bear the names of thousands of other people! Their new names will be sacred, unique, and suit their personalities. They will be given to them personally by Jesus Christ! It does seem reasonable to conclude that these new names may be, in a way, similar to those the Israelites gave to many of their people. Jesus called John *Son of Thunder*. Jesus knew John so thoroughly that he could give him a name that truly reflected who he was. This explains just how well Jesus knows each individual who is faithful to him, which will make these names very special names indeed! Perhaps an appropriate name for a particular woman loved by God will be *Daughter of Heaven!* Someone else may be named *Son of Splendor!* People should make an effort to know the Lord Jesus so they are sure to receive a new name for all eternity. What amazing promises Jesus has for those he loves!

The new special name is given to us at the end of the thousand years when we are transformed for the second time (our Third Phase of Body) from our millennial bodies to our new superglorified bodies. We will have new names, ready for the New Earth and the New City of Jerusalem. This is the final beginning (that never ends because it's outside of time) in our new heaven, sent down to us by God.

YAHWEH'S NEW NAME

Not only are his faithful believers privileged to receive a new name, but Christ informs us that he also gives himself a brand new name! "He who overcomes, I will make him a pillar in the temple of my God, and he shall go out no more. I will write on him the name of my God *(Yahweh*, in Hebrew) and the name of the city of my God, the New Jerusalem, which comes down out of heaven from my God. And I will write on him my new name" (Rev. 3:12).

It is likely that Jesus gives himself the new name when he makes all things new at the conclusion of the thousand year rest period, the seventh millennium, the Kingdom Age.

OLD NAMES & OLD MEMORIES

It is unlikely that we will retain our present earthly names. The names we have now were created in the fallen state/universe. It makes sense that they, like everything else from this universe, will be left behind forever—except for the life experience in this universe, of course. That will always be with us, in memory or in some form or another.

It's true that some Christians argue we will not be able to retain the memories of our lives on the fallen earth once we've been spiritually transformed, but that idea diminishes and reduces Christ's sacrificial act because it makes life on the fallen earth pointless. If we can't remember who we were and can't remember our sinful experience on the fallen earth, what it was like to be separated from God in some way, shape or form, you've then got to ask what was the point of the entire exercise of living on the earth in the first place? Why send Christ to die for humanity if we're not even going to remember who we were and the reason for it?

Reward Number 4
HIDDEN MANNA & A PRECIOUS WHITE STONE BEARING OUR NEW NAMES

Revelation 2:18

"And to the angel of the church in Thyatira write, 'These things says the Son of God, who has eyes like a flame of fire, and his feet like fine brass...'"

CORRUPT

The message from the fourth angel is given to believers in the company in the city of Thyatira. John again verifies that the writings are proclaimed by the Son of God, for John says he has "eyes like a flame of fire" and his feet "are like fine brass." (This description was given to us in Revelation 1:14–15 and in this passage from Revelation 2:18.) Such a description would only relate to Jesus, the Christ!

THYATIRA

Turning to Thyatira in history: it was a city in Asia Minor within the borders of Mysia and Ionia, a little south of a river called Lycus, a Macedonian colony (one of many, it seems). It boasted a temple to the sun-god Apollo and apparently a temple to Artemis as well. Because of its water, Thyatira was one of the best places for dyeing cloth (even to this day), as Acts 16:14 makes clear when it points out that Lydia was *a seller of purple fabrics* from Thyatira. The modern city of *Akhisar* rests on the ancient city site in the territory that is now known as Anatolian Turkey.[14]

Revelation 2:19

"'I know your works, love, faith, service, and your patience; and as for your works, the last are more than the first.'"

CHRIST KNOWS THE FAITHFUL

Jesus knows of the love from those who believe: their patience; their helpfulness to others; their faithfulness in spreading the Word; their service; and their perseverance. They are placing themselves last and others first, and Christ has recognized that.

Revelation 2:20

"'Nevertheless I have a few things against you, because you allow that woman Jezebel, who calls herself a prophetess, to teach and beguile my servants to commit sexual immorality and eat things sacrificed to idols.'"

NEVERTHELESS!

Undoubtedly, the Thyratirian church allowed the heathen to corrupt them with idol worship and sexual immorality, led specifically, it seems, by a woman Christ called *Jezebel.*

Historically, the name *Jezebel* was an unflattering nickname for *all that was detestable*, based on the woman spoken of in the Old Testament, 1Kings 16:31; 18:13; 2Kings 9:7; 22; 2Kings 9:30–37. The name is more than likely used here to describe a woman and her followers who were influencing the Thyratirian church, causing them to follow false teachings and support and practice immoral behavior, similar to how the historical Jezebel led Israel into idolatry.[15]

In our day, it's easy to apply the sexually immoral behavior of our culture to this verse. Clearly, many of us have been lead astray by the modern day *Jezebel*: in a general sense, the media, politicians, and celebrity hold a portion of the blame, but at the end of the day the blame falls squarely on ourselves as individuals. Our Anything Goes culture (or lack thereof) is a reflection of our society's heart. It's a simple enough step (certainly not a big leap) to go from the idolatry in the days of Thyatira and apply that to our modern age—money, greed, self-indulgence, self-worship, a celebrity obsessed culture. These are the idols and gods of our day.

We forget that we were bought at a price. (Christ gave so much for us!) You are therefore encouraged to break free from the slavery to fame and celebrity, greed, sex—whatever it is that you're enslaved to—and humble yourselves before the Lord. Break free from the dark and broken things of humankind! "Do you not know that the unrighteous will not inherit the kingdom of God? Do not be deceived. Neither fornicators, nor idolaters, nor adulterers, nor homosexuals, nor sodomites, nor thieves, nor covetous (those desiring that which is another's), nor drunkards, nor revilers (those who use abusive language), nor extortioners will inherit the kingdom of God" (ICor. 6:9–10).

Revelation 2:21

"'And I gave her time to repent, and she does not want to repent of sexual immorality.'"

GIVEN TIME TO REPENT

Jesus Christ gives sinners time to change their ways from sexual and ethical immorality, which (historically, every time) corrupts a church (as in the case with Thyatira). Sexual and ethical immorality corrupts a culture, a nation, a world power, and leads to its destruction. Clearly, the cycle is about to repeat itself. As Rome fell because of its moral and ethical corruption, so shall the world powers of our day fall.

Christ has given the woman in question and her followers' time to repent of their immoral ways—he is a patient and forgiving God, and because of that it's clear that he must deeply love us all, but even so, his patience can run out.

Revelation 2:22

"'Indeed I will cast her into a sickbed, and those who commit adultery with her into great tribulation, unless they repent of her deeds.'"

THE CONSEQUENCES

The Son of God warns the Thyatrian church: if they continue in sexual immorality and stubbornly determine not to change their ways but continue to follow Jezebel and her followers they will, in fact, force his great wrath upon them—unless they repent. What's most amazing here is even at this point, with his patience all but gone, the Father is still willing to forgive them! Nevertheless, should they not repent, there will be consequences for their behavior. They will suffer, as surely as Jezebel is going to suffer.

This can be applied to our day and culture sure enough, to the masses of our morally bankrupt world—and there will be terrible consequences at the end of this Age when the dreadful and bloody Tribulation is brought upon the unrepentant.

Perhaps the consequences of our immoral behavior are at hand,
for great earthquakes shake the land!
Massive rains flood the rivers and the land!
Violent hurricanes and tsunamis (tidal waves) sweep the land!
Massive tornados rip across the land!
Great winter blizzards and ice storms cover the land!
Excessive summer heat bakes the land!
Forest and brushfires burn the land!
Volcanoes erupt and destroy the land!

What does all this mean? An increase in natural disasters is spoken of in Revelation. It is doubtful that these bizarre and destructive weather patterns and destructive events are merely a coincidence, byproducts of nature and humanity!

Return to God and he shall bless the land. "If my people who are called by my name will humble themselves, and pray and seek my face (search for me), and turn from their wicked ways, then I will hear from heaven, and will forgive their sin and heal their land" (2Chron. 7:14).

Revelation 2:23

"'And I will kill her children with death. And all the churches shall know that I am he who searches the minds and hearts. And I will give to each one of you according to your works.'"

HE WHO SEARCHES MINDS & HEARTS

Obviously, in relation to the verse, Jesus has lost his patience with Jezebel and her wicked followers. I'd argue that he's lost his patience with the modern equivalent of Jezebel and her followers in our time too. We are bringing the judgment of God down upon our own heads because we do not repent. All Christ's faithful should know that Jesus is the one who searches minds and hearts—and we will know, soon enough. All the churches will know, for God is going to bring a noticeable and devastating judgment on us, the modern Jezebel and her followers, because we would not repent of our sins. John is calling to us! We should know the punishment for sin is death. Therefore, we should not pick up the ways of the ungodly. God will punish the unrepentant, as well as reward the faithful.

It's important that we understand here that the faithful are made righteous by the blood of Jesus and that is our reward. We should remember here that we are saved by the grace of Christ and not by works or by what we think, say or do. Good works are the end result of our salvation, the direct result of Christ being in our lives. They will be noticeable: in your private and public behavior; in the things you choose or choose not to do. They are the reflection and fruit of who you are in Christ, and as such you will find reward or acknowledgement from Christ.

Revelation 2:24

"'Now to you I say, to the rest in Thyatira, as many as do not have this doctrine, who have not known the depths of Satan, as they say, I put on you no other burden.'"

GOD WITH US

God says to the company in Thyatira (and this applies to all the corrupt religious organizations abounding on the earth from the time of Thyatira until today) that if they repent of their immoral behavior and refrain from following the evil ways of Satan they shall be forgiven and blessed!

He also says he will give them no other burden—this shows us the compassion of Christ toward his faithful servants when they follow in obedience, and of course this can be applied to us today.

I think it's important to remind ourselves here that the Godhead keeps track of all we accomplish and do. Nothing is overlooked! The reason this is brought up now is simply because God knew exactly what was going on in the hearts of the Thyatira church and the people of its city—his relationship with each individual was intimate, just as it is today. Every act and every thought is known and recorded, for he is Emmanuel, God with Us, the indwelling Christ who lives, moves, and has his being in us. Our bodies are the temple of God. Therefore, all is witnessed by him.

Revelation 2:25
"'But hold fast to what you have till I come.'"

HOLD FAST

Jesus encourages the church and its people to hold on very dearly to whatever knowledge they have of Jesus. They must hold fast to what they have until the Son of Man comes with the clouds—what could be more encouraging than that?

This *holding out* can only be accomplished by *holding onto* Christ, who will in turn *hold on to you* (and never let you go), for he is quite aware how difficult holding out will turn out to be in this life, and of course that is part of the point. Let *him* hold *you* fast until he returns, not Lucifer!

Revelation 2:26
"'And he who overcomes, and keeps my works until the end, to him I will give power over the nations...'"

GOD'S GOOD GRAVY

To those who hold fast, Jesus offers yet another wonderful promise. This can be directly applied to the Church entire, to all believers throughout history: he will give them authority over the nations. This promise will be fully realized during the thousand year reign with the Son of Man during the Kingdom Age. Like all governmental systems (like God himself, who is *the* system), there will be a hierarchy of order and power. This brings us back to the words *reward* and *works*.

This is put simply, but you'll get the idea: it's true that the closer you are to the Lord now the more your life will reflect the nature of the Savior now, bearing fruit in this life—in public/private behavior, volunteering, feeding the hungry, clothing the naked, etc. Why? Answer: by opening yourself up to Christ so that he can power you up and live through you; by serving Christ and living a Christ-like life.

It's also true that the closer you are to the Lord now, the closer you will be with him in the seventh millennium—in an authoritative sense, your position within the *governmental hierarchy*. The stronger your love and devotion is for Jesus now (faith and good works), the greater your position of authority and responsibility will be when he reigns in the Kingdom Age (and beyond, into the Holy Age), for he makes us "...kings and priests to his God and Father, to him be glory and dominion forever and ever" (Rev. 1:6).

It should be pointed out here once again that none of these rewards and positions of responsibility have anything to do with salvation—these rewards of authority and responsibility are merely a reflection of how you chose to live your life in faith, in action, in choice. The act of salvation is the act of grace through and because of Christ, and of course this is our greatest reward and it is reward enough. Everything and anything else that follows, like positions of authority and responsibility, are merely more of God's good gravy.

Revelation 2:27

"He shall rule them with a rod of iron; they shall be dashed to pieces like the potter's vessels, as I also have received from my Father.'"

THE WAY & THE TRUTH

Through the seventh millennium, humanity's last 1,000 years in (perfect) time, Jesus and his government will rule the world wisely, strictly, and with abundant love—the same way his Father rules in heaven. He and his Father are One in love.

Reward Number 5
TO RULE THE NATIONS UNDER JESUS CHRIST, THE SON OF GOD.
This is a satisfying promise!

Revelation 2:28
"'...and I will give him the morning star!'"

THE BRIGHT & MORNING STAR

In the figurative sense the Morning Star is a symbol of Jesus Christ, whom we shall receive!

In one short verse the Savior gives his greatest blessing to all who follow him. Remember always, and treasure, this great promise and most wonderful blessing. He says, "I GIVE YOU THE MORNING STAR!" He faithfully announces this with all his love. This is an exciting, thrilling, and hopeful promise—and it isn't merely an emblem for lofty position and responsibility, for *he* is the Morning Star! "I, Jesus, have sent my angel to testify to you these things in the churches. I am the root and the offspring of David, the bright and morning star" (Rev. 22:16).

"The mystery of the seven stars which you saw in my right hand...the seven stars are the angels of the seven churches" (Rev. 1:20). From this verse we gather from the Son of God that these seven stars, the angels, and the churches symbolize the Seven Spirits of God, representing Jesus himself, for he has the Seven Spirits.

ONE BIG STAR

It's not a big leap to suggest that the seven stars signify one big star. This enormous star is the manifestation of God, who is Jesus Christ, the Bright and Morning Star. Of course, I'm not suggesting that the *big star* is God—that God is *in form* similar to a star or planet. But considering the supernatural nature of everything we're discussing, the fact that these things are quite beyond our comprehension and powers of description, it's not unreasonable to suggest that this alludes to something of God that is in fact quite literal!

Reward Number 6
TO RECEIVE THE MORNING STAR!

Revelation 2:29
"He, who has an ear, let him hear what the Spirit says to the churches.'"

LISTEN!

Four times Jesus declares that people must listen and understand what the Spirit says. It must be vitally important for everyone to listen and understand, for this statement is repeated over and over. Obey the Lord and let your heart keep his commands and live! Gain wisdom! Gain understanding! Gain enlightenment! Listen to the covenant and instruction of Christ and glory in his name! Your survival depends on your belief in Christ.

* * * * *

SOURCES:

1. *Ephesus; Ancient/Classical History,* The History Net,
   <http://www.ancienthistory.about.com>.
   Ephesus, <http://www.PBS.org> and <http://www.turizm.net>.
   Ephesus, pg. 366-367, The New Unger's Bible Dictionary, Moody Press (1988).
   The Seven Churches, Or The Things Which Are, Revelation, Gray's Home Bible Commentary; *Revelation,* Henry's Concise Commentary, The Bible Library Delux, version 5.0. suite, CD-ROM, Ellis Enterprises, Inc. (2,000).
2. *The Cult of Selfishness,* Christians Living by Faith Movement (2002),
   <http://www.accsoft.net>.
3. *Nicolaitans,* C. M. Kerr, International Bible Standard Encyclopedia, Online Edition, <http://www.studylight.or>.
   Nicolaitans, pg. 921, The New Unger's Bible Dictionary, Moody Press (1988).
   The Seven Churches, Or The Things Which Are, Revelation, Gray's Home Bible Commentary; *Revelation,* Henry's Concise Commentary, The Bible Library Delux, version 5.0. suite, CD-ROM, Ellis Enterprises, Inc. (2,000).
4. *Ecumenicism; Where Do You Draw the Line?* Deception in the Church (1998),
   <http://www.deceptioninthechurch.com>.
   The United Religions: Globalist and New Age Plans, Lee Pen, SCP Journal VOL. 23:2-23:3 (1999) *The United Religions: Globalist and New Age Plans,* Lee Pen, SCP Journal VOL. 23:2-23:3 (1999); "An earlier version of this story appeared in "The United Religions Initiative - A Bridge Back to Gnosticism," published in December 1998 by the New Oxford Review. You may order the complete story from the Review, or subscribe to the Review, by calling (510) 526-5374, or by writing to the New Oxford Review, 1069 Kains Ave., Berkeley, CA 94706. Additionally, it also has been published as part of "The United Religions Initiative: Foundations for a World Religion" (Part 1), published in May 1999 by the Journal of the Spiritual Counterfeits Project, Vol. 22:4-23:1. The information in this extract is a small portion of the information printed in the SCP Journal. You may order the complete story from the Journal, or subscribe to the Journal, by calling (510) 540-0300, or by writing to the Spiritual Counterfeits Project, Post Office Box 4308, Berkeley, CA 94704, or by visiting the SCP web site, <http://www.scp-inc.org>.""

Ecumenicism, Southwest Institute for Orthodox Studies, an Orthodox Apologetics Ministry; Orthodox Christian Information Center, <http://www.orthodoxinfo.com>.

United Religions Initiative, <http://www.uri.org>, The United Religions Initiative, P.O. Box 29242 San Francisco, CA 94129, USA.

5. *Tree of Life,* James Josiah Reeve, International Bible Standard Encyclopedia, Online Edition, <http://wwww.studylight.org>.

6. *Tree,* pg. 1306; *Vegetable Kingdom,* pg. 1340, The New Unger's Bible Dictionary, Moody Press (1988).

The Garden of Eden; Genesis Chapter 2, Gray's Home Bible Commentary, The Bible Library Delux, version 5.0. suite, CD-ROM, Ellis Enterprises, Inc. (2,000).

7. *Smyrna,* The Perseus Digital Library, Gregory Crane, Editor-in-Chief, Tufts University, <http://www.perseus.tufts.edu> @ Ancient Sites, Classics 63, Archeology and Architecture of the Greco-Roman World, Internet Resources, Beth Severy, <http://www.macalester.edu>.

Smyrna, pg. 1204, The New Unger's Bible Dictionary, Moody Press (1988).

8. *The Martyrdom of Polycarp,* Early Christian Writings, <http://www.earlychristianwritings.com>.

Smyrna; Polycarp, pg. 1204, The New Unger's Bible Dictionary, Moody Press (1988).

9. *Modern Martyrdom or Persecution Stories, VOL. 2,* Roger's Baptist Church (2002), <http://www.gospelweb.net>.

Martyrdom Continues in Modern Persecutions, Msgr. John Duncan, Our Lady of Carmel Parish, Carmel (2002), The Catholic Diocese of Lafayette-in-Indiana, <http://www.dioceseoflafayette.org>.

30 Missionaries Died in 2,000 While Fulfilling Ministry, Human Rights Without Frontiers, (2002), <http://www.hrwf.net>.

Jesus Freaks; Stories of Those Who Stood for Jesus, the Ultimate Jesus Freaks, DC Talk & The Voice of the Martyrs, Bethany House (1999) & The Voice of the Martyrs, <http://www.persecution.com>.

10. *Crown—Stephanos,* #4735, pg. 66; *crown—Diadema/Diadem,* #1238, pg. 22, Greek Dictionary of the New Testament, Strong's Exhaustive Concordance of the Bible/Dictionary of the Hebrew and Greek Words, Hendrickson Publishers.

11. *The Five Points of Calvinism* by Herman Hanko, Homer Hoeksema, and Gise J. Van Baren, Reformed Free Publishing Association (1975), all rights reserved, the Protestant Reformed Churches in America (unofficial home page web site), <http://www.prca.org/index.html>.

Exposition of the Orthodox Faith (Book I), St. John of Damascus, Orthodox Christian Information Center, <http://www.orthodoxinfo.com>; from John of Damascus, *Exposition of the Orthodox Faith,* Post Nicene Fathers, Schaff Edition, Volume IX, Series II, translated by The Rev. S. D. F. Salmond, D.D., F.e.I.s., Principal of the Free Church College, Aberdeen. (1898). *Holy Ghost,* J. Forget, transcribed by W. S. French, Jr., The Catholic Encyclopedia, Vol. VII, Online Edition, Kevin Knight (2002), <http://www.newadvent.org>.

Holy Spirit, pg. 583-584, The New Unger's Bible Dictionary, Moody Press (1988).

Holy Spirit, Microsoft Encarta Encyclopedia (2002).

The Four Spiritual Laws, Dr. Bill Bright, Campus Crusade for Christ (1965); internet version, including graphics, 1995, by Campus Crusade for Christ

International, <http://www.campuscrusade.com> or
   <http://www.ccci.org> or <http://www.greatcom.org>.
12. *Pergamos; world history* (2002), <http://www.infoplease.com>.
   Pergamos/Thyatira; Cities of Revelation, (2002),
   <http://www.luthersem.edu>.
   Pergamum, pg. 986; *Thyatira,* pg. 1279, The New Unger's Bible Dictionary,
   Moody Press (1988).
   Pergamum, Microsoft Encarta Encyclopedia (2002).
13. *Manna,* pg. 813, The New Unger's Bible Dictionary, Moody Press (1988).
   Manna, contributed by Marshal R. Crosby, Microsoft Encarta Encyclopedia
   (2002).
   What is the Hebrew Meaning of the Word Manna? Rabbi Joanne Yocheved
   Heiligman (1999), Ask A Rabbi, Jewish.com, <http://www.jewish.com>.
14. *Pergamos/Thyatira; Cities of Revelation,* (2002),
   <http://www.luthersem.edu>.
   Thyatira, pg. 1279, The New Unger's Bible Dictionary, Moody Press (1988).
   Akhisar (Thyatira), <http://www.akhisar.com>.
15. *Jezebel,* pg. 690, The New Unger's Bible Dictionary, Moody Press (1988).
   Jezebel, David Francis Roberts, International Bible Standard Encyclopedia,
   Online Edition, <http://www.studylight.org>.

Further reading:

Life the Movie: How Entertainment Conquered Reality, Neal Gabler, Knof
   (1998).
Psychology as Religion: The Cult of Self-worship, Paul C. Vitz, Wm. B.
   Eerdman's Publishing Company (1994).
So Great Salvation, Charles C. Ryrie, Moody Press (1997).
The Holy Spirit, Billy Graham, Word Publishing (2002).
Mere Christianity, C.S. Lewis, Macmillan Publishing Company (1943).
The Pursuit of God, A.W. Tozer, Christian Publications, Inc. (1982; first
   publication, 1948).
Institutes of the Christian Religion/One-Volume Edition, John Calvin (1599);
   translated by Henry Beveridge, Wm. B. Eerdmans Publishing Co. (1995).
Martin Luther, Selections From His Writings, Martin Luther (1463-1546), edited
   by John Dillenberger, Anchor (1958).
The Way of Agape, Nancy and Chuck Missler, Koinonia House (1994).

CHAPTER 3
Dead, Faithful, Lukewarm

Revelation 3:1

"And to the angel of the church in Sardis write, 'These things says he who has the Seven Spirits of God and the seven stars: 'I know your works, that you have a name that you are alive, but you are dead!'"

THE DEAD

Christ continues by speaking to the fifth angel (the minister to) the church of Sardis. The first thing John does is confirm that it is Jesus who speaks, for the Son declares once again the all-important fact that he has the Seven Spirits of God and the seven stars! Then John tells the company in Sardis that they appear alive in Christ, but he knows they are, for all intents and purposes, dead.

SARDIS

Before going on, let's turn for a moment to the city of historical Sardis: the capital of the Kingdom of Lydia, the city lay about 50 miles east of Smyrna. It sat on the side of a mountain called *Mount Tmolus,* which gave the impression to the ancients that the city was unconquerable. This was untrue, of course. It was sacked by invading armies twice. The city's beginnings stretched back to the Iron Age. Sardis means *prince, song of joy,* or *that which remains.* Trade routes, gold mines, and textile and jewelry factories powered its economy and reputation, making it one of the richest cities in Asia. Like all seven cities mentioned by John, it had a famous temple—Artemis (or Diana)—and pagan religions and cults prevailed. A community of Christians began to form there in the first century. Much later, in 1402, Sardis was completely destroyed by Tamerlane, the Conqueror. Archaeological excavations began in 1910. The city itself was not uncovered until 1958.[1]

EARNEST EFFORTS

Jesus knew of their earnest efforts, just as he knows the efforts of all believers everywhere in the world today. They had established themselves within the community of Sardis as a Christian church—not an easy feat for the time, but like the other churches they were having some troubles. Specifically, they were building up the name of Jesus, but not necessarily living up to his name. That doesn't sound too bad when compared to the other churches and their troubles.

BUT! BUT! BUT!

John tells them that as far as Christ was concerned they were as if dead! Now, that's trouble. Serious trouble. They were involved in worldly things belonging to Satan and involved with the things of God, a double life made them dead toward Christ. The Spirit was not reflected in their lives in any way! The devil's purpose is to deceive the elect of God and it seems he succeeded with the church of Sardis. He leads God's faithful along a similar path of destruction today.

THE DESTRUCTIVE PATH OF SATAN

Because Satan is an important character in End Time events, I'd like to focus on this dark being for a moment so that we have a better understanding of who and what and why he is: *Satan* is a Hebrew word for *adversary*. In the New Testament he is known as the *devil* (Greek, *diabolos*).[2] Isaiah 14:12 calls him *Lucifer* (in the literal, *day star* or *light bearer*).[3] When I talk of Satan you must remember that I'm not referring to a mythical character here, but a real spiritual being, an angel, the most powerful angel ever created by God, in fact.

As far as the scriptural doctrine of Satan is concerned in regard to his origin, nature, history, kingdom, and works—the who and what and why he is—what is revealed within the Holy Scriptures is probably all we *need* to know. We can only understand him, in the most limited way, through biblical text. That's true in regard to all angels.

His story is a sad, strange, and sinister one: created by God and given much power, beauty, and authority, he surrendered to pride and then challenged the authority, power, and position of the Holy Father, intending to replace God. He was, therefore, cast from the Father's heaven and bound to this earth in a fallen state separated spiritually from God for eternity.

Satan is a major Christian doctrine. He is a powerful spiritual being, scripturally second only to Christ in power, alien in design to humanity, and he is actively involved in human and angelic life. The earth is considered his kingdom, for he is called the dark prince of this world, and his sphere of influence and power seems to fill this fallen world/universe/reality. It's doubtful his influence reaches beyond that. He is not like God. The devil is not all-powerful. He cannot be in all places at once. He cannot create anything out of nothing. In fact, he cannot create. He is not sexual in the human sense of male and female sexuality, but it's possible that he, and angels/demons, can have sexual relations with human beings by manifesting themselves into human form. What's most clear biblically is that he is *masculine* in the sense of *male in character*. He hates God first, humanity second, and is driven by a purpose so clear and single-minded it would be safe to say it's *insect-like*: the destruction of humanity.[4]

Ultimately, the devil cannot and will not escape this fallen earth and his fallen position. His destruction is complete. But even so, he continues to war with God, humanity, and the angels, fighting to the bloody and bitter end: "And war broke out in heaven: Michael and his angels fought with the dragon (who is the Evil One); and the dragon and his angels fought, but they did not prevail, nor was a place found for them in heaven any longer. So the great dragon was cast out, that serpent of old, called the devil and Satan, who deceives the whole world; he was cast to the earth, and his angels were cast out with him" (Rev. 12:7–9). The devil has been in a Great War with God. Anyone who works for God is an enemy of Satan. Beware, companions of Christ, for Satan is out to harm you, desiring to win you over to him.

Revelation 3:2

"'Be watchful, and strengthen the things which remain, that are ready to die, for I have not found your works perfect before my God.'"

SUPPORT THE WEAK

From the ends of the earth Jesus cries to those in Sardis and his people throughout time, "Watch out! Strengthen yourself and help support those who are weak in Christ." It should be clear here that because of their corrupt nature, the heart of the Sardis church was hardly beating. There were no genuine good works, or fruit, or reflection of the Holy Father in their church or lives. Deep troubles indeed.

Revelation 3:3

"Remember therefore how you have received and heard; hold fast and repent. Therefore if you will not watch, I will come upon you as a thief, and you will not know what hour I will come upon you."

HOLD FAST & REPENT

As displeased as Jesus is with the Sardis church, he tells them to hold fast and repent. He wants to forgive them and bless them (clearly, he loves them), and he will do just that as long as they repent. He does this because he is holding fast to them.

This applies to all Christians, of course. Like the Sardis church, we must hold fast to the Truth and the valuable things we have learned about Jesus, and to live up to what we know. If we as Christians are falling into sinful behavior, if we're allowing sinful habits to develop, if we're choosing to lead lives that reflect the lives of the unsaved instead of our Father, then we must change our ways and repent, for we cannot serve two masters.

TWO MASTERS

We follow either Christ or Satan. It's that cut and dry, really. Following Jesus is not a religion, as such, but a relationship, and an eternal one at that. It's important to remember what Jesus offers us. His gift is priceless. When compared to Christ, Satan's gifts are worthless. They mean nothing and offer nothing and you gain nothing from them. You are then encouraged to overcome darkness and stay with the light.

You might say that you do not know Satan or that you don't believe in God, or that you don't believe in either one, but that doesn't really matter in the end—you can deny that gravity exists all you want when you jump out of a plane—after all, you can't see it, feel it, hear it—and then, when you jump, gravity will take hold of you and you will fall. Gravity is an absolute fact. Like God. This is what a good chunk of life is all about—either we accept Christ and are saved or we knowingly or unknowingly accept Satan and are lost.

THE GRAVITY OF THE SECOND COMING

At this point, we should take the time to remind ourselves about the gravity of the situation: the Second Coming of the Son of God is at hand! We are too quick to believe that he cannot come in our lifetime. We live careless lives—and of course the careless behavior of our modern times ties in well with biblical prophecy: "...scoffers will come in the last days (possibly you), walking according to their own lusts, and saying, 'Where is the promise of his (Christ's) coming? For since the fathers (our ancestors) fell asleep (died), all things continue as they were from the beginning of creation'" (2Pe. 3:3–4).

But Jesus says, "...be ready, for the Son of Man is coming at an hour when you do not expect" (Mat. 24:44). "...of that day and hour (of the coming of the Lord) no one knows, not even the angels of heaven, but my Father only" (Mat. 24:36).

According to God's timetable/calendar, Christ is to return in the Father's year 2001. Remember, that doesn't mean *our* year 2001 because our calendars are inaccurate and out of sync with the Father's timetable. Nevertheless, we can recognize certain prophetic happenings that will suggest to us that we are getting close to *his* year 2001. Be awake so that you can survive, for the greatest event of all time is close at hand!

A verse for our day could read like this: "In the days before Christ's Great Second Coming the people of the earth continued with 'life as usual'—sleeping and eating, going out to restaurants and drinking in bars, marrying, making love, divorcing, working, playing, gambling in great casinos, driving here and there, flying across the skies, scoffing and laughing about the return of Christ— until the beginning of the end began!" Therefore, we must watch and be prepared! The gravity of the return of the King is at hand!

Revelation 3:4

"'Nevertheless you have a few names in Sardis who have not defiled their garments; and they shall walk with me in white, for they are worthy.'"

A FEW

John announces that there were a few in the church who were Christ-like. They walked with the Son in declining Sardis. Undoubtedly, they genuinely lived for and reflected Christ, but their numbers must have been very small indeed.

Because of their faithfulness, the Lord gives an amazing promise to them: they will walk with him in white.

The reference to the color white is straightforward here: forgiveness, purity, holiness, power, a reflection of the Son. But there's also a connection to our star as well, the bright and shining sun and its life-giving rays. What a beautiful and accurate picture that is for the saved in Christ, shining and burning so bright!

Revelation 3:5

"'He who overcomes shall be clothed in white garments, and I will not blot out his name from the Book of Life; but I will confess his name before my Father and before his angels.'"

THE BOOK OF LIFE

The Book of Life covers all the saved prior to the death and resurrection of Christ, as well as all saved in Christ thereafter— from the beginning of time until its end. We who overcome the devil and know and love Jesus, clothed in the blinding white righteousness of his grace, will find our names written in the Book of Life.

The Book of Life is a figurative expression in Scripture that came out of the methods and customs of genealogical recording by the Jews, so it is likely that the book mentioned here isn't a book as we understand books. It's a spiritual book of some sort, concurrently a symbol of record-taking that suggests the salvation of the saved in Christ is in some way recorded, or perhaps more accurately and simply, God knew before the foundation of the world who would accept or reject him, and a literal documentation of everything in life, from the moment of salvation to every thought and action from birth to death. Throughout the New Testament the Book of Life is used as a direct reference to the righteous that are going to inherit eternal life (Phil. 4:3; Rev. 3: 5; 13:8; 17:8; 21:27).[5]

ONGOING DEBATE

It should be noted here that there is ongoing debate in regard to salvation and the saving grace of Christ and whether or not one can have his or her name removed or *blotted out* from the Book of Life. It is a subject that has been long quarreled about in Christian circles. Can someone who is genuinely saved by the grace of Christ *lose* her or his salvation? Does a Christian have eternal security in the promise of Christ or is her or his salvation conditional? When Jesus says, "I will not blot out (or remove) your name from the Book of Life," he is saying this to those who have overcome. If my interpretation of Scripture is correct, I believe this means that if you turn against Christ your name will be removed from the Book of Life. This concept is called *conditional salvation.* Without getting too deep into it, conditional salvation argues that only those who are obedient to the calling of God will enter the kingdom of heaven (Matt. 7:21). Simply put, if a Christian deliberately turns against Christ, actively resisting his Spirit and choosing to sin with great intent, abandoning the faith altogether that Christian will lose his or her salvation. The reason for this is simply because there is an element of responsibility on the part of the person saved. It's not that you have to do something to save yourself or that you can do something to save yourself— you can't. Only Christ can save you and his grace is freely given, but once you're saved you have to do something and that something is the condition: you must have a persevering and lifelong faith that inspires personal action in obedience to Christ, believing that all actions in life have eternal consequences. That's why I strongly encourage you to stick to your guns when you accept him as your Savior, producing lifelong perseverance in faith and good works, as I believe Christ only saves those who faithfully follow his path.

To be fair, the other side of the salvation argument is called *unconditional salvation* or *eternal security*, arguing that once you're saved, you're always saved. It still calls you to responsibility and action, but at the end of the day even if you choose not to do these things you're still saved, regardless. Simply put, the main argument for eternal security is that at the moment of genuine repentance (I think the word *genuine* is important here) a person is justified through Christ and ultimately sealed by the indwelling Holy Spirit (Acts 3:19; Rom. 3:28; 8:15). This means that once you're sealed there is no removing the seal because the seal is, in essence, the Holy Spirit who now exists within you. He's regenerating you, sanctifying you, transforming you, even adopting you, and since the blood and sacrifice of Christ forgives all sin, past, present and future, once Christ forgives you, he forgives you once and for all—there is no reason to do it again, and so the arguments for eternal security start to become clear.

Now, if you step back and look at the whole picture, I believe conditional salvation and unconditional salvation are similar in almost every respect but for one key element: What about the Christian who rejects Christ, abandoning the faith, the end result being that his or her name is removed from the Book of Life?

Perhaps the answer is as simple as this: the person did not genuinely repent in the first place and therefore was not saved.

When all's said and done, I believe fair and full exploration of this topic is vital, but since it will require concentrated study and prayer, I will not pursue it with more depth here. What is said about salvation and the grace of Christ throughout this manual is basic, but it is believed sufficient for the purposes of this book. Even so, a deeper understanding is vital and that is why I encourage you to explore the subject on your own so that you can make an informed decision.[6]

ENTANGLED IN THEOLOGICAL DEBATE

The issues of eternal security versus conditional security aside, instead of getting entangled in endless theological debate, focus on what's most important. If you are a Christian, no matter where you are in life, no matter how well or unwell that life is going, live a life worthy of the calling you have received, persevering in faith and producing good works.

EXAMINE YOUR HEART

John is writing to Christians here who have, in regard to their lifestyles, fallen away from Christ, and he is admonishing them. These references to removing names from the Book of Life are also warnings meant to encourage the Christian community to be aware of apostasy within the Church, those who call themselves Christians but are not. For the genuine believers caught in sin, John is sternly telling them to examine their hearts in regard to their salvation, demanding they get their lives back in gear with Christ.

THE OTHER BOOKS OPENED

There are other books that will be opened: the books in question are the divine records of the works of the unsaved which will be opened during the Great White Throne Judgment (Rev. 20: 12; 15), and based on those *records* the lost will suffer eternal punishment. (For related information on the Book of Life and the other books, turn to Chapters 13:8, under the heading *All Will Worship* and 20:22, under the heading *The Dead, the Angels & the Books.)*

You must understand that when Jesus speaks his word it is forever. On Judgment Day, when Jesus stands before God and his holy angels, he will speak and confess to God that we know him. We will walk away free men and women, for our life-long sins will no longer be held against us. We are washed clean by the blood of the Lamb which was spilled while he was hanging on the cross. Forever we are with Christ, the Son of and Savior of Man. His wonderful countenance beholds the upright! The morning stars sing together, and all the people of God shout for joy! This is a promise we cannot overlook! Let his left hand be under our head and his right hand embrace us!

Reward Number 7
**FOR THE REMAINING FAITHFUL,
OUR NAMES ARE NOT REMOVED FROM
THE BOOK OF LIFE!
WE ARE CLOTHED IN WHITE GARMENTS!**

Revelation 3:6

"He who has an ear, let him hear what the Spirit says to the churches."

UNDERSTAND!

For the fifth time, the Son requests that everyone hear and understand the Spirit. Christ desires that people heed what he says, for he is the truth, spread throughout the world.

Revelation 3:7

"And to the angel of the church in Philadelphia write, 'These things says he who is holy, he who is true, he who has the key of David, he who opens and no one shuts, and shuts and no one opens...'"

FAITHFUL

John brings our attention to the sixth angel of the company in Philadelphia, the faithful followers of Jesus Christ.

PHILADELPHIA

Before moving on, let's take a look at this ancient historical city: much like its neighbors, Philadelphia was a commercial success and cultural center. Built in the second century by Attalus II Philadelphus, a king of Pergamum who evidently named the city after himself, it was located about 28 miles southwest of Sardis and 100 miles west of Smyrna. During John's time it had a large Christian population. The city fell to the Turks around 1379 A.D. Before that it had always been Roman. Earthquakes tend to plague the area, not to mention the city itself. Today, the original Philadelphia site is close to the city known as *City of God*.[7]

THE KEY OF DAVID

John explains that the one speaking to him is holy. Only Jesus is holy! The one speaking to him is true. Only the Son is true! The one speaking to him has the key of David.

In Scripture, the word *key* is often used as a symbol of power and authority, but Isaiah 22:22 speaks literally of *the key of David* being given to Eliakim, the adviser to the king. The key held an enormous amount of responsibility and power in ancient Israel and therefore it makes sense that in the Book of Revelation Jesus is said to have the key of David—he, being of the line of David (a clear indication that he is worthy to hold the key), wields an enormous amount of responsibility and power (Matt. 16:19; 18:18).[8] Only Christ has the key of David which unlocks the truth and the life! The Son, the manifestation of God, is our Lord. He made heaven and the heavens of heaven with all their hosts, the earth and all things in it, and the seas and all that is in them! Stand up and praise God who gives you life!

Revelation 3:8

"'...I know your works. See, I have set before you an open door, which no one can shut; for you have a little strength, have kept my word, and have not denied my name.'"

THE OPEN DOOR OF TRUTH

The Lord announces that he knows the work of his loyal subjects. He has set before these people *an open door of truth* that can never be closed. He is the open door. Christ understands that his loved ones have little strength, and still, they keep his Word and do not deny his name, for deep down they know that his door cannot be shut.

Many nations throughout time have demanded by force that the Door of Truth be shut, but Jesus announced, "No, this cannot be accomplished." He has absolute authority over the human race. No nation has the strength to close this door, for the Son of God, through the Holy Spirit, keeps it open with power, strength, and glory.

Revelation 3:9

"'Indeed I will make those of the synagogue of Satan, who say they are Jews and are not, but lie—indeed I will make them come and worship before your feet, and to know that I have loved you.'"

WORSHIP AT THE FEET

Within the Philadelphian church a group of individuals thrived who were not true believers. They seemed to be involved in satanic activities, literal or otherwise. (If you're not for Christ, you're against him.) Most certainly, their behavior led the church astray. Because of this, Christ promised the faithful within that these particular people would recognize who he loved by having them, the unbelievers, worship at the feet of the faithful—it's unmistakable here that the Lord is displeased and, as is always the case, there are inevitable consequences as a result of sinful disobedience and destructive or self-destructive choices. You never really get away with it. In the case of the unrepentant at the church of Philadelphia, the cost for their unrepentant behavior would be high and ultimately humbling.

CONSEQUENCES FOR SINFUL ACTION

Part of the purpose of this verse is to inform all humanity through all time that for every sinful action (or inaction) there are direct and very real consequences: you choose to jump off the highest diving board in your county and then repent of the action midway, you will be forgiven by the grace of Christ, but you will still have to deal with what you chose to do—in this case, like it or not, you are going to hit the water hard. In modern times this is often referred to as *owning it* or *carrying it.* The words *accountability* and *responsibility* will serve just fine here too.

There are many today who may think the word accountability means *the practical application of the business of accounting*, or perhaps *having an ability to count well*, the point trying to be made here being that the true definition of the word goes largely ignored in our society. As an example, there are many people who say they are Jews and Christians. They go to synagogue and church, celebrate all the right holidays, eat the right foods, listen to all the right music, even dress *right.* For all intents and purposes, they are Christian and Jewish, but their hearts do not reflect the Most High God to which they have been called, and neither does their internal and probably external behavior. Like some of the members within the church of Philadelphia, they are living a lie. Similarly, they will be held accountable.

THEY WILL BOW DOWN

Christ says that, indeed, he makes these people, even some of the elect, come forward to bow down before the feet of the true disciples of Christ. The unrighteous will come to realize that the Most High loves those who love Christ, one way or the other. God's Son declares that he does not know the unjust because they do not know him.

During the last days, before the return of Christ our Lord, many ministers, priests, pastors, preachers, and rabbis will lead their flocks astray. They will lead with untruth in their hearts and celebrity in their eyes, looking for pomp, glory, and riches, relying on attention-grabbing publicity stunts and melodramatic theatrics (performance centered sensational behavior) to sway their congregations. They will change the meaning of the word *accountability* to mean something more like *anything goes and nothing matters,* and even rewrite, delete, and censor Scripture—this is happening in churches and synagogues across the world.

This verse then clearly applies to the End Times, most particularly when the Jewish, Christian, and other religious leaders favor the Antichrist during the Great Tribulation.

What good is the day of the Lord to the Christian apostate and the unrepentant? It is darkness and not light! It is as though they flee from a bear and run into a lion! Regardless, they will bow down.

Revelation 3:10

"'Because you have kept my command to persevere, I also will keep you from the hour of trial which shall come upon the whole world, to test those who dwell on the earth.'"

JESUS ASSISTS THE FAITHFUL

Christ's promise to the faithful in the Philadelphian church—to keep them from the hour of trial which shall come upon the whole world—was much more than a simple blessing here, for Jesus knew, of course, just how intense and horrifying the future-event in question was going to be: the Great Tribulation. To say that the Philadelphian church would not partake in this historical event was a great act of mercy. They were not going to partake in that event because of where they were in the timeline.

THE HOUR OF TRAIL

But we who are living today, obviously not members of the ancient church in Philadelphia (although, we may wish that we were!), may be facing the time which Christ spoke of in this verse. We may indeed be the ones who are tested by the *hour of trial*. But rest assured, as he did with the Philadelphian church, he will assist the faithful! Jesus' promise to the Philadelphians applies to the faithful in the End Times as well: he keeps his faithful from the hour of trial coming upon the whole world. That doesn't mean, of course, that his faithful won't face a chunk of that trial, but the last and final hour of it (three-and-a-half years), certainly the worst of it, they will not face. Why? Answer: because those who believe in him will be raptured and escape the horrors of the Tribulation.

Daniel 9:27 tells us, "Then he (the Antichrist) shall confirm a covenant with many for 'one week' (referring to the seven year Tribulation, also mentioned as the 'hour of trial'); but in 'the middle of the week' (a period of three-and-one-half years) he shall bring an end to sacrifice and offering." Although this verse has very specific meaning in prophecy concerning the Antichrist and the ritual sacrifices in the Jewish Temple, which I'll get to in later chapters, it's very possible here that *end to sacrifice and offering* is an indirect reference to his faithful being removed from the earth (the rapture of the living Saints, the Fourth Rapture) so that they don't have to face *the final hour* of the Great Tribulation, the final three-and-a-half years of the seven years of the terrible affliction.

THE FINAL HOUR

I'd like to take a moment here, a pause to breathe, hope, and pray: let us ask that we be worthy to escape the terror coming upon the world, *the hour of trial.* Let us pray that we escape the wrath of the devil through his son, the Antichrist, and that we stand before the Son of Man at the time of the Fourth Rapture. Be ready, for seven Great Tribulation years are before us and they come quickly—even at this generation's doorstep. We stand to face the hour of trial. Jesus says, "For then there will be great tribulation, such has not been from the beginning of the world until this time, no, nor ever shall be" (Mat. 24:21).

THE GREAT TRIBULATION

I'll focus on *the hour of trial* in greater detail in Chapters 6–22, but a brushstroke of what's to come seems wise at this point: the hour of trial will be the seven years of the Great Tribulation, which will, among many other things, include the murder of all believers in Jesus Christ and their families who are left behind because they were unprepared for the coming of God's Son. (*Left behind* is a modern Christian term for those not ruptured in the Fourth Rapture, those not supernaturally removed from the earth by Christ to escape the final hour, the last three-and-a-half years of the Tribulation.) They will be left behind and then slaughtered by the Antichrist, who begins his most evil deeds in the middle of the seven year Tribulation. "...Then the saints (all Christians who are left behind, the number likely equaling one-half of all the believers alive today; the number is calculated from the parable of the ten virgins, Mat. 25:1–13) shall be given into his (the Antichrist's) hand for a time (one year) and times (a second and third year) and half a time (half a year)" (Dan. 7:25b).

This is alarming news! Three-and-one-half years of unspeakable oppression await Christians, Godly Jews, and all humanity, those who are not prepared for the Second Coming of the Lord. The people who repent during that time will be hunted down for their belief in their God. They will not be able to buy or sell anything because they will not take *the mark of the beast* whose number is 666. (Some form of biometrics like a computer chip beneath the skin, retinal or iris scan, etc. We will study this in more detail in further chapters, specifically, in Chapter 13:8, under the heading *Dialogue to Destruction; the mark and biometric systems.*)

THE UNHOLY TRINITY

"Here is wisdom! Let him who has understanding calculate the number of the beast, for it is the number of a man (the Antichrist). His number is 666" (Rev. 13:18).

Why three sixes? The Antichrist represents the unholy trinity:

(1) Satan, the father.

(2) The Antichrist, the son.

(3) The False Prophet, the unholy spirit.

They are one in 666. (We will study this in more detail in further chapters, specifically, in Chapters 6:5, under the heading The *Black Horse & His Rider; the mark of the Antichrist* and 13:18, under the heading *Calculate the Number of the Beast*).

Revelation 3:11

"'I am coming quickly! Hold fast to what you have, that no one may take your crown.'"

BEHOLD!

Christ instructs John to write and observe because his mighty return comes sooner than we all realize.

Quickly (Greek, *tacheos*, meaning literally *without delay* or, interestingly and appropriately enough, *by surprise and suddenly*)[9] is the right word indeed, and you must remember that when Jesus says, "Quickly!" these are words spoken beyond or outside of time, so quickly for him is very different from quickly for us. Still, *by surprise* applies directly and perfectly: "I am coming by surprise!"

GOD'S PERSPECTIVE OUTSIDE OF TIME

Now, words like *quickly* and terms like *beyond time* and *outside time* have been used quite a bit, but we haven't examined this concept in detail. To have a better understanding of just what *beyond time* might be like, let's try to do that now. C.S. Lewis tackled this in his book *Mere Christianity* in great detail and you are encouraged to read his book and his explanation of God and time, as well as the work of John Jefferson Davis of the American Scientific Affiliation. I'll sum up their ideas here.

C.S. Lewis suggested that life is not pre-set. If God knows everything we're going to do then it would seem pre-set because he knows everything we're going to do—how can we then have free will? Lewis argues that God isn't just seeing into the future like a psychic. God actually exists beyond or outside of time. Since that is the case, his perception and understanding of reality differs from ours in a big way. As we think we understand it, God exists in something like a constant state of *now*. Because of that, Lewis said, tomorrow is visible to God the same way that today is visible to us. This means God would not remember what you did yesterday, nor would he remember what you were going to do tomorrow because from God's perspective outside of time tomorrow and yesterday don't apply. They don't exist. It is only *now*. When God watches you do something yesterday, today or tomorrow, he's watching you do it *now*. This led Lewis to conclude that God does not know what you're going to do until you've done it and in this way free will can indeed be purely free, even though it exists *within* the paradigm of God and all Creation.[10]

But if that's the case, Davis argues in his paper *Theological Reflections on Chaos Theory* that if time and humanity exist *within* the Creation of God (and clearly it does and we do) then God *has to know* everything that is going to happen to us in time, from beginning to end, and in a way we have yet to fully understand this is also true. Davis reaches this conclusion: what it seems to amount to is that God's perspective outside of time allows him to not know what we're going to do before we do it and to know what we're going to do before we do it at the same time, and thus humanity does indeed have genuine freedom of will in a controlled kind of way. Davis compares it to random behavior within an ordered universe, or chaos within order, which is similar in concept, suggesting that random free will can exist within an ordered universe, for indeed we have genuine behavior that appears random, and *is* essentially random, within our chaotic but ordered and designed universe.[11]

QUICKLY MEANS *NOW*

That being the case, a word like *quickly* will have a very different frame of reference for God, and even though we can't truly understand the subtle and likely infinite variations of the meaning (for God and from God's perspective), we can understand it enough to say when Jesus says he's coming quickly he probably means he's coming now.

The experience is different for humanity, of course, for even though Jesus said he was coming quickly and to him it means he's coming now, it might seem like a long time coming to us.

JESUS COMES QUICKLY AFTER DEATH

But Jesus also knows that human life is short, and because of that there is yet another perspective to think about when Jesus says he's coming quickly: it's quite likely that he was also referring to death, for after you have died Jesus will come quickly indeed.

That's why it is imperative for you to hold fast to Christ as time flows ever forward, for it is likely that *this* is the generation that will face the now returning King.

Time is running out! The great deception is upon us! Predictions are beginning to happen! Christ is the lamp and he lights the darkness! He is a shield of light to all who trust in him!

"How can I survive the horror of the Tribulation," you may ask? Answer: by being prepared, and at this point that would lead to being caught up in the Fourth Rapture. The unbelievers run against a shield of darkness held by the Evil One. He is the shield of darkness to all who trust in him. He wraps his black cloak of darkness around them, but Christ wraps his brightness around you protecting you forever.

Revelation 3:12

"'He who overcomes, I will make him a pillar in the temple of my God, and he shall go out no more. I will write on him the name of my God and the name of the city of my God, the New Jerusalem, which comes down out of heaven from my God. And I will write on him my new name.'"

THOSE WHO OVERCOME

Jesus is reaching beyond the Philadelphian Christians here, to all the saved throughout time, while focusing on those who prevail over affliction and persecution, most specifically, those who are martyred for Christ during the Great Tribulation.

Jesus proclaims that he makes *a pillar* of those who overcome and places them in the mighty, most holy temple of God—*pillar* is figurative here, but the idea isn't. It's literal, as you shall see in a moment.

He also says they do not *go out* anymore. This suggests that their salvation is secure in Christ forever. They become *literal* and *permanent* structures *within* him.

These righteous believers are told that they will always have an important position in his shrine, the new holy city of Jerusalem. Not only that, but they are worthy to receive God's name and it will be written on their person, as well as having the name of the new illustrious city of Jerusalem, sent by God from his First Heaven.

How important and loved believers shall feel, for they shall not only carry the name of the Holy Father on their person, but they shall also carry the name of God's city. As an extra blessing, Jesus writes on them his new exciting name! Clearly, believers, and especially those who die for Christ, are given great rewards.

The trees in the fields of heaven clap their hands joyously!

Reward Number 8
IN GOD'S TEMPLE
YOU RECEIVE THE NAME OF GOD,
THE NAME OF THE NEW CITY OF JERUSALEM,
AND CHRIST'S NEW NAME!

Revelation 3:13

"He who has an ear, let him hear what the Spirit says to the Churches."

LISTEN TO THE SPIRIT

Again, the word of the Lord comes to John. Six times Jesus has earnestly cautioned all people to hear the Spirit and listen to what he says to believers and humanity throughout the ages. It is vital to listen, for he is the Living God who has all knowledge and understanding and is steadfast forever. His dominion endures for all eternity.

Revelation 3:14

"'And to the angel of the church in Laodicea write, 'These things says the Amen, the Faithful and True Witness, the Beginning of the creation of God.'"

LUKEWARM

John writes down everything told to him by the seventh angel. This angel represents the lukewarm congregation who followed Christ in the ancient and thriving town of Laodicea in Asia Minor.

LAODICEA

Here's a nutshell of its history: a beautiful and wealthy city, it was located on the highway to Ephesus. It wasn't far from Colossae, a mere 12 miles. The city was named after Laodice, the wife of Antiochus II (261–246 B.C.). Around 66 A.D. or earlier it was destroyed by an earthquake and then rebuilt by Marcus

Aurelius. Today, there's nothing but a heap of ruins there. The Turks call it *Eski-hissar*, which means *old castle*.[12]

FAITHFUL & TRUE, THE AMEN

Again, Jesus confirms that it is he who speaks, for these things are said by the Faithful and True Witness, the beginning of the creation of God. But, interestingly, before he calls himself these things he refers to himself as the *Amen.*

I'd like to clarify the meaning of this word *Amen.* John uses it time and time again, a word which today is often used in houses of worship and prayer. The Hebrew and Greek definition is close to *true, faithful,* and *most assuredly* when translated into English. (Hebrew: *truly, so be it, truth.* Greek: *surely, so be it, verily.*) The word can be used at the beginning of a sentence to give emphasis to what is going to be said. Our Lord Jesus Christ often did this when he spoke—it was translated as *truly* or *verily.* It can also be used at the end of a sentence. In both Jewish and Christian tradition the word usually follows a prayer or a Scripture reading.[13]

There is a higher sense to the word. Many people do not realize that when they speak this word they are actually calling out the name of Christ, for some translations of the word read *God of Life,* and since it's more than evident in Genesis, Chapter 1, that Jesus is the life, it's a reasonable conclusion: *Amen* means *Christ.* Jesus is the Amen, the faithful, true witness, the God of Life!

On occasion some have confused the word *Amen* with *Ammon, the hidden one,* the ancient Egyptian deity known as the sun-god of life. There is no historical evidence that the two words are interrelated, although, in Egyptian mythology *Amen* is an alternate spelling for *Amun.*[14]

Revelation 3:15

"'I know your works, that you are neither cold nor hot. I could wish you were cold or hot.'"

NEITHER HOT NOR COLD

Jesus states that he knows these Christians. They have what can be referred to as *the Laodicean Condition,* a *lukewarmness* and *worldliness* that flows against the heartbeat of Christ. In their work, in their very hearts, they are neither cold nor hot. They're apathetic, indifferent, unmotivated, unconcerned, and perhaps even bored. Jesus would be happier if they were one or the other, hot or cold, for to be in between is of the very worst kind!

Jesus' words apply the Church at the end of the Human Age. He's speaking to those within the Christian Church today, those who ride the fence, the wishy-washy, indecisive, ineffectual, and spiritless—however you want to label it. He is speaking to those who have compromised in some deeply profound way. The future Apostate Church will be rich, cultured, ritualistic, and self-satisfied, and it will at that point be so influenced by the world and its ways that Christ himself will fall out of favor. (Does this sound familiar?)

KNOCK, KNOCK, KNOCKING

In Revelation 3:20 Jesus says he is standing outside, knocking. This is a visual aid, of course, referring to the hearts of the lost, but there is a prophetic layer to it: the door he's knocking on is also the door of the future Apostate Church, the Church that exists today, for the contemporary Church is in the process of removing Jesus from worship. He is even now unpopular in many churches, an embarrassment for some, and obsolete and useless to others. There will come a time when he will no longer even be allowed inside his Church—and that is why he stands outside his Church, knocking.[15]

Jesus desires that his followers be on fire for him, that they burn with an intense desire to seek his face, but many of his flock are not prepared to spread the Word or even allow their lifestyles to reflect a life dedicated to Christ. Some are embarrassed by their faith and draw back rather than mention his name, while still others fear rejection, humiliation, the whole gamut of human emotions and psychologies. They allow themselves to indulge in obvious unchristian behavior: making love to this one and that one, making a mockery of wedlock, committing adultery, casual attitude toward divorce, thinking they are wise, superior, flawless, seeking fame, fortune, and power. But know that true wisdom and true power to overcome these fears and psychologies is fear of the Lord!

ARE YOU LIVING A DOUBLE LIFE?

When you read about the Laodicean church, most certainly if you're a Christian, you have to ask yourself, "Am I living a double life?" If you are, I strongly encourage you to leave the carnality of the world and take to Christ.

"If then you were raised with Christ, seek those things which are above, where Christ is standing at the right hand of God. Set your mind on things above, not on things on the earth (aim to be Kingdom minded). For you died (in Christ, when you accepted him and were forever reborn), and your life is hidden with Christ in God. When Christ who is our life appears, then you also will appear with him in glory (the rapture). Therefore put to death your members (immoral lifestyles, psychologies, possessions and obsessions of worldly things and friends, etc.), which are on the earth: fornication, uncleanness, passion, evil desire, and covetousness (wanting what belongs to others), which is idolatry (worshiping anything other than God the Father, as in, people, idols, etc.)" (Col. 3:1–5).

"...You should no longer walk as the Gentiles walk, in the futility of their mind, having their understanding darkened, being alienated from the life of God, because of the ignorance that is in them, because of the blindness of their heart, who, being past feeling, have given themselves over to lewdness, to work all uncleanness with greediness... Put off, concerning your former conduct, the old man which grows corrupt according to the deceitful lusts, and be renewed in the spirit of your mind... Put on the new man who was created according to God, in true righteousness and holiness. Therefore, putting away lying, let each one of you speak truth with his neighbor, for we are members of one another. In your anger do not sin: do not let the sun go down on your wrath, nor give place to the devil. Let him who stole, steal no longer, but rather let him labor, working with his hands what is good, that he may have something to give him who has need. Let no corrupt word (or curse words) proceed out of your mouth, but what is good for necessary edification, that it may impart grace to the hearers. And do not grieve the Holy Spirit, by whom you were sealed for the day of redemption. Let all bitterness, wrath, anger, clamor (raising your voice in anger and frustration) and evil speaking be put away from you, with all malice (don't threaten to harm anyone, but rather love them). And be kind to one another, tenderhearted, forgiving one another, even as God in Christ forgave you" (Eph. 4:17–32).

"...The wrath of God is coming upon the sons of disobedience, in which you yourselves once walked when you lived in them. But now (that you are a follower of Christ Jesus) you yourselves are to put off all these: anger, wrath, malice (doing harm to others), blasphemy (speaking with disrespect about God), and filthy language out of your mouth. Do not lie to one another, since you have put off the old man (you are now reborn in Jesus) with his deeds, and have put on the new man (you have become a spiritually transformed believer in Christ) who is renewed in knowledge, according to the image of him (Jesus) who created him...but Christ is all and in all (and therefore in you, for you are the temple of God) ...But above all these things put on love, which is the bond of perfection (the best thing to do)" (Col. 3:6–10 and 14).

PURSUE THE GOOD THINGS OF GOD

Watch the workers of iniquity, lest they tear believers like a lion and trample their lives to the earth, laying their honor in the dust! In the grave who will thank them? Instead of pursuing the things of this dark world, pursue the good things of God. Study his work and be close to him. Study in a house of worship or by having a thorough relationship with him at home, or by walking together with him on the mountainsides. Let the mountains be the walls to your cathedral, the grassy meadows its floor, the sky its roof, and let the wind whisper utterances from the hosts of heaven. You will find Jesus is there, in every tree, flower, and blade of grass—and in you! He is in all. "I AM THAT I AM," says the Lord. Honor him, and give thanks for life daily. Since life can stop at the next heartbeat and bring Jesus quickly to you, realize that it is a privilege to be alive. Thank God for everything given to you. Tell him that you love him, praise his holy name through Christ Jesus, and be blessed!

Revelation 3:16
"'So then, because you are lukewarm, and neither hot nor cold, I will vomit you out of my mouth.'"

THE LUKEWARM BELIEVER

This is one of the strongest, most graphic visual aids used in the New Testament. We should heed what the visual aid is telling us. Christ makes it very clear what he thinks of the lukewarm believer by saying that he will vomit him or her out of his mouth. Jesus can't stomach them. They make him sick. By using this expression, he demonstrates just how dissatisfied he is toward those who are neither cold nor hot in their belief.

This concerns our modern Church and society, for both are as lukewarm as can be. Jesus must have a heavy, tearful heart and a sick stomach while he stands at the door of the Church, nation, and world, knocking as his people willingly slip into the hands of Satan and darkness.

Revelation 3:17
"'Because you say, 'I am rich, have become wealthy, and have need of nothing,'—and do not know that you are wretched, miserable, poor, blind and naked—'"

TREASURES OF HEAVEN

Christ tells the rich Laodicean's, who obviously have need for nothing (because they have so much in regard to material things), that they do not realize just how wretched and loveless they are! Blinded by their wealth and egos, they are unable to see the truth, and because of that they are heading for destruction. Instead of being faithful and honorable, they are naked and shameful before God. "But those who desire to be rich fall into temptation and a snare, and into many foolish and harmful lusts which drown men in destruction and perdition (ruin)" (1Tim. 6:9).

In our modern world there are many churches similar to the Laodicean church, companies of God too rich for their own good. They have it all financially, have gained what so many live for in this world today, that so-called security, which is really an illusion here on earth, just smoke and mirrors, for security in this life comes and goes when it pleases like leaves blown in the wind. In the end death takes us all! But the Laodicean's security of the soul through Christ—the only sure security in all human life and the most important (there is a certain amount of irony here)—they have forgotten, even abandoned. They have forgotten their God.

SECOND PLACE

When the Lord becomes second place and the First Love is gone, in his eyes they are unrighteous, selfish, poor, and wicked. They miss the treasures and blessings of heaven, for, sure enough, the Father wants to bless them, but because of their sinful behavior he cannot—it is like a wall, a barrier to his presence and love. "A little that a righteous man has is better than the riches of many wicked. For the arms of the wicked shall be broken, but the Lord upholds the righteous" (Ps. 37:16-17). "Here is the man who did not make God his strength, but trusted in the abundance of his riches, and strengthened himself in his wickedness" (Ps. 52:7).

"Now a certain (rich) ruler asked him (Jesus) saying, 'Good Teacher, What shall I do to inherit eternal life?' So Jesus said to him, 'Why do you call me good? No one is good but one, that is, God. You know the commandments: 'Do not commit adultery. Do not murder. Do not steal. Do not bear false witness. Honor your father and your mother.' And he (the rich ruler) said, 'All these things I have kept from my youth.' So when Jesus heard these things, he said to him, 'You still lack one thing. Sell all that you have and distribute to the poor, and you will have treasure in heaven; and come, follow (and believe in) me.' But when he heard this, he became very sorrowful, for he was very rich. And when

Jesus saw that he became very sorrowful, he said, 'How hard it is for those who have riches to enter the kingdom of God! FOR IT IS EASIER FOR A CAMEL TO GO THROUGH THE EYE OF A NEEDLE THAN FOR A RICH MAN TO ENTER THE KINGDOM OF GOD'" (Luke 18:18–25).

It isn't impossible, of course. There are wealthy people who go to Jesus' glorious kingdom, but it does seem that they are in the minority. Abraham and Job, among others, are good Old Testament examples of wealthy men who followed God's ways and entered into the Kingdom of God, for they always placed riches last and placed God first in their hearts and lives.

Revelation 3:18

"'I counsel you to buy from me gold refined in the fire, that you may be rich; and white garments, that you may be clothed, that the shame of your nakedness may not be revealed; and anoint your eyes with eye salve, that you may see.'"

THE COUNSEL OF CHRIST

Jesus has made it perfectly clear just how much the behavior of the Laodicean church displeases and angers him. Their behavior makes him sick—and *still* he is quite prepared to forgive them if they repent and open themselves to the life changing power of the Holy Spirit. His love for his own is so complete!

As Jesus speaks to the Laodiceans, he of course is speaking to Christians throughout time, encouraging us to take the counsel of Christ: for those of us who have fallen into the Laodicean Condition, he instructs us to buy from him "gold refined in the fire" that we may be rich and pure in spirit, because our spirit is so obviously the opposite; white garments to cover the nakedness of our shameful behavior; and salve for the eyes, for clearly we have been blinded by our sin and have blinded ourselves.

The fact that Jesus has to say this to Christians is quite telling, indicating just how far the Laodiceans fell and how far we today have fallen (and will continue to fall). But even having fallen so far, he expresses his love for them (and us) through his wise counsel for spiritual rebirth or new growth.

LET YOUR EYES BE UPON JESUS

Let your eyes be open upon Jesus that you may see, for you can be naked to worldly things and not recognize the sins in which you indulge. Sin surrounds us at every turn, but the wise take the counsel of Christ, making him their First Love. They do not abandon him, but abandon the ways and things of this fallen world! And they will shine like the brightness of the stars in eye-opening-and-glorious-white—assuredly, as has been said before, this whiteness is the radiant brightness of the Spirit! Look at what Scripture says and see: "Those who are wise shall shine like the brightness of the firmament, and those who turn many to righteousness (are) like the stars forever and ever" (Dan. 12:3)!

Revelation 3:19

"As many as I love, I rebuke and chasten. Therefore be zealous and repent."

LOVE, REBUKE & CHASTEN = LOVE

Jesus loves all of his children, but when sin is embraced by them he will respond like a Father. He will reprimand, correct, and discipline. He will in fact do whatever he has to do, whatever it takes, even die for you—that's how much of a Father he is to us. That's how much he loves you! He hopes that you will repent of your sin.

You are encouraged to follow the Lord's ways to avoid the certain suffering and pain that sinful action and choices bring on. Be filled with the Spirit of the eternal Lord. Pray that you are more Christ-like each day. Overcome the weaknesses of the devil by laying your weakness at the feet of Christ, who is light. "You are all sons of light, and sons of the day. We are not of the night, nor of darkness" (Thes. 5:5). Be eager to change your ways. Let the Lord be your fortress, your deliverer, your strength. He is your rock and there is no unrighteousness in him! He is the God of Life!

Revelation 3:20

"'Behold, I stand at the door and knock. If anyone hears my voice and opens the door, I will come in to him and dine with him, and he with me.'"

AT THE HEART'S DOOR

What Jesus is saying in this verse is, "OBSERVE—I STAND AT THE DOOR OF YOUR HEART AND KNOCK."

What a beautiful expression of love! He is telling us that he is close at hand to help each one of us, even at the doors of our spirits! He is only a heartbeat away. This can be taken two ways:

(1) He is as close as your next heartbeat, waiting for you to allow his Spirit into your spiritual heart.

(2) Death is as close as your next heartbeat, and that means so is Christ—one way or the other, you will discover just how close he is and how quickly he is coming!

THE MARVEL OF LIFE

Once we have been transformed by the grace of Christ we are temples of God, housing his Spirit. Jesus is that Spirit! "He who has an ear (who listens and understands), let him hear what the Spirit (Jesus) says to the churches..." (Rev. 2:7). This is the marvel of life. Christ is the Spirit and he is part of you, for the real you is spirit. He and you are one! Take the spirit away, and your body ceases to function. Again, observe, as it says in the verse above, that Jesus stands at the door of your heart and knocks. If you hear his voice and open the door he will come *into you* and he will dine and dwell with you and you with him! This is a visual representation of the act of salvation through the Holy Spirit, the actual spiritual transformation of the heart of your original self into something altogether new and amazing: a created being permanently connected to the divine Creator!

CLOSER IS HE THAN BREATHING

There is an old saying: "Speak to him for he shall hear, spirit with Spirit shall meet; closer is he than breathing, and nearer than hands and feet." It is well worth your while to repeat this thought daily, for it reminds you that he dwells within your person, that which is comprised of body, soul, and spirit, and remember, the human body/soul/ spirit is a representation of the Holy Trinity. Taking that thought a step further, your body/soul/spirit is your personal trinity—God and his mystical mathematics/geometry once again!

When you pray you're speaking intimately with God, and you talk to God through his Son, Christ Jesus, who, as has been confirmed, is the Holy Spirit within you. It is not necessary to look up to the stars and hope that God hears your words from millions of light years away, for he isn't millions of light years away at all. He is, in fact, right inside of you, for he has replaced your dead spiritual heart with his living spiritual heart, and that heartbeat you now hear is no longer yours but his! He not only hears your prayers, he hears your innermost thoughts too! He hears within, without, and all about.

He is *that* close, always knocking at the temple door of your heart. If you haven't opened your heart to Christ, you are encouraged to let him come in and transform your spiritual heart. He will transform your physical life here on earth too—life may still be difficult, true enough, and it more than likely will be because you will remain in the fallen state/nature/universe, plus become an enemy of Darkness, but you will know "...the peace of God, which transcends all understanding" (Phill. 4:7). You will want to praise his holy name daily, for he is worthy. Praise him in his firmament! Praise him according to his excellent greatness! Praise him with instruments and a dance! Let everyone that has breath praise God through Jesus Christ!

Revelation 3:21

"'To him who overcomes I will grant to sit with me on my throne, as I also overcame and sat down with my Father on his throne.'"

OVERCOMES

This is a promise to the Laodiceans and to all the saved in Christ—to those who overcome.

Christ surely overcame, as he did all that God expected him to do. He left his holy and perfect heaven and became a created human being, entered into the fallen state/nature/time universe while remaining perfect in nature and never sinned, suffered and died physically and then suffered and *died* spiritually in hell, in our place, removed from his Father—he did all that for every single individual and imperfect sinful human being, and then he triumphantly rose from hell, death, and the fallen state/nature/time universe, raising the very nature of the created human being to the nature of the divine. He did all that for those who turn to him in faith. Jesus was victorious and stands with his Father in his throne in his heaven, the First Heaven, and you can stand with him there!

THREE HEAVENS EXPLORED

Here is wisdom. This seems like a good time to explore the concept of three heavens with a little more depth: the Father's, the Son's, and the Holy Spirit's, the three being One.

THE FIRST HEAVEN

(1) The original Earth and all Creation where the Father dwells is called the First Heaven, the heaven of the Father.

THE SECOND HEAVEN

(2) The New Earth/universe/reality during the Holy Age beyond or outside of time is called the Second Heaven, the heaven of the Son.

THE THIRD HEAVEN

(3) The earth/universe/reality that we exist on, is called the Third Heaven, the heaven of the Holy Spirit.

In the beginning, this earth/universe/reality was formed and then came out of the Father's First Heaven. It was perfect in every way. It was a touch of the First Heaven, a glimpse of the Father's Heaven, until the Fall of Humankind, which then plunged this universe/reality into darkness, altering its very nature.

The Holy Spirit remained within this universe and reality, and that is why it is referred to here as the Holy Spirit's Third Heaven. It should be pointed out that this universe reality is no longer *heavenly* because of its fallen nature/sin.

Once again we see God's holy mathematics/geometry at work! Three wonderful heavens. Here's an example of how the concept works, focusing on the New Earth and New City of Jerusalem: both earth and city are a replica of the Father's holy city and original earth in the First Heaven. John says, "And he (Jesus) carried me (John) away in the Spirit (in and out of time/fallen and spiritual reality) to a great and high mountain, and showed me the holy city, Jerusalem, descending out of heaven from God (a replica of God's great city)..." (Rev. 21:10).

This New City descends from the First Heaven *onto* the New Earth that exists within the Second Heaven. This means, essentially, that during the Holy Age humanity will live on a New Earth that comes out of the Father's First Heaven. It will come from the Father himself.

THE THRONE

Returning to Christ's promise to the Laodiceans and those of us who overcome: the throne of Christ.

First, let's take a quick look at what Scripture says about thrones in general, so that we have a common frame of reference: generally, the throne is used as a symbol of power, dignity, and might (Gen. 41:40). The most important feature of a throne is its elevation: Solomon's throne, for example, was six steps high (1Kings 10:19; 2Chron. 9:18). Throughout Scripture thrones can also represent earthly power as well as spiritual power, celestial beings, archangels, etc. (Col. 1:16).[16]

Understanding the purpose of a throne then, it's clear that Christ's throne is *the* throne of thrones. When we think of the throne, the mental picture in our minds is probably something like Kings and Queens of England sit upon, but that would be incorrect, at least, to some degree. Remember, we're dealing with a totally different reality at this point. The general laws that govern our reality and universe won't necessarily have to apply. More than likely, we'll be dealing with a hyperdimensional reality. Even though the purpose of the throne is clear in symbol, the throne itself is something quite beyond what we understand a throne to be—this *is* the throne of thrones! The throne is described as being mighty, a glorious sight to behold and exceedingly great. (For additional information, refer to Chapter 4:3, under the heading *The Green Throne*.) A mighty river of life flows from it! One walks *into* his glorious throne room. Jesus Christ sits in his throne in the middle of the great city of the New Jerusalem, described as being an enormous square tabernacle! A very large throne is required to be the focal point of this stupendous city (not to mention universe/reality), a throne that Jesus sits *in*, rather than *on* (suggestive of a hyperdimensional state).

Lastly, what Christ is promising us—to sit with him on his throne, as he sat on his Father's throne—is an honor we certainly don't deserve and it is truly beyond our understanding. We will be sitting with him *in* his throne. No one other than God himself will truly *sit* on the throne—the reference to his faithful sitting with him is figurative here. Certainly, we will be a part of the throne, sitting around it, having seats *within* it, but the Seat of Power belongs to Christ and Christ alone, the King of the Universe! He is the only one worthy to sit on the throne. How do you get to sit with or within him? Answer: simply believe in him.

Reward Number 9
TO BE WITH CHRIST IN HIS GREAT THRONE!

Revelation 3:22

"He, who has an ear, let him hear what the Spirit says to the churches."

THE SEVENTH TIME

For the seventh time a resounding call like a trumpet is heard: Jesus cries out loud and clear!

His mighty voice states emphatically that we need to understand and heed what the Spirit (Jesus) says to all people around the world. The great roar of his voice counsels us to wisdom: continue to pay attention to the words of the Spirit!

He cries earnestly, asking everyone to hear what he has to say regarding his seven companies, for they are a reflection of all Christians and all humanity from John's time until the very end of time.

You only have one chance in this life of fallen, broken flesh. You are either saved or unsaved the moment you pass over from life into death and from death into a new reality. "THEREFORE YOU ALSO BE READY, FOR THE SON OF MAN IS COMING AT AN HOUR YOU DO NOT EXPECT" (Mat. 24:44).

Set your face toward the rising sun and prophesy that the King is coming! He is coming for you and for me.

* * * * *

SOURCES:

1. *Sardis,* The History of the Ancient Near East Electronic Compendium, Mark MacDonald-Editor, *Esquire,* (2002),
   <http://www.ancientneareast.tripod.com>.
   Sardis, pg. 1129-1130, The New Unger's Bible Dictionary, Moody Press (1988).
   Sardis, pg. 1082, The New American Desk Encyclopedia, Penguin Group (1993).
   Sardis, Microsoft Encarta Encyclopedia (2002).
2. *Diablos—Satan,* #1228, pg. 22, Greek Dictionary of the New Testament; Strong's Exhaustive Concordance of the Bible/Dictionary of the Hebrew and Greek Words, Hendrickson Publishers.
3. *Satan—Adversary,* #7853, pg. 115, Hebrew and Chaldee Dictionary; Strong's Exhaustive Concordance of the Bible/Dictionary of the Hebrew and Greek Words, Hendrickson Publishers.
4. *Satan (Lucifer),* Graham Brodie, Lambert Dolphin's Resources,
   <http://www.ldolphin.org>.
   Satan, pg. pg. 1132-1133, The New Unger's Bible Dictionary, Moody Press (1988).
   Satan, Genesis; Introduction of Sin, Gray's Home Bible Commentary, The Bible Library Delux, version 5.0. suite, CD-ROM, Ellis Enterprises, Inc. (2,000).
   God and His Angels, Lambert Dolpin, Lambert Dolphin's Resources,
   <http://www.ldolphin.org>.
   The Angels of Revelation (continued/addendum), No. 70 & No. 71, James B. Jordon, Biblical Horizons (1995), <http://www.biblicalhorizons.com>.
5. *The Book of Life,* International Bible Standard Encyclopedia, Online Edition,
   <http://www.studylight.org>.
   Book, pg. 178-179, The New Unger's Bible Dictionary, Moody Press (1988).
6. *Whether Anyone May be Blotted Out of the Book of Life? The Summa Theologica of St. Thomas Aquinas,* Second and Revised Edition (1920), literally translated by Fathers of the English Dominican Province, The Catholic Encyclopedia, Online Edition, Kevin Knight (2002),
   <http://www.newadvent.org>.
   The Book of Life, Sue Perlman, Issues 1:1, Jews for Jesus,
   <http://www.jfjonline.org>.
   The Book of Life, Let Us Reason Ministries (2002),
   <http://www.letusreason.org>.
   The Five Points of Calvinism by Herman Hanko, Homer Hoeksema, and Gise J. Van Baren, Reformed Free Publishing Association (1975), all rights

reserved, the Protestant Reformed Churches in America (unofficial home page web site), <http://www.prca.org/index.html>.
What About Eternal Security? Phil Enlow, Midnight Cry Ministries (2003), <http://www.midcry.org>.
The Armor of God: The Adequacy of Our Helmet, Personal Update NewsJournal, Chuck Missler (1997), Koinonia House, <http://www.khouse.com>.
Exposition of the Orthodox Faith (Book I), St. John of Damascus, Orthodox Christian Information Center, <http://www.orthodoxinfo.com>; from John of Damascus, *Exposition of the Orthodox Faith,* Post Nicene Fathers, Schaff Edition, Volume IX, Series II, translated by The Rev. S. D. F. Salmond, D.D., F.e.I.s., Principal of the Free Church College, Aberdeen. (1898).

7. *Philadelphia,* <http://www.abila.org>.
   Philadelphia, Catholic Encyclopedia, <http://www.newadvent.org>.
   Philadelphia, pg. 999-1,000, The New Unger's Bible Dictionary, Moody Press (1988).
   Philadelphia (ancient cities), Microsoft Encarta Encyclopedia (2002).

8. *Keys, power of,* William Owen Carver; *Judah, kingdom of,* Thomas Hunter Weir, *David, 1-8,* Thomas Hunter Weir, International Bible Standard Encyclopedia, Online Edition, <http://www.studylight.org>.
   Key, pg. 737, The New Unger's Bible Dictionary, Moody Press (1988).

9. *Quickly—Tacheos,* #5030, pg. 71, Greek Dictionary of the New Testament, Strong's Exhaustive Concordance of the Bible/Dictionary of the Hebrew and Greek Words, Hendrickson Publishers.

10. *Mere Christianity; Time and Beyond Time,* pg. 146-149, C. S. Lewis, Touchstone Books (1996; original printing 1943).
    Grace Outside of Time, Personal Update NewsJournal, Chuck Missler, Koinonia House (1994), <http://www.khouse.com>.

11. *Perspectives on Science and Christian Faith* 49, June 1997: 7584, <http://www.asa3.org/ASA/PSCF/1997/PSCF6-97Davis.html>, The American Scientific Affiliation, <www.http://www.asa3.org>
    An Introduction to Chaos Theory; "They may initially appear to be random, but they are not. Beneath the initial sense of randomness lies beautiful order," <http://www.students.bath.ac.uk>.
    Theological Reflections on Chaos Theory; The American Scientific Affiliation, from *Perspectives on Science and Christian Faith,* John Jefferson Davis (1997), <http://www.asa3.org>.

12. *Laodicea,* Bible Places (2002), <http://www.bibleplaces.com>.
    Laodicea, pg. 756-757, The New Unger's Bible Dictionary, Moody Press (1988).

13. *Amen,* #543, pg. 14, Hebrew And Chaldee Dictionary; *Amen,* #281, pg. 10, Greek Dictionary of the New Testament, Strong's Exhaustive Concordance of the Bible/Dictionary of the Hebrew and Greek Words, Hendrickson Publishers.
    Amen, pg. 52, The New Unger's Bible Dictionary, Moody Press (1988).

14. *Amun,* pg. 19; pg. 165-183, Chapter 7, Religion of the Late Period, Handbook of Egyptian Religion, Erman, London, A. Constable & co., ltd, publishers. (1907).

15. *Door,* pg. 315, The New Unger's Bible Dictionary, Moody Press (1988).
    The Seven Churches, Or The Things Which Are, Revelation 2-3, Gray's Home Bible Commentary; *Revelation 2,* Henry's Concise Commentary, The Bible Library Delux, version 5.0. suite, CD-ROM, Ellis Enterprises, Inc. (2,000).

16. *Throne,* pg. 1278-1279, The New Unger's Bible Dictionary, Moody Press (1988).
Chair, Microsoft Encarta Encyclopedia (2002).
Divine Images and Aniconism in Ancient Israel, Theodore J. Lewis, The Journal of the American Oriental Society (1998), <http://www.umich.edu/~aos/>.

Further reading:

Angels of Light, Powers of Darkness: Thinking Biblically About Angels, Satan and Principalities, Stephen Noll, Inter-varsity Press (1998).
Genesis, James Montgomery Boice, Baker Books (1998).
The Eternal Security of the Believer, H. A. Ironside, Loizeaux Brothers Publisher (1986).
Hope for the Troubled Heart, Billy Graham, World Wide Publications (2002).
The Summa Theologiae; A Concise Translation, Saint Thomas Aquinas, edited by Timothy McDermott, Christian Classics (1997).
Suma of the Suma; The Essential Philosophical Passages of St.Thomas Aguinas Summa Theologica Edited and Explained for Beginners, edited and annotated by Peter Kreeft, Ignatius Press (1990).
Institutes of the Christian Religion/One-Volume Edition, John Calvin (1599); translated by Henry Beveridge, Wm. B. Eerdmans Publishing Co. (1995).
Martin Luther, Selections From His Writings, Martin Luther (1463-1546), edited by John Dillenberger, Anchor (1958).
Mere Christianity, C. S. Lewis, Touchstone Books (1996; original printing 1943).

PART II

Chapters Four & Five
THE BRIDGE TO PROPHECY

Chapters Four & Five are considered a bridge to the main body of prophecy. This section of the book will focus on these, as well as additional, prophetic connections (not listed in any specific order): the Green Throne; contrasting realities or the multidimensional and literal experience for John; the Emerald Christ and the importance of the color green; the twenty-four Elders; the Sea of Glass; the Four Living Creatures; Ezekiel/Old Testament prophecy; the scroll; further study of Satan; the genetic code/connection of the Israelites and the Root of David; Kings and Priests; and further study of angels.

CHAPTER 4
The Throne Room of Heaven

Revelation 4:1

After these things I looked, and behold, a door standing open in heaven. And the first voice which I heard was like a trumpet speaking to me, saying, "Come up here, and I will show you things which must take place after this."

THE THRONE ROOM OF HEAVEN

Here's the visual: the angel, while pointing into the heavens, cries out to John, "Look!"

Turning toward the north, John witnesses another superior wonder! He observes a golden door standing wide open in the sky, leading to the magnificent First Heaven, the abode of God and his angels! A brilliant pale emerald light shines through the opening (see Revelation 4:3)! John looks intensely. He sees a man appearing like the sunset, molten gold against billowing clouds, everything hued with a distinct touch of the color emerald!

Watching more closely through the mysterious glow, John witnesses the adoration of the Christ who pauses over the threshold of the mighty temple door. The house is filled with a pale golden cloud. The court is full of the reflection of the Son's glory. Then the sound of the divine is heard, the voice of the Son of God. He tells his servant, "On this day, which is the Lord's, you are in the spirit!" Then, like the sound of seven trumpets, he announces, "Welcome. I am Jesus!" (See Rev. 1:10–11).

GREAT PREDICTIONS ABOUT TO UNFOLD!

John enters the spirit. He is now moving in and out of time, entering two contrasting realities: that of this universe/reality and the universe/reality of the spirit or *the spiritual realm*. As I said in Chapter 1, this is no hallucination. This is a real experience in and out of time.

John is informed by Christ to enter through the open door so that he can see what is to come. Even though this is a real experience, it's likely *the door* is a visual metaphor which tells us that Jesus has given John the ability to see everything that must take place before the Human Age comes to its final conclusion because he has taken John's spirit into a hyperdimensional realm that may be outside of time and space.

What a privilege it is for John—to look two thousand years into the future (by God's timetable/calendar)! He is so greatly blessed. "Surely the Lord God does nothing, unless he reveals his secrets to his servants the prophets" (Amos 3:7). God reveals his secrets to the prophets because he is a just God. He desires always to allow the people of the world to peep into the future so that they are not taken by surprise. He gives them the ability to prepare so that they can survive. Take this prophetic gift to heart: heed the cries of God, for he warns of impending dangers about the most important events ever to take place in the history of mankind.

Revelation 4:2

Immediately I [John] was in the Spirit; and behold, a throne set in heaven, and One sat on the throne.

INSTANTANEOUS & TRANSFORMATION

As should be evident here, there wasn't travel time between the reality of earth and the reality of heaven for John. The angel of the Lord led John through the open *door* into God's domain and the *travel* was instantaneous. As far as we know, at this point in John's experience the laws of nature as we understand them broke down and could no longer be applied—time, velocity, acceleration, mass, force, etc. Or perhaps a more accurate way of saying it is, the laws of nature *changed and expanded.*

God says flesh and blood cannot enter through the gates of heaven (because of sin), so this tells us that John's physical body was not involved with the experiential journey and that this was a journey involving soul/spirit. John himself emphasizes in Revelation 1:10 that he "was in the spirit on the Lord's day." Thus, his spirit had been removed from his physical body. He experienced hyperdimension.

Some argue that John took the same form as Jesus Christ after his transfiguration, just as his believers will take the same form in the raptures soon to come (the Third/Fourth and Fifth/Sixth Raptures), when they will be given special bodies (the Second Phase of Body). What's more likely, I think, is that John remained in spirit throughout his Revelation experience.

THE SUPERGLORIFIED BODY OF CHRIST

It's worthwhile to note that Jesus said to Mary of Magdala, who was seeking him three days after his burial, "Do not cling to me (do not touch me, for I have a special body), for I have not yet ascended to my Father" (John 20:17).

This suggests that Christ's body had transformed into something altogether unknowable in our experience, but that doesn't mean we can't understand it in a limited way. Clearly, the change was profound. This has something to do with his perfection and holiness, a perfection and holiness *in bodily form* that was, in a very real sense, consuming.

There are numerous references in the Old Testament to the awesome and consuming nature of God's presence or body (Ex. 33:23; Dt. 23:12–13; Ezek. 1:27; 8:2; Hab. 3:3–4). Christians look forward to a similar transformation of the body (when living with Jesus in the Second Heaven): "Then we (believers in Christ) who are alive and remain shall be caught up together with them in the clouds (with the dead in Christ, having complete new glorified bodies, body number two) to meet the Lord in the air. And thus we shall always be with the Lord" (1Thess. 4:17).

THE RADIANT JESUS

Close to the angel's side, John sees the wondrous sight before him: the radiant Jesus Christ standing in the glorious heavenly throne room! Remember your Creator in the days of your youth, before the difficult days come! When those difficult days come, you will know that you may turn to him for help with confidence. Fear God and keep his commandments, for this is the whole duty of mankind. God brings every person's work and every secret thing he or she does—whether good or bad—into judgment.

Revelation 4:3

And the one who sat there had the appearance of jasper and carnelian [a sardius stone]. A rainbow, resembling an emerald, encircled the throne.

THE GREEN THRONE

The first object John sees in heaven is the throne.

John uses variations of the color green to describe his account of Christ and his glorious throne. Jasper and emerald are all vibrant variations of green. The light coming from Christ is green.

THE GREEN CIRCULAR RAINBOW

As to the green circular rainbow: rainbows are always associated with the Noahic covenant, "...never again shall the water become a flood to destroy all flesh" (Gen 9:15). But there's more to the rainbow here. It's the symbol of a bridge between the throne and humanity. Christ is the green rainbow bridge. To get to the throne humanity must cross the green bridge that is Christ Jesus. Its circular nature suggests eternity and completion, much like a Celtic knot or circle. Traditionally, the rainbow is a symbol of mercy and love, and sometimes the promise of the grace of Christ toward humanity is attached to it. Like the rainbow of the Noahic covenant, it's an image meant to give us hope.[1]

THE COLOR GREEN

Clearly, green is of importance here, so let's examine it in greater detail:

There are numerous references to green throughout the Scriptures, but more often than not the word does not mean or represent the actual color, and in the King James Version the word *green* was actually mistranslated—it should have been translated as the color *white*. The Hebrew terms are *ra'anan*, meaning *vigorous/flourishing* (Job 15:32; Ps. 52:8) or *fresh as oil* (Ps. 92:10), and *yereq*, meaning, *putting forth* or *sprouting*, a general reference to all food products of the earth (Gen. 1:30; 9:3; Ex. 10:15; Isa. 15:6).[2] Since that's the case, it's understandable why green is used here and why it is the actual color that John saw (as opposed to the color white). You could say that Jesus is the color of life.

John sees a soft, delicate hue of beryl and white before him, what amounts to a glorious greenish light. He is reminded of jasper quartz, with its glittering dark red tints as seen in a carnelian stone (a precious and mystical stone) of translucent chalcedony quartz that is commonly pale-blue and gray.[3]

It's interesting to note that the descriptions of Christ in the book of Daniel are similar: "I (Daniel) lifted my eyes and looked (for in his vision he lies at the Lord's feet), and behold, a certain man (Jesus) clothed in linen, whose waist was girded with gold of Uphaz (the finest gold). His body was like beryl (the color of a precious green gemstone, like the color of an emerald—the glory of God's pale green light flowing from his holy body), his face like the appearance of lightning (all power), his eyes like torches of fire (indicating the strength of the power of the Seven Spirits of God), his arms and feet like burnished (polished) bronze in color (depicting his shining might), and the sound of his words like the voice of multitudes (having great authority)" (Dan. 10:5–6).

EMERALD CHRIST
THE GREEN CREATOR

John beholds a spectacular sight, a lightshow of holiness and color, the Lord Jesus, the Emerald Christ!

Is this why the world he alone created from top to bottom is so beautifully green? From these verses we can gather that green depicts his holiness, and since he is the Creator of the planet there must be a touch of Jesus, the fingerprint of the Creator, in every living tree, plant, and blade of grass, and in fact in the color green itself. Everything he touches glows with beauty and reflects his glory and life, and perhaps the natural reflection is simply green, green, green. What a wonder!

HIS GREEN PRESENCE

We sense his presence everywhere. Jesus is in all! The mountains are joyful together before the Lord! The hills are alive with the presence of Jesus! The Emerald Christ makes his world green. Look around you. Green is everywhere. Jesus is everywhere.

The trees of the forest rejoice before the Lord! We are reminded that the earth and the top of the mountains are his. As far as our mind's-eye can see, Christ is on the distant horizon, just like the rainbow that spans the horizon! The earth is a mountain in which Christ desires to dwell! Out on the mountain tops our God reigns! He lies down in green valleys, and the beauty of the Lord is in the glens and the dales! His name is glorious throughout the earth! The color green, his official stamp of approval!

STANDING WITH JESUS

In Revelation 3:21 we are informed that Jesus stands with God in his throne: "To him who overcomes I will give the right to sit with me on my throne, just as I overcame and sat down with my Father on his throne."

Note that we will stand with Jesus who sits on his throne in the new earth, just as Jesus now stands with his Father who sits on his throne in heaven.

In the First Heaven, God sits on his throne in the throne room while his Son stands.

In the Second Heaven, Jesus sits on his throne in the throne room while his subjects stand—there is an order to everything, a system.

The One standing before John in the throne room of heaven, saying, "Come up here, and I will show you things which must take place after this," is indeed Jesus Christ himself! John sees him in his rightful place, in all of his majesty, splendor, and glory.

Revelation 4:4

Around the throne were twenty-four thrones, and on the thrones I [John] saw twenty-four elders sitting, clothed in white robes, with crowns of gold on their heads.

TWENTY-FOUR

John sees twenty-four smaller thrones encircling the Green Throne. On the thrones twenty-four elders (or *leaders*) prepare to sit. Now, Jesus promises that all of his followers will be there with him in his throne room, for he announces that "To him who overcomes, I will give the right to sit with me on my throne..." (Rev. 3:21).

The twenty-four elders sitting with Jesus around the throne represent:

(1) All believers who overcome.

(2) The twelve apostles and the twelve holy prophets of the Old Testament who overcame and who were also adorned in white garments (see Rev. 3:5).

The white garments depict purity and spiritual light, for they are washed in the blood of the Lamb.

The Savior says, "He who overcomes, and keeps my works until the end, to him I give power of the nations. He shall rule them (my people) with a rod of iron (just as my Father gave me the authority to rule them)..." (Rev. 2:26).

Here, the golden crowns given to the saved in Christ represent the spirit of each individual, including his/her authority and responsibility, as well as eternal life. "...I (Jesus) will give you the crown of life" (Rev. 2:10). This ties in nicely with the seventh millennium, the Kingdom Age, and the authority and responsibility given to the redeemed ruling with Christ at that time (the final 1,000 years in time). The fact that the smaller thrones encircle the Green Throne suggests that they (the elders and all the saved in Christ) sit in counsel with the Lord. What an astonishing privilege and honor!

Revelation 4:5

And from the throne preceded lightings, voices, and thundering. Seven lamps of fire were burning before the throne, which are the Seven Spirits of God.

THE SEVEN SPIRITS OF GOD

From God's illustrious throne come flashes of lightning, rumblings, and deafening thunder, illustrating the power and strength of the Ruler of the Universe! Vocal utterances come from the rolling peals: the voice of the Seven Spirits of the Living God, proclaiming deliverance to the twenty-four elders and all the saved in Christ!

Before the throne, John sees seven sacred golden lamps. Each lamp burns an amber flame of fire. Each flame is a depiction of the holiest of holies, once again the Seven Spirits of Life. In essence, John sees the heart of Jesus Christ, who has the Seven Spirits, standing in the great throne room. The Son speaks and all Creation trembles!

Revelation 4:6

Before the throne there was something like a sea of glass, like crystal. And in the midst of the throne, and around the throne, were four living creatures full of eyes in front and in back.

THE SEA OF GLASS

John witnesses countless millions of believers in Jesus Christ standing in the colossal amphitheater before the great throne. The multitude looks like a wondrous sea of glittering glass, clear as crystal! The light from each individual is the shining love all have for Jesus. The brilliance seen here is the combination of light from each individual, a sea of *living lamplight!*

The *sea of glass* is a term that can be associated with the Old Testament in that there's a loose connection to the *Tabernacle laver* (Ex. 30:18–21) and perhaps even the *molten sea* in the Solomonic Temple (I Kings 7:23–37). Both the laver and the molten sea were used by priests in the preparation for religious rites. They used them primarily to wash the body. Thus, we can conclude that each individual in the sea of glass has been cleansed or washed through the purification of the blood of Christ. That the saved in Christ are called *a sea of glass* also suggests that they've been turned into glorious works of art, having gone through the fiery furnace, reformation, and then fine polishing, designed by the Glassmaker of glassmakers. The polished sea of perfection encircles the throne entire, representing eternity and completion just like the green rainbow bridge.[4]

FOUR LIVING CREATURES

Suddenly, seven trumpets are aired! The Lord brings John's attention to the throne: he sees four *living creatures* in the midst of the throne and around the throne. That these creatures are *in the midst of the throne and around the throne* suggests that we are dealing with things of a hyperdimensional nature.

These four creatures may have a connection with cherubim of the Old Testament, most specifically: "He rode a cherubim and flew" (2Sam. 22:11), and the vision of the four cherubim seen by Ezekiel (Ezek. 1:5–14; 10:1–22). Cherubim are connected with vindication and the holiness of God. That's their job as angels in the angelic order.[5]

Each one is *full of eyes in front and in back!* In fact, each one has seven eyes! Why seven? Answer: because each eye depicts one of the Seven Spirits of God! Revelation 5:6 tells us, "And I saw in the midst of the throne and of the four living creatures, and in the midst of the elders, a Lamb standing as though it had been slain (representing Christ who was crucified on the cross), having seven horns (representing all knowledge and all strength that the Seven Spirits have) and seven eyes, which are the Seven Spirits of God sent out into all the earth."

The seven eyes are said to be in front and behind, giving the four creatures 360 degree vision and dimension. This is a visual metaphor showing us the hyperdimensional nature of Jesus. It also suggests that he is everywhere at once, what could be called the non-locality of Christ. He is omnipresent, fully conscious, fully aware of absolutely everything, seeing all, for he is all knowledge, power, and wisdom!

Without doubt, each creature portrays a different personality of Jesus.

Revelation 4:7

The first living creature was like a lion, the second living creature like a calf, the third living creature had a face like a man, and the fourth living creature was like a flying eagle.

THE FIRST CREATURE
The Lion

The angel clarifies that the first living creature is a portrait of Jesus. The creature resembles a *lion*, an indication of the powerful personality of Christ.

"...Behold, the Lion of the tribe of Judah, the Root of David..." (Rev. 5:5); "... (Jesus) cried with a loud voice, as when a lion roars" (Rev. 10:3). Such statements exhibit the mighty strength of the Lord. The lion was also a symbol of Israel (Num. 24: 9) and the tribe of Judah (Gen. 49:9). The lion is most often linked to royal characteristics and the imagery of kings. It should be clear here that the lion is an extremely powerful symbol of Christ (Rev. 5:5).[6]

THE SECOND CREATURE
The Calf

The second living creature, also having seven eyes in front and behind, is a calf.

Calves are of the ox species and are known to be gentle animals, a clear indication here of the gentle side of God. Jesus said, "But I say to you who hear: love your enemies, do good to those who hate you, bless those who curse you, and pray for those who spitefully use you. To him who strikes you on the one cheek, offer the other also. And from him, who takes away your cloak, do not withhold your tunic (shirt) either. Give to everyone who asks of you, and from him who takes away your goods, do not ask them back" (Luke 6:27–30). The Hebrews considered the *fattened calf* an extraordinary sacrifice to God, so the calf, as it's used in this verse, is not only an allusion to the gentle nature of Christ, but to his extraordinary sacrifice as well.[7]

THE THIRD CREATURE
The Man

The third living creature pertaining to Jesus, also having seven eyes in front and behind, has a face like a *man*. God came as the Son of Man to this earth to conquer death and to save us from eternal damnation, darkness, and hell. "For the Son of Man (who is God as man) has come to save that which was lost" (Matt. 18:11). The term *Son of Man* is taken from Daniel 7:13–14. Daniel is referring to the full nature of the Messiah, the eternal authority, glory, and sovereign power attributed to him; it is also a reference to the full nature of Christ. Jesus the divine and Jesus the man. Son of Man occurs 61 times in the Gospels in reference only to Jesus Christ.[8]

THE FOURTH CREATURE
An Eagle

John sees the fourth living creature characterizing the Son of God. It has seven eyes in front and behind and looks like *a flying eagle*. It is a beautiful picture of God's Spirit, the unseen, the mysterious, the mystical and intimate, knowable, and experiential Being who is spiritually present everywhere.

There are numerous references to the word in Scripture: as an example, God called to Moses saying, "You have seen what I did to the Egyptians, and how I bore you on eagles' wings (representing the Spirit) and brought you to myself" (Exodus 19:4). When the word was translated in the King James Version, eagles *and* vultures were included under the single word, *eagle*, so that in many cases the scriptural references could be either/or eagle or vulture.[9] As it turns out, there are many different species of eagles and vultures in Israel and every one of them, eagle to vulture, are swift (Duet. 28:49), fly high to get to rocky outcrops (Job 39:27–30), and have astonishing vision (Job 39:29). In a scriptural sense, then, the exact species may sometimes be unclear but the meaning most certainly is not.

To recap: the four living creatures reflect four distinct personality traits of Christ. The powerful and royal lion; the gentle and sacrificial calf; the Son of Man who was both perfectly divine and perfectly human; and the eagle representing the Spirit of the world!

Revelation 4:8

The four living creatures, each having six wings, were full of eyes around and within. And they do not rest day and night, saying: "Holy, holy, holy, Lord God Almighty, who was and is and is to come!"

WINGED CREATURES OF THE SPIRIT

The four living creatures, each one depicting the sacred Lamb, are described as having six wings. It's clear that the four creatures are angelic in nature and the wings seal this impression. We always picture wings on angels, but if we saw an angel in its true form, whatever that may be, the human mind probably could not handle what it was seeing because the creature was made for and existed in an entirely different kind of reality. There is no reason why angels should have wings, at least in relation to earthly reality and physics, other than the aesthetic, which is certainly possible. But at the end of the day, angel wings are probably a simple romantic notion invented by dreamy men and women to explain something they do not understand.

On the other hand, the fact that in Scripture angels most often (but not always) appear in human form (Gen. 18:2; 19:1, 10; Luke 24:4; Acts 1:10), the titles given to them have a human element— *sons of God*, for example (Job 1:6; 38:7; Dan. 3:25)—and the fact that they are sometimes described as having birdlike wings seems to suggest that, regardless, there is a resemblance between them and us and our reality, no matter how small.[10] (For further study on angels, turn to Chapter 5:11, under the heading *Angels*.)

As far as the verse we're studying now is concerned, the angel wings represent flight and the power associated with the Holy Spirit, for "Jesus...saw the Spirit of God descending like a dove and alighting upon him" (Matt. 3:16).

KNOWLEDGE AROUND & WITHIN

The four living creatures are full of knowledge *around and within* because they represent Jesus, who has the Seven Spirits of God, but the term also identifies the hyperdimensional nature and power of Christ, his hyperdimensional mind. He has a mind that encompasses *around and within*, what could be the past, the present, the future, and anything and everything in between and beyond, up, down, and all around, including the secret internal knowledge of each individual human heart and the hearts/minds of all creation beyond humanity—remarkable, when you think about it.

CHRIST IS ALIVE AND AWAKE

They do not rest day or night. This suggests a number of things:

(1) Christ is always awake and working. What is he working toward? Answer: the salvation of humanity.

(2) That the creatures are tireless, neither resting nor sleeping, shows us his divine and perfect being.

(3) Each of the living creatures represents four of the infinite characteristics of Christ, the ones that are most pertinent to us and his relationship with us. Each living creature praises the Almighty, saying that he is all in all, and, indeed, he is.

EZEKIEL & THE FOUR CREATURES

We learn that Ezekiel (one of the great Old Testament prophets) was shown four living creatures in a vision/experience that was equally amazing. Because of the similar nature of the four creatures a brief study of it should take place here.

In Chapter 1 of his great writings, inspired by the Lord, Ezekiel gives an awesome, lengthy account of the creatures:

"Now it came to pass...that the heavens were opened and I (Ezekiel) saw visions of God... The word of the Lord came expressly to Ezekiel the priest...and the hand of the Lord was upon him there.

"Then I looked, and behold, a whirlwind (the Spirit of Jesus) was coming out of the north (heaven), a great cloud with raging fire engulfing itself (Spirit of Glory); and brightness was all around it and radiating out of its midst like the color of amber, out of the mist of the fire. (The spiritual fire of the Seven Spirits of God. In reality, Ezekiel is more than likely witnessing Jesus coming through an *opening* in heaven/the sky/our universe and sees the brightness of the Lord Jesus Christ, who has the Seven Spirits of God.) Also from within it (Jesus), came the likeness of four living creatures (each creature portraying Jesus Christ). And this was their appearance: they had the likeness of a man (or the Son of Man). Each one had four faces (describing the four most important personalities of Jesus in relation to humanity), and each one had four wings (probably pointing to the spiritual aspect of Jesus). Their legs were straight, and the soles of their feet were like the soles of calves' feet (depicting the gentle/sacrificial side of Jesus). They sparkled like the color of burnished bronze (the brightness shining from Jesus). The hands of a man were under their wings on their four sides; and each of the four had faces and wings (indicating Jesus as man). Their wings touched one another (they're linked together, forming a whole). The creatures did not turn when they went, but each one went straight forward (gravity does not hold the Son; gravity had little to do with it because we're dealing with creatures that do not have to obey the natural laws of our universe/reality).

"As for the likeness of their faces, each had the face of a man (Jesus as the Son of Man); each of the four had the face of a lion (the powerful and royal side of Jesus) on the right side, each of the four had the face of an ox (the gentle/sacrificial side of Jesus) on the left side, and each of the four had the face of an eagle (Jesus full of the Spirit, for he has the Seven Spirits of God). Thus were their faces. Their wings stretched upward; two wings of each one touched one another, and two covered their bodies. And each one went straight forward; they went wherever the Spirit wanted to go, and they did not turn when they went (trying to describe hyperdimensional creatures that normally exist outside our reality would just be plain difficult).

"As for the likeness of the living creatures, their appearance was like burning coals of fire, like the appearance of torches (the Seven Spirits of Life) going back and forth among the living creatures. The fire was bright (the Seven Spirits of Life), and out of the fire went lightning (depicting the power of Jesus). And the living creatures ran back and forth, in appearance like a flash of lightning.

"Now as I looked at the living creatures, behold, a wheel (again, referring to Jesus) was on the earth beside each living creature with its four faces. The appearance of the wheels and their workings was like the color of beryl (the green glory of Jesus!), and all four had the same likeness. The appearance of their workings was, as it were, a wheel in the middle of a wheel. (Trinity) When they moved, they went toward any one of four directions; they did not turn aside when they went (this is most certainly a figurative reference to Christ, but in a literal sense it could also be a description of an angel in its true hyperdimensional form). As for their rims (Jesus), they were so high they were awesome, and their rims were full of eyes (seven eyes in all), all around the four of them (being the four living creatures, standing for the Seven Spirits of God, showing power, wisdom, knowledge, strength, and omnipresence). When the living creatures went, the (radiant) wheels went beside them (the shining light of Jesus), and when the living creatures were lifted up from earth, the (glowing) wheels were lifted up. Wherever the spirit wanted to go, they went, because there the spirit went, and the wheels were lifted together with them (the Trinity), for the spirit of the living creatures was in the wheels (seen as the flowing green light of Jesus Christ!). When those (the creatures) went, these went; when those (the creatures) stood, these stood; and when those (the creatures) were lifted up from the earth, the wheels were lifted up together with them, for the spirit of the living creatures was in the wheels (again, this is a description of hyperdimensional beings).

"The likeness of the firmament above the heads of the living creatures was like the color of an awesome crystal, stretched out over their heads appearance like a sapphire stone (the exquisite throne of Jesus Christ); on the likeness of the throne was a likeness with the appearance of a man (Jesus the Christ) high above it. Also from the appearance of fire all around within it (the Seven Spirits of Life); and from the appearance of his waist and downward I saw, as it were, the appearance of fire with brightness all around (the Seven Spirits of Life). Like the appearance of a rainbow in a cloud on a rainy day, (the spiritual light of Jesus Christ forming an emerald rainbow above his person), so was the appearance of the brightness all around it. This was the appearance of the likeness of the glory of the Lord (Ezekiel 1:1-28).

This is an extraordinary and vivid description of the Lord Jesus Christ, revealing his spectacular countenance, character, and personality, not to mention the mystery of Christ! This account displays his power, his glory and might, and his endless strength and intelligence.

He makes the clouds his chariot! He walks on the wings of the wind! By his breath a fire lights in our souls like a blowing wind!

Revelation 4:9

Whenever the living creatures give glory and honor and thanks to him who sits on the throne, who lives forever and ever...

GLORY GIVEN

The four living creatures give glory, honor, and thanks to the Son of Man. He is God as man and stands in the glorious throne room in the shrine of Almighty God. He lives forever and ever! John was not the only one who witnessed the four living creatures in his astonishing experiential vision.

Revelation 4:10

...The twenty-four elders fall down before him who sits on the throne and worship him who lives forever and ever, and cast their crowns before the throne saying...

YOU ARE WORTHY

The twenty-four elders (the twelve apostles, the twelve holy prophets of the Old Testament, and the multitude of believers in Christ) kneel before Jesus within the mighty throne. They worship Christ, who lives forever and ever.

They willingly cast their golden crowns of life, authority, and responsibility before him, living up to this verse from Revelation 2:10: "...Be faithful until death and I (Jesus) will give you the crown of life."

What a wonderful example this is for those of us living today! His name should be like honey to our lips! His Spirit is the water to our souls, breathing new life within each one of us! Have mercy on us, God. Come and heal our drifting souls, and let us be amazed at the sacrifice you made for us! Let us realize that you hold our next breath in your hands! Let us realize that you died to save everyone living on earth.

Revelation 4:11

"You are worthy, our Lord and God, to receive glory and honor and power; for you created all things, and by your will they existed and were created."

PRAISE THE LAMB OF GOD

John listens to the great multitude declaring their love for Christ: "You are worthy, Lord Jesus, the Lamb of God, to receive glory, honor, and power from each and every one who believes in you; for you are the Christ, the mighty Savior, the mighty, mighty

Lord, the Bright and Morning Star, the Son of Man, the Creator of everything there is." They cry out, "By your will we exist and were created." They clap their hands, pouring out their love before the face of the Lord God, who is holy and righteous. John witnesses this astonishing scene within the throne room of heaven!

He shall strike the earth with the rod of his mouth; and with the breath of his lips, he shall slay the wicked. He shall recover the remnant of his people and take them under his wing. The belt of his waist is righteousness and faithfulness. Praise the Lord! Call upon his name! His name is exalted. Sing praises to the Son, for he has done excellent things. Cry out his name and be saved, for great is the holy one of heaven and earth.

* * * * *

SOURCES:

1. *Rainbow,* Easton's Bible Dictionary, Online Edition, The HTML Bible, <http://www.htmlbible.com> & <http://www.johnhurt.com>, PO Box 31, Elmwood, TN 38560 USA.
Rainbow, pg. 1062, The New Unger's Bible Dictionary, Moody Press (1988).
Rainbow, Microsoft Encarta Encyclopedia (2002).
2. *White/Green—Yarowq,* #3387, pg. 52, Hebrew and Chaldee Dictionary, Strong's Exhaustive Concordance of the Bible/Dictionary of the Hebrew and Greek Words, Hendrickson Publishers.
Colors, pg. 245-246, The New Unger's Bible Dictionary, Moody Press (1988).
3. *Carnelian Stone,* Nature's Emporium, <http://www.natures-emporium.com>.
Carnelian; Quartz Mineral Data, Mineralogy Database, <http://www.webmineral.com>.
Carnelian; Mineral Kingdom, Sardis, pg. 214, pg. 856, The New Unger's Bible Dictionary, Moody Press (1988).
4. *The Sea of Glass,* ChristianAnswers.com, <http://www.christiananswers.com>.
The Seven Seals, or the Things Which Shall Be Hereafter; Revelation, Gray's Home Bible Commentary; *Revelation,* Henry's Concise Commentary, The Bible Library Delux, version 5.0. suite, CD-ROM, Ellis Enterprises, Inc. (2,000).
Sea of Glass, pg. 1152, The New Unger's Bible Dictionary, Moody Press (1988).
5. *What does the Bible Teach about Angels?* ChristianAnswers.com, <http://www.christiananswers.com>.
Angel; Angels, Fallen, pg. 61-62, The New Unger's Bible Dictionary, Moody Press (1988).
The Angels of Revelation (continued/addendum), No. 70 & No. 71, James B. Jordan, Biblical Horizons (1995), <http://www.biblicalhorizons.com>.
God and His Angels, L. Lambert, Lambert Dolphin's Resources, <http://www.ldolphin.org>.
The Holy Angels, The Orthodox Page in America, <http://www.ocf.org>.
6. *Lions,* Bible Encyclopedia, ChristainAnswers.com, <http://www.christiananswers.com>.

Lion; Animal Kingdom, pg 73, The New Unger's Bible Dictionary, Moody Press (1988).

7. *Bullock,* Bible Encyclopedia, ChristianAnswers.com, <http://www.christiananswers.com>.

Bull, Bullock, Ox; Animal Kingdom, pg. 75 & 187, The New Unger's Bible Dictionary, Moody Press (1988).

8. *Son of Man,* pg. 1211, The New Unger's Bible Dictionary, Moody Press (1988).

The Seven Seals, or the Things Which Shall Be Hereafter; Revelation, Gray's Home Bible Commentary; *Revelation,* Henry's Concise Commentary, The Bible Library Delux, version 5.0. suite, CD-ROM, Ellis Enterprises, Inc. (2,000).

9. *The Eagle in the Bible,* Nelson's Illustrated Bible Dictionary, Thomas Nelson Publishers (1986).

Eagle; vulture, Animal Kingdom, The New Unger's Bible Dictionary, Moody Press (1988).

10. *Angels: Genesis; The Cherubim, Ezekiel,* Gray's Home Bible Commentary; *Genesis,* Henry's Concise Commentary, The Bible Library Delux, version 5.0. suite, CD-ROM, Ellis Enterprises, Inc. (2,000).

Further reading:

Angels of Light, Powers of Darkness: Thinking Biblically About Angels, Satan and Principalities, Stephen Noll, Inter-varsity Press (1998).

Genesis, James Montgomery Boice, Baker Books (1998).

CHAPTER 5
The Scroll & The Lamb

Revelation 5:1

And I [John] saw in the right hand of him [Jesus] who sat on the throne a scroll written inside and on the back, sealed with seven seals!

THE SCROLL

Behold, in the presence of the angel John witnesses the Lamb of God sitting on the throne! In his right hand he holds a scroll written inside and on the back. This information is certainly worth exploring.

A scroll was a book made of *papyrus* or *parchment*—the skin of a sheep or goat. It was rolled up on a wooden dowel. You unrolled the scroll to read it. It usually felt soft and unrolled easily. Writing was set in columns. Traditionally, the columns were on one side only, but in the case of this scroll there is writing on the front *and* back. This would have drawn attention to itself. Anyone from John's time would have realized that this was no ordinary scroll— you just didn't write on both sides. Because of that anomaly people probably would have thought the writer of the scroll had a great deal of power.[1]

The message must be important because it's sealed with seven seals. Similar to writing on one side of the scroll only, tradition dictates that seals were often used instead of a signature. They had the same legal authority. Signature or no, a scroll without a seal would have been recognized as fake, and it could have led to all sorts of bad news for the sender of said unsealed scroll. This scroll is sealed. It is therefore authentic, its authority unquestionable. Add to that the fact that the scroll is sealed seven times, what would amount to seven authentic and authoritative signatures, and you get a scroll that's so unusual it could only mean one thing: extreme power. Seven seals! Clearly, this is the granddaddy of all scrolls.[2] The seven seals represent God's Seven Spirits, another symbol of the unique power of the sender/writer of the scroll.

Revelation 5:2

Then I [John] saw a strong angel proclaiming with a loud voice, "Who is worthy to open the scroll and to loose its seals?"

WHO IS WORTHY?

A heavenly angel appears, calling out with a forceful voice, "Who is worthy to open the scroll, and to loosen its seven seals?"

Revelation 5:3

And no one in heaven or on the earth or under the earth was able to open the scroll, or to look at it.

NO ONE

John is surprised and disappointed (as we shall see a few verses from now), for he learns that out of the innumerable company before the throne in heaven, including the twelve apostles and the twelve holy prophets, no one is worthy to break the seven seals and open the scroll or look upon it! No one in heaven, on earth or even under the earth is worthy.

UNDER THE EARTH

I'd like to focus our attention on the term *under the earth* for a moment, explore what it means in relation to this verse and Christianity:

Undoubtedly, it is a direct reference to hell, the place of eternal punishment for the wicked. Like it or not, this is no mere metaphor. The authors of the Bible thought of it as a real place, no question, and when they used terms like *under the earth* they meant it, and that's exactly where they thought it was—close enough to burn their heels. In modern times this concept has been dismissed by a large number of believers and nonbelievers. Heaps of scholars have concluded that hell is purely figurative.[3] Nevertheless, with the advent of quantum physics, dismissing hell may have been a bit presumptuous.

THE PHYSICS OF HELL

The word *hell* is often followed by or represented by the term *bottomless pit* in Scripture. It is rightly described as *the kingdom of darkness*, for there is no light in a bottomless pit! There are scriptural references to hell being under the earth, but to get a better handle on what is meant by *bottomless pit* we have to ask Chuck Missler's question: Can anything be truly bottomless in the universe? Dr. Missler and physics agree that in this universe a pit (no matter how bottomless) has to have bottom—unless you're dealing with a sphere. A sphere has no bottom. It is simply bottom*less*. Apply the cross-pollination of hyperdimensional planes of existence to the concept and a hellish bottomless sphere within the earth begins to make a frightening kind of sense. Who knows what physical realities and what hyperdimensional-natured horrors await the unrepentant under the earth?[4]

Here is a word of wisdom, for the angel reveals to John that within the center of our globe a great kingdom truly exists, a hyperdimensional hell. It is a region referred to as the underworld, a cross-pollination of realities set aside exclusively for the devil, his fallen angels, and the unrepentant, as real as the molten core of this planet. Do not be counted with those who go down to the bottomless pit, the place of destruction and the land of forgetfulness!

Notice what Christ says about hell in Matthew: "FOR AS JONAH WAS THREE DAYS AND THREE NIGHTS IN THE BELLY OF THE GREAT FISH, SO WILL THE SON OF MAN BE THREE DAYS AND THREE NIGHTS IN THE HEART OF THE EARTH" (Matt. 12:40).

This verifies just where hell is: a bottomless sphere within the earth. It is astonishing to realize that after dying on the cross Jesus, the sacred Son of God, suffered in this hyperdimensional hell at the earth's center. He took on the suffering we deserved solely because he loves us.

THE EVIL ONE UNDER THE EARTH

I have already discussed the Evil One in some detail in Chapter 3, but since we're exploring the term *under the earth* and some of the concepts of hell, both old and new, and since the two are deeply entangled—both hell and Lucifer go hand in hand—further commentary on Satan is necessary here.

We know the most powerful angel ever created, Lucifer, was cast out of God's heaven after the Great War between Lucifer and God. We know the war continues, the outcome known: Jesus Christ returns in victory!

After the Great War, Satan was imprisoned by God on earth. Thus, he is the being through which sin entered the world (because of Adam's act of disobedience). This caused our reality to *fall,* changing everything. Entropy or the degradation of matter and energy to the ultimate state of inert uniformity entered the universe. Death became the natural order of things and humanity had to deal with that horrible fate, not to mention battle Satan and our nature which altered at the fall. Our natures were corrupted and now we have to fight our very own hearts of darkness because the once-natural connection to God has been severed.[5]

A THIRD OF HEAVEN'S ANGELS FALL

But after the Great War one third of God's created and arguably less powerful angels in the angelic order (often referred to as *stars* in Scripture) fell with Satan and all were imprisoned on and within earth. What matters to the living on earth is that we face the fury of Satan and all his fallen angels (sometimes called *evil spirits*, hyperdimensional beings that exist beyond or outside our reality, who enter into our reality at will). These fallen beings understand completely that Christ will come to rule the earth and that their time here on and within the earth has a cutoff point. Knowing this, they are on the rampage. These fallen beings are out to destroy everyone before Jesus returns, take down as many with them as they can. The devil's angels imprisoned here have become formidably wicked, and of course they are invisible and this is why we cannot see them. All hyperdimensional spirit is invisible to our eyes, good or bad.

WHAT THEY ONCE HAD

Realize well then that the devil and his demons do not wish us to have what they once enjoyed in the First Heaven. They are going all out to win us over any way they can. They are very successful in their efforts, but their time beyond which they cannot proceed is almost over. Christ comes with the keys to the gates of the abyss to lock them in the underground chambers of the earth. Their dungeon is the bottomless pit. They are locked into the earth at Christ's command during his great Second Coming, when humanity's six thousand years expire (by God's timetable/calendar).

WHAT WE CANNOT SEE

Praise God that we are not permitted to see Satan. Remember, he's a hyperdimensional creature who exists in the spiritual realm and therefore does not obey the natural laws of this universe; he can come in and out of our reality at will; he can shape-change, be invisible, be visible, etc. Praise God that we cannot see Satan's hideous group of fallen angels, for we would be exceedingly troubled by their frightening and repulsive features. I use the words *frightening* and *repulsive* here because sin and evil corrupts all beauty, and clearly the beauty of these once angelic beings is corrupted indeed.

Now we understand that Christ is the keeper of the keys to the gates of hell. "I AM HE WHO LIVES, AND WAS DEAD, AND BEHOLD, I AM ALIVE FOREVERMORE. AMEN (I AM THE GOD OF

GLORY). AND I HAVE THE KEYS OF HADES AND OF DEATH" (Rev. 1:18). Soon, there will be a great locking-up across the earth!

UNNECESSARY

To spend eternity in hell is unnecessary, for to live in Jesus' kingdom of glory and light is simple: "For whoever calls on the name of the Lord shall be saved" (Rom. 10:13). "...If you confess with your mouth the Lord Jesus and believe in your heart that God has raised him from the dead, you will be saved" (Rom. 10:9). "I (Jesus) am the resurrection and the life. He who believes in me, though he may die, he shall live! (Those who believe in Jesus are raised into perfect life at the time of the Third Rapture. See a complete explanation of the seven raptures in Chapter 1:5, under the heading, *The Order of Raptures*.)

Revelation 5:4

So I [John] wept much, because no one was found worthy to open the scroll, or to look at it.

NO ONE IS WORTHY

John's eyes fill with tears. He is greatly distressed (as well as surprised and disappointed, I bet) to learn that no living soul on earth, including himself (no living thing anywhere in all Creation, as a matter of fact) is worthy to open the book or even look upon it!

From a human standpoint, of course, this is because of the fallen nature of humankind. From the standpoint of the rest of Creation, surely it involves the hierarchy or system in place. Since Christ is God, the Creator, and the scroll carries the weight and seal of Christ, it makes sense that no created being is worthy to open it other than he who made it, the Creator.

Revelation 5:5

But one of the elders said to me [John], "Do not weep. Behold, the Lion of the tribe of Judah, the Root of David, has prevailed to open the scroll and its seven seals."

THE ROOT OF DAVID

Bowing his head, aware of the consequences of sin and his own unworthiness, John cries bitterly. But one of the twenty-four elders announces that John need not be so troubled. "Observe," John is told. "The Lion of the tribe of Judah, the Root of David, has prevailed to open the book and to loosen the seven mysterious seals!"

We have explored the symbolic reference as far as the lion is concerned, but I'd like us to take a quick look at the term *root of David* so that we have a clearer understanding of what it means: the Messiah is called the root of Jesse (Isa. 11:10) because, essentially, he has the genetic code of the Israelites. When *root of David* is used in the Book of Revelation it's also a reference to the Messiah's divine and human nature (Rev. 5:5; 22:16). The Messiah is often referred to as *the seed of Abraham* and *the son of David*, for he is the root or the offspring of David.[6]

Unquestionably, the Lion of the tribe of Judah, the Root of David is Christ himself, the Messiah, the Creator, and because of that he alone is worthy to break the seals and open the scroll. Praise him with high-sounding symbols, the musical harp and the sound of the trumpet! Sing to the Lord with thanksgiving! Praise him, all his angels, his hosts, and you heavens of heavens—for he alone is worthy!

Revelation 5:6

And I saw in the midst of the throne and of the four living creatures, and in the midst of the elders, a Lamb standing as though it had been slain, having seven horns and seven eyes, which the Seven Spirits of God are sent out into all the earth.

THE SLAIN LAMB

Lifting his head triumphantly, John witnesses the Lamb of God, Jesus Christ, standing in the center of the throne room with the four living creatures and the twenty-four elders.

The Son is described as being *the Lamb* because he was the gentle and loving sacrificial lamb for all humanity. In the Old Testament, lambs and young rams are mentioned as an important and consistent part of religious sacrifice (Lev. 4:32; Num. 6:14), and the word *lamb* depicts the coming Messiah and his plan for redemption (Isa. 53:7). In relation to the Book of Revelation, the lamb is the symbol of Christ, the Lion-Lamb (Rev. 5:12–13; 7:9; 22:1; 3). "...having seven horns and seven eyes, which are the seven Spirits of God..." This is a reference to the hyperdimensional character of God, most notably, his omnipotence and non-locality. In relation to the horns: power, authority, strength, honor. In relation to the seven eyes: 360 hyperdimensional vision, all knowing knowledge, and omniscience. The Seven Spirits of God also represents the Holy Spirit sent out to the entire world, he who is present everywhere.[7] "For he made him who knew no sin (God took the Lamb, the sinless Jesus) to be sin for us (he took our sins into himself, and God poured his wrath, not on us, but onto his

Son), that we might become the righteousness of God in him" (2Cor. 5:21). He is the only one worthy to open the seals! He is God's Son, the Lion of the tribe of Judah and the Root of David, meek as a lamb—the only perfect One, the Lamb who was slain.

Revelation 5:7

Then he [the Lamb] came and took the scroll out of the right hand of him who sat on the throne.

A RIGHTEOUS ACT

Now, as you may recall, Revelation is Jesus Christ, so therefore: Christ sits on the throne; he is the four living creatures; he is the Lamb that takes the book from the right hand of the Son of God standing in the throne. In essence, the Lamb takes the book, confirming that Jesus is all in all, the I AM, in control of the entire event.

Revelation 5:8

Now when he had taken the scroll, the four living creatures and the twenty-four elders fell down before the Lamb, each having a harp, and golden bowls full of incense, which are the prayers of the saints.

WORTHY IS THE LAMB

John explains that the Lamb of God takes the scroll/book. The four living creatures and the twenty-four elders fall down before Jesus to worship him. Each believer holds a harp in readiness to play a song of praise to his Majesty, the King of Kings.

The harp and its many forms was a common instrument in Egypt and Mesopotamia from ancient times. Its use in Scripture is correctly translated and defined—for example, the lyre had ten strings and was translated *the harp of ten strings*.[8] In reference to this verse, in the purely figurative sense, the musical instrument is used to suggest that the saved in Christ will worship God with music and song and joy; in a more literal sense, perhaps the multitude will indeed pluck a harp in one of its many and ancient forms.

The golden bowls full of incense symbolize the prayers of every believer, as well as the prayers of the twelve apostles and the holy prophets before the great throne, and the prayers of all the holy angels. Throughout Scripture incense is used as the symbol of prayer. It was burned upon the Jewish altar of incense within the Tabernacle. The Hebrews and the Egyptians burned incense and, by and large, used it only in worship and religious ritual.[9]

Revelation 5:9

And they sang a new song, saying, "You are worthy to take the scroll, and to open its seals; for you were slain, and have redeemed us to God by your blood out of every tribe and tongue and people and nation..."

A SONG OF PRAISE

John reveals that all the saved in Christ assembled with Jesus play heavenly music. They begin to sing a brand new song written for this worthy occasion.

This is their song, sung from their hearts of love (paraphrased): "Only the Lamb is worthy to take the book and to open the seven seals. You, Lord, were slain on the cross to save each one of us that you created before the world. You rescued from Satan all those who believe in you. You alone bought us with your precious blood and now we belong to you forevermore. Every race and language, and all people of all nations, praise your holy name. Praise the name of the Lord. We thank you and we love you, God. You have made us kings and priests and we rule under you on this earth. You are the God of heaven. Amen!"

I believe all singing will come naturally to us when we are with the Lord, and by that I mean, all will have perfect musical voices through the knowledge of God!

Revelation 5:10

...And you [Jesus] have made us kings and priests to our God; and we shall reign on the earth."

KINGS & PRIESTS

John continues to write down everything shown to him by the angel. The gigantic heavenly choir finishes the song of praise. Jesus confirms that he has made the saved kings and priests to God, to him be the glory and dominion forever and ever (Rev. 1:6).

The Lord created the beautiful green earth. He has made all his wonderful people who inhabit his planet. Christ's hands have made you and fashioned you, giving you understanding that you may learn his commandments. It is here on this earth where we will learn and carry out our kingly and priestly duties; on the reformed earth during the Kingdom Age, just after "...he (Jesus) laid hold of the dragon, that serpent of old, who is the devil and Satan, and bound him for a thousand years; and he cast him into the bottomless pit and shut him up, and set a seal on him, so that he should deceive the nations no more till the thousand years were finished" (Rev. 20:2–3)

After the capture of Satan, Jesus sets up his government where the current city of Jerusalem presently stands, and all earthlings believing in the Lord join him at the beginning of his spectacular one thousand year reign—the much talked about seventh millennium, the last 1,000 years in perfect time for humanity. Again, bear in mind that this is mankind's wonderful rest period after having worked for six days. Now it is time for relaxing with the Lord, learning and preparing for the glory of the New Earth (our heaven) and the glittering new city of Jerusalem sent down from heaven by God—here we practice our kingly and priestly responsibilities.

WE ARE EARTHLINGS

I'd like to point out something important here: we must remember that we are earthlings, ultimately designed to live on earth. Even though the New Earth in the Second Heaven will be vastly different from this one in regard to natural laws and reality, and in fact in actual experience, the earth is still our home.

Perhaps we'll wander from the New Earth and explore all Creation, but nonetheless we will always be connected to the earth, for this is from whence we came. In addition, our relationship with Jesus is on this earth, as well as on the New Earth, and that is of course our greatest bond to it.

In truth, we do not belong to God's domain. We don't belong in his First Heaven. Our place is as kings and priests with Jesus on his New Earth in the Second Heaven. "The heaven, even the heavens is the Lord's; but the earth he has given to the children of men" (Psalm 115:16).

DON'T MESS AROUND

Let's pause here briefly and remember that Jesus gives us assurance, for he tells us in the New Testament, "Believe in me, and I will give you eternal life with me in heaven" (paraphrased from John 3:16). Don't mess around and miss out on being a child of God. What a pity to lose out on all the wonders offered to us because we reject the One who died to save us! Being of this fallen and broken world and reality most of us have a mere 75 years in life, if we have that good fortune! After that it's get down to business time: facing death and the realities that follow. We are flowers of the field. We flourish and then, but a moment later, a wind passes over us and we are gone!

A TRUE STORY

To further illustrate what I mean, let me tell a brief true-life story. As a parent, I once spoke to my ski instructor son who worked at Crested Butte Mountain Resort, a ski resort in Colorado on the Western Slope of the Colorado Rockies. We were discussing the lost, those who don't know Jesus as their Lord and Savior. We looked down the steep mountain, toward the town nestled at its base. I said to him, "Wouldn't you say that about eighty percent of the people in this city don't know the saving grace of Christ?" My son's quick reply was, "I would say it's more like 90 percent, Dad!" Oh, what a pity indeed! These wonderful and precious people do not pause for a moment to think about the One who made them, don't spare a thought for the One who gives them life, who loves them and who can save them, for they are like flowers in bloom, clothed in petals and bathed in sunshine—but soon their beautiful petals will dry up and the wind will come and blow them away and time will no longer matter. Clearly, for them, now is the time to get down to business!

Revelation 5:11

Then I [John] looked, and I heard the voice of many angels around the throne, the living creatures, and the elders, and the number of them was ten thousand times ten thousand, and thousands of thousands...

THOUSANDS UPON THOUSANDS

John hears the voices of the four living creatures (each one symbolizing the Lamb of God), the twenty-four elders (the twelve apostles, the twelve holy prophets of the Old Testament, and every believer in Jesus Christ), and the angels. The living creatures announce the number of the heavenly multitude. The number is one hundred million, plus thousands and thousands more, ad infinitum!

The size of the multitude is, of course, incalculable, for they are like the sands of a never-ending sea in number. What a wonderful blessing to know we are not alone and will never be alone.

ANGELS

John observes and writes: he hears the voices of the holy angels gathered around the glorious throne, undoubtedly thousands and thousands, as the throne of God is enormous. They praise the Lord God who made heaven and earth. (You can refer to

Chapter 3:1 and Chapter 4:6–8 for additional information on angels.)

Before moving to the next verse, I'd like to point out that angels are everywhere in the Scriptures. Jesus made it perfectly clear that, 1: he believed in angels, and 2: their number is vast (Matt. 13:39; 18:10; 22:30; 25:31; 26:53; Luke 15:10; 16:22). As I mentioned before, there is hardly any evidence in Scripture to show us what they actually look like or how they actually work— how they're designed to operate. We don't have a clue what the original angelic form is, as we humans cannot understand hyperdimensional beings when we see them in their true form, but we do know they can shape-change, altering their appearance to look like men, and they do supernatural things. They appear magical; at least, they do to us. *Unger's New Bible Dictionary* contends that angels are the supernatural messengers of God, working for an angelic courier service, of a sort—that's their main purpose in light of what is taking place on earth with humanity, at any rate.[10]

NON-ANGELIC HUMANS

Angels are not human. Unlike angels, we know what it means to be human. Whether directly or indirectly, we follow the unholy trinity when we trust in worldly things and look upon money, gold, diamonds, Harley Davidson's, drugs, alcohol, family members, houses, the sun, science, religion, movie stars, sex, images of Saints, Mary the mother of Jesus, Joseph Smith, L. Ron Hubbard, Franklin D. Roosevelt, Democrats, Republicans, Independents, Progressives, the Antichrist (and on and on and on) as our salvation.

That's about as non-angelic as it gets!

But of course we non-angelic beings, we humans, have so much hope in Christ. We can, through the Holy Trinity and trust in the heavenly Father, find salvation. Be with Christ's glory above earth and heaven, where his name alone is exalted! Take his testimonies as a heritage forever, for they are the rejoicing of your heart.

Revelation 5:12

...saying with a loud voice, "Worthy is the Lamb who was slain to receive power and riches and wisdom, and strength and honor and glory and blessing!"

THE ANGELS PRAISE

Thousands upon thousands of holy angles join in with the multitude praising their Creator. All say, "Worthy is the Lamb of God, Jesus Christ, who died for our sakes. He is worthy to receive all power, riches, wisdom, strength, honor, glory and blessings forevermore!"

What a chorus for all heaven and earth to share, transmitted into endless space beyond forever and forever. He is our only hope for eternity! "For what is our hope, or joy, or crown of rejoicing? Is it not even you in the presence of our Lord Jesus Christ at his coming?" (1Thess. 2:19). Lift your hands toward Christ and fear and respect the Lord, for this is the beginning of wisdom.

Revelation 5:13

And every creature which is in heaven and on the earth and under the earth and such as are in the sea, and all that are in them, I [John] heard saying, "Blessing and honor and glory and power be to him who sits on the throne, and to the Lamb, forever and ever!"

PRAISE FROM ALL

John listens to the voice of the kings and priests, the holy angels, and everything else in all Creation: "Good wishes, reverence, adoration, and might be to the Lord who sits on the throne in the throne room of God, and to the Lamb forever and ever." The Lord is in his holy temple. The Lord's throne is in heaven. His eyes are on every place, keeping watch! He loves righteousness! His name is Righteousness! His countenance beholds the upright!

Revelation 5:14

Then the four living creatures said, "Amen!" And the elders fell down and worshiped.

WORSHIP

The word of the Lord fills the ears and heart of John: the four living creatures say, "God of Life!" (Amen) and then the twenty-four elders (the twelve apostles, the twelve holy prophets, and all the redeemed in Christ) fall down and worship the Christ who lives forever. The Lamb is about to open the sacred and most holy scroll and break the first of its seven seals! We will wait in awe!

* * * * *

SOURCES:

1. *Scroll,* Encyclopedia Britannica (2002), Online Edition, <http://www.britannica.com>.
   Scroll, pg. 1148, The New Unger's Bible Dictionary, Moody Press (1988).
2. *Seal/Seals in Antiquity,* Encyclopedia Britannica (2002), Online Edition, <http://www.britannica.com>.
   Seal, Signet, pg. 1150-1151, The New Unger's Bible Dictionary, Moody Press (1988).
3. *On Everlasting Destruction; The Vote for Annihilation,* L. Dolphin, Lambert Dolphin Resources, <http://www.ldolphin.org>.
4. *Hell,* pg. 550-551, The New Unger's Bible Dictionary, Moody Press (1988).
   Physics and the Bible, Personal Update NewsJournal, L. Lambert, Koinonia House, <http://www.khouse.com>.
   On Everlasting Destruction, L. Lambert, Lambert Dolphin's Resources, <http://www.ldolphin.org>.
   Beyond Space and Time, article, Chuck Missler, Koinonia House, <http://www.khouse.com>.
   Stretching the Heavens, article, Chuck Missler, Koinonia House, <http://www.khouse.com>.
5. *Satan,* pg. 1132-1133, The New Unger's Bible Dictionary, Mood Press (1988).
   The Angels of Revelation (continued/addendum), No. 70 & No. 71, James B. Jordon, Biblical Horizons (1995), <http://www.biblicalhorizons.com>.
6. *Covenants Which Can't Be Ignored,* Personal Update NewsJournal, Chuck Missler, Koinonia House, <http://www.khouse.com>.
   Root, pg. 1090-1091, The New Unger's Bible Dictionary, Moody Press (1988).
7. *Lamb,* Bible Encyclopedia, ChristianAnswers.com, <http://www.christiananswers.net>.
   Lamb, pg. 752, The New Unger's Bible Dictionary, Moody Press (1988).
   Lamb, Easton's Bible Dictionary, Online Edition, The HTML Bible, <http://www.htmlbible.com> & <http://www.johnhurt.com>, PO Box 31, Elmwood, TN 38560 USA.
8. *Harp,* Bible Encyclopedia, ChristianAnswers.com. <http://www.christiananswers.net>.
   Harp, contributed by Genevieve Vaughn, Microsoft Encarta Encyclopedia (2002).
   Harp; Music, pg. 893-894, The New Unger's Bible Dictionary, Moody Press (1988).
9. *Incense,* Bible Encyclopedia, ChristianAnswers.com, <http://www.christiananswers.net>.
   Incense, pg. 615-616, The New Unger's Bible Dictionary, Moody Press (1988).
10. *Angel; Angels, Fallen,* pg. 61-62, The New Unger's Bible Dictionary, Moody Press (1988).
    God and His Angels, L. Lambert, Lambert Dolphin's Resources, <http://www.ldolphin.org>.
    Satan (Lucifer), Graham Brodie, Lambert Dolphin's Resources, <http://www.ldolphin.org>.

Further reading:

Angels of Light, Powers of Darkness: Thinking Biblically About Angels, Satan and Principalities, Stephen Noll, Inter-varsity Press (1998).

The Bible Has The Answers, Henry Morris, Martin Clark, Master Books (1995).

PART III

Chapters Six through Twenty-two
THE PROPHECY

Chapters Six through Twenty-two are the heart of the Book of Revelation. The information within the following chapters jumps back and forth in time in relation to End Time prophecy and the series of prophetic events. A generalized rundown of the topics that will be explored is provided here (not listed in any specific order) : the last three-and-a-half years of the Great Tribulation; the Seven Seals; the Four Horses and Riders of the Apocalypse; the rise of the Antichrist Nimrod, the Assyrian resurrected; the Antichrist's control of the European Union; the False Prophet/False Pope; the Catholic, Orthodox, and collective Christian Church in regard to history and future history/an apostate nature; the Roman Empire; three waiting places; the Christian martyrs; the 144,000 sealed Jews; the reformation of the earth/universe/time and reality; a six day reformation process; the removal of the Holy Spirit from the earth during the last three-and-a-half years of the Tribulation; the Children of Israel, and of Jesus, of the tribe of Judah; further study of the fallen nature in light of the reformation of the planet/humanity/and reality into the 1,000 year millennium (and what life will be like); Kingdom Age reproduction; the Seven Trumpet plagues; the Seven Thunder Plagues; the Seven Bowl Plagues; the Locust; classical and quantum physics; the River Euphrates; the Beasts; the mark and biometric systems and *the* global biometric system; modern Babylon/the Harlot and her destruction; Armageddon; New World Order/One World Religion Organization (global inter-faith ecumenicism); 7 Papal Kings; the Two Witnesses; abbreviated biblical genealogies; Christian duty toward Jerusalem and all Israel; the Balfour Declaration; the fundamental beliefs of Islam and its history; how Islam relates to the Arab Nations, the Western and Christian world, and End Time events; the pre-Great Tribulation siege upon Israel by the Hostile Nations/Gog and Magog; Petra; the return of Christ and the threefold nature of his return; the Kingdom Age;, the second death; Satan's final release and the doom for all the lost, angelic and human; Judgment; New Jerusalem, the cubed city; the necessity of planets in the Second Heaven and all realities/dimensions; new Heaven and Earth; living water; three trees of life; plus a wealth of additional information.

CHAPTER 6
The Seven Seals

Revelation 6:1

Now I [John] saw when the Lamb opened one of the seven seals; and I heard one of the four living creatures saying with a voice like thunder, "Come and see."

THE FIRST SEAL IS BROKEN

The prophecy begins.

The Lamb of God, Jesus Christ, breaks the first seal. What is written within involves the Antichrist and the Great Tribulation. It is a period that will last seven years, the final seven years in this fallen reality, the last three horrifying beyond belief. The Great Tribulation commences the moment the Lamb of God loosens the first of the seven seals securing the little scroll/book held in his right hand!

John hears one of the four living creatures shout, "BEHOLD WHAT IS COMING!" The sound is like a thunderclap. We must remember here that the voice of the creature is Jesus speaking, for Revelation makes it very clear that the voice of the Lord is like thunder: "And I (John) heard a voice from heaven, like the sound of many waters, and like the voice of loud thunder (Jesus)..." (Rev. 14:2). By the breath of God, the word is given. Even the clouds turn at his sound!

John's heart trembles and leaps from his chest! Jesus does not restrain his voice to John when he roars, "STAND STILL, PEOPLE OF EARTH, FOR THE *MAN OF SIN* IS ABOUT TO BE REVEALED!"

Behold, through his thunder, the great mystery of the seven seals is unfolding.

Revelation 6:2

And I [John] looked, and behold, a white horse. He who sat on it had a bow; and a crown was given to him, and he went out conquering and to conquer.

WHAT IS WITHIN THE FUTURE

The sky rumbles, sounding like the beat of seven thousand drums. With his right hand, the Spirit of Glory, the Son of the Living God, has broken the first seal. This act is extremely significant because what is written within, on both sides of the scroll, is about to be revealed: the future.

At this point, John is taken out of the timeline of this earth and reality and is, in fact, about to see into that timeline from the outside, observing the future history of humankind! In a way, it's like he's dipping his head into a fast moving stream and opening his eyes and looking around. If that is the case, of course, it is very likely that what he witnessed was nearly incomprehensible to his 96 A.D. brain, other than grasping the most basic and obvious traits of humanity and technology. The rest would be beyond his understanding.

IMAGINE

Let us imagine, for a moment, what John saw: masses of people strangely dressed, living in gigantic cities that tower to the skies; splattered with blood, murder, and chaos, echoing laughter, love, and hope, the cities are buried in wondrous and bizarre technology, breathtaking architecture, a melting pot of humanity, a blur of information, language, and pulsating life. The city streets have *shining chariots* racing and raging and jostling one another in every direction. At night, perhaps the chariots seem like dashing torches! They run like lightning! (See Nahum 2:4). John sees tremendous iron bridges crossing endless waterways loaded with the ferocious chariots zooming past! At night the cities (and the world) glitter like starlight reflected on a motionless pond! During daylight hours, he sees great poisonous-looking dust clouds hovering over the cities like asthmatic giants, teetering over-built coastal terrain, and through it all he hears noise, endless noise. He listens to the hills, for they are *alive with the pound of music,* rhythmic voices singing to music he hardly understands!

John sees that the skies above are crowded with enormous *iron birds* with long tails stretching from east to west and north to south, blanketing the sky! As the lightning comes from the east and flashes to the west so also is the speed of these strange birds! *The flying birds* or *eagles* are crowded with hundreds of people traveling to and fro (see Daniel 12:4). He sees very large *mechanical insects made of metal* that appear like locust, hovering above the earth, shining like iron, spitting fire, traveling at great speeds, and strangest of all, they're filled with people. He sees mountainous *iron boats* moving swifter than wild winds blasting across the high seas, and all without the help of sails. He sees that the countryside is overflowing with strange-looking dwellings piled on top of one another for as far as the eye can see. Wide black broad-ways crisscross the earth and long, shiny *Shongalolas* (thousand-leg millipedes) move at great speed across the lands! Orbiting around the globe, John glimpses manmade objects twinkling like tiny stars and, like the shining Shongalolas, moving at great speed!

What a world to see.

When viewing this brave new world, it is likely John noticed that everything moved very fast. His eyes would have burned with amazement as he recognized that human knowledge and technology had greatly increased (again, see Daniel 12:4). But he would be horrified by it too. It would bring him to tears because there were still masses of starving, naked, and sick, still ongoing wars and rumors of wars. At that point he may have pulled his head out of the stream and shouted in wonder, "What manner of time is this?"

THE WHITE HORSE & ITS RIDER

John sees a powerful rider moving toward him on a shining white horse. The one who sits on the horse has a bow. A crown is given to him.

Because a white horse is mentioned here, traditionally (in some schools of prophecy), the interpretation has been that the rider is Jesus Christ, for Revelation clearly refers to Jesus riding a white horse: "Now I (John) saw heaven open, and behold, a white horse. And he who sat on him was called Faithful and True, and in righteousness he judges and makes war" (Rev. 19:11).

Figuratively and traditionally, the horse is a symbol of war in the Bible because of its strength and use in battle (Deut. 32:13; Ps. 66:12; Isa. 58:14). The horse is also a biblical symbol of conquest (Song of Sol. 1:19).[1] In Zechariah 6:2–7, four horses are mentioned, each one a different color: white, red, black, and patterned/or pale. The white horse symbolizes victory, the red horse war, the black horse famine, and the patterned/pale horse pestilence (and sometimes simply death). These horses are commonly referred to as *the Four Horsemen of the Apocalypse.* As far as this book is concerned, the four horses have similar, as well as nontraditional, interpretations—these will be explored in a moment.

Now, the verse quoted from Chapter 19 does indeed pertain to Jesus the King, who is riding a white horse to victory at the Battle of Armageddon at the end of the great seven year Tribulation. This is part of Jesus' mighty return to the earth on the Lord's Day.

THE WHITE HORSE & ITS RIDER REVEALED
The Counterfeit King

The rider of the white horse mentioned in this verse is another king altogether, a counterfeit king. The word *victory* is not associated with his horse. Because he's a counterfeit king he rides a white horse as well, but instead of finding victory and establishing peace, he makes war during the last days of humankind! This king is spoken of as the conqueror who will reign during the days of the Great Tribulation. He is known as *the Antichrist.* He is the counterfeit king.

THE FALSE CHRIST

Now, from the historical and scriptural perspective, the word *Antichrist* literally means *against Christ* or *false Christ.* But when using the word, John (who was the only one who used it) makes it very clear that there is a difference in meaning to antichrists and *the* Antichrist (1John 2:18), for he says that, "...many antichrists have risen," but "that (*the*) Antichrist is coming." The most accepted and generalized meaning of the lowercase *antichrist* today is *any person who opposes the doctrine and deity of Christ.* She or he can be anyone who tries to replace or equate herself or himself to Christ or proclaims a nontraditional route to Christian salvation by inventing or claiming to use ancient-but-clearly-unchristian dogma, ritual, secrets, oaths, supernatural powers, superior intellect, superior understanding and interpretation of Scripture, including additions, changes, and erasure to the Holy Word of God in any way, shape or form. All of that is lowercase antichrist. *The* Antichrist is the man possessed by Satan himself through his unholy son, armed with satanic powers. He will rise to power and control most of the world, persecuting, destroying, and wiping off the face of the earth, in a clear and successful attempt at genocide, Christians and Jews, as well as the name of God and Christ, his *insect-like* purpose to prevent the restoration of Israel (Acts 1:6) during the seventh millennium, the Kingdom Age.[2]

John could have written about the rider on the white horse in a manner like this: "And I see hell open; and coming from the abyss I observe a white horse. And the Antichrist who sits on him is a counterfeit who wants the inhabitants of the earth to believe that he is the Christ. He is called unfaithful and untrue. He talks peace, but his judgment is unrighteous and he makes war on God and man!"

TO SWALLOW UP THE NATIONS

He is described in this verse as having a bow in his hand, depicting mighty power and strength, as well as violence and destruction. In the Old Testament the word *bow,* as well as *bow and arrow,* is used as a symbol of disaster and disease (Job 6:4; 34:6; Ps. 38:2).[3]

He reaches out to swallow up nation after nation! For the purposes of this book, this moment in End Time chronology will be referred to as The White Horse Period, that period of time which covers the first half of the Great Tribulation, the first three-and-a-half years of the final seven.

During this time the Antichrist will come up with astonishing ideas for peace on earth, and he will deceive many through his craftiness. He will appear as the man for whom the world has been waiting—so they will say! Through his angelic and dark intelligence and purpose he will succeed in convincing many countries of the world to join forces with him. His ideas will seem sound and logical and they will promise great prosperity. The entire world will marvel at his leadership.

Revelation 6:3

When he opened the second seal, I [John] heard the second living creature saying, "Come."

THE SECOND SEAL IS BROKEN

The Lamb of God loosens the second seal. John hears the second living creature call out to him. He says, "COME AND SEE!"

Revelation 6:4

Another horse, fiery red, went out. And it was granted to the one who sat on it to take peace from the earth, and that people should kill one another; and there was given to him a great sword.

THE RED HORSE & ITS RIDER
The Antichrist

John looks and, behold, yet another horse rides directly toward him. This time it is fiery red! Again, the rider on the horse is the Antichrist, but now he is seen in a different light. He is seen, in fact, in his true dark light: from counterfeit victory-white to war-red! The White Horse Period is over and the Red Horse Period has begun.

In the middle of the three-and-a-half years of the Great Tribulation he will reveal his true supernatural nature, and many people will believe in him and regard him as their savior, Christians, Buddhists, Muslims, Hindus—all faiths, as well as atheists (although, indirectly), including the nation of Israel, the nation that waits anxiously for their anticipated deliverer and king of the Jews.

During his time of ministry on the earth (three-and-a-half years or so), Jesus experienced a mighty time—it was a time of power and strength and transformation. His short time here fundamentally changed the world. Likewise, because he is an impersonator, the Antichrist will try to do the same! He will have seven years to accomplish his task, and he will desire that his last three-and-a-half years be as mighty, if not more so, than Christ's.

THE ANTICHRIST & THE ROMAN EMPIRE

The Antichrist as counterfeit king and the ancient Roman Empire: the recorded three-and-a-half years of Jesus' earthly ministry took place during the time when the Roman Empire ruled the world. The counterfeit king will want to do the same— everything the unholy trinity does is in direct imitation of the Holy Trinity.

God's Son will allow the Antichrist to have the authority, and he will rule his newly formed Babylon from its capital city (Rome). Similar to the times of the ancient Roman Empire, he will include countries that were once part of the Empire when Jesus was on earth! It will be very similar to old Rome, fully revived and in power once more, with one vital difference: in the Red Horse Period the Empire will be led not by a mere mortal Caesar, but by the devil's son himself. The ten-country kingdom, what amounts to the ten-valved-heart of United Europe, will become the heart of the most powerful nation on the face of the whole earth!

Within the first three-and-a-half years of the Tribulation (the White Horse Period), the Antichrist will win the confidence of the people globally.

THE RED HORSE PERIOD

Not surprisingly, the Red Horse Period will be a vastly different story. It begins right in the middle of the great affliction when he declares himself God in the great, newly built temple in Jerusalem. (Refer to Chapter 13:14, under the heading *The Temple Rebuilt* and *The Temple & the Image*.) "Therefore, when you see the 'abomination of desolation' (the Antichrist's image) spoken of by Daniel the prophet, standing in the holy place (the new temple in Jerusalem)..." (Matt. 24:15). Demanding world worship, the Antichrist will take peace from the earth. His true warlike colors will be fully revealed! "Worship me as god, or die!" he will demand, and many who refuse will be killed—especially all the living left behind believers in Christ, those who weren't caught up in the Fourth Rapture, just before the Antichrist decreed he is God. They are the unprepared, for the glorious rapture at the first part of

Jesus' Second Coming takes place and they are not removed from this earth in the twinkling of an eye. These Christians will become martyrs, as they will also become extremely faithful to the Son, even to the point of death. They will refuse to bow down to the Antichrist and his image. They will refuse to receive his mark (a global biometric system of some sort like a national I.D. card, an iris scan, or perhaps a chip embedded beneath the skin). They will be killed for rejecting the global biometric system. Hence, brother turns against brother and all Jesus' faithful are forced into hiding to save their lives.

Daniel tells us, "...I saw in the night visions, and behold, a fourth beast (the Antichrist), dreadful and terrible, exceedingly strong. It (the beast) had huge iron teeth; it was devouring, breaking in pieces, and trampling the residue with its feet (for he kills all who do not worship him, regardless of race, culture or creed). It was different from all the beasts that were before it, and it had ten horns (referring to the ten nations, the ten-valved-heart, which controls the beating heart of the European Union)" (Daniel 7:7).

Revelation 6:5

When he opened the third seal, I [John] heard the third living creature say, "Come and see." So I looked, and behold, a black horse, and he who sat on it had a pair of scales in his hand.

THE THIRD SEAL IS BROKEN

When the third seal is broken, John hears the third living creature command, "COME AND SEE!"

THE BLACK HORSE & ITS RIDER
The Mark of the Antichrist

Imagine John's curiosity at this point, called thrice by the Voice of Authority, and so he observes: the Antichrist rides a black horse, depicting the darkest moments in the history of the human race! This is exactly what the son of the devil brings upon all humanity!

The light of prosperity enjoyed by all during the first three-and-a-half years of the Great Tribulation will come to an abrupt end and senseless bloodshed will follow. Similar to Hitler and his Final Solution, the slaughter of millions of Christians and Jews, and anyone else that gets in the way, will become law.[4] This time in human history genocide will be global policy.

The world population will face more horrors, for this is the Black Horse Period. There will be widespread hunger, disease, and pestilence. As mentioned earlier, a global biometric system for identification will be established, and everyone who wishes to buy or sell must accept this system, this *mark* of the Antichrist, or go without the necessities of life: "He (the Beast, the Antichrist) causes all, both small and great, rich and poor, free and slave, to receive a mark on their right hand or on their foreheads, and that no one may buy or sell except one who has the mark, the name of the beast (the Antichrist), or the number of his name (666)" (Rev. 13:16–17).

Through the bleak days of the Black Horse Period during the Great Tribulation, Satan's son will control the earth's food and water supply. Prices will become highly inflated! He will be involved with the World Bank, controlling the monetary system of countless governments. The earth's defense systems will be in his hands. For all intents and purposes, he will have complete control of the earth. But it is only for a limited amount of time. Revelation 19:20 tells us: "...the beast (the Antichrist) was captured (at the return of Christ), and with him the false prophet who worked signs in his presence... These two were cast into the lake of fire burning with brimstone." Therefore Sheol (hell) has enlarged itself and opened its mouth beyond measure; their glory and their multitude and their pomp, and he who is jubilant, shall descend into it" (Isaiah 5:14).

Revelation 6:6

And I [John] heard a voice in the midst of the four living creatures saying, "A quart of wheat for a denarius, and three quarts of barley for a denarius; and do not harm the oil and the wine."

THE GLOBAL FOOD SHORTAGE

In the center of the four living creatures (essentially, Jesus), John hears the Lamb's voice say, "A measure of wheat for a day's wage, and three measures of barley for a day's wage, and do not harm the oil and the wine!"

Before we get into the meat of this prophecy, let's take a look at the history of a denarius. A denarius was a Roman silver coin active in the time of Christ, the daily wage of a labor worker. The name comes from what it was originally equal to: ten donkeys. Sometime later the number of donkeys was raised to sixteen.[5]

Keeping that in mind, we have the image of the Antichrist—the black horse and rider—holding a pair of scales in his left hand. In

Scripture, a balance or scale used for the selling of wheat or barley is a symbol of shortage or global famine[6] (Rev. 6:5; Lev 26:26; Ezek. 4:16–17). That is exactly what it means here.

Combining these lines of thought, when the Black Horse Period is in full gallop there will be famine the likes of which the world has never seen. Strict rationing of the world's food market will be controlled by the Antichrist, and so the cost of food will necessarily rise, and the simple, taken for granted task of gathering food from the local supermarket (especially here in America, as well as Great Britain, Europe, Australia, Canada.) will become a thing of the past. This is a clear warning from Christ that a full day's earnings will buy only a small amount of food, perhaps enough for a day— for those who can afford it. It will require every dollar earned to satisfy our hunger!

If it takes a full eight-hour-day-of-wages to buy food for one day, how then will people meet their basic living expenses like rent, mortgage, clothing, car payments, utilities, telephone, and waste? Expect people to face great hunger, especially if handouts from the government are discontinued—and they will be discontinued, of course, as no favors will be given by the devil's son, the Antichrist. Expect a multitude of homeless. They will far exceed the homeless of today. In the United States the estimated number of homeless comes in at around several million, a number made up of mostly adult males. The percentage of homeless women, children, and young adults is, sadly, steadily increasing.[7]

People will be forced to steal food. People will kill for bread. Isn't it interesting that today food prices are not decreasing but are instead increasing? World hunger is not lessening either. It continues to grow. We are being prepared for worse times ahead. The Black Horse Period is approaching swiftly.

THE OIL & THE WINE

Christ warns Satan not to stop the flow of oil and wine. In fact, the Lord *commands* that the oil and the wine continue to flow. Why? Answer: the oil and wine must continue to flow so that humanity will continue to flow, in spite of the fact that they will have to pay an arm and a leg for these products. Humanity needs these things to, in a very real sense, survive. The Holy Father recognizes this and thus his commandment.

As to the oil: God says, "Do not stop the oil," and here the meaning is layered:

(1) It directly relates to crude oil, world economy, and modern machinery.

(2) Oil is a symbol of the Holy Spirit.

The anointing of oil is an Old and New Testament ritual given to humanity by God through the Holy Scriptures. In general, it symbolizes the Spirit of God that indwells the human heart during the act of (and ever after) salvation. Thus, the Lord is saying the *oil of the Spirit* must continue to flow like the oil and the wine—in order for humanity to survive. This means that the Holy Spirit will continue to anoint or indwell those who call for salvation during this time, as well as continue to protect the planet earth. Last of all, the symbolic nature of oil in Scripture can be attached to food and medicine, and since food will be in short supply and medicine will be in great demand (not to mention economically prohibitive), the symbolism here should be clear enough.[8]

As to wine: Jeffrey J. Meyers of *Biblical Horizons* reminds us in his outstanding essay *Concerning Wine and Beer part 1 and 2* that the joy of Jesus and the shalom of life is in beer, wine, and strong drink just as it is in food and rain and flowers. I encourage you to read his essays in full, but in summary he argues that scripturally alcohol is a gift, a blessing from God to humanity. The Scriptures are clear on how to conduct oneself in public and private life in regard to alcohol and intoxication: avoid drunkenness, moderation, etc. But the Bible never commands us not to drink alcohol, nor does it condemn the substance. Instead, the Bible clearly outlines the use of alcohol in regard to a believer's obedience toward it, as well as its potential for abuse and addiction. Alcohol can ease the suffering in the battle of ordinary day-to-day life and survival, which for many, perhaps even most, is a difficult, even brutal life-experience. It can inspire celebration, joy, and honor toward family, friends and God.[9] As to how alcohol can be applied to the End Times and survival during what will amount to an even more difficult and brutal time for humanity, I think Meyers' logic, scriptural wisdom, and faith, and his clear, levelheaded understanding of alcohol's intent, can be easily applied and understood.

Throughout the Scriptures, alcoholic wine is used for religious ritual, everyday hospitality at home, while traveling, festivals, marriages, parties, etc. (Ex. 29:40; Gen. 14:18; John 2: 3–10). Wine is also figurative of the blood of Christ (Matt. 26:27–29) and the Holy Spirit (Eph. 5:18).[10]

Lastly, "...and do not harm the oil and the wine" suggests the wine of Christ's blood will continue to flow at this point, or in other words, salvation will continue to be offered to the lost.

Revelation 6:7

When he opened the fourth seal, I heard the voice of the fourth living creature say, "Come and see."

THE FOURTH SEAL IS BROKEN

After the fourth seal is broken, the voice of the fourth living creature says, "JOHN, COME AND SEE!"

Revelation 6:8

So I [John] looked, and behold, a pale horse. And the name of him who sat on it was Death, and Hades followed with him. And power was given to them over a fourth of the earth, to kill with sword, with hunger, with death, and by the beasts of the earth.

THE PALE HORSE & ITS RIDER
The Antichrist of Death

John sees a pale horse moving toward him, as if it was seen through the shimmering heat of a hot desert floor! The one riding him is the Antichrist. He is dead toward Christ and Death is his name. And Hell follows with him.

THE PALE RIDER

Throughout the course of the Pale Horse Period, the worshiping of Satan's son will be in full force around the whole world. The False Prophet will be doing wonders through trickery and genuine-but-unholy supernatural powers. He will deceive many millions. Death will stretch itself out across the face of the earth like it has never done before. After the Fourth Rapture (three-and-a-half years into the seven year Tribulation period, precisely in the middle), every Christian and Jew on earth, except the 144,000 chosen messianic Jews supernaturally protected by God, will be hunted down and killed. This will be the most successful genocide in the history of the world!

The Red, Black, and Pale Horse Periods of the Great Tribulation cover a total of three-and-a-half years, the last and final three-and-a-half years of the seven year Tribulation period, and it can be summed up as quite literally hell on earth, for at that point, Satan will exercise authority over the entire world. Great pestilence, worldwide hunger, political and emotional hardships, the actual plagues themselves (which we will explore in greater detail in the chapters further on) equal innumerable deaths. "For then there will be great tribulation, such as has not been since the beginning of the world until this time, no, nor ever shall be," declares Christ in Matthew 24:21.

Revelation 6:9

When he opened the fifth seal, I [John] saw under the alter the souls of those who have been slain for the word of God and for the testimony which they held.

THE FIFTH SEAL IS BROKEN
The Cry of the Martyrs is Heard

When Christ opens the fifth seal, John hears the mournful cry of the martyrs *under the alter*. This term is a symbolic reference to the *waiting place* for the slain martyrs in Jesus Christ and for all the Saints who have passed-on as well. The student of prophecy will call it *Abraham's Bosom/Sheol*. Remember, Abraham's Bosom is a paradisiacal place where all the dead in Christ wait for the Third Rapture when they will receive their first new glorified bodies, phase two of the Phase of Body. The lost remain in Sheol or the antiparadise. While in the waiting place they remain in spirit/soul form. They do not have body, for that body grew old and died on earth.

THE THREE WAITING PLACES

I use the word *waiting* in the literal here, and not only for our benefit, for this paradise exists inside of time and in our reality— *waiting* does indeed happen there. The martyrs, and all those who have gone on to the other side, both the saved in Christ and the lost, are kept in this reality and time even though they are of the spirit. They have no earthly body, for that body was left behind and died, but their souls continue to live within the confines of our universe.

This means the first place of waiting, known as Abraham's Bosom/Sheol, is a genuine location in the universe where time passes. It is split in two, housing the paradisiacal Abraham's Bosom for the saved and the hellish Sheol for the lost. Perhaps it's a distant planet in an entirely different solar system or galaxy. Since there are so many planets and galaxies in the ever expanding universe this conclusion seems reasonable.

The Book of Mathew mentions the Second Rapture, that of the Old Testament Saints and all the saved of God prior to the resurrection of Christ. They waited in the first place of waiting in spirit form, having no body. Approximately four thousand years passed, depending on when they passed-over (by God's timetable/calendar). At the resurrection of Christ, the First Rapture, they were resurrected from the first place of waiting, met the Spirit of the Lord in the air, and were immediately transformed into the Second Phase of Body, the glorified body, and transferred to *the second place of waiting.* They had brand new non-entropic bodies.

They now wait in Paradise, the planet made especially for glorified Saints, the second place of waiting.

Mathew goes on to explain that some of those who were resurrected in the Second Rapture were seen in Jerusalem after the death and resurrection of Christ. Upon his resurrection, three days later, they went into Jerusalem and were seen by many. As I pointed out earlier, these Saints were permitted to return to the earth and be seen in their Second Phase of Body as a witness to the glory and power of Christ. They were then either supernaturally taken to the second place of waiting soon thereafter or with Christ 40 days later at the Ascension to join the millions and millions already there.

The lost continue to remain in the first place of waiting called Sheol or the antiparadise, the one they originally went to in spirit. Of course, the numbers of the lost must also be vast.

GOING TO THE PLACES OF WAITING

All believers who have experienced death since the time of The First and Second Rapture will receive their glorified bodies when the next raptures occur, the Third and Fourth Raptures that take place simultaneously in the middle of the Great Tribulation. They will go through the same process. They will not go to the Father's heaven, the First Heaven, like so many want to believe. They will instead join the Old Testament believers and all the other saved in Christ in the second paradise place of waiting.

When the Third and Fourth raptures occur, the passed-on believers in Christ who have been in the first waiting place in spirit over this period of two thousand years since Jesus' resurrection (by God's timetable/calendar), *and* all living believers, will be transformed into phase two of the Phase of Body by Jesus Christ in the air, and then they will go to the waiting place for glorified Saints, the second paradise place of waiting under God's mighty wing of love. This also applies to Raptures Five and Six that take place simultaneously at the end of the Great Tribulation just before the return of Christ.

When the Seventh Rapture occurs, all the dead lost (the unrepentant) who have been waiting in spirit form in the antiparadise over a period of seven thousand years (by God's timetable/calendar) will be finally transformed into phase two of the Phase of Body (the glorified body). Thcy will gathcr togcthcr with Lucifer in the air at the end of the Kingdom Age and these fallen of God will go out to try and deceive the saved living across the breath of the reformed earth.

To fully appreciate this concept, you have to recognize that there is:

ABRAHAM'S BOSOM/SHEOL
The First Place of Waiting

(1) A *waiting place* for the spirit after death that's split in two, housing Abraham's Bosom for the saved and Sheol for the lost.

As stated in Chapter 1, the first waiting place houses the spirits of all the dead, both the saved and the unsaved. A gulf of some kind separates them. Even so, the Scriptures tell us they can, indeed, see one another. They can't cross the gulf and interact, so it seems that on Abraham's Bosom/Sheol the lost suffer on one side of the gulf while the saved exist on the other side of the gulf in a blessed and heavenly state. How could this work if the first place of waiting is a distant planet? Perhaps it's a planet close to a giant star that has a peculiar spin to it, or perhaps no spin at all, allowing one side, Sheol, to smolder and cause the lost to suffer, while the other side, Abraham's Bosom, remains cool and heavenly.

I will paraphrase the parable told by Jesus in Luke 16 so that we can get a mental image to help us understand: "There was once a rich man who was unrighteous. In life he refused to help a particular righteous man who was poor and always hungry. The poor man died and was taken to paradise, called Abraham's Bosom. The rich man died sometime later and he was taken to paradise as well, but he was placed in a different area called Sheol, the antiparadise, separated from the poor and righteous man by a great gulf. He could not pass over to the other side. The terrain he was in was uncomfortably hot and he was constantly thirsty. Seeing that the poor man across the wide gulf was waiting in a place that was comfortable and pleasing, the rich man yelled to him, begging for a drop of water to cool his tongue, for he was tormented in flame. But the poor man was unable to help him, as he could not cross the gulf either."

A planet by an enormous star may not seem so farfetched after all.

PARADISE

The Second Place of Waiting

(2) A *waiting place* for the glorified body after the raptures! This is called Paradise, a beautiful planet reserved for the glorified Saints that is floating somewhere in the cosmos.

THE REFORMED EARTH

The Third Place of Waiting
(3) A third and final *waiting place for all the saved*: the reformed earth of the seventh millennium, the 1,000 years with Jesus. (God always works in threes, a sure sign of his holy mathematics /geometry.)

WHAT ARE THEY WAITING FOR?

What are the people waiting for in each of these three places? Heaven, of course, which comes *after* the seventh millennium, when the saved in Christ face the Third Phase of Body, the super-glorified body, and enter the Second Heaven and eternity, forever removed from time!

You may think this concept is absurd, for most believe that when we die we go straight to heaven. As nice as that sounds (it makes us feel comfortable and safe, to be sure), that argument or perception doesn't stand well in light of Scripture—as with everything involving God there is a pattern, a design, a system, and he adheres to his systems and patterns. He doesn't break his own rules.

HEAVEN

As far as how going to heaven works, we go to heaven but once, the Second Earth called Heaven, all the saved, all at the same time. This will happen *only* after we have lived with Jesus on the reformed earth for a thousand years! During the millennium of rest we will make ourselves ready to go to the true heaven, for we have a thousand years of study and preparation! At the end of the Kingdom Age we will experience the final transfiguration to the super-glorified body when we experience what is called *the second death that does not hurt*. Then it is to the Second Heaven we go forever: eternal life on the glorious New Earth, witnessing the glory of the New City of Jerusalem.

CRY OF THE MARTYRS

The martyrs mentioned in this verse are specifically those murdered by the Antichrist during the last three-and-a-half years of the Great Tribulation because they did not deny their Lord and

Savior. Failing to take part in the Fourth Rapture made them even more faithful than those who experienced it and were taken away with the Bridegroom! Jesus became their First Love and they were determined not to miss out on him a second time.

At this point in the series of End Time events, in relation to the *cry of the martyrs*, the number of those who are going to die for Christ in this period of time has been reached. Every practicing and believing Christian and Jew on earth has been killed. It will only be a matter of months before the Son of God takes the earth from the dragon. "And the armies in heaven, clothed in pure white linen (a symbolic depiction of purity, righteousness, faithfulness, etc.), followed him (Jesus) on white horses (when he returns to claim earth!)" (Rev. 19:14).

THE BLOODBATH

These martyrs are not deceived by the Antichrist and his associate, the False Prophet, for they soon discover the Beast's falsehood when they face his fury head on. They will try to spread the Truth in order to save others, and they will persuade many not to take the mark of the Antichrist or to worship his image; they will try to persuade people not to get involved with the global biometric system by taking its mark, whatever that will be. (Refer to Chapter 13:8 for related information.)

Because they are Christians, they will be slain—every one of them. There will be no survivors. For Christ's sake, their bodies are killed. They do not accept the Antichrist's mark of death. (Accepting the mark spells certain doom for those who take it.) They do not worship his image. "He (the False Prophet) was granted power to give breath to the image of the beast, that the image of the beast (the Antichrist) should both speak and cause as many as would not worship the image of the beast to be killed" (Rev. 13:15). It will be a bloodbath like no other in the history of the world.

Revelation 6:10

And they cried with a loud voice, saying, "How long, O Lord, holy and true, until you judge and avenge our blood on those who dwell on the earth?"

THE CALL FOR JUSTICE

After their earthly bodies are put to death, the souls of the martyrs will pass to the first place of waiting for their resurrection to come. They will go to Abraham's Bosom, and there they will call out to the Lamb, saying to their Savior, "How long, Lord, holy and true, before you judge and avenge our blood on those who dwell on the earth (referring to the Antichrist, the False Prophet, and their worshipers)?" They will demand justice and Jesus will comply in a mighty fashion!

The Lord roars from on high! He utters his voice from his habitation! He answers the call! Jesus returns to earth and encircles the world in a planet transforming wall of fire, and the Antichrist, the False Prophet, and all the unsaved are consumed by the power and glory that is the Son of God! The unredeemed will call out to Jesus in earnest from *under the altar*, where they are separated from the saved, saying, "We are adrift among the dead!"

Revelation 6:11

Then a white robe was given to each of them [each martyr]; and it was said to them that they should rest a little while longer, until both the number of their fellow servants and their brethren, who would be killed as they were, was completed.

WHITE ROBES

The white robes mentioned here are symbolic of purity and honor. The martyrs have been washed clean by the blood of the Lamb. Christ informs these souls, whose earthly bodies were killed by the wicked and unholy trinity, that they should wait in Abraham's Bosom.

There are two additional things associated with those *under the alter:*

(1) That they have to wait a little while longer suggests that the number of those to be killed will be very great indeed.

(2) The human perspective of tragedy and horror aside, it's clear that God is ultimately in control. This gives humanity the ability to face the tragedy and horror with hope, strengthening their faith.

Revelation 6:12

I [John] looked when he opened the sixth seal, and there was a great earthquake; and the sun became black as sackcloth of hair, and the whole moon became like blood.

THE SIXTH SEAL IS BROKEN

Earthquake, a blackened sun, and a red moon: John is witness to the breaking of the sixth seal, the end of flesh and blood as we know it.

THE CAPTURE OF THE UNHOLY TRINITY

Before exploring the sixth seal in depth, I think it's important that we know exactly where we are in regard to the series of End Time Events.

The sixth seal is essentially the end of the End Times. The end of the seven years of the Great Tribulation has reached its conclusion and time itself, or rather, imperfect and fallen time, is coming to an end via the return of Christ. The capture of the Antichrist and the False Prophet will commence. Jesus will apprehend them and then cast them into the burning lake of fire forever, and he will capture Satan as well. (The devil will not be sentenced to the lake of fire at this point, but will instead be imprisoned within his waiting place, what is called the bottomless pit, for he will have one more appearance to make with the unrepentant, at the end of the 1,000 years.)

Following the eternal confinement of the Antichrist and the False Prophet within the lake of fire (from which there is no escape), and the imprisonment of the devil, Jesus reforms the earth and rests with his saints for 1,000 years. At the end of this period, God's Son loosens Lucifer from his bonds, as well as all the unrepentant. Lucifer will be freed from the Bottomless Pit (hell) for *a little while*. The devil attacks Jesus for the third and final time— the first attack was in heaven, the second attack when the Lord soon returns to earth, and the third at the end of the 1,000 years. Then Jesus will move through the heavens with the keys to the bottomless pit and a great chain in his hand (at the end of the thousand years). He will subdue the attacker, the dragon, that serpent of old, who is the devil and Satan, and he will subdue the unrepentant and cast them into the Lake of Fire to join the Antichrist and the False Prophet who have already been confined there for 1,000 years. (A detailed description of the capture of the Antichrist, the False Prophet, and the Battle of Armageddon can be found in Chapter 19. The capture, sentencing, and carrying out of that sentence—imprisoned within the lake of fire for eternity—of Satan, can be found in Chapter 20.)

Prior to these end of the End Time events (the capture of the Antichrist, False Prophet, and Satan, and the Battle of Armageddon, the reformation of the earth and the beginning of the Kingdom Age, the 1,000 years with Christ), all the saved in Christ will have been raptured. They will not face God's wrath: the global earthquake, the blackened sun, and the red moon, what amounts to the total reformation or re-creation of this planet.

EARTHQUAKE

With these extraordinary events accomplished (again, in reference to the capture of the unholy trinity, the battle of Armageddon, and the end to the Great Tribulation), it will be time for the Lord to bring to pass the mighty worldwide earthquake. Jesus reforms the globe in readiness for the millennial kingdom. At the loosening of the sixth seal, the planet will literally tremble as Christ approaches, setting into motion a massive global quake. All dormant volcanoes on earth will activate, consuming the sinful nature of mankind, as well as the sinful nature of the earth itself with a wall of fire and lava. The volcanic smoke will rise, *black* as bubbling pitch, for miles and miles into the atmosphere, eventually blanketing the planet. The sun will appear like *sackcloth of hair* and the moon *like blood.*

In the fourth chapter of the book of Malachi, Verses 1 and 2, Malachi tells us of the great Day of the Lord: "For behold, the day is coming, burning like an oven, and all the proud, yes, all who do wickedly will be stubble..." Malachi 4:1 continues: "'And the day which is coming shall burn them up,' says the Lord of Hosts, 'that will leave them neither root nor branch. But to you who fear My (Jesus') name, the Son of Righteousness shall arise with healing in his wings... You shall trample the wicked, for they shall be ashes under the soles of your feet on the day that I do this,' says the Lord of Hosts." Clearly, no living thing will survive the reformation of the earth by Christ.

As a note of interest, Malachi 4:1 is quite correct in saying that the ash of the wicked will be under the soles of the feet of the righteous, for they will be above the earth with the Son of God at this point—again, reality and the natural laws as we understand them will no longer apply, or in the least, they will be altered in such drastic and inconceivable ways as to make existing *above the earth*—existing *in outer space*—feasible.

Revelation 6:13

And the stars of heaven fell to the earth, as a fig tree drops its late figs when it is shaken by a mighty wind.

STARS FALL FROM HEAVEN

During of the sixth seal, the *stars* from God's First Heaven fall to the earth! They *drop* down from heaven, even as a fig tree drops its ripened fruit when a strong wind blows.

Now, a fig was a favorite food in the East during John's time, but more importantly, the entire national economy depended on the harvest. If the crop failed it could have brought economic disaster for the nation. Important to the people? You bet, and that's why it's used here. Over time, the tree and its fruit became a symbol of peace, but it should be noted that in John's time the connection to peace hadn't been made yet. Thus, it's quite right that the Lord would use the fig tree in a symbolic nature here, for John and his contemporaries would easily identify with it. For them, the imagery of the fig and its fruit was very powerful.[11]

The *stars* drop and move at lightning speed! John is not referring to literal stars and planets seen in the night sky. This is entirely metaphorical in nature, for the Lord is speaking of his holy angels. Scripture often refers to angels as stars. For example, when Lucifer fell from heaven, it is mentioned that "his tail drew a third of the stars (angels) of heaven..." (Rev. 12:4). The word *heaven* as it is used here in the original Greek (*ouranos*) could also be translated *as the abode of God*, as opposed to a literal reference to the *sky* or *firmament*.[12] This is a direct reference to the First Heaven, which is clearly the abode of the angels. In John 1:51 we read, "And he (Jesus) said to him 'Most assuredly I say to you, you shall see heaven open, and the angels of God (spoken of as stars) ascending (from earth) and descending (from heaven) upon the Son of Man (to witness the Son at his coming).'"

Why are the angels dropping from *the abode of God?* Because they are assembling for the greatest event in the history of the world (other than the resurrection of Christ, of course)! Jesus Christ, the Son of God, returns to rule his masterpiece, the earth, his special glory. He comes to face the unholy trinity and the unrepentant at the Battle of Armageddon and to reform the planet earth. The holy angels come with him to partake in the mighty battle of Armageddon, as well as to witness the reformation of their Lord's great work. The First Heaven will be empty of angels! All God's angels will be here, millions and millions and millions of them! "When the Son of Man comes in his glory, and all the angels with him, then he will sit on the throne of his glory (this very earth)" (Matt. 25:31). "For the Son of Man will come in the glory of his Father with his angels, and then he will reward each according to his works" (Matt. 16:27). And so the stars fall to the earth and the Son's Word is bathed in heaven!

Revelation 6:14

Then the sky receded as a scroll when it is rolled up, and every mountain and island was moved out of its place.

GREAT COSMIC DISTURBANCES

At the loosening of the sixth seal, John says that the firmament above, which we call *heaven,* recedes like a scroll rolled up! This seems to be a literal reference to the atmosphere of the planet. John is referring to a gigantic cosmic disturbance here. As the physical earth is reformed the atmosphere will be reformed as well, which makes a great deal of sense since it's been so polluted by the machinery and technology of humanity, a direct result of our lack of stewardship. Humanity has been unable to responsibly manage and take care of the earth as God commanded. The *sky receding* is close in concept to *terra-forming,* the *deliberate alteration of the atmosphere of another planet.*[13]

Now, whether or not humanity will need to breath oxygen, in the sense that we rely on it for life, is arguable. Since the earth and atmosphere will be reformed and cleansed, their original perfect nature restored, surely the physical makeup of gases and things of that nature will be different from the gases in our world and reality today. It is worthwhile to note that oxygen is the most volatile and dangerous gas on the planet, at once sustaining life as it takes life. Every breath of oxygen is necessary to the human body, promoting healthy life, but simultaneously it is harmful and most destructive.[14] The devastating consequence of the byproduct of oxygen (called free radicals) in our system is a link to disease and possibly even the aging process—knowing this then, surely, in a new and perfect world, the *air* that we breathe will not have the same destructive effects to the transformed human body (phase two of three of the Phase of Body, the glorified body). It's even likely that it won't be *necessary* to sustain life, and if that's the case, the gas itself will be irrelevant and perhaps won't exist at all. But since this is purely speculative, who's to say?

The firmament or atmosphere will be removed or replaced, and all by the word of Jesus Christ. The Lord speaks the word and it is so, for mighty is the word of the Son of God, the great Creator of everything there is! If he wanted to, he could place actual stars like our perfectly ordinary sun and a red supergiant and star clusters and gas clouds together and have them spell the wonderful name of the Son of God: *Jesus!* Spread across the sky, glowing with brilliance we have never seen before!

Every mountain and every existing island will be altered during the reformation of the earth. Jesus will stand and test the strength of the earth! The land mass will be altered from pole to pole, from the mightiest mountain to the fairest valley. It's quite possible that with the Second Advent of Christ and the reformation of the nature of this reality/universe/time the earth's tilt may be altered, affecting temperature. There will be less water covering the planet. (Much of the water will return to the atmosphere, creating a perfect climate greenhouse effect similar to pre-Flood earth). Seas the size of the Pacific and Atlantic will not exist. Of course, less water will give more land for a population that will number in the billions. It is likely that the solar system will be affected, as well as our galaxy and the universe entire—and it should be clear here that these will be wonders beyond our imagining and understanding. Indeed, the reformed earth shall be a planet worthy to be called *The Lord's*. (Just to make it clear, this reference to the reformed earth is not the New Earth, otherwise known as Heaven, which is made and taken out of the First Heaven at the end of the 1,000 years.)

The reformation of the earth is also found in Isaiah, which reads, "The earth is violently broken, the earth is split open, the earth is shaken exceedingly. The earth shall reel to and fro like a drunkard, and shall totter like a hut; its transgression (those who have violated God's laws) shall be heavy upon it, and it (the earth) will fall (be reformed), and (the violators will) not rise again. It shall come to pass in that day that the Lord will punish on high the host of exalted ones, and on earth the kings of the earth. They will be gathered together, as prisoners are gathered in the pit, and will be shut up in the prison (called the bottomless pit); after many days (a thousand years, during the rest period of the saved) they will be punished.

"Then the moon will be disgraced and the sun ashamed; for the Lord of hosts will reign on Mount Zion and in Jerusalem, and before his elders, gloriously (after the reformation of earth)," (Isaiah 24:19-23).

THE COMING MILLENNIUM

Since I'm on the topic of the reformed earth, I'd like to briefly remind ourselves here that the reformed earth exists during the seventh millennium or the Kingdom Age, the last 1,000 years for humanity on this planet and the final 1,000 years in time or perfect time for all humanity. When the last year of that perfect 1,000 rolls to a stop and time ceases to exist—at least, for humanity—it will not be the end of this old earth, for this old earth has an eternal purpose. (Refer to Chapters 5:3, 14:10, 20:14–15 for more detailed information.)

The coming millennium is a perfect Age in every detail and it will commence as soon as the Son of God touches his feet to the Mount of Olives in Jerusalem! Finally, the sacred day is reached: Jesus' feet touch the Mount of Olives, facing Jerusalem. (As a side-note, the city is not rebuilt or reformed like the earth—it simply appears whole and perfect, made out of nothing by his most holy presence. We'll study this concept further on.) Instantly, the mount splits in two, making a very large valley! Half the mountain moves toward the north and half toward the south! Living waters flow between the split mount. Jesus Christ has returned and all his Saints with him, for Jesus is King over all the earth! Then the time will be right and life will be without sin for a thousand years, and the earth will have been reformed and made perfect. The reformation of the earth happens prior to Christ's return to the Mount of Olives—the seventh millennium begins precisely when his feet touch the Mount, and the earth will live up to its name once again as the Third Heaven. (It will be like it was before the Fall of Man, in a state of perfection.)

Of course, the question remains: When will this great reformation of the earth take place? I discussed God's timetable/calendar in regard to the return of Christ and the incorrect human calendar, so I won't go into that here. Suffice it to say, the significance of the true year 2,000 should loom always before our very eyes for two reasons:

(1) That will be the time when Christ returns, this earth is reformed, and the seventh millennium begins.

(2) By his calendar the year 2,000 may nearly be upon us, so we should always be in a steady form of readiness—but only he knows the year, the day, and the hour!

Revelation 6:15

And the kings of the earth, the great men, the commanders, the rich men, the mighty men, every slave and every free man, hid themselves in the caves and in the rocks of the mountains...

FLEE TO THE MOUNTAINS

As we study verses 16-18, it's important to understand exactly where we are in the series of End Time events: the sixth seal has been loosened; the raptures of the Saints have taken place, meaning, Jesus' faithful are not found on earth (the number of the Christian martyrs is complete); the protecting influence of the Holy Spirit of God has been removed from the earth (we'll study this event in greater detail in Chapter 7:1, under the heading *The Removal of the Holy Spirit*); the only people left alive on the earth at this point are the hopelessly unrepentant whose fates will have been sealed. The earth is about to be reformed and the unrepentant will have no choice but to flee to the caves and the rocks of the mountains.

Revelation 6:16

...and said to the mountains and rocks, "Fall on us and hide us from the face of him who sits on the throne and from the wrath of the Lamb!"

HE WHO SITS ON THE THRONE

Regardless of power, wealth or class, small or great, all will run to the hills trying to find shelter from he who sits on the throne. They will call to the rocks to fall down and hide them from the face of He Who Comes, but the rocks will not heed their cries. Instead, the earth will begin to be transformed and the very rocks the unrepentant cry out to will melt or explode as a wall of lava and flame engulfs the world and all the living in it. It is too late now. The die is cast. Their doom is eternally sealed.

Revelation 6:17

[And the people say] "For the great day of his wrath has come, and who is able to stand?"

HAILSTONES COULD BE METEORITES

The Scriptures tell us that as the earth is reformed it will be bombarded with hailstones weighing hundreds of pounds.

It's quite possible that these *hailstones* could be meteorites let loose from the heavens to rain down on the planet—if this is so, the devastation will be extraordinary and absolute.

To give us a clearer picture of just how devastating meteorites can be, I'd like to examine meteorites in more detail here: typically, a meteor is small, solid, and enters the atmosphere from outer space. Throughout history there have been all sorts of meteors, fireballs, comet-like meteors, some that explode in the upper atmosphere creating an explosive, booming sound, and of course shooting or falling stars. Sometimes hundreds of meteors can occur simultaneously. These are often called meteor showers.[15]

Meteors burn up as they fall to the earth and end up as harmless dust, but a meteor that reaches the surface of the earth is called a *meteorite*. Meteorites slam into the earth with awesome force, sometimes leaving huge craters that permanently scar the surface of the planet.

Large meteorites can devastate the world, impacting environment, human government and all life. Astonishingly, the largest one ever found weighs 60 metric tons.[16] The force of impact from a meteorite that weighed 60 metric tons, what would be considered a Major Collision or Major Collider, would spew molten rock and lava around the impact site and far into the atmosphere.

Dust and poisonous gases (produced by the collision when it vaporized minerals in the ground) would darken the sky for months, probably years. The debris cloud would cut off sunlight, killing off masses of plant life and eventually other forms of life, including human life.[17]

Keeping that in mind, if these *hailstones* sent by God are indeed meteorites, or if they are similar to meteorites even in the smallest possible way, the planet will indeed be obliterated and reformed. (We'll look into the possibility of Major Collision meteorites during the final three-and-a-half years of the Great Tribulation in Chapter 8, under the headings of the first three plagues.) I'd like to point out here that if the hailstones are meteorites, they aren't meant to be planet killers, for the Lord does not want to break the earth apart, but to instead destroy the last remnants of unrepentant humanity and then to reform/re-create the earth. Thus, the great rocks will pound the earth and the Lord will swallow up the remaining unrepentant in his meteoric fury.

IT IS DONE

The Lord thunders in the heavens, and Jesus Christ utters his voice! Lightning strikes from his moving hands! The bottom of the waters is seen and the foundations of the world are uncovered! The great day of his wrath has come and the end is near. It's here and now. Clearly, there will be no place to hide, for every inch of the earth will be radically and violently transformed by lava, fire, and (potentially) meteorites. At that point, Christ will say, "IT IS DONE." The loosening of the sixth seal will be complete!

Oh, if they had only recognized Christ, for righteousness and justice are the foundation of his throne. Mercy and truth go before his face. Blessed are the people who know his joyful sound! They will walk in the light of Jesus' countenance, for he is the glory of their strength.

THE CONCLUSION OF THE SIX SEALS

To survive these events take note as I summarize: the end of the human race as we know it happens at the conclusion of the Great Tribulation, shortly after the capture of the Antichrist and the False Prophet, who are then thrown into the lake of fire forever. Soon thereafter, Satan's army is destroyed by the Lord at Armageddon. Christ himself locks up the devil in the depths of the bottomless pit beneath earth's crust for the final one thousand years in time. The unholy trinity is bound and powerless and the reformation of the earth and atmosphere is accomplished.

The seventh seal is coming. It is the final act that establishes his glorious millennial kingdom of holiness, during which he rules the reformed earth, the Kingdom Age, the final thousand years of rest, the final thousand years in time, for the saved in Christ!

* * * * *

SOURCES:

1. *Listing of the Word 'Horses' in the King James Version,* GospelMessage.com, <http://www.gospelmessage.com>.
Horses, pg. 588-589, The New Unger's Bible Dictionary, Moody Press (1988).
2. *Antichrist,* The Catholic Encyclopedia, Volume I, Online Edition, Kevin Knight (2002).
Antichrist, Columbia Encyclopedia, <http://www.Bartleby.com>.
Antichrist, pg. 81-82, The New Unger's Bible Dictionary, Moody Press (1988).
Antichrist; An Alternate Ending, article, Chuck Missler, Koinonia House, www.khouse.com.
3. *Bow and Arrow,* pg. 181, The New Unger's Bible Dictionary, Moody Press (1988).
4. *The Holocaust History Project,* <http://www.holocaust-history.org>.
Final Solution, Simon Wiesenthal Center Multimedia Learning Center, <http://www.motlc.wiesenthal.com>.
5. *Aureus; Denarius,* Encyclopedia Britannica, Online Edition, <http://www.Britannica.com>.
Denarius; Metrology, pg. 841-846, The New Unger's Bible Dictionary, Moody Press (1988).
Roman Empire; Coinage and Taxes—Denarius, Microsoft Encarta Encyclopedia (2002).
6. *Balances; Scales,* pg. 140, The New Unger's Bible Dictionary, Moody Press (1988).
7. *Homelessness in America,* National Coalition for the Homeless, edited by Jim Baumohl, NCH Publications (2002).
Homelessness, contributed by James D. Wright, Microsoft Encarta Encyclopedia (2002).
8. *Oil,* Easton's Bible Dictionary, Online Edition, <http://www.biblelearn.com>.
A Biblical Theology of the Holy Spirit, part 1 - The Holy Spirit in the Old Testament, Prairie Bible Institute & Steven C. Ibbotson (2002), <http://www.instructor.pbi.ab.ca>.
Holy Spirit, pg. 583-584, The New Unger's Bible Dictionary, Moody Press (1988).
9. *Concerning Wine and Beer part 1 and 2,* Jeffrey J. Meyers, Studies in Worship, No. 48 (c) Biblical Horizons (November, 1996) and No. 49 Copyright (c) Biblical Horizons (January, 1997), <http://www.biblicalhorizons.com>.
Lara Butler; a letter discussing consumption of beer, wine, and alcohol within the Christian community and in light of Scripture (2002).
10. *Wine,* pg. 1366-1368, The New Unger's Bible Dictionary, Moody Press (1988).

11. *Fig; Vegetable Kingdom,* pg. 1325-1331, The New Unger's Bible Dictionary, Moody Press (1988).
    Fig, Fig-tree, E. W. G. Masterman, International Bible Standard Encyclopedia, Online Edition, <http://www.studylight.org>.
12. *Heaven—Ouranos,* #3772, pg. 53, Greek Dictionary of the New Testament, Strong's Exhaustive Concordance of the Bible/Dictionary of the Hebrew and Greek Words, Hendrickson Publishers.
    Star, pg. 1219; *Angel; Angels, Fallen,* pg. 61-62, The New Unger's Bible Dictionary, Moody Press (1988).
13. *Terra-forming Mars,* Sci-Tech Inserts, <http://www.typc.co.za/Sci-tech>.
    Imagine Living on Mars; the Farthest Suburb, David Tenenbaum, special to ABCNEWS.com/sci-tech (2003), <http://www.abcnews.com>.
    Mars Terra-forming, Astrobiology: The Living Universe, Adrian Hon, Katherine Harris, David Sewell,
    <http://www.ibiblio.org/astrobiology/index.php?page=terraform01>.
    NASA Warms to Living on Mars, Leander Kahney, Wired News (2,000), <http://www.wired.com>.
14. *The Dark Side of Oxygen,* <http://www.greatamericanproducts.com>.
    Oxygen Free Radicals and Aging, part 2, <http://www.intelegen.com>.
    Oxidants, Antioxidants, and the Degenerative Diseases of Aging, Ames BN, Shigenaga MK, Hagen TM Proc Natl Acad Sci 1993;90:7915-7922.
    The Oxygen Battlefield, Gary Null, PhD, GNN, <http://www.garynull.com>.
15. *Meteor; Meteor Shower,* contributed by David D. Meisel, Microsoft Encarta Encyclopedia (2002).
    Meteors and Meteor Showers: How They Work (1999),
    <http://www.space.com>.
16. *Meteors, Meteorites & Impacts,* Bill Arnett (2002),
    <http://www.seds.lpl..arizona.edu>.
    Meteor; Meteor Shower, contributed by David D. Meisel, Microsoft Encarta Encyclopedia (2002).
    Meteorites.com, <http://www.meteorites.com>.
17. *Meteor; Meteor Shower,* contributed by David D. Meisel, Microsoft Encarta Encyclopedia (2002).

Further reading:

Cosmic Pinball: The Science of Comets, Meteors, and Asteroids, Carolyn Sumners, Carlton Allen, Carl M. Allen, McGraw-Hill publisher (1999).

CHAPTER 7
The Sealed Of Israel

Revelation 7:1

After these things I [John] saw four angels standing at the four corners of the earth, holding the four winds of the earth, that the wind should not blow on the earth, on the sea, or on any tree.

FOUR ANGELS

John now explains that he sees *four holy angels of God.*
One stands at the north corner of the earth.
One stands at the south corner.
One stands at the east corner.
One stands at the west corner.
What an amazing sight to behold! These four holy angels are symbols of the four holy creatures representing the Lamb, so in essence Jesus stands at the four corners of the world. He is in control. Even so, as far as earth and humanity is concerned, he is about to let loose the reins.

THE REMOVAL OF THE HOLY SPIRIT

The word "wind" is also used here as a symbol of the Holy Spirit, indicating that he is about to be removed from all that he controls in nature, the earth, the sea, the trees, etc. Without the Holy Spirit here, there is no hope for life on earth, for the Lord holds back the winds.

Let's explore this concept more closely.

THE HOLY SPIRIT IN DETAIL

The Holy Spirit is a distinct person who does distinct things. The Scriptures make it clear that he, like the Father and Son, is an intelligent, self-aware being with a mind of his own (Matt. 3:16–17; 28:19; John 14:16–17; 15:26; 1Cor. 2:10; 12:11); he is undoubtedly called God, as the Father and Son are called God (Acts 5:3–4; 28:25–27; Heb. 10:15–17; 2Cor. 3:17–18); and he is one of the Three, an integral part of the mysterious Oneness of the Holy Trinity. Like Jesus Christ and the Holy Father, the Holy Spirit is not metaphorical. He exists, real as you and me. He is not some sort of wispy ghost, just the *spiritual essence* or *spiritual presence* of God.

We know that as far as the saved in Christ are concerned, the Holy Spirit is here to instruct, reconcile, generate, sanctify, and comfort believers (John 3:5–6; 14:16–17; 16:13–14; 1Pet. 1:2). His main job is the transformative act of salvation.

On a broader scale, the Holy Spirit concentrates on all humanity all of the time, primarily in the form of conscience. He is humanity's Great Teacher. He comforts humanity *and* convicts humanity of sin. He educates and guides us, encouraging us toward salvation. He inspires all of us to create. He fills each and every one of us with things like laughter, unending love, and hope eternal. Every painter, musician, actor, writer, poet, lover, politician, husband, father, wife, mother, child, family—every human being—motivated by good has been inspired by him to do that good. In fact, the good in everyone, the saved and the unsaved alike, comes solely from him. And lastly, and this is important in relation to the verse we are now studying, the Holy Spirit is the *protective seal* on the earth. He keeps the planet together. He keeps the planet going. He keeps a tap on nature, the seas, trees, the winds that blow. Without his influence in the world and on the hearts and minds of humanity, removal of the Holy Spirit would mean total chaos in nature and something akin to global sociopathic behavior in humanity.[1]

HOLDING BACK THE FOUR WINDS

Christ *holds back the four winds,* essentially removing the protecting and inspiring Holy Spirit—and the wicked will suffer for it, for chaos will rule.

This occurs near the end of the final three-and-a-half years of the Tribulation, after the Fifth and Sixth raptures and prior to the bowl plagues, leaving only the Antichrist, the False Prophet, and the unrepentant, whose fates will, at that point, have been sealed, on the earth without the protecting and nurturing seal of the Holy Spirit.

Revelation 7:2

Then I [John] saw another angel ascending from the east, having the seal of the living God. And he cried with a loud voice to the four angels to whom it was granted to harm the earth and the sea...

THE SEAL OF THE LIVING GOD

John views a fifth mighty angel of God. He ascends in all his glory from the eastern corner of the earth, having the seal of the Living God. He appears like the rising sun in the morning! Who can this be but the divine manifestation of God himself? John hears Jesus call out to the four angels to whom authority has been given to harm the land and the sea of the earth. The five *angels* represent but one Person: the Son of God! Christ, the living God, speaks from on high!

Revelation 7:3

...Saying, "Do not harm the earth, the sea, or the trees till we (the Father, the Son, and the Holy Spirit) have sealed the servants of our God on their foreheads."

THE SERVANTS OF GOD

Before the protecting, nurturing, inspiring, and convicting seal of the Holy Spirit is removed from the earth and the hearts and minds of humanity, Jesus commands that his faithful within the tribes of Israel be sealed first.

This is probably a metaphor to illustrate that God will preserve these servants of God from the plagues and the violence of the Antichrist and his perpetrators. They will be protected supernaturally from any and all violence. The servants of God mentioned here are very special to the Father, and come what may he will defend them with his divine love and protection.

Undoubtedly, this is a direct reference to the 144,000 Jews, the servants of God, but it's also true that all believers faithful to him in this time are included in this sealing. The 144,000 Jews and the remaining Christian believers will not be harmed by the plagues— for they will have the mark of Christ within them. They have not taken the mark of the Beast. (Remember, all who take the mark of the Beast will face the suffering caused by the plagues.) The 144,000 Jews will be so supernaturally protected that none of them will die, while on the other hand, the remaining Christians, although protected from the plagues, will all be martyred. They will not be protected from death in regard to natural death and death caused by Man: gunshot wounds, torture, accident, disease, etc.

Christ will not allow this dispensation to end while the servants of God, along with the left behind believers (those who were not taken in the Fourth Rapture because they were unprepared), are alive and active on the planet. This means that the *four winds* will blow on earth for a little while longer. The Holy Spirit has not yet been removed.

Nevertheless, at this point in the Tribulation Jesus will be ready to consume all life on the earth. He announces that before he brings this to pass, the sealing of his chosen of Israel must first be accomplished. Take note, for John is now seeing into the middle of the great and dreadful Tribulation.

Revelation 7:4

And I [John] heard the number of those who were sealed. One hundred and forty-four thousand of all the tribes of the children of Israel were sealed:

THE CHILDREN OF ISRAEL

The word of the Lord comes to John, and the Lord mentions the number of God's very special people who are chosen by the Son of Man: 144,000 of all the tribes of the children of Israel! They are called *the sealed of Israel*, and they are worthy to receive the blessed emblem of the living God, for in Christ they take shelter! In him they trust!

THE TWELVE TRIBES OF ISRAEL

To properly understand this and the subsequent subject matter, we should have a basic understanding of what is meant by *the twelve tribes of Israel:* the word *Israel* means *having power with God* or *God's fighter*. This is in reference to Jacob, the man who had the name given to him by God through his angel, and to whom God said, "...for you have striven with God and with men and have prevailed" (Gen. 32:28). In its early years the nation was something like an enormous extended family called *the house of Israel*. It was divided into genealogical branches or tribes. (Tribal grouping in ancient nations and cultures was common; the Edomites, Ishmaelites, Arabs, etc.). The Hebrew tribes were established by the twelve sons of Jacob/Israel. They were the *twelve tribal fathers of the Jewish people*. The tribes were originally nomadic, living like gypsies scattered throughout the other twelve tribes. The Holy Father changed all that when he gave them the land of Canaan. He divided it up by the number 12 and the division of 12, according to their tribes, clans, and father's houses. The Jewish people, having then been adopted into a remarkable covenant with Jehovah God (Ex. 19:5) were instructed to establish a permanent kingdom in Canaan based on those twelve tribes.[2]

In regard to verses 4–8, it should be clearer now that the 144,000 sealed servants of God are divided by the twelve tribes of Israel—12,000 from each tribe—and how important historically this is in relation to the Jews and their relationship with God. Likewise, the number 12 is playing an important, albeit most mysterious, role here too. The number 12 and the division by 12 is part of God's holy mathematics/geometry.

JESUS, OF THE TRIBE OF JUDAH

Christ Jesus is of the tribe of Judah. Obviously, the tribe of Judah is an important one and should be explored here historically in regard to this verse, the twelve tribes, and Jesus Christ: when the Jews were lost for 40 years in the desert, Judah had an official post or position on the east side of the Tabernacle, facing toward the sunrise, appropriately and prophetically enough (Num. 2: 3–9; 10:14). According to rabbinical authority, Judah's flag was green (the color of Life!), with the symbol of the lion (Christ Jesus!). When compared to the other tribes, Judah was in a way more independent or radical. They were the tribal revolutionaries. Now, when Judah established David as king of all Israel and moved to Jerusalem, the other tribes didn't like that very much. As a result, they tried to form their own governments. At that point, the days of Judah as a tribe was over, for it became Judah the kingdom, and years and years of warring followed. Finally, the kingdom of Judah, the entire country of Israel, was taken over by the king of Babylon, who then went on to destroy the holy Temple and took the twelve tribes of the Jewish people into captivity. The nation Judah no longer existed (2Kings 24-25; Jer. 34–41).[3]

The connection to Judah and its importance in reference to Christ, who is of the line of David, of the tribe of Judah, should be clearer now: "But one of the elders said to me (John), 'Do not weep. Behold, the Lion of the tribe of Judah, the Root of David (Jesus), has prevailed to open the scroll...'" (Rev. 5:5).

The angel reveals the names of each tribe to John. It is important that the twelve tribes be named, and it is imperative to the plan of God that an identical number of his chosen be from each tribe, totaling 144,000. They are not only Jews, but they also believe in the Savior Jesus Christ, the Messiah, with all their hearts. As mentioned before, these 144,000 will live in the times of the end, during the seven years of the Great Tribulation. Arguably, all of them now surely live, and perhaps you're acquainted with one or two of them—what an honor indeed! They will all reside in Israel at the time they are sealed, and as I've said before, all will be protected supernaturally by his divine force. The Antichrist, as much as he will try, cannot harm them, or the plagues, or even death, for Christ will put his seal upon them. Unlike the left behind Gentile Christians (who will all be martyred), these precious few cannot be killed by the Antichrist.

Revelation 7:5

...of the tribe of Judah twelve thousand were sealed; of the tribe of Reuben twelve thousand; of the tribe of Gad twelve thousand...

TWELVE THOUSAND FROM EACH TRIBE

Twelve thousand are sealed from each of the tribes of Judah, Reuben, and Gad. The Lord God has opened their ears and they are no longer rebellious and do not turn away. He covers them with the shadow of his hand!

Revelation 7:6

...Of the tribe of Asher twelve thousand; of the tribe of Naphtali twelve thousand; of the tribe of Manasseh twelve thousand...

Twelve thousand are sealed from each of the tribes of Asher, Naphtali, and Manasseh. The Lord comforts his faithful, and they understand him, for they follow after righteousness. They seek Christ and look to the Rock from which they were hewn! They know that God has chosen to live in them, for they believe they are his temple.

Revelation 7:7

...Of the tribe of Simeon twelve thousand; of the tribe of Levi twelve thousand; of the tribe of Issachar twelve thousand...

Twelve thousand are sealed from each of the tribes of Simeon, Levi, and Issachar. God's chosen listen to him and give ear to him. "I delight to do your will, O my God, and your law is within my heart" (Ps. 40-8).

Revelation 7:8

...Of the tribe of Zebulun twelve thousand; of the tribe of Joseph twelve thousand; of the tribe of Benjamin twelve thousand were sealed.

Twelve thousand are sealed from each of the tribes of Zebulin, Joseph, and Benjamin. And finally, amen.

A NEW SONG

Three-and-a-half years after the sealing of the 144,000, near the end of the seven years of the Great Tribulation, but prior to the bowl plagues—a few weeks before the return of Christ—Jesus rescues each one from the wicked Antichrist, for as has been said they are supernaturally protected from bodily harm, the plagues, even death.

At this point they will be ruptured from the earth without ever facing death (the Sixth Rapture). "Then I (John) looked, and behold, the Lamb (who is Jesus Christ) standing on Mount Zion, and with him one hundred and forty-four thousand (Jews, the servants of God), having his name and his Father's name written on their foreheads. And I heard a voice from heaven, like the voice of many waters, and like the voice of loud thunder (it is the Son saying, 'My chosen are worthy to be sealed!'). And I heard the sound of harpists playing their harps. They (Jesus' chosen) sang, as it were, a new song before the throne, before the four living creatures (signifying the Lamb), and the elders; and through the knowledge of God, no one could learn that song except the one hundred and forty-four thousand who were redeemed from the earth (by Jesus). These are the ones who were not defiled with women, for they are virgins. These are the ones who follow the Lamb wherever he goes. These were redeemed from among men, being first fruits to God and to the Lamb. And in their mouth was found no falsehood, for they are without fault" (Rev. 14:1–5).

It's unlikely that the 144,000 are virgins in the literal sense of sexual intercourse. What *virgin* probably implies here is that the 144,000 may have been sexually active in marriage, but they did not indulge in adultery or fornication, which would mean in the eyes of God they remained whole and true *virgins* by clinging to one spouse and being sexually obedient and self controlled.

In addition, the term *defiled by women* is not a judgment on women or the female sex. When the word *defiled* is translated from the original Greek (*moluno*)[4] it is used in the figurative, as in, *to soil, to soil by sin*. It is a direct reference to sinful sexual disobedience, which of course applies to both sexes, male and female—clearly then, the 144,000 will be an assortment of sexually obedient men and women.

Revelation 7:9

After these things I [John] looked, and behold, a great multitude which no one could number, of all nations, tribes, peoples, and tongues, standing before the throne and before the Lamb, clothed with white robes, with palm branches in their hands...

A GREAT MULTITUDE BEYOND NUMBER

The angel presents more to John. He observes a great multitude that no one can number, made up of all the nations, tribes, people, colors, and tongues standing before the shining throne of God and the Lamb. These are the martyrs from the Great Tribulation, as well as all past martyrs who died for God and the anointed One throughout the six thousand year history (by God's timetable/calendar) of the human race.

In righteousness they are given white robes, a symbol of purity. They are also given palm branches.

In John's time the palm tree and palm frond (palm branches) were symbolic of the righteous enjoying prosperity (Ps. 92:12), and that's exactly what the great multitude is experiencing here. The palm branches are also meant to pay tribute to Jesus, for the great multitude is repeating history, or venerating history, probably waving palm fronds just like the multitude did when Jesus rode the donkey into Jerusalem days before his crucifixion (Zech: 9:9; Mat: 21:1-11). There is also a likely relationship between the color green, as palm branches are a stunning and glowing green, a clear and colorful representation of life and God's creative process within life, the fingerprint of the Green Creator. God's holy geometry is also evident here, for palm fronds are beautiful, but they're also complex in design. Lastly, palm branches were considered a symbol of victory, thus when Jesus rode the donkey into Jerusalem the multitude waved palm branches—victory, hosanna in the highest! In the prophetic sense of Christ's victorious return that is how it is meant here.[5]

These countless thousands of faithful believers chose to suffer death rather than renounce their relationship with their Lord. They come from all walks of life, every avenue, alleyway, and path, all the saved in Jesus Christ, loving each other and worshiping their God through the Son.

As you may recall, Jesus has a brightness of pale green illuminating from his sacred body! He *is* the Emerald Christ, the Green Creator! Thus, these people within the great multitude will shine like stars of light, probably with a hue of green! With the sound of the trumpet they praise him. They honor him with tumbrels and harps! They dance joyously! (As a joyous side-note, I'm sure all people in heaven can play musical instruments, sing, and dance, for the knowledge of God is in them!)

Revelation 7:10

...And [the great multitude] crying out with a loud voice, saying, "Salvation belongs to our God who sits on the throne, and to the Lamb."

PRAISE FROM THE MARTYRS

John now listens to the Tribulation martyrs and all the martyrs from humanity's long and bloody past. They break out with a mighty praise song, saying, "Salvation belongs to our God who sits on the throne, and to the Lamb." They honor Christ, who died on the cross to give them eternal life. He is their great and wondrous Savior.

Revelation 7:11

All the angels stood around the throne and the elders and the four living creatures, and fell on their faces before the throne and worshiped God...

PRAISE TO THE LAMB

The angels stand around the throne and the four living creatures and the twenty-four elders (representing the twelve apostles, the twelve Old Testament prophets, and all the Saved in Christ). They all sing praises to the Lord. Bless his holy name! All the heavenly hosts fall on their faces before God to worship him.

Revelation 7:12

...[The heavenly hosts] saying, "Amen! Blessing and glory and wisdom, thanksgiving and honor and power and might, be to our God forever and ever. Amen."

AMEN & AMEN!

"Jesus! Blessings, glory, wisdom, thanksgiving, honor, power, and might be to Jesus, our Lord, forever and ever!" What blessed words are given to their sacred God, who alone is worthy to stand in the mighty throne room in heaven?

Revelation 7:13

Then one of the elders answered, saying to me [John], "Who are these arrayed in white robes, and where did they come from?"

A QUESTION

John is asked by one of the twenty-four elders, "Do you know who these people are, dressed in white robes, and where they come from?"

Revelation 7:14

And I [John] said to him, "My lord, you know." So he said to me, "These are the ones who come out the great tribulation, and washed their robes and made them white in the blood of the Lamb."

AN ANSWER

John responds, "Sir, you know."

The elder explains: "These people are the ones that came out of the Great Tribulation."

It seems this is a reference to the Great Tribulation martyrs and the martyred throughout the millennia. If that then is the case, this great multitude is great indeed, enormous in number. Their robes are washed clean by the blood of the Lamb, who died so they may live and be pure in heart.

Revelation 7:15

"Therefore they are before the throne of God, and serve him day and night in his temple. And he who sits on the throne will dwell among them."

WITH CHRIST FOREVERMORE

The speaker continues, "This is the reason why they stand before the holy throne of God: they will serve him day and night and Jesus, who is in the throne room, lives with them for eternity."

The phrase *day and night* has a literal and metaphorical meaning here. Literal in the sense of time: Christ will dwell with humanity on this earth, once it has been reformed, so there will be literal day and night for 1,000 years. Metaphorical in the sense of timelessness: eternity, for after the 1,000 years they will serve Jesus, who is the *Temple*, forevermore outside of time on the New Earth.

Revelation 7:16

"They shall neither hunger anymore nor thirst anymore. The sun shall not strike them, nor any heat."

A NEW REALITY

The speaker announces, "This great multitude of faithful believers in Jesus will never hunger anymore, nor thirst anymore, and they have no need of the light of the sun, nor its heat."

This suggests that after the seventh millennium (the Kingdom Age), the New Earth and its reality will be startlingly different from the reality we now know and experience, and of course it has to be—we will be in spirit, soul, and body, having the superglorified body. Time will no longer exist. The laws of nature as we have come to understand them will be radically altered and different, and we will not be enslaved to them as we are now.

It's quite likely that the people in the great shrine on the New Earth and reality will not depend on a mighty star for heat and light, but even so it is believed a mighty star—one much larger than our present sun—will exist in spite of the new reality and physics. What's more, I am led to believe that seven moons will revolve around the New Earth, reflecting the light and glory of Jesus Christ, similar to how our present sun reflects its light on our single moon! Could it be that the New Earth rotates around a supergiant, non-entropic star, just as the present earth rotates around its own (entropic) star, and at *night* seven moons light up the heavens instead of one? The seven moons would follow the principles of the Seven Spirits of God and God's holy mathematics/geometry, so it's not an unreasonable conclusion. We glory in our moon now. Imagine how we would glory in seven moons! Perhaps there is a *heavier* purpose for seven moons, as the new earth will be so gigantic—yes, the New Earth will be much, much larger than the present earth. If this is the case, clearly we will be dealing with new gravity and physics, and that's only if the natural laws as we understand and experience them will continue to apply. If they don't, we're in unimaginable, unexplored territory—with God, all things are possible and always, always, beyond imagination!

Revelation 7:17

"For the Lamb who is in the midst of the throne will shepherd them and lead them to fountains of the waters of life. And God will wipe away every tear from their eyes."

THE SHEPHERD'S PROMISE

John is told by the speaker, "The Lamb of God, seen in the center of the throne, died on the cross to save each one gathered before him. He returned to life to fill all believers with his Spirit and lead them to living fountains of water to drink. He wipes away all tears of sadness from their eyes, and they are happy forevermore, even forever and ever."

This is a wonderful promise for humanity. Waters of life! Every tear wiped away! Eternal hope and happiness! For the Lamb that was slain will shepherd his sheep.

The speaker departs and Chapter 7 concludes.

In the next chapter, John witnesses the Son of Man break the seventh seal. Afterwards there is great silence in heaven, and then seven plagues will be poured upon the earth. The plagues begin shortly after the rapture of the Saints (the Fourth Rapture), just after the first three-and-a-half years have come to a close. The first plague takes place right in the middle of the seven years. We are at the halfway mark of the Great Tribulation!

* * * * *

SOURCES:

1. *Exposition of the Orthodox Faith (Book I),* St. John of Damascus, Orthodox Christian Information Center, <http://www.orthodoxinfo.com>; from John of Damascus, *Exposition of the Orthodox Faith,* Post Nicene Fathers, Schaff Edition, Volume IX, Series II, translated by The Rev. S. D. F. Salmond, D.D., F.e.I.s., Principal of the Free Church College, Aberdeen. (1898).
   Holy Ghost, J. Forget, transcribed by W. S. French, Jr., The Catholic Encyclopedia, Volume VII, Online Edition, Kevin Knight (2002), <http://www.newadvent.org>.
   Holy Spirit, pg. 583-584, The New Unger's Bible Dictionary, Moody Press (1988).
   Holy Spirit, Gray's Home Bible Commentary; *Holy Spirit,* Henry's Concise Commentary, The Bible Library Delux, version 5.0. suite, CD-ROM, Ellis Enterprises, Inc. (2,000).
   The Twelve Tribes of Israel, Goldblum Seedman Corporation (2002), <http://www.yahveh.com/home.asp>.
   Tribes of Israel, Twelve; Jews, contributed by Jay M. Harris, Microsoft Encarta Encyclopedia (2002).
2. *Jewish Culture and History,* David Dickerson (2002), <http://www.ddickerson.igc.org>.
   The Twelve Tribes of Israel, Goldblum Seedman Corporation (2002), <http://www.yaveh.com>.
   Tribes of Israel, Twelve; Jews, contributed by Jay M. Harris, Microsoft Encarta Encyclopedia (2002).
3. *Defiled—Moluno,* #3435, pg. 49, Greek Dictionary of the New Testament, Strong's Exhaustive Concordance of the Bible/Dictionary of the Hebrew and Greek Words, Hendrickson Publishers.
4. *Palm Tree,* Bible Encyclopedia, ChristianAnswers.com (2002), <http://www.christiananswers.net>.
   Palm Tree, pg. 957-958, The New Unger's Bible Dictionary, Moody Press (1988).
   Palm Tree, contributed by Marshal R. Crosby, Microsoft Encarta Encyclopedia (2002).

CHAPTER 8
The Seventh Seal

Revelation 8:1

When he [Jesus] opened the seventh seal, there was silence in heaven for about half an hour.

THE SEVENTH SEAL IS BROKEN

From heaven the Lord views the earth! Holding the little book, he looks down from the height of his sanctuary. Six seals attached to the scroll/book have been opened. The Lamb is about to break open the seventh seal, introducing the mystery of the *seven trumpet plagues*. A complete silence in God's mighty heaven follows, lasting about one-half hour! The mention of time here informs us that the scroll is of great consequence. We know this because of that which silences heaven: the act of opening the seventh seal. The information within the scroll is significant and powerful enough to in fact make heaven pause!

The loosening of the seventh seal spells the beginning of the end for this dispensation, the Human Age—the end of all flesh as we know it, in a mere three-and-a-half years! This is a sacred moment, worthy of pause in all heaven and Creation. As well it should be, for all humanity, all beasts and creeping things, all birds of the air—all life—is to be completely removed from the face of the whole earth!

A CONTROVERSIAL TOPIC

I'd like to explore a rather controversial topic connected with the conclusion of the End Times and the beginning of the Kingdom Age: some modern eschatologists argue that a small number of sinful people will escape the wrath of God at the end of the Human Age, somehow surviving the return of Christ and the subsequent reformation of the earth. If this is the case, human beings that continue to have the sinful nature we have today will manage to exist throughout the restful thousand year period alongside Jesus Christ and his Saints. Sin must exist in the newly recreated world, so the argument goes, because Christ says he will rule the nations with a rod of iron, the hinge-pin of their argument.

First, let's see why Christ says he will rule the nations with a rod of iron.

SCHOOLING

It has nothing to do with sin and everything to do with schooling. He intends to teach and prepare redeemed humanity for eternity. Jesus will be a strict School Master! Humanity may be redeemed and living with Christ in a newly remade and perfect earth in a perfected state, but regardless we will have a lot to learn. We will have to be educated, preparing us for the wonders of the coming eternity. That education will take some discipline and time. Christ will indeed rule us with a rod of iron as we will learn and prepare for 1,000 years.

THE PHYSICS OF THE REFORMED EARTH

Now let's tackle the second part of the argument. The Scriptures do speak about Satan and the unsaved being released for *a little while* at the end of the seventh millennium, but the meaning seems unambiguous here—there's nothing to suggest that the unsaved have been living alongside the redeemed for 1,000 years, sinning, warring, corrupting, and being so disobedient that they force Jesus to rule the nations with a rod of iron. It's clear that *a little while* means that the unsaved will be in the first place of waiting (Sheol, the antiparadise) for a long time, the length of the thousand years, and then they will be released for a little while upon the reformed earth, the final attempt by both Satan and the fallen to corrupt the Saints; the last battle between good and evil.

You also have to remember that at this point the old earth will be reformed and made perfect, the nature of the universe entire and time itself (potentially) made perfect with it. It follows that everything that was imperfect, but specifically, the fallen nature of humanity, no longer exists and could not exist within a perfect state of existence, for the knowledge and the presence of God will be on the reformed earth. If fallen human nature continued to exist within the perfected state of the earth and universe, everything would continue to be in an imperfect state because it would be, in a sense, *infected* by it. This would mean that everything is as it was, in a fallen state, and Christ makes it clear that will not be the case.

Nothing can be holy and perfect while imperfection remains, which the Father makes plain throughout Scripture. It is impossible for sin to exist alongside Christ and the redeemed, absolutely impossible for it to *get into* that state or place, for the seventh millennium is a Holy Age, completely free of sin, the fallen nature of humanity, and the deceptions of Satan (Rev. 20:3).

The seventh millennium or the Kingdom Age is a time when the world will be completely free of sin, and Scripture supports this: "For indeed the gospel was preached to us (the saved) as well as to them (the unsaved); but the word which they (the unsaved) heard did not profit them, since they were not united by faith with those who heeded it. For we who believe do enter that rest, as he has said, 'So I (God) swore in my wrath, they (the unrepentant) shall not enter my rest'" (because of sinful disobedience) (Heb. 4:2–3). "...Between us (the saved) and you (the unsaved) there is a great gulf fixed, so that those who want to pass from here to you cannot, nor can those from there pass to us," (Luke 16:26).

When all is said and done, surviving the reformation of the planet will not be possible. Global waves of lava and flame, smoke and ash filled darkened skies, global weather patterns of a supremely violent nature, world reshaping earthquakes, and what will likely be a bombardment of meteorites slamming into the surface of the earth; not only that, but the reformation goes well beyond the surface of the planet earth, for it is an actual transformation of reality itself. Matthew 24: 35 says, "Heaven and earth will pass away..." This transformation of reality will undoubtedly have an effect on every aspect of the universe, from the largest spiraling galaxy right down to the tinniest atom and subatomic particle—literally, the physics of the universe will change. If God reforms the earth, time, and reality into a perfected state, how then can a handful of people made up of matter, energy and nature that is imperfect continue to exist? (For more information on this subject, refer to Chapter 5:3, under the heading *What is Under the Earth*.)

Whatever fallen nature that exists anywhere on earth prior to the reformation of the planet, be it human, fish, fowl, cockroach, virus, subatomic particle, will be obliterated into nonexistence or its nature radically altered into perfection.

Lastly, the Holy Scriptures make it quite clear that a human being must be raptured and receive a glorified body to enter into the Kingdom Age, and thus they will be immortal. Mortals cannot live during the 1,000 years alongside Christ.

The only way that anything from this fallen universe and reality could survive the return of Christ and the ensuing changes to the world and all reality would be by a direct act of God, who, for whatever reason, would supernaturally protect a handful of the unsaved from the reformation of the planet. But this opposes Scripture, the purpose of the Great Tribulation and the plagues, and the reformation of the planet, for Christ makes it perfectly clear that he intends to wipe off the face of the earth all that remains in a fallen state of existence, but most specifically, the unrepentant dark heart of humanity.

All forms of humanity thereafter, saved or unsaved, will be in a new form. They will be either transformed into spiritually glorified bodies, phase two of the Phase of Body (the saved in Christ), or remain in spirit until the end of the 1,000 years (the unrepentant). In either case, humanity will no longer exist in the fallen body state.

I'd like to quote physicist Lambert Dolphin: "...every time a miracle was performed, God dramatically altered the physics on earth. Example, when he cursed the earth, he changed the physics."[1] How then, after all that comes to pass during the Great Tribulation and the return of Christ could God allow a handful of diehard sinful survivors to cross the street of reality and enter into the thousand years of rest? The answer is simple: he won't. There will be no mortal survivors at all.

SING HEAVEN & EARTH

After the return of Christ and the reformation of the earth there will be no form of life found upon the face of the earth. The earth shall be empty! Mortal humankind shall be no more, gone forever, and the reformed earth shall long for inhabitants!

Sing heaven and earth, for it comes to pass that Jesus renews our days as of old, without sin. The Son announces, "I am God, your God, with you!" Behold, seven times seven trumpets shall be aired before Jesus Christ sets his feet on the earth at the very spot where he left 2,000 years ago (by God's timetable/calendar)! All of his immortal Saints, having glorified bodies, shall follow with perfect hearts! The earth shall be glad, for it will again be filled with people! It was created for inhabitants and so it will be full of laughter! For behold, Jesus has reformed the heavens and the earth. Hallelujah! The earth is to have life once more!

Adam was the beginning of fallen flesh and nature. The final end of fallen flesh and nature comes at the conclusion of the Tribulation. Never again is humankind of flesh and blood as we know it! The last sinner consumed by the global earthquake, the great fire, and the mighty hail ends the reproduction of fallen nature life forever.

KINGDOM AGE REPRODUCTION

But know this: even though the redeemed will have the second glorified body (which probably won't have to depend on food, water, oxygen for its survival), reproduction of life continues in the Kingdom Age, for Scripture tells us: "The nursing child shall play by the cobra's hole, and the weaned child shall put his hand in the viper's den (during the thousand year rest period on the reformed earth)" (Isaiah 11:8).

This is a rather interesting detail, for the earth, universe, and time will be perfected along with humanity. Within this perfection the human population will be sexually active and the cycle of birth will continue as well, although, from the point of view of this book the entire process should be much less complicated, painless, and far more rewarding and pleasing.

The earth's population will greatly increase during the new second Age, the Kingdom Age. But it seems likely that people will neither marry nor be given in marriage in the way we are traditionally accustomed! Couples will be brought together by the express will of God. They will be sexually active, joined as one for 1,000 years. (Remember, there will be no death during the thousand years. Humanity will be immortal, phase two of the Phase of Body, with one more phase to go.) They will raise enormous families—it will be the kind of marriage that many people wish for now, intimate, sexually pleasing, and satisfying and blessed, and filled with support and love, not to mention a nature that not only reflects the Creator but is connected to him in his holy perfection and goodness!

THE PAUSE IN HEAVEN

As I mentioned earlier, *a thirty minute pause* alludes to the importance of the contents within the seventh seal, but it is also linked to a deep and profound respect for life. The saved are silent. The holy angels are silent. God the Father, the Son and the Holy Spirit are silent. Time is symbolically set aside so that those in heaven can pray for the last lost souls on earth whom Jesus loves. He loves all sinners, for he adores his creation. Earnest prayer is given as the end of an Age is foreseen. Heaven is solemn indeed!

Revelation 8:2

And I [John] saw the seven angels who stand before God, and to them were given seven trumpets.

PRELUDE TO THE SEVEN TRUMPETS

The introduction to the plagues of the seven trumpets!

Seven angels, each one portraying Christ who has the Seven Spirits of God, stand before the Lamb. (Jesus has complete authority and control of this event.) "I am the seventh seal, the trumpets, the churches, the angels, and the heavens! I am the Christ and the Lamb. I am who I am!" The angels are given seven trumpets, each one signifying the voice of Christ. "I (John) was in the spirit on the Lord's Day, and I heard behind me a loud voice (Jesus), as of a trumpet..." (Rev. 1:10).

Revelation 8:3

Then another angel, having a golden censer, came and stood at the altar. He was given much incense, that he should offer it with the prayers of all the saints upon the golden altar which was before the throne.

PRAYERS FROM HEAVEN

The angel of the Lord reveals yet another holy angel. He stands at the enormous altar to the throne. He carries with him a golden vessel used for burning incense, the censer. He is given much incense, a symbol of prayers from heaven. (We studied the history of incense in Chapter 5:8, under the heading *Worthy is the Lamb*.) The angel offers his bowl of incense/prayers upon the golden altar that is before the throne. These are the prayers of the great multitude. They pray for the final living souls of humankind, male and female, of every tongue, race, and creed, those who are about to face the plagues poured out upon them by Christ during the last three-and-a-half years on this earth.

Revelation 8:4

And the smoke of the incense, with the prayers of the saints, ascended before God from the angel's hand.

JESUS HEARS THE PRAYERS

From the angel's vessel, John sees the vapor of the incense of prayers ascending before God. All loving thoughts said for the lost by the multitude reach Jesus and are heard: "God of Hosts, you listen to the outpouring prayers in the secret place of thunder! You stand in the congregation of the mighty in heaven and you judge among the gods on earth! The lost walk about in darkness and the foundations of the earth are unstable at your presence!—have mercy, Father, have mercy!" There is still a chance for mercy and salvation for those who haven't taken the mark of the Beast.

Revelation 8:5

Then the angel took the censer, filled it with fire from the altar, and threw it to the earth. And there were noises, thundering, lightings, and an earthquake.

Clay Houseman

THE VESSEL IS FILLED
WITH THE SEVEN SPIRITS OF GOD

"And from the throne proceeded voices, lightning, and thunder. Seven lamps of fire were burning before the throne, which are the Seven Spirits of God" (Rev. 4:5).

Jesus, who has the Seven Spirits of the Living God, casts the prayer vessel to the earth. The prayers for mercy have been heard and they were not ignored—again, prayers of mercy for those who have not accepted the mark of the Beast. There is still time for them to be saved. There is still hope. But the time for mercy and repentance will soon come to an end.

The censer is filled with fire from the altar of God. The prayers have been heard, mercy has been given, yes, and now time is up. The prayers of mercy are replaced with the Seven Spirits of God and the censer is thrown to the earth. The presence of God is coming to the earth with voices, lighting and thunder—and the earth shakes with the expectancy of Christ's presence. When the actual presence of Jesus literally approaches the earth the planet rumbles. Accordingly, the planet faces a mighty earthquake, the introduction to the great sorrows that are to befall humanity.

The Son of Man announces, "Out of the seven plagues of the trumpets that are about to befall the human race, all shall be calamity and shall break forth onto all the inhabitants of the earth!" He utters his judgments against the remaining world population. They burn incense and pray to other gods and worship the works of their own hands. A great moral decline exists, and those who sow wickedness reap the wrath of God! Galatians 6:7 says, "Do not be deceived, God is not mocked; for whatever a man sows, that he will also reap."

Revelation 8:6

So the seven angels who had the seven trumpets prepared themselves to sound.

THE TRUMPETS PREPARE TO SOUND

Behold, the time comes when the Lamb of God prepares to sound the seven trumpets! The resounding call of the trumpets shall signify the seven voices of Jesus Christ himself. Out of the depths of heaven the Lord will be heard!

Revelation 8:7

The first angel sounded: And hail and fire followed, mingled with blood, and they were thrown to the earth and a third of the earth was burned up. And a third of the trees were burned up, and all green grass was burned up.

THE FIRST PLAGUE

With the seventh seal broken open, the first of the seven angels of the seven trumpets steps forward like an emerald pillar of smoke! He blows his trumpet, sharp and clear in tone: the first spirit of the Seven Spirits of God. Heaven stands still! Jesus gives the word, for he is the Word, and he says, "Let hail and fire, mixed with blood, fall upon the earth!" And it is so.

The first plague: mighty hailstones and coals of fire mixed with blood are said to come hurling down from the heavens, causing a third of the earth to be set on fire, destroying a third of plant life around the globe! The reference to hailstones and fire and blood may refer to a devastating shower of smaller, but no less deadly and destructive meteorites. These would not be considered major collision meteorites. It also seems likely that the mention of blood here is a metaphor referring to the murders of many thousands of innocent believers in Christ, the Tribulation martyrs. The hail and fire or shower of meteorites is, in part, punishment for their murders. Now, here's an interesting thing: most meteorites are considered to be fragments of either asteroids or comets, but since comets are more like *dirty snowballs* with cores of ice and dust,[2] perhaps the first trumpet plague is a combination of the two, a shower of comet ice (*hailstones*) and asteroid meteorites (*coals of fire/blood*) that bombard the world.

Persuasively, scientists now scan the skies, expecting an event like this to happen—it's just a matter of time, they argue, for it has happened before. It will happen again.[3] Perhaps the Holy Father set the major colliders on a path for the earth eons ago—*Target: Earth and the Great Tribulation.*

Whatever the case may be, the first plague (of potentially smaller ice and rock meteorites) will burn up a third of the earth's trees and all grass! Around the world the color green in nature will be a thing of the past, as plant life begins to burn and then fail. (The skies would be full of burning smoke from the fires caused by the destruction, thus plant life, which thrives on sunlight, will find it difficult to grow). The blast of the first trumpet is a strike on all vegetation.

An immediate world famine would follow. After this first plague it is very likely that no atmospheric vapor will fall upon the face of the earth—it won't rain. When the plague is completed, weather patterns and global climate will be greatly altered. If the plague is indeed the impact of a number of smaller meteorites smashing into the surface of the earth, the ensuing fire and smoke would certainly affect global weather and climate. Everyone will wail and weep. Their voices will be heard as far as the North Star as the green grass withers away! Likewise, the animals will cry out, for there will be no more grass to eat and they will face extinction! All of the earth's green grass will be scorched and the globe will have the appearance of a dead planet—fitting, for a population dead toward Christ!

Revelation 8:8

The second angel sounded: And something like a great mountain burning with fire was thrown into the sea, and a third of the sea became blood.

THE SECOND PLAGUE

The second angel, portraying the second spirit of the Seven Spirits of God, blows his trumpet, and heaven and all its host gasp! Christ's voice is heard: "Let the seas of the earth become blood!" And it is so!

The second plague: metaphorically, Jesus is the *burning mountain*, for he is the *Rock* who has the fire of the Seven Spirits of Life. The literal interpretation to the burning mountain and the blood is probably a Major Collision with a meteorite, what appears to be a colossal burning mountain thrown into the sea. Again, if it turns out to be a meteorite it wouldn't be a planet killer, but this one would be much more powerful than the smaller shower of meteorites from the first plague. The meteorite would strike the ocean with tremendous impact, causing a global tsunami or tidal wave which would inflict destruction undreamed of along coastlines. It could potentially reach hundreds of miles inland, killing millions, as well as a tremendous amount of marine life, not only because of the force of impact, but because of the poisonous gases created at the impact site.[4] The blood refers to the blood of the martyrs and what will happen to the sea, for a third of the sea is said to become *like blood*. Loudly, Christ proclaims, "If it is spilled blood of the believers in God that you desire, then blood you will have!"

Revelation 8:9

And a third of the living creatures in the sea died, and a third of the ships were destroyed.

MARINE LIFE DIES
SHIPS DESTROYED

A third of the marine life in the ocean depths will die from the impact of the burning mountain. The stink from dead fish in the seas and along the shorelines around the world will be unspeakable! The aforementioned tsunami/tidal wave—the granddaddy wave of the Age—will swallow one third of all vessels on the sea, many of them controlled by the world government of the Antichrist. Depending on the size of the burning mountain/potential meteorite, the wave itself could likely reach a height of many hundreds of feet,[5] a massive wall of water that would destroy everything in its path. Those who flee shall not get away! Ships' crews will drown in bloody waters. Though they hide in submarines at the bottom of the sea there will be no escape from the energy within the wave created from the impact.

Revelation 8:10

Then the third angel sounded: And a great star fell from heaven, burning like a torch, and it fell on a third of the rivers and on the springs of water.

THE THIRD PLAGUE

The Son calls a third time like the voice of a trumpet, which is the third spirit of the Seven Spirits of God. The heavenly Son says, "Let the fresh water of the earth become bitter!" And it is so!

The third plague: a *great flaming star* falls from heaven. Another bombardment from the skies! Again, metaphorically, the *star* that burns bright can be represented as the Seven Spirits of Life—Christ himself. In Revelation 22:16, Christ tells us that he is the *Bright and Morning Star*. In a very real sense, Christ is personally moving upon the fresh waters. If this isn't purely a supernatural event, what I call Super Nature, the tool he chooses to use may be another meteorite. This one would collide with a land mass. It could strike a well populated area, and if it did the end result would be a total devastation chain reaction: no chance of survival at ground zero, hundreds of thousands dead, the destruction beyond the impact crater complete and far reaching. Lethal dust and gas injected into the atmosphere during the impact would cut off sunlight for months and the poisonous gases produced from the collision would contaminate water, making it undrinkable. It would have an effect on rivers, lakes, and even wells. A worldwide food and water shortage would ensue. (Refer to

Chapter 6:17, under the title *It is Done* for more information on how poisonous gases are produced at the impact site.)

Revelation 8:11

The name of the star is Wormwood. A third of the waters became wormwood, and many died from the water, because it was made bitter.

WORMWOOD

The name of the *star* is *Wormwood.*

Several plants native to Europe yield a bitter extract known as *wormwood.* Generally, the plants can be found growing in wastelands, usually desert-like. The word means *bitterness,* and it's usually associated with calamity and injustice.[6]

The devastating plague will contaminate water everywhere. Drinking it, of course, will be out of the question. Times will be desperate because water will be scarce. People will drink the contaminated water, and young and old will become violently ill. Many will fall and never rise again. Death will seek them and find them—it must be remembered here that God will lead the Martyrs, and especially the 144,000 servants of God, to fresh water untouched by the plague. They will be supernaturally protected from and guided through these events!

Revelation 8:12

Then the fourth angel sounded: And a third of the sun was struck, a third of the moon, and a third of the stars, so that a third of them were darkened. A third of the day did not shine, and likewise the night.

THE FOURTH PLAGUE

Jesus informs John to apply his heart to understanding and hear the words of his mouth! Sounding the fourth trumpet, in reference to the fourth spirit of the seven Spirits of God, he says, "Let there be disturbances of the heavenly bodies!" And it is so!

The fourth plague: sunlight, moonlight and the stars are darkened.

After the first three plagues it's possible that the atmosphere will be filled with smoke, ash, poisonous vapors, and radiation similar to the aftermath of a global nuclear attack.

I'll quickly sum up the results of a global nuclear war here so that we can get a visual on just how devastating these three plagues are going to be: a large-scale nuclear attack would affect global climate, what scientists often call a *nuclear winter.* The nuclear explosions would throw vast amounts of dust and smoke into the atmosphere (similar to the impact site of a Major Collision meteorite). The dust and smoke would block sunlight for months, destroying plant life. Subfreezing temperatures in various parts of the earth would follow. It's possible that the ozone layer might be affected as well, allowing the sun's ultraviolet radiation to, essentially, microwave-oven the surface of the earth. It's even possible that the subfreezing climate and the heat from the ultraviolet radiation could happen simultaneously, both heating up and freezing various parts of the planet.[7] What this graphic nuclear war image tells us is that the global climate will be chaotic, life on earth will be nightmarish, and survival will be difficult.

When you apply this model to the first three plagues as potential meteorites and their deadly aftermath, it should be fairly clear what is taking place during the fourth plague: a third of the sun, moon, stars, and a third of the daylight and light at night is *struck* or *in a perpetual twilight*. Could this be because of the aftereffects of the meteorite blasts, the smoke, ash, poisonous vapors, and radiation they projected into the atmosphere? It would encircle, as well as darken, the globe. It would quite literally mean the end of human civilization, and that end could certainly come in a short amount of time, less than three-and-a-half years.

The meteorite and nuclear bomb data is compelling, but at the end of the day this could simply be referring to something we don't understand, an event of Super Nature. What's most clear from verse 12 is that the firmament (outer space and the planets) will feel the direct touch of the hand of God. It is not unreasonable to conclude that all of this is a supernatural event where Christ makes the sun go down at mid-afternoon, strikes the moon and it dims, stretches to the stars and they do not shine—in effect, supernaturally altering the way the universe works. After all, the Creator of the Universe is behind all of this. I believe this is the truth of it. Jesus has the power to accomplish the task without meteorites and nuclear bombs.

Whatever the case may be, these events will terrify the remaining inhabitants of the earth. The Antichrist and the False Prophet, with all their trickery and unholy supernatural power, will be unable to rectify the situation because Christ is in control. All humanity will cry out in great alarm.

Revelation 8:13

And I [John] looked, and I heard an eagle flying through the midst of heaven, saying with a loud voice, "Woe, woe, woe to the inhabitants of the earth, because of the remaining blasts of the trumpet of the three angels who are about to sound!"

THREE WOES TO COME

Here we have a definite warning from the Son of Man, whom John describes as an "eagle flying through the center of heaven." (We discussed Christ in relation to the *eagle* in Chapter 4:7, under the heading *The Fourth Creature: An eagle*.) He says, "Great sorrow!" shouting this three times, stressing its importance, and then continues, "Watch out people of the earth. Deep suffering, affliction, and grief come to everyone by the way of the next three trumpets which are yet to be heard!"

The final three-and-a-half years of the Great Tribulation will overflow with events that lead to the end of humanity as we know it. The events will overlap one another, but the very end won't happen until the return of Christ. Still, you have to ask: If these three plagues didn't finish the job what nightmares are to come?

* * * * *

SOURCES:

1. *Creation Science Evangelism: FAQ on Hugh Ross; A Statement Concerning the Ministry of Dr. Hugh Ross,* Bolton Davidheiser, Logos Publishers, 1993; Lambert Dolphin's Resources, <http://www.ldolphin.org>; *An Open Letter to Dr. Hugh Ross,* Lambert Dolphin's Resources, 1989, <http://www.ldolphin.org>.
2. *Meteors and Meteor Showers: How They Work* (1999), <http://www.space.com>.
    Meteors, Meteorites & Impacts, Bill Arnett (2002), <http://www.seds.lpl..arizona.edu>.
    Meteor; Meteor Shower, contributed by David. D. Meisel, Microsoft Encarta Encyclopedia (2002).
    Meteorites.com, <http://www.meteorites.com>.
3. *Meteor; Meteor Shower,* contributed by David. D. Meisel, Microsoft Encarta Encyclopedia (2002).
4. *Meteors and Meteor Showers: How They Work* (1999), <http://www.space.com>.
    Meteors, Meteorites & Impacts, Bill Arnett (2002), <http://www.seds.lpl..arizona.edu>.
    Meteor; Meteor Shower, contributed by David. D. Meisel, Microsoft Encarta Encyclopedia (2002).
    Meteorites.com, <http://www.meteorites.com>.
5. *TSunami—Giant Tidal Waves; Impact of Asteroid; Terrestrial Impact Craters,* Sefydlaid Morien Institute (2003), <http://www.morien-institute.org>.
    New Wave Supercomputers Catch Big Wave, TERRADAILY (2002), SpaceDaily, "Your portal to space," <http://www.SpaceDaily.com>.
    Meteors, Meteorites & Impacts, Bill Arnett (2002), <http://www.seds.lpl..arizona.edu>.
    Meteor; Meteor Shower, contributed by David. D. Meisel, Microsoft Encarta Encyclopedia (2002).
6. *Wormwood; Vegetable Kingdom,* pg. 1341, The New Unger's Bible Dictionary, Moody Press (1988).

Wormwood, Microsoft Encarta Encyclopedia (2002).
7. *Nuclear Winter,* Columbia Encyclopedia, sixth edition (2003), <http://www.encylopedia.com>.
Meteors, Meteorites & Impacts, Bill Arnett (2002), <http://www.seds.lpl..arizona.edu>.
Meteor; Meteor Shower, contributed by David. D. Meisel, Microsoft Encarta Encyclopedia (2002).

Further reading:

Cosmic Pinball: The Science of Comets, Meteors, and Asteroids, Carolyn Sumners, Carlton Allen, Carl M. Allen, McGraw-Hill publisher (1999).
Path Where No Man Thought: Nuclear Winter and the End of the Arms Race, Carl Sagan & Richard Turco, Random House (1990).

CHAPTER 9
The Locust From The Bottomless Pit

Revelation 9:1

Then the fifth angel sounded: And I [John] saw a star fallen from heaven to earth. To him was given the key to the bottomless pit.

THE FIFTH PLAGUE
The First Woe

The writer notes that the fifth angel, portraying the fifth Spirit of the Seven Spirits of God, sounds his trumpet. It is Jesus the Christ! Jesus gives the word, for he is the Word.

The fifth plague: John sees a *star* falling from heaven. Jesus is the *Bright and Morning Star*. The Lord himself descends from heaven and he has the key to the bottomless pit.

That this angel holds the key confirms that the star is Christ (and not a potential meteorite), for only Christ has the keys to hell. Christ alone has the authority to unlock the gates of the bottomless pit so that the plagues will occur; Christ alone has the authority to lock up the devil in the pit of the abyss. This verse is not only a metaphorical reference to Christ, but also a direct reference to his literal presence on the earth.

Before accomplishing the task of locking the devil within the abyss at the end of the Tribulation, Jesus must bring about the first two woes/plagues, the fifth and sixth plagues of the trumpets, and to do that he must unlock the bottomless pit.

As a reminder, as far as the series of End Time events concerning the last three-and-a-half years of the Great Tribulation goes and where these plagues fall within it, the three plagues of the Woes will happen near the end of the seven years. The plagues themselves begin in the middle of the seven year Tribulation and then from that point on continue, one plague after another, some overlapping, twenty-one plagues in all, *slam! slam! slam!* until the return of Christ.

Revelation 9:2

And he opened the bottomless pit, and smoke arose out of the pit like the smoke of a great furnace. So the sun and the air were darkened because of the smoke of the pit.

THE SMOKE OF THE PIT

Let's examine this verse from the literal perspective: Jesus has descended from Heaven with the keys to the bottomless pit and has unlocked it—that place called hell and death, the prison-place residing within the bowels of the earth in both the literal physical and hyperdimensional sense of reality. (Refer to Chapter 5:3, under the heading *Under the Earth* for more information on this subject.) He liberates Lucifer's fallen from the abyss and the way is open for them to ascend out of the pit through dense black vapor like smoke ejecting from a great furnace or volcano. These hyperdimensional beings will enter our physical reality/universe.

In verse 14 of this chapter, God says, "...Release the four angels (representing the devil's fallen angels) who are bound at the great river Euphrates!" It's interesting to note that the river flows through the country of Iraq that once marked the original boundary to the Garden of Eden, and we know that Satan deceived Adam in the Garden and caused the Fall, thereby ushering sin into our reality—this raises some provocative questions: Does this verse point the way to the literal gates to hell? Is hell accessible by way of a vent through the earth's crust, perhaps in the vicinity of the River Euphrates? I contend that this verse is, indeed, showing us something quite extraordinary and literal, a complex process involving multiple and overlapping realities reduced to a simple visual metaphor, and in regard to these fallen angelic beings and what they do to humanity, it will be very literal indeed.

Some biblical scholars suggest the smoke from the pit may be a reference to the smoke, ash, poisonous vapors, and radiation that would exist because of the first three plagues. Others suggest this is simple visual metaphor indicating evil. When these fallen beings do appear on earth, I believe a hellish and very literal smoke will announce their arrival, and after studying the Scriptures I've come to the conclusion that they will indeed enter into our world through an actual vent of some kind near the Euphrates River.

Revelation 9:3

Then out of the smoke locusts came upon the earth. And to them was given power, as the scorpions of the earth have power.

THE LOCUST

John is quite literally seeing beings from another world, fallen angels, otherwise known as evil spirits or demons, or in the modern vernacular, aliens—all of these terms refer to the same thing. What's important to realize is that they are super intelligent, super powerful, and supernatural, and there's nothing benign about them. These are not the friendly Extra Terrestrials you find in the movies. They are part of the army of the Evil One. These creatures are beyond our experience and understanding, the worst of it being, not their hyperdimensional appearance and processes, but their nature and purpose, which is wholly evil. They are inhuman and virtually impossible to understand, other than their main purpose, the destruction of humanity.

In relation to John's description of the locust, he can only explain what he sees by using the knowledge and experience of his time. Apparently, they look something like locusts, having grotesque insect-like features. They're given a power that is similar to the sting of scorpions.

Scorpion stings are painful to humans, but not fatal; the sting of one species in the United States is fatal to young children and potentially fatal to adults. The poison a scorpion injects into a victim is a *neurotoxin*. It attacks the nervous system. The tissue around the sting is damaged, which causes swelling. The body itches all over. Victims have said it feels like hundreds of mosquito bites that you want to scratch. The tongue may puff up and saliva may overproduce. This could potentially block the airway and lead to death. The lungs may have an adverse reaction, making it difficult to breath or they may fill with blood. This could lead to respiratory distress and death. In serious cases *anaphylactic shock* takes place. As a result, immediate death is likely.[1]

If the stings from the supernatural locust are even remotely similar to the sting of a scorpion, the human body will suffer greatly.

Revelation 9:4

They were commanded not to harm the grass of the earth, or any green thing, or any tree, but only those men who did not have the seal of God on their foreheads.

THE UNSEALED SUFFER

The locusts/hyperdimensional demons are allowed to hurt and torment those who do not have the seal of God on their foreheads. This means those who have not been saved by the grace of Christ and have instead taken the seal of Satan, the mark of the Beast, will suffer, for they worship the Antichrist and his image.

Remember, those who have taken the mark have sealed their fates. Once someone accepts or allows him or herself to be inducted into the global biometric system, once someone swears allegiance to the Beast—because that's what receiving the mark amounts to—there is no chance of repentance or salvation. (Refer to Chapter 13: 8 for related information on biometric systems.) In contrast, the 144,000 Jews chosen by God and the Christian Martyrs—those who continue to live, at any rate; many of the Christian martyrs will have been executed at this point—will have complete protection from the demonic spirits/plagues.

These fallen angelic beings have an enormous amount of power, but there is a limit to what they can do. They are not given power to harm the grass or plant life—there will be less than two thirds existing on the planet at this point, and clearly, humanity and animal life will be hungering for it. The command may also be intimately connected with Christ as the essence of life and the color of his light reflecting that essence: Green, the Emerald Christ. Plant life in general is full of the color green, the color of life, similar to our Lord. He is in all that lives, for God says, "I AM THE ESSENCE OF LIFE." His throne room is full of the color green. The fallen angels may, in fact, be forbidden to harm any plant life because the plants continue to reflect the Creator, unlike humanity, for there is no Christ (or another way of saying it could be, there is no *green*) within them!

Revelation 9:5

And they were not given authority to kill them, but to torment them for five months. Their torment was like the torment of a scorpion when it strikes a man.

FIVE MONTHS OF TORMENT

The thoughts of men and women will be depraved continually, having lost the knowledge of God. Because of this, Jesus allows the hellish demons to torment the remaining world population for five months. The demons do not have authority to kill at this point.

Revelation 9:6

In those days men will seek death and will not find it; they will desire to die, and death will flee from them.

DEATH WISH

When the fallen angels strike at those without the seal of the Living God, the unrepentant will want to literally die, for the terror and the pain the creatures bestow will be extraordinarily great. It's possible that the locust will sting them repeatedly and so they will be in constant pain. Truly, their suffering will be beyond compare. Many will try to take their lives—but death will flee from them. This is no mere metaphor here. Death will be supernaturally prevented, and at this point we're getting into some very disturbing territory: if death is prevented, this means, of course, that no unsealed/unsaved human being will be able to die for a period of five months. It's possible that no natural death—no drug overdose, no gunshot, no drowning, no burning in flames—will work effectively. What that means for those who attempt suicide or get into a car accident or are trapped in a burning house or are starving to death or are super-dehydrated is utterly beyond human comprehension and experience. If this turns out to be the truth of it, the results will be horrifying.

Revelation 9:7

The shape of the locusts was like horses prepared for battle. On their heads were crowns of something like gold, and their faces were like the faces of men.

FALLEN UNHOLY ANGELS

John explains that the shape of the dreadful demons is something like horses prepared for battle with faces of men. Some argue they have humanlike features because these fallen hyperdimensional beings were once holy angels. They have something like golden crowns on their heads. This could be a metaphor that suggests they have the power and authority of kings given to them to torture humanity for five full months, what will amount to an eternity for the population of the earth!

Revelation 9:8

They had hair like women's hair, and their teeth were like lions' teeth.

LONG HAIRED DEVILS

John describes these demonic beings as having long hair. There is a verse in the New Testament that focuses on the subject of hair in reference to men and women and God apparently desiring an obvious distinction between the sexes: "Does not even nature itself teach you that if a man has long hair, it is a dishonor to him? But if a woman has long hair, it is a glory to her; for her hair is given to her for a covering" (1Cor. 11:14–15). How this verse relates to these long haired devils has less to do with the length of hair and more to do with *dishonor*. These beings are not human. They do not have to deal with human sexuality/gender issues. But they understand honor. If these creatures do have something like human hair and if they wear it long, it would be worn that way solely in order to defy and dishonor God, following the broken pathway of the fallen nature.

Relating this to humanity, long hair on men can be looked upon in many cultures as dishonorable, suggesting that the individual is wild, reckless, dangerous, animal-like. Conversely, there are cultures that find long hair on men honorable. To them it signifies strength and masculinity.[2] That being the case, perhaps the long hair on these locusts is metaphor combined with the cultural perceptions from John's time. By describing these creatures as men having long hair like women, it would be clear to early Christians that the locusts were dishonorable and defiant, and thus wild, reckless, dangerous, and animal-like.

LIONS' TEETH

John describes the locusts as having teeth like the teeth of lions, another cultural perception from John's time. While not forgetting that what John saw was beyond his experience, knowledge, and powers of description—for he was in fact trying to describe Godlessness and pure evil—the teeth are probably metaphorical in nature here. Still, these beings may indeed have teeth. If it turns out that they do, then the teeth will probably be used for biting and not for eating. These are supernatural, hyperdimensional beings. Surely, human food won't be on the menu.

Turning to metaphor once again, it's also probable John was trying to show us that the more corrupt and defiant people are the more they look like wild and dangerous animals—and how grotesque the fallen angels look! This ties in well with John's lesson here. It gives us a clear picture of the corrupting nature of evil, for when these angels lived in God's First Heaven, before their fall from his most holy grace, they were beautiful beyond imagination.

Revelation 9:9

And they had breastplates like breastplates of iron, and the sound of their wings was like the sound of chariots with many horses running into battle.

IRON & WINGS

These beasts are soul and spirit without flesh and blood. They come from a different universe and reality. They are not only alien to the human race, but far more advanced. In his great vision John describes these beasts from hell wearing iron armor—heavy, ugly, frightening stuff. Could it be that we are only permitted to see the armor covering of the immortal demons, their true hyperdimensional shape hidden from our eyes? Could the armor that John described be a strong force field generated around them? That might explain why John referred to it as breastplates of iron.

Their wings (possibly another word for *spirit*) are described as sounding like chariots with many horses running to battle, or perhaps the sound of revving engines or many waterfalls or a mighty wind—of course the possibilities are endless here, especially in light of hyperdimensional beings. As I said before, hyperdimensional beings will impact our existing reality. The result of that impact may sound like a jet plane breaking the sound barrier or chariots with many horses running into battle.

Revelation 9:10

They had tails like scorpions, and there were stings in their tails. Their power was to hurt men [the world population] five months.

HELL'S ANGELS

These are indeed peculiar creatures: part locust, horse, scorpion, lion, and even having the faces of men with long hair. As I said earlier, what John witnessed was probably so difficult for him to understand that the best he could do was resort to simple visual metaphor, but still, I have to ask: What if these peculiar creatures are closer in form to John's description than we know or want to admit?

FALLEN ANGELS vs. HELICOPTERS

Along those lines, there are some students of prophecy who are convinced that John was trying to describe a modern helicopter with human pilots at the helm. We have human faces, stinging bullets, thundering sound, and even a green insect-like appearance, since many military helicopters around the globe are painted in camouflage-green.

This is an interesting idea, certainly, but I must point out that the Scriptures make it very clear that the locust are not man-made machinery, but are in fact supernatural beings from hell. In light of the supernatural events that will be taking place during the last three-and-a-half years of the Tribulation, the locust-as-helicopter theory seems a bit prosaic to me—similar to the theory that God may use meteorites as plagues to reform the earth, as opposed to supernatural and therefore unexplainable events in nature.

It's important to remember that the locusts don't have to be something as believable as helicopters at all. They could be something clse altogether unbelievable, and unimaginable. We tend to use arguments like the meteorite and helicopter because they are things known to us. Known things make us feel better. If we understand them, we think we have some kind control over them. The unknown does the opposite. It shatters the illusion of control and all we're left with is the Truth.

Whatever the form of the locusts may be, these fallen beings are given the ability to hurt people for five long months. After the five months have passed, these bizarre and intelligent beings will return to the bottomless pit, for the time of their plague on earth is limited.

Revelation 9:11

And they had as king over them the angel of the bottomless pit, whose name in Hebrew is Abaddon, but in Greek he has the name Apollyon.

ABADDON & APOLLYON

John verifies where the demons come from and who controls them! They follow the king of all demonic beings, the fallen angel: Satan, the devil, the Evil One, for his name is given as *Abaddon*, (in Hebrew, meaning, *destruction*) and *Apollyon* (in Greek, meaning, *destroyer*, or *the angel of the bottomless pit*).[3]

Revelation 9:12

One woe is past. Behold, still two more woes are coming after these things.

THE COST OF TAKING THE MARK

With the fifth plague accomplished, John verifies that two more are yet to come. The first horror of the demon locusts is complete. Earthlings have been hunted, attacked, and tortured, and most horrifying of all death has eluded them. Without doubt they have been terribly afraid. They do not turn to Christ, but rather curse his name. At this point in the last three-and-a-half years of the Tribulation—nearing its completion—it is too late for them to find salvation, for all would have taken the mark on their *foreheads* or *on their hands;* they would have been inducted into the global biometric system. (For related information on biometric systems, refer to Chapter 13:8.) By surrendering to the global biometric system they, in effect, pledge allegiance to the Antichrist. This would mean that they belonged to Satan for eternity, their fates eternally doomed and sealed!

"All who dwell on the earth will worship him (the Antichrist), whose names have not been written in the Book of Life of the Lamb slain from the foundation of the world" (Rev. 13:8). We are reminded again in Revelation 13:16 that "He (the False Prophet) causes all, both small and great, rich and poor, free and slave, to receive a mark (of the Antichrist) on their right hand or on their foreheads" (the global biometric system). Christ makes it very clear not to take this deadly mark, for the consequences will not only be high, they will be eternal: "...If anyone worships the beast and his image, and receives his mark...he himself shall also drink of the wine of the wrath of God which is poured out full strength into the cup of his indignation. He shall be tormented with fire and brimstone in the presence of the holy angels and in the presence of the Lamb. And the smoke of their torment ascends forever and ever; and they have no rest day or night, who worship the beast (the Antichrist) and his image, and whoever receives the mark of his name," (Rev. 14:9–11).

Clearly, taking the mark and allowing yourself to be inducted into the global biometric system won't be a viable option if you are to survive the End Times.

Revelation 9:13

Then the sixth angel sounded: And I [John] heard a voice from the four horns of the golden altar which is before God.

THE SIXTH PLAGUE
The Second Woe

The sixth angel, symbolic of the sixth Spirit of the Seven Spirits of God—Jesus himself—sounds, and a voice comes from the four horns of the golden altar.

The sixth plague: the four angles Euphrates; the locust demon horde returns.

In the Old Testament, the altar of burnt offerings had four projections, as well as the altar of incense (Ex. 27:2; 30:2). Each projection was referred to as a *horn*. By taking hold of these horns a criminal would find sanctuary (1Kings 1:50; 2:28; Ex. 21:14). The horns described here are similar in design and purpose to the Old Testament projections, but since almost everything in the Book of Revelation can be symbolically tied to Jesus, it can also be said that he is the altar. Since that is the case, like criminals did in Old Testament days by taking hold of the horns, the unsaved can take hold of Christ and in him will they find sanctuary. In Scripture horns often suggest *honor* and *strength* because various animals have horns. By having horns on the altar we have a direct reference to the honor, strength, and power, and perhaps even the unpredictable animal-like ferocity, of God (Ps. 18:2).[4]

Fittingly, John hears the Lamb's powerful voice come from the *four horns of the golden altar.* The horns represent three things:

1) The power of God.
2) The protection of Christ.
3) The four living creatures spoken of in Revelation 4:7.

But because the horns are animal-like, Christ-like and have the ability to speak, there's a deeper symbol meant to be represented here. Remember that everything in the Book of Revelation ultimately embodies Christ, so the answer should be clear: the horns wholly symbolize Jesus, he who is all power, all protection, and has all knowledge.

Revelation 9:14

...saying to the sixth angel who had the trumpet, "Release the four angels who are bound at the great river Euphrates."

THE FOUR ANGELS EUPHRATES

The sixth angel announces with a loud voice from the four horns (or Jesus announces), "Let loose the four angels bound at the great river Euphrates!" *Angels* as it is used here is not in reference to God's holy angels from the First Heaven, but instead is a direct reference to fallen angels of Satan! This is the reason why they are *bound.* The original Greek (*deo*), a primary verb, reads *to bind,* and it can be used in the literal or figurative: *bind, be in bonds, knit, tie.*[5] Only the fallen, disobedient angels that follow Satan would have to be *bound* for any reason by God.

These four angels are bound at the great river Euphrates. They are confined by Jesus, and they may indeed be literal spiritual beings, but as far as metaphor goes, they represent Satan's army of fallen angels. The number in this army is set by John, for the angel of Jesus reveals to him the exact number that had been cast out of God's heaven during the Great War: "Now the number of the army of the horsemen was two hundred million; I (John) heard the number of them" (Rev. 9:16).

This is the original *one third* of the angels who were cast from the First Heaven after the Great War because of their rebellion. Accepting this as correct, then the number of remaining angels in God's First Heaven should be approximately four hundred million, or two thirds. This gives a full count of the six hundred million angels created by the Holy Father up until he formed the earth.

Both Dr. Lambert Dolphin and Dr. Chuck Missler have said in regard to angels that we do not know whether God continues to create them or not, but because he had a population of six hundred million angels in heaven back in the beginning, before the Great War in Heaven, it's likely he requires that amount now. It is fitting that God creates all things in abundance, for his mind is limitless.

Revelation 9:15

So the four angels, who had been prepared for the hour and day and month and year, were released to kill a third of mankind.

NUMBER SYSTEMS

We already examined the four angels bound at the river Euphrates in the previous verse, so let's explore the time period, or number system, mentioned here: one hour, one day, one month and one year. Since it's a number system, we should consider it a mathematical problem to solve, keeping God's holy mathematics/geometry in mind.

One day = 1.
One month = 30.
One year = 365.
Calculate one day + one month + one year.
1 + 30 + 365 = 396.
Add the numbers in 396 together:
3 + 9 + 6 = 18.
Continue by adding the numbers in 18 together.
1 + 8 = 9.

As it turns out, the number 9 is considered by many interpreters of Scripture and Scripture prophecy as the number of judgment and death. One of the compelling arguments for reaching this conclusion is the number of Greek words in the Bible derived from the root word meaning *judgment (dikay)*. It turns out to be exactly 9.[6]

Now, in regard to the hour mentioned in the 396 number system, some biblical scholars argue that the sense of the word in the original Greek does not refer to a literal point in time, but instead is a reference to the entire period because the word suggests *preparation* instead of *literal time*. The hour would then mean "a time has been prepared" for the four angels to be released, particularly, one day, one month and one year or 396 days.

There is an additional line of reasoning, much more complicated and because of that I won't get into great detail here, but I will briefly address it: the number system refers to a much lengthier period of time, spanning many hundreds of prophetic years, the idea being that a "day" should be interpreted as a "year."

Using 30 day months, 1 year (360 days) + 1 month (30 days) + 1 year + 1 hour (1/24th of a year or 15 days) equals 391 years and 15 days. Intriguingly, those who support this theory claim there are historical connections that strengthen the argument.

Additional theories aside, it's clear that the number system in question is used in direct reference to a time during the Great Tribulation, and in that sense it remains a very short period of literal time indeed, that is, 396 days.

With that said, calculating one hour + one day + one month + one year in literal time, when reduced to the final number the solution to the number system turns out to be 6, as opposed to 9-- the final number when the hour is not added to the number system. But still, the number of death and judgment can be reached by simply inverting it. As I argue in 13:18, because Satan has a penchant for distortion and uses (unholy) imitation and reversal, it's reasonable to conclude that he would invert the number 6 to 9 and we can apply that logic here.

One hour = 60.
One day = 1.
One month = 30.
One year = 365.
Calculate one hour + one day + one month + one year.
60 + 1 + 30 + 365 = 456.
Add the numbers in 456 together:
4 + 5 + 6 = 15.
Add the numbers in 15 together:
1 + 5 = 6.

Invert the 6 and you get 9, the number of death and judgment. Bear in mind that biblically 6 is considered the number of man. When the number is inverted it represents death and judgment. Thus, it's more than clear why the answer is 6 when you add the hour to the 396 number system. In a sense, 6 and 9 equal the same thing in meaning: the death and judgment of man, which is apropos considering the time period we're talking about, i.e., the Great Tribulation.

I'd like to point out here that most biblical scholars recognize that numbers and number systems/codes in the Bible have symbolic meaning. They can be considered keys to opening and understanding prophecy.[7] I refer to these numbers/number systems as *God's holy mathematics/geometry*, but I'd also like to make it perfectly clear that when I use this phrase I am not referring to the Gnostic concept of *sacred geometry* or any of its modern counterparts. Gnosticism is, in part, a religion that claims salvation can be attained with the help of numbers and number systems in the Bible. This knowledge is found in pagan number systems/sacred geometry throughout the world. Pagan systems wind up in the stars and all nature, the pyramids, Atlantis, including the Bible via so-called Christian Gnosticism, a heretical splinter group that broke from Christianity ages ago. The term *gnostic* comes from the Greek word *gnosis* meaning *knowledge*.[8]

NUMEROLOGY

The number 9 is also embraced as the number of judgment, finality and death by those who practice modern Christian numerology. Numerology is a pseudoscience that attempts to interpret the occult by using numbers, number systems, and their symbolism. (The number 9 has a variety of different meanings, depending on what school of Numerology you're studying.) It's based on a set of rules designed by the Greek philosopher and mathematician Pythagoras, the basic idea being that everything in the universe is made up of numbers and consists of geometrical figures that can be interpreted symbolically. If you are wise and specialized enough to figure them out you can control your destiny.[9]

Like almost everything involving sacred geometry and numbers, from the Gnostics to modern numerologists, it's all about power and control—*your* power and control. This can lead to elitism. There's nothing quite like being part of a specialized group requiring specialized secret knowledge that only you can attain through specialized secret rituals to put you above the common seeker of Truth! Power, control, and pride is what it all finally boils down to, and of course that's the seductive and lethal beauty of Gnosticism and everything else like it. This, of course, contrasts greatly with Christianity in regard to humility, selflessness, and the power and control of Christ. There is nothing you can do to save yourself. There is no secret ritual, no specialized number or number systems that can save you.

I am neither a Gnostic Christian nor a numerologist, and I do not support their belief systems, but I do find the study of numbers, number systems, and their symbolism within the Bible a worthwhile and revealing endeavor. It has lead to some startling conclusions and evidence[10] that points to a clear pattern of holy mathematics/geometry within the framework of the physical universe and even the Bible itself, most of which is very compelling—and even though this may be considered by some biblical scholars as much of a pseudoscience as numerology, I believe without a doubt that God is the greatest mathematician in the universe and that he uses numbers and number systems. He undoubtedly relies on mathematical blueprints and patterns, from

DNA, the building blocks of life, to the construction of the universe, to prophetic dates and mysteries concerning the End Times and the return of Christ in the Book of Revelation. That being the case, these numbers and number systems within the Bible should be taken seriously and studied, a task to which I have applied myself for many years. (See Chapter 13, in the text under Verse 18, for a full explanation of Satan's unholy number.) They are tools that can guide you toward a deeper understanding and relationship with Christ, but by no means do they usurp the power and glory of the grace of Jesus Christ. He alone has the authority and power to save.

A SECOND TIME

The four angles Euphrates are released and the locusts return.

I am absolutely convinced that the second demon horde is the same fighting force that appeared for five months—similar to the first demon horde, they are released from the bottomless pit. This tells us that they are one and the same. They will be released a second time, 13 months (396 days) later.

Like the voice of a trumpet, Jesus gives the word, for he is the Word. He says, "Now it is time! The demons of hell will kill a third of the wicked inhabitants of the earth!" The multitude of fallen angels prepares to do battle a second time—after torturing people for five months and then returning to hell; they have been kept in readiness for a period of three hundred and ninety-six days and one hour, exactly one year, one month, one day, and one hour later. What a mighty God we have who plans things with such precision! They are turned loose on the earth for a second wave. The demon horde will assault sinful earthlings once again.

Whether or not these beings are the identical fallen angels from the First Woe, spoken of as locusts, is debatable, of course, but the most important thing to remember is that a second wave of hyperdimensional beings will be released from the bottomless pit upon the earth and humanity, and they will have the power not only to sting this time, but to kill.

Death will not elude humanity this time. Many of the unrepentant will be consumed. These supernatural beings are only able to destroy those who follow the Antichrist and have his mark, those within the global biometric system!

The remaining Christians who have escaped death from the Antichrist thus far, as well as the 144,000 Jews who have the living seal of God, have divine protection from the demonic army.

When the plague is over, the second wave of locusts will return to the bottomless pit. They must return because it is from whence they came. They will be driven by something like instinct, what could be called *demonic instinct*. The bottomless pit is where they belong, for the Lord has placed them there forever. They have no choice but to return, as the Lord authorizes their coming and going.

Interestingly, John does not mention the length of time these beings will remain on the earth. It seems reasonable to suggest that it won't be long because if they're not held back and restricted they would end up killing every human on earth. It's likely that the return of Christ will be at hand when this occurs. Time will indeed be short.

Revelation 9:16

Now the number of the army of the horsemen was two hundred million; I [John] heard the number of them.

TWO HUNDRED MILLION

Lucifer's great army of demons will spread across the length and breadth of the entire earth (for the second time) to torment and kill a third of the living! John reveals that the number of the army is 200,000,000 strong. Now, do the math: if one fallen angel succeeds in killing but one person, the demonic horde will succeed in killing 200,000,000. The world population will have reached many billions by this time, and since a third will be killed the number of fatalities could potentially reach two billion or more. It is certainly possible.

Even so, billions of the world's population will escape death, as the earth is greatly populated.

Revelation 9:17

And thus I [John] saw the horses in the vision: those who sat on them had breastplates of fiery red, hyacinth blue, and sulfur yellow, and the heads of the horses were like the heads of lions; and out of their mouths came fire, smoke, and brimstone.

THE LOCUST RETURN

John's account of the second wave is certainly extraordinary, and as far as metaphor goes, the images do their job: this will be a most frightening, and deadly, event.

John reveals sulfuric vapor discharging from what could be massive vents in the earth—near the Euphrates River? Through the gases, fumes, and steam he views an endless column of millions of horses with *dead* riders emerging out of what could potentially be the gates of hell. The riders are considered dead because these creatures lack the light of the Son who gives life. They are of darkness. They are Satan's own—released by the power of Christ, for he is in control. Once again, the reference to riders and horses here may be John's inability to describe what he witnessed, for a supernatural being would have no need of a horse, but then again, the opposite argument is also valid. Perhaps the riders of this dark storm appear on horses or something like horses—I lean toward literal horses, but for all we truly know they could be riding dragons!

John declares that these spiritual devils will have breastplates of fiery red, dark blue, and sulfur yellow—the colors of fiery hell. The horses and riders will be themselves enflamed. The hell-ridden horses will have heads like lions, and out of their mouths issue fire, smoke, and sulfur, for dragons they seem to be.

Surely, John's description of the second wave is similar enough to the demons described in the first great sorrow (the locusts) to suggest that these are the same beings. Unquestionably, they come from the same place, the bottomless pit, and power is given to them like the scorpions of the earth: power to hurt mankind and this time the power is deadly.

HORSES vs. TANKS

Like the helicopter argument, there are some students of prophecy who argue that John was trying to describe tanks and modern weapons of warfare. As I said before, based on Scripture the only conclusion you can make is that the demon horde as described by John is a literal army of hyperdimensional beings, not tanks and helicopters. They will be an alien invasion of fallen angels!

It should be clear here that during the invasion the whole world will be in disarray. Everyone will flee from the fury of the demons and their horses. Though they hide in the thickets and climb rocks, the inhabitants will be revealed because of the mark they have taken. Every city, every town, every village, every encampment will be found and destroyed. There will be no escape for the unrepentant.

Revelation 9:18

By these three plagues a third of mankind was killed—by the fire and the smoke and the brimstone which came out of their mouths.

FIRE, SMOKE & BRIMSTONE

By these three the unholy trinity of Satan—one-third of the population of the world will be killed by the fire, smoke, and sulfur flowing from the mouths of the horses. Because the population of the earth has pledged allegiance to the unholy trinity they will be killed, for they belong to the family of Lucifer. The unholy trinity will be responsible for the murder of many millions. Death catches up to the *living dead toward Christ* in the form of these fallen angelic beings.

It's likely the demon horde will be released in groups of 9 or multiples of 9, marching in all directions like an army of ants from their underground command center. (See Chapter 13, Verse 18, for further explanation of the number 9 as Satan's unholy number, as well as further study into God's holy mathematics/geometry.) I reach this conclusion because this information is brought to our attention in the 18th verse in Chapter 9.

18 = 9 because 1 + 8 = 9.

18 + 9 = 27.

27 = 9 because 2 + 7 = 9.

27 + 18 = 45.

45 = 9 because 4 + 5 = 9.

It's the number of judgment and death; and it's an important power-number within the unholy/satanic system of numbers. It's a safe bet that the demon horde will use the number 9 in some significant way, perhaps even as they deploy.

Nothing is accidental when written by the hand of God!

Even though the weapons of modern warfare argument is worth considering, I'm convinced the fire, smoke, and brimstone that issues out of the mouths of these creatures will be supernatural in nature. These are real demons from hell with hyperdimensional powers.

Revelation 9:19

For their power is in their mouth and in their tails; for their tails are like serpents, having heads; and with them they do harm.

MOUTHS & TAILS

What we know: each horse seems to be, potentially, a *devil* unto itself, a *fallen angel from the bottomless pit*; the hell-ridden horses will have some kind of power (or weapon) that comes from their *mouths*; the mouths issue fiery flames and smoke; they will also have a tail like a snake and a head that *strikes out*. Once again, this could be metaphor, but it seems reasonable to conclude, given the supernatural nature of the events, that it's a literal reference to something of a hyperdimensional and thus entirely alien nature!

The beasts hurt and kill with their *mouths* and with their *tails.* They and their *riders* take millions of unrepentant people with them.

The creatures will appear everywhere on the globe. They will come from under the earth in various places, deploying in groups or multiples of 9. The *central vent* will be located somewhere around southern Iraq and the Euphrates River. Remember, we're dealing with creatures that exist in an entirely different reality/dimension, so they could, in fact, *appear* from out of nowhere anywhere on the planet if they wanted to.

Furthermore, the fact that there seems to be a crosspollination of realities/universes concerning the spiritual hell and this planet—the center of this planet is a multidimensional place that houses the actual physical bowels of this planet and at least two converging realities at exactly the same time, the reality of earth's molten core and the reality of spiritual hell—the fallen angels can indeed rise or appear to rise from vents from within the earth's crust.

THE GATE TO HELL

We realize from Revelation 9:14 that the *physical entrance* to hell, possibly the *central vent,* lies directly under the water flow of the Euphrates River. When I say *physical entrance* or *vent* I mean a genuine *gate* or *location* that can take you from this world into the literal underworld of the earth, as well as the literal spiritual underworld of hell: "...Release the four angels (Satan's army) who are bound at the great river Euphrates." Of course, a river of water could not prevent beings of a hyperdimensional nature from entering into our universe. The central vent may be hidden from our eye by the waters of the Euphrates, it's true, but the only reason it holds back the demon horde is simply because God holds them back. If there is a literal vent there must be a *spiritual seal* over it that prevents humanity from discovering its location and existence while, at the same time, prohibits the demon horde from being released.

There's no chance that someone could ever find the central vent because of its hyperdimensional/spiritual nature and because of God's protective seal. It couldn't be found because God would not permit it. It's true that the Scriptures point to the vicinity of the Euphrates riverbed, north of the boundary of the original garden given to the first human couple, but a detailed map, of course, is not provided. (Refer to 9:14, under the heading *The River*

Euphrates and Chapter 16:12 for more information on this subject.)

TWO REALITIES TO THE DARK DOMAIN

As I stated in Chapter 5, the dark domain or hell/the bottomless pit is a cross-pollination of hyperdimensional planes of existence where the literal molten core of our planet and the spiritual reality converge so that it becomes a bottomless, eternal, and hellish sphere called the lake of fire.

When the bottomless pit is referred to as a *prison* or *a place that binds Satan*, the implication being that it's a prison Satan and his demons *can be released from*, the Scriptures are describing two different realities: the lake of fire, having an eternal connection, and the prison called the bottomless pit, which has a connection to time. The two may be one and the same, but somehow separated by eternity.

The lake of fire is a permanent place of eternal damnation, time ceases to exist, and there is no getting out once you've been sentenced there. No one resides within the lake of fire at this point in time. The Antichrist and the False Prophet will be imprisoned in the lake of fire at the end of the Tribulation. No one else will be sentenced there until Judgment Day, after the 1,000 years of rest.

The bottomless pit, when it is referred to as a *prison*, functions in time. Those who have been sentenced there can be released from it, even though it is within the bowels of the earth and has a hyperdimensional reality to it. The fallen angels reside in the bottomless pit now.

Do not confuse *Sheol/Hades* with the *lake of fire/bottomless pit/hell* and the prison that is called the bottomless pit. Abraham's Bosom/Sheol is nowhere near planet earth.

It is mentioned in Revelation 19:20 that "these two," the Antichrist and the False Prophet, are cast alive into the lake of fire burning with brimstone (sulfur).

Then we are informed that, "He (Jesus) laid hold of the dragon, that serpent of old, who is the devil and Satan, and bound him for a thousand years; and he cast him into the bottomless pit…" (Rev. 20:2-3). "Now when the thousand years have expired, Satan will be released from his prison (the bottomless pit)…" (Rev. 20:7).

And then, finally: "The devil who deceived them was cast into the lake of fire and brimstone" (Rev. 20:10).

You have to understand that after the return of Christ the devil will be bound or imprisoned within the place called the bottomless pit for the duration of the 1,000 years, fully conscious of time. He is released at the end of the rest period, the Kingdom Age, and goes to war one last time with God. He loses the battle and then is finally thrown and eternally imprisoned into the place where the Antichrist and the False Prophet were confined a thousand years before, the eternal lake of fire! And there they will be tormented day and night forever and ever.

During the seventh millennium Jesus will rule this present (but at that point reformed) planet with his faithful, while his enemy, the devil, will be confined in the prison known as the bottomless pit, conscious of time. The Evil One will be separated from his wicked trinity, the Antichrist and the False Prophet, for they will be in hell, the lake of fire—once you've entered into the reality of the lake of fire, escape or release is eternally impossible, for we have discovered that after a thousand years the Antichrist and the False Prophet are still there, quite alive. They haven't been annihilated or blasted into eternal oblivion. They continue to exist. (Existence is eternal!) But John explains in Revelation 20:7 that there's a prison-place called the bottomless pit from which Satan can indeed be released. Could the bottomless pit be located in the mantle of the earth, the layer surrounding the planet between the earth's crust and the core? (For more information on the subject of the bottomless pit and the lake of fire, refer to Chapter 5:3, under the heading *Under the Earth*.)

Revelation 9:20

But the rest of mankind, who were not killed by these plagues, did not repent of the works of their hands, that they should not worship demons, and idols of gold, silver, brass, stone, and wood, which can neither see nor hear nor walk.

THE SURVIVORS DO NOT REPENT

After the fiery demons of the devil's army return to the depths, John observes that the survivors do not repent. Humanity will continue to go its merry way into oblivion, seeking immorality in all its names and forms: sexually, satanic worship of idols/images of gold, silver, brass, stone, wood, celebrity, the self, none of which can see nor walk, hear or speak, for none of them are alive. Humanity will continue to worship a man on earth as their god, even as the opportunity for repentance still remains—God is patient and gracious and will go as far as ever he can go to save you. But most of the survivors at this point would have taken the mark of the Beast, their fates sealed. Still, the grace of Christ is extended for those few who may have not taken the mark.

DEATH, THE HORIZON

Only God, who is the Beginning and the End, the One who created humanity, is to be worshiped. "Jesus said... 'I AM THE RESURRECTION AND THE LIFE. HE WHO BELIEVES IN ME, THOUGH HE (his body) MAY DIE, HE (his soul and spirit) SHALL LIVE'" (John 11:25).

What many people of the world don't realize is that death is like the horizon: there is so much beyond what one can see!

THE FUNDAMENTAL TRUTHS OF CHRIST

I've been focusing on a lot of dark and frightening concepts, so it would be good to pause here a moment to remind ourselves about the fundamental truths of Christianity: Jesus Christ came into this broken, fallen world, lived a perfect and sinless life, fully human, fully God, and then like a sacrificial lamb died, suffering in our place so that we might be saved from God's wrath, rising three days later from hell and death, alive again and reaching out to all humanity, taking all that would come with him (2Cor. 5:21).[11] "I came that they might have life, and might have it abundantly," said the Lord (John 10:10).

LISTEN & RECEIVE

Listen to the seven trumpets! Receive this wisdom. What the Lord has called you to do he has also gifted you to do! Where your heart longs for you to be is where you need to be, for you have a good feeling about that place and you will find happiness there. Listen to your heart, know what he has called you to do, and do it there, even if it means a 2,000 mile move. Dependence on the Lord is the beginning of knowledge. Praise God for his mighty acts, and for what he does for you! Praise God for his excellent greatness! Praise God and the Son in their sanctuary! Praise Jesus in the firmament of his power!

Revelation 9:21

And they did not repent of their murders or their sorceries or their sexual immorality or their thefts.

THEY DO NOT TURN

In spite of the fear caused by the plagues during these dark times, humanity will continue to resist the grace of Christ. People will not turn from their immoral ways, continuing to murder, dabble in sorcery (from the literal to the figurative), sexual immorality, theft, you name it, and the hearts of the inhabitants of the world will become deceitful above all matters, desperately wicked, and the end of the world will draw nigh.

* * * * *

SOURCES:

1. *Scorpion*, Microsoft Encarta Encyclopedia (2002).
2. *Hairstyle History,* The Costume Gallery, <http://www.costumegallcry.com>.
   Hairdressing, Microsoft Encarta Encyclopedia (2002).
   Hair, pg. 515-517, The New Unger's Bible Dictionary, Moody Press (1988).
3. *Destruction—Abaddon,* #6, 9, 10, pg. 7, Hebrew and Chaldee Dictionary; *Destroyer—Apollyon or The angel of the bottomless pit, i.e. Satan,* #623, pg. 14, Greek Dictionary of the New Testament, Strong's Exhaustive Concordance of the Bible/Dictionary of the Hebrew and Greek Words, Hendrickson Publishers.
4. *Horns,* Easton's Bible Dictionary, Online Edition, The Unbound Bible, Biola University, <http://unbound.biola.edu/>.
   Horn, Horns, pg. 587-588, The New Unger's Bible Dictionary, Moody Press (1988).
   Horns; The Tabernacle and Its Furniture, Exodus, Gray's Home Bible Commentary, The Bible Library Delux, version 5.0. suite, CD-ROM, Ellis Enterprises, Inc. (2,000).
5. *Bound—Deo,* #1210, pg. 21, Greek Dictionary of the New Testament, Strong's Exhaustive Concordance of the Bible/Dictionary of the Hebrew and Greek Words, Hendrickson Publishers.
6. *9, the Number of Judgment, Biblical Numerology,* Christian Apologetics & Research Ministry, <http://www.carm.org>.
7. *Biblical Numerology,* Christian Apologetics & Research Ministry, <http://www.carm.org>.
   Number (number & arithmetic, notation of numbers, numbers in Old Testament history, round numbers, significant numbers, gamatria, literature), William Taylor Smith, International Bible Standard Encyclopedia, Online Edition, <http://www.studylight.org>.
   Genesis 5 & 11: Chronological-Theological Reflections, James G. Jordan, *Biblical Chronology,* Bible Horizons (1994), <http://www.biblehorizons.com>.
   Evidence of Design; Beloved Numerologist, article, Chuck Missler, Koinonia House, <http://www.khouse.com>.
   Biblical Numerology, Christian Apologetics & Research Ministry, <http://www.carm.org>.
   Number, pg. 928, The New Unger's Bible Dictionary, Moody Press (1988).
8. *Gnostics, Gnostic Gospels, & Gnosticism,* Early Christian Writings, <http://www.earlychristianwritings.com>.
   Gnosticism, J. P. Arendzen, transcribed by Christine J. Murray, The Catholic Encyclopedia, Vol. VI, Online Edition, Kevin Knight (2002), <http://www.newadvent.org>.
   Bogus and Refuted 'Christian' Apologetics, Evidence for God from Science, <http://www.GodAndScience.org>.
9. *The History of Numerology,* Kathy Bradley, <http://www.oxy.edu>.
   Number, pg. 928, The New Unger's Bible Dictionary, Moody Press (1988).
   Numerology; Divination, Microsoft Encarta Encyclopedia (2002).

10. The evidence would include the author's research and conclusions written in the text in regard to numbers and number systems (God's holy mathematics/geometry) within the Bible, as well as the evidence within the following web sites and books, which you are encouraged to peruse:
The Numerical Bible: Hebrews to Revelation (1932), F. W. Grant, Kessinger Publishing Company (1942).
Genesis 5 & 11: Chronological-Theological Reflections, James G. Jordan, *Biblical Chronology,* Bible Horizons (1994),
<http://www.biblehorizons.com>.
Evidence of Design: Beloved Numerologist; "Chuck Missler explores the subject of hidden numerical codes and repetitive sequences in the Bible," Chuck Missler, Koinonia House, <http://www.khouse.com>.
Cosmic Codes; Hidden Messages from the Edge of Eternity, Chuck Missler, Koinonia House Inc., publisher (1998).
Biblical Numerology; A Basic Study of the Use of Numbers in the Bible, John J. Davies, Baker Book House (1995).
Biblical Numerology, Christian Apologetics & Research Ministry,
<http://www.carm.org>.
11. *Jesus Christ,* pg. 682-687, The New Unger's Bible Dictionary, Moody Press (1988).
Exposition of the Orthodox Faith (Book I), St. John of Damascus, Orthodox Christian Information Center,<http:// www.orthodoxinfo.com>; from John of Damascus, *Exposition of the Orthodox Faith,* Post Nicene Fathers, Schaff Edition, Volume IX, Series II, translated by The Rev. S. D. F. Salmond, D.D., F.e.I.s., Principal of the Free Church College, Aberdeen. (1898).
Jesus Christ 2, James Orr, International Bible Standard Encyclopedia, Online Edition (2003), <http://www.studylight.org>.
Holy Ghost, J. Forget, transcribed by W. S. French, Jr., The Catholic Encyclopedia, Vol. VII, Online Edition, Kevin Knight (2002),
<http://www.newadvent.org>.
Holy Spirit, pg. 583-584, The New Unger's Bible Dictionary, Moody Press (1988).
Holy Spirit, Microsoft Encarta Encyclopedia (2002).
The Four Spiritual Laws, Dr. Bill Bright, Campus Crusade for Christ (1965); internet version, including graphics, 1995, by Campus Crusade for Christ International, <http://www.campuscrusade.com> or <http://www.ccci.org> or <http://www.greatcom.org>.
The Five Points of Calvinism by Herman Hanko, Homer Hoeksema, and Gise J. Van Baren, Reformed Free Publishing Association (1975), all rights reserved, the Protestant Reformed Churches in America (unofficial home page web site), <http://www.prca.org/index.html>.

Further reading:
The History of Hair; Fashion and Fantasy Down the Ages, Robin Bryer, Philip Wilson Pub Ltd. (2,000).
The New International Dictionary of New Testament Theology, Colin Brown, Zondervan (1986).
The Holy Spirit, Billy Graham, Word Publishing (2002).
So Great Salvation, Charles C. Ryrie, Moody Press (1997).
Mere Christianity, C.S. Lewis, Macmillan Publishing Company (1943).
The Pursuit of God, A. W. Tozer, Christian Publications, Inc. (1982; first publication, 1948).

Institutes of the Christian Religion/One-Volume Edition, John Calvin (1599); translated by Henry Beveridge, Wm. B. Eerdmans Publishing Co. (1995).

Martin Luther, Selections From His Writings, Martin Luther (1463-1546), edited by John Dillenberger, Anchor (1958).

CHAPTER 10
The Angel & The Little Scroll

Revelation 10:1

I [John] saw still another mighty angel coming down from heaven, clothed with a cloud. And a rainbow was on his head, his face was like the sun, and his feet like pillars of fire.

PRELUDE TO THE THIRD WOE

Christ himself is about to release the final calamity upon the world! John faces the Lord standing in his spectacular throne room, and he comes face to face with yet "another mighty angel coming down from heaven."

The angel is clothed with a white cloud, an indication of holiness and glory. From the historical perspective, in regard to the climate, from May through September there were literally no clouds at all in the hot desert-like region, so few in fact that if clouds formed it was considered almost miraculous—clouds were *that* rare, as were rains in this season (I Samuel 12:17–18). It makes sense that over time clouds developed a symbolic attachment to the divine. Throughout Scripture, clouds are often used to show the power and wisdom of God (Pss. 135:6-7) and his divine presence (Ex. 16:10; 33:9; Num. 11:25; Job 22:14).[1]

John understands that the One he sees moving toward him is undoubtedly Jesus. In righteousness, the Son appears with a "rainbow...in appearance like an emerald," (Rev. 4:3). "I AM THE RAINBOW," says Jesus, "I AM THE PROMISE." He is the Emerald God, the Green Creator of the heavens and earth!

Like the cloud clothing the mighty angel, the rainbow is used here as a symbol of holiness and glory, multihued with the awe-inspiring colors of Christ's mercy and love. The rainbow is traditionally associated with a promise because of the Noahic covenant, and so accordingly this rainbow is the symbol of a promise, that of Christ and his grace, which reaches backward in time toward Noah and beyond and forward in time to the present and beyond. (For additional information on the rainbow, go to Chapter 4:3, under the heading, *The Green Throne Room*). "...His countenance (the brightness of his face) is like the sun shining in its strength" (Rev. 1:16). "His feet were like fine brass (great shining columns), as if refined in a furnace..." (Rev. 1:15). He is a pillar of fire, for he is the radiant Christ!

Revelation 10:2

He [Jesus] had a little book open in his hand. And he set his right foot on the sea and his left foot on the land...

THE SEA & THE LAND

Jesus is standing in readiness to release the Third Woe (the seventh plague), and in his right hand he continues to hold the little scroll/book with writing on both sides. The book now has seven opened seals: "And I (John) saw in the right hand of him who sat on the throne a scroll written inside and on the back, sealed with seven seals" (Rev. 5:1).

Now that the seven seals are loosened, Jesus opens the scroll/book and reads the contents within. John listens and is astonished! Completing the readings, the Son rises in all his glory. The "mighty angel who comes from heaven" approaches earth. He places his right foot on earth's sea and his left foot on earth's land. This suggests that he alone has absolute dominion and authority over the green planet earth and all its inhabitants!

But Satan's kingdom is of this earth too—because he is bound to it. Humans are of this earth because we belong to it, and we choose whom we shall follow. If we do not choose Christ, the Creator of earth, then we choose Lucifer, who is bound to it. Without Christ we automatically belong to the prince of this world! "For we do not wrestle against flesh and blood, but against principalities, against powers, against the rulers of this darkness, against spiritual hosts of wickedness in the heavenly places" (Eph. 6:12).

Revelation 10:3

...And [the mighty angel] cried with a loud voice, as when a lion roars. When he cried out, seven thunders uttered their voices.

THE SEVEN THUNDERS

Nearing the completion of the six plagues of the trumpets, Jesus' voice is heard like the roar of a lion with deep volume and intensity. (Refer to Chapter 4:7, under the heading *The First Creature; the lion* for related information about the lion.) He tells John that the inhabitants of the world are against him. He says, "Why do my people reject me?" With his love he created them. He desires to have everyone live with him in his great kingdom. Because of this rejection they cannot share his domain, and, consequently, they must also suffer seven additional plagues spoken of as *the thunders.*

At the sound of his cry (for, in truth, his heart is breaking), *seven mighty thunders* prepare to utter their voices. As the trumpet depicts the voice of Jesus, so thunder depicts his voice of authority, for John tells us in Revelation 6:1 that he heard one of the four living creatures (Jesus Christ) speak "with a voice like thunder." In Psalm 30:3, David informs us, "The God of glory thunders." The Most High thunders loudly in the heavens when his voice is heard.

In relation to the climate of the region, thunder was rarely (if ever) heard in the hot summer months, so just like clouds forming an attachment to the divine, over time thunder developed a similar attachment [2] (Prov. 26:1). It makes a great deal of sense that the Hebrews looked upon thunder as the voice of God, assigning divine power and divine vengeance to the sound (Ps. 81:7; Job 37:2; 4–5; 40:9, Ps. 29:3; 1Sam. 2:10; 2Sam. 22:14).[3] The use of the word in regard to this verse should be clear.

Jesus Christ, having the Seven Spirits of God, speaks seven thunderous times, and John hears the words of his Master. Now, once again, he is astounded that seven more plagues are to befall mankind, even while the inhabitants of earth continue to suffer from the plagues of the trumpets. The voice of the Lord warns of seven more extreme plagues/calamities that will soon take place on earth. The plagues of thunder are part of the second terrible sorrow/Woe that will bring to an end the sixth trumpet plague! When the Seven Spirits speak, the severity of the plagues is revealed.

Revelation 10:4

Now when the seven thunders sounded, I [John] was about to write; but I heard a voice from heaven saying, "Seal up the things which the seven thunders uttered, and do not write them."

THE SEVEN THUNDERS SEALED

John obediently prepares to write down the facts regarding the plagues of the thunders, for he was allowed to see into them, and surely, what he saw was vivid indeed. Of course, symbolically, Jesus is the seven thunders and he controls them, but something extraordinary happens next.

Jesus instructs John not to reveal to the world what the seven thunders will be in reality: "Seal up what the seven thunders have said and do not write it down. Do not reveal the meaning of it to humanity."

In the beginning of the Book of Revelation John was instructed, "What you see, write in a book and send it to the seven churches which are in Asia (and into the entire world)" (Rev. 1:11). Why must John now do the opposite and the thunders be sealed?

THE GOOD ROTTWEILER

The simple answer, and what probably amounts to the simple truth, is that the seven thunders are so bizarre, incomprehensible, and horrifying that John would have had great difficulty trying to describe them. Comparably, it would be like showing a loving and faithful Rottweiler a computer chip and asking the great headed dog to explain what it is and what it does. After a moment the dog might simply lean his body against you and nudge you with his head: *Food?* Clearly, the dog wouldn't have a clue why you held a computer chip instead of a nice doggy snack.

It's probably safe to say that John would, like that good Rottweiler, simply stare at the thunders, lost in their wonder. Furthermore, because the seven thunders are probably going to be so horrific, it's likely that John would have struggled emotionally when revealing to humanity what was in store for them, and thus God prevented him from revealing it to us. Obviously, the seven thunders will be much worse than a computer chip, although some may say that's arguable. They will be terrible, destructive, and powerful, a literal phenomena in nature, reality, and experience. All understanding of what the seven thunders are stop there because the seven thunders are sealed.

INTERNALIZING THE WORD OF GOD

Nevertheless, James B. Jordon suggests in his essay *The Seven Thunders: An Interpretive Suggestion* that the seven thunders can be, in a way, *unsealed.* How? Answer: because the voice from heaven tells John to seal the message of the seven thunders and then instructs him to eat the little scroll. By absorbing the information within the little book, Jordon argues, John can reflect on the seven thunders. Having internalized them he can—and here's Jordon's point—prophesy on them.[4] This relates to all Christians, for like John we are called to prophesy. Others argue that once we have absorbed and internalized the Word of God we can literally unseal the seven thunders and explain them. This is certainly an intriguing possibility, but thus far the arguments or evidence is purely speculative. Thus, the seven thunders remain fully sealed, and it's likely there they will remain until we hear and see the seven thunders ourselves.

SEVENS

During the last three-and-a-half years of life in this Age, the earth's population must endure the seven plagues of the trumpets, the seven plagues of the thunders, and the seven plagues of the bowls. Three sets of plagues, twenty-one plagues in all, and everyone of them take place in three-and-a-half short years. It should be clear that the Seven Spirits of God are represented in the set of sevens and three sets of seven represents the Holy Trinity, reinforcing God's holy mathematics/geometry.

As I have discussed previously, in the last three-and-a-half years of the Great Tribulation all left behind believers will be slain by Satan's unholy trinity. The great slaughter is accomplished when the period of the second great sorrow/Woe is in progress. (For additional information on the martyrs, refer to Chapter 6:9, under the heading *The Blood Bath*.) This will be the time when Jesus releases the "four angels who are bound," just before the introduction of the seven unknown thunders and subsequent seven bowl plagues, for these final fourteen plagues are kept strictly for the wicked. (The living 144,000 must be ruptured before the thunder and bowl plagues begin so that there will no longer be a living soul that is saved or can be saved on earth. It is likely that the last living faithful *to die* on the planet will be the Two Witnesses, thus ending the slaughter of the martyrs. This means that the Fifth and Sixth Raptures, the raptures of the martyrs and the 144,000 Jews, occur shortly after the resurrection of the Two Witnesses.)

Revelation 10:5

The angel whom I [John] saw standing on the sea and on the land lifted up his right hand to heaven.

HAND TO HEAVEN

John watches the powerful *angel* (Jesus) standing on the sea and on the land of the earth. He is the great God of Glory, the perfect Christ. His feet are on fire. His face shines like the midday sun! His hands are lifted upward to his Father's mighty heaven and to his heaven. Lightning strikes from the palms of his hands! Jesus, the Most High himself, prepares to establish himself on earth forever.

Revelation 10:6

...And [the angel] swore by him who lives forever and ever, who created heaven and the things that are in it, the earth and the things that are in it, and the sea and the things that are in it, that there should be delay no longer.

THE OATH

The angel swears by Jesus' name and the name of his Father who lives forever and ever, the Creator of heaven and everything that is in it—Jesus is making the oath.

I'd like to examine the importance of oath-taking in relation to this verse, Christianity, and Judaism so that we understand just how serious this is: for the Jews, an oath meant *to call upon God.*

In Hebrew, an oath could also mean *a sworn covenant* (Gen. 26:28), *an appeal to God* (Ex. 22:11), and it could sometimes be attached to the sacred number seven (Gen. 21:30). An oath, be it public or private, consisted of *a promise* and *an appeal* to God. God was actively involved in the process, a literal participant in the oath taking. Because of that an oath was considered absolutely, perhaps even eternally, binding. There were always three people involved when an oath was taken: the one who took the oath, the one who accepted the oath, and God, the One within the oath. You did not break an oath. You did not *bear false witness*, and if you did it was not taken lightly (Ex. 20:7; Lev. 19:12; Duet. 19:16–19). In fact, the punishment for breaking an oath was severe.[5]

As far as Christianity and oaths go, Matthew 5:33–37 suggests that Christians should know no oath at all. A yea and nay are oath enough. In other words, when a Christian says yes or no it is just like an oath in the Jewish sense of the word.[6]

DELAY NO LONGER

Jesus swears an oath that he will delay no longer.

John sees his Master standing on the world proclaiming his oath with a voice like a roaring lion. Jesus swears this oath on God who created heaven and the things that are in it, on the earth and in it, on the sea and the things that are in it—essentially, he is covering all his bases here, making it crystal clear that he means business, for he is swearing upon everything, including himself, the I AM. He is letting all his Creation know that his oath will stand faithful and true.

Revelation 10:7

But in the days of the sounding of the seventh angel, when he is about to sound, the mystery of God would be finished, as he declared to his servants the prophets.

SECRETS & MYSTERIES

Jesus concludes by saying, "The plague of the trumpet of the seventh angel is about to happen. The third sorrow is going to unfold upon the inhabitants of the earth. The third sorrow does not begin until I blow the seventh trumpet. When I do, the mystery of God will be finished, as I declared to my servants the prophets!"

Behold, the seventh trumpet is ready to be aired, the trumpet of his consuming wrath. (The sounding of the seventh trumpet, which introduces the seven bowl plagues and the end of the Age, is described in detail in Chapter 16.)

The term *mystery of God* is used here in reference to something God has, thus far, not revealed to us. It appears to be in reference to a complex and mostly unknowable blueprint involving humanity, what I like to call the Big Picture, but above and beyond that the mystery remains.

In Scripture the word *mystery* usually indicates a secret that *will be* revealed, and since we are also informed that the *mystery is finished* or *complete*, this suggests at the point of completion the mystery of God will indeed be revealed to us. It's quite likely that at the end of the End Times God will tear open the fabric of this universe and reveal the blueprint of the Big Picture to us, the mystery of God revealed. Many biblical scholars believe the term *mystery of God* applies to very specific mysteries within Christianity.[7]

What's most important here, I think, is to realize that this particular mystery of God *will be* revealed—it is promised.[8]

Revelation 10:8

Then the voice which I [John] heard from heaven spoke to me again and said, "Go, take the little book which is open in the hand of the angel who stands on the sea and on the earth."

THE LITTLE BOOK

Before John describes the nature of the third fateful and deep sorrow/Woe, the voice of Jesus speaks to him once more, telling John to take the little book that Jesus holds in his right hand while standing upon the sea and on the land of the earth. John knows written in the little scroll/book are the secrets of the seven thunders, an addition to the second sorrow/Woe.

Revelation 10:9

So I [John] went to the angel and said to him, "Give me the little book." And he said to me, "Take and eat it; and it will make your stomach bitter, but it will be as sweet as honey in your mouth."

BITTER & SWEET

Approaching Jesus, John is ready to take the little book. There are writings on the inside and the outside of the scroll/book. (Refer to Chapter 5:1, under the heading *The Scroll* for related information.)

The book is described as *little*. This is directly related to time: it all begins and ends in an extraordinarily condensed or *little* period of time. Twenty-one plagues in a mere three-and-a-half years, and at least fourteen of those plagues, the seven plagues of the thunders and the seven plagues of the bowls, will occur at the tail-end of the last three-and-a-half years, perhaps in as short a period as two weeks. This is, of course, estimated. It could be a month, or a few months more, give or take. Whatever the case may be, the main point here is that the last fourteen plagues will take place in a very short period of time indeed.

John looks at the nail-scarred hand stretched out to him. Jesus tells his servant to take the book and eat it, warning him that the eating of the book will taste as sweet as honey in his mouth but it will upset his stomach.

Honey is used in Scripture to suggest sweet conversation (Song of Sol. 4:11), the Word of God (Pss. 19:10; 119:103), and pleasure (Prov. 25:15; 27). The use of honey here seems to be in the sense of pleasure, but it's a false pleasure, one that is short lived. It is a direct allusion to the first half of the Great Tribulation, a so-called time of sweet peace and restoration.[9]

In regard to the bitter taste and nausea that immediately follows, clearly, this represents the last half of the Great Tribulation.[10]

In the figurative language of the Scriptures *eating the book* or *eating a book* translates into comprehension of the written material. The information has been absorbed or downloaded, if you like. John ate the book and absorbed its contents, a book/scroll filled with information about the End Times and thus he could comprehend its meaning and, if need be, employ the knowledge toward his survival.

This can be applied to the Book of Revelation, for as you read it you will absorb it and comprehend its meaning so that when the End Times come you can apply what you have learned toward *your* survival.[11]

Revelation 10:10

Then I [John] took the little book out of the angel's hand and ate it, and it was as sweet as honey in my mouth. But when I had eaten it, my stomach became bitter.

JOHN EATS THE BOOK

Obediently, John takes the little book and begins to eat it! As he chews (and as promised), it tastes as sweet as honey in his mouth. Soon as he swallows, his stomach becomes greatly upset!

Ezekiel the prophet also mentions a scroll to be eaten: "'But you, son of man, hear what I say to you. Do not be rebellious like that rebellious house (Israel); open your mouth and eat (and digest) what I give you.' Now when I looked, there was a hand stretched out to me; and behold, a scroll of a book was in it. Then he spread it before me; and there was writing on the inside and on the outside, and written on it were lamentations and mourning and woe. Moreover he said to me, 'Son of man, eat what you find; eat this scroll, and go, speak to the house of Israel.' So I opened my mouth, and he caused me to eat that scroll. And he said to me, 'Son of man, feed your belly, and fill your stomach with this scroll that I give you (and digest the words).' So I ate, it was in my mouth like honey in sweetness." (Eze. 2:8–10 and 3:1–3).

EZEKIEL

I'd like to point out that the Book of Ezekiel is an Old Testament book of prophecy full of supernatural visions and apocalyptic imagery, similar to the Book of Daniel. It is directly and deeply related and connected to the Book of Revelation.

Ezekiel was one of the captives of Israel banished to Babylonia in 597 B.C., 11 years before the fall of Jerusalem. From 597–86 people considered him the prophet of doom, and later, after the fall of Nebuchadnezzar II, he was known as a *comforter and inspirer* to the people of Israel. There are roughly 12 Old Testament prophecies directly related, connected and made complete in the Book of Revelation. A number of them can be found in the Book of Ezekiel.[12]

Revelation 10:11

And he [the angel] said to me [John], "You must prophesy again about many peoples, nations, tongues, and kings."

GO, TELL IT ON THE MOUNTAIN

Again, Christ asks John to prophesy about things that must shortly come to pass before his Second Coming. This is similar to the time of Ezekiel when he was told to prophesy to the nation of Israel. This can be directly applied to present day believing Christians, to all the saved in Christ: go, tell it on the mountain! Tell the world! Prepare! Be ready! Absorb! Internalize! Prophesy so that you and everyone can survive!

Let the Lord roar! Let the Lord thunder! "He is the Lord our God; his judgments are in all the earth. He remembers his covenant (his oaths and promises) forever, the word which he commanded, for a thousand generations" (Psalms 105: 7–8).

The sixth trumpet has blown, the Second Woe has passed. The Lord is about to blow the seventh trumpet and reveal the Third Woe, the seventh plague. (For related information on this subject, refer to Chapter 16:1, under the heading *The Seventh Trumpet.*)

* * * * *

SOURCES:

1. *Israel; Climate,* Library of Congress Country Studies, <http://www.lcweb2.loc.gov>.
   Israel, contributed by Bernard Reich, Microsoft Encarta Encyclopedia (2002).
2. *Rain,* International Bible Standard Encyclopedia, Online Edition, <http://www.studylight.org>.
   Rain, pg. pg. 1061-1062, The New Unger's Bible Dictionary, Moody Press (1988).
3. *Thunder,* International Bible Standard Encyclopedia, Online Edition, <http://www.studylight.org>.
   Thunder, pg. 1279, The New Unger's Bible Dictionary, Moody Press (1988).
4. *The Seven Thunders: An Interpretive Suggestion,* James B. Jordan, copyright © Biblical Horizons, No. 66 (1994), <http://www.biblicalhorizons.com>.
5. *OATH (Semitic),* Maurice A. Canney, James Hastings, ed. Encyclopedia of Religion and Ethics, Vol. IX, <http://www.dabar.org>.
   Oath, International Bible Standard Encyclopedia, Online Edition, <http://www.studylight.org>.
   Oath, pg. 930-931, The New Unger's Bible Dictionary, Moody Press (1988).
6. *Taking Oaths; Matthew 5:33-37* and *The Keeping of Vows,* Calvary Chapel, <http://www.calvarychapel.org>.
   Oath, pg. 930-931, The New Unger's Bible Dictionary, Moody Press (1988).
   Oaths, A. Vander Heeren, transcribed by Rosalie Nesbit , The Catholic Encyclopedia, Volume
   XI, Online Edition, Kevin Knight (2002).
7. *Mystery of God,* J. A. Mchugh, transcribed by Douglas J. Potter, *Dedicated to the Sacred Heart of Jesus Christ,* The Catholic Encyclopedia, Volume X, Online Edition, Kevin Knight (2002).
   Mystery, Bible Dictionary, BibleLearn.com, <http://www.biblelearn.com>.
   Mystery, pg. 896, The New Unger's Bible Dictionary, Moody Press (1988).

8. *Promise,* W. L. Walker, International Bible Standard Encyclopedia, Online Edition, <http://www.studylight.org>.
   Promise, pg. 1039, The New Unger's Bible Dictionary, Moody Press (1988).
9. *Honey,* WebBible Encyclopedia, <http://www.christiananswers.net>.
   Honey, pg. 585, The New Unger's Bible Dictionary, Moody Press (1988).
10. *Bitter,* WebBible Encyclopedia, <http://www.christiananswers.net>.
    Bitter, pg. 173, The New Unger's Bible Dictionary, Moody Press (1988).
11. *The Seven Thunders: An Interpretive Suggestion,* James B. Jordan, copyright © Biblical Horizons, No. 66 (1994), <http://www.biblicalhorizons.com>.
12. *Countdown to Exile IV; Ezekiel and the Structure of History,* Biblical Chronology, James B. Jordan, Vol. 8, No. 12, Biblical Horizons (1996), <http://www.biblicalhorizons.com>.
    The Prophet Ezekiel, article, Chuck Missler, Koinonia House, <http://www.khouse.com>.
    Ezekiel, Jos. Schets, transcribed by Sean Hyland, The Catholic Encyclopedia, Volume V, Online Edition, Kevin Knight (2002), <http://www.newadvent.org>.
    Ezekiel, pg. 390-391, The New Unger's Bible Dictionary, Moody Press (1988).
    Ezekiel; Book of Ezekiel, Microsoft Encarta Encyclopedia (2002).

CHAPTER 11
The Two Witnesses

Revelation 11:1

Then I [John] was given a reed like a measuring rod. And the angel stood, saying, "Rise and measure the temple of God, the altar, and those who worship there."

THE MEASURING ROD

John is given a measuring rod and told to measure the greatness of Jesus' throne room. It consists of God's sanctuary, the great altar before the holy throne, and the massive amphitheater, the assembly place for the innumerable company of Saints who stand before Christ.

The Hebrews called the tool a measuring *rod* or *reed* probably because they used lengths of sweet cane. It became known and used as *a measure* (Ezek. 40:3; 5; 42:16–19). The length of a measuring rod was about 11 feet.[1]

Revelation 11:2

"But leave out the court which is outside the temple, and do not measure it, for it has been given to the Gentiles. And they will tread the holy city underfoot for forty-two months."

DO NOT MEASURE THE WORLD COURT

The angel tells John not to measure the outside of the Temple or the Outer Court. This has a twofold meaning.

(1) It is directly related to the Tabernacle and the Temple of Solomon, often called *the place of the deity* or *house of Jehovah.*

Both were reproductions of the heavenly Tabernacle that exists within the First Heaven. The Outer Court was given to the Gentiles, for Gentiles and any kind of unclean objects were allowed in the Outer Court of the Temple. The purpose for this was basically to keep the Gentiles and unclean objects *out* of the Tabernacle. The Outer Court worked like a pressure valve—by allowing the Gentiles into this area the pressure was removed from the Inner Temple; it kept the Gentiles satisfied or distracted enough so that they would not enter the Inner Tabernacle and thereby desecrate it. The Outer Court protected the Inner Temple. It was the border to the Inner Temple which lead to the Holy of Holies.[2]

(2) The Outer Court represents fallen humanity and the Antichrist. They are not allowed within the Inner Court because they are unclean. This is why John is not permitted to measure the Outer Court. It embodies the Antichrist and fallen humanity. They are unworthy of not only measurement, but the actual act of measurement. Expanding on that idea, the Outer Court as it's used here can also symbolize the planet earth. The entire planet is the Outer Court because it exists in a fallen, entropic state. It belongs to the devil and to those who support him. Salvation can be found, not on the planet, the fallen Outer Court, but only deep within the divine Inner Temple that is Jesus Christ.

At this time in the Great Tribulation the Gentiles and Jews will not seek God and for that reason, as well as the reasons listed above, they will not enter into the Inner Temple.

The Antichrist and the unrepentant tread upon the holy city (in relation to the earth, as well as the city of Jerusalem and the Temple) for 42 months, or three-and-a-half years. This is a direct reference to the final three-and-a-half years of the Great Tribulation and the sinful, unworthy behavior of the lost.

Revelation 11:3

"And I will give power to my two witnesses, and they will prophesy one thousand two hundred and sixty days, clothed in sackcloth."

THE TWO WITNESSES

The Lord tells John that he is sending Two Witnesses to the earth during the last three-and-a-half years of this dispensation.

Most biblical scholars and students of prophecy agree, and strongly too, that the Two Witnesses will undoubtedly be Jewish, the literal Old Testament Elijah and Enoch. Some scholars disagree, suggesting they will be men *like* Elijah and Moses; others suggest that they will be two Jewish men inspired by the Holy Spirit, similar to John the Baptist; and still others claim the Two Witnesses will be angels, seraphim or cherubim.[3]

I support the traditional Elijah and Enoch interpretation.

Both men did not face physical death on the earth, but were whisked away into the spirit by God, experiencing a living rapture similar to the Fourth and Sixth Raptures. Because of this they must face physical death, and thus they return to earth in bodily form just before Christ's return.

THEY MUST FACE DEATH

Because Christ is going to rapture the living in the Fourth and Sixth Rapture, and those involved in the Fourth and Sixth raptures will never face physical death, some ask: Why can't that apply to Elijah and Enoch?[4] Answer: the reason they must face death is so that Scripture might be fulfilled; and because they are tied to the time from whence they came, pre-Christ. All human beings that existed before the time and salvation of Christ had to face physical death—for Jesus had to be the first resurrected. Scripture tells us that the punishment for sin is death. Although God *took them away* because of their godliness and righteousness, they were sinners, for they were part of the fallen nature. Because of Adam's sin, God said to him, "In the sweat of your face you shall eat bread till you return to the ground, for of it you were taken; for dust you are, and to dust you shall return" (Gen. 3:19). God took both men to Abraham's Bosom without experiencing death, planning their return to earth at the end of our Age. God kept the sting of death from them, but they will return to earth to complete their lives and their deaths. That Elijah and Enoch will die a physical death thousands of years after their living rapture is unimportant, but because they are inexorably tied to that time they must face what everyone from their time faced, and that's physical death. They simply cannot escape it.

PLAGUE REDUNDANCY & MID-TRIB DEATH

Some eschatologists believe the Two Witnesses will be martyred in the middle of the Tribulation, as opposed to near the end of the Tribulation, as I argue in this manual. This is an interesting interpretation based on a number of concepts, which I will briefly address here.

(1) *Plague Redundancy* claims God wouldn't want the Two Witnesses, who will have the power to turn water into blood, among other things, to *duplicate* or *repeat* his End Time plagues.

(2) Belief that the Lord will be in the process of setting up his millennial kingdom during the last three-and-a-half years of the Tribulation, the implication being that the work of the Two Witnesses will have to be completed by then.

(3) Because everyone will *see* the deaths of the Two Witnesses, it is believed that an operational satellite system for television and technology must be in working order; at the same time humanity must continue to have a celebratory spirit, the argument being that at the end of the Tribulation no one would have the desire, let alone the energy, to celebrate anything.[5]

Although these ideas are well intentioned and certainly worthy of further discussion and debate, it's likely that plague redundancy won't be an issue—is God really concerned with one-upmanship? The Scriptures make it very clear the entire last three-and-a-half years of the Tribulation will be filled with plagues, martyrdom, war and Armageddon (as opposed to Christ prepping for the millennium), and a global satellite network does not necessarily have to fully function or even exist at the end because of advancing new technologies, as well as good old fashioned broadcasting through the airwaves. If you've got a bent coat-hanger and radio and TV are still on the air, with or without satellites, you're probably going to get some kind of reception, surely enough to get the message that the Two Witnesses have been killed.

Lastly, in regard to humanity having a celebratory spirit, it can be argued that humanity always manages to unearth the spirit of celebration, even in the midst of terrible events—when the Two Witnesses have been killed near the end of the Tribulation there *will be* worldwide relief and celebration because humanity will be convinced that the Two Witnesses were the cause of all their suffering. For those who survive, the death of the Two Witnesses will bring such great relief *that they will find a way to* celebrate, either figuratively, within their hearts, or literally by exchanging food stuffs, water, clothing, alcohol, dancing in the streets. In light of how humanity has celebrated from the release and victory over horror in the past this conclusion does not seem unreasonable.

When all is said and done, Plague Redundancy falls squarely on the shoulders of personal (subjective) interpretation and some scriptural inaccuracy.

A PROMISE OF THINGS TO COME

We are informed that "Jesus answered and said to them (his disciples), 'Indeed, Elijah is coming (just before his return), and will restore all things (by witnessing the truth)" (Matt. 17:11).

Malachi writes, saying, "Behold, I (God) will send you Elijah the prophet before the coming of the great and dreadful day of the Lord (the Second Coming of Jesus)" (Mal. 4:5). "And it came to pass, when the Lord was about to take up Elijah into heaven (Abraham's Bosom) by a whirlwind (the Spirit of God), that Elijah went with Elisha from Gilgal," (2Kings 2:1). "Then it happened, as they continued on and talked, that suddenly a chariot of fire (the Spirit of Jesus) appeared with horses of fire (referring to the Seven Spirits of Life) and separated the two of them; and Elijah went up by a whirlwind (the Spirit) into heaven (Abraham's Bosom)" (2Kings 2:11).

I strongly believe that Elijah's transformation into the spirit without facing physical death is a promise of things to come: the rapture of the living. Its example inspires us with such great hope.

If Elijah represents the rapture of the living Saints, it follows that there must be a representative of the rapture of the dead Saints. That representative is Moses, the man of God who died and who was buried by God himself in a valley in the land of Moab, as described in Deuteronomy 34:6.

ONE & ONE = THREE

Those who have an ear to hear, listen: when Jesus was transfigured on the high mountain before Peter, James, and John (Mark 9:1–5) they saw Elijah and Moses with him. One man who had never faced death, representing the Fourth and Sixth living raptures of the Saints preceding the end of the Age, and one man who had faced death, representing the rapture of the dead Saints, the Second, Third, and Fifth Raptures. Christ standing in the middle represents his own rapture, the First Rapture. He is the living conduit between the two, which suggests that only he is able to resurrect all Saints, whether dead or alive, on earth or in Abraham's Bosom and Paradise.

ELIJAH

In post-biblical Judaism Elijah's return to earth is anticipated. It is celebrated every Passover. Elijah is looked upon as an invisible participant in the celebration. His return heralds the coming of the Messiah—this concept is embraced primarily because of his living translation (2Kings 2:11; supported in Mal. 4:5–6). Jesus did not agree with this conclusion, for he made it clear that the herald of the coming Messiah was John the Baptist, the man who was the spiritual fulfillment of Elijah. John the Baptist was said to have come "in the spirit and power of Elijah" (Matt. 11:14, 17:11–13; Mark 9:13; Luke 1:17).[6] In light of this information, when Elijah does return the reaction from the Jewish community and an Apostate Dominant Christianity in general will be, to say the least, interesting, especially in regard to what the Book of Revelation describes taking place *after* he returns.

ENOCH

In regard to Enoch, Genesis 5:24 says, "Enoch walked with God (for he was a righteous man); and he was not (similarly to Elijah, he was translated into the spirit by God and taken away to Abraham's Bosom, experiencing a living rapture), for God took him." "By faith Enoch was taken away (translated from this life) so that he did not see death, and was not found (on earth), because God had taken him; for before he was taken (in his translation) he had this testimony, that he pleased God," (Heb. 11:5).

Enoch was born in about the year 3034 B.C. He lived 300 years in length and during those years he was very close to God.[7]

It should be clear that these two prophets never experienced physical death, for God's plan was to keep their deaths until the latter days, "And as it is appointed for men (and women) to die once, but after this the judgment" (Heb. 9:27). They will simply appear on earth as mortal men, more than likely the way they looked at the time they were taken to Abraham's Bosom. Their flesh and blood physical bodies will be exactly the same as any other human being living on earth (and at that point you could say that they will be pretty old)!

SACKCLOTH

Elijah and Enoch will clothe themselves in sackcloth, a sign of complete humility and loyalty to God. This could be figurative in nature, but in ancient times prophets and those who practiced self-denial as a part of their personal or spiritual discipline literally wore sackcloth (Isa. 20:2).[8] The Two Witnesses will probably wear sackcloth or something like sackcloth to show the world just how sincere and devoted they are as they deliver their message. Their time will be short, a period of only three-and-one-half years, the one 1,260 days mentioned by John, a total of three years, five months, and fifteen days!

Jesus gives the Two Witnesses great power while they prophesy to humanity during the last days. They make a humble plea for people to change their ways and accept Jesus Christ as their Lord and Savior. They warn the world's population not to take the mark of the Beast. They advise the inhabitants not to follow the evil ways of the Antichrist and to leave their immorality behind. They emphasize the fact that Jesus' second great coming is about to be fulfilled, and remember, they are on earth while the world is being struck by plague after plague. They are God's witnesses to the last of the living.

MAGICAL TECHNOLOGY

Scripture says that all humanity across the globe will see the Two Witnesses and hear their message. This will happen by way of television, radio, cell phones, the Internet: in a word, technology.

The saved in Christ who lived ages ago may have believed that Jesus would return in their lifetimes, but the world was not technologically advanced enough. The world has the technology to make those prophecies possible now. In fact, we take these unbelievable and genuinely miraculous, even magical, technologies for granted, having accepted them into our lives with unabashed and unequaled abandon.

We have all the technology we need: radio and television have long since invented; the computer chip and micro-processing; satellites picking up world events instantaneously; global positioning systems; global tracking devices; the Internet and Email; cell phones and instant and wireless communication; and there's more radical and almost Godlike technology just around the corner like advanced biometric technology and the integration of man and machine; nanotechnology, silicon-based quantum dot quantum bits, and subatomic quantum natured computer systems; artificial intelligence; epidermal computer chips; even a brain chip called *Soul Catcher*, a nanodot technology being researched right now by British Telecom and the United States that implants behind the eye, attached directly to the nerve cells entering the brain, recording everything you see, hear, smell, and experience, with the ability to instantly download the recorded data onto your home computer.[9]

The stuff of science fiction? Fantasy? It's like magic! But it's real. Because of our rapidly advancing technologies you could easily say the period is ripe for the Two Witnesses.

That being the case, it's a good bet that it's also the right time to prepare for Jesus' Second Coming, for the time is at hand! You must have a survival plan. Put yourself in readiness so that you will survive. "Blessed is he who reads and those who hear the words of this prophecy, and keep those things which are written in it; for the time is near" (Rev. 1:3).

Revelation 11:4
"These are the two olive trees and the two lamp stands standing before the Lord of the earth."

OLIVE TREES & LAMP STANDS

Elijah and Enoch are equated to two olive trees. Why? Answer: in ancient times the importance of the olive tree was similar to the national importance of the fig tree, in regard to economics and need—as it is today still. (See Chapter 6:13, under the heading *Stars Fall From Heaven* for related information on the fig tree.) The harvest of olive trees continues to be a vital part of Israeli agriculture. The olive tree was also a symbol of peace, prosperity, and wealth.[10] The olive tree is deeply embedded within Israel's history and culture. There are references to the tree in the New Testament in regard to Christ as the olive tree (Romans 11:11–24). This makes it clear that Elijah and Enoch are Jewish, of the lineage of Israel, of the lineage of David, and of the lineage of Jesus Christ.

The Witnesses are also equated to two lamp stands. (For related information on the symbolic significance of lamp stands, refer to Chapter 1:12, under the heading *Seven Golden Lamp stands.*)

Since they are with Jesus (in fact, standing before him, the Lord of the earth), and Jesus is the Light of the World and has the Seven Spirits of God, Elijah and Enoch are bathed by the light and holiness of God. This tells us that they have been given the authority to do what they're going to do, signed, sealed, and delivered by God. It is, indeed, accurate and correct to describe them as lamp stands casting the light, which is the Christ Light, onto the world. They are godly and Christ-like, and they faithfully stand for their mighty God of heaven, Jesus Christ.

Revelation 11:5

"And if anyone wants to harm them, fire proceeds from their mouths and devours their enemies. And if anyone wants to harm them, he must be killed in this manner."

MOUTHS OF FIRE

Like the sound of a lion, John hears Jesus say with a loud voice, "If anyone tries to harm my loyal subjects, watch out, for the power of the Lord works through Elijah and Enoch. They utter my judgments against the people concerning all their wickedness."

The description of fire coming from the mouths of Elijah and Enoch is probably a visual depiction of their power, but still, considering the supernatural nature of the last three-and-a-half years of the Tribulation, it's quite possible that when they strike their enemies a power literally comes from their person. They could generate the energy God has given them and direct the force much like a laser beam or a lightning bolt, a theatrical laser beam from the eyes notwithstanding—but who's to say? The possibilities are limitless when the Lord is involved, even theatrical, mythical beams from the eyes!

Revelation 11:6

These [the Witnesses] have power to shut heaven, so that no rain falls in the days of their prophecy; and they have power over waters to turn them to blood, and to strike the earth with all plagues, as often as they desire.

THE GLOBAL DROUGHT

During their time on the earth the Two Witnesses will have power to do virtually anything, as many times as they wish. They will have the power to strike the earth with any kind of plague they can think of—and it should be clear here that these two men will not be careless or offhand when it comes to how they go about choosing and then administering those plagues, and surely they won't be concerned with Plague Redundancy.

The punishment they administer to sinful earthlings during the concluding years on earth will be unbearable. The remaining inhabitants of the earth will curse God. They will hate the Two Witnesses and blame them because their mighty acts will cause great suffering and pain.

They will have power over water, earth, and sky. In fact, it's reasonable to conclude that they will have power over all reality. It's important to remember here that what the Two Witnesses choose to do is *in addition to* the twenty-one plagues that befall humanity during the last three-and-a-half years, which is remarkable. Truly, with the number of events, many of them overlapping, plus everything the Two Witnesses throw at the world, there will be no time to rest *in between*, no time to catch one's breath, just *slam! slam! slam! slam! slam! slam!* Clearly, it will be a chaotic and dreadful time.

This verse specifically mentions the ability of the Two Witnesses to stop rainfall. This will cause global drought. Green grass (all plant life) will wither away, what is left of it at any rate, for the first plague of the trumpets that devastated the world with mighty hail and fire, mingled with blood burned up much of the green grass. Grass (and all plant life) does indeed recover quickly after it has been burned, but with the atmosphere already filled with ash, smoke, poisonous gases, and radiation (from the first three plagues) and sunlight having a difficult time cutting through that intense cloud cover, coupled with subfreezing and superheated temperatures and the lack of rain caused by global climate changes, as well as by the actions of the Two Witnesses, whatever greenness tries to recover and return will wither away and then vanish entirely. By the end of the last three-and-a-half years it's quite possible that there won't be a green blade of grass left on the planet.

The Two Witnesses will stop rainfall over the three-and-a-half years—indeed, there will be global drought and famine and much death. While they are on the earth there will be no more precipitation until the final plague occurs, which is referred to as *hail*, but this hail may have nothing to do with precipitation at all. This mighty hail is sent by God to obliterate all flesh off the face of the earth just days before Christ sets up his kingdom on this very planet!

POWER

To make matters even worse, the Two Witnesses will have the power to contaminate the earth's available water supply, including stored, bottled, and well water. They can turn water to blood—or something like blood. This could be metaphorical in nature, but once again, it doesn't have to be. The verse doesn't say that they will turn all water into blood, but only that they will have the power to do so, which suggests that there will be—and must be— water remaining. If all the water is turned into blood all humanity would die before the end of the three-and-a-half years, and the Scriptures make it very clear that a large portion of unrepentant humanity, as well as the Antichrist and the False Prophet, will continue to survive right until the very end. Water will become more precious than gold, diamonds, real estate, you name it.

What drinking water and food is still available will be completely controlled by the Antichrist and his agents. "...So I (John) looked, and behold, a black horse, and he who sat on it (the Antichrist, whose name is death) had a pair of scales in his hand (referring to the Beast's rationing of the world's food and water supply). And I heard a voice in the midst of the four living creatures saying, 'A quart of wheat for a denarius (a day's wages), and three quarts of barley for a denarius...'" (Rev. 6:5–6). This, of course, will make it all the more difficult to survive.

The Two Witnesses have great power, just as Jesus has great power. Divine favor is completely removed from the face of the earth by the will of Elijah and Enoch through Christ.

Revelation 11:7

When they [the witnesses] finish their testimony, the beast that ascends out of the bottomless pit will make war against them, overcome them, and kill them.

ELIJAH & ENOCH FACE DEATH

During the time the second great sorrow/Woe is in progress (the sixth plague), when Jesus opens the gates to the prison called the bottomless pit for the second time and releases Satan's gigantic army of demons (locust) to kill one third of the unrepentant, the

Two Witnesses will be testifying on the earth! The first six plagues will have transpired while these Godly men witness to the lost and carry out all the plagues they can come up with. Many people will blame them for the plagues they created and possibly for the twenty-one plagues as well. They will be greatly hated.

No person on earth will have the power to harm them, for they will be supernaturally protected by the Holy Spirit! Nonetheless, near the end of the seven year Tribulation and all the plagues, when their work is finished (just before the second army of demons/locust is scheduled to return to its prison), it is God's plan to allow the spirits of evil to conquer Elijah and Enoch. They are overcome by the demons (locust) and their physical fallen-natured bodies will be killed. Elijah and Enoch will finally face death.

The Two Witnesses will be slain by the creatures of the devil—I'm convinced it will take something extraordinary and supernatural to end their lives. Satan will claim this as his victory and have a moment of satisfaction, potentially having killed the very last saved in Christ on the entire planet, but God receives all the glory three-and-a-half days later. As stated in Chapter 10:4, under the heading *Sevens*, "the living 144,000 must be raptured before the thunder and bowl plagues begin so that there will no longer be a living soul that is saved or can be saved in Christ on earth. It is likely that the last living faithful *to die* on the planet will be the Two Witnesses, thus ending the slaughter of the martyrs. This means that the Fifth and Sixth Raptures, the raptures of the martyrs and the 144,000 Jews, occur shortly after the resurrection of the Two Witnesses."

Revelation 11:8

And their dead bodies will lie in the street of the great city which spiritually is called Sodom and Egypt, where also their Lord was crucified.

IN THE STREETS

John is shown the Witnesses' dead bodies lying in the streets of Jerusalem. As the Godly men will be blamed for many plagues, including the three-and-half-years of worldwide food shortage and drought, the people will jeer at the lifeless bodies. It's likely that this will transpire in the warmer summer months, when the weather is exceedingly hot, remembering, of course, that the atmosphere of the planet will be filled with debris. The global climate will be unpredictable. The two dead bodies left lying in the burning, heated streets of Jerusalem will, of course, rapidly decompose.

Revelation 11:9

Then those from the peoples, tribes, tongues, and nations see their dead bodies three-and-a-half days, and will not allow their dead bodies to be put into graves.

TELEVISION & 3 ½

John explains that everyone on earth, except for the blessed and supernaturally protected 144,000, will glory in the deaths of the Witnesses, and not only that, but will see them as well. Television will play an important role here, even if it isn't being distributed by satellites, but broadcasts through the airwaves; radio and other advanced technologies will also be involved. One way or another, the world's population will see the bodies of the Two Witnesses lying on the ground in the holy city for a period of three-and-a-half days!

Once more there is something significant about the number three-and-a-half: Christ witnessed to the world for three-and-a-half years at the beginning of mankind's fifth millennium! The Antichrist rules the earth for three-and-a-half years at the end of mankind's sixth millennium! Mankind's final span of life on this earth is entwined within the number three-and-a-half, the last years of the Tribulation. It's fitting that Elijah and Enoch, who gave their testimonies for approximately three-and-a-half years during the latter half of the Great Tribulation, lie dead on the ground for three-and-a-half days! That is one day for each year they witnessed to the masses while living on earth.

Revelation 11:10

And those who dwell on the earth will rejoice over them, make merry, and send gifts to one another, because these two prophets tormented those who dwell on the earth.

THE WORLD REJOICES

The entire world will have enormous hatred for the two prophets and they will delight in their deaths. The world will rejoice! The dead bodies of the two faithful Witnesses will be left to rot in the heat of the sun for the entire world to see. People will make merry and send gifts to one another because Elijah and Enoch are dead. As I pointed out earlier, it's likely that the reference to making merry and sending gifts is both figurative and literal here, for the world will be in such a shocking state of chaos at that point that throwing a party and going to the mall to buy party gifts would be near-to-impossible. Thus, because of the strength of their celebratory spirit, feeling they have *conquered the evil of the Two Witnesses and survived*, humanity will rejoice within, which will in turn motivate them to make merry and give gifts to one another (if they can). Indeed, for those who can dance there will be dancing and celebration in the devastated streets, in the blasted homes, in the plague-ruined countryside.

By painting this picture of celebration and gift giving John is also making it very clear just how much hatred they have for the Two Witnesses and just how relieved they will be when they die: in the heart of darkness and destruction humanity will rejoice.

Even after the death of the Two Witnesses people will fear them, for no one touches them! They will jeer at the bodies. They will dance around the bodies. But they will not mutilate the bodies or drag them through the streets. The world will rejoice for 84 hours, gloating with pleasure and grinning over their victory in destroying their worst enemies, or so they believe.

Little do they realize what is in store for them when Jesus introduces the seventh trumpet, loosening the last seven plagues of the bowls, finally bringing to an end the Age of sin and brokenness, separation, and loneliness. Their hollow victory over the death of the Two Witnesses is their final celebration before their own deaths and eternal destruction!

Revelation 11:11

Now after the three-and-a-half days the breath of life from God entered them, and they stood on their feet, and great fear fell on those who saw them.

WONDER

The nations will see a wonder of wonders, captured on television, cell phones, laptops, the Internet, all technologies! Our sovereign, omniscient, omnipotent God miraculously resurrects the faithful men! Into their nostrils he breathes the breath of life, and Enoch and Elijah instantly become living and beautiful beings! Their rotting carcasses turn into whole, perfect, and young bodies and the two Godly men glory in a radiant light given to them by the Spirit of Jesus Christ forever and forever! They experience a personal resurrection! The people of the earth will see the holy men stand up! What a miracle of miracles for every eye to behold!

Imagine two dead bodies resurrected after lying in the hot, sizzling sun for three-and-a-half days! Now, all will know that the Lord God of heaven is with the Two Prophets—and what's more, this amazing spectacle of the raising of the two Saints will occur in your lifetime, for it is this generation who will witness the coming of the Lord!

Revelation 11:12

And they [all the people] heard a loud voice from heaven saying to them, "Come up here." And they ascended to heaven in a cloud, and their enemies saw them.

EVERYONE HEARS

Humanity will be dumbstruck over the miracle of their resurrection, of course, and then yet another marvel transpires! The sky over Jerusalem suddenly blackens and lightning strikes and loud thunder cries out in the heavens. The sound of a voice is distinctly heard. The Spirit of Christ Jesus roars from on high! His voice is heard from his holy habitation like *Pocahay,* as the North American Plains Indians would say, which means *a roaring wind?* Everyone throughout the world will hear the voice and understand.

Because God relies on patterns and his holy mathematics/geometry, I think it's possible, even likely, that the Lord may command the witnesses to, "COME UP HERE!" seven times (seven being the holy number) in the Hebrew tongue first, and then following that with seven languages of the world. It's also quite possible that when he speaks everyone everywhere will simply hear his voice and understand it. The voice will be instantly and universally translated supernaturally.

The Lord speaks, and just as Jesus ascended into heaven, Elijah and Enoch will also ascend. Parting from the crowds, they will move upward gloriously, viewed by the entire world! Their enemies, witnessing the mighty hand of the Lord at work, watch until the witnesses disappear into an open tunnel of greenish light through the clouds!

NEARING THE FINAL HOUR

This extraordinary event will take place at the end of the terrible second sorrow/Woe. The death of the Two Witnesses happens during the very final days left to humankind.

During the final three-and-a-half years of the Tribulation the Antichrist rules one-fourth of the earth and has powerful influence over the remainder of the world; Elijah and Enoch witness for a period that is a little short of three-and-a-half years (1,260 days), leaving a very brief period between their ascension to Paradise (in the form of the Second Phase of Body, the glorified body) and the great, glorious Second Coming of the Lord Jesus Christ. During this period of time, Jesus will introduce the last plagues of the third sorrow/Woe, which will completely annihilate all life from the earth.

Revelation 11:13

In the same hour there was a great earthquake, and a tenth of the city fell. In the earthquake seven thousand people were killed, and the rest were afraid and gave glory to the God of heaven.

A TENTH OF THE CITY FALLS

Immediately after the Two Witnesses return to Paradise, God's supernatural influence and presence causes a tremendous movement of the earth, shaking the entire city of Jerusalem. His voice rumbles from the darkened sky and a tenth of the city is destroyed. Seven thousand souls perish in the earthquake!

John sees that some of the unrepentant are greatly disturbed and they actually give the God of Heaven credit for the miraculous events. They do this because they are afraid. Yet, even while some will give God credit for these miraculous acts, most will continue to bow down to the Antichrist and his image regardless—and of course the fates of those who have taken the mark of the Beast are sealed. For them, survival is no longer an option.

Revelation 11:14

The second woe is past. Behold, the third woe is coming quickly.

BEHOLD

This is the conclusion of the second sorrow/Woe (the sixth plague). The third sorrow/Woe (the seventh plague) is coming quickly.

That the words *coming quickly* are used here to suggest that the final three-and-a-half years are almost at an end. Everything to come will be compressed into a very short period of time. It's interesting to note that the original Greek word for *coming* (*aperchomai*) can be translated *to come or go*, which suggests compression of time. Similarly, *quickly* in the original Greek (*tachu*) can be read *without delay, by surprise, suddenly,* and *readily*.[11] In light of the compression of time these two words were indeed well chosen.

Revelation 11:15

Then the seventh angel sounded: And there were loud voices in heaven, saying, "The kingdoms of this world have become the kingdoms of our Lord and of his Christ, and he shall reign forever and ever!"

THE SEVENTH TRUMPET
The Third Woe!

The seventh plague: the plague of the bowls.

Loud and clear, the seventh trumpet is heard, coming from the seventh angel, who is the seventh Spirit of the Seven Spirits of God (Jesus Christ). This seventh trumpeting is a warning call from the Son of the Mighty God, proclaiming to the world that the third sorrow/Woe, which officially introduces the seven bowl plagues (as recorded in Chapter 16), is about to begin.

VOICES

Before the plagues of the bowls commence, John hears the voices of the Seven Spirits of God! Seven mighty voices like the sound of seven rushing waterfalls: "The kingdom of this world shall become the kingdom of the Lord Jesus Christ who reigns for a thousand years and henceforth forever and forever on the New Earth!" With the trumpet fading in the distance, Christ proclaims officially that his awesome return in person is about to commence—time is indeed running out.

Revelation 11:16

And the twenty-four elders who sat before God on their thrones fell on their faces and worshiped God.

WORSHIP

While standing in the throne room before the greatness of his Christ, John sees the twenty-four elders, representing Jesus' twelve apostles, the twelve great prophets of the Old Testament, as well as the innumerable company of the saved in Christ, worshiping the Lord and Savior. Clearly, John wants us to understand that this is not only a holy and sacred moment, in which God must be honored and must receive credit and glory, it is vitally important—the plan and mystery of God is nearly complete. Humility is essential.

Revelation 11:17

[The elders are] saying, "We give you thanks, O Lord God Almighty, the One who is and who was, because you have taken your great power and reigned."

THE ONE WHO IS & WAS & WILL BE

John listens to the saved in Christ giving thanks to their Lord God, the One who is and the One who was. (For more information on this subject, refer to Chapter 1:4, under the heading *Welcoming the Seven*.)

He is the One who is to come, for he returns as the King of this earth. Jesus says, "I AM THE ALPHA AND THE OMEGA, THE BEGINNING AND THE END" (Rev. 1:8a). "I AM THE ALPHA AND THE OMEGA, THE FIRST AND THE LAST" (Rev. 1:11a). "I AM HE WHO LIVES, AND WAS DEAD, AND BEHOLD, I AM ALIVE FOREVERMORE" (Rev. 1:18a).

Revelation 11:18

[The elders continue] "The nations were angry, and your wrath has come, and the time of the dead, that they should be judged, and that you should reward your servants the prophets and the saints, and those that fear your name, small and great, and should destroy those who destroy the earth."

THEY SAY

The heavenly multitude says, "The earthly nations should give the glory due to Jesus' name and give to him praise, strength, and honor! They should worship Christ!"

They say, "The wrath of God has come to bring about the extinction of all flesh and blood once and for all."

They say, "The time for the final judgment of the unrepentant that are dead toward Christ has come."

They say, "Believers in Jesus are not judged for their sin, for by their faith they are washed in the blood of the Lamb."

They say, "Those who destroy the earth shall be likewise destroyed."

STEWARDSHIP OF THE EARTH

I think it's important to note here that stewardship of the earth, our responsibility to care for the planet, is mentioned. This suggests that the lack of humanity's stewardship toward the planet is cause for destruction! Some may argue this as purely figurative, but I strongly disagree. Stewardship of the earth and all its animal life carries much more weight than merely the allegorical. The truth is, *stewardship of the earth as Christian duty* is not allegorical and *it is not a new concept*, as some secular and even some Christian proponents like to argue today. Stewardship of the planet has always been and is, in fact, an essential part of a

Christian's calling, made clear in both the Old and New Testament. It is not a modern concept that Christians have finally grafted into Christianity, jumping on to the humanists' save-the-earth-and-go-Green bandwagon at the last minute, better late than never. Genesis 1:26–28 is a fine example: God entrusted the earth to Adam and Eve and all humanity.

If you love God you will be moved by his most Holy Spirit to love what God loves, and it's very clear the Lord loves his Creation. It is our responsibility, nay, our very duty, to love and care for the earth and everything in it. Stewardship of the earth has been part of Christian duty from the very beginning. It should be part of all Christian duty now.

Revelation 11:19

Then the temple of God was opened in heaven, and the ark of his covenant was seen in his temple. And there were lightnings, noises, thunderings, an earthquake, and great hail.

THE END OF THE AGE IS COMING

John witnesses Christ open the great way to God's massive shrine in heaven. Inside, through the emerald brightness coming from Christ, John sees the sacred Ark of his Covenant. This is directly related to the Hebrew Ark of the Covenant which held the two stone carvings of the Ten Commandments, the terms of God's covenant with Israel—it was also called *the ark of the testimony* and *the ark of God* (Numb. 10:33; Ex. 25:16; 1Sam. 3:3; 4:11). The Ark of the Covenant was the symbol of the Lord's literal presence on earth. It was, indeed, an ark of great power (Josh. 3:11–17; 4:7; 11, 8).[12]

The use here also suggests that this is the same ark only made new and complete through Christ. This ark brings together the old and the new covenant, Jew and Gentile, through Christ the living conduit.

Christ displays an awesome degree of power here, for when the Ark of his Covenant is seen there are flashes of lightning, thunder, noises, earthquake, and hail. (The voices of the Seven Spirits of God are powerful.) These are clearly visual metaphors in relation to his power as the supreme and only God. They are also more than that, for they are prophetic visions or images of the End Times, especially in regard to the earthquake and the great hail (the global earthquake and potential bombardment of meteorites during the reformation of the earth).

As Chapter 11 comes to a close, Jesus is about to speak, and when he does, behold, the last seven plagues administered to mankind shall be released, terminating this dispensation!

But now we will have to pause for a moment and wait to hear what the Lord Jesus says, as Revelation 12:1 takes us, like John's journey, back and forward in time.

* * * * *

SOURCES:

1. *Rod,* International Bible Standard Encyclopedia, James Orr, Online Edition, <http://www.studylight.org>.
   Rod, pg. 1085-1086, The New Unger's Bible Dictionary, Moody Press (1988).
2. *Tabernacle,* Executive Committee of the Editorial Board, Eduard Konig, Jewish Encyclopedia.com,
   <http://www.jewishencyclopedia.com/index.jsp>.
   Tabernacle, International Bible Standard Encyclopedia W. Shaw Caldecott , James Orr, Online Edition, <http://www.studylight.org>.
   Temple, pg. 1258-1264, The New Unger's Bible Dictionary, Moody Press (1988).
   Temple (sanctuary, Jerusalem), Microsoft Encarta Encyclopedia (2002).
3. *Eight Good Reasons Why Enoch Must Be One of the Two Witnesses!* Bob Wunderlich, The Xcellent Files, Apocalypse Soon, <http://www.apocalypsesoon.org>.
   Lesson 19: The Temple, the Two Witnesses, and the Seventh Trumpet (11:1-19), Studies in Revelation, Lehman Stauss, Litt.D. F.R.G.S., <http://www.bible.org>.
   The Two Witnesses, David Guzik, Calvary Chapel.com, <http://www.calvarychapel.com>.
   The Unveiling of Jesus Christ; The Two Witnesses, A. E. Knoch, Biblical Studies, Concordant Publishing, <http://www.concordant.org>.
4. *The Two Prophets of Revelation 11* - May 25, 2001, Jimmy Humphrey, Christian Steps, <http://www.christiansteps.com>.
5. *Questions and Answers to Prophecy,* Calvary Prophecy Page, Pastor Malone (1998), <http://www.calvaryprophecypage.com>.
6. *The Details of Passover Are Overwhelming—How Do I Begin?* Seder Tips, Rabbi Raphael Rank;
   Elijah's Cup, Temple Beth El of Greater Buffalo, <http://www.uscj.org>.
   Passover; Festivals, pg. 406-422, The New Unger's Bible Dictionary, Moody Press (1988).
   Passover, contributed by Saul Lieberman, Microsoft Encarta Encyclopedia (2002).
7. *Enoch,* A. C. Grant, James Orr, International Bible Standard Encyclopedia, Online Edition, <http://www.studylight.org>.
   Henoch (Greek, Enoch), A. J. MAAS, transcribed by Don Ross , The Catholic Encyclopedia, Online Edition , Kevin Knight (2002), <http://www.newadvent.com>.
   Enoch, pg. 363-364, The New Unger's Bible Dictionary, Moody Press (1988).

8. *Sackcloth,* pg. 1097-1098, The New Unger's Bible Dictionary, Moody Press (1988).
9. *Biometrics; Where Are We In Bible Prophecy?* John L. Terry, III CEC, CalvaryChapel.com, <http://www.calvarychapel.com>.
   PERSONAL COMPUTING: The Melding of Mind With Machine May Be the Next Phase of Evolution, Rob Fixmer, The New York Times, <http://www.nytimes.com>.
   The End of Death: The 'Soul Catcher' Computer Chip, Robert Ulhig, The Electronic Telegraph, CNI News (England), <http://www.rense.com>.
10. *The Olive Tree,* G. W. E. Masterman, International Bible Standard Encyclopedia, Online Edition <http://www.studylight.org>.
    Olive; Vegetable Kingdom, pg. 1324-1337, The New Unger's Bible Dictionary, Moody Press (1988).
    Olive Trees, Microsoft Encarta Encyclopedia (2002).
11. *Coming—Aperchomai,* #565, pg. 14, Greek Dictionary of the New Testament, Strong's Exhaustive Concordance of the Bible/Dictionary of the Hebrew and Greek Words, Hendrickson Publishers.
12. *Ark of the Covenant,* Willhelm Lotz, International Bible Standard Encyclopedia, Online Edition, <http://www.studylight.org>.
    Ark, pg. 102-103, The New Unger's Bible Dictionary, Moody Press (1988).
    Ark of the Covenant, Microsoft Encarta Encyclopedia (2002).

CHAPTER 12
The Woman, The Child & The Dragon

Revelation 12:1

Now a great sign appeared in heaven: a woman clothed with the sun, with the moon under her feet, and on her head a garland of twelve stars.

TWO THOUSAND YEARS AGO

The entire vision revealed to John in this chapter is multilayered with multiple meanings that change from verse to verse, and that being the case I'd like to start with the first layer: the period of time when Jesus Christ was about to be born.

MARY

A great wonder is revealed to John. He witnesses a privileged maiden, the chosen woman, the human mother of Jesus Christ: Mary. She is *clothed with the sun*, for the brightness of her face (a brightness that is powered by the Holy Spirit) is overwhelming to his eyes! The sun is a symbol of Jesus Christ: "...His (Jesus) countenance was like the sun shining in its strength" (Rev. 1:16); in reference to Christ's coming (Mal. 4:2), the glory of Christ (Matt. 17:2; Rev. 1:16; 10:1), the Savior (John 1:9; Mal. 4:2), etc. The woman in this verse is about to give birth to Immanuel, *God with us*.

John also sees the *moon under her feet*. In the figurative language of the Scriptures the moon often represents the glory of God. The moon is also mentioned in relation to the Second Coming of Christ[1] (Isa. 13:10; Joel 2:31; Matt. 24:29; Mark 13:24). In Revelation chapter 6:12 the moon was said to become like blood, and that's a direct reference to the plagues and the last three-and-a-half years of the Tribulation. In this verse, the meaning also suggests the glory of God and the glory of Christ.

The woman wears a *garland of twelve stars*.

A *garland* was thought of as a crown, usually made out of the natural things of the forest and garden. In John's time they were often used by pagans in rituals or celebrations involving or honoring Nature. The original Greek word (*stemma*) could be translated *wreath*. Since garlands are usually made up of natural materials like twigs and berries this leads us to conclude that Mary, the mother of Christ, is in a symbolic sense the Mother of Nature—after all, she is wearing a garland on her head, a natural, earthy, organic crown. Furthermore, because the Holy Spirit is part of the process of motherhood and Nature, and we know that the Holy Spirit is the guardian and protecting seal of the earth and all nature, Mary also symbolizes the Mother of Earth. When you combine the Holy Spirit's protecting character toward the earth and all nature, his direct involvement with humanity, and the birth of Jesus Christ, you find the truest and deepest meaning of Mary's crown: the Mother of Humanity.[2]

The garland is also made of twelve stars. The implication here is that, yes, nature mother and mother to humanity Mary may be, but she comes exclusively from God's chosen people, the twelve tribes of Israel. She is to marry Joseph, who is of the line of David, who is of the line of Abraham, the father of the Jewish race.

To understand this verse, as well as the rest of the Book of Revelation and the Bible itself, we have to understand the genetic and spiritual connection here: for any of the prophecy to be valid Jesus had to be from the line of David, the tribe of Judah, of the Jewish people. The following text will examine Jewish genealogy and how it relates to Christ more deeply.

BIBLICAL GENEALOGIES

Matthew 1:1–16 gives a full account of the genealogical line of Christ, from Abraham to Christ. Matthew goes on to state in 1:17, "So all the generations from Abraham to David are fourteen generations, from David until the captivity in Babylon are fourteen generations, and from the captivity in Babylon until the Christ are fourteen generations." Clearly, we have a very consistent God, for each period covers two balanced sets of seven generations, which of course symbolize the Seven Spirits of God! There are three sets of fourteen generations representing the Father, Son, and Holy Spirit!

It's important to understand that Bible genealogies do indeed contain gaps and omissions. They are abbreviated. Because of that you cannot use the genealogical lists to date the age of the earth or humanity. Thus, they are not reliable tools in relation to dating the age of the earth/humanity—the total length of time from the creation of Man to the Flood and from the Flood to Abraham is not scripturally documented. (It is, of course, well documented in regard to God's timetable/calendar, which is understood as 6,000, that is to say, it falls into the pattern of 2,000: 2,000 + 2,000 + 2,000 = 6,000 + 1,000 = 7,000—by God's timetable/calendar.) Furthermore, the ancient Semitic languages used words like *beget* and *father* and *bare* and *son* in a rather wide-ranging fashion. Here's an example of what I mean: to *beget a son* could easily have meant to *beget a child* or *grandchild* or even *great-grandchild*. It could have even been used in reference to distant relatives, and thus you get gaps, omissions, genealogical abbreviation.[3]

Biblical genealogies are broad outlines of genealogical history. The accounts are accurate, the records stable and consistent, the genealogical connections not in doubt nor their validity and integrity questioned, but rather than listing all the names one after another for pages and pages and pages, which would have amounted to an endless and unbroken genealogical line that may have given us the ability to date the age of the earth, abbreviation was the name of the game.[4]

The genealogical line of Christ as stated in the Book of Matthew may not name every name in the genealogical line, but it is factual and accurate in relation to its definite Jewish genetic ancestry and the spiritual connection/promise of God to the Jews, validating that Jesus was from the line of David, of the tribe of Judah, of the Jewish people. In that regard it is a reliable, useful, and most trustworthy tool.

Additionally, in relation to genealogical balance and God's holy mathematics/geometry, Matthew 1:1–17 reveals the balanced number patterns of 7, 3, and 14.

PRAY FOR THE NATION OF ISRAEL

Lastly, blessed are they who pray for the nation of Israel, chosen by God, for they are his special people from the time of Abraham to this day! How important they must be when we realize that God chose a Jewish maiden for his Son to be born on this earth!

The Christian worships Jesus, who was born of a Jewish woman in Bethlehem, in the land of Israel, of the line of David. "Behold, the Lion of the tribe of Judah..." (Rev. 5:5). "I (Jesus) am the Root and the Offspring of David..." (Rev. 22:16). Jesus is deeply rooted in the Jewish nation, genetically, spiritually, and prophetically, for he is the Jewish Messiah, as well as the Messiah to the entire world. This genealogical connection is vital, the basic building block in understanding Christ, Judaism, Christianity, and Revelation prophecy.

CHRISTIAN DUTY TOWARD ISRAEL

While I'm on this topic, I'd like to point out that, like loving and caring for the earth and God's creation, loving the land of Israel is also part of the duty of Christians, for it's a direct reflection of a Christian's love for the Lord. It is a Christian's duty to not only love Israel, but support Israel as well, in prayer and other means. (In relation to war, Israel must always be supported and defended). "Pray for the peace of Jerusalem: may those who love you be secure" Psalm 122:6.

In the past, nations that hate the Jews have paid a high price for their hatred, for God is against those who are against his chosen people! The Lord will remove his blessing from a nation that does not support or defend Israel. The nation that resists, fights against or hates Israel, God himself will fight against.

EZEKIEL 38 & 39
A Pre-Tribulation Event

We're going to leave the verse for a moment. I will return to it, of course, for there is a connection here, but it's a little distanced. I will have to go beyond the beginning of the Tribulation to a number of years pre-Tribulation to make the connection.

I've been discussing hostility toward Israel and because of that this is a good place to explore this topic.

Chapters 38 and 39 in Ezekiel refer to *Hostile Nations* that will invade the land of Israel in the *latter days*. The Scriptures make it very clear that any nation who is hostile toward Israel will pay a hefty price. These Hostile Nations fare no better, for God will destroy them completely.

But here is a word of wisdom! Chapters 38 and 39 in Ezekiel are not a scriptural reference to the battle of Armageddon, as so many in prophecy circles believe. This is the battle *prior to* the beginning of the Tribulation, the battle that inaugurates the seven year reign of the Antichrist. Once the battle is complete, the world will yearn for peace and they will find it in the man known as the Beast, and then the seven years of the Great Tribulation will begin, the first three-and-a-half years being peaceful, the last and final three-and-a-half years being utter chaos and hell on earth. When the seven years are finished the battle of Armageddon will commence.

Let's explore this concept in greater detail. Following are some abbreviated accounts found in Ezekiel 38 and 39 describing the destruction of the Hostile Nations.

EZEKIEL'S HOSTILE NATIONS

"Therefore, Son of Man, prophesy and say to Gog (leader of the Russian Commonwealth), thus says the Lord God: 'On that day when my people Israel dwell safely in peace (prior to the Last Days), will you not know it? Then you will come from your place out of the far north (northern Russia), you and many peoples with you (all of your allies will comprise a force of many millions) ...you will come up against my people Israel like a cloud, to cover the land.

"It will be in the latter days (or nearing the Last Days of this Age and time) that I will bring you against my land, so that the nations may know me, when I am hallowed in you, o Gog (a reference to the Russian leader), before their eyes" (Ezekiel 38:14–16).

"'...And it will come to pass at the same time, when Gog (the Russian leader and his allies) comes against the land of Israel,' says the Lord God, 'that my fury will show in my face.... Surely in that day there shall be a great earthquake in the land of Israel.... And all people who are on the face of the earth shall shake at my presence. The mountains shall be thrown down, the steep places shall fall, and every wall shall fall to the ground. I will call for a sword against Gog (the Russian leader and his armies) throughout all my mountains (of Israel),' says the Lord God. 'Every man's sword will be against his brother (ally will turn against ally). And I will bring him to judgment with pestilence and bloodshed (the Russian hoard will face sickness, infection, disease, death); I will rain down on him (the Russian leader), on his troops, and on the many peoples who are with him, flooding rain, great hailstones, fire, and brimstone. Thus I will magnify myself and sanctify myself, and I will be known in the eyes of many nations. Then they will know that I am the Lord'" (Ezekiel 38:18–23).

"...Behold, I am against you, o Gog, the prince of Rosh (leader of the Russian army) ...and I will turn you around and lead you on, bringing you up from the far north (referring to the Commonwealth of Russia) and bring you against the mountains of Israel. Then I will knock the bow (weapons) out of your left hand, and cause the arrows (bullets) to fall out of your right hand. You (Russian leader) shall fall upon the mountains of Israel (while leading your armies), you and all your troops (the armies of your allies, the Arabs, the Germans, and the Turks) and the peoples who are with you; I will give you to birds of prey of every sort and to the beasts of the field to be devoured. You shall fall on the open field; for I have spoken,' says the Lord God. 'And I will send fire on Magog and on those who live in security in the coastlands (the Arab nations who join forces with Russia). Then they shall know that I am the Lord... the holy One in Israel" (Ezekiel 39: 1–7).

"'Then those who dwell in the cities of Israel will go out and (set on fire and burn the weapons...and they will) make fires with them (Russia and her allied forces weapons) for seven years" (Ezekiel 39:9).

Now, this section is probably referring to irradiated weapons of warfare; the metal is lethal to the touch and *burns for seven years.* People in the area will also be trying to clean up the contaminated weaponry and land—the *seven* years mentioned here is the seven years of the Great Tribulation, the last seven years on earth. We'll study this more deeply in the following paragraphs.

In a nutshell, what Ezekiel 38 and 39 are referring to is a war between Israel and Russia (Gog and Magog), and Russia's allies, specifically, Germany, Turkey, Iran, Iraq, Ethiopia, Libya—they will be a great hostile power controlled by Satan (Rev. 20:8). In Ezekiel 38:2, Magog is also identified as a land—the home or country of Gog.

In later rabbinic literature Gog and Magog became symbols for any force or group, military or political, that opposed what they called *authentic religion or its believers.*[5] But on the whole, most biblical scholars believe Gog and Magog relates specifically to Russia and the Russian president.[6]

Ezekiel 38:5–6 lists Russia's allies: "Persia (Iran and Iraq), Ethiopia, and Libya are with them, all of them with shield and helmet; Gomer (Germany) and all its troops; the house of Togarmah from the far north (Turkey) and all its troops—many people are with you."

It is interesting to note that Germany is referred to as an undivided nation (no longer broken in half by a brutal wall). Today, these countries have deep and powerful economic ties with one another, as well as rising anti-Semitism—and for some it is almost policy.[7] In Germany it once *was* policy, legal and binding.[8] This is mentioned as a reminder that what seems impossible today can be very possible tomorrow.

Ezekiel 39:9 mentioned *seven years.*

WHAT SEVEN YEARS IS THIS?

This a direct reference to the seven year period of the great and terrible Tribulation! The war with the Hostile Nations referred to in Ezekiel 38 and 39 happens, not at the end of the Great Tribulation (as some incorrectly think of as Armageddon), but as a war just before the Antichrist declares his kingdom on earth.

The pre-Tribulation war against Israel by Gog and Magog and her allies comes to a sudden and miraculous end because God intervenes and destroys them. This will be recognized by the world as an act of God. It will not be nuclear warfare between Israel and Russia and her allies. Nuclear weapons may indeed be fired, there will be an earthquake of great magnitude and other natural phenomena, but God will miraculously intervene and end the war.

After the Hostile Nations have been destroyed and Israel is spared, the world will be in total disarray politically and socioeconomically, and as a result of the destruction Islam will no longer have a stronghold over the nations. Its influence as a world power will greatly diminish. (This is Islam's Great Fall.) Because everyone, regardless of religious faith (or lack thereof), will know that the Hostile Nations were destroyed by the hand of God, fear will motivate them to elect a world leader to bring lasting peace in the Middle East and the world. The Antichrist will use this knowledge to his advantage—religion will play a hand in his election.

Ezekiel continues: "'It will come to pass in that day that I will give Gog (the Russian leader) a burial place there in Israel, the valley of those who pass by east of the sea; and it will obstruct travelers, because there they will bury Gog and all his multitude...'" (Ezekiel 39:11). We can gather from this that, without doubt, God destroys those who go against the land of Israel, but there are other implications here as well.

Ezekiel explains that the bones of those killed in the war on Israel will need to be marked if someone stumbles upon them and then they will need a *cleansing* (Ezekiel 39:12–16). Most biblical scholars believe the reference to *cleansing the land and the bones,* and the fact that it takes months to do this, indicates nuclear warfare between Gog and Magog and Israel. This is a reasonable conclusion, of course, even if the war is won by a miraculous act of God. Since it's likely that a nuclear strike will occur, the lethal byproduct will remain after the miraculous intervention of God. Thus, the *contamination* will be a direct result of nuclear warfare and (almost certainly) the supernatural intervention of God.

America and the British Commonwealth are mentioned in the prophecy: "Sheba (the Arabian Peninsula), and Dedan (northwestern Arabia), the merchants of Tarshish (England and the British Empire), and all their young lions (America, once part of the British Empire; Canada; Australia; New Zealand; and South Africa) will say, 'Have you come to take plunder? Have you gathered your army to take booty, to carry away silver and gold, to take away livestock and goods, to take great plunder?'" (Ezekiel 38:13).

This begs the question: Does Israel dip its foot into oil in the land of Megiddo? Is that another reason why Magog and its allies have come to plunder Israel? If so, we are talking big stuff here!

The nations mentioned above will be on friendly terms with Gog and Magog, or Russia. They will object to the invasion of Israel, but they will not offer Israel manpower and technological assistance.

They choose not to support or defend Israel and, therefore, they lose God's blessing.

There are a number of reasons why this happens: first, it is the will of the Lord, for God himself protects his people and he wants the world to know it. They are his chosen and he plans to receive the glory; second, a number of these countries may have already lost their blessing from God because they did not or do not support Israel. The British Empire was one!

GREAT BRITAIN'S GREAT FALL

I'd like to follow this line of thought here: historically, whenever a nation removes its support, breaks a promise, or turns its back on Israel, the nation in question suffers, falls from power and ultimately loses God's blessing. An example of this can be seen quite easily and most recently with Great Britain.

During World War I the British government issued the Balfour Declaration,[9] which initially showed Britain's support for the Jewish people. It meant, basically, that the British stood behind the Jews one hundred percent in regard to establishing their own Jewish nation in Palestine. The Balfour Declaration wasn't a treaty as such, but something more along the lines of a promise, a simple formal letter that showed the world that Great Britain approved, but by no means was it legally binding. Interestingly, one of the most powerful forces behind the Balfour Declaration at the time were Christians and Bible prophecy.[10]

Now, in 1922 Britain was given control over Palestine. At that point, it became Great Britain's job and duty to set up a Jewish nation. Making that happen, of course, wasn't going to be easy or simple. Why? Answer: Britain had prior agreements with France and Russia (among other nations) that ultimately made nation building difficult. Additionally, Britain had made promises to those involved with Arab independence.

Great Britain was genuinely concerned for Israel, but nonetheless things began to almost immediately unravel because of one dramatic fact: establishing a nation of Israel was never Britain's goal. In fact, Britain never planned to fulfill any of the agreements. The long-term and undisclosed goal of Britain was primarily strategic, its main interest in the Arab lands, i.e., the oil.

Arab hostility toward the Jews increased and continual Arab rioting finally caused Britain to issue its White Paper[11] in 1939 (also known as the MacDonald White Paper). The two most important policies of the Paper were:

(1) To permanently restrict/limit Jewish immigration to Palestine.

(2) Prove it was not British legal policy that Palestine should become a Jewish State or nation.

The British abandoned Palestine on May 15th, 1948, essentially leaving the future of Jerusalem, the Jews, and the nation of Israel up in the air—left to the winds of fate, a dangerous gamble, a foolish roll of the dice, and a serious miscalculation.

The days of Britain as a world power were over.

It can be argued that the British Empire's power had steadily begun to decline for much of the first half of the twentieth century because they dropped the ball (with no intention of picking it up and continuing to play the game) in regard to setting up the Jewish nation and homeland. The White Paper and British abandonment of the Jews, of course, sealed their fate. When the British Empire no longer supported Israel and chose to kowtow to political maneuverings, resorting to political betrayal by breaking their promise and turning their back on Israel, God removed his blessing and the days of Britain as a world power were over—this conclusion is indeed debatable, and certainly there were other factors involved that led to the fall of the British Empire, the loss of God's blessing would certainly have made Great Britain's Great Fall inevitable. This conclusion seems reasonable in light of Scripture and Jewish history.[12]

AMERICA'S GREAT FALL

This would explain why, in part, the United States of America, a young lion of Great Britain, stands back and does not support Israel during the blockade and war, simply because of its lineage— its ties—with Great Britain. But it does not explain why the Americans turn their back on Israel so willingly, leaving the Jews to the mercy of the Hostile Nations, especially in light of the fact that the United States has traditionally been an ally of Israel. Many scholars have speculated that America will be facing internal problems such as economic disaster, civil war, or Islamic jihad— and those all may play a role, in one form or another—but in 2009 the U.S. administration took a surprisingly hostile turn toward Israel. Today, it appears as if the U.S. may be deliberately sabotaging its ties for geopolitical/sociopolitical reasons just like Great Britain did in the early twentieth century—and if that is the case, the United States of America will lose its blessing from God (if it hasn't lost it already). Since America's new Middle Eastern policy seems determined to target Israel as the bad guy, this may be part of the answer that has eluded eschatologists for generations.

THE PRE-TRIBULATION WAR IS A SIGN

Let us return to the Gog and Magog war on Israel.

We don't know how long it will take to prep for the war. A number of months or years may pass before war is officially declared. (I believe the actual military preparation will be short.)

Russia and her allies attack Israel and the rest of the world does not support or defend her.

The attack begins and at that point God rains down his fury upon the army of Gog and Magog and utterly destroys them. Israel is spared.

The line "brother turning against brother" seems to suggest that some kind of confusion or delusion (panic) will sweep across the armies and aid in their demise.

The point here is that the pre-Tribulation war is a sign. Students of prophecy will know that the Great Tribulation is about to begin, for soon after the destruction of Gog and Magog and their armies the world will shout for peace, and then the Antichrist will give it to them. The time of the Antichrist immediately follows the downfall of the Hostile Nations against Israel.

Considering the turn of events in our world today, God, in Christ, indeed comes in our lifetime! It's hoped that the connection I talked about earlier is clear: national and prayerful support of Israel is imperative. It is a Christian's supreme duty.

Revelation 12:2

Then being with child, she [the woman] cried out in labor and in pain to give birth.

JEWISH MOTHER OF JESUS

John notes that the Jewish maiden chosen for the most important event of all time is impregnated through the power of the Holy Spirit. We are told in Matthew 1:18, "Now the birth of Jesus Christ was as follows: After his mother Mary was betrothed (engaged) to Joseph, before they came together, she was found with child of (through) the Holy Spirit" (Matt. 1:18).

Centuries before Christ was born, Isaiah said: "For unto us a Child is born, unto us a Son is given; and the government will be upon his shoulder. And his name will be called Wonderful, Counselor, Mighty God, Everlasting Father, and Prince of Peace. Of the increase of his government and peace there will be no end" (Isaiah 9:6–7). The child of course is Jesus the Christ!

The virgin engaged to Joseph was ready to give birth, for she cried out in labor and in pain to deliver a Son, Immanuel, God with

304

us on earth! An angel informed the maiden that God found favor with her and that she had conceived a Son in her womb; she and Joseph would call him Jesus. She was told that he would become very great and she was to call him the Son of the Highest, as the Lord God gives him his throne. This is an allusion to the thousand year rest period on the earth and the coming New Earth/reality called Heaven, or the Second Heaven, where he reigns forever.

THE VIRGIN BIRTH

It should be noted here that modern critics of the virgin birth suggest that it is entirely metaphorical. Some of them support the idea that God *entered* a man who was conceived as any other human, which lead to the conception of Jesus who was conceived through normal human sexual intercourse, the natural father being Joseph, and if not Joseph, any another human male would do.

This suggests that Jesus was simply a man who transcended his fallen nature and became divine. The concept is not supported in Scripture, neither in Old Testament prophecies, New Testament doctrine, or apocalyptic prophecy and is considered by most Christians as heretical.

There are also a number of rather extreme critics who equate the Immaculate Conception to rape, suggesting that Mary, the Mother of God, had no choice in the matter and was, in consequence, a victim of the forceful sexual manipulations of God. If you're a reasonable human being who isn't empowered and motivated by hate and ignorance it should be clear that the Holy Scriptures present the Immaculate Conception as being a sacred honor. Out of all women in Creation Mary was chosen to give birth to the Son of God. The radical and deeply insulting concept of *immaculate rape* obviously runs contrary to the Scriptures, as well as to the hearts and minds of Christians and the true nature of Christianity.[13]

The Gospels make it very clear that God impregnated Mary, which of course means that she remained a virgin in the human sense of sexuality. The pregnancy had to be a miraculous act.

Revelation 12:3

And another sign appeared in heaven: behold, a great, fiery red dragon having seven heads and ten horns, and seven diadems [crowns] on his heads.

THE DRAGON!

The angel of Jesus shows another sign to John: he displays Lucifer as a great *fiery red dragon*. This is a direct reference to the Antichrist, the son of Satan. Remember, he and his son maintain that they are one, in unholy imitation of the Holy Father and Son who are, indeed, One. The dragon has *seven heads*, a symbol of control. This further suggests that he controls a place with *seven mountains* or *an undulating terrain consisting of seven hills*. Chapter 17 tells us about these hills: "Here is the mind which has wisdom: the seven heads are seven mountains (or hills) on which the woman sits" (Rev. 17:9).

THE WOMAN IS THE OWRO

The *woman* mentioned in 17:9 is a symbol of a new religion found in the last seven years of our age, what will amount to the worship of the Antichrist through the One World Religious Organization (OWRO). It is not referring to Mary, the mother of the Son of God.

John states that the seven heads have *ten horns*. This informs us that the dragon controls ten leaders of ten different nations from the place with seven hills: "The ten horns which you saw are ten kings..." (Rev. 17:12a). In Verse 1 of Chapter 13, John says, "Then I stood on the sands of the sea. And I saw a beast (the Antichrist) rising up out of the sea, having ten horns (the ten nations) and seven heads (the seven mountains or hills)." It is interesting to note that before the ten countries form into one nation there are more than ten that desire to join the community. With some shuffling around, ten nations end up structuring this new union. They become the ten-valved-heart of all the nations that form the one union of nations.

The Antichrist will thoroughly control ten leaders of the ten countries that are the heart of the unified nation. Could this be the Union of Europe? We shall find out!

A SECRET REVELATION

John reveals a secret revelation in this same verse: the fiery red dragon, Lucifer, wears *seven crowns*. This is an astonishing announcement because it clearly suggests that the Seven Spirits of God—the power source of God, so to speak—were bestowed upon him when he was an angelic servant of God! This would explain why Satan is so powerful. Clearly, he is not *all* powerful, but it seems that he is very powerful indeed, perhaps the most powerful being God ever made. He is the only creation God gave that kind of power to, essentially giving him part of the very power source of God. Or perhaps more accurately, God gave him the ability to *tap into that Power Source,* the Seven Spirits of God, making him second only to Christ in power.

This verse reveals another rather deep and dark secret: Lucifer was entrusted with the Seven Spirits! The prince of darkness, the dragon, God's *right hand angel/creation* in the First Heaven who stood with God *before the throne,* glorious in his power and nature, *stole* what God had given him. Scripture mentions the Seven Spirits *before the throne* in Revelation 1:4: "...Grace to you and peace from him (Jesus) who is and who was and who is to come, and from the Seven Spirits who are before his throne." This strongly suggests that Lucifer had been in the same place or position of authority as the Seven Spirits before the throne, the Seven Spirits of God!

Of course, we know he abused that power, thinking if the angels in heaven worshiped God, who had the Seven Spirits, they should worship him too. After all, he also had power from tapping into the Seven Spirits. He not only demanded worship from all the heavenly angels, he desired to be above the Creator, the Source of all his power! He believed he could become greater than God. He failed to realize (blinded by his pride and lust for power) that the Holy Father exercises authority over everyone and everything!

When all is said and done about Satan, when all that power and pride and mystery is set aside, he is seen for what he is: nothing more than a thief.

THE THIEF IS CAST OUT

Lucifer was then cast out of heaven, "How you are fallen from heaven, O Lucifer, son of the morning" (Isaiah 14:12). "How you are cut down to the ground, you who weakened the nations! For you have said in your heart: 'I will ascend into heaven, I will exalt my throne above the stars of God (the angels of God); I will also sit on the mount of the congregation on the farthest sides of the north (a depiction of the throne itself); I will ascend above the heights of the clouds, I will be like the Most High!'" (Isaiah 14:12–14).

What this information tells us is that Lucifer was cast out of the First Heaven while still retaining the partial power or ability to tap into the Seven Spirits!

But here is good news: Satan cannot keep the power of the Seven Crowns/Spirits, for he is not Almighty God or Jesus Christ, the Son of God. He is a created being and has no authority over the Holy Trinity. Everything that was, everything that is, and everything that is to come is created by the Godhead. "I AM THAT I

AM," says the Lord. It is not possible for a created being to create, and clearly, Satan does not have that power or authority, even though he may be able to tap into the power of the Seven Spirits of God. What was given to Lucifer and then stolen will be returned to the Father by the authority of God himself. The Father is in absolute control.

WRONG SELF DETERMINATION

It's true that we're dealing with stuff of a sublime nature here, and by that I mean, our understanding of it is limited; perhaps it's all we *need* to know.

Still, our incomplete understanding of how and why Lucifer could fall into sin while existing in a perfect universe *closerthanthis* to a divine and holy God should be explored here. Graham Brodie calls it *wrong self determination.* This term suggests that to have genuine free will Lucifer had to exist in a similar state of probation just like pre-Fall humanity.[14] (For related information, refer to Chapter 3:1, under the heading *The Destructive Path* and 5:3, under the heading *What is Under the Earth*, as well as in Chapter 2:7, under the heading *The Tree of Life Foretold.*)

What's clear from questions and even answers like these is that the Big Picture is much, much bigger than we realize, and that being the case many questions concerning Satan and his fall from grace are, at this point in our existence, unanswerable and unknowable. What we do know has been gathered from methodical study of the Scriptures.

THE CROWN WITHIN US

Jesus promises each one of us a *crown*. Each of us has one spirit of life. "...be faithful until death, and I will give you the crown of life," he announces in Revelation 2:10b. John refers to the spirit within us as a crown. "These things says he (Jesus) who has (seven crowns signifying) the Seven Spirits of God..." (Rev. 3:1). This seems to suggest that we human creations have but one spirit of the Seven Spirits of God, that which was given to Satan from God as a gift that he abused and then, in a sense, stole.

Revelation 12:4

His [the dragon's] tail drew a third of the stars of heaven and threw them to the earth. And the dragon stood before the woman who was ready to give birth, to devour her Child as soon as it was born.

A THIRD FALL

John witnesses Lucifer—that serpent of old, that great red dragon who is the devil and Satan—draw "a third of the stars of heaven (the angels in God's heaven, the First Heaven)..." (Refer to Chapter 6:13, under the heading *Stars Fall from Heaven* for related information.) These angelic beings joined forces with Lucifer during the Great War in heaven. The Godhead was victorious, as we know, and God cast Lucifer and the fallen angels out of his domain. The Creator planned for them to be confined to this world forever. One third of the angels were cast out of the First Heaven.

TO DEVOUR

Never again are Satan and his angels permitted to return to the First Heaven. I'd like to point out here, however, that some biblical scholars argue Satan can return to the First Heaven and confront God whenever he pleases—this conclusion is based mostly on the Book of Job. Elsewhere is Scripture it is very clear that Satan can never return to the First Heaven, so perhaps the reference in Job is metaphorical in nature, and by that I mean, since humanity can *come before the Lord* through prayer, it seems reasonable to conclude that Satan can *confront God* through similar means and method, without having to literally re-enter the First Heaven.

Whatever the case may be, the devil, not giving up his fight, continues his war with the Lord on earth, and that's the picture John is painting here: the dragon recognized that God would come to earth through his Son, Jesus. Therefore, as Mary, the mother of God, the chosen woman who followed the ways of God, she who was "clothed with the sun and the moon under her feet," the most honored mother, gave birth to the Son of God, the devil waited with mouth wide open, ready to devour the Christ, the divine manifestation of God in the flesh who was coming to destroy sin and the devil. The birth of the Christ meant God was going to change the very nature of his human creations, raise them to a higher state of being through his grace and divine purpose, raising them to a position higher than the angels, transforming them into creations that genuinely reflected and were directly connected to the divine, the Seven Spirits of God!

Everything Satan had, humanity was going to get through Christ!

Genesis 3:15 says, "...I (God) will put enmity between you (Satan) and the woman (the church of Jesus Christ) and between your seed (the Antichrist) and her seed (Jesus the Christ). He (Jesus) shall bruise your head (by sentencing him to death in the lake of fire), and you (Satan) shall bruise his (Jesus') heel (by his death on the cross)." What we can gather from these verses is that, clearly, there has been continuous battle between Jesus Christ and Satan from the time the Evil One was cast out of heaven.

Revelation 12:5

She [the woman] bore a male Child who was to rule all nations with a rod of iron. And her Child was caught up to God and his throne.

THE BIRTH OF JESUS

John continues to paint the picture of the birth of Jesus, and he delights at the wonder of it: an angel of the Lord informed Joseph, "...She (the virgin Mary) will bring forth a Son and you (Mary and Joseph) shall call his name Jesus (*Savior*), for he will save his people from their sins" (Matt. 1:21).

The One born is meant to rule all nations on earth strictly and wisely ("with a rod of iron") until the end of the earth, and beyond the end of the earth! He came to give his creations eternal life so that they would never perish: "Neither shall anyone, including the devil, snatch them out of my hand," Jesus declares in John 10:28.

Joseph's wife gave birth to the child and she was protected from the Evil One when Jesus Christ was born. She was, in fact, protected by the Holy Spirit who is present everywhere. Speak to him and he shall hear. Spirit with spirit shall meet. Closer is he than breathing and nearer than hands and feet: "I AM WHO I AM!"

The child is caught up to God and his throne: Jesus faces crucifixion, death and resurrection, returning to his throne in heaven to find reconciliation with his Holy Father, victorious over death and Satan.

Revelation 12:6

Then the woman fled into the wilderness, where she has a place prepared by God, that they should feed her there one thousand two hundred and sixty days.

INTO THE WILDERNESS

After seeing the great power given to Lucifer and seeing him thrown out of heaven with many millions of heavenly angels, and the outcome; after seeing the glory of the birth of his Lord by the honorable mother, and the wonder of it; after witnessing these marvels and astonishing events, John is shown yet another awesome picture, this time looking far into the future.

ONE WOMAN = THREE WOMEN

The allegorical nature of *the woman* in this verse changes in meaning. Let's peel the layers away:

(1) Mary, the Mother of Jesus.

(2) The future Apostate Dominant Church under the banner of the OWRO, embodied primarily by the corrupted Holy Roman Catholic Church.

(3) The 144,000 Jews, a very special branch of the Church—for two millennia the Church survived persecution and great affliction caused by the prince of this world (and, conversely, persecuted and afflicted many in the name of Christ, to Christianity's shame), and now this woman before John, the last Church of Christ found at the conclusion of our dispensation, finds herself in the heart of the Great Tribulation. This branch of Christianity is shown fleeing into a wilderness, pursued by the soldiers of the Antichrist and the powers of darkness.

The 144,000 Jews firmly believe in Jesus Christ as their Messiah, as foretold by the Old Testament prophets. These believers have been supernaturally protected from the ensuing plagues and even from death itself, and they take rest in a place that has been specially prepared and preserved for them in a wilderness.

The woman flees to a desert place or mountainous terrain, and God is with her. For 1,260 days (three-and-a-half years) she hides from the raging dragon and demonic angels.

WHEN YOU SEE THE ABOMINATION

God's Son warns in Matthew 24:15–27: "...when you see the 'Abomination of Desolation' (the image of the Antichrist erected in Jerusalem at the time when he declares himself God) spoken of by Daniel, the prophet, standing in the holy place (the newly built Temple in Jerusalem), then let those who are in Judea (the 144,000 Jews) flee to the mountains (the rest of the left behind believers, as well as any Jews believing in the Lord who are not counted in the 144,000, whether in the land of Israel or around the world, will hide in the countryside, and of course, every one of them will be hunted down and killed). Let him who is on the housetop not go down to take anything out of his house. And let him who is in the field not go back to get his clothes," says Jesus.

After the Fourth Rapture, the saved in Christ who remain on earth—the martyrs, excluding the 144,000—should instantly flee for their lives, for, quite literally, the devil himself will be on their heels. This is a warning to those believers who will have to face the last three-and-a-half years of the Tribulation. It would be wise not to return home or seek out their loved ones at this desperate time, for that course of action would more than likely lead to their quick capture and death. In any case, travel anywhere without the mark, the global biometric system, will be difficult and dangerous. For example, purchasing fuel for a vehicle and even food will be near-to-impossible without being a part of the system. Escape will only prolong the inevitable: they all will be caught and martyred.

"But woe to those who are pregnant and to those who are nursing babies in those days (trying to escape will be especially difficult for the expectant mother and those with infants). And pray that your flight may not be in winter or on the Sabbath. For then there will be great tribulation, such as has not been seen since the beginning of the world until this time, no, nor ever shall be. And unless those days were shortened, no flesh would be saved; but for the elect's (the 144,000 chosen servants of God) sake, those days will be shortened."

The Sabbath is mentioned here because of the many rules that must not be broken on the Sabbath for orthodox Jews—having to flee on the Sabbath would have been difficult. Having it fall in the season of winter would only make escape harder. The point here, of course, is that it's going to be an unpleased and difficult period.

FALSE CHRISTS & TIMES/DATES

"Then if anyone says to you, 'Look, here is the Christ!' or 'There!' do not believe it! For false Christs and false prophets will rise and show great signs and wonders to deceive, if possible, even the elect. See, I (Jesus), have told you beforehand. Therefore, if they say to you, 'Look, he (Christ) is in the desert!' do not go out; or 'Look, he (Christ) is in the inner rooms!' Do not believe it."

This verse has a meaning that is layered in relation to false Christs and time/dates:

(1) It spans the entire Church Age.

(2) It is an indicator that the End Times are fast approaching—when many false Christs appear throughout the world the End Times are near.

(3) It focuses specifically on the last three-and-a-half years of the Tribulation when *the* false Christ rises to power.

CHRIST IS SELF-EVIDENT

When the genuine Christ appears it will be self-evident: Jesus says, "For as the lightning comes from the east and flashes to the west, so also will the coming of the Son of Man be." There will be no mistaking the return of Christ, for the skies will announce his coming with ominous clouds rolling in, darkening the day. The sun and the moon will appear to turn blood red. The winds will roar. Jesus tells us that his coming will be announced by heaven itself, therefore we are not to be fooled. He will appear in the sky for all to see.

Following this line of thought, John describes the glorious return of Christ in Revelation 19:11–12: "Then I (John) saw heaven opened, and behold, a white horse (John sees Jesus descending on the white horse). And he (Jesus) who sat on him was called Faithful and True, and in righteousness he judges and makes war. His eyes were like a flame of fire (the power of the Seven Spirits of Life), and on his head were many crowns (this is allegorical in nature, but in any case, at least as many as seven crowns, representing the Seven Spirits of God, which are the Seven Spirits of Life)..." (Rev. 19:11–12).

Even though everyone in the world will *see* the returning Christ, the Lord will have a very specific destination in mind: the valley of Armageddon near Jerusalem—not Salt Lake City or any other city or place anywhere else in the world, as a matter of fact. The Scriptures make this utterly clear. During the battle, near the conclusion of the Tribulation of seven years, the Lord will appear, and once again his return will be unmistakable: Matthew confirms this in Chapter 24, Verses 29–30, "Immediately after the tribulation of those days the sun will be darkened, and the moon will not give its light; the stars (referring to the holy angels of First Heaven) will fall from heaven (to witness the great event of the returning Christ and the reformation of the earth), and the powers of the heavens will be shaken (by the Son, for the very nature of our heavenly stars and planets and universe, i.e., reality, will be transformed into perfection). Then the sign of the Son of Man will appear in heaven, and then all the tribes of the earth will mourn..."

Revelation 1:7 assures us, "Behold, he (Jesus) is coming with clouds, and every eye will see him, even they who pierced him..."

Matthew Chapter 24, Verse 31: "And he will send his angels with a great sound of a trumpet, and they will gather together his elect from the four winds, from one end of heaven to the other." Etc.

The Scriptures make it more than clear that it's easy to discern between the genuine return of Christ and a false returning Christ.

When you apply this to men and women calling themselves the embodiment of Christ today, returned or otherwise, reincarnated, channeled, brought back by a UFO, showed up quietly in 1914, whatever the case may be, it's a rather small and reasonable step to go from there and say that anyone who calls him or herself the Christ or a Christ and yet doesn't appear in the manner in which the Scriptures give explicit detail is obviously not the genuine Christ. (In Chapter 19, Armageddon and the coming of the Lord are explained in full detail.) You do not have to be a brain surgeon or a rocket scientist to identify the return of Jesus Christ. It will be absolutely unmistakable and humanly impossible to imitate, as clear and as simple to recognize as the dawning of a brand new day.

Revelation 12:7

And war broke out in heaven: Michael and his angels fought with the dragon; and the dragon and his angels fought.

THE GREAT WAR & SATAN REVISITED

We have now returned to the Great War in God's heaven (the First Heaven). This verse is speaking directly about those events. Earlier in this chapter I mentioned that we have a limited understanding of what took place in relation to the Great War, but even so, I will continue to explore some related concepts here.

To gain a better understanding of the Great Heavenly War we really have no choice but to continue to examine the nature of Lucifer: we know that Satan was the most powerful and most beautiful angel God had created and that he chose to be independent of God; he was given a great deal of power and then decided to usurp the power from the Power Source. He was called the great, exalted *Son of the Beautiful Morning*, the angelic being who was said to be "full of the understanding of what is true," and perfect in beauty. His pride demanded that he rise above the level of the congregation, higher than the heights of the clouds, and above the north, which represents heaven. This in turn led to the Great Battle in God's First Heaven.

The original appearance or form of Satan and angels was discussed in Chapters 3:1, 4:8; 5:3 and 5:11, but this description of Satan from Ezekiel is fascinating, and telling, and it helps us peer into a corner of that mysterious Big Picture: "You were the seal of perfection, full of wisdom (for he was given the Seven Spirits before the throne) and perfect in beauty. You were in Eden, the garden of God. (In fact, he was in the First Heaven. As you may recall, this Third Earth's Eden was merely a copy of the First Heaven's glorious garden.) Every precious stone was your covering: the sardius, topaz, and diamond, beryl, onyx, and jasper, sapphire, turquoise, and emerald with gold (nothing could have been more breathtaking). The workmanship of your (Lucifer's) timbrels and pipes was prepared for you on the day you were created." Clearly, his literal appearance/original form was too wonderful to comprehend.

"...I (the Lord) established you. You were on the holy mountain of God (the Lord's sacred throne); you walked back and forth in the midst of fiery stones. (The *fiery stones* are the Seven Spirits of Life before the throne. Again, it seems clear that God had given Satan the ability to tap into his very own Power Source.) You were perfect in your ways from the day you were created, till iniquity was found in you... You became filled with violence within, and you sinned, therefore I cast you as a profane thing out of the mountain of God (out of the First Heaven)... Your heart was lifted up because of your beauty. You corrupted your wisdom for the sake of your splendor... You...shall be no more forever" (Ezekiel 28:12–19).

Scripture vividly states, "And he (Jesus) said to them (his apostles), 'I saw Satan fall like lightning from heaven (to this earth, where the multidimensional underworld became his kingdom)!'" (Luke 10:18).

Lucifer was removed from heaven like a thunderbolt of lightning! Many scholars believe this reference is entirely metaphorical, and perhaps that is indeed the case, but conversely, considering the supernatural nature of the event we're discussing it is plausible, even true, that Satan fell from heaven in a way that was similar to lightning, that when he *entered into* our dimension and universe it impacted the nature of this universe and reality in a way that could be heard—sonic booms—and seen—like lightning.

This leads me back to the verse and John's description of the Great War. We will focus specifically on the archangel Michael here.

THE ARCHANGEL MICHAEL

It should be made clear that nowhere in Scripture does it say that Michael is allegorical in nature, unless you take the stand that most everything in the Bible is metaphor. The Bible and its authors did not take that view. I do not take the allegorical position either—as far as the Bible is concerned, Michael is a real hyperdimensional angelic being created by God.

Michael means *who is like God?* He is one of the chief princes or archangels (Dan. 10:13; Jude 9) in the angelic order, and he is actually called *the prince of Israel* (Dan 12:1). From this we can gather that there is a definite angelic order or structure, a system of government and power. He is a special guardian of the Jews and will always defend them, especially in regard to what they will face during the Great Tribulation (Jer. 30:5). The angel Michael will be the *supernatural protection to the 144,000 Jews* that I discussed earlier. This seems to be his primary purpose. In the Old Testament, Michael is clearly the guardian of the Jewish people. In the New Testament we discover Michael fought against Satan during the Great War in the First Heaven and that he is deeply involved with the Christian Church, taking a direct part in the struggles of the Church. Interestingly, Jude 9 and 2Peter 2:11 tell us about a confrontation between Satan and Michael in which Michael was almost reverential toward Satan. He showed the Evil One a great deal of respect. If Satan has the ability to tap into the Seven Spirits of God, what would give an extraordinary amount of power to a created being, respect toward Satan would seem a wise choice. I'd argue Michael never let his eyes or his guard down when facing him. This helps us understand who or what we're dealing with a little better.[15]

THE NORTH STAR POINTS THE WAY

Following a fascinating side-note, there's an ancient belief that the North Star points toward the headquarters of God. Ideas like this were not unusual in John's time and many people subscribe to the belief today. Some ancient cultures thought the Milky Way Galaxy, our brilliant spiral galaxy that you can see wrapping around our nighttime sky, was *the pathway to heaven.* Taoists regard the North Star as the Center, the Source of the Universe, calling it *the Gateway to Heaven.* And some contemporary biblical scholars refer to the North Star as *God's Throne Room,* agreeing with the ancients and modern day Taoists, at least in concept.

But here's where it gets really interesting: the North Star is named Polaris, and as it turns out, it isn't a single star at all; it's actually a triple star system that looks like one star. Three stars that look like one star from planet earth—a coincidence? Not likely. It's an example of God's holy mathematics/geometry at work! One and three; three are one. Strangest of all, the earth's axis is aligned with Polaris and there appears to be a dark void around the star, a so-called *empty space*, what some scholars have suggested may be the visible result of the War in Heaven (Isaiah 14) and the *empty space* mentioned in Job 26:7.

Since that is the case, I ask, is it possible that the headquarters of God or the literal *pathway to God and his First Heaven*—wormhole, black hole?—is in the direction of the North Star? Ancient beliefs tend to have kernels of truth imbedded deep within them, and it does make a kind of enchanting sense in regard to the north representing heaven and the use of the star in Scripture, which can sometimes refer to or be called a pathway to Christ.

Revelation 12:8

But they did not prevail, nor was a place found for them in heaven any longer.

DRIVEN OUT OF THE FIRST HEAVEN

Lucifer fought with all his cunning and all his strength. He was out numbered two to one by the angels, with God directly behind them. He could not prevail. Victory was the Lord's. Thus, he was driven out of the First Heaven. When the spiritual dust settled, they were gathered together and shut up in the prison of this earth/reality/universe! Through conceit, Lucifer lost it all.

This is noteworthy, of course, because it can be applied to all of us, a moral lesson for us to always remember and try to put into practice. Arrogance leads us to this same fate. We face the same test.

OPEN YOUR HEART BY FAITH

Jesus is at the door to your spiritual heart, asking you to let him in. Be strong in your faith. Open the door and ask him in. "God is our refuge and strength, a very present help in trouble. Therefore we will not fear, even though the earth be removed, and though the mountains be carried into the midst of the sea; though its waters roar and be troubled, though the mountains shake with its swelling.... The Lord of hosts is with us (his faithful). The God of Jacob is our refuge" (Psalms 46:1–3, 7).

"Now faith is the substance of things hoped for, the evidence of things not seen. But without faith it is impossible to please him, for he who comes to God must believe that he is, and that he is a rewarder of those who diligently seek him" (Heb. 11:1, 6).

By faith, Noah prepared the great ark.

By faith, Abraham obeyed God by seeking out the place he would receive as his inheritance.

By faith, Abraham's wife Sarah conceived at ninety years old and from her seed was born as many descendents as there are stars in the skies!

By faith, Joseph made mention of the departure of the children of Israel from the land of Egypt hundreds of years before it transpired.

By faith, Moses renounced Egypt, not fearing the wrath of the king.

By faith, he passed through the Red Sea.

By faith, the walls of Jericho fell.

By faith, we are saved!

Oh, we of little faith. Where is our hope without firm faith in God through Christ Jesus?

Revelation 12:9

So the great dragon was cast out, that serpent of old, called the devil and Satan, who deceives the whole world; he was cast to the earth, and his angels were cast out with him.

EARTH & SATAN FOREVER LINKED

What took place after the Great War should be pretty clear at this point, so I won't go over it again, but I would like to focus on the relationship between Lucifer and the planet earth: the two will forever be linked. Because this old earth has been corrupted by Satan and the fallen nature, and even though Jesus purifies its surface and perfects time (potentially) and the universe for his one thousand year reign during the Kingdom Age, sadly, it will never be free of the Evil One. In fact, it will turn into his eternal prison. God's plan is to separate his universe/reality (the First Heaven, the Second Heaven, and whatever else there may be) from sin (the fallen nature) and anything that has been tainted by sin (this world and its fallen nature). He does that by *rolling up* the earth, moon, sun, and planets, in fact, our entire universe, and puts it beyond the reach of his faithful for eternity! In light of quantum physics and the broadening knowledge of the bizarre behavior of our universe, the unlimited possibilities, rolling up the universe entire is a concept that is in fact quite credible, understandable, and very doable—certainly, in relation to God. Without a doubt, the Evil One and this earth are inescapably and forever linked.

A CREATED BEING ALTERED

With all this talk about Satan and his power and that even the holy angels treat him with respect, we should remind ourselves that Satan himself is a created being, just like the angels who follow him—just like, in fact, you and me. All were created by God.

It seems clear that wickedness or sin (the fallen nature, which is not only contrary to God, but separated from, or *as separated* from God as anything in Creation can be from its Creator) altered Lucifer's form. All his great power aside, he lost his splendor and beauty. This is a clear indication that separation from the Creator affects all created things. The more sinful one becomes (or the further one moves away from the Creator), the more *un-Godlike* one's appearance becomes! This is seen with people on earth. Though they may be handsome in the beginning because of their fallen nature and sin (as well as the fallen nature and makeup of the universe), attractive features vanish—in most cases, the darker our thoughts, the more we resemble them, and for those who try and appear to succeed in hiding their darkest hearts and thoughts behind beauty, the *Dorian Grays* of our world, even they, like everything else in this broken universe, cannot hide their darkness forever—dark hearts will eventually break under the weight of their own corruption. Even if their outward beauty somehow makes it to the last, in the end their sinful dark hearts will take them in death.

Revelation 12:10

Then I [John] heard a loud voice saying in heaven, "Now salvation, and strength, and the kingdom of our God, and the power of his Christ have come, for the accuser of our brethren, who accused them before our God day and night, has been cast down."

THE POWER HAS COME

A voice from heaven is heard like mounting thunder. The words come from the Lord. He tells John that Lucifer has been removed from heaven and has been cast down in defeat, and salvation, strength, the kingdom of God, and the power of Christ have come.

Satan was cast down and defeated by Christ Jesus, who came as a man to remove the curse of sin and death. He took on all the sins of humankind so that we would be free under grace. For us he died, rose from the dead, and was resurrected by his Father forevermore. All who believe in Christ, by faith, are also resurrected in like manner, living forever with him. This is the great promise of Jesus, the victor.

Revelation 12:11

They overcame him by the blood of the Lamb and by the word of their testimony, and they did not love their lives to the death.

OVERCOME

Jesus tells John that the believers overcome the devil by the blood of the Lamb and by the word of their testimony. The phrase *and they did not love their lives to the death* has a twofold meaning:

(1) It concerns all the martyred for Christ throughout the Church Age, those who did not put themselves and their lives first.

(2) The Tribulation martyrs, for they will not try to save their lives by denouncing their God. The faithful martyrs are true to Jesus. Their conviction in Jesus Christ becomes extraordinarily strong in view of the fact that they are left behind because of the lukewarm nature of their faith. In the heat of what will be horrific

persecution, by faith they will reach out to him and be saved! "Awake! Stand up! The Son has covered the martyrs with the shadow of his hand that they shall not die in the abyss!"

Revelation 12:12

"Therefore rejoice, O heavens, and you who dwell in them! Woe to the inhabitants of the earth and the sea! For the devil has come down to you, having great wrath, because he knows that he has a short time."

A SHORT TIME

The heavens and everything in them rejoices because the Evil One has been vanquished, imprisoned in the universe/reality of our earth. The word *heaven* in the original Greek (*ouranos*) reads as *the abode of God*,[16] and it's interesting to note here that it is used in the plural, which suggests the hyperdimensional nature of Creation. Creation is layered like God: there is a First Heaven, a Second Heaven, and our universe the Third Heaven, and of course that means there's potential for many more layers or realities/universes to exist. Infinite potential aside, I am absolutely convinced that there are only three layers, three realities/universes, a direct reflection of the Trinity.

The Son warns the people on earth, for the devil has been banished from heaven and is now locked forever into our world with all his fallen demonic angels. Christ tells us that Lucifer's anger is great. He is determined to bring the world's population down to his wicked level. Apparently, Satan does not wish to spend eternity within the lake of fire, the bottomless pit, alone, and he is well aware that time is short.

As a note of interest, even though Satan is a spiritual creature and multidimensional it's highly likely that he is stuck in imperfect time like the rest of humanity and this universe. He is not God, who is timeless and omnipresent and omniscient, that is to say, beyond time, existing everywhere in Creation at once. Neither is he all-knowing. Satan has probably had to suffer through the years, watching the second hand tick ever so slowly forward, forward, forward for millennia until the return of Christ. If that is the case, his agonized watching of the second hand is nearly over, for the clock of time rapidly advances to the final years when Satan's time, and ours, actually runs out! Undoubtedly, he is a desperate creature.

Revelation 12:13

Now when the dragon saw that he had been cast to the earth, he persecuted the woman who gave birth to the male Child.

SATAN PERSECUTES THE CHURCH

The devil has got nothing to lose. He is fully aware that he is no longer a citizen of God's kingdom. He is, in fact, experiencing what it is like to be separated from the presence of God, or as separated as a created being can be from its Creator, similar to us. We long to be connected to God. Imagine how it must be for Satan who once was directly connected to God, knowing that he will never have that again and that we will. This must cause him to stamp his feet in a maddened rage.

Thus, he has made a special point of persecuting the Jews and the Church of Jesus Christ, as well as corrupting them and using them to persecute themselves and the world. He has constantly afflicted the righteous since the origin of mankind. He left his lair like an enraged dragon and has been devouring humanity ever since, by the millions and the billions—the time is long and the number is vast. Watch out, inhabitants of the world! He places his black cloak around the people and snatches them into darkness! Let the Son place his bright wings around us and take us into the light and everlasting life.

Revelation 12:14

But the woman was given two wings of a great eagle, that she might fly into the wilderness to her place, where she is nourished for a time and times and half a time, from the presence of the serpent.

THE 144,000 IN HIDING

This is a direct reference to the last three-and-a-half years of the Great Tribulation, *a time and times, and half a time*. Satan, through his son the Antichrist, will set his sights on the 144,000 chosen servants of God who are of the Church of Christ. They are the *woman* in this verse. These believers will be the only remaining congregational body of Jesus.

The rest of the saved in Christ will be scattered, hunted, and slaughtered to the last.

By the power of the Holy Spirit, the 144,000 will be supernaturally protected. The phrase *two wings of a great eagle* is probably referring to the supernatural protection of the Spirit, as the Spirit guides the 144,000 who have the seal of God to the place mentioned as the *wilderness*.

PETRA

It is quite likely that this wilderness is in the vicinity of *Mount Hor*, and even though this location, known as Petra, has traditionally been embraced as the prophetic wilderness the 144,000 escape to, no one knows precisely or if indeed it will be that place. But in light of the historical and scriptural evidence all arrows seem to point to Petra.

John discloses that the Lord, through the Holy Spirit, leads the 144,000 Jews to this special wilderness area, possibly through a maze of canyons, to a hiding place of times gone by. He does this in order to protect them from the *killer* who is "dreadful and terrible, exceedingly strong... (with) huge iron teeth...devouring, breaking in pieces, and trampling the residue with his feet" (Dan. 7:7). This can be taken literally and can be summed up by saying the Antichrist will *stamp his feet with rage!*

In this desert terrain, the 144,000 will be absolutely protected from the presence of the serpent, the plagues, and even death itself for three-and-a-half years! This miraculous escape from the Antichrist will occur in the middle of his reign, right under his nose, at the time he declares himself god in the sacred temple in Jerusalem. This event starts the final countdown for the final forty-two months of all fallen flesh and nature on earth!

A HIDDEN & ANCIENT CITY

Could the hidden and ancient city, Petra, situated in Jordan, be this wilderness and hiding place where these supernaturally protected servants of God flee? Is this the reason why Israel and Jordan signed a peace treaty in the latter part of 1994, making it possible for Jewish citizens to freely cross the border? Whatever the case may be, the prince of darkness will certainly be hunting God's chosen Saints, and knowing their whereabouts he will seek to destroy them! The serpent, working through the Antichrist, will come up with an evil and destructive plan. To carry out his deed he will send forces to the wilderness. Before going on, I'd like to pause here and explore this barren and empty region, walk through the streets of Petra itself.

Petra (it's about fifty miles south of the Dead Sea) is famous for its Hellenistic tombs carved in rock. *Petra* means *rock* in Greek (Latin *petrae*). That's what it is: a city carved in rock. Not much is known about Petra (nothing concrete, at any rate, other than historical tradition) until around 312 B.C., when the Arab tribe of the *Nabataens* made Petra their capital. They were brilliant tradesmen and craftsmen. Through their ingenuity and good business sense Petra became a center for trade in spice, cloth, and incense, exporting and importing goods via camel caravans. The Nabataens were also remarkable hydraulic engineers, for they developed advanced systems for transporting water into Petra, as well as systems designed to remove flood waters. They still function today. Pompey, the Roman general, conquered Petra in 64 B.C. The culture and architecture of the city was forever altered at that point, as Rome had a massive influence on the rock city. As time moved forward and empires came and went and earthquakes ravaged the area, Petra changed and grew and rebuilt and was forgotten by the outside world for hundreds of years.

It's about a mile long and half a mile wide, but only about one percent of the city has been excavated and investigated since its rediscovery. Excavations are ongoing. The surrounding rock cliffs have tombs and buildings cut right into them. Arguably, it's most famous features are the *Khazneh* or *Treasury*, that reaches a height of 130 feet; the Roman theatre that can seat 4,000 people; and *Ed Deir*, a temple 165 feet wide, 148 feet high, with a door 23 feet high. To enter this mysterious and ancient city you have to find your way through a canyon of rose-colored limestone walls. The walls rise hundreds of feet. The main entry is through a narrow fissure in the eastern ridge, known as the *Siq*. When you near the end of the Siq and enter the city, the first thing you see is the Khazneh.

The city has been preserved by God for over two thousand years. Petra is significant in regard to its rock-hewn structures and its place in God's plan with the Jews and Christians. It was rediscovered in the nineteenth century. It hadn't been seen by outsiders for more than 500 years.[17] It's likely God was preserving Petra for the end of our Age.

Revelation 12:15

So the serpent spewed water out of his mouth like a flood after the woman, that he might cause her to be carried away by the flood.

THE HUMAN FLOOD

Petra's well preserved ruins are about 2,700 feet above sea level and 95 miles southeast of Jerusalem, 50 miles south of the Dead Sea, and about 55 miles from the *Gulf of Aquaba*. This is not an impossible distance for 144,000 people to flee in a short period of time, especially in our advanced times when much of the distance could be covered by modern transportation—*two wings of a great eagle* could certainly apply to helicopters or aircraft.

When the Antichrist *stamps his feet and roars with rage* because the servants of God have escaped him, he will devise a wicked plan to destroy the company in one gigantic sweep! The schemes of the schemer are evil indeed! He will plan to *flood* the entrance to the narrow gorge in Petra with a massive army, his intention: to kill every one of the 144,000!

Revelation states that he "spewed water out of his mouth like a flood after the woman, that he might cause her to be carried away by the flood." This is a visual indicator informing us that the Antichrist will gather an enormous army to annihilate Jesus' own! He will be able to easily arrange this, as much of the world's military might will be under his control. With all his knowledge and cunning the Antichrist will prepare an attack on the Jews in hiding. There appears to be no hope for them, as they will probably be unarmed, vastly outnumbered, and there will be no escape!

Revelation 12:16

But the earth helped the woman, and the earth opened its mouth and swallowed up the flood which the dragon had spewed out of his mouth.

THE HUNGRY EARTH

But Jesus Christ will cause the earth to open a large crevasse like a mouth. The *great flood waters* of the Antichrist will be swallowed up by the hungry earth! The army will be completely obliterated, disappearing into the depths. The mighty power of the Son of Man will overcome the wicked deeds of Lucifer. The Lord of Hosts sweeps down to defend his people! What a wonder to behold! Jesus is all power, all strength, all wisdom, and all knowledge. Great is the might of the Lord!

Revelation 12:17

The dragon was enraged with the woman, and he went to make war with the rest of her offspring, who keep the commandments of God and have the testimony of Jesus Christ.

A DECLARATION OF WAR

After the earth swallows the flood of soldiers and their weapons of warfare, the Antichrist will be unable to harm the 144,000 in any way. (It's certainly arguable, but perhaps a divine force-field will encircle Petra and the surrounding area.) Thus, it's doubtful Satan will return to Petra. He will know that any and every attack will be defeated. Because of this supernatural intervention by Christ via Michael the archangel, Satan, the devil, working through his son, the Antichrist, will be greatly humiliated and extremely enraged. The Beast will turn his head from Petra and look to the rest of the world. Stamping his feet with madness, he will go out to harm believers, and vast numbers of the unrepentant on earth will support him!

He makes a declaration of war on the rest of the Church, the Christians that were left behind, those who were not taken in the Fourth Rapture; he declares war on the Jews and all other people who do not support him.

The Antichrist will strike out for three-and-a-half years and succeed in killing all the saved in Christ! John tells us in Revelation 6:9 that when Jesus opened the fifth seal, he sees "under the altar the souls of those who had been slain for the word of God and for the testimony which they held." John continues in Verse 10 of Chapter 6: "And they cried with a loud voice, saying, 'How long, O Lord, holy and true, until you judge and avenge our blood on those who dwell on the earth?' Then a white robe was given to each of them; and it was said to them they should rest a little while longer, until both the number of their fellow servants and their brethren, who would be killed as they were, was competed." As mentioned before, it will be a bloodbath.

SO SUDDENLY FAITHFUL

It seems clear why the left behind believers will become so suddenly faithful, to live for Christ even to the point of death. It's true that before the rapture they will be lukewarm in faith, but afterwards they realize what is taking place. They know they missed Christ's great calling (the Fourth Rapture); they know that only three-and-a-half years remain; they understand that fallen-natured life will be completely coming to an end, and quickly.

Their end comes quickly too. As brother turns against brother, all the saved in Christ will be hunted and found. Their earthly bodies will be killed, solely for being faithful to Jesus Christ.

None living in the Middle East will flee to the wilderness, or Petra, for that sacred place is reserved for the 144,000. (Perhaps no living soul beyond the borders of Petra will be able to get in, no matter how hard they try. This may even apply to dangerous animal life!)

In spite of the mass murder of believers in Christ, it will be a hollow victory for Satan, for he will be completely overshadowed by the return of Christ Jesus, whose glorious resurrection overcame death. Every believer slain by Satan stands to live spiritually with Jesus forevermore in his wonderful New Earth that he created for himself and his people even before the foundations of the world!

This is our great hope—to live forever, even forever and ever, with him when we get to Glory.

* * * * *

SOURCES:

1. *Moon,* C. E. Shenk,, International Bible Standard Encyclopedia, Online Edition, <http://www.studylight.org>.
   Moon, pg. 883-884, The New Unger's Bible Dictionary, Moody Press (1988).
2. *Garland—Stemma,* #4725, pg. 67, Greek Dictionary of the New Testament, Strong's Exhaustive Concordance of the Bible/Dictionary of the Hebrew and Greek Words, Hendrickson Publishers.
   Garland, International Bible Standard Encyclopedia, Online Edition, <http://www.studylight.org>.
   Garland, pg. 458, The New Unger's Bible Dictionary, Moody Press (1988).
3. *Genealogy 1-7; Genealogy 8, part 1 & 2,* Philip Wendell Crannell, International Bible Standard Encyclopedia, Online Edition, <http://www.studylight.org>.
   Genealogy; Abbreviated Genealogy, pg. 462-464, The New Unger's Bible Dictionary, Moody Press (1988).
4. *Genealogy,* contributed by P. William Filby, Microsoft Encarta Encyclopedia (2002).
   Genealogy; Abbreviated Genealogy, pg. 462-464, The New Unger's Bible Dictionary, Moody Press (1988).
   Genealogy 1-7; Genealogy 8, part 1 & 2, Philip Wendell Crannell, International Bible Standard Encyclopedia, Online Edition, <http://www.studylight.org>.
   The Genealogy of Jesus Christ, Louis Matthews Sweet; *Genealogy 1-7; Genealogy 8, part 1 & 2,* Philip Wendell Crannell, International Bible Standard Encyclopedia, Online Edition, <http://www.studylight.org>.
   Genealogy of Christ, A. J. Mass, transcribed by Thomas M. Barrett, *Dedicated to Ann Kracke,* The Catholic Encyclopedia, Volume VI, Online Edition, Kevin Knight (2002), <http://www.newadvent.org>.
   Genealogy in the Bible, A. J. Mass, transcribed by Thomas M. Barrett, *Dedicated to those preserving their family history, The* Catholic Encyclopedia, Volume VI, Online Edition, Kevin Knight (2002), <http://www.newadvent.org>.
   Whether Christ's Genealogy is Suitably Traced by the Evangelists? The Summa Theologica of St. Thomas Aquinas, Second and Revised Edition (1920), literally translated by Fathers of the English Dominican Province, Online Edition, Kevin Knight (2002), <http://www.newadvent.org>.
5. *Gog and Magog,* Emil G. Hirsch, Mary W. Montgomery, JewishEncylopedia.com, <http://www.jewishencylopedia.com>.
   Gog, pg. 490; *Magog,* pg. 804, The New Unger's Bible Dictionary, Moody Press (1988).
6. *The Magog Invasion,* Chuck Missler, article, Koinonia House, <http://www.khouse.org>.
   The Roots of War, part 2; the Magog Identity, article, Chuck Missler, Koinonia House, <http://www.khouse.org>.
   Russia, key Scriptures/current events and links, Prophecy Central, <http://www.bible-prophecy.com>.

Gog, pg. 490; *Magog,* pg. 804, The New Unger's Bible Dictionary, Moody Press (1988).

7. *Anti-Semitism in the Arab World,* Anti-Defamation League;
   Global Anti-Semitism: Selected Incidents Around the World in 2002, Anti-Defamation League, <http://www.adl.org>.
   The New Anti-Semitism: The Transformation of Hate, Professor Stephen Scheinberg, National Chair, League for Human Rights, Professor of History, Concordia University, Montreal, Canada (2001), <http://www.bnaibrith.ca>.
   A New Anti-Semitism? Chief Rabbi Professor Jonathan Sacks, Institute for Jewish Policy Research, Anti-Semitism and Xenophobia Today, <http://www.act.org.uk>.

8. *The Holocaust History Project,* <http://www.holocaust-history.org>.
   Final Solution, Simon Wiesenthal Center Multimedia Learning Center, <http://www.motlc.wiesenthal.com>.

9. *The Balfour Declaration,* Jewish Virtual Library, The American-Israeli Cooperative (2003), <http://www.us-israel.org>.

10. *Balfour Declaration,* Microsoft Encarta Encyclopedia (2002).

11. *British White Paper of 1939,* The Avalon Project at Yale Law School, The Lillian Goldman Law Library in Memory of Sol Goldman, <http://www.yale.edu>.
    What was the Macdonald White Paper of 1939? Palestine Facts, <http://www.palestinefacts.org>.

12. *The Case for Jerusalem,* John Loeffler, World Affairs Editor, Personal Update NewsJournal (1998), Koinonia House, <http://www.khouse.com>.
    Behind the Middle East Crisis, John and Carol Loeffler, Personal Update NewsJournal (2002), Koinonia House, <http://www.khouse.com>.
    Can the Bible Be Taken Literally? A Response to Lenny Flank, Helen Fryman,, Lambert Dolphin's Resources, <http://www.ldolphin.com>.

13. *Why a Virgin Birth?* Chuck Missler, Personal Update NewsJournal, (1998), Koinona House, <www.khouse.com>.
    The Virgin Conception of Christ: A Redemptive-Historical Interpretation, Peter Leithart, Biblical Horizons, <http://www.biblicalhorizons.com>.
    Virgin Birth, Louis Matthews Sweet, International Bible Standard Encyclopedia, Online Edition, <http://www.studylight.org>.
    Creation and the Virgin Birth, Impact, No. 30, Henry M. Morris, Ph.D. (1975), Institute for Creation Research, <http://www.icr.org>.
    Virgin Birth of Christ, A. J. Maast, transcribed by Douglas J. Potter, *Dedicated to the Immaculate Heart of the Blessed Virgin Mary,* The Catholic Encyclopedia, Volume XV, Online Edition, Kevin Knight (2002).
    Isn't the Virgin Birth of Jesus Christ Mythological and Scientifically Impossible? Daryl E. Witmer, AIIA Institute, ChristianAnswers.net, <http://www.christiananswers.net>.
    Mary, pg. 822-823, The New Unger's Bible Dictionary, Moody Press (1988).

14. *Satan (Lucifer),* Graham Brodie, Lambert Dolphin's Resources, <http://www.ldolphin.org>.
    The Eternal Purpose of God; Satan - (Lucifer), Created: 23 - Jan - 1997.
     Last modified: 26 - Apr – 2,000, Copyright © 1998, Graham Brodie, Lambert Dolphin's Resource Page, <http://www.ldolphin.org
    Tree, pg. 1306; *Vegetable Kingdom,* pg. 1340, The New Unger's Bible Dictionary, Moody Press (1988).
    The Garden of Eden; Genesis, Gray's Home Bible Commentary, The Bible Library Delux, version 5.0. suite, CD-ROM, Ellis Enterprises, Inc. (2,000).

What Does the Bible Teach About Angels? ChristianAnswers.com, <http://www.christiananswers.com>.
God and His Angels, L. Lambert, Lambert Dolphin's Resources, <http://www.ldolphin.org>.
The Holy Angels, The Orthodox Page in America, <http://www.ocf.org>.
The Angels of Revelation (continued/addendum), No. 70 & No. 71, James B. Jordon, Biblical Horizons (1995), <http://www.biblicalhorizons.com>.

15. *St. Michael, the Archangel,* Fredrick, G. Holweck, transcribed by Sean Hyland, The Catholic Encyclopedia, Volume X, Online Edition, Kevin Knight (2002), <http://www.newadvent.org>.
   Angel; Angel, Fallen, pg. 61-62, The New Unger's Bible Dictionary, Moody Press (1988)

16. *Heaven—Ouranos,* "the abode of God," #3772, pg. 53, Greek Dictionary of the New Testament, Strong's Exhaustive Concordance of the Bible/Dictionary of the Hebrew and Greek Words, Hendrickson Publishers.

17. *Sela,* W. Ewing, International Bible Standard Encyclopedia, Online Edition, <http://www.studylight.org>.
   Petra, pg. 995-996, The New Unger's Bible Dictionary, Moody Press (1988).
   Petra, A Brief History, The Levant, Al Mashriq, Cultural Riches from the Countries of the Eastern Mediterranean, <http://www.almashriq.hiof.no>.
   Ancient Petra, The History of the Ancient Near East Electronic Compendium, <http://www.ancientneareast.tripod.com>.
   Petra, Microsoft Encarta Encyclopedia (2002).
   Petra, the Great Temple Excavation, Brown University, Copyright© 1999 Brown University, <http://www.brown.edu/Departments/Anthropology/Petra/excavations/history.html>.
   Petra, Los City of Stone, American Museum of Natural History, <http://www.amnh.org/exhibitions/petra/>.

Further reading:

The Summa Theologiae; A Concise Translation, St. Thomas Aquinas, edited by Timothy McDermott, Christian Classics (1997).
Suma of the Suma; The Essential Philosophical Passages of St. Thomas Aquinas Summa Theologica Edited and Explained for Beginners, edited and annotated by Peter Kreeft, Ignatius Press (1990).
A Peace To End All Peace; The Fall of the Ottoman Empire and the Creation of the Modern Middle East, David Fromkin, Harold Hold and Company (1989).
Angels of Light, Powers of Darkness: Thinking Biblically About Angels, Satan and Principalities, Stephen Noll, Inter-varsity Press (1998).
Genesis, James Montgomery Boice, Baker Books (1998).
Petra, Fabio Bourbon, Barnes & Noble Books, Publisher (2,000).

CHAPTER 13
The Beasts From The Sea & The Land

Revelation 13:1

Then I [John] stood on the sand by the sea. And I saw a beast rising up out of the sea, having ten horns and seven heads, and on his horns ten crowns, and on his heads a blasphemous name.

FROM UNDER THE SEA

John is now shown the Antichrist, the son of Satan, "rising up from out of the sea." The sea represents:

(1) The sea of humanity.

(2) The fallen, entropic nature of the earth and reality.

(3) The fallen, dark hearts and nature within humanity. Since the Beast is the father of sin and the fallen, entropic nature, the fact that he rises up from the sea shows us that he influences the sea as well as poisons it because he exists within it, i.e., he influences and corrupts earth/nature/humanity. Additionally, rising up out of the sea suggests that he comes from a much deeper, darker place beneath or below the sea.[1]

The Beast also points to the ancient king, Nimrod. There are a number of reasons for reaching this conclusion, which I will pursue here.

HISTORICAL NIMROD

Let's take a brief look at Nimrod before going on: in the Book of Genesis he was described as "the first potentate (or emperor/king) on earth," as well as being a "mighty hunter in the eyes of Yahweh (God)" (Gen. 10:8–9). He is identified as the son of Ham and the grandson of Noah. Nimrod was an Assyrian (this is important as we are informed that the Antichrist is an Assyrian), considered a builder of empires. His lands included large areas of southern Mesopotamia. Genesis 10:8–11 says, "And the beginning of his kingdom was Babel (Babylon) ... in the land of Shinar. From that land he went to Assyria and built (the renowned city of) Nineveh ..." (Gen. 10:8–11). He has been associated with the Mesopotamian god Ninurta, the legendary Mesopotamian hero Gilgamesh, and King Shamshi-Adad I, the founder of the Assyrian empire (1813–1780 [?] B.C.). He is most famous for building the tower of Babel.[2]

THE TOWER OF BABEL

Tower of Babel: Nimrod instructed his people to build a tower to reach to heaven. In Genesis 11:1–9 the Scriptures tell us that the tower was raised on the plain of Shinar in Babylonia by the descendants of Noah. Nimrod believed he could build a tower that would reach to heaven. His goal: to conquer heaven, similar to Lucifer's goal and his tower of pride that lead to the Great War in Heaven and his being cast to earth in fiery shame and destruction. As Lucifer's pride hurt, disappointed, and angered God, Nimrod's pride did the same thing. In his righteous anger, God caused a confusion of languages among the builders of the tower, bringing its construction to an end forever. Read Genesis 10 and 11: "Now (in those days when Nimrod built the Tower of Babel) the whole earth had one language and one speech. And it came to pass, as they journeyed from the east, that they found a plain in the land of Shinar, and they dwelt there. Then they said to one another, 'Come, let us make bricks and bake them thoroughly.' They had brick for stone, and they had asphalt for mortar. And they said, 'Come, let us build ourselves a city, and a tower whose top is in the heavens; let us make a name for ourselves, lest we be scattered abroad over the face of the whole earth (by the Lord of heaven)'" (Gen. 11:1–4). God scattered these people and their different languages across the face of the earth, and thus a world filled with different languages was born![3] It's possible that the account in Genesis may have been the famous temple-tower of *Etemenanki* (which indeed did fall), and was later restored by King Nabopolassar and his son Nebuchadnezzar II of Babylonia.[4]

NIMROD THE MIGHTY HUNTER

Nimrod was the polar opposite of God's ideal for a king. Being labeled *a mighty hunter* in Genesis is not meant in a positive sense. The term has traditionally been interpreted as *his prey was man*— clearly not a flattering name for a king, mighty hunter or not. Take that a step further and another connection is made: Nimrod was not Man at all but beast, perhaps even king of the beasts. As beast he hunted Man. Thus, the term *mighty hunter* can be interpreted to mean *a mighty hunter of man*.

NIMROD THE ANTICHRIST

The Antichrist is Beast, and similarly his prey is Man.

Now, I'd like to point out, in all fairness to the beasts of this world, that I am not comparing them to him, for that would insult the animals of this world and their great beastly lives.

NIMROD THE ASSYRIAN

Let's examine the coming Antichrist in light of this information.

(1) The Book of Revelation refers to the Antichrist as an Assyrian—this ties in quite nicely with the historical Nimrod, indeed an Assyrian.

(2) The nature of Nimrod as hunter-king and beast-hunting-man is identical to the nature of the Beast whose prey is Man. Nimrod is identical in pride and purpose, both in spirit and in body, because he is the spirit of hell personified in the flesh of the son.

(3) Even though there is no historical record of the death of Nimrod, that the Beast rises from the sea might tell us how Nimrod died. Here's why: whenever the Bible refers to the dead rising, the dead are always described in the figurative language of the Scriptures as rising from the place in which they died or were buried, land or sea. It makes sense scripturally that if Nimrod drowned, when he resurrects as the Beast, the Antichrist, the figurative language of the Scriptures would say he rose from the sea. The Beast rises from the sea.

(4) This leads us to unholy imitation. We know that the unholy trinity imitates the Holy Trinity in regard to number systems, but there is also unholy imitation in design: Jesus Christ came to earth as a man; the unholy trinity duplicates the act in Nimrod. Jesus Christ was resurrected and returns; the unholy trinity duplicates the act in the Antichrist, the return of Nimrod.

MODERN NIMROD

In relation to our modern world, Nimrod's way of thinking seems to fit like a glove. We live in a time when self-absorption is king and it is reaching to heaven, looking to conquer. Of course, pride in humanity is nothing new, but in our day and age the worship of the self seems to have leveled the playing field in the sense of global community. These days, it seems that anyone within global society, regardless of station, will do anything, from the foolish to the profane to the tragic, for a few seconds of celebrity, fame, and fortune.

Additionally, in our modern times crime and violent crime/murder is historically unparalleled: from 1960 to 1996 the crime rate in the U.S. steadily rose a remarkable 313%, and globally crime and violent crime/murder show no signs of slowing.[5] Couple those numbers and realities with the fanatical Islamic movement and their suicide brigades, with promises of self glory and worship, and perhaps the Father and his Son are ready once more to destroy our latest Tower of Babel and scatter us over the face of all the earth with plagues and supernatural wonders through the Great Tribulation. The time of the *mighty hunter* does indeed appear to be upon us.

SEVEN HEADS, HORNS & CROWNS

In the latter days, after the hand of God completely destroys the *hostile forces* that will go against the land of Israel, Satan's son will surely reign from a region having *seven heads*. This is a figurative in nature, describing a city built on seven mountains or hills—the seat of power from which the Antichrist rules. He will fully control *ten horns*, alluding to ten countries—potentially, the ten-valved heart that pumps the body of United Europe. Each of these nations has a leader and these leaders are spoken of as *ten crowns*, all of whom look to the Antichrist as king. (For related information on the meaning of horns and crowns, refer to Chapters 5:6, 9:13 and 12:3.)

A BLASPHEMOUS NAME

The Antichrist and his ten leaders from ten separate countries will work together against God, similar to how Nimrod and his leaders worked together against God during the infamous king's reign centuries ago. They will blaspheme the name of the Lord—and their mocking abuse will indeed reach heaven. The Antichrist (a.k.a., Nimrod, who ruled part of the earth almost four thousand years ago), is given much power in Europe and across the world. Some scholars have suggested that he may use the same name when he returns to power: Nimrod. This is possible, but surely he could just as well disguise it within an anagram or some such clever linguistic device, or use an entirely new name altogether. Whatever the case may be, the name will be blasphemous to God and everything that is good.

In Scripture, the word *blasphemy* usually means *speaking evil of God* or *to curse the name of God* (Isa. 52:5; Rom. 2:24). Along the same lines, there are two clear identifying characteristics to something or someone that is blasphemous:

(1) Assigning evil to God.

(2) Giving the attributes of God to a created being, any created being, and of course in this case that applies directly to the Antichrist.[6]

Keep an eye out for names with references to *the Mighty One*, or *Christ*, and even *David*, for the Antichrist will strengthen himself through confusion, manipulation, and impersonation. Remember, he is a copycat, an imitator of all that is holy.

Revelation 13:2

Now the beast which I [John] saw was like a leopard, his feet were like the feet of a bear, and his mouth like the mouth of a lion. The dragon gave him his power, his throne, and great authority.

LEOPARD

John sees that the Beast, who is the Antichrist, has great power, for he resembles and has the strength of a *leopard*. This informs us that some of the nations he controls will include part of North Africa and the Arabic countries, for the leopard is their symbol.

In the animal kingdom the leopard is well-known and well-respected as a mighty hunter. Clearly, the figurative use of the leopard here is fitting![7]

BEAR

The Beast is also cunning and cannot be trusted, as he has the feet of a *bear*, which tells us that he controls part of Eastern Russia. The bear is the symbol for that region of the world. In Scripture, bears are used to represent craftiness (Lam. 3:10), ferocity (2Sam. 17:8; Prov. 17:2; Hos. 13:8), and danger (1Sam. 17:34).[8]

LION

The Beast roars with great authority and his mouth resembles the mouth of a *lion*. This leads me to believe that the Antichrist's European kingdom will reach as far as the British Isles, for the symbol of Great Britain is the lion. In Scripture, the lion can represent great strength, cruelty, and greed, and in this case the imitation of the royal characteristics of Jesus Christ, the Lion.[9]

The Antichrist will be Christ-like in form, royal and powerful in appearance, whilst his true hellish nature remains hidden from the world. Indeed, his true nature will reflect the nature of the Beast!

THREE ANIMALS = UNHOLY IMITATION

It's worthwhile to note that the Antichrist is described in a number pattern of 3. This is the unholy trinity's imitation of the Holy Trinity's use of the number 3 and its pattern.

That the Antichrist is described as having a multiple-nature (three separate beasts) is possibly a reflection of the multidimensional nature of the Beast himself. The figurative language of the Scriptures is informing us in the most simple of ways about the complex nature of a hyperdimensional being.

It should be evident in this verse that the dragon is a symbol of the Evil One who will be powering this multi-natured creature, the Antichrist, giving him his throne and authority. Of course, their support for one another can in no way be similar to the support of the Trinity. Satanic *support* is tenuous at best, evil and hateful, a dark competition—once again, the exact opposite of the Holy Trinity.

Let us remember that this verse is describing the kingdom of the Antichrist during the Tribulation, which will encompass the same boundaries as those of old Rome. (This is in reference to the old Roman Empire of Jesus' time, revived, and within it the Antichrist is given great authority.)

DANIEL & FOUR BEASTS

Now listen, for this is a word of wisdom! Daniel 7:3–6a tells us: "Four great beasts came up from the sea! (and become mighty on the earth), each different from the other." (They each become part of the Antichrist's new kingdom covering the boundaries of the old Roman Empire.)

SEASON OF THE LION

Britain—the Season of the Lion: "The first was like a lion (referring to the Commonwealth of Britain that grew into a mighty nation), and had eagles' wings. (Spiritually, *wings* can convey Godly principles; this is also a potential prophetic nod toward the United States because it once was a part of the British Empire.) I watched till its wings were plucked off. (The countries forming its great empire were plucked off one by one after the Second World War. This plucking of wings included America, which was plucked off over two hundred years ago.) ... and it was lifted up from the earth ... "

SEASON OF THE BEAR

Russia—the Season of the Bear: "... Suddenly another beast, a second, like a bear ... It was raised up on one side, and had three ribs in its mouth between its teeth. And they said thus to it: 'Arise, devour much flesh!'" This applies to the Soviet Union, its leaders—Lenin, Stalin, Khrushchev, Brezhnev, et al.—and its form of Communistic government during the Twentieth Century, which took peace from the earth.

The Soviet Union was responsible for the murders of many, many millions of people; some scholars argue the Soviet Union might have killed more people than any other government in history. In a general and political sense, the Soviets despised the God of heaven because Satan had them by the tail.

The reference to three ribs probably relates to the carnage or violence the bear inflicted upon humanity. It is interesting to note that the Hebrew word for *rib* is used here (*ala*): in the literal sense the word could mean *rib* or *the side of a person*, but in the figurative it could mean *part of an object* or *part of the sky*, as in, *a quarter of the sky*. With the proliferation of nuclear arms the potential meaning could relate to three parts of the sky: *the bear had three parts of the sky in its teeth.* It isn't too much of a stretch to argue that during the Cold War the Soviet Union controlled three parts of the sky.[10] Unsurprisingly, we find another pattern of three.

SEASON OF THE LEOPARD

The Arab Nations—the Season of the Leopard: "After this I (Daniel) looked, and there was another (beast), like a leopard." This is, as mentioned earlier, a direct reference to the Arab countries of North Africa and the Middle East.

To fully understand how and why the Arab nations fit into this puzzle of prophecy we'll have to have a basic review of Islam, the giant motivator/generator of the Arab peoples and Muslims, as well as briefly examine how it stands in regard to Christianity and Judaism, briefly exploring some of the arguments and debates.

This is a complex subject that requires study, so you are encouraged to explore the truth of it yourself by reading the Qur'an (Koran), the Islamic holy book, and other credible source material.

ISLAM

The Islamic faith is the central religion of the Arab nations and binds them altogether. The word *Islam* means *surrender* or *submission* in Arabic—or more accurately, *submission to the will of God*. The word is related to the Arabic word for peace (*Salem*), but it doesn't literally mean *peace*. A follower of Islam is called a *Muslim*, which in Arabic means *one who surrenders to God*. Islam's central teaching is that there is only one all-powerful, all-knowing God and that this God created the universe. He is called *Allah*.

Attaining peace is one of the goals of all Muslims, but peace can only be attained through true obedience, or more accurately, blind submission to the will of Allah, what amounts to a lifelong and constant struggle/battle to attain peace, justice, and equality.

At first glance the Islamic God comes across as just about indistinguishable in relation to the God of Judaism and Christianity. This is due, in part, because Muslims worship one God. The fact that they have incorporated fundamental components of Judaism and Christianity within Islam also strengthens this perception.[11]

Because of this many people believe the God the Muslims worship is the same God the Jews and Christians worship. Many believe Islam, Christianity, and Judaism are part of the same religion. In regard to monotheism and official Church doctrine the Catholic Church seems to think this is so, concluding that in general all three religions are more or less part of the same whole and they undoubtedly do worship the One True God. But this is almost certainly in error: what Islam basically amounts to is something of a mixture of religions, namely, Hinduism, Buddhism, Mythraism, Greek mystery cults, Judaism, Christianity, and Allah, the Moon-god, a pre-Islamic pagan god and sect. Archeological evidence has been building for the last hundred years or so that strongly supports the conclusion that Islam is a mixture of religions, the actual pagan Moon-god idols exist, and there's a considerable amount of historical and credible linguistic data to back it up, further corroboration Allah did not come from the Bible and that the worship of Allah was not passed to the Muslims via Judaism and Christianity, as Islam claims.[12] This conclusion does not seem unreasonable or intolerably biased in the Christian sense.

Muslims refute the evidence in question as religiously biased and unpersuasive.

You are encouraged to explore the historical and archeological evidence on your own to make an informed decision.

UMMA

Muslims have a demanding monotheism and their dedication to it is most remarkable. All Muslims are equal before Allah. (In regard to the origin of the word *Allah*, the word probably comes from the compound Arabic word *al-ilah*, or *the god*. *Allah* is not Hebrew in origin. If it had been borrowed from the Hebrew Bible, as Muslims claim, clearly it would have Hebraic origin. It does not because it is purely Arabic.[13] This fact effectively shows the clear and obvious path from whence the word came: the heart of Arabic culture/religion.) Because of this they belong to an extremely loyal community, what they call the *umma*—class, race, nationality, even differences in the way each sect within Islam applies Islamic Law are said to be beneath them, or in other words, Muslims are apparently extremely tolerant of differences within their own faith. *The five pillars of Islam,* the ritualistic core of the Muslim faith, are the essential religious duties required of every adult Muslim: the profession of faith (*Shahabad*), prayer (*salat*), almsgiving (*zakat*), fasting (*sawm*), and pilgrimage (*hajj*).[14]

JIHAD

There is an extremely important and essential component to Islam and that's the spiritual struggle against evil, what is called *jihad.* Jihad is the duty of all Muslims. There are four ways to fulfill a jihad: by heart, tongue, hand, and finally sword. In a general sense, and to mainstream or *moderate/liberal Muslims*, jihad is in reference to the inner spiritual battle, as opposed to a literal violent struggle with unbelievers. It is their way to fight against passion, ignorance, addiction, sexual immorality, etc. In other words, it's how they battle against sin.

But it also has a literal interpretation as well. It is their duty to literally spread the word of Islam through one's tongue (similar to Christianity); to choose to do good and avoid evil with one's hand (in regard to *other* Muslims); and to wage war against non-Muslims with the sword.

This last method of jihad is, of course, practiced with great passion and duty today by the fanatical arms of Islam in regard to suicide bombings and global terrorist activities. The mainstream, moderate branches of Islam, the more tolerant branches, tend to try to focus on the inner spiritual jihad, but they have some difficulty dealing with or ignoring the written law of jihad to wage war against non-Muslims with the sword.

There are some mainstream/moderate/liberal Muslims, like the *Imami* and *BohoraIsmaili-Shiites*, who simply will not follow and do not allow hostile jihad—but *only* because they believe the person lawfully capable of encouraging, starting, and supporting a hostile and violent jihad is their *imam* or spiritual leader.

Islamic Law states that all nations throughout the world must surrender to Islamic rule, whether or not they surrender to its faith. Until this actually comes to pass—and that literally means one Islamic World—every adult male Muslim is expected, and commanded, to take part in unmistakably hostile and violent jihads against non-Muslim peoples and nations. The Qur'an without doubt states that those who die in this type of jihad—specifically—will instantly become martyrs of their faith and will be rewarded with a special place in heaven.[15]

KAFIR & AHL AL-KITAB

Ideally, there are only two kinds of non-Muslim enemies: *Kafir* (nonbelievers in Islam) and *ahl al-kitab* (*people of the book*). Buddhists and Hindus would be considered kafir. They would have to convert to Islam or face execution. Once a kafir is converted to Islam, to renounce the faith would be considered a capital offense punishable by death. Jews, Christians, and followers of Zoroastrianism are considered people of the book. (Zoroastrianism is a monotheistic religion of ancient Persia. There are about 30,000 Zoroastrians living in Iran and the religion has a following of about 270,000 people worldwide. It appears to be a religion Muslims are somewhat tolerant toward.) If these people of the book (Jews, Christians, and Zoroastrians) would submit to Muslim political authority they could avoid or even end a hostile jihad. People of the book are allowed to keep their original faith but they would forever be called *dhimmi*, a protected non-Muslim, reduced in social status, something similar to a second citizen, and they would have to pay a poll tax.[16]

MUHAMMAD

The moral character, sincerity, and integrity of Muhammad have been debated for centuries. There are plenty of negative scholarly opinions and conclusions about the man, some that are extremely biased because of ignorance in regard to the religion of Islam and certainly because of personal hatred toward Islam and Muhammad, the man, the warrior, the prophet. Likewise, scholarly opinions can also be equally pro-Islam and pro-Muhammad, having a bias that is sympathetic and even, in some cases, blindingly fanatical and without doubt dangerous. This kind of scholarly loyalty to Muhammad and the Islamic religion often includes an intense hatred for Jews and Christianity. Both sources are unreliable at best. There are numerous sources out there, however, that give a more unbiased view of Muhammad's life and character, motives, sincerity, integrity.

Here's his back-story in brief: Muhammad, the founding father/prophet of Islam, was born around the year 570 A.D. He was a merchant for many years. Around the age of 40, in the city of Mecca, the pre-Islamic center for pagan worship, Muhammad started preaching his new religion, called *Islam*. He'd had a religious experience in a cave where he believed Allah commanded him, through the angel Gabriel, to recite the verses of Allah, what would eventually become the Qur'an.

Islam broke in a fundamental way from the existing moral and social codes in Arabia at the time in that the new religion taught a strict monotheism, forever separating itself from the pantheon of gods that dominated Arabic culture.

Muhammad continued to receive messages from Allah for 23 years until his death in 632. He increased his sphere of influence and power through force, an active military leader for ten years. Muslim scholars argue Mohammad's main reason for warfare was defensive and he always insisted on humane rules of warfare. He died at the age of 63 of an unknown sickness and had, at that point, united most of Arabia by religious conversion and conquest.[17]

MUHAMMAD, JESUS & WARRIOR CODES

Islam claims Muhammad was the last in a long line of prophets and messengers, concluding that God sent various codes/systems of laws through human messengers/prophets, among them Moses and Jesus. In general, Muslims do not look upon Jesus as the Son of God but as a prophet of Allah. Some Muslims believe Jesus was indeed the Son of God but not the *only* Son of God, and so on. There are a variety of interpretations within the Muslim community in regard to Jesus.

Muslims believe the various codes/systems of laws came in the form of the Hebrew Bible and the Christian Bible, which were made complete in and by the Qur'an, the holy book of Islam—the Hebrew and Christian Bibles are looked upon as a set of holy books, but holy books that have been altered. This means the Hebrew and Christians Bibles are distorted in nature and filled with error, while the Qur'an is free from error or distortion of any kind. It is considered flawless. There are about 1 billion followers of Islam on all five continents, and as it turns out, it is one of the fastest-growing religions in the world.[18]

HISTORIES

In all fairness, it should be remembered that Judaism and Christianity have histories of their own in regard to lack of religious tolerance and warrior-like brutality. The Jewish Wars, the Christian persecution of pagan religions and Christian heretics, the Crusades, the Roman and Spanish Inquisitions, to name but a few. The fundamental difference here is that, practiced by Christians or not, concepts like forgiveness, love thy brother, turn the other check, and ultimately a deeply personal, intimate, and loving/love centered relationship with God that literally transforms the believer from savage warrior (fallen humanity) to peaceful warrior/gentle shepherd (regenerated humanity) *is* the heart and soul of Christianity, the actual written doctrine of Christ, while clearly in regard to Islam, written or otherwise, it is not.

FANATICAL ISLAM

Within the fanatical branch of Islam their hearts are filled with hatred for God's chosen people, the Jews, as well as the Gentile nations of the world. From the Christian perspective they are spiritually led by Satan, and collectively the devil has their souls in his possession and under his dominion—this isn't said *because* they're Muslims who worship Allah, Moon-god or no, but clearly, like all humanity, because they have fallen short of the Glory of God and are under the domain of the Fallen One and need the saving grace of Christ.

Of course, Muslims do not believe they are spiritually led by Satan but in fact conclude the opposite: anyone who isn't a Muslim is spiritually led by Satan.

SHARIA LAW

Sharia Law is the basis of all law in Islam. It gives Muslims the power and ability to make judgments against kafir and ahl al-kitab, the enemies of Islam, those who do not follow the teachings of Muhammad or the laws of Allah. The judgments are based on the Qur'an and the hadiths. In its purest form Sharia Law is a wide-ranging and sophisticated legal system that, when read as a whole, is meant to be something much more than just inflexible rules interpreted and controlled by the personal beliefs and motives of Muslim clerics. In spite of this, the fact remains that the written laws are indeed extreme and if strictly adhered to, as many Muslim clerics and believers choose to do, submitting blindly to the will of Allah, the results are often deadly. Strictly interpreted Sharia Law consists of punishments like stoning, amputation, mutilation, and beheading, as well as instant death for anyone found guilty of blasphemy against the prophet Muhammad or the Qur'an; becoming a Christian or a Jew would be considered the highest form of blasphemy; under Sharia Law conversion from Islam to another faith is punishable by death; women are treated more like cattle and property because females have deficient brains; rape and physical abuse against women is hardly considered a crime; marriage and divorce practices within Islamic society are dominated by and favor men (the *mustahil* custom, for example, which insists that a divorced woman must consummate a marriage with someone else, a hired gigolo, beforc she remarries); the code of conduct for women in regard to behavior and clothing is stringent; homosexuality is punishable by death via beheading, stoning and hanging, all of which take place in the modern Islamic world (Saudi Arabia, Iran, et al) with a sickening regularity today; and honor killings by parents of children that have "dishonored" the family are substantiated and even praised.[19]

This is merely a brushstroke of Sharia Law. I encourage you to study it on your own so that you can be well informed.

WHAT WE CAN GATHER

What we can gather from this information is that Christians must not teach hate or spread fear even though what we face may indeed be hate-centered and frightening. We must put ignorance aside and seek to understand Islam and Muslims so that we can be prepared should we have to face hostile jihad and so that as true servants of Christ, who do not embrace violence and hatred, we can reach out to them with respect, love, and faith with the hope of guiding them toward the truth so that each and every one of us can survive.

OUR MOST SACRED DUTY

Even so, radical Islam is indeed at war with Israel and the West—and, quite frankly, the world entire. There is no end to this war in sight, and as Revelation makes clear, escalation is what's coming. Because of this we must bear in mind what I said in the paragraph above, but also remember that Christians have a solemn duty toward Israel. Should Islamic fundamentalists attack Israel we must stand firm with Israel, shoulder to shoulder, and defend her, for it is our most sacred duty.

THE EXPECTED ONE

We have now reached the period of *the Expected One,* the Messiah, the Savior. To the Muslim, the Promised One is the 12th Imam. To the Christian, the One is Jesus Christ, he who will rule on the earth for a thousand years with his Saints and into eternity. To the Jew, the One is Moshiach, their savior, who will be anointed as king. Each faith believes the coming of the One is eminent.

It's important to note that the Muslims are determined to take over the world in readiness for their savior, the Mahdi, he who demands a violent path to conquer the world. The goal is to eliminate all Jews and Christians, and anyone else who resists, facilitating the arrival of the 12th Imam. President Mahmoud

Ahmadinejad of Iran is preparing for this right now. He is determined to wipe out Israel and bring down the Great Satan (America), creating worldwide bloodshed and war to raise the Mahdi to power.

The Jewish, Christian, and Muslim faiths will be deceived, of course, for the Great Antichrist will suddenly step in and convince the earth that he is the True One the world has been waiting for. He will rule the earth for seven years. Many Muslims, Christians and Jews will believe that the Great Antichrist is the Messiah/Mahdi, for he will have amazing knowledge, wisdom and power, and will set himself up as God in the holy place.

The Savior expected by the Jews and Christians will come, seven years after the Antichrist has risen to power.

AFTER THIS: THE SEASON OF THE BEAST

The Season of the Beast: Daniel 7:7 tells us: "After this (it's important to note the first two words stated in this verse, as they are very meaningful, for they refer to the sequence of events—Britain, Russia, the Arab Nations—*after this* comes the Antichrist) I saw in the night visions, and behold, a fourth beast, dreadful and terrible, exceedingly strong. It had huge iron teeth; it was devouring, breaking in pieces, and trampling the residue with its feet. It was different from all the beasts (or Seasons and their kingdoms) that were before it, that is Britain, Russia, the Arab Nations, and it had ten horns (referring to the Antichrist's control of his kingdom of ten nations)... . And there was another horn, a little one, coming up among them ... And there, in this horn, were eyes like the eyes of a man, and a mouth speaking pompous words (the *little horn* reference here is signifying the False Prophet)."

The Season of the fourth beast follows the Season of the third beast, the Leopard *(the Arab Nations)*, the Season that we are now in! The fanatical branches of the Arab Nations and radical Islam have engaged in acts of terrorism for decades, for the *Season of the Leopard* is upon us and it is rushing toward its climax with the hostile nations Gog and Magog and their siege on Israel. (Remember, the Gog and Magog siege on Israel is not to be confused with the war of Armageddon at the end of the Tribulation.) The first war with Iraq (1991), the war in Afghanistan against the Taliban/Al-Qaeda (2001), the second war with Iraq (2003), global acts of terrorism, Islamic terrorists bent on hostile jihad intending to bring down Israel and the might of America and western civilization with deeds of destruction against innocent civilians—all are forerunners to this mighty pre-Tribulation invasion against Israel by the Arab Nations who will join forces with Russia and her allies (*the hostile nations*). The invasion will be a clear indicator that the period of the fourth beast is about to arrive, the *Season of the Beast*.

The Season of the Leopard ends when this great army is totally destroyed by the hand of God! After this the fourth beast appears and the final Season in our dispensation begins, a period of seven years: the Great Tribulation. The words *after this* should ring in our ears, reminding us that we are now living through the Season of the Leopard!

Revelation 13:3

And I [John] saw one of his [the beast's] heads as if it had been mortally wounded, and his deadly wound was healed. And all the world marveled and followed the beast.

A DEADLY WOUND

Now it comes to pass that while the Antichrist rules the European Union (and as his power expands across the globe), he receives a *deadly wound*. This may refer to an assassination attempt. Someone probably realizes who he really is (the Antichrist) and attempts to assassinate him.

The reference to one of the Beast's heads being wounded also suggests that the attempt may somehow damage the face or head of the Antichrist. The fatal wound will not kill the Beast, however. The wound will appear to *heal miraculously*—either *on site*, which would probably come across as a supernatural healing, or perhaps in the hospital, with a more believable outcome, that of a miraculous *survivor story*.

As far as speculation goes, perhaps the assassin will be a Christian or a Jew motivated out of an understanding of what the Antichrist is—the deed probably will come across as a political and religious assassination attempt to the rest of the global population. This will help turn the world's population against Christians and Jews even more. It will also convince many that the Antichrist is more than just human. His miraculous healing, whether on site or in recovery at a hospital, will inform the world that he is a very special and powerful man, even godlike. This will lead to most of the global population embracing him as messiah and literally worshiping at his feet.

In reality, of course, no miracle takes place at all—no *God-given miracle*. It will be miraculous in the sense of the supernatural, but it will be a dark and unholy miracle. Most people will not realize that the Antichrist died as a man when he lived as Nimrod four thousand years ago! They will not realize that the Assyrian has reappeared on earth again as a fully grown immortal man who cannot die a second time. (It seems reasonable to conclude that the Antichrist will not be *born* as a normal human child, growing up into adulthood, as many scholars of prophecy and Hollywood moviemakers like to claim. Instead, because he is an imitator of Christ, he should appear or *resurrect* similar to Christ, in appearance fully who he was in body at his death 4,000 years ago. When he receives the wound that should be fatal, he lives. Jesus Christ also received a wound and died, and yet he lives. Unholy imitation is clear here.)

Revelation 13:4

So they worshiped the dragon who gave authority to the beast; and they worshiped the beast, saying, "Who is like the beast? Who is able to make war with him?"

GLOBAL WORSHIP

Men and women bow down and worship the Antichrist who is powered by his father the devil (the dragon)—this is worship of one man on a global scale.

John hears the people of the world say, "No one is as great as the *mighty one.* He withstands a blow to the body that spells certain death. Yet he survives! We cannot go against him. In him we see a mighty hunter before the Lord!" The people will believe that he is their hope and their god. Because of the miraculous healing, some who call themselves Christians and Jews may be led astray.

None of the left behind believers mentioned in Matthew 25, and none of the 144,000 Jews, worship the Great Deceiver.

Revelation 13:5

And he [the beast] was given a mouth speaking great things and blasphemies, and he was given authority to continue for forty-two months.

THE GREAT MOUTH

Satan, the Evil One, gives his son great knowledge, strength, ability, and wisdom. Of course, it can't be genuine wisdom, for only genuine wisdom comes from God.

In Scripture wisdom is a definite characteristic of God related to divine knowledge.[20] But Satan retains the ability to tap into the Seven Spirits of God and this gives the dragon the ability to be, in some ways, very wise, and so through the great mouth of the devil the Beast speaks mightily against the Lord God of Heaven.

But he only has the authority to do this for 42 months, a mere three-and-a-half years, the second half of the seven years of Tribulation. Lucifer, who's tapping into the power source that is the seven crowns before the throne, who passes that power on to aid his son, will not retain that power once he is imprisoned a second time in the depths of the bottomless pit. Christ will take away his seven crowns forever!

Revelation 13:6

Then he opened his mouth in blasphemy against God, to blaspheme his name, his tabernacle, and those who dwell in heaven.

THE GREAT MOUTH SPEAKS

John is now seeing far into the future, witnessing a scene that takes place right in the middle of the 84 months of the Antichrist's reign, at the time when the Antichrist proclaims he is god on earth. The Beast demands that all humanity worship him and bow down to his speaking image standing in the holy place, the newly erected sacred temple in the city of Jerusalem. He will give life or something like life to the image. (Refer to 13:14, under the heading *The Image & the Temple* and Chapter 17:14, under the heading *The Temple Reconstruction* for related information.)

John hears him open his great mouth. He speaks against the Holy Trinity and his great mouth will be full of the words of Satan. He blasphemes the holy name of God, the sacred holy tabernacle, and everyone and everything that lives in heaven.

It should be pointed out that Satan has succeeded in putting the blasphemy and vulgarity of his words in our mouths in regard to national and worldwide language today—in books, film, television, the stage, and most notably in everyday conversation. It isn't much of a stretch to imagine a political world leader standing before the world arena speaking out in an unabashed and public display of blasphemy.

Revelation 13:7

It was granted to him to make war with the saints and to overcome them. And authority was given him over every tribe and people, tongue, and nation.

WAR ON THE SAINTS

It is now shown to John that Jesus Christ allows the Antichrist to declare open warfare on all the left behind believers in the Lord, the saved in Christ who were not taken in the Fourth Rapture.

Those whose faith was halfhearted or lukewarm before the Fourth Rapture will now be hunted into extinction. The Antichrist is granted power to overcome them until every last one of them is killed! Jesus will not capture the Antichrist, end the flesh of fallen humanity or reform the heavens and this earth until that last Christian martyr's earthly body dies.

This brings to light an interesting question: Is it possible that God's Two Witnesses, Elijah and Enoch, are the last of the martyrs to die, concluding the terrible bloodbath, as discussed in Chapter 10:4, under the heading *Sevens*, and Chapter 11:7, under the heading *Elijah & Enoch Face Death*? If that is the case, once they have been murdered there will not be a living Christian left on the planet except for the 144,000 Jewish believers in Christ.

TIME OF THE MARTYRS

Let's review the time of the martyrs as it may pan out:

(1) At the turn of the middle of the Tribulation the One World Religion Organization (OWRO) based in Rome is destroyed by the Antichrist and then the Antichrist sets himself up as God within the Temple in Jerusalem, demanding all to worship him. It's likely that he will outlaw all world religions, including Judaism and Christianity, of course. The 144,000 immediately flee to the wilderness and the Antichrist is unable to destroy them.

(2) The Antichrist is assassinated, possibly by a zealous Jew or Christian.

(3) Recovering miraculously and now enraged, the Antichrist declares war on all Jews and Christians; the slaughter begins and is carried out for most of the following three-and-a-half years. The Antichrist will have authority over every race, every language, and every nation on earth.

After the events mentioned above—at the turn of the middle of the Tribulation—there will be a great band of global resistance numbering in the millions from the remaining Christians and Jews who will eventually be martyred. The Church will have to go completely underground at that point, and any and all who are unsympathetic to the cause of the Antichrist, Jews or Christian alike, will be hunted.

Revelation 13:8

All who dwell on the earth will worship him, whose names have not been written in the Book of Life of the Lamb slain from the foundation of the world.

DIALOGUE TO DESTRUCTION
The Mark & Biometric Systems

All the inhabitants of earth will worship Satan through the Antichrist and the False Prophet. For their own gains or out of fanatical devotion and loyalty or politics and fear, men and women will take the Beast's *mark* on their foreheads or on their right hands. In light of advances in biometrics—automatic methods for identifying people based on biological or behavioral characteristics (fingerprinting is arguably the most recognized method of biometrics)—it's doubtful this is figurative.

Facial analysis/animation/recognition and facial thermography systems technology is steadily advancing, while epidermal microchips placed beneath the skin, specifically in the location of the hand, make a great deal of sense in regard to everyday use when shopping and for personal identification and global tracking. In the United States pets and even some children have been microchiped, their location monitored on a regular basis so that if lost or abducted they can be found by GPS. The British and U.S. military are experimenting with microchip technology implanted in the neck of soldiers for tracking, locating, and identifying bodies, as well as microchips implanted in the brain meant to increase soldier memory and brain power, foreshadowing the cyborg-super-soldier.

Verses 16–17 refer to placing the mark on the *hand* and the *forehead*, which could have easily been a figurative reference for the eye. Individual identification can be processed through the retina, the innermost layer of the eye. Retinal scans are in use today. The pattern formed by veins beneath the surface of the retina is unique to each individual, making them a reliable biometric tool. Nonetheless, the amount of cooperation required for a retinal scan by the person being scanned is high, so this tool is ineffective for global applications. Retinal scanners are also prohibitively expensive.[21]

The iris (the colored part of the eye surrounding the pupil), however, is totally unique in every human (both irises, in fact), and it is an accurate tool for the identification of individuals. As far as the technology goes, the accuracy and speed of iris-based identification has been extremely promising. It is entirely feasible and cost effective to develop large-scale recognition systems using individual iris information, and in fact this technology is being implemented today in schools and office buildings in the U.S. It will eventually become commonplace. The iris can be much more easily imaged than the retina, requiring much less or even no direct involvement on the part of the individual. The technology allows for *scanning of individual irises within a crowd.* Individuals could easily be scanned and identified while they continued to shop in malls, buying, selling, walking, driving their cars, attending large-scale sporting events, movies, theatre, political rallies.[22] With or without an epidermal microchip placed in the hand for convenience and global tracking, this could easily be the biometric system to which John was referring to when he called it the *mark.*

How a system like this could *seal the fate* of those who *accept* it was explored in more detail in Chapter 9:4, under the heading *The Unsealed Suffer,* Chapter 9:12, under the heading *The Cost Of Taking The Mark,* as well as in Chapter 14:9-11, but I'd like to restate the basic cause here: obviously, it's not the technology that seals the fate of those who take it, for of course it is simply a clever, efficient, and sophisticated global identification tool, a wonder of invention. An individual seals his or her fate the moment he or she *chooses* to take the mark. An individual would be, in a sense, swearing allegiance to the Antichrist and all that he stands for when they choose to be inducted into the global biometric system. If you do not take the mark or worship the Beast you will not be *let into* the system. This means you would not be able to earn money or hold a bank account, or credit cards. That, in turn, would mean you couldn't buy food, gasoline, water. You would be outside the system and likely an enemy of the State. The point is, it isn't the technology that's destructive. It's the choice.

ALL WILL WORSHIP

All will worship the Antichrist. Most will want to and some will be forced to unless they choose an existence *underground,* which would lead to certain death. The *all* refers to those who do not have their names written in the very sacred Book of Life of the Lamb who was slain. (Refer to Chapter 3:5, under the heading *The Book of Life* for related information.)

This verse is telling us that the all-knowledgeable God knows everyone who is against him and everyone who is for him "... from the foundation of the world," a clear indicator that God the Father knew before the creation of the world who would choose salvation and who wouldn't, as well as showing that Christ's salvation reaches through all time, covering all sin and therefore all humanity. The blood of Christ does not merely cover and reach to a specific and superior *chosen few* ordained before the creation of the earth, as some Calvinists emphasize, commonly called the doctrine of Unconditional Election,[23] which suggests that God made some people within humanity specifically designed to reject him and burn in hell. This Calvinistic concept is age-old and to this day remains highly controversial and much debated in Christian circles. All of this falls under the design of God, his Master Plan (the Big Picture), suggesting that everything— *everything*—is under his control.

Revelation 13:9
If anyone has an ear, let him hear.

AN EARFUL

This is a warning to the reader, one that is repeated numerous times. It is also an appeal to the lost heart of humanity, to every single human being created, to anyone "who has an ear," which in the figurative language of the Scriptures suggests that Christ is reaching out to every human being and that in fact his grace reaches out and covers everyone—all they need to do is reach out to him in faith and acknowledge him. Christ is giving the lost the opportunity to repent. Through his writings, John instructs the world to listen to what Christ says, for time is running out.

Revelation 13:10
He who leads into captivity shall go into captivity; he who kills with the sword must be killed with the sword. Here is the patience and the faith of the saints.

LOVE ABOUNDS

Whoever leads one into captivity goes into captivity. The person who kills in like manner is killed. In other words, we will all get our just rewards for our wrongdoings, whether it be tomorrow, years ahead, or in the life to come—no one gets away with anything. The laws a Christian follows are strict, but they are not extreme or embrace violence of any kind, and the way to overcome is through love, obedience, and the love and grace of Christ.

Loving does not lead one into captivity.

Love suffers long and is kind.

Love does not envy, is not puffed up, thinks no evil, does not rejoice in iniquity, but rejoices in the truth.

Love never fails.

Love abounds, as Jesus is love.

Here is the patience and the faith of the Saints, and of course this applies to those who will suffer in captivity and those who will go under the sword during the Great Tribulation. Indeed, they will have to be patient and faithful—even unto death.

Revelation 13:11

Then I [John] saw another beast coming up out of the earth, and he had two horns like a lamb and spoke like a dragon.

FROM UNDER THE EARTH

When John sees the second person associated with Satan coming up from under the earth he is referring to the False Prophet, a different *beast* but of the same species as the devil's son. Similar to the Antichrist (who came from under the sea), "Coming up from out of the earth" suggests that, like the Antichrist, he had lived before as a man who lead an active, godless life on this world. It's arguable, but he may have lived during the time of Nimrod. He could very well have been his right-hand man. Similar to the discussion about Nimrod having a watery death, when the previous life of the False Prophet had come to an end, it's reasonable to suggest that he probably died on solid ground. Like the Antichrist, he will reappear from hell as an immortal man, not born as an infant and growing to adulthood, but resurrected as a fully functional adult. His first life/time on earth was wicked indeed, and he almost certainly played an important role in history like (and probably alongside) Nimrod. He worked against the God of heaven then and he will work against the God of heaven when he returns, for he belongs to Satan's unholy and imitating trinity!

He will appear to be Christ-like, for he is described as having *two horns like a lamb*, which symbolically represents his *gentle and Christ-like nature*. Of course, this gentle nature will be a light coating of paint, concealing his true dark and hellish colors. When he speaks he roars like a dragon, for the False Prophet and the Antichrist are attached to and powered by their father, Satan. He will have the mind of the Lawless One, as the Antichrist will have the mind of the Lawless One.

The dragon/Satan speaks through False Prophet, obviously, but there is another aspect to this: it suggests that the False Prophet is a powerful orator. Like a magical dragon from the mists of legend he will be able to place people under his spell just through speaking. His public speaking skills will be unmatched.

Daniel also describes the False Prophet in the last days. He writes, "I was considering the horns (that is, the ten horns of the beast's kingdom controlled by the Antichrist, forming the union of Europe), and there was another horn, a little one, coming up among them (the False Prophet), before whom three of the first horns were plucked out by the roots. (This suggests there will be some shuffling around of the nations in Europe. Possibly 13 nations form the union in the early stages. If three are plucked out, then only ten remain.) And there, in this horn, were eyes like the eyes of a man, and a mouth speaking pompous words" (Dan. 7:8).

In Scripture, the *budding* or *sprouting* of a horn (as the horn described in Daniel *coming up among them*) is figurative of the revival of a nation or power, in this case, the revival or resurrection of the False Prophet (Ps. 132:17; Ezek. 29:21; Ps. 75:4-5).[24]

Revelation 13:12

And he exercises all the authority of the first beast in his presence, and causes the earth and those who dwell in it to worship the first beast, whose deadly wound was healed.

THE AUTHORITY OF THE FIRST BEAST

Halfway through the Tribulation the False Prophet exercises all the authority of the first Beast, the Antichrist. He does mighty miracles, convincing humanity to worship the Antichrist, whose deadly wound heals miraculously. People marvel at the Antichrist. The False Prophet will convince them through supernatural and unholy power and his penchant for public speaking, and so all will be deceived. Those whose names are not written in or are blotted out of the Lamb's Book of Life will worship Satan through these two men, and they will worship the Antichrist as their god.

Revelation 13:13

He performs great signs, so that he even makes fire come down from heaven on the earth in the sight of men.

FIRE IN THE SKY

The False Prophet, who at this point in the wheel of the Great Tribulation—mid-Tribulation—will be the head of the One World religion that worships the Antichrist. He may be referred to as the Pope. Whatever the case may be, he does astonishing things like literally make fire come down from heaven onto the earth! Everyone witnesses these miracles, capturing the scenes on laptops, PCs, Macs, palm pilots, cell phones, and new and advancing technologies.

The reference to *fire coming down from heaven* may suggest his great political power and his ability to potentially *rain down nuclear fire* on his enemies, but in light of the supernatural nature of the time and events, it seems likely that he will perform what appear to be genuine supernatural acts powered by the unholy.

Revelation 13:14

And he deceives those who dwell on the earth by those signs which he was granted to do in the sight of the beast, telling those who dwell on the earth to make an image to the beast who was wounded by the sword and lived.

THE TEMPLE REBUILT

The False Prophet/False Pope of the global OWRO finds it easy to deceive the earth's population through these supernatural signs and wonders. The Antichrist allows him to perform these spectacles—they will be very convincing, and people around the world, from the most ignorant and gullible fool to the most educated and skeptical scientist, will have little choice but to shake their heads in wonder and belief.

The OWRO will have already been well established in the first three-and-a-half years. At the midpoint of the Tribulation, the Jewish Temple rebuilt and fully functional, the Antichrist will declare himself God on earth.

The Jewish Temple must be rebuilt *prior to* or *early into* the first three-and-half-years of the Great Tribulation. This will be no easy feat as the Dome of the Rock, the world famous Islamic mosque, rests on the building site of the original Temple today. Regardless, Jewish custom and biblical prophecy insist the new Temple must be rebuilt on the original site in Jerusalem. There is no middle ground here. Because of that, how the Temple gets rebuilt is unknown at this point in time, but both building scenarios are plausible, the latter (early into the Tribulation) suggesting the Antichrist supports the reconstruction of the Temple under the banner of the OWRO and world peace, gathering the support and cooperation of a much reduced-in-power Islam. (Remember, Islam's Great Fall will occur after the destruction of the Hostile Nations and the war with Gog and Magog, a pre-Tribulation event indicating that the Tribulation is imminent.) The former (prior to the Tribulation), suggesting either a similar scenario of collaboration with a weakened Islam or a violent solution like the destruction of the Dome of the Rock via terrorism or natural collapse. Is it possible the great earthquake that destroys the Hostile Nations when they attack Israel topples the Dome of the Rock, signaling Islam's Great Fall and Temple reconstruction?

THE TEMPLE

Historically, the Romans destroyed the second Jewish Temple some 1,930 years ago. Muslim conquest 600 years later resulted in the construction of the *Al Aqsa* mosque and the golden domed Dome of the Rock. In the summer of 1967, during the Six Day War, Israel retook the Old City of Jerusalem, including the Temple Mount. The Israelis gave political authority to the *Waqf* in order to show respect to Muslim religious sites and ease political tensions— the relationship has been shaky at best ever since, its future uncertain and unclear. Adding to the tensions, Israeli archeologists identified a 35-foot wide bulge near the southern end of the retaining walls of the Temple Mount. The bulge has been there since the first half of the twentieth century, but it has now started expanding at what the Israeli archeologists call an alarming rate. To make matters worse, a controversial Israeli archeological tunnel runs along the base of the western retaining wall, and even though the tunnel doesn't breach the Temple Mount itself or the Al Aqsa mosque, there is concern that the entire site may collapse.[25] If that were to happen, the end result could be the reconstruction of the Jewish Temple. I'd like to note, however, that Jordanian sources report there is no immediate danger of collapse, contradicting Israeli reports on the issue,[26] which, if nothing else, demonstrates the political/religious tensions between both sides and their inability to communicate.

THE TEMPLE & THE IMAGE

The Temple must be fully functional for most of the first three-and-a-half years of the Tribulation. This will allow the reintroduction of the sacrifice that was practiced by the Jews in the days of the Old Testament in the sacred Temple in Jerusalem. This must take place in light of Scriptural prophecy. It will inaugurate the merciless reign and global worship of the Antichrist in the middle of the Tribulation, allowing the Antichrist to set himself and his image up within the Temple as God. The Jews will believe in this man, the Antichrist, and announce that he is the messiah for whom they have been waiting!

Once the Antichrist has declared himself god on earth, the False Prophet instructs all people to make an image of the Antichrist, some sort of physical construction of the Antichrist that is placed in Jerusalem. Some argue John was trying to describe a giant television screen or holographic image, but many biblical scholars believe this is not figurative in nature, but literal: a statue of the Antichrist's image is indeed erected. This verse also seems to suggest that perhaps every home worldwide has a statue of the Beast. It is possible that families will be encouraged to make their own *home versions* of the image and worship it there. This could be a throwback to a more ancient time when idols were in many homes and that would add up since the Antichrist and the False Prophet existed previously in a world when idol worship was common and inspired by genuine evil. That every household will have its own personal image could also be a reference to television or some sort of technology that *places* the image of the Beast within a home via television, home computers, holographic imaging, et al. Whatever the case may be, it seems clear that the presence of the Beast and his image will be everywhere.

WOUNDED BY A SWORD & LIVED

The Antichrist is referred to as the *beast who was wounded by a sword and lived.* This seems to indicate that the assassination attempt involves a knife or sword-like weapon, but of course John may have used the word *sword* because it was one of the weapons of choice in his time. Be it a dagger or a bullet from a gun, the weapon that someone uses to assassinate the Antichrist will in all likelihood pierce his head, and this should end his life instantaneously, but of course it does not. Interestingly, some scholars suggest the word *sword* suggests decapitation. It's true that men and women can survive massive head wounds, from bullet wounds to steel rods entering and exiting the skull and brain—human survival from fatal wounds such as these is not uncommon and many have been well documented and they are rarely looked upon as genuine medical miracles.[27] But no human being can survive a beheading. An immortal man, however, can survive such a wound. If the Antichrist wanted to stop the human world from spinning, all he'd have to do is lose his head and survive. The False Prophet could pick it up and then put it back in place right then and there and lo and behold! The Antichrist lives! Now, that would get world's attention. Decapitation does seem to make a horrible kind of sense, and again, because of the supernatural nature of the time and events, something as outrageous and fantastic as this isn't out of the question.

Revelation 13:15

He was granted power to give breath to the image of the beast, that the image of the beast should both speak and cause as many as would not worship the image of the beast to be killed.

THE IMAGE LIVES

The unrepentant people of the earth will more than likely make a larger-than-life statue of the Antichrist and the False Prophet is granted power to give life to the image so that the great sculpture breathes and speaks. Again, some suggest this refers to a giant television screen or holographic image, but many biblical scholars feel this is not figurative in nature but literal: a genuine sculpture/statue somehow comes to life. Humanity is technologically sophisticated in this day and age. They are hard to trick. It seems highly doubtful that they wouldn't be able to recognize inventive technology from a genuine supernatural event. In any case, those who do not bow down and worship the image are killed, be they Christian, Jew, Islamic, atheist, Mormon, et al. The people who refuse to worship the Antichrist will most certainly be made up of the left behind believers who didn't partake in the Fourth Rapture, the 144,000 sealed Jews, and as I said, anyone else who resists.

Revelation 13:16

He causes all, both small and great, rich and poor, free and slave, to receive a mark on their right hand or on their foreheads.

THE MARK REVISITED

The time comes for the False Prophet to demand that every living being on earth receive the mark of the Antichrist, either on their right hands or on their foreheads. (Refer to 13:8 for related information.) This edict is on pain of death. If you don't accept the global biometric system you will not be able to buy or sell anything (see Chapter 13:17), your property will be confiscated, and then you will likely be hunted down and killed.

KEEP OUR BEARINGS

To keep our bearings: forcing the global biometric system upon humanity will occur after the Fourth Rapture, when all believers who have missed that rapture will become extremely faithful in Christ; when the Antichrist sets himself up as god; when the False Prophet rules the OWRO and erects the image of the Antichrist in Jerusalem with the rebuilt and fully functional Jewish Temple. There should be less than three-and-half years left on earth at this point, and of course the unrelenting succession of plagues are about to begin and absolute chaos and anarchy is about to rule. The plague-riddled dominoes are going to fall.

If it were a lifetime before the return of Christ's Second Coming many of the left behind Christians might be tempted to fall into the trap of the Antichrist and receive the devil's mark, although, considering that they witnessed the Fourth Rapture and, what's worse, knew they missed it and now know what's coming, it seems unlikely that many would doubt or even be angry with God at that point, at least, enough to want to take the mark. Every believer will know, without doubt, that in less than four years Jesus will establish his millennial kingdom on earth. To receive the mark, to get into the biometric system for any reason at that point, would be unthinkable, and of this they will be well aware.

Believers will be hunted down and killed, locked in prisons for ten days, torture. The worldwide bloodbath will ensue. The saved in Christ will attempt to stay alive as long as possible during the three-and-a-half-year world reign of the Antichrist, their mission: to try to save the unrepentant. It will cost them their lives, even though they will be protected supernaturally from the plagues and also by sympathetic friends within the biometric system, those who have taken the mark but wish to help. They will hide in dens, caves, sewers, every place conceivable, but sooner or later all will be hunted, found, and killed until there are no Christians and no Jews left alive on the face of the whole earth but for the 144,000!

Soon afterward, Jesus Christ returns and captures the Antichrist and the False Prophet and throws them into the lake of fire, where they will remain for eternity. The dragon, Satan, the Evil One, will be securely sealed into the prison that is the bottomless pit. Jesus will exclaim, "IT IS DONE!" and he will usher in the thousand years of rest and tranquil peace, free from emotional disturbances, agitation, hate, etc.

Daniel confirms that Jesus comes to put a stop to the Antichrist, the False Prophet, and the devil's ways, for he sees things in a night vision and records: "I watched then because of the sound of the pompous words which the horn (the False Prophet) was speaking; I watched till the beast (the Antichrist) was slain, and its body destroyed and given to the burning flame (in the lake of fire)" (Dan. 7:11).

Revelation 13:17

And that no one may buy or sell except one who has the mark or the name of the beast, or the number of his name.

THE GLOBAL BIOMETRIC SYSTEM

The False Prophet, the third person of the unholy trinity, will act as head of the Antichrist's sacred rites and practices, and one of the most important roles he'll play is judge and executioner: whoever does not bow down to his strict and extreme so-called moral laws will be judged and sentenced to death. He will demand the worship of the Antichrist as god and acceptance of him as the messiah, the earth's anticipated king and deliverer, passing a decree that forbids anyone to buy or sell except those supporting the Great Deceiver by taking his mark or his name on their right hands or on their foreheads, and those who refuse the False Prophet will judge and execute. I discussed in more detail the biometric system earlier in this chapter (13:8) and the end results of not being a part of that system, the mark of the Beast, so I won't go into that here.

Revelation 13:18

Here is wisdom. Let him who has understanding calculate the number of the beast, for it is the number of a man: His number is 666.

CALCULATE THE NUMBER OF THE BEAST

We're entering into numbers and number patterns again, or what could be called God's holy mathematics/geometry. Jesus gives this explanation concerning the number of the beast: "Here is the word of wisdom to those who understand. Calculate the number of the Beast (the Antichrist), for it is the number of a man, and his number is 666!"

Many biblical scholars tend to believe the number adds up to a name, suggesting that in fact John had a name in mind—by placing a numerical value to the letters that make up the name, and assuming that the writer thought in Hebrew and Aramaic and then calculated, the answer turned out to be 666. This is often referred to as *Gematria*, a highly complicated system of numbers and calculations linked to names, words, and even ideas the Jews and some early Christians practiced. The number 666 is the only clear example of it in the Bible. The meaning of this biblical number has been debated for centuries, the potential name it may refer to unknown. Some scholars point out that because the number falls short of the sacred number 7 it suggests imperfection and incompleteness, a valid argument.[28] The reference to the word *calculate* in the verse suggests to count, add, multiply, divide— plain and simple arithmetic, but of a much more sublime nature!

As has been pointed out, numbers and number systems or patterns are necessary and important to the divine nature of God. (Refer to Chapter 1:19, under the heading *Numbers & Patterns* for related information of God's holy mathematics/geometry.) A system of mathematics is required. He is the Master Mathematician and he is precise and accurate in the use of numbers and calculations. To him, each number is meaningful and layered. Certain numbers are holy. For instance, the number 3 denotes the Godhead, the Father, Son, and Holy Spirit. 7 is the holy number, and then there are patterns of 7, as in the Seven Spirits of God. Three-and-a-half is meaningful, as we have discovered. The number 40 and number 9 are significant as well. What we can gather from this information is that God is conforming to a set system of principles or rules—and remember, this mathematics/geometry should not be connected with numerology, the occult number system involving the practice of trying to foretell the future or the unknown.

Now, given Satan's fondness for distortion, unholy imitation, and a contemptuous reversal of the good things of God, it seems reasonable to conclude that he would quite naturally invert 666 to 999—after all, he is resentful of any number system placed upon him by God, he is the opposite of all that God is, and he is dead toward the Savior. Everything associated with the prince of this world depicts death, of course, as he is without the Life, but by inverting 666, the meaning of the number goes far beyond mortal death: 999 becomes the numerical antithesis of the holy transformation of humanity's nature through the grace of Christ and the power of the Holy Spirit, and thus 666 not only represents Satan's son, the Antichrist, but its hostile twin, 999, represents eternal death and separation from God.

Furthermore, each 6 within the number represents a person within the unholy trinity: 6 (Satan); 6 (Antichrist); 6 (False Prophet).

And, lastly, we know that 3 represents the eternal living Holy Trinity in heaven (everlasting Life); 6 represents living humankind on earth (fallen-natured physical death); and 9 represents Satan (eternal and spiritual death), and since there is always a hidden 9 found in numbers associated with the devil, when we calculate 666 the one and only thing that's clear is we're dealing with a number system that is, for all intents and purposes, beyond our total understanding.

Even so, we are told to calculate the number of the Antichrist, so let us do just that!

The number 666 adds up to 18.

6 + 6 + 6 = 18.

The two numbers in 18 add up to 9!

1 + 8 = 9.

Invert the three sixes and calculate again.

9 + 9 + 9 = 27.

The two numbers in 27 add up to 9!

2 + 7 = 9.

Once more, you arrive at the number 9, for the Antichrist spells eternal death whichever way you look at it.

Of course, I reduced 666/999 to a rudimentary number system here so that you can, in the very least and most unfussy way, understand what I'm trying to get at. (If you wish to go beyond my calculation and get more complicated, by all means, I encourage you to do so.) But since we know the entire 666/999 system is largely incalculable in human terms and understanding, the question we're left with is: Why did John ask us to calculate the number of the beast in the first place? What was he really asking us to do? The answer is pretty simple: it's not the computation or even the answer that matters, it's what 666 *means*. It's a symbol. We know that 666 means/symbolizes the Antichrist; inverted as 999 it represents eternal death and separation from God; and because it falls short of the sacred number 7, it points to imperfection and incompleteness in regard to the human condition.

Once the meaning has been calculated, the answer that John wants us to find is fairly easy to understand and even recognize: to survive the End Times; to avoid eternal death by embracing eternal life through Christ—that's the most important message in 666, whether or not one goes further with the calculations in regard to biblical prophecy and God's number systems. But should you notice 666 appearing in many places/systems or sense its presence, recognizing the signs of 666 in the world, specifically in relation to biblical prophecy and sweeping immorality, or should you calculate the potential name of the number through biblical Gematria and land a living political figure bullseye—that should be a good indicator that the End Time's are at hand!

"Blessed is he who reads and those who hear the words of this prophecy, and keep those things which are written in it; for the time is near" (Rev. 1:3).

* * * * *

SOURCES:

1. *Sea,* pg. 1149, The New Unger's Bible Dictionary, Moody Press (1988).
2. *Nimrod,* Edward Mack, International Bible Standard Encyclopedia, Online Edition,
<http://www.studylight.org>.
Nimrod, pg. 923-924, The New Unger's Bible Dictionary, Moody Press (1988).
Nimrod, Microsoft Encarta Encyclopedia (2002).
3. *The Tower of Babel,* T. G. Pinches, International Bible Standard Encyclopedia, Online Edition,
<http://www.studylight.org>.
The Confusion of Tongues; The Biblical Bases of Modern Science, Henry M. Morris (1984), Lambert Dolphin's Resources, <http://www.ldolphin.org>.
4. *Nimrod,* Microsoft Encarta Encyclopedia (2002).
5. *United States: Uniform Crime Report -- State Statistics from 1960 -2000,* The Disaster Center,
<http://www.disastercenter.com>.
The United States of Murder, BBC News, BBC Online Network (1998),
<http://www.news.bbc.co.uk>.

A True Murder Mystery: Killings Are Up Again, Time Inc, Time.com (2000), <http://www.time.com>.

World Incarceration and Murder Rates, <http://www.acsu.buffalo.edu>.

Murder Rates on the Rise in Oakland, Other Cities, Kim Curtis, Associated Press, San Diego Union-Tribune (2002), <http://www.signonsandiego.com>.

6. *Blasphemy,* T. Ress, International Bible Standard Encyclopedia, Online Edition, <http://www.studylight.org>.

Blasphemy, pg. 174, The New Unger's Bible Dictionary, Moody Press (1988).

7. *Panthera pardus; Leopard,* Leeann Bies, University of Michigan, Museum of Zoology, Animal Diversity Web, <http://www.animaldiversity.ummz.umich.edu>.

Leopard, Microsoft Encarta Encyclopedia (2002).

Leopard, The Columbia Encyclopedia, Seventh Edition (2002), <http://www.bartleby.com>.

Leopard, pg. 768, The New Unger's Bible Dictionary, Moody Press (1988).

8. *Ursusa arcto; Brown Bear, Grizzly Bear,* Liz Ballenger, University of Michigan, Museum of Zoology, Animal Diversity Web, <http://www.animaldiversity.ummz.umich.edu>.

Bear, contributed by John Seidensticker, Susan Lumpkin, Microsoft Encarta Encyclopedia (2002).

Bear, Animal Kingdom, pg. 63-66, The New Unger's Bible Dictionary, Moody-Press (1988).

9. *Lion,* Alfred Ely Day, International Bible Standard Encyclopedia, Online Edition, http://www.studylight.org.

Lion, Animal Kingdom, pg. 63-73, The New Unger's Bible Dictionary, Moody Press (1988).

10. *History and Culture of Russia: The Soviet Era,* Interknowledge.com, http://www.interknowledge.com.

Russia, contributed by Kurt E. Engelmann, W. Bruce Lincoln, Bruce Parrott, Dominic Lieven, Microsoft Encarta Encyclopedia (2002).

Rib—Ala, #5967, pg. 89, Hebrew and Chaldee Dictionary; Strong's Exhaustive Concordance of the Bible/Dictionary of the Hebrew and Greek Words, Hendrickson Publishers.

11. *Islam,* A Shi'ite Encyclopedia, < http://www.al-islam.org>.

Islam, contributed by Ahmad S. Dallal, Microsoft Encarta Encyclopedia (2002).

Islam (concept), Gabriel Oussani, transcribed by Joseph P. Thomas, The Catholic Encyclopedia, Volume VIII, Online Edition, Kevin Knight (2002), <http://www.newadvent.org>.

A Definitive Reply to Islam, Terjis T. Alajaji, Orthodox Christian Information Center, <http://www.orthodoxinfo.com>.

Muhammad's Mecca, pg. 26-45, Chapter 3: Religion In Pre-Islamic Arabia, W. Montgomery Watt, OUP Pakistan; 1 Ed edition (December 1, 1980).

12. *The Sword of Allah,* Chuck Missler, article, Koinonia House, <http://www.khouse.com>.

Notes on the Background of Islam, The Islamic Invasion, Dr. Robert Morey, Harvest House Publishers (1992); Lambert Dolphin's Resouces, <http://www.ldolphin.org>.

Islam; The true Origin of 'Allah': The Archaeological Record Speaks, New
 Covenant Ministries, Box 120, S-671 23 ARVIKA, Sweden (2001),
 <http://www.nccg.org>.
Morey's Moon-god Myth, Shabbir Ally, Islamic Awareness,
<http://www.islamic-awareness.org/Quran/Sources/Allah/Moongod.html> &
 <http://www.islaminfo.com/new/>.
*Reply To Dr. Robert Morey's Moon-God Myth & Other Deceptive Attacks On
 Islam,* Shabbir Ally, Islamic Awareness, <http://www.islamic-
 awareness.org>.
13. *"Allah" is the Name of a "Moon-god" Alleges a Christian Research and
 Education Foundation,* Akbarally Meherally,
 <http://www.mostmerciful.com>.
Responses to Akbarally Meherally's Site; Allah is the Name of the Moon-god,
 Andrew Vargo, <http://www.answering-islam.org.uk/>.
Allah, The Holy Koran, (its meaning rendered in English), Grand Shaykh,
 Professor Hasan Qaribullah, Dean of Umm Durman Islamic University &
 Shaykh, Ahmad Darwish, <http://www.Allah.com>.
Allah, A Shi'ite Encyclopedia, <http://www.al-islam.org>.
Islam; The True Origin of 'Allah': The Archaeological Record Speaks, New
 Covenant Ministries, Box 120, S-671 23 ARVIKA, Sweden (2001),
 <http://www.nccg.org>.
The Sword of Allah, Chuck Missler, article, Koinonia House, www.khouse.com.
A Definitive Reply to Islam, Terjis T. Alajaji, Orthodox Christian Information
 Center,
<http://www.orthodoxinfo.com>.
14. *Umma,* A Shi'ite Encyclopedia, <http://www.al-islam.org>.
Islam, Spread Of, contributed by Norman Itzkowitz, Microsoft Encarta
 Encyclopedia (2002).
Islam (concept), Gabriel Oussani, transcribed by Joseph P. Thomas, The
 Catholic Encyclopedia, Volume VIII, Online Edition, Kevin Knight (2002),
 <http://www.newadvent.org>.
15. *The Islamic Jihad; The Imperative of Holy War,* Boaz Ganor, Jerusalem
 Center for Public Affairs, Survey of Arab Affairs, <http://www.jcpa.org>.
Jihad, Microsoft Encarta Encyclopedia (2002).
Notes on the Background of Islam, The Islamic Invasion, Dr. Robert Morey,
 Harvest House Publishers (1992), Lambert Dolphin's Resouces,
 <http://www.ldolphin.org>.
The Sword of Allah, Chuck Missler, article, Koinonia House,
 <http://www.khouse.com>.
16. *Kafir; Jihad,* Microsoft Encarta Encyclopedia (2002).
Kafir; Jihad, A Shi'ite Encyclopedia, <http://www.al-islam.org>.
17. *Mohammed and Mohammedanism,* Gabriel Oussani, transcribed by
 Michael T. Barret, *dedictated to the poor souls in Purgatory,* The Catholic
 Encyclopedia, Volume X, Online Edition, Kevin Knight (2002),
 <http://www.newadvent.org>.
Muhammad (prophet), contributed by Fazlur Rahman, Microsoft Encarta
 Encyclopedia (2002).
Muhammad, A Shi'ite Encyclopedia, <http://www.al-islam.org>.
Mohammad, contributed by Ahmad S. Dallal, Microsoft Encarta Encyclopedia
 (2002).
18. *Islam,* A Shi'ite Encyclopedia, <http://www.al-islam.org>.
A Definitive Reply to Islam, Terjis T. Alajaji, Orthodox Christian Information
 Center,

<http://www.orthodoxinfo.com>.

Islam, A Shi'ite Encyclopedia, <http://www.al-islam.org>.

Islam, contributed by Ahmad S. Dallal, Microsoft Encarta Encyclopedia (2002).

Islam (concept), Gabriel Oussani, transcribed by Joseph P. Thomas, The Catholic Encyclopedia, Volume VIII, Online Edition, Kevin Knight (2002), <http://www.newadvent.org>.

19. PUNISHMENT FOR NON-MARITAL SEX IN ISLAM Examples of convictions under Sharia law, Religious Tolerance.org, Copyright © 2002 by Ontario Consultants on Religious Tolerance, originally written: 2002-SEP-1, latest update: 2002-SEP-26, Author: B.A. Robinson, <http://www.religioustolerance.org/isl_adul1.htm>.

Afghan Couple 'Stoned to Death' Over Love Affair, from correspondents in Kunduz, AFP, news.com.au, copyright 2010, News Limited (August 16, 2010), <http://www.news.com.au>.

Zahid, Pakistan, circa 1986: Jesus Freaks, dc Talk & The Voice of the Martyrs, Bethany House Publishers (1999) & The Voice of the Martyrs, <http://www.persecution.com>; *Martyrdom of Hriday Roy,* Religion Today & The Voice of the Martyrs (2003); *Students Freed from Kenyan 'Torture',* *Gray* Phombeah, BBC News world edition, BBCi (2003), <http://www.news.bbc.co.uk>.

Woman Executed in Afghanistan, Associated Press News Service, 1997-MAR-30.

Afghanistan Execution for Adultery, New York Times News Service, 1996-NOV-06.

U.S. Women Protest Stoning Verdict by Nigerian Court. Activists decry 'barbaric' aspect of Sharia law, Jim Fisher-Thompson, U.S. Department of State, International Information Programs at:
<http://usinfo.state.gov/regional/af/a2082903.htm>.

Sharia Law and Australia, On Line Opinion, Australia's E-journal of Social and Political Debate, Sebastian De Brennan - posted Wednesday, 22 March 2006,
<http://www.onlineopinion.com.au/view.asp?article=4282>.

20. Wisdom, pg. 1369, New Unger's Bible Dictionary, Moody Press (1988).

21. Brave New Whorl; ID Systems Using the Human Body Are Here, But Privacy Issues Persist, Rajiv Chandrasekaran, Washington Post Staff Writer, The Washington Post, The Biometric Consortium,
<http://www.biometrics.org>.

Biometrics, contributed by Anil Jain, Microsoft Encarta Encyclopedia (2002).

Facial Recognition Projects; Department of Defense Counterdrug Technology Development Program Office, <http://www.dodcounterdrug.com>.

Biometrics; Where Are We In Bible Prophecy? John L. Terry, III CEC, <http://www.calvarychapel.com>.

22. Iris Recognition, Eye Ticket Corporation, <http://www.eyeticket.com>.

Iris Recognition Basics, Iridian Technologies, <http://www.iridiantech.com>.

Biometrics, contributed by Anil Jain, Microsoft Encarta Encyclopedia (2002).

How Iris Recognition Works, John Daugman, Ph.D., OBE, University of Cambridge, The Computer Laboratory, Cambridge BC2 3QG (2000), <http://www.CL.cam.ac.uk> or white papers @ Itpapers.com, <http://www.itpapers.com>, a product of CNET Networks.

23. The Five Points of Calvinism by Herman Hanko, Homer Hoeksema, and Gise J. Van Baren, Reformed Free Publishing Association (1975), all rights reserved, the Protestant Reformed Churches in America (unofficial home page web site), <http://www.prca.org/index.html>.

24. *Horn, Horns,* pg. 587-588, The New Unger's Bible Dictionary, Moody Press (1988).

25. *Battle of the Bulge,* Jerry Golden. "Report" (2002), Jerusalem, Israel; *Recent Developments in the News Regarding the Temple Mount,* Lambert Dolphin's Resources,

<http://www.ldolphin.org>.

The Bulge on the Southern Wall of the Temple Mount Becomes Larger-Archaeologists Say that the Southern Wall Will Soon Collapse Together with the Mosque-The Temple Mount Faithful to Sharon: Let it collapse! This is the Hand of G-d! Temple Mount and Land of Israel Faithful Movement, Jerusalem, Israel, <http://www.templemountfaithful.org> & *Recent Developments in the News Regarding the Temple Mount, Lambert* Dolphin's Resources, <http://www.ldolphin.org>.

26. *Jordanian Architects Will Fix Al Aqsa Bulge,* TJT Staff, The Jerusalem Times (independent Palestinian weekly), <http://www.jerusalem-times.net> & *Recent Developments in the News_Regarding the Temple Mount,* Lambert Dolphin's Resources, <http://www.ldolphin.org>.

27. *Medical Miracles,* BBC News, <http://www.news.bbc.co.uk>.

'Luckiest Man' Survives Nail Gun Shot to Head; Others Have Even Survived Pierced Brains, Michael S. James (2003), ABC News, ABCNEWS.com, <http://www.abcnews.go.com>.

The Phineas Gage Information Page, web site maintained by Malcolm Macmillan, School of Psychology, Deakin University, Victoria, Australia, <http://www.deakin.edu.au>.

An Odd Kind of Fame: Stories of Phineas Gage, Tranel D., N Engl J Med 2001, The New England Journal of Medicine, <http://www.nejm.org>.

28. *Number; Gematria,* William Taylor Smith, International Bible Standard Encyclopedia, Online Edition, <http://www.studylight.org>.

Further reading:

The Holy Qur'an, S.V Mir Ahmed Ali, Tahrike Tarsile Qur'an, Inc., Second Edition (1995).

The Qur'an Translation, Abdullah Yusuf Ali, Tahrike Tarsile Qur'an, Inc., Fourth U.S Edition (1999).

Concise Encyclopedia of Islam, H. A. R. Gibb, J. H. Kramers, Brill Academic Publishers (2002).

The Two Faces of Islam; The House of Sa'ud, from Tradition to Terror, "an informed and sympathetic history of Islam," Stephen Schwartz, Doubleday, a division of Random House, Inc. (2002).

Islam Revealed; A Christian Arab's View of Islam, Anis Shorrosh, Thomas Nelson Publishers (1988).

The Islamic Invasion, Dr. Robert Morey, *Allah—the Moon- God; the Archeology of the Middle East,* Harvest House Publishers (1992).

Famous South African Crimes; Hendrik Verwoerd—murder in parliament, Rob Marsh, Ampersand Press (1991) or <http://www.africacrime-mystery.co.za>.

CHAPTER 14
The Lamb & The 144,000

Revelation 14:1

Then I [John] looked, and behold, the Lamb standing on Mount
Zion, and with him one hundred and forty-four thousand, having
his name and his Father's name written on their foreheads.

ON THE MOUNT

John sees Jesus is standing on the Mount of Zion.

Historically, the term *Zion* was a specific geographical reference
to the rock cliff between the *Kidrom* and the *Tyropeoean* valleys of
Jerusalem. The term expanded over time to include the western
ridge of early Jerusalem, and then eventually the entire city. In
modern terms Zion is a literal reference to *the city of Jerusalem.* In
a theological and prophetic sense, Zion is layered in meaning: Zion
as King David's City, the city that David conquered, making it the
capital of the kingdom of Israel (1Chron. 11:5; Ps. 2:6; Isa. 2:3);
Zion as the Millennial City, the future capital of the nation of Israel
during the Kingdom Age (Isa. 1:27; Joel 3:16; Zech. 1:16-17; Rom.
11:26); Zion as the Heavenly City, the New Jerusalem on the New
Earth within the Second Heaven (Heb. 12:22–24; Rev. 21–22).[1]

THE TRANSLATION OF THE 144,000

The 144,000 Jewish servants of God are supernaturally
protected from the Antichrist and the plagues during the final
three-and-a-half years of the Tribulation—this verse focuses on the
end of it all, just before the return of Christ, the moment when the
144,000 will be translated from their fallen-natured bodies in the
twinkling of an eye into their super-glorified bodies (the second
body of the Phase of Body). They will be caught up in the air with
Jesus and appear with the Lamb on Mount Zion!

Each one of the 144,000 will have the Father's name written on
his or her forehead.

The reference to the *forehead* and *marking the forehead* here is
likely figurative in nature, although, some ancient Asian/Eastern
nations had the custom of literally coloring or marking the face,
forehead or body. The custom seems to have been adopted into
ancient Hebraic society. As an example, in Ezekiel 9:4–6 we're told
that a Hebrew letter should be placed on the forehead of those who
mourned the abominations of Israel so that they might be spared.

Marking the forehead in Scripture can also signify devotion to and the sealing of the servants of Christ or the servants of Satan.[2]

THE TRANSLATION OF THE MARTYRS

A moment before the rapture of these living saints (the Sixth Rapture), the rapture of the dead in Christ will have occurred: the Tribulation martyrs meet Jesus in the air, for the dead precede the living. The second part of Jesus' return to the earth will be complete!

This is confirmed in 1Thessalonians 4:16, which tells us, "For the Lord himself will descend from heaven with a shout, with the voice of an archangel, and with the trumpet of God. And the dead in Christ (the Tribulation martyrs) will rise first. Then we (the 144,000 Jews for Jesus) who are alive and remain shall be caught up together with them (the Tribulation martyrs) in the clouds to meet the Lord in the air. And thus we shall always be with the Lord."

The Fifth and Sixth Raptures happen almost simultaneously, a few weeks, perhaps months, before the literal physical/spiritual return of Christ to the earth.

Revelation 14:2

And I [John] heard a voice from heaven, like the voice of many waters, and like the voice of loud thunder. And I heard the sound of harpists playing their harps.

THE VOICE

John hears the voice of Jesus. It is like the wondrous sound of seven rivers flowing; like the skies rumbling after seven thunderclaps! The Highest is about to make an announcement: "Prepare to hear another seven mighty voices of the Seven Spirits of God. Receive my words, and write down what you hear." These *voices* will begin in verse 6 of this chapter. They suggest that Christ will speak but seven more times and then it will be finished—as we shall soon discover!

John describes the great company of 144,000 with harps in their hands. A praise song is about to begin and their beautiful music is heard in Zion. They shine like the rising sun on a brand new day. They sing to the Lord. All heaven plans to celebrate the saving of God's chosen people from the Antichrist's hands. It is time to sing! A time to embrace! A time to love! A time to dance! Let it be known that all the reborn are gifted to sing, love, and dance beautifully, for the knowledge of God is in them!

Revelation 14:3

They [the 144,000] sang as it were a new song before the throne, before the four living creatures, and the elders; and no one could learn that song except the one hundred and forty-four thousand who were redeemed from the earth.

THE SONG

Standing before the Son of God, before the four living creatures and the elders, and all the saved in Christ, John witnesses a marvelous celebration. The 144,000 sing a new song of praise and admiration to Jesus Christ. There is nothing in this verse to suggest that this is not literal as opposed to allegorical. It seems that indeed the 144,000 will literally sing and play music in celebration. A musical celebration of worship and thanksgiving makes a great deal of sense here. All heaven will hear the song *of the 144,000 servants of God* known only to them. The fact that they have their own unique song illustrates just how extraordinary they will be to the Lord.

In Scripture, and in the figurative, *songs* or *singing* is indicative of joy and the absence of sorrow.[3] It should be clear here how this relates to the song mentioned in this verse.

Revelation 14:4

These are the ones who were not defiled with women, for they are virgins. These are the ones who follow the Lamb wherever he goes. These were redeemed from among men, being first fruits to God and to the Lamb.

REDEEMED FROM AMONG MEN

God considers the 144,000 redeemed among men because of their obedience and faith. Chapter 7:8, under the heading *A New Song,* explored this in more depth. Return to Chapter 7 for more detailed information on this subject.

GENTILE WISHFUL THINKING

Some Gentile cults and religions believe that they *are* or *will be* a part of this very special company of people, the 144,000 Jewish believers. The 144,000 as a number and as a blessed group of people are central to their cult/religious belief systems, but the fact of the matter is if they are not Jewish they stand no chance of belonging to the gathering of 144,000! As I pointed out in Chapter 7, and as Scripture makes more than clear, multiples of 12,000 are used to fill the 144,000 and each multiple is taken from the 12 tribes of Israel, the Jewish nation, chosen by God himself. The Scriptures do not suggest *in any way* that this applies to a so-called *lost tribe of Israel,* or what the bogus theory amounts to: a Gentile branch of the Israel nation that was *lost* as it wandered to America or some other part of the world. This is a false, heretical doctrine based on the concept of *Two Houses of Israel,* what is known as *Christian Emphramism,* the belief that when a person is saved in Christ he or she finds salvation, in part, because of a direct literal Jewish genetic connection made through Ephraim, the second son of Joseph who supposedly spread Jewish DNA throughout the entire world population. This means that when one is saved in Christ he or she is naturally genetically Jewish, or even more radically, that once a person is saved in Christ he or she *becomes* fully, even genetically, Jewish. This is absolute nonsense and inaccurate historically (in regard to the Jewish nation and their history), scientifically (in regard to genetics), and theologically (in regard to translation of the Scriptures, salvation, and biblical prophecy). In his wisdom the 144,000 were chosen by God before the foundation of the world to govern the earth during his thousand year reign of peace, and every one of them is 100% of the Jewish genetic line, each from one of the existing 12 tribes of Israel and not an imaginary *lost tribe.*[4]

God has indeed spoken through his Holy Word. Without doubt people cannot choose themselves for this honored position, no matter how badly they want it. What a non-Jewish or so-called *lost tribe* making up any or all of the 144,000 amounts to is a false sense of superiority and a boatload of Gentile wishful thinking.

Revelation 14:5

And in their mouth was found no falsehood, for they are without fault.

WITHOUT FAULT

The verse is not suggesting in any way that the 144,000 are perfect or sinless or some such thing. Their human imperfection is covered by the blood and grace of Jesus. Human and fallen-natured they will be, but they will almost certainly lead exemplary lives, the Spirit of Christ living powerfully through them in voice, thought and deed. "Pleasant words are like a honeycomb, sweet to the soul and healthy to the bones" (Prov. 16:24).

Revelation 14:6

Then I [John] saw another angel flying in the midst of heaven, having the everlasting gospel to preach to those who dwell on the earth—to every nation, tribe, tongue and people.

EVERY NATION, TRIBE, TONGUE & PEOPLE

In this chapter, verses 1–5 centered on the very end of the seven year Tribulation period, specifically focusing on the 144,000 and their living rapture (the Sixth Rapture) from earth.

Verse 6 returns to the beginning of the Great Tribulation.

John sees an angel that symbolizes the Son of God. The angel has the everlasting gospel about him to preach to all those who live on the earth, further illustrating that Christ Jesus is the essential living conduit for humanity, reaching out to every nation, tribe, tongue, and people.

It's interesting to note that the angel who is preaching this message is said to be *in the middle of heaven*. This being *in the middle* shows us, once again, the central importance of Christ. Christ is in the center of everything and everything is in the center of Christ. There is no center without Christ. All is central to Christ, the Center Point, he who is the center and equally distant from the exterior of all Creation.

Each angel is a figurative representation of Jesus Christ. When they speak it is Christ who is speaking. You could phrase it, "The seven voices of God from the seven angels." The seven angelic voices are the seven voices of the Seven Spirits of God—Jesus Christ. As was said in 14:2, under the heading, *The Voice*, "They (the seven voices of the angels) suggest that Christ speaks but seven more times, and then it will be finished..."

Revelation 14:7

[The angel] saying with a loud voice, "Fear God and give glory to him, for the hour of his judgment has come; and worship him who made heaven and earth, the sea and the springs of the water."

SEVEN VOICES & SEVEN ANGELS

The first of the seven angels (Jesus Christ) speaks with a loud voice.

Use of words like *loud* always indicate authority and power that point to Christ, saying, "The secret of the Lord is with those who fear me. The fear of the Lord is the beginning of wisdom! I bless those who fear the Lord, small and great, those who delight in God's commandments. Those who fear and trust in me find that I am their help and their shield! People need to fear God and give glory to him, for the "hour of his judgment,' the Great Tribulation, is upon them. Worship the One who made you, O heaven, earth, land, sea, and fresh water!"

Psalms 119:73–74 says, "Your (God's) hands have made me and fashioned me; give me understanding that I may learn your commandments. Those who fear you will be glad when they see me, because I have hope in your word."

Revelation 14:8

And another angel followed, saying, 'Babylon the great is fallen, is fallen, which has made all nations drink of the wine of the wrath of her fornication."

THE FALL OF MODERN BABYLON

The second angel appears, portraying the second Spirit of the Seven Spirits of God, Jesus Christ!

When he speaks, he says to John, "The corrupt city of modern Babylon is fallen." This is a reference to the literal city and its destruction, what will probably be modern Rome—this is no metaphor. It is repeated twice, suggesting the importance of the announcement and the certainty of Babylon's doom.

The angel continues to say, "This city houses the church that has become the New World Order and Religious Center on earth, the Church that is led by the False Prophet appointed by the Antichrist." He is the great fornicator who brings the wrath of God upon the Church.

Babylon's meaning here is layered.

(1) Prophetically, the term is used to suggest the *confusion* and *chaos* brought about during the centuries-long Gentile domination of the world and the confusion and chaos that will occur politically, religiously, as well as in regard to world climate and supernatural experience during the End Times (Luke 21:24; Rev: 6:16).

(2) Babylon is the herald to the Apostate Dominant Christian Church in the Great Tribulation (Rev. 17:5–18).

(3) It also represents political Babylon (Rev 17:15-18), which as we know turns on the Christian Church in the middle of the Tribulation (apostate or not) and utterly destroys it, murdering the minority of genuine Christians that remain within the apostate Church.[5]

The word *fallen,* as it's used here, broadly applies to all three figurative Babylons—prophetically, religiously and politically Babylon has fallen or become corrupted. In a narrower sense, the word is associated to the fall and destruction by the Antichrist of the modern Christian Church, the apostate harlot.

ONE WORLD RELIGION ORGANIZATION

During the first three-and-a-half years of the Great Tribulation, the One World Religion Organization is the only *recognized* religious body on earth. Within that great body Christians are still free to worship God and Jesus Christ, and other world religions are free to do so as well, for the organization will combine *all* religions. It will be ecumenical in every sense of the word. During this time, Christianity will join together with other world religions and completely lose its genuine Christian Spirit, adopting an apostate nature. This kind of interfaith-ecumenicism is indeed being embraced by much of the Church today.[6]

To create an organization that incorporates all the religions of the world under one roof will be tricky to say the least, but because the puppet leader will be the False Prophet/False Pope and the puppeteer will be the Antichrist—and the Evil One the puppet master—the One World Religion Organization will indeed come together and appear to function reasonably well for the first three-and-a-half years.

The False Prophet will allow freedom of worship for a time. In fact, it will be his aim to gain control of all religion and eliminate the worship of the true God, as well as all other beliefs and forms of worship. At the end of the first three-and-a-half years he will declare the Antichrist, the actual son of Satan, god and demand that he be worshiped as god on earth!

At that point the Antichrist attacks modern Babylon/OWRO and she falls. The seat of the Christian Church in the city of Rome, the Holy Roman Catholic Church, along with the rest of Christianity, will be swept off the face of the earth. This will be a literal attack on the city which reduces it and the One World Religion Organization to ashes. Afterward, it is demanded of all remaining Christians to renounce their faith or die.

A world church exists today and its power is growing. It is forming through Islam and the Catholic Church, as well as other Christian and religious denominations. There is widespread political and religious movement toward globalization between government and religion. Institutions like the New Age Movement, the World Bank, and politicians within the European, American, and world political system are preparing the way for one world government and religion.

The United Religions Initiative, or URI (its goal is to become the United Religions, or UR), is a good example: URI was founded in 1995, having its first Global Summit in 1996 and its Charter Signing in 2000. Its intention is to become the spiritual equivalent of the United Nations, one organization for all the religions of the world to take shelter under, one banner, one voice.[7] They have aggressive ongoing inter-faith projects and grassroots inter-faith Cooperation Circles and Affiliates in over 60 countries.

It is also wise to watch well intentioned Christian organizations like the World Council of Churches, for example, an international organization of more than 320 Protestant, Anglican, Old Catholic, and Orthodox churches that promotes healthy ecumenicism within Christianity. Even though the council's constitution affirms the Lord Jesus Christ is God and Savior according to the Holy Scriptures, seeking to bring together all Christians under the glory of the one God, Father, Son and Holy Spirit,[8] it has been argued, organizations like the World Council of Churches inherent danger in their system, that of becoming so big and unwieldy, while retaining a good deal of ecumenical authority, that moral collapse and compromise is inevitable—the nature of the beast, so to speak. Even though the decisions of the council cannot in any practical way be enforced at this point in time, the authority of the 150-member central committee is powerful, influential, and vast. There is the possibility that an organization like the World Council of Churches has been infiltrated by secret pressure groups with aggressive agendas involving global interfaith-ecumenicism. However the organization can be supported and praised but a keen and watchful eye should be kept on them.

In point of fact, these movements and organizations are preparing the way for the Antichrist because of their globalized nature and agendas, whether those involved know it or not. Some within these institutions may have good intentions, but as we all know, the road to hell is paved with good intentions.

Revelation 14:9

Then a third angel followed them, saying with a loud voice, "If anyone worships the beast and his image, and receives his mark on his forehead or on his hand..."

IF

A third angel (Jesus), representing the third Spirit of the Seven Spirits of God, speaks.

Jesus announces with a loud voice of authority, "If people worship the Antichrist and his image, and receive his mark on their forehead or on their hands, watch out, for this is the mark of death!" (Refer to Chapter 13:8 for related information.)

Revelation 14:10

"He himself shall also drink of the wine of the wrath of God, which is poured out full strength into the cup of his indignation. He shall be tormented with fire and brimstone in the presence of the holy angels and in the presence of the Lamb."

PLAGUES OF THE MARK

Once more, Jesus makes it very clear that people who receive or *take* the mark of the Beast, those who become a part of the global biometric system, shall also drink of the wine of the wrath of God which will be poured out in full strength into the cup of his indignation! The *marked ones* will face all the horrors of the plagues released upon them during the last three-and-a-half years of the Great Tribulation. Above and beyond suffering the physical horrors/plagues, they will have to pay an eternal price, for they will be tormented in the presence of the holy angels and Jesus forever!

The use of the word *presence* is interesting here, especially in light of the original Greek (*enopion*), which when translated can be interpreted a number of ways.

(1) *In the face of*, literally or figuratively; *before, in the presence (sight) of*. If this is literal, this would seem to suggest that the holy angels are involved in some fashion with the lake of fire/hell, perhaps as boundary sentinels. (The possibilities concerning the holy angels and their duty in relation to the lake of fire are, of course, endless.)

(2) The Greek word can signify a fixed position in place, time, or state in relation to *at, between,* and *under.* As it is defined here, it is rarely used with verbs of motion and then not to indicate direction, except *elliptically.*

ELLIPTICAL BOTTOMLESS PIT

This is fascinating in light of the earlier description of the lake of fire and the bottomless pit as a spherical and therefore bottomless eternal hell. (An *ellipse* is an oval, a closed plane curve generated by a point moving in such a way that the sum of its distances from two fixed points is a constant.) Since *under* as well as *elliptical motion/direction* is attached to the definition, coupled with the word being an indicator of a fixed position in place, time, or state, we seem to be crossing into a hyperdimensional crosspollination of realities in relation to time and state with elliptical qualities that point to a bottomless place *under* in relation to place—written around 96 A.D. on the Island of Patmos! This may be something of a stretch in relation to the Greek word and its potentially layered hyperdimensional meanings, of course, and there may not be definitive empirical evidence to support this theory, but there's enough circumstantial evidence to hint at them and that alone is rather remarkable.[9]

Revelation 14:11

"And the smoke of their torment ascends forever and ever; and they have no rest day or night, who worship the beast and his image, and whoever receives the mark of his name."

LOST FOREVER

John confirms here that those who worship the Beast and receive his mark will face punishment that leads to physical death and, ultimately, eternal death and torment—and remember, the moment someone accepts the mark the fate of that person is sealed and she or he is lost forever.

Revelation 14:12

Here is the patience of the saints, who keep the commandments of God and the faith of Jesus.

THE PATIENCE OF THE SAINTS

These times call for patient endurance on the part of those who obey God's commandments and remain faithful to Jesus. Since they are not ready for the Fourth Rapture, they are sought after and killed. Because of their great faithfulness toward the Lord, their reward is eternal life.

Revelation 14:13

Then I [John] heard a voice saying to me, "Write: Blessed are the dead who die in the Lord from now on." "Yes," says the Spirit, "that they may rest from their labors, and their works follow them."

BLESSED MARTYRS

The fourth Spirit of the Seven Spirits of God, the fourth angel (Jesus), speaks: "John, you must write concerning the Tribulation martyrs. How blessed they are to die in the name of the Lord during the last three-and-a-half years of the Tribulation."

The Lord honors those who sacrifice their lives for the lives of others or who die for him. Because we live in a world plagued with modern martyrdom in the guise of Islamic suicide bombers, I feel that I need to make it clear here that God honors these Christian martyrs because they're willing to die for the love and life of Christ. They do not commit suicide nor do they try to kill people in the process. Islamic martyrdom involves a suicidal sacrifice in the name of Allah and Islam and the murder of many innocent people.

This is why these Christian End Time martyrs hold a special place in God's heart, for they will face unimaginable persecution and horror, and in the thick of it they will love as Christ loves, being faithful to him, even unto death.

The voice of the fourth Spirit continues: "Yes, you may rest with me from your labors for a thousand years on earth. And your works of faithfulness follow you to the new Holy Age in my glorious heavenly kingdom, the New Earth."

Revelation 14:14

Then I [John] looked, and behold, a white cloud, and on the cloud sat One like the Son of Man, having on his head a golden crown, and in his hand a sharp sickle.

JESUS, THE HARVESTER

John looks and observes a pure white cloud, and on the cloud he sees the Son of Man wearing a golden crown, illustrating that he is the King of Kings.

In his right hand he holds a sharp sickle! The sickle indicates *gathering a harvest* (Mark 4:29), or in this case, the harvest of souls.[10] That he holds the sickles tells us he is in complete and total control of the harvesting process.

Jesus is the Reaper of souls, and there's nothing grim about it, unless you're counted with the lost.

Revelation 14:15

And another angel came out of the temple, crying with a loud voice to him who sat on the cloud, "Thrust in your sickle and reap, for the time has come to reap, for the harvest of the earth is ripe."

THE TIME HAS COME

A fifth angel comes out of the temple, the fifth Spirit of the Seven Spirits of God, Jesus Christ.

Like a roaring lion, he cries to the One sitting on the white cloud. He (Jesus) says, "I thrust my sickle and reap, as the harvest of the earth is ripe. The time has come to end this Age."

The harvest metaphor here was appropriate for the time in which it was written, for the importance of agriculture and the workings of agriculture were well understood by almost everyone. It still works today, of course, but in a reduced kind of way because the intimate knowledge, process, and power of agriculture is lost on most of the modern population.[11]

Revelation 14:16

So he who sat on the cloud thrust in his sickle on the earth, and the earth was reaped.

THE HARVEST OF SOULS

"...and they will see the Son of Man coming on the clouds of heaven with power and great glory" (Matt. 24:30b). Jesus prepares to end the world as we know it, for its cup overflows with sin and it is ready to be harvested.

Revelation 14:17

Then another angel came out of the temple which is in heaven, he also having a sharp sickle.

A SECOND HARVEST

The sixth angel portraying Jesus, the sixth Spirit of the Seven Spirits of God, comes from the temple in heaven.

The Spirit of the Lord is seen holding a sharp sickle in readiness.

His voice is heard saying, "My glory is about to unfold."

The second angel is Jesus Christ, of course, the Harvester of Souls. Using the same metaphor twice, a *second sickle*, may suggest that the harvest of souls is going to be particularly thorough.

Revelation 14:18

And another angel came out from the altar, who had power over fire, and he cried with a loud cry to him who had the sharp sickle, saying, "Thrust in your sharp sickle and gather the clusters of the vine of the earth, for her grapes are fully ripe."

THE GATHERING

The seventh angel, the seventh Spirit of the Seven Spirits of God (Jesus), comes from the altar, having power over fire.

The fire represents the Seven Spirits of Life. "Seven lamps of fire were burning before the throne, which are the Seven Spirits of God" (Rev. 4:5); it is also used here as a symbol of the Lord's presence (Ex. 14:19; Num. 11:1; etc.).[12]

Once again, the angel is described as coming out of the altar, which indicates that this is Jesus Christ, for it is his altar.

Clay Houseman

Now, in ancient times the vine was one of the most important sources of revenue and wealth in the East—in Scripture, the plant, grapes, and alcoholic wine are mentioned frequently. Like the fig, palm, and olive tree, the local populace would have understood the symbolism of the vine because of its national/agricultural importance. Its use here would be understood by most everyone.[13]

The seventh Spirit (Jesus) gives a resounding call, like deafening thunder, while grasping the sharp sickle. Jesus announces, "I am ready to thrust my sickle and gather the clusters on the vines of the earth (the nations of the world), for the grapes (humanity) are fully ripe."

The word *ripe* represents this apostate generation that does not know the Lord or the great works that he has done. It also suggests that things get pretty ripe here on earth, in the sense of sin and wickedness. Humanity has reached the time of their end because the Lord sees that their wickedness is great upon the earth.

Revelation 14:19

So the angel thrust his sickle into the earth and gathered the vine of the earth, and threw it into the great winepress of the wrath of God.

THE WINEPRESS

Jesus thrusts his sharp blade to the earth, delivering the final judgments of the bowls, which includes the transformation of the earth. This action will end the six thousand years of sin (by God's timetable/calendar) as Jesus shows great wrath toward the unholy trinity of Satan.

Winepresses extract juice from grapes, but the interesting thing about ancient winepresses is that they were huge and made out of solid rock (Isa. 5:2; Matt. 21:33). They were made so well some of them still exist today. The vats had two levels: the upper level where the grapes were *trodden upon* or *crushed*; the lower level caught the juice. The act of treading upon or crushing the grapes was a pretty violent act, and it took place on something huge and made out of solid rock—a powerful and useful metaphor here. The violent use of the winepress is found elsewhere in Scripture: Isaiah 63:6–3 where Jehovah is pictured taking holy vengeance against the ungodly nations by *treading upon them.*[14]

Revelation 14:20

And the winepress was trampled outside the city, and blood came out of the winepress, up to the horses' brindles for one thousand six hundred furlongs.

THE BATTLE OF ARMAGEDDON

This verse jumps ahead to the end of the Great Tribulation, summing up John's eyewitnesses account of the end of humanity's sinful/fallen-natured life. It is the return of Christ at the battle of Armageddon, the final battle on the old earth before its reformation. (For a detailed account of the battle of Armageddon turn to Chapter 19.)

Jesus returns and overthrows the Antichrist and the False Prophet outside the holy city of Jerusalem during this battle. The blood from the mangled dead runs so deep that it reaches the height of a horses bridle. It covers a distance of 240 miles, from one end of the valley to the other! There's nothing in this verse or passage to suggest John meant this metaphorically.

The Lord God announces, "IT IS DONE."

The inhabitants lift themselves up against the Lord of heaven. All people are weighed in the balance and found wanting! They have praised a man as god and have gods of silver and gold and wood and stone and self, and none of them see or hear or live. The Christ who holds their breath in his hands and knows all their ways they have not glorified, and he returns with the winepress of his wrath.

* * * * *

SOURCES:

1. *Zion,* E. W. G. Masterman, International Bible Standard Encyclopedia, Online Edition, <http://www.studylight.org>.
   Zion, pg. 1388-1389, The New Unger's Bible Dictionary, Moody Press (1988).
2. *Forehead,* H. L. E. Luering, International Bible Standard Encyclopedia, Online Edition, <http://www.studylight.org>.
   Forehead, pg. 439, The New Unger's Bible Dictionary, Moody Press (1988).
3. *Singers/Singing,* James Millar, International Bible Standard Encyclopedia, Online Edition, <http://www.studylight.org>.
   Music, pg. 893-896, The New Unger's Bible Dictionary, Moody Press (1988).
4. *Christian Ephramism: Where is the Spiritual Birthright?* Robert Somerville, <http://www.awarenessministry.com>.
   Thy Kingdom Come, Thy Will Be Done; The Prayer Offered Most Often Is About To Be Answered ("The 144,000 Called"), Ron Graff & Lambert Dolphin, <http://www.ldolphin.org > & Prophecy Central, <http://www.Bible-prophecy.com>.
   The Next Holocaust & the Refuge in Edom, Chuck Missler, article, Koinonia House, <http://www.khouse.org>.
5. *Babylon,* pg. 134-135; *Mystery,* pg. 896, The New Unger's Bible Dictionary, Moody Press (1988).
   The Mystery of Babylon, Chuck Missler, article, Koinonia House, <http://www.khouse.org>.

Ecumenicism; Where Do You Draw the Line? Deception in the Church
(1998), <http://www.deceptioninthechurch.com>.

6. *The United Religions: Globalist and New Age Plans,* Lee Pen, SCP Journal
VOL. 23:2-23:3 (1999); "An earlier version of this story appeared in "The
United Religions Initiative - A Bridge Back to Gnosticism," published in
December 1998 by the New Oxford Review. You may order the complete
story from the Review, or subscribe to the Review, by calling (510) 526-
5374, or by writing to the New Oxford Review, 1069 Kains Ave., Berkeley,
CA 94706. Additionally, it also has been published as part of "The United
Religions Initiative: Foundations for a World Religion" (Part 1), published in
May 1999 by the Journal of the Spiritual Counterfeits Project, Vol. 22:4-
23:1. The information in this extract is a small portion of the information
printed in the SCP Journal. You may order the complete story from the
Journal, or subscribe to the Journal, by calling (510) 540-0300, or by
writing to the Spiritual Counterfeits Project, Post Office Box 4308,
Berkeley, CA 94704, or by visiting the SCP web site, <http://www.scp-
inc.org>."

Ecumenicism, Southwest Institute for Orthodox Studies, an Orthodox
Apologetics Ministry; Orthodox Christian Information Center,
<http://www.orthodoxinfo.com>.

United Religions Initiative, <http://www.uri.org>, The United Religions
Initiative, P.O. Box 29242 San Francisco, CA 94129, USA.

Some International Examples of Organizations of the Ecumenical Movement,
Richard J. Fears, Department of Philosophy and Religious Studies, Ball
State University, <http://www.rfears@gw.bsu.edu>.
Association of Christian Colleges and Universities, New Delhi, India.
 Christian Peace Conference, Brussels, Belgium. Council of World
Missions, London, United Kingdom. Ecumenical Association of Third
World Theologians, Manila, Philippines. Ecumenical Coalition on Third
World Tourism, Bridgetown, Barbados. International Christian Youth
Exchange, Berlin, Germany. International Federation of Action of
Christians for the Abolition of Torture, Paris, France. Organization of
African Instituted Churches, Nairobi, Kenya. United Bible Societies,
Reading, England. World Alliance of Young Men's Christian Association,
Geneva, Switzerland. World Association for Christian Communication,
London, United Kingdom. World Council of Churches, Geneva,
Switzerland. World Student Christian Federation, Geneva, Switzerland.
 World Vision International, Monrovia, California, USA. World Young
Women's Christian Association, Geneva, Switzerland. A Few United States
Examples of the Ecumenical Movement:
National Council of Churches of Christ 1950 CE.
*Some Organic Mergers of national bodies resulting in these new national
denominations:*
United Church of Christ 1957 CE.
United Presbyterian Church 1962 CE.
Consultation on Church Union proposed 1960 CE.
United Methodist Church 1968 CE.
Presbyterian Church (USA) 1983 CE.
Evangelical Lutheran Church of America 1987 CE.
Resurgence within Roman Catholic Church, Vatican II (1962-65 CE).
Resurgence of inter-faith relationships.

7. *United Religions Initiative,* <http://www.uri.org>, The United Religions Initiative, P.O. Box 29242 San Francisco, CA 94129, USA.
Faith in Dialogue, Leaders from World's Myriad Religions Gather at Stanford in Hopes of Transcending Beliefs, Borders with Spiritual 'U.N.', Richard Scheinin, Mercury News Religion and Ethics Writer, San Jose Mercury News, June 23, 1997, page 1A, The Mercury News, MercuryNews.com, <http://www.bayarea.com>.
The Case Against the United Religions Initiative, Lee Pen; *The United Religions: Globalist and New Age Plans,* Lee Pen, SCP Journal VOL. 23:2-23:3 (1999); "An earlier version of this story appeared in "The United Religions Initiative - A Bridge Back to Gnosticism," published in December 1998 by the New Oxford Review. You may order the complete story from the Review, or subscribe to the Review, by calling (510) 526-5374, or by writing to the New Oxford Review, 1069 Kains Ave., Berkeley, CA 94706. Additionally, it also has been published as part of "The United Religions Initiative: Foundations for a World Religion" (Part 1), published in May 1999 by the Journal of the Spiritual Counterfeits Project, Vol. 22:4-23:1. The information in this extract is a small portion of the information printed in the SCP Journal. You may order the complete story from the Journal, or subscribe to the Journal, by calling (510) 540-0300, or by writing to the Spiritual Counterfeits Project, Post Office Box 4308, Berkeley, CA 94704, or by visiting the SCP web site, <http://www.scp-inc.org>."

8. *Constitution; World Council of Churches,* <http://www.wcc-coe.org>.
World Council of Churches, Microsoft Encarta Encyclopedia (2002).

9. *Presence—Enopion,* #1799, pg. 29, Greek Dictionary of the New Testament, Strong's Exhaustive Concordance of the Bible/Dictionary of the Hebrew and Greek Words, Hendrickson Publishers.

10. *Sickle,* James A. Patch, International Bible Standard Encyclopedia, Online Edition, <http://www.studylight.org>.
Sickle, pg. 1192-1193, The New Unger's Bible Dictionary, Moody Press (1988).

11. *Sickle; Harvest,* James A. Patch, International Bible Standard Encyclopedia, Online Edition, <http://www.studylight.org>.
Sickle, pg. 1192-1193, The New Unger's Bible Dictionary, Moody Press (1988).

12. *Fire,* W. L. Walker, International Bible Standard Encyclopedia, Online Edition, <http://www.studylight.org>.
Fire, pg. 425-426, The New Unger's Bible Dictionary, Moody Press (1988).

13. *Vine,* E. W. G. Masterman, International Bible Standard Encyclopedia, Online Edition, <http://www.studylight.org>.
Vine, pg. 1353-1354, The New Unger's Bible Dictionary, Moody Press (1988).

14. *Wine; Wine Press,* pg. 1366-1368, The New Unger's Bible Dictionary, Moody Press (1988).
The Seven Thunders; An Interpretive Suggestion, No. 6, Biblical Horizons, James B. Jordan, <http://www.biblicalhorizons.com>.
Thunder, pg. 1279, The New Unger's Bible Dictionary, Moody Press (1988).

Further reading:

Babylon Mystery Religion, Ralph Woodrow, Ralph Woodrow Evangelistic Association (1966).

CHAPTER 15
Seven Angels With Seven Plagues

Revelation 15:1

Then I [John] saw another sign in heaven, great and marvelous: seven angels having the seven last plagues, for in them the wrath of God is complete.

PRELUDE TO THE FINAL SEVEN

John views *seven powerful angels* in all their great and marvelous glory. Each one holds a golden bowl in their right hand.

The *angels* signify the Seven Spirits of the Holy God—Jesus Christ. Each Spirit/angel brings before the inhabitants of the earth a worldwide plague with the fury of God in it!

This is the prelude to the final seven *bowl judgments*. They will bring an unquestionable end to the human race's six thousand year Age (by God's timetable/calendar). John will witness all seven bowl plagues.

HOW MANY REMAIN?

This leads me to ask: How many people will still be alive at this point, after having faced so many catastrophes already—the plagues of the trumpets, the plagues of the unknown thunders, not to mention the plagues of the Two Witnesses? Remember, chaos will rule during the last three-and-a-half years because of the overlapping nature and rapid sequence of the plagues, one after another, *slam, slam, slam!* You'd think that life would almost be extinct! But the truth of it is, no—life finds a way to survive, for God has endowed within life a great ability to continue to exist, even under the most extreme and unnatural conditions. This means near the end of the Tribulation a portion of humanity continues to exist, millions, in fact. This is due in part because the world will be saturated with billions and billions of humans in the final days—it should be more than evident that today's world population has reached the point where it could easily meet End Time prophecy population numbers!

When it's all over, for the first time since it began all life will be wiped off the face of the earth, from the largest living animal to the smallest single cell, right down to the atom and beyond—any life that is of the fallen nature will be absolutely removed, including (potentially) fallen time.

CALCULATE THE NUMBER OF THE SAVED

In regard to how many will be saved in Christ at the end of the Tribulation, no one can calculate the number. It must be vast, of course, along the lines of billions and billions!

I'd like to point out that the great number of the saved in Christ will include the millions upon millions of children born throughout the course of the *rest period*, the seventh millennium, the Kingdom Age. Remember, reproduction shall continue during the Second Age. Each couple joined together by God shall be fruitful and multiply for a millennium, obeying God's law: "Then God blessed them (mankind), and God said to them, 'Be fruitful and multiply; fill the earth and subdue it...'" (Gen. 1:28).

THE AGES REVISITED

As you may recall, the reformed earth of the Second Age of humankind (the Kingdom Age) shall be perfect in the second phase of this earth, and it must be filled with his creation! This command to increase in number is meant for the first two Ages on this earth.

The First Age, the Human Age, is the age of sin.

The Second Age, the Kingdom Age, is an age free of sin for 1,000 years.

The Third Age, the Holy Age, is experienced on the New Earth for eternity, "For in the resurrection (when the godly are transfigured from the Second Phase of Body, the glorified body, to the Third Phase of Body, the super-glorified body, to dwell on the New Earth to begin the Third Age) they (experience a higher form of life and) ...are like the angels in heaven" (Matt. 22:30).

The Third Age makes it complete.

SECOND AGE CHILDREN REVISITED

Because so many children will be born into the sinless state of existence during the Kingdom Age some biblical scholars argue it's possible that Satan's final release upon the world at the end of the Second Age will sway them to the dark side. Those born into the millennium, the argument goes, may be susceptible to the lure of the Evil One and the hordes of fallen angels and the souls of the unrepentant simply because they've never experienced sin before. A state of probation may exist for them as well. Their free will may fall under God's divine law and need to be tested as it was for Adam and Eve in the Garden and Lucifer in Heaven—the potential to choose to fall while existing in a perfect state may exist for them; and this may explain why Satan is released one last time, for assuredly he believes he can sway the children of the Second Age. He'd done it before, he could do it again.

I believe he will try and fail and that none of the children of the Second Age will fall. It seems highly unlikely that anyone existing in the Kingdom Age will fall to the call of the dark lord, for truly all the Saints and all the children of the Second Age will be covered by the blood and grace of Christ, a permanent and irremovable state of being.

WHAT OF THE LOST?

During the 1,000 years the lost will remain in Sheol, the antiparadise. Remember, that many of them did not believe in the devil but, of course, Satan believed in them, and he took billions with him. This is why John sees billions of unsaved resurrected souls during the Seventh and final Rapture, the rapture set aside only for the lost. They are said to be like the sands of the sea in number! Sadly, instead of meeting Jesus in the air—who is life and love—they gather with Lucifer in the air at the end of the Second Age, he who is death and hate! John tells us in Revelation 20:7: "Now when the thousand years have expired, Satan will be released from his prison (called the bottomless pit) ..." The unsaved are raised from Sheol, raptured in the twinkling of an eye into the Second Phase of Body, the glorified body, finding themselves with Lucifer in the air above the reformed earth. Revelation 20:8: "...And (the heathen, who join with Gog/Satan in the land of Magog) will go out to deceive the (godly) nations (living with their King, Jesus Christ) in the four corners of the earth..." The Evil One will gather with the unrepentant souls in the north and then they will spread across the reformed/recreated earth in an attempt to delude God's people, everyone who had previously experienced fallen nature/time but were saved in Christ and those born into perfect nature/time during the 1,000 years, the children of the Second Age. This will be the last and final attempt by Satan to sway the Saints, and of course the Evil One and all the unrepentant fail.

Revelation 15:2
And I [John] saw something like a sea of glass mingled with fire, and those who have the victory over the beast, over his image and over the number of his name, standing on the sea of glass, having harps of God.

VICTORIOUS SEA OF GLASS

The angel of Jesus shows John something resembling a *sea of glass mingled with fire.*

The sea of glass is the innumerable company of Saints standing before the throne of Jesus glowing as if on spiritual fire, powered by the Seven Spirits of God—*tapping into* the seven flames/Spirits of God, the very Power Source of God! The multitude includes all the saved in Christ from the beginning of time and the creation of humanity, including those victorious over the Antichrist, his image, and his mark, the Tribulation martyrs and the 144,000. (For related information on the sea of glass, refer to Chapter 4:6, under the heading *The Sea of Glass*.)

The Saints, along with the holy angels, are given harps of God. (For related information on harps, turn to Chapter 5:8, under the heading *Worthy is the Lamb*.)

Revelation 15:3

They sing the song of Moses, the servant of God, and the song of the Lamb, saying: "Great and marvelous are your works, Lord God Almighty! Just and true are your ways, O King of the nations."

THE SONG OF MOSES

They sing the *Song of Moses*, a praise song to the Son of Man, their wonderful Savior and God who is encircled by an emerald rainbow.

The song of Moses relates to the original song of Moses sung in the Old Testament, prior to the death of Moses (Duet. 32:1–43); both songs reflect deep praise, but it's the link with the Old and New Testament here that is most important—the living conduit of Jesus Christ reaches out to the Old World and the New World, bringing Old and New together, both Jew and Gentile.[1] Their words are heard throughout heaven: "Great and marvelous are your works, Lord God Almighty, Jesus the Christ. Just and true are your ways, King of the believers in you."

Revelation 15:4

"Who shall not fear you, O Lord, and glorify your name? For you alone are holy. For all nations shall come and worship before you, for your judgments have been manifested."

JESUS ALONE IS WORTHY

"Who does not fear you, Lord, and glorify your name? For you alone are holy. All nations come and worship before you during your thousand year reign on earth, for your judgments are revealed and your promises have been kept."

Whosoever is wise will observe these things and they will understand the Lord. Awaken the dawn by singing and give praise to his outstanding glory. His mercy is above the heavens and his truth reaches to the clouds.

Revelation 15:5

After these things I [John] looked, and the temple of the tabernacle of the testimony in heaven was opened.

THE TABERNACLE OF TESTIMONY

The Temple of the shrine, which is the Tabernacle of the testimony in heaven (the original Tabernacle from the First Heaven), opens for the Lord's somber descent!

John observes every believer in the Lord since the creation of humanity standing before the Creator. Jesus is ready to cast the final plagues upon the earth, bringing an end to life as we know it and ending this dispensation. The Tribulation believers, the Christian martyrs, and the rest of the innumerable company have finished their praises in song.

The final seven plagues of the Great Tribulation are about to be unleashed on what seems to be a totally unrepentant humanity. At this point in the last three-and-a-half years of the Tribulation, other than the supernaturally protected 144,000, every Christian will be dead, including the Two Witnesses, Elijah and Enoch. (The "taken" are with Jesus). This will leave only the unsaved to face the final seven plagues of the bowls.

Revelation 15:6

And out of the temple came the seven angels having the seven plagues, clothed in pure bright linen, and having their chests girded with golden bands.

OUT OF THE TEMPLE

Out of the Temple come the *seven angels* who are the Seven Spirits of God (Jesus). John sees his Lord ready to release the seven last plagues.

"And in the midst of the seven lamp stands (the Seven Spirits of Life) One like the Son of Man, clothed with a garment down to the feet and girded about the chest with a (belt resembling a) golden band" (Rev. 1:13).

The reference to the *chest girded with a golden band* suggests complete authority and strength in Christ Jesus, the One who is the Son of Man.

Revelation 15:7

Then one of the four living creatures gave to the seven angels seven golden bowls full of the wrath of God who lives forever and ever.

A CREATURE GIVES

One of the four living creatures, possibly the creature characterizing Jesus as Man, presents the seven angels (the Seven Spirits of God/Jesus Christ) with seven golden bowls. Each bowl is full of the wrath of Almighty God.

Jesus Christ takes the seven golden bowls in readiness to pour out the plagues upon the last of wicked humankind and the followers of the dark prince of this world.

At this time on the earth the Left Behind martyrs will have been entirely consumed. They no longer exist in the flesh! Their souls wait *under* the altar of God in the place of waiting known as Abraham's Bosom. At this point only a few weeks remain.

Revelation 15:8

The temple was filled with smoke from the glory of God and from his power, and no one was able to enter the temple till the seven plagues of the seven angels were completed.

THE GLORY OF GOD

The great and wondrous temple of God is seen emitting the brightness of Christ, the Spirit of Glory and of God, what will probably amount to something like a smoke the color of pale-green—he is, after all, the Emerald Christ, the Green Creator.

The word *smoke* (Greek, *kapnos*) indicates the presence of God. When his presence appeared above the Mercy Seat in the Old Testament Tabernacle within the Holy of Holies it was described as *smoke-like* or *vaporous.*[2] Perhaps there is something of a more literal nature going on here of which we are unaware. Whatever the case may be, the last seven plagues are about to be poured upon the world and they will be severe, indeed. The plagues identify the very end of our first dispensation, the last few weeks of the final three-and-a-half years of the Great Tribulation.

* * * * *

SOURCES:

1. Song of Moses (Exodus 15); The Seven Vials; Revelation, Gray's Home Bible Commentary; *Song of Moses, Exodus 15,* Henry's Concise Commentary, The Bible Library Delux, version 5.0. suite, CD-ROM, Ellis Enterprises, Inc. (2,000).

Moses, song of, James Orr, International Bible Standard Encyclopedia, Online Edition, <http://www.studylight.org>.

Song, pg. 1209, The New Unger's Bible Dictionary, Moody Press 1988).

2. *Temple,* pg. 1259-1264, The New Unger's Bible Dictionary, Moody Press (1988).

Smoke—Kapnos, #2586, pg. 39, Greek Dictionary of the New Testament, Strong's Exhaustive Concordance of the Bible/Dictionary of the Hebrew and Greek Words, Hendrickson Publishers.

The Mercy-seat, W. Shaw Caldecott, International Bible Standard Encyclopedia, Online Edition, <http://www.studylight.org>.

CHAPTER 16
The Seven Plagues Of The Bowls

Revelation 16:1

Then I [John] heard a loud voice from the temple saying to the seven angels, "Go and pour out the seven bowls of the wrath of God on the earth." Heaven gasps!

THE SEVENTH TRUMPET!
Introduces the Final Plagues of the Bowls

The voice of the Son of God speaks to seven angels holding seven golden bowls round about the temple! Once more, these angels represent the Seven Spirits of God/Jesus Christ. In actual fact, Jesus, who has the Seven Spirits, speaks from the altar. He calls out to John, "I am about to pour out the seven bowls of God's wrath onto the whole earth, ending forever corrupt flesh and thoughts and deeds, for the seventh angel airs his trumpet and the mystery of God's plan is to be fulfilled, as I declared to my servants the prophets!"

Revelation 16:2

So the first went and poured out his bowl upon the earth, and a foul and loathsome sore came upon the men who had the mark of the beast and those who worshiped his image.

A FEW WEEKS LEFT

At the introduction of the first bowl plague there will only be a few short weeks left in the last three-and-a-half years of the seven year Tribulation.

All the Saints of God will have been murdered or raptured by this time; including the Two Witnesses, potentially Elijah and Enoch—put to death by the demons released from the prison-place known as the bottomless pit. The bowl plagues (as well as the seven plagues of the thunders, which of course happen prior to the bowl plagues) are kept strictly for the lost of the world.

During this period of time it will come to pass that people will long for death and it will be slow in coming! Give ear, all inhabitants of the earth, for Christ whistles for the birds and they come at his calling, and they rest in the desolate valleys ready for the great supper of the unrepentant.

THE FIRST BOWL PLAGUE
The Third Woe

The first angel, representing Jesus and holding a golden bowl, pours out the first of the bowl plagues upon the earth.

Foul and loathsome sores break out upon all men and women who have taken the Antichrist's mark, those within the global biometric system, the same people who believe in the Antichrist and worship his living image erected in the sacred Jewish temple in Jerusalem!

It seems likely that these sores will be boil-like, inflamed and pus-filled, and they will almost certainly have an unpleasant odor. Each one may cause a swelling of the skin one inch in diameter or larger.

To clarify, there are several kinds of boils: simple boils, carbuncles or large boils, and malignant pustules—in relation to what these sores will be or be like, you can take your pick.

When the word *boil* is used in Scripture it isn't a singular reference to boils but, in fact, represents all kinds of disease that plague the skin—this means the boils referred to in this verse could be just about anything. The original Greek word used here (*helkos*) can be interpreted *ulcer-sore*, which leads me to think these sores will indeed be boil-like. Of course, that these sores will be unlike anything we've ever encountered medically because they could and probably will have a supernatural aspect to them is not outside the realm of possibility![1] Whatever the case may be, people will endure much pain because of these sores, and even though they try to cure their pain there will be no relief. It's probable the painful sores will cover their entire bodies, from the soles of their feet to the crowns of their heads, and nothing will give them relief or comfort.

Revelation 16:3

Then the second angel poured out his bowl on the sea, and it became blood as of a dead man; and every living creature in the sea died.

THE SECOND BOWL PLAGUE

Jesus, as the second angel, pours out the second bowl onto the earth's oceans, causing the seven seas of the world to turn into coagulated blood that smells like death. The earths people have to face this while still trying to overcome the plague of the boils.

The reference here to blood could be figurative, but because of the supernatural/miraculous nature of the events there's no reason why the second plague couldn't be literal coagulated blood. The original Greek word (*haima*) can be more exactly defined as *flour-like* or *like ground flour*.[2] If it isn't a literal transformation from saltwater into dead blood, the word suggests that it is very much like thick, dead blood. Whatever the case may be, clearly, every living creature (that continues to exist) in the great oceans die because of the blood, and they wash upon all the shorelines of the earth. Imagine, at this point, the stench of billions and billions of decomposed fish. Many fish will already be dead because of the earlier plagues. Total chaos around the earth will follow as nature completely breaks down and even transforms. Those hiding at the bottom of the sea in nuclear submarines (or *underwater vessels* from John's perspective) will not escape the wrath of God, for the oceans will be wholly unnavigable!

Revelation 16:4

Then the third angel poured out his bowl on the rivers and springs of water, and they became blood.

THE THIRD BOWL PLAGUE

Jesus, as the third angel, pours out the third bowl plague upon the rivers, lakes, and fresh water sources of the world. All the fresh water that remains on earth turns into blood, like the blood of a dead body. The wicket have to face this calamity while trying to accept the deployable conditions of the oceans.

Once again, the use of the word *blood* here could be figurative. It is the same Greek word that can be more precisely translated as *flour-like* or *like ground flour*—regardless, because of the supernatural/miraculous nature of the events, it certainly could be literal coagulated blood!

Some water must escape the plagues of blood or humanity would cease to exist before the end of the Tribulation. That being the case, it's reasonable to conclude that some water systems will not be affected, possibly deep aquifers and stored bottled water.

Revelation 16:5

And I [John] heard the angel of the waters saying, "You are righteous, the One who is and who was, the Holy One, and who is to be, because you have judged these things."

JESUS ALONE IS RIGHTEOUS

"I am righteous and I am your God. I am the one who is, from the beginning. I am the one who was, when I died on the cross to save mankind from eternal damnation. And I am the one who is to come, for I rose from the dead and went to my Father in heaven, and I am soon to return. But each one now on earth has forsaken me. I meet the standards of what is right and just. I am alive forevermore. All believers in me, in like manner, have been resurrected and now wait in Abraham's Bosom and Paradise for my coming to earth, where they will live with me. Yes, my actions are righteous, and I do judge these things."

THE ANGEL OF THE WATERS

It's worthwhile to note that the angel speaking here is referred to as the *angel of the waters.* Of course, at the highest level of metaphor the angel symbolizes Jesus Christ, but it also reveals the angelic hierarchy to us, what amounts to the angelic chain of command. This angel's job in the angelic hierarchy is to literally care for the waters of the earth, and even though the water the angel cares for is destroyed, the angel praises God for it, confirming that the judgment upon the waters is righteous and the total destruction of the waters of the earth is a blessed and holy act.[3]

Revelation 16:6

"For they [the unrepentant] have shed the blood of saints and prophets, and you have given them blood to drink. It is their just due."

BLOODY JUSTICE

"The unrepentant spilled the blood of believers and prophets from the beginning of human existence. Therefore, I give them blood to drink, for it is their just due."

Jesus speaks to the hearts of those who did not, do not, and will not honor God. They have forsaken Christ, rejecting him and all he has to offer; rejecting even the most basic kernel of goodness. They have taken to other gods and have filled the earth with the blood of the innocent. Behold, the day will come when the Lord breaks these people as one breaks a potter's vessel. He fills their stomachs with dead blood! They cry out, saying they thirst for fresh water to drink.

Humanity will find it nearly impossible to find water to drink and wash their bodies. Whatever plant life remains, if any does remain, will vanish as the earth becomes an environmental disaster and wasteland! For three-and-a-half years the planet has been bombarded by (potential) meteorites, and most certainly the global climate will have been drastically altered, super-cooling and superheating wide sections of the earth so that by the time the third bowl is poured on the planet it will hardly be fit to sustain life—and that's *all* fallen natured life—for very much longer.

Revelation 16:7

And I [John] heard another from the altar saying, "Even so, Lord God Almighty, true and righteous are your judgments."

THE JUDGMENTS ARE TRUE

John hears Jesus' powerful voice come from the altar of God. The voice is described as *another,* indicating the Seven Spirits of God, and he says, "Even so, I am the Lord God Almighty. My judgments are true."

Because of the holy nature of Christ these judgments are righteous and holy. This is difficult to understand from our perspective. We don't understand because of our fallen nature, which battles constantly with God's divine nature. Our fallen nature does not understand his nature and is even resistant to it, and that would include resistant to understanding it. Additionally, we cannot see into the Big Picture. We are, in fact, somewhere *in* the Big Picture and that makes our perspective skewed and limits our understanding of it. All we are afforded to see is Christ Jesus, the candle shining bright in an immense big picture of darkness.

Revelation 16:8

Then the fourth angel poured out his bowl on the sun, and power was given to him to scorch men with fire.

THE FOURTH BOWL PLAGUE

Jesus, as the fourth angel, pours out his fourth bowl on the sun and it causes the surface temperature of much of the earth to become superheated.

Refer to Chapters 8:12, under the heading *The Fourth Plague,* 11:8, under the heading *In the Streets,* and 11:16, under the heading *The Global Drought* for related information on global climate, superheated temperatures, and the ozone.

Because this plague occurs weeks or even days before the earth's and fallen-natured mankind's end, the reference to the sun may be more literal than we suspect here. Indeed, it could refer to the actual sun scorching the earth, and not because of holes in the ozone or a dysfunctional magnetic field and magnetosphere. Catastrophic changes within the body of the sun itself could cause lethal and destructive forms of radiation, gravity, or massive solar flares that could damage the planet.

Those on the earth, in the sky, and even those outside the earth in spinning space stations encircling the world (*those who build layers in the sky,* from John's perspective) will find no escape. Alas, the presence of Christ melts the earth! Once again we're at a Super Nature level here where anything, even the improbable and unbelievable, is possible.

SCORCHED AGAIN

It will not be scorched like this again until 1,000 years after its reformation, when the earth is transformed one final time into the bottomless pit for all lost souls and fallen angels after Judgment, the planet's core taking on its hyperdimensional eternal duty of the lake of fire/hell.

Revelation 16:9
And men were scorched with great heat, and they blasphemed the name of God who has power over these plagues; and they did not repent and give him glory.

THE GREAT HEAT

Whatever comes to pass regarding the sun, clearly, the great heat becomes unbearable and lethal. Still suffering from the lack of water from the third plague, people will burn, blister, become blind, and many will die.

All who worship Satan and blaspheme the name of God and his power—the only remaining humans on the planet—will face the final bowl plagues. They will go anywhere and do anything to find relief, but their efforts will be in vain. They don't change their evil ways nor do they give God glory, for their hearts are fully corrupted at this point and no goodness can be found in them.

Revelation 16:10
Then the fifth angel poured out his bowl on the throne of the beast, and his kingdom became full of darkness; and they gnawed their tongues because of the pain.

THE FIFTH BOWL PLAGUE

Jesus, as the fifth angel, pours out his fifth plague of the bowls upon the throne of the Antichrist. He says, "Behold, I punish them and bring catastrophe on the people of the world."

This plague focuses on Satan's kingdom and domain, and since his domain covers the entire earth it seems likely that the planet will be plunged into total darkness! No light comes from the sun, the moon or the stars—only darkness. We have moved into uncharted and unknowable territory here, dealing with events of a Super Nature.

The verse makes a reference to a *pain* that is *because of*, or *within*, or *caused by* the darkness. This is veiled, of course, for we do not know what it refers to—perhaps the inhabitants of the world will *gnaw their tongues* because they will only know fear and discomfort in the darkness. Speculation aside, darkness is most appropriate, for the Antichrist is the son of the devil, the king of the kingdom of darkness!

Revelation 16:11

They blasphemed the God of heaven because of their pains and their sores, and did not repent of their deeds.

THEY CONTINUE TO CURSE GOD

The unrepentant people of the world whose fates have been eternally sealed because they accepted the mark of and worshiped the Beast continue to curse the name of God. They are incapable of doing anything else at this point, for their hearts are in darkness as complete and total as the darkness around them.

We know the plagues overlap one another, but this verse seems to reveal further disturbing evidence: some of the plagues will continue. For example, there is no scriptural indication that the plague of the sores comes to an end. This may mean when another plague arrives the plague of the sores continues. It may be that some of the plagues overlap and continue unabated until the return of Christ. Still suffering the heat, they have to suffer total darkness. Many will die from fear.

Revelation 16:12

Then the sixth angel poured out his bowl on the great river Euphrates, and its water was dried up, so that the way of the kings from the east might be prepared.

THE SIXTH BOWL PLAGUE

Jesus reveals to John the plague of the sixth angel, who is the sixth Spirit of the Seven Spirits of God, Jesus Christ. Heaven hears Jesus say, "The sword of the Lord shall devour them, from one end of the land to the other!" God's Son pours out the sixth plague upon the earth. The plague of the darkness ends and the bloody water of the great River Euphrates dries up completely. This will give the nations and the armies of the East (China) the opportunity to march over and attack Israel. It will give the enemies of God a final opportunity to support the Antichrist within his capital, Jerusalem. They will gather together in the valley of Armageddon for the final war of this dispensation between good and evil. During that battle the Antichrist and whatever human followers remain— the number will certainly be in the many millions—plan to destroy the Almighty, but he dissolves them with the glory of his return!

THE RIVER EUPHRATES

The Euphrates River rises in the mountains of southwest Turkey. It flows through Syria and Iraq where it joins the Tigris and forms the *Shatt al Arab*, empting into the Persian Gulf.

Today, it divides the two nations of Iraq and Iran.

The Euphrates runs parallel to the Tigris River. When both rivers enter Iraq they are never more than 100 miles apart. The Euphrates forms the western boundary in northern Iraq called *Al Jazirah* (Arabic for *the Island*). The Tigris forms the eastern boundary. After flowing within 25 miles of the Tigris, the Euphrates splits in two, coming together again 110 miles downstream. In Greek the word Euphrates means *sweet water.* The Assyrian name means *the stream* or *the great stream*.[4]

94 percent of the river's water originates in the Turkish highlands. Major modern cities on the Euphrates and the Tigris include *Ar Raqqah, Dayr az Zawr* in Syria, *Karbala', Al Hillah, An Najaf* and *Baghdad* in Iraq—all of which depend on this single water source. The Euphrates is important solely for its water supply. Turkey, Syria, and Iraq all compete for its water in regard to irrigation, hydroelectric power, and simple need. Making matters worse, Iraq has to deal with a high salt content in Euphrates water because of what's happening upstream, i.e., discharges of sewage, industrial chemicals and pesticides.[5]

TRIBULATION EUPHRATES

Clearly, the Euphrates River is of major importance to Turkey, Syria, and Iraq, among other nations. Were the earth's climate to drastically change, every country that depends on water from the Euphrates would be on the verge of total collapse. During the final years of the Tribulation that will be the case.

In relation to the River Euphrates and the Tribulation, the flow of water will greatly decrease during the last three-and-a-half years because of the plagues. Potential meteorites, global climate changes, super cooling because of intense cloud cover and debris in the atmosphere, superheating because of significant loss of ozone and perhaps even a catastrophe within the sun, and the plague of no rainfall from the Two Witnesses—this will all lead to global drought.

At the end of the three-and-a-half years the river's water will still be flowing, but the water flow could be so low as to prove useless and utterly undrinkable, and of course it will probably be undrinkable anyway because of the plagues and direct human intervention. The Antichrist and his nations and armies will need an unobstructed path to gather in Israel for the Battle of Armageddon, the final war against Christ, and so the River Euphrates will completely dry up as a miraculous act of God *so that the way of the kings of the east may be prepared*.

HYPERDIMENSIONAL EUPHRATES

The Euphrates River was a natural dividing line in ancient times. To cross it meant much more than simply crossing a river—to cross the boundary of the Empire and enter a different world.[6]

When that ancient fact is applied to the future fact, that of the armies of the East crossing the dried-up riverbed of the Euphrates and marching toward Jerusalem, the ancient perception of the river as boundary and its meaning is the same. What we have here is the collision of the past and future at the same point of the natural dividing line. Thus, the dividing line, the Euphrates River, is hyperdimensional in the sense of place and time.

Place: When the armies of the East cross the natural border and leave the boundary of the Empire they are leaving the natural world behind and entering a different world in the sense that soon they will face the hyperdimensional person of Jesus Christ and the literal transformation of the world and all reality. All will meet in or around Jerusalem for war, a mass converging of multiple hyperdimensional realities and beings in one place.

Time: When the army crosses the dividing line it will be like stepping across a preprogrammed timepiece that immediately starts the final countdown for the end of the world.

200,000,000 MAN ARMY

After the introduction of the sixth bowl plague the Antichrist immediately declares war on God at the Battle of Armageddon. The remnants of humanity in the nations of the East, those dwelling beyond the great River Euphrates—primarily China, among others—collaborate with the Antichrist.

Even after millions of deaths because of the plagues, a large Chinese population would still exist. In the Book of Revelation the army that crosses the dried Euphrates is estimated to be

200,000,000 strong. The only country on earth that could meet that number is China.

In 2,000, the total estimated active personal strength of the Chinese military, the People's Liberation Army (PLA), reached 2.5 million: 1.8 million ground forces, plus numerous reserve and paramilitary units. Some estimates are as high as 2.8 to 3 million, easily the world's largest army. The available manpower for the PLA between the ages of 15-49 is 370,087,489 (2002 est). Those fit for military service of the same age: 203,003,036 (2002 est).[7]

Should China require an army of 200 million today they could pull it off without breaking a sweat.

China joins with the Antichrist, whose seat of power will be in Israel.

The Antichrist will have the largest and most abundant water reserves in Israel and all the world! Knowing what was coming, and in spite of the global drought and plagues, the Antichrist will be prepared. He'll have water reserves to supply his needs and the needs of his vast army. Thus, water will also be a motivator on the Euphrates dependent nations like Turkey, Syria, Iraq, and China. The Antichrist will be able to supply their countries with water—if they join his war effort.

And deep sorrow finds them, for when the war is ended they are consumed by the birds shadowing the valley.

Revelation 16:13

And I [John] saw three unclean spirits like frogs coming out of the mouth of the dragon, out of the mouth of the beast, and out of the mouth of the false prophet.

UNCLEAN SPIRITS

At this point in the series of events we're nearing the very end of the Tribulation.

Three *unclean spirits* come from the dragon, their father the devil, and the Antichrist, who is the Beast, and False Prophet, the second Beast.

The unclean spirits are three unholy angels from the kingdom of darkness. Although the spirits are described as frog-like in appearance this description may be figurative in nature, suggesting that they are *unclean* and perhaps *small in form.*

But the spirits in question are literal. They are very real. These won't be gifted human orators or strange phenomena within nature. (A plague of frogs, as some have argued.) These are genuine fallen angels performing signs and wonders which the Antichrist and the False Prophet use to convince the remaining human population to follow them into the Battle of Armageddon, a battle that essentially amounts to suicide. The *frogs* are magical, supernatural, frightening, and very convincing.

I'd like to make it clear that even though the Antichrist will be mighty beyond compare (because of the power given to him by the devil who can tap into the Seven Spirits of God, the Power Source of God), he is unable to prevent the collapse of world order. The remaining eastern nations, as well as the nations of the world, are greatly affected by the disastrous chain of events of the last three-and-a-half years. The world will be in total disarray. To marshal the last of humanity, the Antichrist will have to do something *unusual* to pump up the masses one final time. The magic powers of the unclean spirits will do the job! Humanity will marvel and be completely captivated by, as well as fear, the power and supernatural nature of the three unclean spirits brought forth by Satan. The wonders that they do will help to motivate China and the nations to gather their armies together and cross the dry riverbed of the Euphrates to assist the Antichrist. The unclean spirits may even convince them that the earth is being threatened by aliens from outer space—Jesus Christ, a Returning Space Alien with his (heavenly) army.

Revelation 16:14

For they are spirits of demons, performing signs, which go out to the kings of the whole world, to gather them to the battle of that great day of God Almighty.

THE FROGS

These unclean spirits once served God in heaven, but of course they are no longer angels of beauty, for they serve their leader Lucifer, that serpent of old who is the devil and Satan, their unholy king. They lost their original beauty long ago, for as I have discussed, evil corrupts beauty and turns it into ugliness beyond compare.

The reference to *frogs* is probably metaphorical here. The true shape or form/appearance of these creatures is for all intents and purposes unknown, but interestingly enough, there are historical accounts of demonic spirits described as *frog-like, lizard-like, reptilian humanoids that live under the earth,* obviously of the amphibian and reptile family.[8]

A PERSONAL DEMONIC ATTACK

On occasion, in regard to demonic attack or possession, people who are *possessed* or *attacked* by fallen spirits sometimes describe them as frog-like or lizard-like.

Fallen angels/spirits can literally attack humans and try to *possess* or *control* their bodies. I, myself, had a personal encounter with a lizard-like demon, an actual attack on my body and soul—to say that I believe these three unclean spirits will appear frog-like or lizard-like is an understatement. My experience was of the worst and most horrific kind and I can say, without doubt, lizard-like in appearance is as factual as gravity, a description that's unfortunately dead on the nail.

Many cultures use similar verbal descriptors for evil spirits. This is not coincidence. There is a *common thread* that connects them all—frogs and lizards are generally disliked or thought of as unclean in many parts of the world and so, like the serpent, they have become common descriptors for evil spirits, but I argue there is an ancient truth to them that we, in all our logic and reason, have incorrectly, and most arrogantly, brushed off as myth, the horrific stuff of dark fairytales.

A REAL AFRICAN FAIRY TALE

What should be clear by now is that many of the events that take place during the Great Tribulation will indeed be magical, supernatural, mythic and even fairytale-like, so we shouldn't be surprised if there is more than a grain of truth to these global descriptions of evil spirits or successful or unsuccessful demonic attempts at possession or attack. I come from Africa where voodoo and witchcraft, curses and demons, are as common as apple pie and baseball in America. I come from a much older world where the grains of supernatural truth are larger, heavier, and often observable. Because of my personal encounter, I can describe evil spirits as most definitely lizard-like. Their eyes are blood red and produce a bright-colored flush—a red glow falls from them. From their perspective they may even *see in red* or *only in red*. Their temples puff out like adders and *smoke* or *puffs of steam ejects* or *blasts* from their swollen temples. From their mouths come harsh, screeching, piercing whines that produce deafening noise of a relatively high pitch. This may sound like a monster from an African fairy tale, but it's a real monster that I witnessed with my very own eyes.

As far as other cultural descriptions are concerned, demons are traditionally amphibious, or scaly, or covered in something like scales, and they appear to have a humanoid form. I'd like to point out here, as a reminder, that even though the Scriptures clearly attest to the reality and validity of demons, what they really look like is never described in any detail in the Bible.[9]

I believe these three *unclean frogs* will turn out to have an appearance similar to the one that I saw and described above. It doesn't seem unreasonable to conclude that given the supernatural and unpredictable nature of End Time events my conclusion is more than possible. It is fact.

However it turns out, these three unclean spirits or frogs captivate the attention of the world and give the Antichrist the power he needs to ally the world population for the last battle on earth.

Revelation 16:15

"Behold, I am coming as a thief. Blessed is he who watches, and keeps his garments, lest he walk naked and they see his shame."

AS AN UNEXPECTED THIEF

The mighty Lord Jesus confronts John, saying, "Observe, I am coming a second time, unannounced, like a thief in the night. Blessed are those who watch and keep their clothes, so they may not go naked and be shamefully exposed."

The Lord uses phrases like *coming as a thief* in regard to his Second Coming to make it perfectly clear that his return will catch most everyone off guard!

This is also a reference to the Fourth Rapture, an event that will also catch people off guard. Both events have an unexpected, even unexpected thief-like aspect to them.

Jesus also warns us that we must not be *naked to the truth,* for the truth sets us free from slavery to the fallen nature, freeing us from our shame—and if you're prepared, his grace will free you from having to face the devil himself during the last three-and-a-half years of the Great Tribulation. Thus, we must cover ourselves in the grace and peace of Christ because he's our survival plan.

If you're unprepared and distracted the end result in regard to your lack of preparedness is going to be rather revealing.

NAKED SEXUAL IMMORALITY

The reference here to *nakedness* also seems to reflect the sexual nature of the End Times, what will amount to a world culture of rampant sexual immorality. The lack of modesty and the acceptance of immoral sexual behavior (sexual disobedience) in our society today is a sure sign of the moral decline of global society and a strong indicator that the End Times are nearing.

Rampant sexual immorality is, of course, nothing new, but the nature of the world during the End Times will encourage nakedness, immodesty, and sexual immorality in extreme forms, which is why the verse says humanity walks about *naked* and *shameful* before the Lord. Of course, from the perspective of the sexually disobedient there will be nothing immoral or shameful about it, and certainly nothing new.

Revelation 16:16

And they gathered them together to the place called in Hebrew, Armageddon.

ARMAGEDDON

John is told that the people of the earth will gather themselves together in a place called *Armageddon*, that long, wide valley pointing like a finger toward the city of Jerusalem. The word is Greek, derived from the Hebrew (*har Megiddo*), which means *hill* or *city of Megiddo*. The historical Megiddo was located on the southern rim of the *Plain of Esdraelon*, a place known as the *Battlefield of Palestine*. Over the centuries *Armageddon* came to mean *the place of terrible and final conflict*. Today, the word is attached to locations and battles all over the world that have nothing to do with the real place and original meaning.[10]

The Battle of Armageddon: before the return of Christ, the Antichrist, with the False Prophet/False Pope, the three evil *frog-like* spirits, and the remaining human population, gather in Israel (Isa. 10:28–32). Massive armies cross the dry riverbed of the Euphrates, motivated by thirst, fear, and the wonder of three unclean spirits, their intention: to go to war with God. Remember, it's possible that the Antichrist, the False Prophet, and the unclean spirits may convince humanity that Jesus is an alien from outer space coming to attack the earth. They will retreat to Megiddo, the valley of Armageddon, after the events of Zechariah 12:2–9 and 14:2 have taken place, and within the valley of Armageddon all of them will be utterly consumed, not by an outer space alien, but by God, Jesus the returning Christ.

HOPE AT THE END OF THE WORLD
FOR THE UNBELIEVER

Armageddon is not the end of the world, as many biblical scholars claim. It is the end of this world in regard to the fallen nature of life, but this planet will carry on forever as the mighty and bottomless lake of fire, the eternal prison-place for the Evil One, the fallen angels, and the unrepentant.

The unbeliever may say this is distressing, to say the least. Where is our hope if we are all to perish? Our hope is in Jesus Christ! It should be clear by now that Christ has been patient, giving the unrepentant time, reaching to them for their salvation, but he will at some point finally lose patience—he will reach as far and as long as he ever can reach and then one day he will finally pull his hand away.

The unbeliever may also say that it is cruel for our children to perish and not have the chance of long life, but most Christians believe that there is an *age of accountability* where young children reach an age at which they are in the position to make a true decision to accept or reject the Spirit of Christ. No one knows the age, but it seems reasonable to conclude that it is a matter between God and the individual. Many Christians tend to think the age of accountability falls around the age of 13, but again, this is arguable. Whatever the case may be, before that age all children fall under God's protection and so therefore those children will be raptured in the Fourth Rapture with the living believers in Jesus. They will escape the wrath of the Son of God. As for living a long life, they will indeed live a long and happy life with the Lamb of God—for one thousand years on this earth and then for eternity with him in the Second Heaven.

ARMAGEDDON ALIENS & ALIEN ABDUCTION

In our logical, rational, and scientific times it's interesting to note that belief in aliens and alien abduction is widespread. Numerous alien cults exist throughout the world. Believers in aliens and alien abduction range from well respected scientists to your basic home-grown kid from Kansas living in a trailer with her dog. The country of France released a government report that endorsed the reality of UFOs on May 31, 2010, concluding that UFOs are real and possibly extraterrestrial in origin.

I bring this up now because I want to explore the *Jesus as attacking alien* concept.

As I stated earlier, when Christ returns the Antichrist, the False Prophet, and the three fallen angels may have convinced humanity that the returning Christ is *an alien* coming to *abduct* the rest of humanity as a way to motivate them to join the Battle of Armageddon.

Hollywood, television, and print media have done a splendid job convincing us that aliens are real and that alien abduction takes place every day, it's true, but media can't take all the credit. It doesn't fully explain why such a deep belief or faith in alien visitation exists today.

Personal alien encounters and abductions occur many times a day all over the world! The 1992 Roper Survey reported that at least 2% of the population within the United States claimed to have been abducted by aliens from outer space. This means in 1992 over 5 million Americans believed they were abducted by aliens, resulting in over 6,000 abductions taking place every day. Using those figures, the number for the entire planet would be something close to one hundred million people! If these numbers are correct, as the late and great scientist Carl Sagan suggested, this means personal alien abductions by beings from another planet have been taking place about every three seconds for the last couple of decades.[11]

You might think numbers like this would turn the most ardent *UFOlogist* into a raging skeptic, but that is not the case—why? The answer is difficult to nail down. For whatever reason, the belief or faith in aliens and alien abduction around the world runs as deep as belief and faith in God. This increase in the belief of alien existence is fascinating and timely, for the belief of alien existence and visitation around the world suggests that we are, indeed, nearing the End Times.

GOD IS FOR CHILDREN
ALIENS ARE FOR GROWNUPS

Thousands of people have no problem accepting the existence of aliens today. There is no doubt in their minds that aliens exist. When asked about God—if he exists—they dismiss the reality of God offhand, labeled the stuff of myth and childhood. God is for children. Aliens are for grownups. It seems that it is easier in our modern culture to believe in unseen, unproven, unknown UFOs and alien visitations that are most often extremely negative experiences than it is to believe in a loving God. There are even radical and heretical priests and pastors within the Christian Church that make this claim today, asserting that Christ was an alien and not the Son of God, a simple case of mistaken alien identity.

In light of this information it isn't much of a stretch to imagine that humanity will be primed to believe and accept that the returning Savior is an alien from another planet or dimension. Jesus, the extra terrestrial.

After the Fourth Rapture people may claim that Christ, the Christians, and the Jews had been working together for centuries, an alien conspiracy theory of truly epic proportions. Thus, the rapture of the living Christians in the middle of the Tribulation may be referred to as *alien abductions.* The *abductees* may be looked upon as enemies of the earth and humanity instead of kidnapped victims. They would see Jesus as an alien invader and abductor, an enemy worth fighting against at the Battle of Armageddon.

FORMS OF LIFE IN THE UNIVERSE

I think it's important to point out that I believe there are no other forms of intelligent alien life similar to humanity in this entropic, fallen universe. There is but one form of life in the universe and that life consists of the Family of God, the Father, Son, and the Holy Spirit, the angels, both holy and fallen, and humanity and all life on earth.

If aliens are perceived to be real in any way it's likely that they're not physical beings who've traveled billions of light years to earth in spaceships, but are in fact hyperdimensional beings posing as distant space travelers, merely fallen angels in disguise.[12] Since the Holy Scriptures make it very clear that Satan can appear in different forms, this conclusion does not seem unreasonable. I don't believe aliens or extra terrestrials or beings from other planets exist in any form anywhere in this universe other than in the form of fallen angels. The irony, of course, is that the fallen angels *are the real aliens,* for they are not of this world, and humanity will fight with them against the so-called alien invader from outer space who has come to wage war at the Battle of Armageddon.

Revelation 16:17

Then the seventh angel poured out his bowl into the air, and a loud voice came out of the temple of heaven, from the throne, saying, "It is done!"

THE SEVENTH BOWL PLAGUE

With the conclusion of the Battle of Armageddon and the Antichrist's armed forces completely annihilated, the only people left alive on earth will be the regular citizens, all of whom have become exceedingly corrupt through the Evil One they worship. Now that Lucifer's unholy trinity and the armies of the world have been sent to the Land of Forgetfulness, Jesus, as the seventh angel, being the seventh Spirit of the Seven Spirits of God, releases the final seventh bowl into the air.

Heaven exclaims, "Prepare yourselves, people of the earth, for it is done!"

This final plague on earth spells doom to all earthly fallen-natured flesh forever, right down to the subatomic particles!

Revelation 16:18

And there were noises and thundering and lightning; and there was a great earthquake, such a mighty and great earthquake as has not occurred since men were on the earth.

THE REFORMATION OF THE EARTH
The Destruction of the Last of Fallen Natured Humankind

Lo and behold, John hears deafening noises. Lightning proceeds from the holy Temple in heaven, electric-like discharges, and tremendous sounds like peals of thunder, depicting the power and strength of the Voices from the Seven Spirits of God—the end of the world as we know it is coming in the form of the Son of God. His holy presence alone causes a catastrophic global earthquake as he approaches the planet. (For related and much more detailed information on the reformation of the earth refer to Chapter 6.) Then he reaches out and moves the earth to and fro, shaking the massive planet. Not since the Father and Son and the Holy Spirit created the world has there been such a tremendous quake, and the lost who continue to exist will be doomed as the very shape and nature of the earth transforms right down to the atom and beyond.

Revelation 16:19

Now the great city was divided into three parts, and the cities of the nations fell. And great Babylon was remembered before God, to give her the cup of wine of the fierceness of his wrath.

THE NATIONS FALL

The intense earthquake causes the area where Jerusalem stood (mentioned by John as *the great city*) to divide into three parts, a clear representation of the Trinity. The city is absolutely destroyed by the reformation of the planet: (potential) meteorite strikes, global earthquake, a wall of lava and fire encircling the planet, plus the actual *changing* of the nature of life right down to the molecular level.

Christ returns to the exact spot from whence he departed 2,000 years before, returning to a newly made Mount of Olives. Every other city and every nation on earth falls and disappears as though they had never existed! Modern Babylon will be remembered by God as Jesus pours out his wrath upon the terrain where the proud city once stood on seven hills (Rome).

Revelation 16:20

Then every island fled away, and the mountains were not found.

THE PLANET IS ALTERED

The planet is altered in great and awesome ways. John sees every island disappear. Massive mountains are gone. Christ is preparing the globe for the new order—not the senior President Bush's new order planned in 1992; not President Obama's new order in 2009; not the Antichrist's new order established through the Great Tribulation. It is Christ's New Order. It begins with his new kingdom in the seventh millennium!

The earth is transformed into a glorious paradise similar to the First Heaven, as it was originally meant to be when it was first created as the Third Heaven long ago, before its Fall into the sinful nature. Nothing that retains the fallen nature can be allowed to enter into this restful paradise. "For the word of God is living and powerful, and sharper than any two-edged sword... And there is no creature hidden from his sight, but all things are naked and open to the eyes of him to whom we must give account" (Heb. 4:12a, 13).

Revelation 16:21

And great hail from heaven fell upon men, each hailstone about the weight of a talent. Men blasphemed God because of the plague of the hail, since that plague was exceedingly great.

THE PLAGUE OF HAIL

The Lord thunders in the heavens and enormous *hailstones* fall from the sky. Once again, this might be referring to meteorites and ice rocks jettisoned from the *dirty snowball* core of comets. (Refer to Chapter 6 for much more detailed information on the reformation of the earth and the possibility that the hailstones are meteorites.) Every hailstone is a talent in weight, about a hundred or more pounds.

Whatever the hail turns out to be, it lays waste to the last people who have thus far escaped death, those who have somehow survived the worldwide earthquake and the encircling wall of fire and lava, and though they cry to the mountains to hide them, the mountains cannot help them, and so with their last dying breaths they blaspheme the God of Glory because of the final plague.

Jesus reforms the earth and removes all fallen-natured life from the face of the planet!

"I AM THE EARTHQUAKE! I AM THE WALL OF FIRE AND LAVA! I AM THE HAILSTONES! I AM!" declares the Lord.

When the last of unrepentant humanity passes from existence, cursing their Creator, Jesus Christ finally shouts, "IT IS FINISHED!"

The first Human Age of human life on earth will be over forevermore!

The seven bowl plagues are complete!

Christ is ready to introduce the Second Age to all believers of the old world.

As a note of interest, the Scriptures make it clear that the Saints witnessed the *great ending* from the sky above. None were on the earth when Christ reformed the planet. With the heavenly angels they all witness Jesus reform the earth, and of course we're talking about hyperdimensional realities here and Super Natured events, the spiritual and physical worlds melting into one another while Christ reforms the earth.

All will be ready to live on this same-but-totally-reformed-and-transformed planet for one thousand years! The saved will not be of flesh and blood as we know it, for they are transfigured when they are resurrected and have new bodies just like Christ when he reappeared after his death on the cross. The Saints will be in the Second Phase of Body, the glorified body!

SIX DAYS OF REFORMATION

Christ spends six literal days reforming the earth for his Kingdom Age, and on the seventh day he rests with all his faithful believers!

When his work is concluded, his precious feet touch down upon the Mount of Olives—the *new* Mount of Olives—and at this point the Saints hovering above join Jesus on the reformed Earth and the holy angels return to the First Heaven, the Father's Heaven. The Kingdom Age in perfect nature and (potentially) perfect time begins!

The seventh *day* will last one thousand years. After that the Saints will follow him into eternity and God only knows what. His Word is complete and the world will be bathed in his glory and his light will shine forever!

* * * * *

SOURCES:

1. *Diseases,* pg. 305-308, The New Unger's Bible Dictionary, Moody (1988).
   Boil (1), Alex Macalister; *Boil (2),* W. L. Walker, International Bible Standard
   Encyclopedia, Online Edition, <http://www.studylight.org>.
   Boil/sore—Helkos, #1668, pg. 27, Greek Dictionary of the New Testament,
   Strong's Exhaustive Concordance of the Bible/Dictionary of the Hebrew
   and Greek Words, Hendrickson Publishers.
2. *Blood—Haima,* #129, pg. 8, Greek Dictionary of the New Testament,
   Strong's Exhaustive Concordance of the Bible/Dictionary of the Hebrew
   and Greek Words, Hendrickson Publishers.
3. *Angels, I & II,* John Macarteny Wilson, International Bible Standard
   Encyclopedia, Online Edition, <http://www.studylight.org>.
   Angel; Angels, Fallen, pg. 61-62, The New Unger's Bible Dictionary, Moody
   Press (1988).
4. *Euphrates,* pg. 381, The New Unger's Bible Dictionary, Moody Press (1988).
   Euphrates, George Frederick Wright, International Bible Standard
   Encyclopedia, Online Edition, <http://www.studylight.org>.
   Euphrates, from *Hitchcock's Bible Dictionary* (late 1800s), Hitchcock, The
   Hyper Dictionary, compiled by Chris Knight,
   <http://www.hyperdictionary.com>.
5. *Euphrates,* contributed by Shaul Cohen, Microsoft Encarta Encyclopedia
   (2002).
   Syria, Iraq Stress Historical Rights to Waters of Tigris, Euphrates, Syria-Iraq,
   Economics (1998), Arabic News.com, <http://www.arabicnews.com>.
   *A SCRAMBLE FOR WATER RESOURCES IS UNDER WAY IN THE MIDDLE
   EAST,* Republic of Turkey Ministry of Foreign Affairs,
   <http://www.mfa.gov.tr/MFA_tr/>.
   Israel's Chronic Water Problem, Ministry of Foreign Affairs,
   <http://www.israel-mfa.gov.il>.
6. *Euphrates,* pg. 381, The New Unger's Bible Dictionary, Moody Press (1988).
   Euphrates, contributed by Shaul Cohen, Microsoft Encarta Encyclopedia
   (2002).
   Euphrates, George Frederick Wright, International Bible Standard
   Encyclopedia, Online Edition, <http://www.studylight.org>.
   Euphrates, from *Hitchcock's Bible Dictionary* (late 1800s), Hitchcock, The
   Hyper Dictionary, compiled by Chris Knight,
   <http://www.hyperdictionary.com>.
7. *China; military,* CIA World Fact Book 2002, <http://www.cia.gov>.
   China's Army Marks 70th Anniversary, CNN/Reuters, Beijing (1999),
   <http://www.cnn.com>.
   China's Military Capabilities, CheckPoint (2001), text source: Frank W.
   Moore, Institute for Defense and Disarmament Studies (2,000),
   CheckPoint, <http://www.checkpoint-online.ch>.
   World's Largest Army Not Necessarily Strongest, CNN/Military Affairs
   Correspondent Jamie McIntyre (1998; posted online 1999),
   <http://www.cnn.com>.
8. *The History of the Devil and the Idea of Evil From the Earliest Times to the
   Present Day,* Paul Carus (1900), Online Edition, J. B. Hare, Sacred-texts,
   The Internet Sacred Text Archive, <http://www.sacred-texts.com>.

Pseudomonarchia daemonum, Johann Wier (1583); *Dictionnaire Infernal,* Collin de Plancy (1863); *Goetia,* S. L. MacGregor Mathers (1904); compiled by Krista M. Baker, *Delusions of Grandeur,* <http://www.deliriumsrealm.com/delirium/index.asp>.

The History of the Devil and the Idea of Evil From the Earliest Times to the Present Day, Paul Carus (1900), Online Edition, J. B. Hare, Sacred-texts, The Internet Sacred Text Archive, <http://www.sacred-texts.com>.

Unclean Beasts Issuing from the Mouths of the Dragon, the Beast, and the False Prophet, Artist unknown; English, probably London, about *1255-1260*; Tempera colors, gold leaf, blue, green, red and brown washes on parchment; MS. LUDWIG III 1, FOL. 34V, The Collections, the Getty Museum, <http://www.getty.edu>.

9. *Armageddon,* pg. 103, The New Unger's Bible Dictionary, Moody Press (1988).
10. *The Demon-Haunted World,* Chapter 4, Carl Sagan, Random House (1995).
11. *Demons in Alien's Clothing,* Ron Patton, article, Illuminati Conspiracy Archive, <http://www.conspiracyarchive.com>.
12. *The Return of the Nephilim?* article, Chuck Missler, Koinonia House, <http://www.khouse.com>.

Further reading:

Dictionary of Deities and Demons in the Bible, Karel van der Toorn, Bob Becking, Pieter Willem Van Der Horst, Wm. B. Eerdmans Publishing Co.; 2nd edition (1999).

Biblical Demonology, Merril F. Unger, Kregel Publications (1995).

Demons, David G. Reese, The Anchor Bible Dictionary, ed. David Noel Freedman, Doubleday (1992).

Alien Encounters, Chuck Missler, Mark Eastman, Koinonia House (2003).

CHAPTER 17
The Scarlet Woman & The Scarlet Beast

Revelation 17:1

Then one of the seven angels who had the seven bowls came and talked with me [John], saying, "Come, I will show you the judgment of the great harlot who sits on many waters."

DESTRUCTION OF MODERN BABYLON

Chapter 16 described the end of the Human Age, focusing on the conclusion of the Great Tribulation just before the return of Christ, the reformation of the earth, and the establishment of his millennial and restful 1,000 year kingdom.

Chapters 17 and 18 take us back to the middle of the Tribulation, concentrating on the fall of modern Babylon, the apostate Christian Church which includes the seat of power within the city of Rome.

Revelation devotes two chapters to modern Babylon's fall and its total obliteration, a sure sign that God disapproves of its ways!

Now, John explains that one of the seven angels, having one of the seven bowls, comes forward to speak to him. As should be more than clear now, the angel is also a symbol of Christ. Jesus is the seven angels! He is the seven stars, the seven churches, the seven spirits! "I AM WHO I AM! I AM EVERYTHING THERE IS!" Revelation is Jesus, the Christ! Let the eternal light of the Son of God shine forever, amen!

Jesus beckons John, saying, "Come, I will show you the judgment of the great harlot who sits on many waters."

In the figurative language of the Scriptures the word *harlot* typically refers to an *idolatress* (Isa. 1:21; Jer. 2:20; Ezek. 16:13–63; etc.).[1] That's how it's meant here, in the sense that there's a general falling away from Christ and a turn toward *idol worship* within the Christian Church, what amounts to a blending and acceptance of foreign religious practices via global inter-faith ecumenicism and self worship. It can also be interpreted literally, in the sense that salvation can be bought for a price, for the Christian Church will have prostituted herself to the world and become whore-like.

There is also an historical connection to the Catholic and Orthodox Church in regard to the worship of statues/Saints/icons, common practice within both the Catholic and Orthodox body. This suggests that the movement toward corruption and an apostate nature in the Church began long, long ago.

The word *waters* indicate those who make up the Church scattered around the globe. It also pertains to all humanity and the influence of the harlot upon them.

Revelation 17:2

"With whom [the harlot] the kings of the earth committed fornication, and the inhabitants of the earth were made drunk with the wine of her fornication."

THE WINE OF HER CORRUPTION

Jesus continues saying, "Willingly, she allowed herself to be corrupted by the rulers of the earth (spoken of as *kings*), and the masses of the earth are easily led and intoxicated with the wine of her corruption."

In a very real sense the Church sells her soul to the devil. It's reasonable to argue that some of those involved will probably have good intentions, at least, initially. They will convince themselves that global inter-faith ecumenicism is what God wants and supports. After all, God is a God of love and tolerance is he not? Of course, this is simply a way for them to justify their will over the will of God, what amounts to ignorance, lack of judgment, dangerous self-absorption, pride/ego, and justification for sinful/immoral behavior, religious, sexual, or otherwise. They claim to be Christians without having to accept and obey the teachings of Christ, a practice that's becoming more and more common today in the Christian world. What it amounts to, really, is a sort of Anything Goes Christianity. It's Christian Gumbo for the soul, a mix of leftovers and whatever else you can find in the religious kitchen thrown in—everything except faith in and obedience to Christ. But the truth of it is, it might taste good and spicy, but it won't do your soul any good, and so in their arrogance they will think the Lord Jesus Christ is with them.

Revelation 17:3

So he [the angel] carried me [John] away in the Spirit into the wilderness. And I saw a woman sitting on a scarlet beast which was full of names of blasphemy, having seven heads and ten horns.

MODERN BABYLON
The Beginning of the Tribulation

John is carried away into the *wilderness*. This is a Greek word (*eremos*), referring to *wild country/wild wood* or *an uninhabited, sterile land unable to support human life, a place of desolation* (Ps. 107:4; Job 24:5; Deut. 32:10).[2] It means the woman who rides the Beast is in a desolate place morally and spiritually.

John sees a *woman* sitting on a *scarlet-colored beast.*

The woman is the symbol of the harlot Christian Church, the Apostate Dominant Church that exists during the Great Tribulation. That Church is forming now. The apostate nature of the Christian Church that will exist in the first three-and-a-half years of the Tribulation is taking hold within the Church today via global inter-faith ecumenicism, the increase in specialized and fracturing dogmas/splinter groups within Christianity, a steady decline or an exceptionally loose interpretation of Judeo-Christian ethics and moral values, and the relentless driving force of politics and power. There are powers within Christianity today that are moving the Church at an even, unbroken pace away from the true nature and heart of Christ. In the not-so-distant future the Christian heart will be so far removed from the true Heart of Christ that authentic believing Christians will have little choice but to move *underground.* In fact, this postmodern Christian underground movement has already begun.

THE UNDERGROUND

Many genuine Christians have become dissatisfied and untrusting of their local Christian organizations. They have started looking for more likeminded followers of Christ, those who are not caught up in the complex web of religious dogma, heresy, and immorality that has spread through the modern Church—and they're quietly finding one another. They are choosing to leave their ethically and morally corrupt church bodies and in a sense go *underground.*

During the last three-and-a-half years of the Tribulation Christians will have no choice but to literally go underground in order to survive.

There will be strong believing Christians within the apostate Christian Church for the first three-and-a-half years of the Tribulation, of course, and they will be raptured in the Fourth Rapture. Likewise, there will be many indifferent or lukewarm Christians influenced by the apostate nature of the Church. They will not partake in the Fourth Rapture. They will then be martyred for Christ. Of course, there are many in the Church who won't be genuine Christians at all.

THE SCARLET DRAGON & THE WOMAN

The scarlet dragon is the red dragon, the devil.

The woman is the apostate Church and she is riding the dragon. This tells us that the dragon controls the Church through the dragon's son, the Antichrist, as well as through his False Prophet.

The reference to blasphemous names is meant to show us just how evil the dragon, the Antichrist, and the False Prophet are, revealing how much hatred they have for Christ. We are also told that the scarlet dragon is *full* of blasphemous names. This informs us that the arrogance and hatred within the unholy trinity has filled them to capacity—their blasphemy is within and without them, in every way possible complete.

The *seven heads* represent the seat of power for the apostate Church. The city of Rome is the seat of power for the Catholic Church which historically represents the seat of power for all Christianity. Rome sits on seven hills. Thus, the scarlet dragon (Satan) will rule the woman (the apostate Church) through Rome (the Catholic seat of power) via the Antichrist and the False Prophet by uniting the religions of the world under the banner of the False Prophet's One World Religion Organization.

The *ten horns* symbolize the ten nations ruled by the dragon— United Europe, or the ten-valved-heart that pumps life into all the nations of United Europe.

Revelation 17:4

The woman was arrayed in purple and scarlet, and adorned with gold and precious stones and pearls, having in her hand a golden cup full of abominations and the filthiness of her fornication.

PURPLE & SCARLET

The woman is the symbol of the apostate system (forming within the Church today) that is the Christian Church at the beginning of the seven year Tribulation.

It's more than likely *purple and scarlet, gold and precious stones and pearls* are allegorical references to a generalized and widespread corruption within the Christian Church. At the same time, the colors point to the specific seat of Christian power in Rome, the Catholic Church, the Vatican, St. Peters, the residence of the Pope.

How so? Answer: purple and scarlet can be called the *colors of Catholicism.*

That this verse refers to the exact colors is not an accident or coincidence. Arguing that Catholicism simply took two colors from the many colors mentioned in Scriptures and decided to use them is patently absurd because where the colors came from is so obvious: purple was the color of Roman Emperors. As time wore on and the papacy became more and more powerful, gaining significant wealth and power, the popes started wearing clothing dyed purple, and the color-connection to imperious Rome was complete. It even came with the imperial Roman Emperor attitude. Others within the Church, motivated by similar desires (power, wealth, social status), mimicked the example by wearing purple robes. In regard to the papacy, here are but a few cases in point: Pope Innocent III (1198-1216) sat on a purple throne, his horse draped in scarlet; Pope Boniface VIII (1294-1303) said he was Caesar, the Roman Emperor, and wore a crown covered with more than 200 jewels, including rubies, emeralds, sapphires, and large pearls; Pope Paul II (1464 to 1471) adopted the color scarlet in 1464, another symbol of wealth and power. On special occasions popes, cardinals, and bishops don golden miters and golden vestments, all made of real gold and golden thread. Popes also sometimes wear ermine, an expensive fur.[3]

During the End Times, those who are in favor of the dragon and have positions of power within the Church will dress themselves in such finery and color, having usurped a once noble branch of the genuine Christian Church, the Catholic Church.

NAME OF THE OWRO

The name of the One World Religion Organization is of course unknown, but global inter-faith groups with names like the United Religions Initiative (U.R.I.) are certainly strong contenders. If nothing else, they are credible gauges on which to base name-theory.[4]

Potential names aside, it's clear that the Christian Church, specifically, Catholicism in regard to Rome, falls beneath the banner of the OWRO and together they are responsible for abominations against God.

The *woman's cup* in this verse is full of the filthiness of her corruption. This suggests that the Church in general has fallen into total corruption and sinful disobedience.

Revelation 17:5

And on her forehead a name was written: "Mystery, Babylon the Great, the mother of harlots and the abominations of the earth."

NEW WORLD RELIGIOUS ORDER

In the sight of God a title is give for the new organization and the name is placed upon the *woman's forehead*. (For related information on marking the forehead/body, refer to Chapter 14:1, under the heading *On the Mount*.) God is labeling the apostate Church, and you could paraphrase it like this: "The New World Order (OWRO) is a *mystery* organization operating from the seven hills, representing modern Babylon the Great. She is the mother of prostitutes."

The word *abominations* is used to describe corruption, immoral behavior, and the apostate nature of the woman at the beginning of the Tribulation, but it also refers to the historical record of the woman, i.e., the Holy Roman Catholic Church (and to a lesser degree, collective Christianity) in regard to violence and warfare in the name of Christ, heretical theology, and idolatry over the centuries. Because of its long history the Holy Roman Catholic Church shoulders much of the burden and responsibility.

THE MYSTERIOUS HISTORICAL RECORD

She is called a *mystery* for a number of reasons:

(1) From John's perspective the modern Church would nearly be unrecognizable as a Christian institution. This would include all aspects of the Church entire, but specifically the Catholic Church. She would truly be a mystery to John.

(2) The word suggests secrecy and things that are baffling or unexplainable, and since much of the modern Church is involved in unbiblical secrets—rituals behind closed doors, addendums to the Bible filled with so-called elite knowledge involving specialized incantations, rites, behavior, clothing, theology, and dogma—and since secrets by their very nature promote mystery and elitism, and sometimes even baffling or unexplainable behavior, it should be clear that she's apart from God and the Antichrist controls her, for all things apart from God are secretive, baffling, and unexplainable, and all things involved with the Antichrist are exceedingly wicked.[5]

THE ERA OF THE HARLOT

The era of the harlot, the Apostate Dominant Christian Church, comes about at the beginning of the Great Tribulation. The old religious order, primarily Catholicism, with its headquarters on the seven hills, is reformed by the man who is (more than likely) the chosen president of the European Union, the Antichrist. The figure who has unquestioned authority over the One World Religious

Organization will be the False Prophet, probably disguised as the Pope. With cooperation from the ten nations forming the ten-valved heart of the union of Europe, the old religious order falls under (in a global sense) and changes into (in the political/seat of power sense) the One World Religion Organization. It will be recognized as the only formal religious body on earth.

In the first three-and-a-half years all the religions of the world will fall beneath its banner under the guise of cooperation, unity, and world peace.

In the last three-and-a-half years of the Tribulation the One World Religious Organization demands the worship of the Antichrist and his image. It becomes the only world religion and all other religions, including Christianity and Judaism, are banned on pain of death.

Revelation 17:6

I [John] saw the woman, drunk with the blood of the saints and with the blood of the martyrs of Jesus. And when I saw her, I marveled with great amazement.

BLOOD DRUNK

The reference to both the Saints and the Tribulation martyrs here indicates two separate moments in the history of the Christian Church: the Saints martyred for Christ throughout the centuries, and this would include the saved in Christ murdered by the Christian Church in the name of God; and the saved in Christ who are martyred during the last three-and-a-half years of the Tribulation.

It's also reasonable to conclude that one of the reasons John marvels with such great amazement here is simply because, mystery though she may be, he recognizes her enough to know that the religious organization *drunk with blood and lust* is none other than the Christian Church entire—the Church he helped start.

Revelation 17:7

But the angel said to me, "Why did you marvel? I will tell you the mystery of the woman and of the beast that carries her, which has the seven heads and ten horns."

I AM WILL TELL: BE PREPARED

Jesus says to John, "Why are you so amazed? I will tell you the mystery of the woman and the Beast that has seven heads and ten horns that is in control of her."

The question asked by Jesus can be interpreted in a less literal way. Instead of, "Why are you so amazed?" it could be read as, "You shouldn't be so surprised." The difference here may seem slight, but it points to a sobering reality: the importance of being prepared and having a survival plan.

This could apply to John in the sense of had he been more prepared he would not have marveled so. Had he been more focused on Christ and less focused on himself none of what he was seeing would have surprised him because Christ would have prepared him for it—that's a powerful lesson given the fact that John was so devoted to Christ!

It also teaches us that devoting your life to seeking the truth through Christ is a crucial act of preparation. Christ is our survival plan, but devotion to him is, in part, how you prepare, in the sense of preparing for the world to come and in the more immediate sense of preparing for the world we exist in now, so that we can survive whatever life throws our way. If you're prepared in Christ, instead of acting in surprise or marveling or panicking or responding in anger you will react in such a way that communicates without doubt that your survival is sure, in both daily life and life eternal.

This lesson can be applied to the saved in Christ throughout the ages and the Left Behind Saints who have lead indifferent and unprepared lives in regard to their faith. They will marvel when these prophecies begin to unravel before their eyes; and they will survive the End Times because they are saved in Christ, but their earthly bodies won't survive, for they will be martyred because they were not prepared.

How do you escape being a martyr in the End Times? Believe in Jesus the Christ and be ready for his mighty return! Prepare!

Revelation 17:8

"The beast that you saw was, and is not, and will ascend out of the bottomless pit and go to perdition. And those that dwell on the earth will marvel, whose names are not written in the Book of Life from the foundation of the world, when they see the beast that was, and is not, and yet is."

THE SECOND COMING OF THE UNHOLY SON

The Beast John sees is the Antichrist, son of the red dragon, the devil.

Jesus says that he *was*, for he lived once as (potentially) Nimrod, the Assyrian, when he ruled the world in times gone by. Then Jesus declares that he *is not*, for he died (possibly a water related death—refer to Chapter 13:1, under the heading *Nimrod, the Antichrist* for more detailed information), and then his immortal soul was cast into the prison-place known as the bottomless pit. "Yet *he is*," for in the latter days he returns to rule once more. He ascends out of the abyss to destroy God's way of life on earth through lies and corruption. This is the second coming of the unholy son!

MORTALLY WOUNDED

After his second unholy coming the Antichrist is *mortally wounded,* but he will not die. Those who dwell on earth whose names are not written in the Book of Life from the foundation of the world will marvel at him. When they see the Antichrist that *was*, and *is not*, and *yet is*, they will bow down and worship him as God. Remember John's words, "I saw one of his (the Antichrist's) heads as if it had been mortally wounded, and his deadly wound was healed. And all the world marveled and followed the beast" (Rev. 13:3).

Human beings are appointed once to die; after death we cannot die again, for we have shed the mortal body and released our immortal essence (our soul) that exists within the mortal body. Clearly, this is not the case with the Antichrist who will appear to have a mortal human body. But he won't have a human body because he isn't human, and this is why the wound to his head does not harm him and all the world marvels at his supernatural being, he who emerges from *under the sea* and once again rules much of the world!

Revelation 17:9

"Here is the mind which has wisdom: The seven heads are seven mountains on which the woman sits."

THE WISE MIND

The angel is telling us that we need wisdom. We are like children who do not understand what we read, for we have not yet been schooled in the wisdom of the Lord. We need to mature and grow up in Christ so that we can understand.

How do we do that? How does the mind understand and receive that wisdom which we so desperately need? Jesus said, "Ask and you shall receive!" The Holy Spirit is here to lead you on the path of Truth. He is your Teacher, if you will only let him into your heart: "For this reason we also, since the day we heard it, do not cease to pray for you, and to ask that you may be filled with knowledge of his will in all wisdom and spiritual understanding; that you may walk worthy of the Lord, fully pleasing him, being fruitful in every good work and increasing in the knowledge of God" (Col. 2:9–10). Seek and you shall find wisdom. Devote yourself to Christ and you will learn and survive.

SEVEN HEADS

The seven heads are seven mountains or hills, but we are told that the seven heads belong to the Beast. This informs us that the place of seven mountains or hills (the seat of power for the False Prophet) will be controlled by the Beast and that *the woman* who houses the apostate Christian Church will have its headquarters in the vicinity of those hills. In the figurative language of the Scriptures the place is called Babylon, but we know it today as modern Rome!

Revelation 17:10

"There are also seven kings. Five have fallen, one is, and the other has not yet come. And when he comes, he must continue a short time."

7 PAPAL KINGS

Jumping a verse ahead, we are informed that there are in fact *eight kings*. The eighth king is the Antichrist.

The *seven kings* mentioned here are likely papal kings; seven Bishops of Rome. Of the seven we know that five ruled the Great System/Church before the Affliction. They were pre-Tribulation popes.

We don't know whether or not the five popes followed in sequence or if they were scattered throughout the centuries. It does seem reasonable to argue that the reference is sequential, for it suggests something like a papal countdown, one that could be recognized by scholars of prophecy who are paying attention—but this is purely speculative.

Five religious heads *have fallen*, indicating these popes die before the commencement of the Great Tribulation.

One *is* suggests that he rules the Church prior to the Tribulation as the sixth pope.

The other, being the seventh, is *still to come*. When he comes he will be the last pope of the Great Order of the Vicars of Christ upon the earth. He will be known as the False Prophet/False Pope, the seventh pope, making God's holy mathematics/geometry complete. He governs in power only a *short time*—seven years to be precise (the Tribulation period). Soon after he takes control of the New World System (in the middle of the Tribulation), the False

Prophet/False Pope alters his character from Christ-like lamb to Satan-like dragon, "for the lamb speaks like a dragon (Rev. 13:11). His rule is short because God's Son returns and casts him into the lake of fire at the end of the Great Tribulation.

This we know, for John says, "I saw another beast (the False Prophet) coming up out of the earth, and he had two horns like a lamb (indicating his great power, his Christ-like appearance, his authority as head of the New World System) and spoke like a dragon (for he is controlled by Satan)" (Rev. 13:11). "Then the beast (the Antichrist) was captured, and with him the false prophet... These two were cast alive into the lake of fire burning with brimstone" (Rev. 19:20).

Revelation 17: 11

"The beast that was, and is not, is himself also the eighth, and is of the seven, and is going to perdition."

THE EIGHTH KING

The Beast *that was*: suggests a previous life on earth, perhaps in the guise of King Nimrod.

The Beast that *is not:* refers to his time locked up in the prison-place known as the bottomless pit after his death.

The Beast that *is himself the eighth:* the Antichrist, who controls and dominates the earth when he is released from the pit, having risen again!

The Beast that *is of the seven:* he gives the seven papal kings power. Even though he is of the seven papal kings, he is not a pope. The seventh king is the False Prophet, a False Pope placed in power by the eighth king, the Antichrist.

And it comes to pass that the Beast declares himself god on earth, forcing all inhabitants to worship him through the power and influence of the False Prophet, the False Pope who governs the One World Religion Organization.

Some in current eschatological circles suggested that Pope John Paul II was the sixth king/pope. It's likely that this concept was embraced because of his great age. After his death, many people felt the one who replaced him and claimed the papal throne would be the *seventh king*, the False Prophet who takes his orders from the *eighth king*, the Antichrist—and this would introduce the beginning of the Great Tribulation.

But the pope who replaced John Paul II, Pope Benedict XVI (Cardinal Joseph Ratziner) is in fact quite elderly, and thus the connection with Pope John Paul II being the sixth king/pope seems unlikely. Of course, because so much of this papal prophecy is veiled, it is almost impossible to pinpoint exactly where we are within it. Perhaps Pope Benedict is the sixth king. This would mean, if accurate, that the seventh king, the False Prophet, is the next pope in line.

It's important to remember that the Scriptures make it clear that the eighth king, the Antichrist himself, will appoint the seventh king, the False Pope. This means that the seventh king cannot come into the picture until the Antichrist is already in control of Europe, at least, to some degree, and he must have a commanding influence within the Holy Roman Catholic Church.

It's clear the answer lies with God, who is waiting until the time is right for Satan's False Pope to be appointed. But watch out readers, for I am convinced the time of the end is nearer than you can ever imagine. These two immortal men, the Antichrist and the False Pope, are likely already here waiting in the darkened wings of the theatre, listening for their cue, prepared to make their grand and destructive entrance. Indeed, they are like vultures waiting patiently for their prey!

Revelation 17:12

"The ten horns which you saw are ten kings who have received no kingdom as yet, but they receive authority for one hour as kings with the beast."

TEN HORNS, TEN KINGS

Jesus explains to John that the ten horns are ten kings of ten nations that form into one great body. Since the ten nations or the ten-valved heart that pumps life into the nations ruled by the Beast will cover territory similar to the old Roman Empire some two thousand years ago, we know this is referring to the United Nations of Europe that will be controlled by the Antichrist at the beginning of the seven year Tribulation! The headquarters for this newly formed nation will be Rome. It becomes the capital city of not only Catholicism, Eastern Orthodoxy, and collective Christianity and all the world's religions under the banner of the One World Religion Organization (Babylon), but of the governing world itself, for it will be the Antichrist's initial seat of power—for the first three-and-a-half years of the Tribulation.

The Son of God informs John that the leaders of the ten nations have power over their countries, but ultimately the Antichrist demands and receives total control from them. The political system will be mind-bendingly corrupt, of course, the politicians making a deal with the devil—and even though that isn't unusual behavior for politicians, the difference here is that they'll make a deal with the devil incarnate.

The reference to *one hour* indicates a period of real time in which these ten kings find the authority they seek: one short hour. The Antichrist will in fact allow them to *speak their minds and power-up their political machinery* at a special conference that wraps up in exactly 60 minutes!

Revelation 17:13

"These are of one mind, and they will give their power and authority to the beast."

ONE HOUR

During the one hour conference, the kings of the ten nations find what they're looking for: the Antichrist gives them power and authority, but only because they are of one heart and mind.

Revelation 17:14

"These will make war with the Lamb, and the Lamb will overcome them, for he is Lord of Lords and King of Kings; and those who are with him are called chosen, and faithful."

WAR WITH THE LAMB

The conference lasts one hour. Why so short? Answer: they are of one mind and purpose and they have all the power and authority they need. At that point, it's simply a matter of choosing to power-up the engine of destruction. Turn it on and let it go to work.

Not much will need to be said, other than voicing total commitment. The inevitable decree is: "All this I will give you, if you will bow down and worship me" (Matt. 4:9). And the ten kings give quick reply: "You are god and we worship you." The engine starts running. Remember, the Antichrist is able to make good on his deal by providing genuine power, wealth, and celebrity to these kings. He is a supernatural being, miraculous in nature. Perhaps he will cause a great spiritual light to shine from his body. Or maybe he will simply exude supreme power and authority. Whatever the case may be, he will convince the politicians and they will commit to him and his cause and the engine of destruction will motor-up. It stands to reason if anyone resists (doubtful), he or she will face death; some of these people will be motivated out of fear as well as greed.

The ten kings and countries, what amounts to the heart of the newly formed nation of United Europe and the politicians who've made the New Deal with the old devil, make war on the Godhead of Heaven, for during the meeting the Antichrist proclaims that he is the messiah the world has been waiting for. Most will believe he is god on earth, and then he will move his seat of power from Rome to Jerusalem, destroy the Roman city, and set himself up as god on earth within the Jewish Temple!

Revelation 17:15

Then he [Jesus] said to me [John], "The waters which you saw, where the harlot sits, are peoples, multitudes, nations and tongues."

THE CORRUPTED WATERS

Jesus tells John the great harlot sits on *waters.* This indicates that the woman, the great harlot, will completely deceive and corrupt the world with her immoral behavior. Before the Great Tribulation can begin Christianity in general will reach a state of apostasy, what will amount to waning influence of genuine Christianity throughout the world because of an abandonment of traditional Christian belief and practice, a process well on its way within the Church entire today.

Revelation 17:16

"And the ten horns which you saw, and the beast, these will hate the harlot, make her desolate and naked, eat her flesh and burn her with fire."

TEN HORNS TURN AGAINST THE HARLOT

The ten horns represent the leaders of the ten nations who attended the one hour conference with the Antichrist. They followed the Antichrist and worship him as the true living god on earth. It's important to point out here that when they do this they abandon any and all political ties and personal beliefs. The Antichrist is the only one with authority and power, and the only one worshiped! This occurs at the end of the first three-and-a-half years of the Tribulation.

At the beginning of the last three-and-a-half years of the Tribulation all agree to destroy the One World Religion Organization , the center of religion for the world. They power-up their engine of destruction and target the harlot located on the seven hills in the city of Rome, the OWRO that houses the Catholic/Orthodox/ Protestant Christian Church, as well as all other faiths, all of which have become completely corrupt under the authority of the Antichrist and the False Prophet/False Pope.

The Antichrist and the False Prophet/Pope want to eliminate all the religions of the world by doing this, but their desire to destroy Rome is personal, for Rome historically and traditionally represents the heart of the Christian Church entire.

THE HARLOT BURNED WITH FIRE

The Antichrist and the False Prophet/Pope insist the city of Rome must be annihilated. They make her desolate and naked. They eat her flesh and burn her with fire.

This could be a reference to a nuclear explosion. The Bible says: "The kings of the earth who committed fornication and lived luxuriously with her will weep and lament for her, when they see the smoke of her burning, standing at a distance for fear of her torment, saying 'Alas, alas, that great city Babylon, that mighty city! For in one hour her judgment has come'" (Rev. 18:9–10).

In defiance of Almighty God and influenced by the Antichrist, the ten kings arrange to have their god worshiped in Jerusalem, claiming the city as their new world capitol and new world center of the only religion: worship of the Beast. Breaking their vow with the Jewish nation (a vow made three-and-a-half years previously, under the banner of the OWRO), they prohibit Temple sacrifices and the Antichrist sets himself up as god in the new sacred Temple—this can only be accomplished by removing the One World Religion Organization from the face of the earth.

After the destruction of Rome, thousands will perish, for anyone who does not choose to worship the Beast, regardless of faith or the lack thereof, will die. Jews and Christians will be hunted down and slaughtered into extinction, and at that point the misled world, losing its religious and spiritual core in Rome, will turn to the Antichrist and willingly worship him as god. Some will probably be motivated out of fear and self preservation, but many will believe that the Antichrist is God / Buddha / Jesus Christ / Krishna / Muhammad / David Koresh / Gurdjieff / Elvis, et al.

Revelation 17:17

"For God has put it into their hearts to fulfill his purpose, to be of one mind, and to give their kingdom to the beast, until the words of God are fulfilled."

ONE EVIL HEART

John is informed that the destruction of the OWRO and Rome is God's judgment for her many sins as the apostate center of world religion, but this is also a specific judgment upon the Holy Roman Catholic Church. She is being called to account for the crimes against humanity perpetrated in his name over the centuries and, in relation to the End Times, for her apostate nature and corruption during the Tribulation so that God's words are fulfilled.

Revelation 17:18

"And the woman whom you saw is that great city which reigns over the kings of the earth."

THE HOLY CATHOLIC CHURCH

Jesus announces to John, "The woman you see is that great religion of modern Babylon which reigns over the nations of the earth."

I will follow this line of thought into the next chapter.

* * * * *

SOURCES:
1. *Harlot/Whore,* pg. 536-537, The New Unger's Bible Dictionary, Moody Press (1988).
2. *Wilderness—Eremos,* #2048, pg. 32, Greek Dictionary of the New Testament, Strong's Exhaustive Concordance of the Bible/Dictionary of the Hebrew and Greek Words, Hendrickson Publishers.
3. *Empire and Papacy,* IMS (Internet Medieval Sourcebook), Paul Halsall, ORB sources editor, <http://www.fordham.edu.com>.
   Imperial Popes, Mary Ann Collins, Catholic Concerns (2002), <http://www.catholicconcerns.co>.
4. *United Religions Initiative,* <http://www.uri.org>, The United Religions Initiative, P.O. Box 29242 San Francisco, CA 94129, USA.
   Faith in Dialogue, Leaders from World's Myriad Religions Gather at Stanford in Hopes of Transcending Beliefs, Borders with Spiritual 'U.N.', Richard Scheinin, Mercury News Religion and Ethics Writer, San Jose Mercury News, June 23, 1997, page 1A, The Mercury News, MercuryNews.com, <http://www.bayarea.com>.
   The United Religions: Globalist and New Age Plans, Lee Pen, SCP Journal VOL. 23:2-23:3 (1999) *The United Religions: Globalist and New Age Plans*, Lee Pen, SCP Journal VOL. 23:2-23:3 (1999); "An earlier version of this story appeared in "The United Religions Initiative - A Bridge Back to Gnosticism", published in December 1998 by the New Oxford Review. You may order the complete story from the Review, or subscribe to the Review, by calling (510) 526-5374, or by writing to the New Oxford Review, 1069 Kains Ave., Berkeley, CA 94706. Additionally, it also has been published as part of "The United Religions Initiative: Foundations for a World Religion" (Part 1), published in May 1999 by the Journal of the Spiritual Counterfeits Project, Vol. 22:4-23:1. The information in this extract is a small portion of the information printed in the SCP Journal. You may order the complete story from the Journal, or subscribe to the Journal, by calling (510) 540-0300, or by writing to the Spiritual Counterfeits Project, Post

Office Box 4308, Berkeley, CA 94704, or by visiting the SCP web site, <http://www.scp-inc.org>."

5. *Mystery,* pg. 896, The New Unger's Bible Dictionary, Moody Press (1988). *Mystery,* D. Miall Edwards, International Bible Standard Encyclopedia, Online Edition, <http://www.studylight.org>.

Further reading:

The Gospel According to Rome, James G. McCarthy, Harvest House Publishers (1995).

The Decline and Fall of the Roman Church, Malachi Martin, G. P. Putnam's Sons (1981).

Vicars of Christ, Peter de Rosa, Poolbeg Press (1988).

A History of Christianity, Paul Johnson, Simon & Schuster (1976;1995).

The Catholic Source Book, Peter Klein (Editor), Rev. Peter Klein, Harcourt; 3rd edition (1999).

CHAPTER 18
The Fall Of Babylon The Great

Revelation 18:1

After these things I [John] saw another angel coming down from heaven, having great authority, and the earth was illuminated with his glory.

ANOTHER ILLUMINATED ANGEL

Jesus, who has authority over all things that exist, described here as yet *another angel coming down from heaven,* once more makes his appearance by illuminating the earth with his splendor.

The word *illuminated* refers to the all encompassing nature of Christ, he who guides humanity toward enlightenment by way of his salvation. That the earth is illuminated with his glory suggests in the literal sense that the earth will be bathed in the light of his glory. In the figurative sense it means that everything on earth will be exposed by the light of his glory. The word *with,* can also be interpreted *in the midst of,* as in, the earth was illuminated *in the midst of Christ.* This indicates the earth (and all earthly reality) resides within Christ or the reality that is Christ. The illumination by Christ of the earth comes from within and without, a clear reference to the omnipresence and omniscience of Christ. He is the Bright and Morning Star outside the earth! He is the Bright and Morning Star shining from within the earth! He is the Bright and Morning Star shining from within your heart! He is like the light of the morning when the sun rises! He is like a morning without clouds! He is like a clear day shining after a rain!

Revelation 18:2

And he cried with a loud voice, saying, "Babylon the great is fallen, is fallen, and has become a dwelling place of demons, a prison for every foul spirit, and a cage for every unclean and hated bird!"

BABYLON HAS FALLEN

We now know John's description of modern Babylon as *the woman/the harlot riding the beast* is a direct reference to the One World Religion Organization, but it also points to the Apostate Dominant Christian Church, the Holy Roman Catholic Church in particular, that falls under its banner. It also refers to the seat of power for the entire global organization which will be held by the False Prophet/False Pope in the city of Catholic Rome.

That Babylon has fallen tells us that this is the literal end of Rome, the Vatican, and St. Peters Cathedral, probably by way of a nuclear device. The fact that *fallen* is repeated twice here makes it perfectly clear: the city's destruction is absolute and in no doubt.

Furthermore, the city has become *a habitation of demons*, which reveals God's holy perspective toward Babylon: the city has become unholy and thus its destruction is not only complete it is virtuous and even beneficial in the eyes of God. The reference to *demons* is figurative in the sense of the corruption and immoral behavior of humanity; and literal in the sense that since the OWRO is powered by the Antichrist and the False Prophet/False Pope literal demonic spirits and power reside there; the Holy Roman Catholic Church (and perhaps to a lesser degree collective Christianity) have also become fouled with demonic spirits. This is why the verse refers to it as *a prison for every foul spirit and a cage for every unclean and hated bird*. The city, the OWRO, and the Holy Roman Catholic Church is infested with demonic activity, both spiritual and/or otherwise, as the human population there hastens after other gods and indulges in immoral behavior.

Revelation 18:3

"For all the nations have drunk of the wine of the wrath of her fornication, the kings of the earth have committed fornication with her, and the merchants of the earth have become rich through the abundance of her luxury."

SHE CORRUPTS THE WORLD

Jesus explains here that the entire planet will be corrupted by her immorality, having indulged in modern Babylon's great falling away—in the sense that the Christian Church in general will have fallen away from Christ, having become apostate in nature, the way the Christian Church is becoming today.

As a reminder, for the first three-and-a-half years (the White Horse Period) the face of Christianity is pious and good, reflecting the politically correct nature of the One World Religious Organization, embracing world peace, tolerance, and love. In appearance, the Catholic, Orthodox, and collective Christian Church under the OWRO will seem to reflect the nature of Christ, but beneath the thin veneer of religion they are exceedingly corrupt and thus they help to corrupt the nations of the world. The merchants of the earth become wealthy through the abundance of the organization's luxuries, enormous wealth, and her corrupt nature.

CAPITALIST & MARXIST
SPIRITS WITHIN THE CHURCH

To gain some insight into how this corrupting spirit found itself within the Church entire it's necessary for us to take a look at a snapshot of Church history.

The first and most important thing you need to realize is the ancient Christian Church was not wealthy by any means and the concept of living for wealth was not embraced or encouraged. In fact, that kind of thinking was not a part of ancient Christianity. It would have been entirely alien, even unnatural, for an early Christian to think of living for wealth and material gain.

The reason for this is simply because early Christianity taught the original Christian concept of *individual salvation:* an individual is saved through a sinner's prayer of repentance and then the Spirit of Christ inspires faith, hope and charity within the individual, which leads the individual to love thy neighbor as thyself and motivates each individual to live a selfless life of radical generosity. Furthermore, the early Christians believed the Second Coming was imminent. That's part of the reason why they practiced what might appear to us today as an early form of socialism, but as time went on and they understood that Jesus would not return in their lifetimes, they learned how to earn a living and own property within a secular capitalistic system that celebrated selfishness, greed and personal reward without living for the accumulation of wealth and material gain—and this is what Christians in capitalistic societies continue to do.

Today, there are some in the Christian Church that teach a concept called *collective salvation.* It claims that Jesus was something of a socialist who forced the care of others onto the early Christians. One's individual salvation depends on the collective salvation of the world and ultimately the development of a welfare state. As well intentioned as collective salvation may appear to be, it is a heretical concept birthed in Marxism. The defining difference between individual salvation and collective salvation and capitalism and Marxism is the matter of choice and force. In a capitalistic society based on the free market individuals are motivated by the ability of the individual to achieve capital based on effort and ability, and within that system they can choose to either be selfish and greedy or to live for others as Christ intended. In a Marxist society the collective is forced to live as the government commands—choice and the individual no longer apply;

individual salvation necessarily converts to collective salvation and Jesus Christ is reduced to Benevolent Dictator.

ACCUMULATION OF WEALTH & MATERIAL GAIN

As the number of converted Christians from higher social status and wealth increased within the early Church, the desire to accumulate wealth and material gain increased. Whether intentionally or unintentionally, the wealthy converts brought it with them and it began to creep into the Church and take hold.

Theodosis declared Christianity the official religion of the Roman Empire in 378 A.D. He placed the Church smack-dab in the center of the secular world of governing and thereby cemented the secular spirit within the Church, and the power that came with it allowed the Church to rule over most of Europe like a Roman Emperor.

The Church became extraordinarily wealthy and powerful, and the power-elite within the Church reflected this wealth and corruption in their behavior, which for some had become dangerous. A good portion of that wealth and power came from bribes, black market sales, extortion, and the buying and selling of church office, criminal acts that helped bring about the Protestant Reformation in the sixteenth century.[1] It was hoped by some that the Protestant Reformation would, at least in part, eradicate the secular spirit that now dominated and governed the Church entire, returning Christianity to its ancient roots. Regrettably, that was not entirely the case.

In contrast, it should be pointed out that Amintore Fanfani suggests that Catholicism as a religion and moral code—making a very clear distinction between the Catholic Church as an organization and Catholicism as religion/moral code—was not historically responsible for the secular spirit that dominates the Church entire today. He argues the secular concept did not enter Christian thought as a *life-determining idea* prior to the Middle Ages, probably somewhere in the sixteenth century, as opposed to much earlier in Christian history. He lays the blame fully on the Protestant Reformation. The corruption that came with the spirit in question, he contends, falls not on individual Protestants but squarely on the shoulders of Protestant doctrine.[2] His argument is well taken, and certainly valid to a degree, but the historical facts paint a very different picture—Christian dogma aside, the human heart is ultimately to blame.

Having taken centuries to embed itself within the Holy Roman Catholic Church, the spirit of apostasy is well formed within it and the rest of the body of Christ today. The Christian Church entire is dominated by the old monstrous beast, the secular spirit that adorns the Church with luxuries, enormous wealth, and a corrupt nature—thus, in the eyes of the Lord, the OWRO, established at the beginning of the Tribulation with the support of the Holy Roman Catholic Church, is sinfully wicked.

Revelation 18:4

And I [John] heard another voice from heaven saying, "Come out of her, my people, lest you share in her sins, and lest you receive of her plagues."

A WARNING TO THE FAITHFUL

John hears Jesus warn the faithful residing within the city of Rome in the middle of the Great Tribulation: "Come out of the great city, my faithful people who love and believe in me, lest you are caught up in her great sins and have to share her affliction, for her misfortune is sudden destruction, fire, and death!"

This is a real warning, similar to the warning given by God just before the destruction of Sodom and Gomorrah. It is likely that the Son of God gives this warning to the genuine Christians living in Rome through his Two Witnesses who may exist in the world at this time.

They tell them to get out of the city for two reasons:

(1) Its corruption may corrupt and kill you.

(2) Its corruption is going to destroy the city, which will kill you.

Those who heed the warning survive the soul-corrupting nature of the city by leaving the area; and they escape the literal (potential nuclear) destruction of the city. Many of them will not face death, for they will partake in the Fourth Rapture almost immediately or shortly after Rome's destruction.

Remember, the Fourth Rapture is the rapture of the living faithful and prepared Christians who exist within the collective body of Christ, even while the apostate Church itself falls under the banner of the OWRO during the first-three-and-half years of the Tribulation.

Those who are not taken in the Fourth Rapture, the genuine but indifferent, unprepared, and lukewarm Christians, may escape the destruction of Rome, but they will not escape death. They will be martyred for their Christian faith soon thereafter.

Revelation 18:5

"For her sins have been heaped up to heaven, and God has remembered her iniquities."

SINS UP TO HEAVEN

In the hands of the unholy trinity the Holy Roman Catholic Church has been so thoroughly corrupted that her sins reach up to heaven. Her sin has been piling up for centuries and now it has finally caught up with her, for she is guilty of a long, sinful, and violent past. Heaven knows her sin, and God takes into account the iniquities in which the great body has participated.

IMAGES & ICONS

The Lord is certainly displeased with the Church and the earth's people for having worshiped images/Icons. The Lord of Hosts says, "You shall have no other gods before me. You shall not make for yourself a carved image... You shall not bow down to them nor serve them" (Exo. 20:3–5), and clearly the Catholic and Eastern Orthodox Church and much of the collective Christian Church has, for centuries, had something of an addiction to bowing and praying to images/Icons.

Judaism, a variety of denominations within Protestantism, and Islam forbid images/Icons of God across the board, but images of holy persons, Saints, or of Jesus and Mary are objects of worship in Catholicism, as well as in Eastern Orthodox Christianity.[3] This is but one part of the sin that has been building up to heaven over the centuries.

I should point out that Catholic and Orthodox Christians defend the veneration of images/Icons by citing *correct translation/interpretation* of the Old Testament Hebrew, New Testament Greek, and ancient cultural practices in regard to kissing, bowing, and honoring people or images/Icons, arguing that modern culture has:

(1) Lost the meaning behind these actions, which were common and practiced in the Bible.

(2) The concept of Icon has been lost to much of the modern world.

(3) There is a difference between honoring someone with kisses and respectful bowing and literal worship, suggesting the veneration of Icons is simply a form of honor toward the Saints. Orthodox Christians and Catholics agree on just about everything in regard to the principle of the veneration of images/Icons, but they have differences of opinion. For example, the Orthodox don't like solid, three dimensional statues. Catholicism, on the other hand, uses statues in worship but maintains the statues are not usually venerated. They're simple visual aids and decorations.[4]

THE 787 SEVENTH ECUMENICAL COUNCIL

Nevertheless, in 787 the *Seventh Ecumenical Council of the Catholic Church* ordered the excommunication of anyone who rejected the veneration of images/Icons: "Those who do not so hold (to the veneration of images/Icons), let them be anathema (banned or cursed)." The declaration was comparable to *ban or curse them and maybe they'll go away.* Despite the fact that a Christian faced excommunication if she or he rejected the veneration of images/Icons, the 787 Council did not represent the entire Christian Church and those banned or curse did not go away, as was evident later in Church history.[5]

By choosing to venerate images/Icons the Catholic and Eastern Orthodox Church participated in something clearly laid out in the Bible as sinful and continue to do so to this very day. It has nothing to do with good intentions and it doesn't matter if it genuinely assists one in regard to daily faith. The Lord found it sinful then. He finds it sinful now. End of story. Thus, I conclude, like those willing to face excommunication, that the 787 Council in regard to venerating images/Icons was most idolatrous.

ANOTHER EXAMPLE

As another example of God's displeasure with the Holy Roman Catholic Church, the False Prophet/False Pope is called the *Holy Father.* In fact, the term Holy Father is applied to the pope today. The label comes from a long and ancient tradition within the Catholic Church, but even so, it is clear from Scripture that this phrase is abhorrent to God when placed on anyone else but him, for only God is the Holy Father, not any man or woman, and that includes the pope. The Son of the Father of the Universe commands, "Do not call anyone your (holy) father; for One is your (Holy) Father, he who is in heaven" (Mat. 23:9).

Examples of the sin and corruption within the Catholic Church, the Eastern Orthodox Church, and the collective Christian Church could go on and on. Indeed, their sins are heaped up to heaven.

Revelation 18:6

"Render to her just as she rendered, and repay her double according to her works; in the cup which she has mixed, mix double for her."

RENDERINGS

"Give her as much torture and grief as the glory and luxury she gave herself."

Satan will be in full control of the city and the religion, and the Church will be an abomination in the eyes of God. Yes, her sin has been building up over the centuries, but during the first three-and-a-half years of the Tribulation her sin and corruption will peak, and Christ will show great wrath.

Revelation 18:7

"In the measure that she glorified herself and lived luxuriously, in the same measure give her torment and sorrow; for she says in her heart, 'I sit as queen, and am no widow, and will not see sorrow.'"

THE HARLOT QUEEN

"In the way that she glorifies herself and lives luxuriously, in the same measure give her torment and sorrow, for the city says in her heart 'I am queen and no widow. I am wealthy. I am in need of nothing and will never mourn.'"

This is a direct reference to the Catholic Church, for Mary, the Mother of God is called *Queen of the Universe*, and in the sense that God impregnated her through the power of the Holy Spirit she is, to be sure, not looked upon as a widow. The Catholic Church is also extraordinarily wealthy. Thus, the Catholic Church has no need and because of that she may feel she will never mourn. Nonetheless, because of her historical and Tribulation corruption and immoral behavior/apostate nature she will see sorrow, she will mourn, and she will be a widow.

Revelation 18:8

"Therefore her plagues will come in one day—death and mourning and famine. And she will be utterly burned with fire, for strong is the Lord God who has judged her."

ONE HOUR REVISITED

"Therefore her punishment comes in one time, in one day, in one hour—death, mourning, and famine. The great city is utterly consumed by fire, for mighty is the Lord God who has judged her!"

Most biblical scholars conclude that the reference to *one hour* and *fire* strongly suggests destruction via nuclear detonation.

Revelation 18:9

"The kings of the earth who committed fornication and lived luxuriously with her will weep and lament for her, when they see the smoke of her burning."

THE KINGS WEEP FOR THE HARLOT

"And the nations of the earth who commit corruption and live luxuriously with her sob and grieve for her when they see the smoke of her burning."

Those who have prospered from her corruption will weep at her destruction. Many will weep simply because of their love for the city, their hearts broken at Rome's judgment—and so the world mourns over the destruction of modern Babylon.

It's likely that some of the world population will not support the destruction of Rome, but they will have no way of preventing it, of course, for the power of the Antichrist is global and overwhelming. The earth cries over her sudden destruction and the loss of the so-called everlasting city. She meets her end quickly!

Revelation 18:10

"Standing at a distance for fear of her torment, saying, 'Alas, alas, that great city Babylon, that mighty city! For in one hour your judgment has come.'"

FEAR OF HER TORMENT

"The people in the vicinity are terrified at her torment and stand far off crying, 'Great grief for that mighty city of power! In sixty minutes her doom came.' Everyone watching throughout the world is staggered."

Television and advancing technologies play a leading role in this event, for the scene is captured and spread around the globe, similar to the way the whole world watched in horror as New York was devastated by the destruction of its Twin Towers.

The verse refers to people standing at a distance in fear of her torment. This fear, distance, and the short period of time seems to suggest that Rome is indeed destroyed by a nuclear device, as opposed to this being a miraculous event. This is a reasonable conclusion since the destroyer of the city is not God but the Antichrist. Of course, it could still turn out to be supernatural, a dark and an unholy supernatural act, but the Antichrist turning to a nuclear device instead of the supernatural seems like something the Antichrist would do. It's pedestrian enough, and perhaps more to the point, easy enough to accomplish, and if anyone was going to take the easy way out it would be the Antichrist. Whatever the case may be, the life threatening effects of (in all probability) fallout radiation causes all to *stand at a distance.*

Revelation 18:11

"And the merchants of the earth will weep and mourn over her, for no one buys their merchandise anymore."

MERCHANTS MOURN

"And the merchants of the earth cry and mourn over the annihilation of the metropolis, for no one can buy her goods anymore."

With the absolute destruction of Rome, the OWRO, and the Catholic seat of power, the merchants who profit from her excess and corruption will mourn. Truly, if Rome was destroyed today those who thrive upon the Church would face devastating economic loss—this is what happens in the near-future.

The Antichrist will also have something to say to the merchants and the religious industry they profit from: he will outlaw the sale of anything having to do with Catholicism, Orthodoxy, the Protestant Church, and Christ. These merchants will indeed be out of a job, and they will know it without doubt, for they watch the city and the religion that made them rich, burn. Therefore, they weep and mourn at their loss.

Revelation 18:12

"Merchandise of gold and silver, precious stones and pearls, fine linen and purple, silk and scarlet, every kind of citron wood, every kind of object of ivory, every kind of object of most precious wood, bronze, iron and marble;"

MERCHANDISE OF CATACLYSM

"All merchandise of every kind that profited the sellers is completely obliterated and gone forever."

Here's a little intriguing, and telling, fact that points to Rome: the vegetation of the central and southern lowlands of Italy in general is Mediterranean in nature. The vegetation in these regions are trees such as the olive, orange, lemon, palm, and *citron.*[6]

Revelation 18:13

"And [every kind of] cinnamon and incense, fragrant oil and frankincense, wine and oil, fine flour and wheat, cattle and sheep, horses and chariots, and bodies and souls of men."

EVERYTHING GONE

"All vehicles, animals, bodies and souls of men and women are forever gone from Rome. Everything is gone in one hour!"

By listing goods that are integral components of Catholic worship (incense, fragrant oil, wine), as well as food stuffs (flour, wheat, cattle, sheep), and the mention of transportation and bodies and souls, suggests that the total and absolute destruction of all life in Rome affects all aspects of life all over the world, another tie-in to the merchants and their loss.

Revelation 18:14

"The fruit that your soul longed for has gone from you, and all the things which are rich and splendid have been lost to you, and you shall find them no more at all."

GONE FROM YOU FOREVER

"The good things we long for in you are gone. All the things that are rich and splendid in you are no more, never again to be found. All is gone in you forever, and only in an hour!"

The *fruit that your soul longed for has now gone from you* seems to suggest that at one point in her long history the Holy Roman Catholic Church was once on the path of Truth, but somewhere along the way she lost the fruit her soul longed for, as well as the reason why she longed for it in the first place—a corrupt, immoral, and apostate nature replaced the heart of the Church. She lost her First Love.

She is told that she will find that longing and fruit *no more*, and what's worse, this pronouncement is absolute. This seems to suggest that not only will she and her city be *gone from you* in the sense of imminent destruction, but that she and her city will be gone forever, never to return.

Revelation 18:15

"The merchants of these things, who became rich by her, will stand at a distance for fear of her torment, weeping and wailing."

WEEPING & WAILING

"The merchants who became rich from the great organization stand at a far distance, terrified at her torment. They sob and cry."

Here we have a second reference to *distance*: after the first hour of a nuclear explosion, radioactivity dissipates slowly, resulting in long-term danger to all life. In fact, the danger may exist for many years, contaminating land, buildings, foods, and water.[7]

If Rome is destroyed by a nuclear device it is certain that her days as the seat of religious and economic power and influence will be *gone from you* in a flash that will last forever.

Revelation 18:16

"And saying, 'Alas, alas, that great city that was clothed in fine linen, purple, and scarlet, and adorned with gold and precious stones and pearls!'"

ALAS, ALAS!

"They will say, 'What a pity! The great mother city that was clothed in fine linen, purple, and scarlet, and that was adorned with gold, precious stones, and pearls is no more."

This verse illustrates Babylon's immense wealth, now lost forever, and again, there is a clear connection here to Catholicism in regard to the colors of purple and scarlet and jewelry made up of precious stones and pearls.

Revelation 18:17

"'For in one hour such great riches came to nothing.' Every shipmaster, all who travel by ship, sailors, and as many as trade on the sea, stood at a distance."

COME TO NOTHING

"In one hour, such great riches came to an end. Every sea captain, all who travel by ship, every sailor, and as many as trade on the sea will stand their distance too, waiting in awe."

It's very interesting that this verse refers to sea captains and ships *standing at a distance* and *witnessing* the destruction of Rome. This is strong evidence in support of the destruction of the city of Rome by nuclear detonation, for only a nuclear explosion could be seen from the Tyrrhenian/Mediterranean Sea. Indeed, were sailors and their captains looking toward the Italian west coast they would easily see an atomic blast—and true enough, they would watch in horror and awe. You have to understand that when an atomic bomb explodes a fireball creates shock and heat waves that destroy everything in its path-radius. The fireball rises up and sucks up debris to form a massive mushroom cloud. The cloud can reach a height of six to eight miles above the surface of the earth, visible day or night, and once it stabilizes it can retain its shape for well over an hour.[8]

Revelation 18:18

"And [they] cried out when they saw the smoke of her burning, saying, 'What is like this great city?'"

BABYLON, THE GREAT CITY

"They will cry out when they see the smoke of the great city burning, saying, 'There was nothing as fine as this city.'"

Even though the Antichrist orders the destruction of Rome and the collective Christian Church, many people throughout the world will be greatly affected by this mandate. They will obey, out of fear or fanatical devotion to the Beast, but lots of people will still understand the horror and tragedy of what has just taken place: the great city of Rome and all its glory has been laid waste by what very well may be a nuclear bomb.

Revelation 18:19

"They threw dust on their heads and cried out, weeping and wailing, and saying, 'Alas, alas, that great city, in which all who had ships on the sea became rich by her wealth! For in one hour she is made desolate.'"

DUST IN THE WIND

"With dust above their heads, they mourn aloud in great grief, crying, 'That mighty city, in which all who had ships on the sea became rich by her great wealth! She was disintegrated, leaving no trace.'"

The continual reference to ships and the sea seems to also suggest the global wealth and trade the city and religion promoted.

The use of the word *sea* also suggests the *sea of humanity*. Babylon influenced the sea of humanity and now that she's been disintegrated—*gone from you forever*—the sea of humanity mourns.

Revelation 18:20

"Rejoice over her, O heaven, and you holy saints and apostles and prophets, for God has avenged you on her!"

HEAVEN APPROVES

John perceives: "The world weeps, while heaven rejoices and approves! Be glad of the annihilation of the city that was led by Satan's trinity, you holy apostles, prophets, and all true believers in Jesus Christ, for God avenges you on her!"

Revelation 18:21

Then a mighty angel took up a stone like a great millstone and threw it into the sea, saying, "Thus with violence the great city Babylon shall be thrown down, and shall not be found anymore."

NOT FOUND ANYMORE

The angel described here as *a mighty angel* represents, of course, Jesus Christ.

He takes up a rock that has the appearance of a great grinding stone and throws it into the sea, saying, "In this way, with violence, the great city of modern Babylon was thrown down, because of her great iniquity. She is gone forever!"

To fully appreciate the metaphor here you have to understand that a *millstone* was a heavy stone device used for grinding grain into fine powder or flour. This focuses on two aspects of the Church entire:

(1) The historical record of the Holy Roman Catholic Church (and, to a lesser degree, collective Christianity) in regard to crimes against humanity—the Holy Roman Catholic Church has been grinding the bones of humanity into dust for centuries with its heavy and corrupt secular spirit in the form of wealth, power, violence, and widespread immorality.

(2) The apostate nature of the Holy Roman Catholic Church and collective Christianity as the Church entire, having become a secular and apostate millstone that has ground Christ out of Christianity.

Revelation 18:22

"The sound of harpists, musicians, flutists, and trumpeters shall not be heard in you anymore. No craftsman of any craft shall be found in you anymore, and the sound of a millstone shall not be heard in you anymore."

THE SOUND OF THE MILLSTONE IS SILENCED

Jesus continues to explain, "The sound of music is not heard in her again. No craftsman of any skill is found in her. The sounds of food factories are not heard in her anymore."

The reference to the millstone here, the second in this series of verses, is layered:

(1) The words *musicians* and *craftsman* suggests that what beauty and goodness exists within the Holy Roman Catholic Church and its long history will also be wiped out because of her iniquity—every aspect of the Holy Roman Catholic Church, the good, the bad and the ugly, is going to be absolutely destroyed.

(2) The musical instruments also point to her orgiastic immorality, suggesting that the age-old party is over.

(3) The secular spirit of corruption within the Holy Roman Catholic Church and collective Christianity has been brought to an end; its days of grinding humanity into dust and Jesus Christ out of Christianity have been silenced forever. With the destruction of the OWRO, Babylon is finished.

Revelation 18:23

"The light of a lamp shall not shine in you anymore, and the voice of bridegroom and bride shall not be heard in you anymore. For your merchants were the great men of the earth, for by your sorcery all the nations were deceived."

HEAVILY MEDICATED CHRISTIAN SORCERY

"'No light shines ever again on the seven hills. The voices of honeymooners are never heard in the city again. Her merchants were the great men of the earth, but by her sorcery all the earth was deceived."

The original Greek word for *sorcery* (*pharmakeia*) can be interpreted in the medicinal sense ala *medication.* This could be rephrased *medicated.* Replace the word *sorcery* with the vernacular and you get: the nations were *heavily medicated by her deception.* It has the same meaning in sense, suggesting *control, manipulation, deception.* The word can also describe literal *magic* or *sorcery,*[9] which may point to literal occultism practiced within Babylon, suggesting that the Holy Roman Catholic Church (and, to a lesser degree, the collective Christian Church) used the occult to deceive the nations.

Knowing human nature, both meanings for the interpretation of the word *sorcery* are probably true here. The Church had a medicating effect, prescribing political, economical, and social secular *drugs* to control, manipulate, and ultimately deceive the nations; and the Church dabbled in authentic sorcery.

Revelation 18:24

"And in her was found the blood of prophets and saints, and of all who were slain on the earth."

BLOOD OF ALL THE SLAIN ON EARTH

"In her was found the blood of the prophets, believers, and all who were slain on earth."

The blood of prophets and believers shed and *all who were slain* is a direct reference to the innocents killed primarily by the Holy

Roman Catholic Church in the name of religion and God throughout the centuries, what amounts to the wanton murder of genuine believers in Christ and innocent unbelievers, heretics, pagans, witches, warlocks, Jews, and on and on, ad infinitum, ad nauseam. The Orthodox and collective Christian Church are not except from this litany of destruction.

Clearly, God is not only remembering modern Babylon and her Tribulation atrocities, but the 2,000 years of violence the Church has done in his name.

He is also aware of her wealth, pomp, and ceremony, for "that great city that was clothed in fine linen, purple, and scarlet, and adorned with gold and precious stones and pearls" (verse 16) paraded herself around as queen for centuries while she ignored many peoples and nations who were suffering from hunger, economical hardship, and disease.

He is aware of the *mystery* of the organization (possible occult attachments), as well as the worship of images/Icons.

Christ brings every work into judgment, including every secret thing, whether it is good or evil—the apostate Holy Roman Catholic Church, Orthodox Church, and collective Christian Church have come under his judgment, along with any other religion in the One World Religion Organization.

BABYLON, BABYLON REPEATED

The description of Babylon is repetitive and written about at length. Why? Answer: the repetition is an awareness tool. It cannot be ignored. Furthermore, the amount of time given to the nature of Babylon, her Great Fall, and its repetitive nature in Revelation text shows us that Babylon is a matter of great consequence.

Since the apostate spirit can be clearly seen in the Church entire today, and the fact that this spirit has taken many centuries to root, it's reasonable to argue that we are standing at the doors of the Great Tribulation! The Church will soon be taken over by the OWRO, powered by the Antichrist, controlled by the False Prophet/False Pope and his evil demons and worshipers, and they will bow down to the Antichrist for power, glory, authority, and greed. They will think like Satan, for there will be no light of Christ in them, and they will consent to completely destroy the core of all religion with the nuclear destruction of the One World Religion Organization.

At the start of the last three-and-a-half years, Babylon, the Holy Roman Catholic Church, is destroyed by those she embraced and sold her soul to: the Antichrist and the False Prophet/False Pope. They burn her like the thousands of innocent witches and warlocks she'd burned centuries ago, and unlike them she will not rise from ashes in glory.

* * * * *

SOURCES:

1. *Wealth, Church History, and Morality, Reverend* David Zampino (2002), <http://www.gold-eagle.com/editorials_02/zampino060802.html>. Reverend David Zampino holds degrees in history and theology and is currently working on his doctorate. His areas of expertise include Early Church history, liturgy, and American Political history. *Imperial Popes,* Mary Ann Collins, Catholic Concerns (2002), <http://www.catholicconcerns.com/> *Edict of Milan (313 A.D.),* Medieval Sourcebook: *Galerius and Constantine: Edicts of Toleration (311/313),* Internet Medieval Sourcebook, Part of ORB, Online Reference Book for Medieval Studies; The Internet History Sourcebooks Project is located at the History Department of Fordham University, New York. The Internet Medieval Sourcebook, and other medieval components of the project, are located at the Fordham University Center for Medieval Studies, Paul Halsall, ORB sources editor, <http://www.fordham.edu>. *History of the Orthodox Church,* Life of the Orthodox Church, Serbian Orthodox Diocese of Raska and Prizren, <http://www.kosovo.com/orthodoxy.html>, plus this additional source information kindly provided by the Servian Orthodox Diocese of Raska and Prizren: introductory surveys of the history and doctrines of Eastern Orthodoxy may be found in ERNST BENZ, The Eastern Orthodox Church, *Its Thought and Life* (1963; originally published in German, 1957); TIMOTHY WARE (KALLISTOS WARE), *The Orthodox Church* (1963, reprinted with revisions, 1984); JOHN MEYENDORFF, *The Orthodox Church: Its Past and Its Role in the World Today,* 3rd rev. ed. (1981; originally published in French, 1960), with special attention given to 19th- and 20th-Century history; and DEMETRIOS J. CONSTANTELOS, *Understanding the Greek Orthodox Church: Its Faith, History, and Practice (1982).* Top of Form

2. *Catholicism, Protestantism, and Capitalism,* originally published: London, 1935; IHS Press 222 W 21st St. Suite F-122, Norfolk, VA 23517, *Catholicism, Protestantism & Capitalism, part 2,* Dr. Peter Chojnowski (1999), The Angelus, Volume XXII, Number 11, A Journal of Roman Catholic Tradition, 2918 Tracy Avenue, Kansas City, Missouri 64109 USA, Society of Saint Pius X Canada, <http://www.sspx.ca> & <http://www.angeluspress.org>. *The Veneration of Icons in the Tradition of the Byzantine Rite,* Byzantine.net, <http://www.byzantines.net/moreinfo/venerateIcons.htm>. *Veneration of Images,* Adrian Fortescue, transcribed by Tomas Hancil , The Catholic Encyclopedia, Volume VII, Online Edition, Kevin Knight (2002), <http://www.newadvent.org>. *Is Venerating Icons Idolatry?* Timothy Copple (2002), Orthodox Christian Information Center, <http://www.orthodoxinfo.com>. *Idolatry,* Microsoft Encarta Encyclopedia (2002).

3. *Idolatry,* J. Wilhelm, transcribed by Douglas J. Potter, *Dedicated to the Sacred Heart of Jesus Christ,* The Catholic Encylopedia, Volume VII, Online Edition, Kevin Knight (2002), <http://www.newadvent.org>.

4. *Veneration of Images,* Adrian Fortescue, transcribed by Tomas Hancil, The Catholic Encyclopedia, Volume VII, Online Edition, Kevin Knight (2002), <http://www.newadvent.org>.
   The Veneration of Icons from *The Orthodox Companion,* Reverend David F. Abramtsov, Copyright © 1999 OrthodoxNet. All rights reserved, <http://www.orthodoxnet.com>.

5. *The Seventh Ecumenical Council of Nice, A.D. 787,* The Decree of the Holy, Great, Ecumenical Synod, the Second of Nice (Labbe and Cossart, Concilia. Tom. VII., col. 552); introduction and translation taken from *Decrees of the Ecumenical Councils*, ed. Norman P. Tanner, <http://www.piar.hu/councils/ecum07.htm#CANONS>.
   The Second Council of Nicaea, Dedicated to the Immaculate Heart of Mary, The Catholic Encyclopedia, Volume VII, Online Edition, Kevin Knight Copyright © (2009), <http://www.newadvent.org>.

6. *Citron Wood; Vegetable Kingdom,* pg. 1325-1330, The New Unger's Bible Dictionary, Moody Press (1988).
   Citron, Microsoft Encarta Encyclopedia (2002).

7. *Nuclear Weapons,* contributed by Samuel Glasstone, Microsoft Encarta Encyclopedia (2002).

8. *Nuclear Fallout,* Microsoft Encarta Encyclopedia (2002).

9. *Sorcery—Pharmakeia,* #5331, pg. 75, Greek Dictionary of the New Testament, Strong's Exhaustive Concordance of the Bible/Dictionary of the Hebrew and Greek Words, Hendrickson Publishers.

Further reading:

The Gospel According to Rome, James G. McCarthy, Harvest House Publishers (1995).

The Decline and Fall of the Roman Church, Malachi Martin, G. P. Putnam's Sons (1981).

A History of Christianity, Paul Johnson, Simon & Schuster (1976;1995).

Martin Luther, Selections From His Writings, Martin Luther (1463-1546), edited by John Dillenberger, Anchor (1958).

Triumph, The Power And The Glory Of The Catholic Church, H W Crocker, III, Random House (2002).Bottom of Form

Catholicism, Protestantism, and Capitalism, Amintore Fanfani, Giorgio Campanini (Preface), Charles Clark (Preface), I H S Press (2003).

CHAPTER 19
Hallelujah!

Revelation 19:1

After these things I [John] heard something like a loud voice of a great multitude in heaven, saying, "Alleluia! Salvation and glory and honor and power belong to our God."

HEAVEN REJOICES

John hears the heavens and all that is in them singing joyously over the destruction of Babylon, the One World Religious Organization that housed the apostate Holy Roman Catholic Church, collective Christianity, and the remaining religions of the world.

The great multitude includes all nations, tribes, people, and tongues. They stand before the throne and the Lamb, clothed in white robes, carrying palm branches. The saints of God cry: "Hallelujah! Salvation, glory, honor, and power belong to our God, who sits upon the throne, and to the Lamb!" Every angel, the twenty-four elders, and the four living creatures fall on their faces before the throne to worship Christ, saying, "Amen! God of Glory! Blessing, wisdom, thanksgiving, and might be to our God forever and ever."

Revelation 19:2

"For true and righteous are his judgments, because he has judged the great harlot who corrupted the earth with her fornication; and he has avenged on her the blood of his servants shed by her."

THE GREAT HARLOT JUDGED

The innumerable company continues to express the holiness and righteousness of God's judgment upon the great harlot, saying, "True and righteous are Jesus' judgments. He has judged the great prostitute, who corrupted earth with her fornication. Christ has avenged the blood of his believers shed by her."

The term *Christ has avenged* is referring to the centuries of corruption, murders, and crimes against humanity in the name of religion and God perpetrated by the Holy Roman Catholic Church and to a lesser degree the Orthodox and collective Protestant Christian Church. It's also a reference to what is likely to be a more restrained version of corruption, murder, and crimes against humanity during the first three-and-a-half years of the Tribulation under the banner of the One World Religious Organization. Of course, once Babylon is destroyed in the middle of the Tribulation out-and-out slaughter of genuine believers will commence, the end result being a genocidal bloodbath.

With the destruction of Babylon, the King's wrath will be like the roaring of a lion, and know it well: his favor is like the dew on the grass!

Revelation 19:3

Again they said, "Alleluia! Her smoke rises up forever and ever!"

HALLELUJAH!

God in heaven is pleased with the holy and righteous judgment, and so all the saved in Christ sing, "Hallelujah! The city's smoke rises up forever and ever!"

Because of the potential for nuclear destruction, *her smoke rises up forever and ever* brings to mind a massive mushroom cloud and long term radioactive fallout.

It also shows us just how lasting and absolute the nature of the judgment is, for the smoke will be seen by all forever burning and it will never be forgotten.

Death confronts the world on the day of Babylon's calamity. All nations and people will say to their neighbors, "Why has this happened to the great city?" The Two Witnesses will answer, "Because they abandoned the covenant of Christ made by the Lord their God and this is why the city has been destroyed!"

Revelation 19:4

And the twenty-four elders and the four living creatures fell down and worshiped God who sat on the throne, saying, "Amen! Alleluia!"

AMEN & HALLELUJAH!

Once more the twenty-four elders and the four living creatures fall down to worship God who stands in the magnificent throne. They cry, "God of Glory, the faithful and true witness, the commencement of creation! Amen! Hallelujah!" The Lord says, "I AM THAT I AM!"

Revelation 19:5

Then a voice came from the throne, saying, "Praise our God, all you his servants and those who fear him, small and great."

SMALL & GREAT

A voice (not Jesus) comes from the throne and cries out, "Honor God, all of you who are his servants, his believers, and those who fear him, both small and great."

In this case, it isn't the voice of Christ, but one of the redeemed Saints.

That the voice *came from the throne* suggests that, yes, it's coming from the throne of Jesus Christ—he who is the ultimate and true King—but because of his grace the saved in Christ sit with him on the throne. Thus, they can speak from the throne with power and authority.

Revelation 19:6

And I [John] heard, as it were, the voice of a great multitude, as the sound of many waters and as the sound of mighty thunderings, saying, "Alleluia! For our Lord God Omnipotent reigns!"

SOUNDS

The great multitude sounds like the roar of rushing waterfalls and peals of thunder! They shout, "God of Glory! The Lord Omnipotent reigns!"

He is worthy to receive honor and glory, for he is King of Kings and Lord of all. The Christ of heaven exercises sovereign power and has absolute authority over everything. Praise him, those who stand in the courts of the house of the Son! Sing praises to his name!

Revelation 19:7

(they say) "Let us be glad and rejoice and give him glory, for the marriage of the Lamb has come, and his wife has made herself ready."

THE FOURTH RAPTURE

In Chapter 18:4, under the heading *A Warning to the Faithful*, I pointed out that the end of modern Babylon/OWRO happens in the middle of the Great Tribulation and soon thereafter Christ comes for his bride, which is the commencement of the Fourth Rapture. When Jesus returns as the Bridegroom he takes away half of all the genuine saved in Christ on earth, those who will not reflect an apostate nature or a lukewarm indifference or half-heartedness, for Christ is their survival plan and they are prepared!

Thus, we must ask: What can we do to escape the things that must come to pass? How can we be saved? How do we survive? What is our survival plan?

The path of the just is like the sun that shines ever brighter until the perfect day! But the way of the unjust is like darkness. They do not know what makes them stumble! Go and humble yourself so that you may be called into the marriage of the Fourth Rapture. Expect Christ's return and escape the sting of death.

Escape becoming a martyr.

Escape being hunted, tortured, and slain.

Our survival plan is Christ. Believe in him and you will escape the things that must come to pass. Open his worst-case scenario survival handbook, the Book of Revelation, and study it so that you can survive the End Times!

THE MARRIAGE COMMENCEMENT

Prior to the Man of Sin's proclaiming himself god on earth, the innumerable company of Saints in Abraham's Bosom and Paradise declare, "Let us be glad and rejoice and give Jesus glory, for the marriage of the Lamb has come to the one half of all living Christians (called his *wife*, those taken in the Fourth Rapture). His wife is full of the Glory of God and prepares herself for the Lord, his brightness in them takes away evil and darkness."

Revelation 19:8

And to her it was granted to be arrayed in fine linen, clean and bright, for the fine linen is the righteous acts of the saints.

THE BRIDE

The *bride* is dressed in fine white linen, clean and bright, for she has been made pure in Christ, cleansed by the blood of the Lamb.

The term *fine linen* illustrates the righteous behavior and the state of being for the prepared believers. They are of exceptional quality, for while on the corrupted earth they were strong in faith, spirit, and mind, the saved in Christ who earnestly pursued a relationship with Jesus Christ, those who not only *know* the Path, but *walk* it and *talk* it.

Revelation 19:9

Then he said to me [John], "Write: Blessed are those who are called to the marriage supper of the Lamb!" And he said to me: "These are the true sayings of God."

THE BRIDE IS BLESSED

The voice (not Jesus) that comes from the throne announces, "The Bride is blessed, these living believers in Jesus who are called to the marriage supper of the Lamb. These are the true sayings of God Almighty."

The bride is blessed for a number of reasons:

(1) She will be taken away in the Fourth Rapture before the Antichrist can harm her.

(2) She never faces fallen-natured physical death. One moment she is alive on earth and the next she meets Jesus in the air, transforming into the Second Phase of Body, the glorified body, without going through the cocoon of death—what a privilege!

A moment before the Fourth Rapture they could have been aging in bed. The next moment, they are healthy and young, standing with Jesus in the air! An instant before they could have been working in a field or in a factory or office, climbing a mountain, sitting in a theater, driving a car or flying in a plane. Suddenly, they are lifted up into the air, glowing with the love of Jesus Christ! He will then immediately take them to Paradise in the Second Phase of Body, the glorified body, where they wait far from planet earth in time—three-and-a-half years—for the return of Christ to the earth, the Battle of Armageddon, and the reforming of the planet. At the appointed time they leave Paradise and arrive with Christ above the world to witness God's greatness. They view the colossal battle and earth's reformation, after which they come down to live with their Mighty King on earth for a thousand glorious years!

Revelation 19:10

And I [John] fell at his (speakers) feet to worship him. But he said to me, "See that you do not do that! I am your fellow servant, and of your brethren who have the testimony of Jesus. Worship God! For the testimony of Jesus is the spirit of prophecy."

MYSTERY MAN

It's made clear in this verse that the voice coming from the throne is not Jesus Christ but a redeemed Saint. He has the power and authority of Christ because it comes from the throne, but he is not Christ the King. He's actually something of a mystery man, probably an Old Testament or New Testament Saint—a servant of God. John makes the mistake of falling at his feet to worship him. The servant of God instantly reprimands John by saying he must not do this, for he is a fellow servant, one of billions of brothers and sisters who holds to the testimony of Jesus.

What is meant by the term *the testimony of Jesus is the spirit of prophecy?* The entire Bible was inspired by the Holy Spirit who is "the spirit of truth" (John 16:12) and the spirit of prophecy who convicts us of sin, righteousness, and the judgment *to come* (John 16:8-11). This means that the Bible encompasses the *spirit of* and always *points to* the return of Christ, for Jesus cleanses us of our sin, fills us with his righteousness, and saves us from judgment— he is the center of all biblical prophecy and all Creation. Since prophecy in biblical terms usually means a message from God inspired by the Holy Spirit, the author of the Bible, we see that the inspired biblical testimony of Jesus is by its very nature prophetic, always pointing to the return of Christ as an historical fact, even while it remains for us future fact, indicating the return of the once and future king.

Revelation 19:11

Now I [John] saw heaven opened, and behold, a white horse. And he who sat on him was called Faithful and True, and in righteousness he judges and makes war.

THE ONCE & FUTURE KING
The Second Coming

The first appearance of Christ as the Lamb of God took place some two thousand years ago when he came to this earth as the Son of Man. He taught the world how to genuinely love (for he is Love), reflecting the self-denying and sacrificial nature of the perfect sacrifice for all of fallen humanity separated from God: "For God so loved the world that he gave his only begotten Son, that whoever believes in him should not perish but have everlasting life" (John 3:16).

At the Second Coming the Future King does not come as he came before, reflecting the nature of sacrificial Lamb.

He returns as the King of Heaven coming to conquer the leaders of the earth and all that sin represents and is.

He returns to destroy the destroyer and the unholy trinity.

He returns to clean up the earth and begin the new glorious Second Age of one thousand years of rest on this (reformed) planet with his Saints and the established Jewish millennial kingdom and government.

THE THREEFOLD RETURN OF CHRIST

The return of Christ has a threefold purpose, having three parts to it. The number 3 is sacred and falls within God's holy mathematics/geometry, for it reflects the Holy Trinity!

PART I

(1) The first part of the return of Christ is known as the rapture of the dead in Christ and the living who believe in him—this is the Third and Fourth Raptures that take place in the middle of the Tribulation.

The dead and the living meet Jesus in the air above the earth so that in a literal sense Christ will indeed have returned to earth. This will be in secret or veiled, for he comes quietly, like a thief unseen.

The rest of the human world does not see this part of his return. They do not see and probably won't be aware of his presence. They will experience it in the sense that they're witness to a phenomenally strange event which will greatly affect the world, but above and beyond that they will be blind to it. Those who partake of the Third and Fourth Raptures are transformed into the Second Phase of Body, the glorified body.

PART II

(2) The second part of the return of Christ involves the rapture of the martyrs killed by the Antichrist in the last three-and-a-half years of the Tribulation and the rapture of the living 144,000 chosen Jews for Jesus, the Fifth and Sixth Raptures.

They meet the Lord in the air so that once again in a literal sense Christ will indeed have returned a second time to the earth. Once again, this is done in secret, for his presence will not be seen and probably not sensed by any living humans even though he will have literally returned.

Similar to those raptured previously, the martyrs and the 144,000 are transformed into the Second Phase of Body, the glorified body.

PART III

(3) The third and final part of the return of Christ occurs when he reveals his presence to the world in the form of his literal person in the sky with great noise and great glory.

The scene will be dramatic and holy and nothing short of astonishing, clearly no longer secret, but totally and completely unveiled. He comes to defeat the unholy trinity and every eye sees him. As was pointed out in Chapter 12:6, under the heading *False*

Christ's & False Times/Dates, there is no mistaking the return of Christ, for the fabric of our universe and reality will be torn apart as he reveals himself to the world.

THE SIXTH BOWL PLAGUE CALLED ARMAGEDDON!

At this point in the verse, John is taking us into the period of the sixth bowl plague at its climax.

In the region of Megiddo, near Jerusalem in the nation of Israel, the Antichrist gathers his armed forces in preparation for war against the mighty Lord Jesus Christ and his faithful army of believers (who are with Christ as witnesses, not warriors). The armies of the world will receive news of an impending invasion from outer space, the potential global perception claiming *Jesus is an invading alien.*

The technologically sophisticated military of the Antichrist, the greatest ever to assemble in the history of humankind, gathers together from the four corners of the globe. All of the Antichrist's troops, his military advisors, political entourage, and the millions from the great eastern nations come like a storm, covering the land like a cloud. They primarily come from China, traveling west, crossing the dry riverbed of the Euphrates!

The Son meets the onslaught of Satan's wicked military might on his own, riding a white horse.

The reference to a *horse* here is, of course, probably allegorical in nature, but once again because of the supernatural nature of the event it's not improbable that Christ could return on a white horse; and so the Battle of Armageddon commences.

The outcome is clearly summarized: "And the rest (of Satan's army) were killed with the sword which proceeded from the mouth of him who sat on the horse. And all the birds were filled with their flesh" (Rev. 19:21).

TARGET: JESUS CHRIST

The colossal force of the Antichrist comes in defiance to fight the Creator of heaven and earth. Their target: Jesus Christ! They will desire to destroy the *alien assembled in the sky.* Tanks, rockets, missiles, jets, nukes, and all the latest advanced weaponry and machinery are poured into the war of Armageddon. The strength of the world's armed forces, under the direction of the son of Lucifer, will be utterly staggering. Nothing is able to withstand the great power of the people of the earth—so they will say. No, not even the Heavenly Invader. Most of them will be confident of victory. They are prepared to meet him and defeat him in the clouds, this Stranger from another planet.

Clay Houseman

TARGET: ISRAEL

Over the battleground mighty clouds gather. At this point in the last-three-and-a-half years of the Tribulation the land of Israel will be unbearably hot and the skies will be free of clouds—seeing clouds will shock the gathering armies.

Because many of the verses associated with the return of Christ suggest that the sky will be free of clouds at first, the Middle East might be dealing with massive ozone depletion and superheated atmosphere caused by the plagues. Of course, it must be remembered that natural and scientific explanations may not apply here, for it is far more likely that the events in question will be Super Natured and therefore unexplainable.

Ominous clouds, dark and heavy, roll and turn and hang low over the entire valley of Armageddon. Bolts of lightning come from the east, striking and flashing to the west! The world's forces below are indeed afraid, as the Son of Man targets his mighty strength on the military organization of the Antichrist. Jesus comes with staggering power! There are deafening thunderclaps, and within the peals of thunder singing voices are heard! The forces of the Antichrist will hear in the thundering the sound of the Seven Spirits of God and they will be much terrified! The howling wind blows with staggering strength with the movements of the Spirit of God.

There is sudden and widespread panic in the hearts of the soldiers! Millions of *birds* come from apparently out of nowhere, helping to darken the skies, for "where the carcass is, there the eagles gather together!"

"That day is a day of wrath, a day of trouble and distress, a day of devastation and desolation, a day of darkness and gloominess, a day of clouds and thick darkness, a day of trumpet and alarm against the fortified cities and against the high towers" (Zeph. 1:15–16).

This battle transpires between God, Satan, and the inhabitants of the world at the very end of the Tribulation. The sun appears blood red and the moon is as dark as sackcloth. This leads us to an interesting possibility: before the return of Christ *something* may happen to our solar system's star. The sun will be red in color and there will be no light from the moon at night; the moon will apparently not be reflecting light from the sun. If this turns out to be the case, clearly it will be designed and controlled by the Lord, a Super Natured event. On the other hand, it may simply be because of the cloud, debris, and bird cover reducing or filtering the sun and moonlight—I believe this is the truth of it.

In any case, the mention of both the sun and the moon indicate a period of at least twenty-four hours or longer of widespread anguish to the masses assembled in the war zone. At that point, the stars (angels) *fall* from heaven to witness the grandeur of Christ's supreme strength and inevitable victory.

JESUS APPEARS

And behold, One like the Son of Man comes with the clouds of heaven, for the great day of his wrath has come, and who is able to stand? Suddenly, the clouds form an immense tunnel into the darkened skies and the earth seems to vanish as heaven opens (crosspollination of hyperdimensional realities), and the Antichrist, the False Prophet/False Pope, and all unrepentant humanity see a magnificent magnified white horse! Mounted on the horse is a magnified Christ Jesus, called Faithful and True. He passes his righteous judgment on the world!

Revelation 19:12

His eyes were like a flame of fire, and on his head were many crowns. He had a name written that no one knew except himself.

EYES OF FIRE

At Jesus' coming there is a brilliance never before witnessed by humanity—the blinding light could be compared to a giant star's supernova. John describes it like this: "His head and hair were white like wool, as white as snow, and his eyes like a flame of fire" (Rev. 1:14); "And his feet (were) like (the brightness of) fine brass" (Rev. 2:18).

Jesus not only returns in overwhelming light, but also with great wrath—the fact that his eyes are described as flames of fire make this more than clear. On his head are *many crowns*, seven to be precise, each one a representation of the Seven Spirits of Life. Surely this is allegorical in nature, similar to the flaming eyes, but given the supernatural nature of the event, anything is possible. Each crown stands for life eternal, and Jesus says, "I am coming quickly! Hold fast to what you have, that no one may take your crown (of life)" (Rev. 3:11). (Remember, every human being has this crown of life, which is but one Spirit of God. Jesus has seven crowns of life, or to be precise, the Seven Spirits of God!)

He also has a name that no one knows except himself. The meaning behind this is veiled, but we can unearth some possibilities: similar to the nature of the scroll with the seven seals and writing on both sides, that his name is known only to himself suggests a similar show of power, authority, and importance. It also compels us to look at who this person is, this Savior with the name known only to himself.

Revelation 19:13

He was clothed with a robe dipped in blood, and his name is called the Word of God.

THE ROBE & THE WORD

At the Battle of Armageddon, the Antichrist's armed forces see Jesus above them, clothed with a robe as though dipped in blood.

(1) The blood represents his shed blood on the cross.

(2) The blood of all believers/martyrs throughout the Tribulation shed by Satan.

(3) The blood of all believers/martyrs shed throughout human history.

(4) The blood spilled by the Holy Roman Catholic Church and, to a lesser degree, the Christian Church entire, throughout human history.

(5) A broader association with all death associated with violence or murder of the innocent—that Christ Jesus wears the robe dipped in blood tells us that his holy and precious blood covers and saves them all.

(6) The righteous and holy wrath of Christ and the consequences of sin.

(7) The Word became flesh when the Son of God dwelt among us, thus the Word bled on the cross for each individual. The Saints will call his name the *Word of God*, for in the beginning was the Word and the Word was with God and the Word was God! We will behold his glory as the only One sired by the Father, named Jesus the Christ.

There is nothing in this verse to suggest that the name referred to here, *the Word of God*, is the secret or veiled name known only to Christ.

Revelation 19:14

And the armies in heaven, clothed in fine linen, pure white linen, followed him [Jesus] on white horses.

THE HEAVENLY ARMY

The heavenly army accompanies God's returning Son. It is made up of all the saved in Christ from the foundation of the world.

They leave Abraham's Bosom/, the first place of waiting, every one of them transformed into the Second Phase of Body, the glorified body, no longer existing in spirit/soul; they leave the second place of waiting, called Paradise, in the Second Phase of Body. All come to witness the great battle. When it's over they will settle down on the reformed earth with their God in their glorified bodies like their Master.

They are clothed in fine linen. Although this word is a literal reference to clothing, it's quite likely that John was trying to describe the light that radiated from their glorified bodies. They're clothed in holy and perfect brightness, reflecting the Spirit of Glory and of God.

The *linen* is described as being white, clean, and pure, telling us that they reflect the righteous and perfect nature of God.

These are all the transformed Saints, as well as the Tribulation martyrs and the 144,000 chosen of God. Apparently, they follow Christ on gleaming white horses, and again, this could be metaphor, but because of the supernatural nature of the events that the heavenly army rides literal white horses is not improbable.

Revelation 19:15

Now out of his mouth goes a sharp sword, that with it he should strike the nations. And he himself will rule them with a rod of iron. He himself treads the winepress of the fierceness and wrath of Almighty God.

THE SHARP SWORD

Out of Jesus' mouth, the Word is spoken: "...these things says he who has the (words as) sharp (as a) two-edged sword (Rev. 2:12).

The reference to the *sharp sword* is layered:

(1) It represents the Holy Word of God, the Bible, and Jesus Christ, for both cut to the heart of the sinner.

(2) It's a symbol of the nature of Christ at his return.

(3) It's a reference to the power of the Word.

The Word of Jesus breaks the might of the Antichrist. His Word shakes the mighty wilderness! By his Word he strikes the nations beneath him. By his speaking the Word, it becomes so! "I AM IS THE WORD!"

THE POWER OF THE WORD I AM

As an example of the power of Christ's Word, there are potentially two hundred million people or more gathered for the Battle of Armageddon whose target is Jesus, and by his Word alone they are destroyed. The Lord consumes them with the breath of his mouth! Behold, the glory of God comes from the skies and his voice is like the sound of seven great rivers! The voice of his thunder is in the whirlwind, the mighty Spirit of God! He looks upon the earth and it trembles at his presence! He touches the hills and they quake! He casts the Antichrist's throne to the ground—all by his Word alone.

All humanity is indeed afraid because they are in the presence of the true and Mighty God, "I AM THAT I AM."

THE ROD OF IRON

The reference to Jesus ruling the nations with *a rod of iron* directly applies to the millennial reign of Christ during the Kingdom Age, the next and perfect Age. It will be 1,000 years of peace and rest for the Saints on the reformed earth in perfect nature and (potentially) time.

The reference to *ruling with a rod of iron* has everything to do with training the Saints in the ways of holiness and nothing to do with disciplining sin or fallen-natured behavior. Jesus rules with a rod of iron because the Saints have 1,000 years of learning and study to do. The study will be intense, for we are training for existence in eternity.

Many people incorrectly believe after death everything will be, in a complete way, *instantly understood and known*, and even though this will probably be true in regard to some of the broader concepts and perceptions because fallen human nature is transformed into perfection, reflecting the nature of the divine Trinity—naturally, the new true divine nature will have a much deeper understanding and connection and because of that we will, indeed, know a lot more about Creation than we do now—but when it comes to actual existence in a holy eternity the Saints are going to have to go *back to school*, as it were, for all they will *know and understand* is existence from the fallen-natured perspective. Jesus will have to teach and prepare redeemed humanity for eternity within the Holy Age and that will take some time—a thousand years, in fact.

The process is probably going to be much more complex than anyone realizes. Because many of us live in societies where instant gratification is the norm we immediately apply that to the afterlife. We expect it. We demand it. We feel entitled to know everything there is to know instantly—it would certainly make everything easier. But this education is not about *easy*. To exist in eternity after the 1,000 years I believe we are going to need a thorough understanding of a much deeper and more complex knowledge and experience. You won't be able to pop it in the heavenly microwave and cook it up in seconds like Jiffy Knowledge. You won't be able to instantly download it into our new natures and brains. No, it's going to take something much more sublime and elegant than instant gratification. It's going to take a skilled loving Carpenter to train his apprentices. We must all learn righteousness.

The meaning of *the winepress of the fierceness and wrath of Almighty God* is certainly clear here, an image strengthened by the fact that Christ himself is said to be the One who crushes or destroys the grapes. (Refer to Chapter 14:19, under the heading *The Winepress* for related information.) Obviously, on his return, no one escapes his wrath.

Revelation 19:16

And he has on his robe and on his thigh a name written: "KING OF KINGS AND LORD OF LORDS."

KING OF KINGS, LORD OF LORDS

On his robe and on his thigh, the great Lord of all has a title written: "KING OF KINGS AND LORD OF LORDS."

Having his name written on his thigh comes from the historical Old Testament practice of *swearing an oath upon the thigh*. It was customary to put a hand under the thigh when taking an oath. It is often referred to as the *bodily oath*.[1]

In relation to this verse, the fact that the name is written on or tattooed to the thigh of Christ makes it very clear just how deeply held Christ's oath is: it's permanent in an eternal sense.

Behold, this is his name, by which he is also called: "THE LORD OF RIGHTEOUSNESS, KING OF THE EARTH." The mind of Christ is righteousness and this prophecy comes from God.

Revelation 19:17

Then I [John] saw an angel standing in the sun; and he cried with a loud voice, saying to all the birds that fly in the midst of heaven, "Come and gather together for the great supper of God..."

THE SUN ANGEL

John is shown *an angel*, which of course represents Jesus because he is referred to as *standing in the sun*. "...His countenance was like the sun shining in its strength" (Rev. 1:16b).

Jesus Christ, the Son of God, is often associated with the sun, he who is like pure sunlight. He is the Rising Dawn, our eternal sunrise. But he is also like the mighty sun in relation to the star's power: the sun has an enormous field of gravity, energy, and size.[2] This tells us that Jesus has the strength of the sun.

The angel also stands in a place where no mortal could stand—in the sun—but he isn't merely standing on it. He's standing *within* it. This suggests a number of things: Christ is the power source of all that enormous energy; he is the Creator of the star; he is the Star in the center of the human solar system and existence; and he is the Center of everything and everything is in the Center of Christ.

He prepares the *birds* that fly in the midst of heaven and announces, "Come and gather together for the great supper of the great God."

THE BIRDS ARE CALLED

The Greek word used for birds (*orneon*) means a literal *birdling* or *fowl. Midst of heaven (mesouranema)* can be translated *mid-sky,* pertaining to the sky above, or perhaps more accurately, *mid-heaven,* as in, *celestial.*[3]

The birds may have some, as yet to be discovered meaning; they may be hyperdimensional beings. The reason this is suggested is simply because the verse seems to suggest that the birds are real things that fly *in the middle of heaven.* It's reasonable to ask then, what earthly bird would fly in heaven? Of course, these could simply be metaphor describing genuine birds of the earth, but if that isn't the case then these birds may turn out to be something else altogether, something from Super Nature. The argument is made stronger, when one realizes these birds not only fly in the middle of heaven, but they are designed to eat up everything on the earth, all the life that's left. They have been specifically prepared for the *Great Supper of God* that immediately follows the Battle of Armageddon, eating all the flesh that's left before or perhaps even during the sequences that follow, the total reformation of the earth.

I believe the birds are indeed literal birds of the earth, billions in number. They survive because they're supernaturally protected from the plagues. After they do their work, the birds and all fallen natured life will be utterly consumed and destroyed by the reformation of the earth.

Revelation 19:18

"That you [the birds] may eat the flesh of kings, the flesh of captains, the flesh of mighty men, the flesh of horses and of those who sit on them, and the flesh of all people, both free and slave, both small and great."

THE BIRDS WILL EAT

The birds are called from the midst of heaven to eat the flesh of the world's forces after the Battle of Armageddon. They will eat the flesh of kings, leaders, captains, foot soldiers and mighty men and women, and not only those destroyed at the Battle of Armageddon, but all the people remaining on the earth, both free and slave, small and great, and all animals—every living thing. The birds appear in such great numbers that they will blacken the sky!

Revelation 19:19

And I [John] saw the beast, the kings of the earth, and their armies, gathered together to make war against him who sat on the horse and against his army.

LOST

The verse jumps backward in the sequence of events here, returning to Armageddon and the vast army, their number is like the sands of the sea.

The army prepares to make war against Jesus, he who sits on the regal white horse. Indeed, they may feel a sense of premature victory over the incoming so-called *Invading Alien* because of their vast resources, numbers, and advanced technology, but all is lost, for Jesus is the One who rides the white horse and he is Master of all. The victory goes to him. By the power of his Word the world forces find themselves utterly powerless! He targets the Antichrist and alone he conquers!

It mustn't be forgotten that the last three-and-a-half years of the Tribulation will be intensely chaotic because of the plagues— perhaps humanity won't be feeling as confident as one presumes. Fear may be all that drives them; fear of the Invading Alien and his alien space army; fear of the Antichrist.

The plagues will certainly cause global chaos, and that chaos will increase as the three-and-a-half years near their end. By that point, surely the entire world will be in a sort of modern and historically unequaled Dark Ages—modern civilization will have steadily fallen apart for three-and-a-half years, which means that nearing the Battle of Armageddon it is very likely global communications will be down and ignorance and fear will be in fine working order.

Revelation 19:20

Then the beast was captured, and with him the false prophet who worked signs in his presence, by which he deceived those who received the mark of the beast and those who worshiped his image.

These two were cast alive into the lake of fire burning with brimstone.

END OF THE LINE

Jesus meets the world's military might and faces the Antichrist and the False Prophet/False Pope at the Battle of Armageddon, and he does this without any aid. The Saints and holy angels accompany Christ, but the only One who's going to be directly involved in the Battle of Armageddon is Jesus.

With the voice of a lion he says the Word and a blinding brightness covers the battlefields! In spite of the enemy's number, their strength is naught compared to the power of the Lord! His blinding light paralyzes all and they are struck with fear. They stand helplessly before Christ, the King. The birds of the skies, the beasts of the fields, all creeping things, and all people on earth shake before his presence.

At some distance above, Christ's army of believers, with the holy angels, look down as witnesses, observing his victory!

It is the end of the line for the Antichrist and the False Prophet.

All the unrepentant—the foot soldiers, generals, and politicians—at the disastrous battle scene face death. They perish and are forever lost to the kingdom of darkness. Of course, their fates were eternally sealed the moment they joined the global biometric system and worshiped the Antichrist.

Out of countless millions, only the Antichrist and the False Prophet remain unharmed.

At first, the glorious light of Jesus, like the great sun shining in its full strength, brings the mightiest army in the human history to an instant standstill. All the people who remain in the world witness the battle and fear the power of the light of the Holy Lord.

Remember, the lack of communication and breakdown of technology and governmental systems does not necessarily mean that television viewing will be impossible, for I believe that TV will continue to the very end, allowing survivors to witness the event. This seems reasonable because, even if the network and satellite systems were down on a global scale, good old fashioned local television and radio would probably continue to broadcast. Every eye sees the returning Christ as John predicted, but let me make this clear: the Lord will make sure everyone sees him and I seriously doubt he'll have to rely on television and radio or any human technology to make this happen. One way or another, every eye will see him, whether it's through human technology or a supernatural event. I tend to lean toward the supernatural.

Christ's single Word brings the Beast's forces to a sudden stop. While they are paralyzed, blinded by the light, Jesus takes the Antichrist, who is the son of Lucifer, and the False Prophet, and casts them alive into the eternal lake of fire.

And then he deals with the massive bewildered army of millions.

Revelation 19:21

The rest were killed with the sword which proceeded from the mouth of him who sat on the horse. And all the birds were filled with their flesh.

ARMY OF DEATH

John informs us that after the Antichrist and the False Prophet have been locked away forever, the armed forces are laid waste by the presence and greatness of God.

Jesus speaks the Word and millions cease to exist. Zechariah tells us exactly how the wicked force is destroyed: "And this shall be the plague with which the Lord will strike all the people who fought against Jerusalem: Their flesh shall dissolve while they stand on their feet, their eyes shall dissolve in their sockets, and their tongues shall dissolve in their mouths (by the power of the Lord).... So shall this plague be" (Zech. 14:12 and 15).

Some scholars of prophecy believe this *dissolving* of the flesh is a direct reference to nuclear detonation, that this description is merely metaphor for a great global nuclear strike between humanity, one in which Christ, standing along the sidelines like a football coach, uses to defeat the Antichrist.[4]

It is understandable why some may reach this conclusion (dissolving certainly suggests something like nuclear bombs), but in light of the supernatural events that take place at this point the theory doesn't seem credible—it reduces Jesus to dependence on manmade nuclear bombs to destroy his greatest enemy.

The great army gathered at Armageddon will be consumed by his supernatural shining brightness and power. Jesus will take all the credit and glory! Now, this dissolving may be similar to nuclear detonation, or in other words, it may involve the physics of nuclear detonation—that is certainly plausible. But again, given the supernatural nature of this event it is not at all *necessary*. The glory belongs to the Lord. By his power alone they melt. Simple as that.

At his presence, while sitting upon his white horse, very magnified, the bodies of the great army dissolve and melt away, and all the birds of the air, already gathered, come for their fill and eat the flesh of the lost.

The birds have to be supernaturally protected from the plagues and the dissolving light of Christ Jesus, and then they pick the bones of the Antichrist's dead army clean.

The end of the world's biggest war machine is not the end of all life on earth, no, not yet, not by a long shot, for potentially millions around the globe who weren't directly involved with the Antichrist's great army will still be alive!

TARGET: EARTH

Moments later, through the mighty power of his Word, Jesus destroys all life on the earth, from the largest animal (if any remain at this point), to the smallest living cell (and beyond), altering the very nature of the planet, solar system, and universe, including (potentially) time itself.

He reforms the planet for his kingdom by pouring out the seventh bowl plague.

Zechariah 14 tells us, beginning with Verse 4: "...And in that day (when Jesus is finished, the beginning of the true year 2001, by God's timetable/calendar) his feet will stand on the Mount of Olives, which faces Jerusalem on the east (at the exact same place he departed from the world two thousand years before). And (when his feet touch the Mount), the Mountain of Olives shall be split in two, from east to west, making a very large valley; half of the mountain shall move toward the north and half of it toward the south.... Thus the Lord my God will come (with all his power), and all the saints with you. (For more detailed information on the reformation of the earth, turn to Chapter 6:14, under the heading *Great Cosmic Disturbances*.)

"And in that day it shall be that living waters shall flow from Jerusalem (from the Mount of Olives), half of them toward the eastern sea (now known as the Dead Sea) and half of them toward the western sea (now known as the Mediterranean Sea). In both summer and winter it shall occur. And the Lord shall be King over all the earth (then to the Son of God is given dominion, adoration, and the kingdom, and all people will serve him; his dominion and kingdom will be everlasting; all the faithful believers of the Most High will receive the kingdom and possess it forever, even forever and ever). In that day it shall be—'The Lord is One,' and his name One" (Zech. 14: 4,5b, and 8–9).

Afterward, billions and billions of Saints come down to the reformed earth, phase two of the three phases of this, *the third earth of the Third Heaven,* recreated to reflect the nature it once had before its terrible Fall, and again, notice the sequence. The earth phases began after the original earth in its perfect nature fell into imperfection; before that, it was perfect/non-entropic, constant or *phase less*, if you will. The three phases of the earth begin after the Fall.

THIRD EARTH PHASE I

Phase 1: The fallen earth, this earth in its first phase, entropic in nature.

THIRD EARTH PHASE II

Phase 2: The transformed earth, this earth in its second phase, reformed to its original—Third Heaven—perfection for 1,000 years.

THIRD EARTH PHASE III

Phase 3: The earth as the lake of fire, this earth in its third and final phase, transformed into the eternal prison-place for both the angelic and human lost.

We have another complete sequence of three.

The Saints will study and learn with their Lord, their Great Master for a thousand years, and then beyond that into eternity on the Second New Earth (as opposed to this old earth in one of its three phases), called the Second Heaven. The millions of holy angels will return to their Holy Father's First Earth, called the First Heaven, for the great Day of the Lord will be finished! (For additional information on the concept of three heavens, turn to Chapter 3:21, under the heading *Three Heavens Explored* and the three heavens diagram.)

We will follow the Saints into the new millennium, the Kingdom Age, living on this earth in its second phase as the reformed earth in the next chapter.

* * * * *

SOURCES:

1. *Oaths,* pg. 930-931, The New Unger's Bible Dictionary, Moody Press (1988).
   Weekly Parsha, Jonathan Wolf (February 12, 2003), Oceanside Jewish Center, 2860 Brower Avenue, Oceanside, N.Y. 11572, <http://www.oceansidejc.org>.
   Oaths, Paul Levertoff, International Bible Standard Encyclopedia, Online Edition, <http://www.studylight.org>.
2. *Sun, 2,* C. E. Schenk, International Bible Standard Encyclopedia, Online Edition, <http://www.studylight.org>.

Sun, pg. 1224-1225, The New Unger's Bible Dictionary, Moody Press (1988).

3. *Birds—Orneon,* #3732, pg. 52; *Midst of heaven—Mesouranema,* #3321, pg. 47, Greek Dictionary of the New Testament, Strong's Exhaustive Concordance of the Bible/Dictionary of the Hebrew and Greek Words, Hendrickson Publishers.

4. *Nuclear Weapons in the End Times, Does The Bible Predict A Nuclear Holocaust?* Dennis Pollock, Lamb & Lion Bible Prophecy Ministry, <http://www.lamblion.com>.

The End of the World: What Does the Bible Say?, Neol, Horner, The Good News, a Magazine of Understanding, <http://www.gnmagazine.org>.

Nuclear Weapons in the End Times, David Reagan, BPT, Bible-Prophecy-Today.com (2009), <http://www.bible-prophecy-today.com>.

CHAPTER 20
The Thousand Years

Revelation 20:1

Then I [John] saw an angel coming down from heaven, having the keys to the bottomless pit and a great chain in his hand.

THE KEYS
Target: Satan

Before the Kingdom Age can begin the Son of God will have some tidying up to do. He targets Satan. The Lord captures and confines him in the prison-place called the bottomless pit.

The reference to *chain* suggests that the Great Deceiver is chained and therefore powerless. In the original Greek (*halusis*) *chain* or *chained* can be interpreted as *lifeless, inanimate, without life*. This is a fitting description because the Evil One will be in a sort of *lifeless* or *inanimate* state of existence for 1,000 years, imprisoned within the bottomless pit.

Revelation 20:2

He laid hold of the dragon, that serpent of old, who is the Devil and Satan, and bound him for a thousand years.

CHAINED FOR 1,000 YEARS

The Evil One will be chained within the prison-place known as the bottomless pit for 1,000 years.

"For this purpose the Son of God was manifested, that he might destroy the works of the devil..." [1](1 John 3:8b). After eons of corruption, temptation, destruction, and on and on, Lucifer will finally be imprisoned—but it isn't over for him just yet. He will be released one last and final time before being eternally imprisoned within the lake of fire.

But it is over for the Antichrist and the False Prophet. They have both been thrown into the lake of fire, the eternal and permanent hell—once placed within the lake of fire there is no escape and that means forever.

Revelation 20:3

And he cast him into the bottomless pit, and shut him up, and set a seal on him, so that he should deceive the nations no more till the thousand years were finished. But after these things he must be released for a little while.

SHUT UP

With the Battle of Armageddon over and the Antichrist and the False Prophet confined to their rightful and eternal prison in the lake of fire, it is Satan's turn to be bound, but only for the duration of mankind's seventh millennium. He is shut up for 1,000 years. Overpowered by God's Son, Jesus wraps the chain around Lucifer seven times and takes him to the entrance of the abyss. He unlocks the gates to the prison and casts him into the depths of the pit.

The reference to a *chain* describes the imprisonment of Lucifer through the great *chain-like* power of Christ. Lucifer is captured and bound, or *sealed,* by the power and Glory of Christ. He is no longer able to deceive anyone. The use of the word *seal* seems to suggest in the original Greek (*sphragizo*) not only *to be sealed* or *to seal closely,* but *a thrusting through* by an arrow or some other missile-like object.[2]

NO MORE

The meaning of the verse is clear: the dark lord is totally incapacitated and there he remains for the duration of the Kingdom Age. Lucifer will not be able to deceive the Saints or the children born into the millennium throughout the 1,000 years on the reformed earth. Believers will clap their hands, for they will be ready to live a perfect life on earth without the deceptions of the devil! Work as we know it for the human race comes to a close after six thousand years of toil and hardship (by God's timetable/calendar). The *7th day* of rest for humankind is upon us.

THE DAY OF THE LORD

Each *day* represents a Spirit of the Seven Spirits of God and time.

1 day = 1,000 years (by God's timetable/calendar.)

6 days = 6,000 years (by God's timetable/calendar).

The 7th *day* is of course made up of 10 centuries.

7 centuries symbolize the Seven Spirits of God.

3 centuries symbolize the Holy Trinity!

This is indeed a holy day, for the Son of God will be with his people, resting with his faithful from all their works that they have done. The Lamb who is holy will be hallowed in righteousness and the world will be a wonderful place for the saved in Christ. They remain young for a thousand years because the earth was originally made to be wooed and won by the young!

God's Word informs us that only the Father knows when the *7th day* begins, which introduces the seventh millennium and freedom from the work that we have done. Because of this, the saved in Christ need not be so anxious trying to work out when the *Day of the Lord* will be revealed, for he alone knows the day and the hour. Mankind does not have to tell God like so many try to do. God will tell us.

THE RE-CREATION

Six Days of the Earth's Transformation
The re-creation of the earth—all that is discussed in the following paragraphs—happens *after* the return of Christ, global earthquake, wall of fire, lava encircling the globe, and hailstones that bombard the planet, destroying all the fallen-natured human life that remains and, in fact, all fallen-natured life/reality.

Jesus reforms the heavens and the earth to his liking, the reformation process taking six literal 24 hour days, similar to the original creation.

RE-CREATION DAY 1

Now the Spirit of God hovers over the earth and his Son reforms it. Jesus says, "LET THERE BE AN ADJUSTMENT IN THE LIGHT," and it is so, for new light appears. He sees that the adjustment with our light/sun is good, and he divides this light from the night. This concept suggests that before God alters the universe into perfection he transforms our light source first, the sun—perhaps our original sun will supernova, giving birth to a brand new and non-entropic star. And the evening and the morning is the first day of earth's transformation, making ready for the Second Age!

RE-CREATION DAY 2

Then Jesus says, "LET THE VAPORS SEPARATE TO FORM THE SKY ABOVE AND THE WATERS BELOW," and it is so, the way it was originally meant to be! An adjustment is made to the firmament and to the waters. He calls the firmament a new heaven above, and the atmosphere is cleansed. And the evening and the morning is the second day of the great change, preparing for earth's second Age!

RE-CREATION DAY 3

The Mighty Son of God changes the dry land, calling it the *Good Earth of the Wonderful Golden Age of Rest*. The gathering of the waters is called the New Waters. And Jesus sees that it is good! He says, "LET THE EARTH BRING FORTH FIELDS OF GRASS AND TREES THAT YIELD FRUIT ACCORDING TO THEIR KIND," and it is so! And the evening and the morning of the third day of the reformation of the planet, in preparation for the new perfect Age, is complete.

RE-CREATION DAY 4

On the fourth day, the Son says, "LET THERE BE AN ADJUSTMENT IN THE ARRANGEMENT OF STARS AND PLANETS IN THE GREAT HEAVENS TO DIVIDE THE DAY FROM THE NIGHT. LET THEM GIVE NEW SIGNS AND NEW SEASONS FOR DAYS AND YEARS, AND LET THEM GIVE NEW LIGHT TO THE RENOVATED EARTH," and it is so. The solar system/galaxy/universe will be transformed into perfection. The universe will reflect a perfect nature instead of the imperfect/entropic universe such as the universe in which we now live. God sees that it is good! And the evening and the morning is the fourth day of these great adjustments for humankind, in readiness for the new Age!

RE-CREATION DAY 5

Jesus fills the earth's waters with an abundance of new living creatures and every sort of fish. The skies are filled with every kind of bird! Then Jesus says, "LET THE EARTH BRING FORTH EVERY KIND OF ANIMAL." And the Lord is pleased with his creation, for the animals are all the different species that were created from the beginning. Because of the knowledge and presence of God they reflect the nature of God; they are gentle in the sight of humanity. And God sees that it is good! And the evening and the morning is the fifth day of the new changes of earth, making way for the new dispensation!

RE-CREATION DAY 6

Jesus continues, saying to his Father, "LET US BRING FORTH ALL THE SAVED THAT LIVED ON EARTH BEFORE THE GREAT REFORMATION," and it is so! God's Son brings down from the sky all his believers raptured from the old earth, male and female. They come down from above and hover over the earth after watching their Master transform the great planet.

The first One to touch the newly reformed earth will be Christ himself. The Saints and the angels won't settle on the earth until this happens.

HIS FEET TOUCH THE EARTH

Jesus' feet touch the Mount of Olives and the ground splits open. Sacred waters flow between the Mount and a garden he calls Eden. The waters spread across the land, eastward from the glowing new city he names Jerusalem.

This is a new Jerusalem made out of nothing. It will simply appear. The new city will not be reconstructed using materials from the original old city, for the original Jerusalem is utterly destroyed when the earth is reformed, and of course, the old Jerusalem was constructed out of fallen-natured material.

The Creator makes every tree grow that is pleasant to the sight and good for food. The Tree of Life will be found somewhere in the middle of the new Garden of Eden, and the people will be content. And the evening and the morning is the sixth day. Indeed, it is very good. So this ends the six days of the reconstitution of the earth for the anticipated Kingdom Age!

THE 7th DAY

Now heaven proclaims, "Oh be joyful!" All God's people join their Savior on the wonderful newly reformed earth, singing and dancing joyously, and the seventh millennium, the Kingdom Age, officially begins.

Jesus blesses them, giving them a new command: be fruitful and multiply for 1,000 years, filling the beautifully recreated earth with life.

On the 7th day Jesus rests with his people, and he blesses and sanctifies the 1,000 years because in it he rests from all his work that he has done. And his faithful rest with him.

FOR A LITTLE WHILE

The reference to the dark lord being released *for a little while* suggests that at the end of the 1,000 years of peace and perfection on the reformed earth the Evil One will, indeed, be released from the prison-place known as the bottomless pit one last and final time, but it will be a very short time.

The unrepentant, who have been in the place of waiting Sheol/antiparadise for 1,000 years in spirit/soul, will come with him. Their goal: to tempt the Saints from Christ. The Saints and those born into the *7th day of perfection* will be unaffected by these temptations, for under the grace of Christ they will find refuge and security for eternity. (For related information on this subject, refer to Chapters 8:1, under the heading *Kingdom Age Reproduction* and 15:1, under the heading *Billions & Billions*.)

Throughout the thousand years they will study, learn, and prepare just like scholars for their transfiguration into eternity, for at the conclusion of the Kingdom Age they will be transferred to Heaven itself. They will go to the New Earth which is the Second Heaven that comes down from the domain of God, his First Heaven.

Revelation 20:4

And I [John] saw thrones, and they sat on them, and judgment was committed to them. Then I saw the souls of those who had been beheaded for their witness to Jesus and for the word of God, who had not worshiped the beast or his image, and had not received his mark on their foreheads or on their hands. And they lived and reigned with Christ for a thousand years.

THRONES OF JUDGMENT

John sees the thrones that will appear at the end of our 7th day of rest, the Kingdom Age.

It is possible that these thrones are intended only for the holy heavenly angels, but I think it's more probable that the angels *and* redeemed humanity will sit on the thrones as witnesses to God's judgment on the unrighteous.

Jesus says, "I will confess his (and her) name (all the names of the saved) before My Father and before his angels" (Rev. 3:5b). Because of this encouraging verse we know that judgment is not passed on to the righteous, for they are made worthy through the grace of Christ. The sins of the saved are remembered no more. Their sins have been washed clean by the blood of the Lamb. Only those who believe in the One who gave his blood will receive this honor. "...having now been justified by his blood, we shall be saved from wrath through him" (Rom. 5:9).

BEHEADED TRIBULATION MARTYRS

The Left Behind believers, those who did not participate in the Fourth Rapture and were killed for their witness to Jesus during the last three-and-a-half-years of the Tribulation, stand before their Lord.

Beheaded is a derivative of the Greek word for *axe*, (*pelekizo*), suggesting in the literal *to chop off* (the head), or perhaps more accurately, *to behead*.[3]

The use of this word has caused many scholars to debate its meaning. Some believe the literal act of beheading will be official policy during the last three-and-a-half years of the reign of the Antichrist. Some have gone so far as to suggest that *motorized/computer controlled beheading machines* may be driven all over the world, chopping off Jewish and Christian heads left and right because beheading is a quick and efficient way to kill large masses of people.

Mainstream eschatological critics used to scoff at ideas like this, arguing that the word simply referred to modern weaponry and technologies.

But in light of recent world events involving innocent victims kidnapped by Islamic fundamentalist terrorist groups and their subsequent beheadings, together with the rising tide of Islamic influence in the world where beheading is official Sharia Law and policy, put into actual practice, the concept of the Antichrist beheading Christians and Jews isn't such a stretch of the imagination after all.

LIVED & REIGNED FOR 1,000 YEARS

The verse ends with a nod to the Kingdom Age: the Tribulation martyrs live and reign with Christ during the 1,000 years, learning and studying alongside all the Saints—and so, blessed are they whose hope is in the Lord, for they will inherit the New Earth and will be like trees spreading out their roots! "Now, may the God of hope fill you with all joy and peace in believing, that you may abound in hope by the power of the Holy Spirit" (Rom. 15:13).

Revelation 20:5

(But the rest of the dead did not live again until the thousand years were finished). This is the first resurrection.

THE REST OF THE DEAD

John confirms that the *dead toward the Godhead*, all those who rejected the Holy Trinity from the time of Adam until the end of the Human Age, will not live again until the thousand years have ended. They will exist in the form of spirit/soul in the place of waiting called Sheol/antiparadise.

The Seventh Rapture is their rapture, the transformation of lost souls into the Second Phase of Body, the glorified body; their bodily transformation will go no further, and thus they will be forever incomplete. The unrepentant never experience phase three of the Phase of Body, the superglorified body, into eternity.

This is the first and only resurrection for the lost. It will transpire at the end of the restful millennium when Satan is released from the bottomless pit *for a little while.*

When they show up at the end of the millennium, they enter into the recreated perfected earth reality in their glorified bodies. They will remain imperfect in the sense of connection (or the lack thereof) to the Divine, retaining a fallen nature, and because of that it's possible that when they appear in the recreated earth reality a crosspollination-of-realties-chain reaction may be triggered. This could explain why, in part, their stay is so short. (Refer to Chapter 8:1, under the heading *A Controversial Subject* for related information.)

The reference to *the first resurrection* applies directly to the martyred saved in Christ during the final three-and-a-half years of the Great Tribulation, the Fifth Rapture just before the return of Christ. All of the raptures, Three through Six, fall under the title of *first resurrection*, and I'll explore that concept in the next verse.

Revelation 20:6

Blessed and holy is he who has part in the first resurrection. Over such the second death has no power, but they shall be priests of God and of Christ, and shall reign with him a thousand years.

THE FIRST RESURRECTION

The first resurrection is a broad term that involves all people who believe, namely, the saved in Christ.

The Third Rapture through the Sixth Rapture fall within the borders of the first resurrection as it's used in this verse.

The Saints will receive their glorified bodies shortly before the thousand year period begins in regard to the sequence of raptures and where they fall in that sequence, partaking in rapture Three, Four, Five, or Six.

Blessed and holy are the ones who take part in the first resurrection, for over such the second death has no power! They will become priests of God and of Christ and reign with him for a thousand years, and then on into eternity.

Modern Christians look upon the Fourth Rapture as the first resurrection of the living. This first resurrection of the Saints is indeed the first resurrection/rapture of the living since Jesus went to be with his Father in heaven nearly two thousand years ago, but in the sequence of the raptures it is actually the Fourth, not the First. The resurrection/rapture of Elijah and Enoch are the only two exceptions in regard to living resurrections/raptures that we know of.

The first and only resurrection of the dead toward Christ a thousand years later, the Seventh Rapture of the lost, will be similar in process, for they will receive the Second Phase of Body, the glorified body, but instead of rising with Christ they will rise with Lucifer in the air, fully in sin and the fallen nature, for they trusted in Satan's wickedness.

THE SECOND DEATH

The *second death* is a term that applies to the Third Phase of Body for the saved in Christ, as well as the reality-shift into eternity for the saved in Christ.

Even though it is called *the second death*, it will have no power in the sense of *pain* and *suffering*. It is clearly stated that those who have ears, let them hear what the Spirit declares: "He who overcomes shall not be hurt by the second death" (Rev. 2:11). It is the final transfiguration into the Third Phase of Body, the superglorified body, designed for eternity. At the end of the seventh millennium the second death will be exciting to believers rather than tragic or horrifying. They will be transfigured from this world to the New Earth and the Second Heaven, and they will be given new names! "He who overcomes (those who experience their second deaths), I (Jesus) will make him a pillar in the temple of my God (in the new city of Jerusalem), and he shall go out no more (depicting that those who overcome will always be with the Lord). I will write on him the name of my God and the name of the city of My God, the new Jerusalem, which comes down out of heaven from my God. And I will write on him my new name" (Rev. 3:12).

The verse shifts gears midway through the last sentence, returning to the restful millennium: during the Kingdom Age all believers will be priests of God and of Christ. All will reign with him—everyone involved in the first resurrection and series of raptures, as well as those resurrected in the Second Rapture, including the Old Testament Saints, prophets and all the saved in Christ prior to the death and resurrection of Jesus Christ. What a wonderful relationship! All will belong to Jesus forever!

Revelation 20:7

Now when the thousand years have expired, Satan will be released from his prison.

SATAN WILL BE RELEASED

Satan's final assault upon humanity: when the thousand years have expired, Jesus will unlock the prison-place called the bottomless pit and release Satan from his prison under the earth, according to God's plan.

The dead toward Christ will experience their one and only resurrection, the Seventh Rapture, meeting Lucifer in the air. Remember, Scripture confirms in Revelation 20:5 that "the rest of the dead (the unrepentant) do not live again until the thousand years were finished."

Revelation 20:8

And [Satan] will go out to deceive the nations which are in the four corners of the earth, Gog and Magog, to gather them together to battle, whose number is as the sand of the sea.

THE FOUR CORNERS & SAND OF THE SEA

The nations in the four corners of the earth: this is a reference to millennial families. Families are clearly important to the Lord. They are the most precious things on earth, for in the beginning God said, "Be fruitful and multiply. Fill the earth and subdue it." During the millennium kingdom the reformed earth's population will increase dramatically. God commands this for the Human Age and the Kingdom Age. Since death won't exist, the global population will increase and the world will joyfully turn.

In verse 3 of this chapter, John foresaw that, "After these things he (the devil) must be released a little while"—his last and final time. Satan will go out to deceive the nations scattered over the four corners of the earth. The number of the unrepentant with him, now in the Second Phase of Body, the glorified body (exactly the same Phase of Body the saved in Christ exist in at this point), will number as the sand of the sea.

The sand of the sea: this refers to Satan and his followers who will invade the reformed earth, sweeping across the globe like a fallen-natured virus *for a little while*.

The amount of time could be hours, days, weeks, or perhaps even months; it's likely that the amount of time will fall under a pattern of 3 or 7. I believe it will last three days. Sin and the fallen nature will *enter* the perfect reality of the Kingdom Age, disrupting and perhaps even corrupting the new reality three days. The only reason sin and fallen nature can enter into the new reality of the Kingdom Age is simply because the event is controlled by God.

SATAN'S THIRD & FINAL ACT

This will be the red dragon's third and final conflict against God and his creations, making it a complete and sacred 3!

Why will Satan and the unrepentant be permitted to disrupt sinless humanity and potentially corrupt the perfect Kingdom Age?

The answer lies hidden in the Big Picture, far too sublime for us to form a complete, irrefutable answer here, but we can try to understand the purpose from our veiled perspective.

(1) God conforms to set patterns, number systems, and rules. The reason the lost return to the earth at the end of the 1,000 years is solely to receive their new bodies and to be judged, and to do that they must experience a resurrection similar to the resurrection of the saved. This will be the seventh resurrection since Jesus rose and conquered sin and death for all humanity through his sacrifice and grace. Again, another number system— 7—making it complete. Seven is one of the sacred and holy numbers, standing for completeness, but since these souls will be unrepentant, or *broken* and *incomplete*, they will be resurrected into sin and the sinful nature, as opposed to *out of the sinful nature*, as the saved in Christ were resurrected, and clearly this happens because they did not choose to know the Lord. If you add all the lost from the beginning of the human world and Fallen time the numbers will amount to billions and billions, for broad is the path to Lucifer and narrow is the path to Christ!

(2) God requires of every human soul ever created that they be on earth in readiness for Judgment Day, and by resurrecting the unrepentant into the Second Phase of Body (from the spirit) and allowing them to exist and stand on the reformed earth, he accomplishes this task.

(3) This will be Lucifer's last bid to win believers over to him by encouraging them not to follow the path of Christ. Because God clearly permits this, it's clear that he's adhering to and finally closing a pattern/design/chapter, making it complete.

A LITTLE WHILE REVISITED

The devil and his army of fallen will experience the end of the Kingdom Age for *a little while.* When they're resurrected/raptured into the Second Phase of Body, the glorified body, they will appear in the reality/universe/time of the seventh millennium, the recreated earth, which makes sense since this is the world from which they came. They will enter into the perfected world/reality of the seventh millennium and try to corrupt it.

Fact is, we know it takes only a short while to disrupt and corrupt a world. Satan and the unrepentant won't need 1,000 years to do it, if they can indeed do it. The historical references to back this argument up would fill a book thick enough to stun an ox: from Hitler—a mere 12 years—to Nero to Stalin to Mao, weeks, months, and sometimes years, but on the whole corruption comes quick and easy. There's one more example that shows just how quickly a world can be corrupted, in the mere twinkling of a choice: the Fall of Adam.

Since Lucifer will have billions and billions of corrupted humanity and fallen angels to aid him *a little while*, or from the King James, *a little season* (Greek, *little: mikros/mikroteros*, meaning, *small in size, quantity or number*, and *chronos*, meaning *an uncertain duration of time or season*)[4] is all Lucifer will need—but, once again, the amount of time is unknown. I believe it will be exactly three days in length.

BATTLE READY

The lost will have had 1,000 years of waiting in Sheol/antiparadise to prepare. They will be more than ready to attempt the deed. The saved in Christ will also have had 1,000 years to prepare. Thus, both sides will be prepared to do battle. The difference is, of course, that the saved in Christ will be under the tutelage of Jesus Christ, the Creator of the Universe. The outcome is certain.

In regard to the term *battle*, it doesn't seem likely Satan and the fallen will try to disrupt or corrupt the Saints through violence because there will be no death, but perhaps they will inflict some kind of violence upon the Saints and the world, regardless. I suspect that persuasion will be the weapon of choice for the fallen.

The fallen will try to tempt the Saints to follow Lucifer instead of Jesus, knowing full well they have been preparing for this moment with Christ as their drill sergeant for 1,000 years; knowing the redeemed and the children born to them (potentially the most vulnerable to Satan's persuasions) have been living without sin and the fallen nature for 1,000 years; knowing they have been studying, learning, and preparing for eternity for 1,000 years; knowing they are held in the eternally secure grace of Christ, which makes falling away to the call of darkness impossible.

Knowing all that the Evil One will send his entire force throughout the world, trying to mislead the nations.

Denial must play a huge role in the thinking processes of the fallen.

Their time will be limited, and essentially pointless (in regard to successfully corrupting the saved in Christ, which I think tells us that their time on earth will be ridiculously short), and so the lost will go all out, from one end of earth to the other, with nothing to lose. They will do everything in their sinful repertoire that they can to lead the Saints from Christ. They will attempt to reopen Pandora's Box and corrupt the world. But for the sake of the elect, who are all God's people, Satan's final days will be cut short!

SHORTSIGHTED DENIAL

These *sands of the sea* will come with only one objective: to destroy and take as many Saints with them as possible. I think it will be absolutely impossible to achieve, so perhaps they will resort to simple anarchy and rampant destruction—the release of their final rage and denial. Whatever the case may be, as they go out to practice deceit on a world totally free of sin, Jesus will make ready to defeat them, for he has authority over the wicked and will be victorious.

Lastly, think about this: after 1,000 years of study with Jesus Christ, the children of God will now be ready for the Third Phase of Body, the superglorified body, and existence within eternity, when they will be transported from the reformed earth to heaven for time and eternity. At that point you have to ask, who would give that up? Answer: no one.

The lost will not experience the third transformation of body. Their second death will involve pain and suffering, for they will be cast into the lake of fire for eternity in their glorified bodies, the Second Phase of Body, remaining forever incomplete.

Revelation 20:9

They went up on the breath of the earth and surrounded the camps of the saints and the beloved city. And fire came down from God out of heaven and devoured them.

DEVOURED

In the earlier prophecy concerning Gog and Magog the leader was called *Gog,* referring to the president of Russia. Gog is Satan in this prophecy.

He assembles his army in the north, in the land that once was known as Magog. We understand the place to be Western Asia and the countries that border the Black and Caspian Seas: Russia, Turkey, Iran, Romania, Bulgaria, etc.

After a thousand years imprisoned within the bottomless pit, Lucifer will take over the northern territory, making it his headquarters for a little while. It is not clear why he returns to the northern countries, but the fact that John uses Gog and Magog in relation to Satan and his final earthly domain suggests that he may occupy the area of reformed Western Asia. Perhaps this is done out of some kind of satanic instinct or behavioral pattern we little understand. Some have argued Satan's return to the northern territories has a military objective: the sacking of Jerusalem. I tend to think that's probably the truth of it. Put more simply, Satan's return to Magog is the last act of a desperate being bent on mocking and dishonoring God to the bloody and bitter end.

The devil's own will spread out swiftly from the northern parts of the world to do their spoil. They will swarm over the length and breadth of the recreated earth, surrounding the dwelling places of believers, including those in the beloved holy city of Jerusalem. They will duplicate what the pre-Tribulation Hostile Nations did against Israel—history repeats itself, although this time the forces of the dark lord will be decidedly larger, billions and billions strong; and similar to the conclusion of the siege over Israel by Gog and Magog and the Hostile Nations, the forces of Satan (Gog) and his army of the fallen will be devoured by the wrath of God as a result of fire that comes down from the skies.

The Greek word *pur* can be used in the literal or the figurative as *fire*, but specifically, and perhaps more accurately, it can be translated as *lightning*, or perhaps *fiery lightning*[5]—clearly, a supernatural event.

Revelation 20:10

The devil, who deceived them, was cast into the lake of fire and brimstone where also the beast and the false prophet are. And they will be tormented day and night forever and ever.

UNDENIABLE FIRE!

Finally, Lucifer, who has deceived people from the beginning of Fallen time, and even before that, will be easily overpowered by Jesus Christ. He is caught and then cast into the lake of fire and sulfur. This is the same place where the Antichrist and the False Prophet/False Pope were placed one thousand years prior to this event, for Revelation explains that, "Then the beast (being the Antichrist) was captured, and with him the false prophet... These two were cast alive into the lake of fire burning with brimstone" (Rev. 19:20). This is the eternal prison from which there is no reprieve or escape.

It seems clear here that Lucifer was fated to fail, even with his mighty army numbering as the sands of the sea, for God has authority over him. Perhaps his ability to tap into the Seven Spirits of God, the Power Source of God, and his ability to deny reality or hyperdimensional realities generated enough arrogance to fuel his belief that he could somehow overthrow the Supreme Being, the Creator of Everything.

It's arguable, but it seems likely that there is no other creature in the entire universe and all Creation that is in a bigger state of denial than the devil himself.

Whatever the case may be, once he is cast into the lake of fire, at that point he will be an ordinary created being or fallen angel. In fact, his ability to tap into the Seven Spirits of God will be taken from him well beforehand, when he is locked up into the prison-place known as the bottomless pit at the beginning of the thousand restful years. When he is released the last and final time he will have none of the power of the Seven Spirits of God. He will merely be another lost and fallen angel, exactly like the angels that followed him from the beginning—powerful maybe, but when compared to the power he used to have, weak as a dying ember in a cold fire!

SATANIC SUICIDE MISSION

Satan's final battle with the Saints at the end of the seventh millennium turns out to be nothing more than a suicide mission. He will be utterly defeated and finished and then cast into the lake of fire. The devil's unholy trinity will be together again, tormented day and night forevermore, even forever and ever!

Revelation 20:11

Then I [John] saw a great white throne and him who sat on it, from whose face the earth and the heaven fled away. And there was found no place for them.

GREAT WHITE THRONE

The *Great White Throne judgment* comes to pass.

The angel (Jesus) shows John a massive white throne, a clear visual depiction of God's purity, holiness, and strength. God Almighty will sit on the throne, at whose face the reformed earth and heaven (universe) flee. Jesus will stand by his side.

EARTH & HEAVEN FLEE

The reference to the earth and heaven fleeing from the face of God is more than likely literal here in the sense that the earth and its universe/reality will be removed, or removed as far from the

Creator as a created thing can go/be from its Creator. Considering the hyperdimensional and (potentially) digital nature of this universe and (potentially) all Creation, and of course dealing with God who can indeed do anything, that the universe entire could be *removed* or *flee from the face of God* is not improbable.

It's worthwhile to note, and rather telling, that the original Greek word for fled (*katapheugo*) can be translated *to flee down (away)*, *escape*, or (*pheugo*), *to vanish*. The words *down* and *vanish*[6] could suggest something of a quantum and even digital nature in reference to the earth and heaven flying from the face of God, what amounts to the digital removal of this earth and universe. (Refer to Chapter 1:19, under the heading *Classical & Quantum Physics* for related information.)

The reformed earth and firmament (universe/time/reality) will be relocated for a variety of reasons, two of which are listed here.

(1) The earth and its universe have one final and eternal use as the prison-place for the lost—the third phase of this earth. Once that has been accomplished this entire earthly universe/reality will be removed from the presence of God, tucked into some dark and lonely corner of Creation.

(2) Nearing the end of the seventh millennium sinful humanity spread over the earth and tried to corrupt the Saints, an act which might have corrupted the planet and reality, what would amount to something like a Second Fall. If the planet/reality was not altered in any way, it was still contaminated or touched by evil— that's enough to send it on its way.

Interestingly, there is nothing in Scripture to indicate that a Second Fall takes place at the end of the seventh millennium. Satan and the unrepentant speed across the recreated and perfect earth in corruption, for what I think will be three short, but brilliantly destructive days, and then they face total annihilation. Why won't Satan be able to cause a Second Fall?

(1) Satan will no longer have the power to do it because he cannot tap into the Power Source of God, the Seven Spirits of God; thus, he will be unable to corrupt the Saints as he did with Adam, which caused the perfect nature of the world/universe/time/ reality to alter; the Saints will be under the grace of Christ, so it seems reasonable to conclude that even if Satan retained his original power (but he won't), he wouldn't be able to sway the Saints because of the seal of Jesus Christ.

(2) Clearly, and most importantly, this will be an event controlled by God.

The dragon, that old snake, who is the devil and Satan, will be locked up in the lake of fire by the power of the Lord, along with his son, the Antichrist, and the False Prophet, and all the lost who will be judged, and then this earth/universe/time will be *removed* from the presence of God for all eternity. After seven thousand years (by God's timetable/calendar), the great plan will be complete!

Revelation 20:12

And I [John] saw the dead, small and great, standing before the throne, and books were opened. And another book was opened, which was the Book of Life. And the dead were judged according to their works, by the things which were written in the books.

THE DEAD & THE BOOKS

Before the earth, solar system, and universe are removed from God's presence to become the eternal prison-place for the lost and before it is *rolled up like a scroll* (point and click, drag to the recycle bin, and delete), John sees the vast number of the dead. The reference to the dead here encompasses all humanity, both great and small, the saved and the lost.

The *books* are opened. The original Greek word (*biblion* or *biblos*) can be translated in the literal, as in, *book, scroll*,[7] suggesting some form of writing. It seems that all human information has been in some way *recorded*.

The Book of Life will also be opened. This book will *list* all the names of the saved in Christ. (Refer to Chapters 3:5 and 13:8 for related information.)

To help us understand the purpose of the books the following visual metaphor will be used: when an unrepentant person preparing to face judgment stands before God, the angels, and the Saints, the books will be opened and a liar might say, "No, I never did what they are accusing me of doing," and then a *picture recording* of the very act itself may very well flash across the sky for billions to see!

Of course, this is imagined from the human perspective and understanding—it doesn't have to be a television-like picture spanning the sky for the entire world to see at all, but how it will be accomplished is not what's important. What's important is that it will be accomplished. God will know the heart and mind of the saved and the unsaved, and every act of goodness, every choice of disobedience, every sinful thought, every secret truth will somehow be presented.

The number of the fallen, the lost souls whose fates were sealed upon their deaths on the old earth (who were waiting in Sheol/antiparadise and then released for a little while at the end of the Kingdom Age, the seventh millennium), will number in the billions and billions. Add to that the number of the redeemed and we have billions and billions and billions standing before God Almighty who will sit upon the great white throne.

THE FIRST BOOKS

The first books opened seem to focus on the lifetimes of every individual. They *show* or *have* everything about everyone in them, redeemed and unredeemed. It seems likely that those whose fates were sealed when they died without the grace of Christ will have little use for the books, given that their fates will be sealed. The books will be used to show them their sin and sinful nature—the emptiness of their choices, the tragedy of choosing to live for the self, the opportunities lost because of selfish, self-destructive, and disobedient lives. Although the judgment passed by God will be just, true, and holy, the moment will nonetheless be deeply tragic. God will take no pleasure in it.

The saved will be there as witnesses and as those who receive judgments/rewards based on their good works. The reference to "...judged according to their works..." applies only to the saved in Christ—Jesus will recognize that they are saved through his grace, examine their lives, and reward them according to their good works, ushering them into eternity with God. The books will be opened and their lives examined. Again, these books are probably metaphor, even though the Greek word can be interpreted literally. It's unlikely they're literal books as we understand them.

The holy angels will be present at the judgment as witnesses. They were appointed by God to be our guardians while we lived on this planet as fallen-natured flesh—if this were not so, or without their direct involvement in our lives, the devil could have potentially misled all humankind. Remember, angels are not only messengers of God, they are deeply involved in the lives of humanity as guardians, thus angels must have *records* of every human action committed. It makes sense that they should be our witnesses at the judgment.

THE BOOK OF LIFE

Another book is opened. This is the Lamb's Book of Life containing every name of every believer in Jesus Christ from the foundation of the world.

At this point, all the dead in Christ will be judged. Their names will not be found in the Book of Life, confirming their rejection of God and the Lord Jesus Christ! Jesus says, "He who overcomes shall be clothed in white garments, and I will not blot out his name from the book of life, but I will confess his name before my father and his angels" (Rev. 3:5).

JUDGMENT

John witnesses the great Day of Judgment at the end of seven thousand years of earth's and humanity's history (by God's timetable/calendar). "And it is appointed for men to die once, but after this the judgment," says the Lord (Heb. 9:27).

All humanity will be judged, the saved in Christ as well as dead in Christ. Everyone's lives will be closely examined, but only those who do not know the Lord will be sentenced and condemned after judgment.

The saved in Christ will be rewarded according to their good works and they will not be judged because their sins were washed clean by the blood of their Savior. Their sins will not be known. Jesus will know them because they were by his side for a 1,000 years and, of course, because they are in his grace. After their judgment and reward, they will be transferred to the New Earth.

To all the others Jesus will say, "I don't know you," and thus they will be of this old earth forever, for it will be transformed into its third and final phase as the lake of fire and it will keep them. The newly transformed earth, its hellish reality, and all the unsaved in it are *folded up* and removed from God's presence for eternity!

Revelation 20:13

The sea gave up the dead who were in it, and Death and Hades delivered up the dead who were in them. And they were judged, each one according to his works.

DEATH & HADES

Death and *Hades* come from an earlier period in human existence that at this point in human history no longer exists or applies—they represent the Old World and Ways. Nevertheless, they bring all the dead, the saved and unsaved, before God the Father, for like Death and Hades the dead were born in the Old World and Ways.

The reference to *according to his (or her) works* applies only to the saved. Recognizing the *good works* in the lives of the lost would be utterly purposeless at this point, for their fates will be sealed, their judgment sure, their sentence carried out. Good works will not stand or apply in the heat of hell.

Like the lost, the fates of the saved are sealed as well, but sealed by the grace of Christ. It seems that many of the saved in

Christ will garner *rewards* from Christ for leading faithful lives and having good works in those lives, but clearly those works will not be what saved them from the judgment. Christ alone saves humanity from judgment.

Revelation 20: 14

Then Death and Hades were cast into the lake of fire. This is the second death.

THE SECOND DEATH FOR THE LOST

Death and Hades are symbolically judged, the inevitable sentence is carried out, and they're thrown into the lake of fire where Satan, the Antichrist, the False Prophet, and all the fallen angels reside deep within the bowels of the recreated earth's prison-place. Death and Hades are now eternally dead, the Old World and its Ways gone forever.

The term *second death* in relation *to* death applies only to the unsaved. It is attached to the first painful and frightening physical human death that occurred in the fallen, entropic reality of this old earth and its old ways. It also suggests separation from God, for separation from God is like death or is in fact death. In this case, the death/separation will be eternal. There is also a mathematical connection here: you could refer to the second death as *death* squared. The second death is all the negative associations of the first *death multiplied by itself.*

The second death for the lost will be eternal, but it will not amount to annihilation. The fact that the Antichrist and the False Prophet continue to exist within the lake of fire during the 1,000 years is proof of this. Conscious awareness of the self, the ego I, and physical existence in the Second Phase of Body, the glorified body, is guaranteed since the self or soul—that which is *you*—and the glorified body are eternal by nature.[8]

THE ORDER OF THE JUDGMENTS

No one is certain of the order of judgments, but it seems likely that the fallen angels will face judgment first and then humanity will follow.

The second death applies to humanity and the fallen angels equally.

LEVELS OF TORMENT

It's doubtful that the lake of fire will have *levels* in the classic *Dante* sense of hell and eternal suffering because of the grace of

Christ—without grace all humanity would suffer the same judgment. From that we can gather all suffering will be equal in hell. This is why *good works* in the life of an unrepentant sinner during judgment won't matter. Levels of suffering based on levels of sin means *good sinners* will suffer less than *bad sinners.* This is an incorrect interpretation of sin and the fallen nature, suggesting that sin and the fallen nature are not total, suggesting that some humans aren't as sinful as other humans. Clearly, that is not the case, for all have fallen short of the glory of God.

WISHFUL THINKING HIGHWAY

The Bible doesn't reveal much about hell, but there are common Christian views in the Orthodox, Catholic and Protestant traditions. Alternate views of hell exist as well, such as universalism, conditional immortality, total annihilation, and hell as nothing short of metaphor, among others. The traditional views of hell are the most biblically based. The alternate views of hell turn the consequences of sin down a notch or two or even completely off, what amounts to taking a drive down the Wishful Thinking Highway.[9]

THE ISSUE OF DIVINE MERCY

Even though Scripture makes it very clear what a Christian's duty is in regard to the lost—we must pray for and actively seek their salvation—and we understand the basics—all have fallen short of the glory of God and need the saving grace of Christ—there is much within the issue of divine mercy and punishment that is veiled to us. As James Orr suggests concerning the issue of eternal punishment and God's mercy on the unrepentant, "...in His dealing with sin in the world to come, God's mercy will reach as far as ever it can reach." Additionally, in regard to punishment, he writes, "There is a vast area here for the divine administration on which no light at all is afforded us."[10]

This informs us that the issue of divine mercy and punishment is very complex, relegated to the judgment and mercy of God alone. There remains much about heaven and hell that is veiled to us, but the truth of it burns like an eternal flame in this present darkness: "Salvation is found in no one else, for there is no other name under heaven given to men by which we must be saved" (Acts 4:12) and "That if you confess with your mouth, "Jesus is Lord," and believe in your heart that God raised him from the dead, you will be saved" (Rom. 10:9).

THE SECOND DEATH FOR THE SAVED

The *second death* for the saved in Christ will be an experience quite the opposite of the lost, for their second death will not hurt them or lead to their suffering. Its mathematical equation is *life squared* or *life multiplied by itself*. They will experience the wonderful transfiguration, phase three of the Phase of Body, the superglorified body, and they will then be transferred to the glorious New Earth with Jesus, the Light, forever.

When the judgment is over and the unrepentant are secure in their eternal prison, the earth (now the lake of fire), the solar system, and the universe entire will move away at great speed to the furthest corner of God's Creation, probably not forgotten, but never seen again.

Revelation 20:15

And anyone not found written in the Book of Life was cast into the lake of fire.

THE LAKE OF FIRE

John is informed that anyone not found written in the Book of Life will be cast into the lake of fire, and obviously this applies to all the unrepentant and fallen angels.

In the New Testament, Jesus often uses the word *gehenna* in relation to the consequences of sin—*gehenna* is the transliteration from the Aramaic form of the Hebrew *ge-hinnom*, the equivalent of the word *hell*. It shouldn't be confused with the Hebrew *Sheol* or Greek *Hades,* which describe the *place of waiting* for the unrepentant dead, the antiparadise; *gehenna* or *hell* is a reference to the final eternal and unchanging state of existence for the unsaved. When Jesus spoke about it he meant it literally, not metaphorically—he refers to it as a real place (Matt. 5:2; 29–30; 10:28: 18:9; 23:15; 33; Mark. 9:43; 45;47; Luke 12:5). The word *gehenna* is identical in meaning to *lake of fire*, and interestingly enough the terms *second death* and *lake of fire* are also identical. They describe the eternal state of the unrepentant and the fallen angels who are forever separated from God and cast into a special eternal prison.[11] (For more information on hell, the bottomless pit and the lake of fire refer to Chapter 5:3, under the heading, *Under the Earth* and Chapter 9:19, under the heading *Two Sections to the Dark Domain.*)

NO SEA

As a note of interest, it's likely that the old earth, now the eternal prison-place called the lake of fire, has no sea, let alone water. Perhaps the entire surface will be molten lava, the lake of fire just beneath its cracked and heated surface. (Along similar lines, it's also quite possible that when Christ reforms this old earth for the 1,000 years of peace, the second phase of this earth's three phases, the reformed earth will be without sea so as to accommodate the vast number of Saints.)

We might believe our lives are good and we're good people. We might think we're honest, reliable, thoughtful, and kind to others, but good deeds, good works, and good intentions will not lead us to heaven. Nothing can save us, not even goodness. There is only one possible way to find salvation and that is through the grace of Jesus Christ. We must accept the fact that we're sinners. We must believe that Jesus Christ is our Lord and Savior. We must ask him into our hearts, and then and only then we will be saved and have our names written in the blessed Lamb's Book of Life. (For more information on the Book of Life, refer to Chapter 3:5, under the heading *The Book of Life*.)

* * * * *

SOURCES:

1. *Chain—Halusis,* #265, pg. 10, Greek Dictionary of the New Testament, Strong's Exhaustive Concordance of the Bible/Dictionary of the Hebrew and Greek Words, Hendrickson Publishers.
2. *Seal—Sphragizo,* #4972, pg.70, Greek Dictionary of the New Testament, Strong's Exhaustive Concordance of the Bible/Dictionary of the Hebrew and Greek Words, Hendrickson Publishers.
3. *Beheaded—Axe—Pelekizo,* #3990, pg. 56, Greek Dictionary of the New Testament, Strong's Exhaustive Concordance of the Bible/Dictionary of the Hebrew and Greek Words, Hendrickson Publishers.
4. *Little—Mikros/Mikroteros,* #3398, pg. 48; *Time/Season—Chronos,* #5550, pg. 78, Greek Dictionary of the New Testament, Strong's Exhaustive Concordance of the Bible/Dictionary of the Hebrew and Greek Words, Hendrickson Publishers.
5. *Fire—Pur,* #4441, pg. 63, Greek Dictionary of the New Testament, Strong's Exhaustive Concordance of the Bible/Dictionary of the Hebrew and Greek Words, Hendrickson Publishers.
6. *Fled—Katapheugo/Pheugo,* #5342, pg. 75, Greek Dictionary of the New Testament, Strong's Exhaustive Concordance of the Bible/Dictionary of the Hebrew and Greek Words, Hendrickson Publishers.
7. *Book—Biblion/Biblos,* #975, pg 19, Greek Dictionary of the New Testament, Strong's Exhaustive Concordance of the Bible/Dictionary of the Hebrew and Greek Words, Hendrickson Publishers.

8. *The Second Death; Eschatology of the Old Testament,* James Orr, International Bible Standard Encyclopedia, Online Edition, <http://www.studylight.org>.
The Seven Dooms, continued; Revelation, Gray's Home Bible Commentary; *Revelation,* Henry's Concise Commentary, The Bible Library Delux, version 5.0. suite, CD-ROM, Ellis Enterprises, Inc. (2,000).

9. *Eschatology,* P. J. Toner, transcribed by Michael C. Tinkler, The Catholic Encyclopedia, Volume V, Online Edition, Kevin Knight (2002), <http://www.newadvent.org>.

10. *Punishment, Everlasting; Range of Divine Mercy & Gradation of Punishment,* Orr, James, M.A., D.D. General Editor. "Entry for PUNISHMENT, EVERLASTING, International Standard Bible Encyclopedia, <http://www.studylight.org/enc/isb/view.cgi?number=T7158>, 1915, James Orr, International Bible Standard Encyclopedia, Online Edition, <http://www.studylight.org>.

11. *Sheol,* pg. 1178-1179; *Hades,* pg. 512-513; *Hell,* pg. 550-551; *Gehenna,* pg. 462, The New Unger's Bible Dictionary, Moody Press (1988).
Gehenna, Geerhardus Vos, International Bible Standard Encyclopedia, Online Edition, <http://www.studylight.org>.

CHAPTER 21
The New Jerusalem

Revelation 21:1

Now I [John] saw a new heaven and a new earth, for the first heaven and the first earth had passed away. Also there was no more sea.

PASSED AWAY

The Word of the Lord comes to John like a river, its magnificent flow unceasing. The Lord says, "My son, pay attention to my words. Incline your ear and heart to my sayings. Do not let the New Earth that I shall be showing you depart from the eyes of your heart! Keep it always before you, beating in the midst of your heart. This New Earth shall be life to those who find it, for out of it shall spring the issues of eternal life itself forever!"

The reference to the old heaven and earth as having *passed away* can be applied to the act of literally removing this old earth and its reality from the presence of God. It will be as separated from the Creator as any created thing can be while existing within God's Creation, which it has to do, because, everything that exists, *exists* within God. There is no existing *without him.*

Because of this separation, the lake of fire will be an utterly desolate, lonely, and horrifying place without goodness of any kind in it—not even *good thoughts*. Nothing will exist to inspire thought toward goodness. Emotions like *compassion, love, happiness, hope* will not be able to exist there. All thoughts and emotions will reflect the separation of the place, and in the midst of that dark desolation the human mind will be self aware.

Passing away in the original Greek does not suggest total annihilation, but instead *removal (parerchomai).*[1] This old earth will never be annihilated into nothingness. If Jesus had planned to annihilate the Third Earth (this earth), he would have said so, but in this verse he clearly states that this old earth will be *altered* and then it will *move on.* It seems that the reason the Third Earth is never annihilated is simply because God has a use for it, changing its original design to house the damned within the lake of fire, those unrepentant who have the fingerprint of God within them, for they were made in his image and are therefore immortal and indestructible. For this reason the earth must go on.

Clay Houseman

THE FINGERPRINT OF GOD IN HUMANITY

The *fingerprint* of God or his Spirit within all Creation is undeniable, so it is by its very nature immortal and indestructible, but that does not necessarily mean planets, solar systems, universes, or even our favorite pets for that matter, will exist forever. God may well bless them with eternal existence or even recreate them, even our favorite pets, but that's only because nothing outside of the fingerprint of God and his will is eternal. Indeed, the afterlife may be filled with eons of humanity's favorite pets! But the Bible makes it very clear when compared to other forms of life in Creation that humanity is different.

Our human souls have a unique design. They are made in God's image and thus like God's fingerprint or Spirit, they are immortal and indestructible. Human souls will never annihilate, unlike dogs, for example, which I don't think have eternal souls, although, they do have *spirit* (Hebrew, *nephesh*)[2] in the sense that they are living, breathing, and feeling creatures.

Genesis 1:26 makes this distinction very clear: "Let us make man in our image, after our likeness..." Animals are mentioned in the text that follows, but there's nothing to suggest that they have the same blessing bestowed upon humanity. Cats and birds and fish and lizards, and all the other creatures of the world, were not made in the image of God.

Between the animals and humanity there is an enormous difference in design and purpose. Some attempt to challenge this argument, citing Genesis 2:7, "And the Lord God formed man from the dust of the ground and breathed into his nostrils the breath of life, and man became a living being (or *nephesh*)." It's the same word used in relation to soul/spirit. Because of that they conclude we all exist forever, animals and humanity.

The Hebrew word *nephesh*, or *soul*, is used broadly in relation to life and breath in the Scriptures (Gen. 1:20, 30; 19:17), representing the state of all life. Another way of saying it could be, it represents the state of *basic* life, but when it comes to having an *eternal* soul that retains the self, the ego I, the Bible states that this is given only to human beings and not animals, plants, mountains, stars, galaxies, etc.

The Book of Ecclesiastes has a number of references concerning the death of man and animals and what happens afterward, the conclusion unambiguous: animals return to dust and the soul of man, who has been made in the image of God (unlike the animals), returns to God who gave it (Eccl. 3:21; 12:7).[3]

Angles are indeed eternal, so in that regard humanity is not unique, but what Christ has done to humanity through his sacrifice and grace is so unique it's staggering, essentially Christ becoming a created being himself and then experiencing physical created-being-death, so that he could *take on* the fallen nature of every human creation, to in fact, alter their state of being to reflect the state of being of the Creator, that is, raising the created beings to the level of the Creator, to the level of divinity—motivated entirely out of love for us!

THE FINGERPRINT OF GOD vs. PANTHEISM

It should be pointed out here that I'm not endorsing pantheism, which states that God and Creation are one inseparable thing, a magical force, the Mysterious Awareness; a rock or a tree or a mountain is God and if you touch them you touch God—that's pantheism. In the Christian sense, God is in all Creation because he made it, so a residual *fingerprint of the Creator* exists within it; as the Bible tells us you can see it everywhere because the fingerprint of God is in everything. But the Creator is separated from his Creation because he is the Creator of it and therefore independent from it. His Spirit or *fingerprint* may be recognizable in, and closely identified with his Creation, but regardless, as A. W. Tozer suggests, God is above his Creation simply because he is God. He is the Creator and his creations will forever be less than he.[4]

NEW HEAVEN & EARTH

Jesus now takes his glorious shrine, the New Earth and the new City of Jerusalem, out of the First Heaven right before our eyes! He brings them *down* from the First Heaven, for they were designed in that mysterious place beyond or outside of time known as the Father's Heaven; they were prepared there and have been *waiting* there for the time when God's Son would require them. When the New Earth and the New Jerusalem come down from the First Heaven the former things of this old fallen world will hardly come to mind.

WHAT COMES TO MIND

I'd like to point out that there's a slow-flowing but deceptive and dangerous current of heretical doctrine in some modern Christian theology, probably influenced by pop psychology and various teachings of the East. It argues that when the saved shift into eternity with the Father, Son, and Holy Spirit they are either *absorbed* into the God Force, the Mysterious Awareness, or our memories are *wiped clean* so that we forget our sin, lives, and who we were.[5] This is incorrect, for the fallen state and our individual self, the ego I, will indeed continue after death, and we will remember who we were and what we were rescued from.

Perhaps explicit memory of our sin will be removed, but humanity must retain understanding and memory of what existence was like when we were separated from God or Jesus died for nothing, which is what it would amount to if all the saved in Christ had their memories and individuality wiped clean. Clearly, this concept is not supported scripturally, for even though Jesus died *for the world,* the Bible makes it very clear that he died for each *individual* that makes up the world entire from the beginning of the foundation of that world. This is why, in part, it's called *individual salvation* and not *collective salvation.* Without a doubt the wounded hands and feet of Christ will remind us of his sacrificial act and saving grace; we will know from whence we came and what we were saved from, and why we continue to survive.

We will never forget why Jesus is our Survival Plan.

NO SEA = ONE LARGE PLANET

There will be no sea on the New Earth. The new planet will be larger than this one and it will be landlocked. Perhaps lakes and seas will exist, but surely they'll be small in comparison to the oceans of our world. Since the innumerable company of believers will amount to many billions, a new planet without a sea will be required to house the multitude. Furthermore, the new holy city of Jerusalem will be hundreds of miles long and hundreds of miles wide, and it will rise hundreds of miles into the *sky/atmosphere.* To accommodate humanity and the New Jerusalem the new planet will have to be twice, triple, or quadruple the size of our present earth; maybe it'll be the size of our present sun. Whatever the case may be, it will be one large new world.

THE NEW WORLD'S LAND & MANSIONS

Jesus will give an abundance of *land* to the Saints, and rather large domiciles, what he called *mansions.*

In a figurative sense, *land* and *mansions* helps humanity understand just how rewarding life will be on the New Earth.

But there is much more going on her than just metaphor, for Jesus tells us that, indeed, he will gift the Saints with land and large homes on the New Earth—literally. How much land will be given to the Saints the Lord does not say, but surely the amount granted to each individual will be great—and of course the *amount* of land is not the point nor is what it's used for. If a form of agriculture exists on the New Earth the process would likely be different from agriculture today and the purpose would certainly be pleasure and delight instead of need and survival.

DON'T FENCE ME IN

This has inspired me to follow a purely speculative and romantic notion: the American government once granted 160 acres to its citizens to homestead. Perhaps Jesus will grant 160,000 acres to each of his subjects! The old song *Don't Fence Me In* tells us that we need land, lots of land, land under the starry skies![6] Indeed, I'm convinced it's a human need that God has placed in our hearts. The Irish got it right when they said *land is a man's very own soul!* That human need will be met on the New Earth for all the Saints, for everyone will have land, lots of land, land under the starry skies and it will be a joy to the inhabitants!

A LARGE NEW PLANET OF YOUR OWN

It's also possible that when Jesus promised us land and mansions he meant large new planets—God is lavish! He thinks big! In the Holy Age anything will be possible!

THE NECESSITY OF PLANETS

Residence on planets seems to be necessary for humanity, part of the Great Design and Divine Will. Jesus confirms this with the New (although, undoubtedly much larger) Earth. God requires people to live on planets, even into eternity. Of course, the natural laws of the Second Heaven do not have to and likely won't conform to the natural laws of the universe and reality we know and experience today. A perfect reality/ universe/Heaven will most certainly not obey a single natural law as we understand them.

Perhaps there will be variation on a theme, but certainly not *absolute adherence to.* By way of example, food and water will not be necessary to sustain life. Energy and matter, if we can define them as such, will not be like energy and matter here. Time will not exist.

Furthermore, the Holy Father and his angels dwell on a planet called Earth in the First Heaven. It should be evident that the First Heaven's planet Earth cannot compare in any way to our planet Earth and its physical makeup because it exists in the reality of the First Heaven which is fundamentally different from the reality of the Second Heaven, as well as from the Third. The First Heaven is the dwelling place of God where no beings, other than the holy angels and God himself, exist. We live on the old planet earth now, and when the great division comes believers will live forevermore on the New Earth surrounded by the new firmament—and once again, it is quite clear that we will not be held to the laws of this fallen universe while existing on the New Earth in a New Reality.

Unbelievers will exist forever on, or *in*, a planet too—this present old earth in its third and final phase, surrounded by the existing firmament. Thus, the necessity of planets, or perhaps another way of saying it would be, the necessity of Earths, is unmistakable in the Divine Plan.

A NEW FIRMAMENT

John views an incredible expanse of space above: *a new heaven*. This expanse will be that solid arch or vault of stars spoken of as the firmament, for "God called the firmament (above earth) heaven" (Gen. 1:8a). The starry expanse John sees will be made specifically for the illustrious New Earth and new reality. It will be an entirely new made earth/universe/reality, non-entropic in nature. It will be a living universe that will reflect the perfect, holy, and living nature of its Creator, obeying entirely new natural laws, ruled by Jesus after the conclusion of earth's seven thousand year history (by God's timetable/calendar).

Undoubtedly, this firmament will be manifested by the power and will of God.

Revelation 21:2

Then I [John] saw the holy city, New Jerusalem, coming down out of heaven from God, prepared as a bride adorned for her husband.

OVERWHELMED & IDENTICAL

Surely, John was overwhelmed when God's most holy Son allowed him to witness the new city coming down from on high. Imagine his feelings while watching the awesome, illustrious holy city descend, the glittering New Jerusalem that was prepared and waiting like a bridegroom in the First Heaven, where the Father and his holy angels dwell!

The reference to *bride* and *her husband* is clearly Christ the husband to the bride of his Church, the saved in Christ.

The Saints (Jew and Gentile) have a claim to the city. It is designed for them and they are the main body that will dwell in it—however, it is also clear that other beings, such as angels, will enter the city so that it will indeed be a gigantic and active metropolitan area.

This is literally the city of God as Abraham saw by faith (Heb. 11:8–10) and as described in Hebrews 12:22–24 and Revelation 3:12 and 20: 2, 10.

The Christian Church and the nation of Israel, the Lord's people, the company of *righteous men made perfect*, will exist within the city alongside Christ as the Mediator and God the Father and visiting angels.[7]

The new Heaven and New Earth are an exact copy of the Father's First Heaven and First Earth in almost every way. They are identical, so in a sense, the First and Second Heaven and their Earths are One, linked by the Father and Son!

A STARTLING REVELATION

Human beings will never know the Holy Father's First Heaven.

The Scriptures make it clear that the First Heaven is reserved for the Holy Father and his holy angels.[8] Even though it will not separate humanity from the presence of the Father in the sense that we will be directly linked to him through his Holy Spirit through Christ, humanity cannot and will not exist there.

The reason for this is layered.

(1) Humanity belongs with the Son of Man on earth. As we are earthlings, our place is to worship Jesus on earth, whether it is on this planet or on the New Earth. Our rightful place of existence is on earth with Jesus Christ forevermore.

(2) The human race belongs to Jesus Christ and his Second Heaven, just as the angels belong to Almighty God and his First Heaven—patterns and design, and clearly God is sticking to them.

(3) Inhabitants living in the First Heaven have soul and spirit. This includes God, for he has the Seven Spirits! Inhabitants living in the Second Heaven have body, soul, and spirit. This includes the Son, who also has the Seven Spirits of God.

It seems that the very nature of the First Heaven will be, even then, beyond our comprehension, experience, and the makeup of our superglorified body. If that is the case, how then can the New Earth be identical to the First Earth in God's First Heaven? Fundamentally, or in principle, it will be identical—perhaps another way of saying it is, the New Earth will be a manifestation of the Holy Father's New Earth of spirit and soul that exists within the First Heaven.

We don't understand what soul *is*, other than it is that which makes us who we are, the eternal essence and trigger, or perhaps *software* is a more accurate term, that causes us to have individual life and self, the ego I, made in the image of God and covered in flesh and blood, the body. That being the case, it's nearly impossible to explain how or why this will work, but it seems that the First Earth within the First Heaven of spirit and soul will be copied, or cloned if you like, and then taken into a totally different reality that combines spirit, soul, *and body*, and still identical in every way. The Trinity is similar in concept and perhaps even in function: Three distinct Personalities that are One.

You must remember that at this point we're dealing with things that are far beyond our understanding. Clearly, this is a miraculous act of God. The important thing to focus on here is in a literal sense there will be no separation from the Father, the Son, the Holy Spirit, and the Saints, even though we will never experience the Father's Heaven, the First Heaven.

THE SECOND HEAVEN IS THE NEW EARTH

Why is our Second Heaven spoken of as the *New Earth?* Answer: it is generally accepted that the reason for this is simply because the New Earth follows the present *old* and, at that point, reformed earth (*the first copied earth*) in sequence—old to new, and of course that is certainly correct.

But there is another perspective that is also correct: it relates to *God's First Earth* in the First Heaven. The sequence follows *down* from there.

(1) The First Earth, the abode of the Holy Father and his holy angels.

(2) The Second Earth, the abode of the Holy Son and the Saints.

(3) The Third Earth, the abode of the Holy Spirit and the fallen in the lake of fire.

Since the New Earth is a replica of God's domain, the First Earth, in following the sequence from God's First Heaven to the Second Heaven the planet will indeed be *new*.

The majesty of Earth, God's First Heaven, signifies the Father!

The majesty of the New Earth, Jesus' Second Heaven, signifies the Son!

The majesty of the Third Earth, humankind's present world, signifies the Holy Spirit—and once again, consistent number patterns are clear here! This is one of the reasons why this present earth will not perish or be annihilated. The three will always exist in one form or another.

Clearly, the Great Plan is for the Father's heavenly hosts to live with God in the First Heaven forever and for the Saints to live with Jesus in the Second Heaven forever and for the fallen to exist in the Holy Spirit's realm forever in the lake of fire.

As a side-note of interest, it seems that humanity will be given the right to explore God's great Second Heaven—that would include the universe of the Second Heaven and all of Creation's unimaginable potential. This will certainly be the time when the real *space age* will begin. One may take off on exotic adventures to not only other worlds, but entirely foreign dimensions, universes, and on and on.

Revelation 21:3

And I [John] heard a loud voice from heaven saying, "Behold, the tabernacle of God is with men [the inhabitants of the earth], and he will dwell with them, and they shall be his people. God himself will be with them and be their God."

THE VOICE OF JESUS

A loud voice comes from heaven sounding like the voice of a trumpet and the roaring sea! It is Jesus: "Listen! The shrine of God, the place of worship, the tabernacle, the new city of Jerusalem is coming, and it shall be with the righteous. And I shall dwell with them, for they are my people. I shall be with them forevermore, for I am their God, as Man! I am God with the children of humanity for eternity!"

It should be evident from this verse that the Holy Father, through Christ and his Holy Spirit, will manifest himself within redeemed humanity and be One with them, even though he will *dwell* within the First Heaven. The reference to *the tabernacle of God is with men* (Jesus Christ, the Tabernacle), *he will dwell with them,* and *God himself will be with them and be their God* supports this.

Revelation 21:4

"And God will wipe away every tear from their eyes; there shall be no more death, nor sorrow, nor crying. There shall be no more pain, for the former things have passed away."

JOY ETERNAL

"In this place, I shall give my people only gladness, love, and joy. There shall be no such thing as tears of sadness. No one shall ever die, for life shall be eternal, with youth never ending! Sorrow shall be no more. Each person shall only know contentment. Only laughter shall be heard. All peoples shall be whole, perfect, strong, powerful, loving, harmonious, and overjoyed with happiness, for the former things are passed away and gone forever."

Plainly, the heart of humanity will be altered to reflect the nature of the Creator. There will be no more arguing, belittling, nagging, picking out, scowling, sulking, moodiness, fighting, for his people will have been changed by the grace of Christ and we will pour out love, that magical stuff that is holy perfection.

Revelation 21:5

Then he who sat on the throne said, "Behold, I make all things new." And he said [to John], "Write, for these words are true and faithful."

ALL THINGS MADE NEW

Jesus in all of his greatness announces with joy, "Observe! I make all things, and they stand brand new for everlasting, since nothing wears out in the Kingdom of God! You, my believers, have new, young bodies, for you are the new bride of Christ. You have new names, for you are the family of God. You have a New Earth, for the old one passed away. You have a new shrine, which comes down from heaven. You have new mansions, a wonderful promise from God. All remain new, for my Word is so!"

The Lord says to John, "Write down everything I am telling you, for these words are true and faithful. I am the Word, for I AM that I AM!"

Truth and *faithfulness* are characteristics of God often used in Scripture (Ps. 36:5; 89:2; Isa. 11:5, etc.).[9] They are a significant and vital part of his divine and holy character. They also tell us that Christ keeps his promises. This applies to every aspect of his promises, from forgiveness and redemption for humanity to wrath against sin and the sinful nature—it must be remembered here that the Lord's truth and faithfulness is holy, as is his wrath. Jesus made it very clear he could become angry in a sense that was pure and holy and without sin.

Revelation 21:6

And he [Jesus] said to me [John], "It is done! I am the Alpha and the Omega, the Beginning and the End. I will give of the fountain of the water of life freely to him who thirsts."

IT IS DONE!

"It is done! I am the Alpha and the Omega, the Beginning and the End, the First and the Last. And what you have seen, write in a book and send it out into all the world."

It is done suggests that everything Christ promised in regard to humanity has now come to pass, and not only that, but from here on out everything will be, in the sense of our salvation in Christ anyway, unchanging.

There will be continual spiritual and intellectual growth, of course—God is not static, but is instead dynamic. It makes sense then that within eternity humanity will be similarly dynamic. Reaching some sort of *divine spiritual and intellectual peak* and then coasting there into eternity for eternity, as some scholars believe because of our elevated status through Christ, seems highly unlikely. That there will always be something new to learn or explore is much closer to the truth of it, for God has endowed humanity with curiosity and a deep desire for exploration. It's clear enough that these characteristics reflect the Creator himself.

NATURAL ADVENTURE & EXPLORATION

People are indeed natural adventurers and explorers. Many of us seek new places to go, from the likes of Vasco da Gama and Christopher Columbus discovering *new worlds* on earth, to a vacationer finding different and exciting places to enjoy on holiday, to an astronaut exploring space above. Of course, the search for spiritual truth is the deepest and most satisfying exploration and the Path to genuine salvation always and only leads to Christ. People desire to travel and explore because God has placed it within the hearts of his children. This desire to travel will most certainly continue when God's people are in the Second Heaven! As heirs, they will seek to see their inheritance, which will be the endless worlds of God and all the possibilities of Creation. There is no doubt that all saved humanity will one day walk among the stars! They will walk on the wings of the wind (the Spirit of God)! There will be no end to travel and exploration, for the vastness of Creation is limitless, bottomless, timeless, hyperdimensional. His will is for humanity to perceive his creations so that they will declare the majesty of his works! They are made for his good pleasure, and it is in wonder that people will acknowledge the greatness of the Lord and praise him with the sound of a trumpet!

"But as it is written: Eye has not seen, nor ear heard, nor have entered into the heart of man the things which God has prepared for those who love him" (ICor. 2:9).

THE REVELATION WILL BE COMPLETE

When time merges into eternity the revelation will be complete. It will be done. This is a guarantee, a promise: there will never be another Fall of humanity again and held within the grace of Christ for eternity his righteous promises and judgments and the saved in Christ will endure forever.

He has the highest authority over everyone and everything. He announces, "I give of the fountain of the water of life freely to those who thirst for it." He is saying here, with deep affection, that he gives everlasting life and everlasting love to all who seek him, giving them all the wonderful promises prophesied in these writings, for he indeed is faithful and true.

Revelation 21:7

"He who overcomes shall inherit all things, and I will be his God and he shall be my son [and daughter]."

INHERITANCE

The Lord God makes a covenant by saying, "Those who believe in me and overcome trials and tribulations of life inherit all things."

Christ promises, "Everything that is, is mine; therefore, it is yours also."

Why is this? Answer: Christ explains, "For I am your God. God is my Father. He and I are One. I come as the manifestation of God in the flesh. You who believe in me are of the family of God."

We will inherit what belongs to him because as adopted children we will literally belong to his family. Jesus is telling humanity that through Christ we will be divine. It should be clear here that we will never *be* God or *be equal to* God, but because of his great love for us we will be *like* him.

INHERITANCE DOES NOT MEAN PREEXISTENCE

It should be made clear here that nowhere in the Bible does it suggest humanity existed *before* the foundation of the world in a state of perfection/divinity so that through the grace of Christ we are *returning to* our previous state of divinity—this concept, that all of us existed in perfection/divinity *prior to* our fallen lives is in error and is not supported scripturally. Furthermore, it creates a false sense of superiority, telling us that we are not undeserving children *adopted into* the family of God because of his unconditional love for us, but instead deserving children *brought back into* the family of God because we were already a part of the family of God in the first place, equal to our Lord and Savior Jesus Christ—stop right there, for we are now in the land of heresy. The concept also demeans Christ's sacrificial act of grace and resurrection because it suggests that the act of salvation was not solely motivated by love, but indeed obligation! *He was only doing his job, what he needed to do, what any of us could have done were we in the same position.*

Without doubt, the Scriptures do not support this popular and false doctrine, for all humanity has fallen short of the glory of God. "The saints of the Most High shall receive the kingdom, and possess the kingdom forever, even forever and ever" (Dan. 7:18). "Then the kingdom and dominion, and the greatness of the kingdoms under the whole heaven, shall be given to the people, the saints of the Most High" (Dan. 7:27a). "Then (Jesus) the King will say to those on his right hand, 'Come, you blessed of my Father, inherit the kingdom prepared for you from the foundation of the world" (Mat. 25:34).

The reference to *inherit* or *an inheritance*, and the fact that God says he will look upon the saved in Christ as sons and daughters, unquestionably confirms that humanity will be adopted by God and then raised to the level of divinity—and that, in and of itself, is remarkable.

The Greek word *kleronomeo* can be used in the literal: *to be an heir*, or *to obtain an inheritance*,[10] so that when Paul tells us that we are "heirs of God and joint heirs with Christ," it means we are literal adopted heirs to the Kingdom.

Revelation 21:8

"But the cowardly, unbelieving, abominable, murderers, sexually immoral, sorcerers, idolaters, and all liars shall have their part in the lake which burns with fire and brimstone, which is the second death."

FIRE & BRIMSTONE

Unrepentant humanity shall take part in the lake of fire in the heart of the earth which is burning with fire and brimstone. Indeed, this is a direct reference to the second and eternal death for the lost, those who were not saved.

BROKEN MACHINES

Remember, we are all fallen creations, or if you like, *broken machines*. We cannot repair ourselves. Humanity cannot save itself, no matter how hard it wants to, no matter how hard it tries, but we can be saved from fire and brimstone in eternity.

Jesus, in his perfection and wisdom, reaches to us, and then we, in faith, reach to him and he repairs (or saves) us. The act of salvation comes completely and totally from Christ. From that position of extreme humility we are inspired to do good works and sin no more. Because we are still in the flesh, or rather, because our souls continue to reside within these *broken machines* and reality, sin and brokenness will continue to plague us. Only through reliance on Christ and his Holy Spirit can we overcome our fallen nature (brokenness) and sin no more.

"He (Jesus) is the image of the invisible God, the firstborn over all creation. For by him all things were created that are in heaven and that are on earth... All things were created through him and for him" (Col. 1:15–16). "If you had known me (Jesus), you would have known my Father also; and from now on you know him and have seen him (because you have seen Jesus)" (John 14:7).

Jesus calls to everyone and anyone All the broken machines are welcome, from the worst person imaginable to the nicest goofball in town and all the folks in between, cowardly, unbelieving, murderers, sexually immoral, sorcerers, idolaters, liars, Republicans, Democrats, Independents, Liberals, Conservatives, Progressives, and on and on—all humanity. You are encouraged to change your broken ways and receive the wonderful promises of God, for his promises are faithful and true.

Revelation 21:9

Then one of the seven angels who had the seven bowls filled with the seven last plagues came [to John] and talked with me, saying, "Come, I will show you the bride, the Lamb's wife."

I WILL SHOW YOU

The *angel* referred to here is Jesus Christ, for only Christ would have all seven bowls. This is showing us the great power of Christ.

John hears the Lamb of God say: "Come! It is time! I will show you the bride, the Lamb's wife: the city of the New Jerusalem." The day is here! It has come! The absolute glory of God is to be seen!

The most spectacular scene is about to unfold before John's very eyes.

Revelation 21:10

And he carried me [John] away in the Spirit to a great and high mountain, and showed me the holy city, Jerusalem, descending out of heaven from God...

MOUNTAIN HIGH

John finds that Jesus carries him away to a great and high mountain range. This is extremely holy and shouldn't be ignored.

The mountaintop has spiritual significance: high altitude suggests closeness to God and snow and crisp and clean air often signify holiness.

David says, "I will lift up my eyes to the hills (mountains)—from whence comes my help? My help comes from the Lord, who made heaven and earth" (Ps. 121:1).

From the mountaintop I cry: "Do not keep silent, O God! Let the mountains be joyful together before the Lord of Hosts! The mountains are filled with the Spirit of the heavenly God. How lovely on the mountain are the feet of him who gives us good news! Our help comes from the Lord, the maker of heaven and earth! The signs of the times announce your near coming. The skies alone announced your birth with the brightness of stars. Are the heavens now calling for your return? Was the brightness of the dramatic 1996 *Hyakutake Comet*, which performed its nightly celestial show with a head as large as the moon and a tail stretching halfway across the darkened sky in southern New Mexico, a herald of the nearness of your coming? Was the appearance of the comet *Hale-Bopp* a year later another heavenly signal of your imminent return? Are the skies trying to tell us something? I, like John, stand on the mountaintop in humbled awe!"

FROM THE MOUNTAINTOP

Jesus stretches out his mighty right arm, and with his forefinger pointing to the heavens he tells John, "Son of Man, look with your eyes and hear with your ears, and fix your mind on everything I display to you, for you are brought here so that you will declare to all people everything you see."

John was, surely, overwhelmed by the sight of the structure, so vast was its size, that marvelous city, the holy Jerusalem, descending out of the First Heaven from God, prepared as a *bride* adorned for her husband, Jesus the Christ! "I AM THE NEW CITY OF JERUSALEM!" The city of God (the replica of the Father's city in the First Heaven) will be so colossal that it will fill the sky! It is well to remember that the bridal city is a habitation for the *living bride*, the Saints. No one knows exactly how this will transpire, but since the Scriptures suggest that the city literally *drops down* from the First Heaven, and considering the supernatural nature of the event itself, imagine, if you will, that the city will move ever so slowly down from the First Heaven, as if it were a gigantic, radiant elevator, sparkling like the beauty of a crystal chandelier reflecting the light of a billion suns!

Revelation 21:11

[The city] ...having the glory of God. Her light was like a most precious stone, like a jasper stone, clear as crystal.

THE CITY COMES TO REST

The New Earth has already been sent down from the First Heaven by the Most High.

Now the mighty city follows, and comes to rest on the New Earth.

That the city *has the glory of God* suggests the literal presence of God through Christ will reside within it. The city is identical in nature and connects to the spiritual city and reality of God in the First Heaven.

The reference to *her light* informs us that the city itself will have an internal glow, powered by the glory and the presence of Jesus Christ. The New Jerusalem, the city of God, will appear as a most precious stone, like a jasper stone, clear as crystal, and a pale emerald light will radiate from the city as her crowning glory. "And he who sat there (Jesus) was like a jasper and a sardius stone in appearance; and there was a rainbow around the throne, in appearance like an emerald" (Rev. 4:3).

Green is the color most often ascribed to the light of Christ—the Emerald Christ, the Green Creator!—so it makes sense that the city itself will reflect the same color.

We learn that his *new bride* (the city) will have the brilliance of a jasper stone, so that even though it is described as clear as crystal it will indeed have a soft hue of emerald green.

Revelation 21:12

Also she [the city] had a great and high wall with twelve gates, and twelve angels at the gates, and names written on them, which are the names of the twelve tribes of the children of Israel.

TWELVE

The new city of Jerusalem will be surrounded by a lavish wall of tremendous height.

Twelve pearl gates will stand within the wall, each gate fashioned out of one pearl, as we will soon discover.

At each opening of each gate a holy angel from the realm of the First Heaven will stand triumphantly!

Names will be written on each entrance: the names of the twelve tribes of the children of Israel. This shows us the importance of the Jewish people in the eyes of God, as well as establishes the Jewish nation into eternity by stating that they will inhabit the city with the Saints, for through Christ both Jew and Gentile are united into one new being: "This mystery is that through the gospel the Gentiles are heirs together with Israel, members together of one body, and sharers together in the promise in Jesus Christ" (Eph. 3:6).

In the Old Testament, Ezekiel describes the gates of the new city of Jerusalem. He tells us, "These are the exits of the city. On the north side, measuring four thousand five hundred cubits (the three pearl gates combined on each side of the square city will measure 6,750 feet wide; the gates of the city shall be named after the tribes of Israel), the three gates northward (three pearl gates): one gate for (the tribe of) Reuben, one gate for (the tribe of) Judah, and one gate for (the tribe of) Levi; on the east side, four thousand five hundred cubits, three gates (measuring 6,750 feet wide): one gate for (the tribe of) Joseph, one gate for (the tribe of) Benjamin, and one gate for (the tribe of) Dan; on the south side, measuring four thousand five hundred cubits, three gates (6,750 feet wide): one gate for (the tribe of) Simeon, one gate for (the tribe of) Issachar, and one gate for (the tribe of) Zebulun; on the west side, four thousand five hundred cubits with their three gates (measuring 6,750 feet wide): one gate for (the tribe of) Gad, one gate for Asher, and one gate for Naphtali. All the way around shall be eighteen thousand cubits (27,000 feet, the sum total of the gates); and the name of the city from that day shall be: THE LORD IS THERE (the shrine of the city of the New Jerusalem has Christ in it)" (Eze. 48:30–35).

It should be more than clear that the Jewish nation is very special to the Lord. Remember, woe to the person or nation who condemns his people, the Jews, for it is the Lord whom you condemn.

Revelation 21:13

Three gates on the east, three gates on the north, three gates on the south, and three gates on the west.

THE GATES

There will be three gates on each side of the giant city, each a set of 3, signifying the Trinity and conforming once again to the patterns and number systems of God.

This great and magnificent city is *waiting* to be sent down for Jesus to establish his new kingdom on the New Earth. At this present time, the New Earth and the city are just a thousand years away from descending from heaven (by God's timetable/calendar)!

Revelation 21:14

Now the wall of the city had twelve foundations, and on them were the twelve names of the twelve apostles of the Lamb.

THE WALLS

The wall encompasses the entire city, stretching 1500 miles on each side. Each wall will be supported by 12 foundations that are extremely decorative.

The use of 12 foundations reveals just how truly enormous the walls will be and how God adheres to patterns and number systems. It also shows us the importance of the twelve apostles in the scheme of God's plans. This is similar to the names of the twelve tribes of Israel on each gate. Indeed, the twelve referred to here are the very foundations of the walls themselves, a powerful image. The 12 foundations for the walls more than likely will have little or nothing at all to do with structural engineering as we understand it today.

Revelation 21:15

And he who talked with me [Jesus] had a gold reed to measure the city, its gates, and its wall.

THE MEASURING ROD REVISITED

Jesus holds a golden measuring rod in his right hand to ascertain the dimensions of the mighty city, its gates, its walls, and its foundations. (For related information on the measuring rod, refer to Chapter 11:1, under the heading *The Measuring Rod*.)

Revelation 21:16

The city is laid out as a square; its length is as great as its breadth. And he measured the city with the reed: twelve thousand furlongs. Its length, breadth, and height are equal.

THE SQUARE CITY

The new holy city of Jerusalem will be in the shape of a square. I believe the city will be a massive and literal cube.

Jesus measures the city with his golden measuring rod, finding it to measure one thousand five hundred miles in length (1500 miles wide and high as it is long), forming a transparent, green-hued cube!

A cube can be defined as:

(1) *A regular solid of six equal square sides or six corresponding square faces*. This can be related to the number of humanity—6—and since it is the city of God *for* man (humanity), this seems to add up rather nicely.

(2) *The product got by taking a number three times as a factor,* that is to say, 3 the sacred number which obviously represents the Holy Trinity.

(3) *Raised to the third power,* a mathematical equation that, when applied to this verse, suggests the exponential and infinite nature of God. Furthermore, each of the six sides or faces of a cube is a perfect square, which reflects the perfect and exponential nature of God. Simple elements such as cubes can involve mathematical permutations of brain-numbing complexity, and this, once again, is another example of the complex nature of God—that which is simple and yet is infinitely complex, and of course this can also be applied to the salvation of Christ.

The branch of geometry that deals with the properties and measurement of geometric figures in three-dimensional space is called Solid Geometry, which the cube falls under. Solid geometry extends and reinforces the propositions of plane geometry and is the *necessary* foundation for spherical trigonometry, solid analytical geometry, descriptive geometry, and other forms of mathematics. It is used extensively in mathematics, engineering, and the natural sciences.[11] It is, therefore, no mistake that the city is described as a cube. This is another example of his holy mathematics/geometry at work, for God *extends and reinforces* the city because he is the *necessary* foundation of it. Everything extends and reinforces the geometry of God because God is the necessary foundation of Everything, for he is *the* Solid Geometry— again, that the city of God, the New Jerusalem, is designed as a cube is no mathematical blunder or coincidence. The cubed city is designed as a celebration of God's glory, holy mathematics/geometry, and infinite complexity.

Revelation 21:17

Then he measured its wall: one hundred and forty-four cubits, according to the measure of a man, that is, of an angel.

THE HEIGHT

Decorated with every kind of precious stone imaginable (and surely beyond imagination), the walls are measured at 216 feet, according to the measurement of a human being *and* an angel!

In John's time, measurements were in cubits, the length from an elbow to the middle finger, approximately one-and-one-half feet. The greatness of the walls certainly fits the mightiness of the city!

Clay Houseman

Revelation 21:18

The construction of its wall was of jasper; and the city was pure gold, like clear glass.

JASPER & GOLD

John observes that the construction of the walls will be transparent, green-jasper, and gold, and of course these colors represent the glorious God and maker of all.

(1) Transparent = purity.

(2) Green-jasper = Christ; green depicts life and the Green Presence of Christ in everything, for he is Life.

(3) Gold = the reward for believing in Christ.

The holy city, being the Tabernacle of God, will be alive with the radiant light of life, every crystal-like building and structure illuminated from *within*. His shrine and throne will glow with the light of life.

The city is said to be made of gold so refined that it will appear as clear as glass—again, another reference to transparency! Some scholars argue that all of this is metaphor describing something far beyond John's comprehension and ability, and that could certainly be the case, but likewise, there's no reason why this couldn't be literal either. Indeed, I believe the entire cubed city will be made out of some kind of otherworldly and perfectly refined gold.

Revelation 21:19

The foundations of the wall of the city were adorned with all kinds of precious stones: the first foundation was jasper, the second sapphire, the third chalcedony, the fourth emerald.

THE COLORS OF THE FOUNDATIONS

The illuminating foundations of the holy shrine will be adorned with all kinds of precious stones—again, this could be metaphor describing something beyond human comprehension or in fact literal precious stones.

JASPER

The first foundation is made of jasper. It is first because it represents Jesus, the Christ, for we need to be reminded that: "He (Jesus) who sat there (on the throne) was like a jasper and a sardius stone in appearance, and there is a rainbow around the throne (for Jesus radiates his brightness), in appearance like an emerald" (Rev. 4:3).

Jasper as we know it on earth is an entirely opaque variety of quartz, usually dark-green in color. Sometimes it can be red instead of completely dark-green. The jasper described here may be a combination of the two colors, green and red, which is a fitting, a color-correct description of Christ: green in life and red in sacrifice. On our old earth jasper does not reflect light and it is usually dull and dark. It can present every variety of color, yellow, brown, blackish-white, sometimes green and blue, and also green-chalcedony—what I call *the colors of humanity.* As a precious stone it is somewhat like fine marble.[12]

Revelation tells us that the jasper used in the city's first foundation will be transparent, and that seems to be beyond question, for John says, "... (The city's light was) like a jasper stone, clear as crystal" (Rev. 21:11). It will be prominently green, exquisite, and shining with beauty.

SAPPHIRE

The second outstanding foundation is made of sapphire, a precious stone of great luster, second only to the diamond in hardness and value. It is any of several relatively pure forms of corundum, especially a pure blue form used as a gemstone.[13]

The sapphire foundation will be crystal-clear with hues of sapphire, blue, green, red, et al.

CHALCEDONY

The third foundation is made of chalcedony, a transparent milky quartz with distinctive microscopic crystals arranged in slender fibers like parallel bands. Again, this is another precious mystical gemstone having a great variety of colors, such as pale-blue, grayish, greenish-yellow, and brown. It is a very hard, glassy minera.[14]

The chalcedony foundation will be transparent with hues of pale-blue, gray, green-yellow, and brown, soothing to the eye.

EMERALD

The fourth foundation is made of emerald, a grass-green variety of the mineral beryl, in hardness next to the ruby, and considered a gemstone. It comes in a variety of green colors that sometimes mix with yellow or blue.[15]

The emerald foundation will be transparent with hues of green and an internal glow powered by the glory of God. Of course, emerald represents life and the life of Christ Jesus, the Green Creator.

Revelation 21:20

The fifth [foundation is] sardonyx, the sixth sardius, the seventh chrysolite, the eighth beryl, the ninth topaz, the tenth chrysoprase, the eleventh jacinth, and the twelfth amethyst.

SARDONYX

The fifth glistening foundation is made of sardonyx, commonly called onyx today. It is a striped, semiprecious type of agate with alternate layers of colors that occur in light and dark bands, colored in brown, red, black, white, and grey. It is wonderful to behold.[16]

Undoubtedly, the sardonyx foundation will be transparent, but colored with various belts and veins and sardonyx hues.

CARNELIAN

The sixth foundation is made of a carnelian, or *sardius stone;* in relation to Jesus we are told that, "He (Jesus) who sat...was like a jasper and a sardius stone in appearance..." (Rev. 4:3).

This is a gem of reddish-brown (sometimes so deep red in color that it looks like blood), bright-orange, and reddish-orange. It comes from the chalcedony family.[17]

In relation to the foundation, its color-symbolism should be obvious here: the spilled blood of the Lamb of God. It will be transparent like the other foundations and it will shine like the glory of God.

CHRYSOLITE

The seventh foundation is made of chrysolite, a splendid transparent golden gemstone of lavish beauty. It usually comes in the colors of soft green, yellow, and bright moss-green. It is considered a semi-precious stone. It is often referred to as goldstone.[18]

The chrysolite foundation will be transparent with hues of soft green, yellow, and bright moss-green.

BERYL

The eighth foundation is made of beryl, a mineral essentially made up of aluminum and beryllium silicate, occurring in hexagonal prisms. It is a very hard gem, sometimes mistaken for an emerald gemstone, usually colored blue-green.[19]

Assuredly, the beryl foundation will be transparent, exhibiting overtones of blue-green, yellow, and pink.

TOPAZ

The ninth foundation is made of topaz, a precious clear crystal that has hues of yellow, red, brown, green, pink, and blue. It is often found with granite rocks. In our world, topaz is one third in value to the diamond.[20]

Undoubtedly, the topaz foundation will be transparent and predominantly green, in honor of Jesus, the Life Giver.

CHRYSOPRASE

The tenth glorious foundation is made of chrysoprase, a soft pastel, apple-green see-through crystal quartz, a variety of chalcedony used as a semi-precious stone. It often has a gold-green color.[21]

The chrysoprase foundation will be transparent, reflecting a pastel, apple-green, gold-green hue.

JACINTH

The eleventh foundation is made of jacinth, a crystal of pure orange and a gem of great beauty. It is a precious stone, sometimes found with a reddish tint. It is a variety of zircon, a brown-to-colorless mineral; when heated it transforms into a bright blue-white gem. This is another clear stone with alternating hues of orange.[22]

The jacinth foundation will be transparent with hues of orange, red, and bright blue-white.

AMETHYST

The twelfth foundation is made of glorious amethyst quartz, a glassy, silica-type mineral known for its hardness and enchanting color purple. Sometimes it's more violet than purple. It is often used as a gemstone.[23]

The amethyst foundation will unquestionably be transparent like the other foundations, reflecting its enchanting purple hue.

THE COLORFUL COLLECTION

What can be gathered from this colorful collection is that every color created by God is found within the transparent foundations and the city's surrounding walls. This is not only a clear representation of the glory of God, but the glory of humanity as well, for all the colors of humanity are celebrated here, black, red, brown, white, yellow, and all the colors in between!

The foundations will be breathtaking in beauty, above ground for all to see, and filled with all the colors found in the rainbow and beyond, but clearly the color green dominates. It is prominently embedded into the spectacular base of the new structure. Brilliant green is conspicuous, and of course it makes sense that this is so, for the Creator of the shrine sent down by the Holy Father is none other than Jesus, the Emerald Christ: "... (The light of the city) having the glory of God. Her light was like a most precious stone, like a (green) jasper stone, clear as crystal" (Rev. 21:11).

Revelation 21:21
The twelve gates were twelve pearls: each individual gate was of one pearl. And the street of the city was pure gold, like transparent glass.

THE PEARLS

The twelve colossal gates, three on each side of the cubed city (possibly set apart at five hundred mile intervals) will consist of twelve pearls.

Some scholars argue that this is mere metaphor describing something beyond human comprehension, but it is certainly possible and I'd say even likely that this is literal: the gates are each made out of a single pearl. With God anything is possible! These unbelievable pearl gates will tower to a great height.

THE GOLD

The streets will be made of a gold. Apparently, the entire city is made of gold so refined that it appears like clear glass.

This means that the Tabernacle, the city of God, will resemble a crystal palace-cube filled with color beyond imagination! Again, this could be metaphor describing something outside human comprehension, but considering the supernatural nature of the city itself there's no reason why it couldn't be made out of a refined and otherworldly gold.

Revelation 21:22
But I [John] saw no temple in it [the city], for the Lord God Almighty and the Lamb, are its Temple.

CHRIST, THE TEMPLE

John sees no temple within the city, for the Father, Son, and the Holy Spirit are the living temple!

Now, remember, in the First Heaven God is Spirit.

In the Second Heaven, being the New Earth and new heavens, he is God as Man in Christ Jesus!

This suggests that not only will the Presence of the Father dwell in the city, but the physical Presence of Jesus Christ will exist within the walls of the city itself, and humanity will reside alongside him.

Revelation 21:23

The city had no need of the sun or of the moon to shine, for the glory of God illuminated it. The Lamb is its light.

THE GLORY OF GOD

Although the New Earth seems to have a star and possibly seven moons, the new city will, of course, have no need for them in regard to light and heat, for the glory of God will brighten the planet, as the Lamb Jesus Christ is the Light and Caretaker of the planet. He is the New Earth's Star. There will be no night in the city, for Jesus is its light eternally and forever!

This suggests that, surely, the nature of the universe of the Second Heaven will not be comparable to the nature of our universe now, that indeed the natural laws will be quite beyond our comprehension. That has to be the case, of course, because we live in a fallen, entropic universe now. Planets and stars will exist in the Second Heaven, but in a perfect, non-entropic reality. This guarantees that their purpose and the laws that govern them will be entirely different when compared to the purpose and laws that govern them in this fallen universe.

Revelation 21:24

And the nations shall walk in its (the city's) light, and the kings of the earth bring their glory and honor into it.

HONOR THE CITY

People of all nations who are saved in Christ will walk into the city's light, honoring the city and its Creator and Savior, Jesus Christ. The Lord's eyes will fall on the faithful and they will dwell with him. The Son will walk with them along the streets of gold.

The city will be a metropolis teeming with life! It will be active, dynamic, and alive like the Creator. Humanity's purpose for visiting the city is specifically to worship God. There are scriptural references to positions of responsibility and power within the city (Chapter 2:6, under the heading *God's Good Gravy*), but pilgrimage, worship, and honoring the Lord will surely take precedent.

The New Jerusalem will be the only city on the New Earth.

People will live in their mansions or country estates and towns scattered throughout the new world, perhaps gathered in immense family clans, but they will visit the only genuine city on the planet, the New Jerusalem.

Revelation 21:25

Its [the city's] gates shall not be shut at all by day (there shall be no night there).

ALWAYS OPEN

John is informed that the new city will always be open. This is a lovely picture of the openhearted nature of Christ, as well as a reflection of the unchanging nature of things to come for humanity in regard to salvation—when Christ says that it is done he means that it's done forever; humanity is sealed in the safety of Christ's grace for eternity.

When the New Earth's star sets there will be no darkness, for the wonder of God will constantly light up the shrine. The *night* will capture the greatest glory of the shining light of Christ.

Revelation 21:26

And they [the people] shall bring the glory and the honor of the nations into it [the city].

PILGRIMAGE

Jesus says the congregation of the heavenly New Earth shall bring the glory and the honor of the nations into the holy city. This tells us that humanity will visit the sacred shrine from time to time (even though there will be no time) in pilgrimage to Christ.

The great city will accommodate the pilgrims, for millions will pour into it *daily* to honor their Lord. This informs us that the city/shrine will not be a place of permanent residence, for heaven's population will cycle through it continually, leaving their homes—their *mansions* or possibly *planets*—to witness, praise, and honor their wonderful Savior.

Revelation 21:27

But there shall by no means enter it [the city] anything profane, nor one who causes an abomination or a lie, but only those who are written in the Lamb's Book of Life.

BY NO MEANS

John confirms here that the wondrous city will only be for the faithful believers in God's Son, the saved in Christ, Jew and Gentile. By no means will anything sinful be allowed to enter the city. This tells us that nothing sinful will exist anywhere, inside the city or beyond its walls.

It should be clear that at this point there will be no corruption on the New Earth or in the reality of the Second Heaven. No fallen nature will exist anywhere in the new universe—it would be impossible for anything of a fallen nature (anything certainly fallen in regard to human nature) to be able to exist in the Second Heaven with Christ.

With thanksgiving they will enter his gates. With praise they will enter his courts. Only those whose names are written in the Lamb's Book of Life will walk into the holy city of the Lamb.

* * * * *

SOURCES:

1. *Passed away—Parerchomai,* #3928, pg. 55, Greek Dictionary of the New Testament, Strong's Exhaustive Concordance of the Bible/Dictionary of the Hebrew and Greek Words, Hendrickson Publishers.
2. *Soul—Nephesh,* #5315, pg. 80, Hebrew and Chaldee Dictionary, Strong's Exhaustive Concordance of the Bible/Dictionary of the Hebrew and Greek Words, Hendrickson Publishers.
3. *Do Animals Have a Soul?* Bible Questions, <http://www.biblequestions.org>.
   Whether the Souls of Brute Animals are Subsistent? The Summa Theologica of St. Thomas Aquinas, Second and Revised Edition (1920), literally translated by Fathers of the English Dominican Province, The Catholic Encyclopedia, Online Edition, Kevin Knight (2002), <http://www.newadvent.org>.
4. *The Pursuit of God,* chapter 5, *The Universal Presence,* A. W. Tozer, Christian Publications, Inc., (1982), first publication (1948).
5. *Is There Life After Death?; A Bishop Speaks,* John Shelby Spong, Beliefnet, <http://www.beliefnet.com>.
   Liberal Christian Beliefs; The Afterlife; Current Beliefs of Major Wings of Christianity, B.A. Robinson, Ontario Consultants on Religious Tolerance, ReligiousTolerance.org (2002), <http://www.religioustolerance.org>.
6. *Don't Fence Me In,* words and music by Cole Porter & Robert Fletchers, copyright (1942); from the film *Hollywood Canteen.*
7. *Jerusalem, New,* pg. 680, The New Unger's Bible Dictionary, Moody Press (1988).
   The Seven New Things; Revelation, Gray's Home Bible Commentary; *Revelation 21,* Henry's Concise Commentary, The Bible Library Delux, version 5.0. suite, CD-ROM, Ellis Enterprises, Inc. (2,000).
8. *God's Holy Angels,* Demitri J. George, World Magazine (1978), Antiochian Orthodox Christian Archdiocese of North America: Midwest Region, The

Most Reverend Philip, Metropolitan-Archbishop, The Right Reverend Demetri, Auxiliary Bishop, <http://www.antiochian.org>.
God and His Angels, L. Lambert, Lambert Dolphin's Resources, <http://www.ldolphin.org>.
The Holy Angels, The Orthodox Page in America, <http://www.ocf.org>.
Angel; Angels, Fallen, pg. 61-61, The New Unger's Bible Dictionary, Moody Press (1988).
9. *God,* pg. 480-482, The New Unger's Bible Dictionary, Moody Press (1988).
10. *To be an heir—Kleronomeo,* #2816, pg. 42, Greek Dictionary of the New Testament, Strong's Exhaustive Concordance of the Bible/Dictionary of the Hebrew and Greek Words, Hendrickson Publishers.
11. *Cube; Solid Geometry,* Microsoft Encarta Encyclopedia (2002).
12. *Jasper, mineral,* Microsoft Encarta Encyclopedia (2002).
Jasper; Quartz Mineral Data, Mineralogy Database, <http://www.webmineral.com>.
13. *Sapphire,* Microsoft Encarta Encyclopedia (2002).
Sapphire; Sapphire Mineral Data, Mineralogy Database, <http://www.webmineral.com>.
14. *Chalcedon,* Microsoft Encarta Encyclopedia (2002).
Chalcedony; Quartz Mineral Data, Mineralogy Database, <http://www.webmineral.com>.
15. *Emerald,* Microsoft Encarta Encyclopedia (2002).
Emerald; Beryl Mineral Data, Mineralogy Database, <http://www.webmineral.com>.
16. *Sardonyx,* Microsoft Encarta Encyclopedia (2002).
Sardonyx; Quartz Mineral Data, Mineralogy Database, <http://www.webmineral.com>.
17. *Carnelian,* Microsoft Encarta Encyclopedia (2002).
Carnelian; Quartz Mineral Data, Mineralogy Database, <http://www.webmineral.com>.
18. *Chrysolite,* Microsoft Encarta Encyclopedia (2002).
Chrysolite; Olivine Mineral Data, Mineralogy Database, <http://www.webmineral.com>.
19. *Beryl,* Microsoft Encarta Encyclopedia (2002).
Beryl; Beryl Mineral Data, Mineralogy Database, <http://www.webmineral.com>.
20. *Topaz,* Microsoft Encarta Encyclopedia (2002).
Topaz; Topaz Mineral Data, Mineralogy Database, <http://www.webmineral.com>.
21. *Chrysoprase,* Microsoft Encarta Encyclopedia (2002).
Chrysoprase; Quartz Mineral Data, Mineralogy Database, <http://www.webmineral.com>.
22. *Jacinth,* Microsoft Encarta Encyclopedia (2002).
Jacinth; Zircon Mineral Data, Mineralogy Database, <http://www.webmineral.com>.
23. *Amethyst,* Microsoft Encarta Encyclopedia (2002).
Amethyst; Quartz Mineral Data, Mineralogy Database, <http://www.webmineral.com>.

Further reading:

The Summa Theologiae; A Concise Translation, St. Thomas Aquinas, edited by Timothy McDermott, Christian Classics (1997).

Suma of the Suma; The Essential Philosophical Passages of St.Thomas Aguinas Summa Theologica Edtied and Explained for Beginners, edited and annotated by Peter Kreeft, Ignatius Press (1990).

Angels of Light, Powers of Darkness: Thinking Biblically About Angels, Satan and Principalities, Stephen Noll, Inter-varsity Press (1998).

Genesis, James Montgomery Boice, Baker Books, 1998.

CHAPTER 22
The River Of Life

Revelation 22:1

And he showed me [John] a river of water of life, clear as crystal, proceeding from the throne of God and of the Lamb.

LIVING WATER

Some scholars argue that John was having difficulty explaining what he saw, that the reference to *a river of water of life* was purely metaphor describing something beyond human comprehension, but I'm convinced the river is indeed real. It is *flowing water* or the actual Presence of God *that flows like water*. The most important thing to remember here, of course, is that the Presence of God flows from the city in a literal sense.

The city's pure, glittering *water of life* will flow from *the throne of God and of the Lamb*. It will have the appearance of clear crystal and it will be situated in the center of the Son's holy shrine, for God says, "I AM THE RIVER OF THE WATER OF LIFE."

It will sparkle with brilliance unequaled, and surely its beauty will arouse a peaceful, delightful, and contemplative state of mind. It will be the jewel of the great, hallowed Tabernacle.

Revelation 22:2

In the middle of its street, and on either side of the river, was the tree of life, which bore twelve fruits, each tree yielding its fruit every month. The leaves of the tree were for the healing of the nations.

THE TREE OF LIFE

Imagine for a moment:

Jesus leaves John and the angel on a mountain. He appears at the New City's throne room that houses the seat of Christ. Instantly, the glory of the God of the New Jerusalem comes from the throne, arced by an emerald rainbow, a testimony to his Presence and his Word, which is true forevermore.

A voice from the throne is heard like the sound of seven rushing rivers.

"I AM THE THRONE! I AM THE RAINBOW!"

It is Jesus. He calls out to John, asking him to, "COME AND SEE!"

John views his Master's city glowing with his holy brightness and falls on his face in worship. The angel lifts him up and carries John to the threshold of the throne in the middle of the city where he sees a wide, shining street paved with pure gold so refined it resembles transparent glass!

The golden street spans the sacred waters of the river of life. The bridge is wide and it is made out of one dazzling precious stone!

"I AM THE BRIDGE!" cries our Lord.

The bridge leads to the sacred throne of Jesus Christ, the focal point of the city, where all go to praise his holy name!

In the center of the bridge the tree of life spreads its leafy canopy.

John sees two more trees. They are also the tree of life. They grow on the approach embankment on either side of the bridge's abutment like two blossoming sentinels guarding the entrance to the Tabernacle, the living throne of Jesus Christ.

"I AM THE TREE OF LIFE. I AM WHO I AM! I AM!" says the Son.

Each tree bears twelve different kinds of living fruit every *month!*

Lining the banks of the river are all kinds of glorious trees, producing fruit. Their leaves do not wither and their fruit never fails! Like the three trees of life, they bear fruit every month, for they drink from the same precious water flowing from the most holy sanctuary.

THE MYSTERY REVEALED

The voice of the Spirit of the Lord came to John, saying: "Listen, all who are prepared for the new heaven and you who belong to the New Jerusalem. Here is understanding of what is true and right. Here is the mystery of the tree of life!"

THREE TREES OF LIFE

There will be three trees of life within the great city, as there were three trees in the original Garden of Eden.

(1) The tree that was *pleasant to the sight and good for food.*

(2) The tree *of life.*

(3) The tree *of the knowledge of good and evil* (Gen. 2:9).[1]

All three trees in the New Jerusalem will emit a streaming greenish light.

The three holy trees, of course, represent the Holy Trinity! The *Three* are *One*, and since that is the case it's more than likely, should the trees have roots as we understand root systems, that they'll be joined as one, similar to the roots of an Aspen grove which form one living entity, a living forest of a single tree!

John speaks of the three trees in the singular because they are indeed One.

That the tree supplies *food and medicine for all* is figurative here, or in other words, the eating of its food will only be for pleasure and not survival, similar to *drinking* from the river of life—none of it will be necessary for survival, for the nature of the Second Heaven will be eternal perfection and life. I'm sure the fruit and the water will have a glorious and stimulating taste!

The leaves and the tree, as well as its fruit, symbolize the healing nature of Christ and the good work that he has done with humanity. Of course, there won't be a need for literal medicine to heal the superglorified body.

The Greek word for *leaf* as it is used here is interesting: *phullon* or *phule*, which can be translated *as a sprout, i.e. leaf* and *an offshoot, i.e. race or clan—kindred, tribe*.[2] This suggests that the tree represents the nature of Christ and the glorious act of Christ, his *grafting on* of humanity into the divine nature of God. Thus, we are like branches grafted on to an olive tree. (For related information on the subject of the tree of life, refer to Chapter 2:7, under the heading *The Tree of Life Foretold*.)

Revelation 22:3

And there shall be no more curse, but the throne of God and of the Lamb shall be in it, and his servants shall serve him.

NO MORE CURSE

As sin will not be known and the fallen nature of humanity will have been healed through the grace of Christ there will no longer be a curse upon humanity. The new heaven will be blessed with absolute perfection and total unity with God, for the Son and the wondrous throne of God will exist in it.

Surely, the reality of it is beyond description. Free of the curse, the Saints will serve him gladly with great honor, joy, and love. The path of the just is like the shining sun! They lend their ears to his understanding, their lips keep his knowledge, and their eyes brighten in deep satisfaction with the truth of heaven!

Revelation 22:4

They shall see his face, and his name shall be on their foreheads.

HIS FACE

This confirms it: Christ will literally be with believers on the New Earth. Humanity will see Jesus' wonderful and loving face. They will worship, praise, and converse with him!

And his name shall be on their foreheads shows us just how permanent Jesus' Word is and how blessed the Saints are, confirming once again that humanity will be Christ's adopted children, for the unbreakable seal of Christ is *stamped or tattooed to their foreheads*, an image that suggests absolute permanence. (For additional information on the forehead and marking the forehead refer to Chapter 14:1, under the heading *On the Mount*.)

Revelation 22:5

There shall be no night there: They need no lamp nor light of the sun, for the Lord God gives them light. And they shall reign forever and ever.

CHRIST-LIGHT

Because the Presence of Christ is permanent there will be no evening in the new city of Jerusalem, and no night. Those who dwell within its mighty walls will have no need of a lamp or light from moons and stars, for the great brightness of the Lord God Almighty will give light to his people.

This seems to suggest the New Earth will indeed experience day and night, but that the New Jerusalem itself will never be in darkness because the Son will shine within its walls continually. This *hallowed brightness* will honor God and illuminate the entire holy shrine, penetrating the transparent foundations, walls, and *skyscrapers* constructed of gold, crystal, and the most precious gemstones. The throne will shimmer with a constant and glowing emerald-hue like the emerald rainbow of Christ!

SEVEN SACRED LAMPS BEFORE THE THRONE

There will be seven sacred golden lamps of fire burning before the radiant *sapphire stone* that is the throne of Jesus Christ. The lamps represent the Seven Spirits of Life—the Seven Spirits of God that Jesus has within him.

A continuous pilgrimage of believers will move before the throne having passed through the golden courts and colossal amphitheater. The pilgrims will resemble a *sea of shining glass crystal*. Their superglorified bodies will radiate a greenish life-glow, adding to the vastly illuminated area—God has indeed given them light! The reference to *giving humanity light* is quite literal. Indeed, we shall be like him and thus we shall be *alight like him.*

The Saints will gather to worship their Lord, their Master, their King, their Savior, their Almighty God in Christ Jesus, for he is God as Man. Jesus is *God with them,* and his Word will settle in the heart of the Second Heaven, deep within the New Jerusalem!

Trumpets will sound!

"Behold!" Jesus says, "I have created new heavens and a New Earth, and the former things shall not be remembered or come to mind. Be glad and rejoice forever in what I create. See, I have created the New Jerusalem as a shrine and a great gathering place, and her people are a complete joy."

Revelation 22:6

Then he said to me [John], "These words are faithful and true." And the Lord God of the spirits of the prophets sent his angel to show his servants the things which must shortly take place.

THE TIME IS NEAR

John is told that all the words proclaimed by the Lord Jesus are faithful and true. (For related information on the words *faithful* and *true* refer to Chapter 21:5, under the heading *All Things Made New.*)

The angel confirms to John that the Lord God sent him, for he mentions the Old Testament prophets; this refers to the twenty-four elders mentioned in Chapter 4:4, under the heading *Twenty-Four,* the twelve apostles and twelve holy prophets of the Old Testament: "...around the throne are twenty-four thrones, and on the thrones I (John) saw twenty-four elders sitting, clothed in white robes, with crowns of gold on their heads" (Rev. 4:4). It is well not to forget that these twenty-four elders not only represent Old Testament prophets and the apostles from the New Testament, but also the great innumerable company of believers.

Jesus sent his angel to reveal to his believers, through John, the events that must shortly take place—now, since it seems quite clear that we are in the Season of the Leopard, time is growing short. The return of Christ will soon take place. Remember, he comes quickly.

John hears the words of the Lord reminding all: "BLESSED IS HE WHO READS AND THOSE WHO HEAR THE WORDS OF THIS PROPHECY, AND KEEP THOSE THINGS WHICH ARE WRITTEN IN IT; FOR THE TIME IS NEAR" (Rev. 1:3).

"He (Jesus) who testifies to these things says, 'Surely I am coming quickly'" (Rev. 22:20).

THE MEANING OUTSIDE OF TIME

It must be remembered that the phrase *events that must shortly take place* was stated outside of time by a being (an angel or Christ himself) that exists in and out of time, and so it is not necessarily applicable to our perception of time and the understanding of the word *shortly*.

THE MEANING IN TIME

The phrase *events that must shortly take place* has a subtler meaning: it is referring to the *shortness* of life itself. The phrase not only alludes to the return of Christ, which is coming *shortly* or *soon* in relation to the broader concept of the timeline, but also to the span of human life, for *death* comes *shortly* for all humanity and when it comes Christ comes with it.

This is why we are told to prepare our hearts and minds because either way these *events must shortly take place*.

Revelation 22:7

[Jesus said] "Behold, I am coming quickly! Blessed is he who keeps the words of the prophecy of this book."

BLESSED

"BLESSED ARE THE ONES WHO KEEP THE WORDS OF THE PROPHECY OF THIS GREAT BOOK."

Remember, as I stated in Chapter 1:3, under the heading *Blessed by these Words*, whoever *reads* the words of this prophecy is blessed; whoever *hears* the words of this prophecy is blessed; whoever *understands through study and prayer* is blessed. This is the only book in the Bible that contains a special promise to obedient readers. Study it and be blessed so that you can prepare for the return of Christ who is coming quickly!

That's why it is imperative to realize that the Book of Revelation is your handbook to survival! I cannot emphasize this enough, for all unbelievers and half of the living Christians will be left behind when the Fourth Rapture happens. Millions of Christians will not be prepared, and then they will have to face the terror of the Antichrist, the Great Tribulation, and death in martyrdom.

For those who do not know the Lord now, I pray please do not put it off, thinking that death will find you before the Great Tribulation. Do not die without the Lord, for then it will be too late.

Set your hopes on the Fourth Rapture, the rapture of the living. Be a part of the *bride* who meets the Bridegroom, Jesus, in the air!

Escape the terror and torture of the last days of this Age. The Son of God is coming back sooner than we all believe!

Prepare and survive.

Revelation 22:8

Now I, John, am the one who heard and saw these things. And when I heard and saw, I fell down to worship before the feet of the angel who showed me these things.

DOWN TO WORSHIP

John has seen and heard astonishing things. He is so overcome with humility that he falls down, kneeling at the holy angel's feet. He fell down at the feet of Jesus when he first saw him at the beginning of Revelation, but falling before the feet of an angel is not acceptable, and that is what John has done here.

Revelation 22:9

Then he [the angel] said to me [John], "See that you do not do that. I am your fellow servant, and of your brethren the prophets, and of those who keep the words of this book. Worship God."

WORSHIP ONLY GOD

The holy angel warns John that he must not bow down before him, for he is a fellow servant like John and his brothers the prophets, and of those who keep the words of this Book of Revelation. The angel tells John to worship only Almighty God through Christ Jesus.

This verse informs us that it is totally unacceptable to bow down and worship any angel or human being, or for that matter, *anything* other than God.

Revelation 22:10

And he [the angel] said to me [John], "Do not seal the words of the prophecy of this book, for the time is at hand."

DO NOT SEAL THE PROPHECY

Unlike the time of the plagues of the seven thunders when John was told not to write down what he saw and what they meant, the angel explains to John once more that he must not seal the words of the prophecy of this book. He is told that it's imperative to write down all he has seen and heard so that the entire world will know, for *the time is near* (Rev. 1:3).

The nearness of Christ's coming because of human death or his literal return is indeed closer than your inmost thoughts.

Revelation 22:11

"He who is unjust, let him be unjust still; he who is filthy, let him be filthy still; he who is righteous, let him do right still; he who is holy, let him be holy still."

JUST DESERTS

This verse is emphasizing a solemn truth: the punishment of sin *is* sin, just as the reward for holiness *is* holiness. Thus, in relation to God and his morality, eternal punishment for sin and eternal reward for holiness is the natural and holy order of things. It also suggests that sin and holiness have a natural gravity to them. The closer you get to one or the other the more it pulls you in. Sin crushes you like a black hole. Holiness fills you like love shining from a bright burning star. Both results are the natural and holy order of things in relation to God and his moral law. Finally, it confirms the power of the Book of Revelation, the ultimate worst-case scenario survival handbook. The filthy and unjust will read it and either repent or become even more filthy and unjust, spiraling ever downward in a crash dive they may never pull out of, and likewise, those seeking the Path of Truth and Enlightenment will feel the tug of the Holy Spirit and they will seek the truth with more passion, spiraling ever upward and into the grace of Jesus Christ.[3]

Revelation 22:12

[Jesus says,] "And behold, I am coming quickly, and my reward is with me, to give to everyone according to his (or her) work."

THE TESTIMONY OF CHRIST

In relation to human death and the literal return of Christ the word *quickly* is applicable, for Jesus comes quickly in either case, and his reward comes with him.

The reference to *according to his (or her) work* applies to the saved in Christ and the good works of their lives. Jesus will honor those who pursue good works in life.

Behold, he indeed is coming quickly: "I (Jesus) will kill her children with death, and (the unfaithful, the unrighteous, the unbelievers, and) all the churches (including religious institutions such as synagogues, mosques, and other places of worship) shall know that I am he who searches the minds and heart (for closer is he than breathing, and nearer than hands and feet). And I will give to each one of you according to your works (our works are measured according to our faith)" (Rev. 2:23).

Revelation 22:13

"I am the Alpha and the Omega, the First and the Last, the Beginning and the End."

THE END & THE BEGINNING

Jesus tells us that he is the Son of God, the Alpha and the Omega, the Beginning and the End, or in the case of his return, he is the End and the Beginning, the First and the Last. (For more information on the *Alpha* and the *Omega*, return to Chapter 1:8, under the heading *Jesus, the Beginning & the End*.)

Revelation 22:14

"Blessed are those who wash their robes [in the blood of Christ], that they may have the right to the tree of life, and may enter through the gates into the city."

WASHED IN THE BLOOD

Blessed are those who are washed in the blood of the Lamb and who make every effort to keep the commandments of Christ, that they may have the right to the sacred tree of life and may enter through the mighty pearl gates into the new holy city of Jerusalem.

Revelation 22:15

"Outside are dogs and sorcerers and sexually immoral and murderers and idolaters, and whoever loves and practices a lie."

THE LAKE OF FIRE REVISITED

It is confirmed here, once again, that those who are unrepentant and continue to exist in the fallen nature, practicing or following the ways of sin and disobedience, do not and will not ever enter into the holy city—this includes all sin, for all sin, no matter how *big*, no matter how *small*, is equal in relation to separation from the holiness of God.

The reference to *dogs* can be translated in the original Greek (*kuon*, as *wolf* or *wolves*)[4]—clearly, this is allegory, equating sin, sinners, and the fallen nature to the cruel and unforgiving nature of the animal kingdom.

We know that the lost will not experience the third and final Phase of Body, the transfiguration into the superglorified body, but will instead remain forever incomplete in the Second Phase of Body, the glorified body.

We know that they will not be transferred from this Third Earth to the New Earth, but will instead remain on this old earth in its third phase, deep within its old bowels, the lake of fire, their second and eternal death. The closest they shall ever come to heaven during their lifespan on earth will be now, for the Holy Spirit still dwells here!

The word *outside* (Greek, *exo*, meaning *outside* or *outside of doors,* or literally or figuratively: *away, out, out of,* or *outward,* the latter seeming to suggest *beyond*),[5] implies that sin is by its very nature outside of God and never in the center. It is just plain *out there,* naturally moving away from that which is good. Indeed, it will be *removed beyond* the presence of God at the end of all things.

Revelation 22:16

"I, Jesus, have sent my angel to testify to you these things in the churches. I am the Root and the Offspring of David, the Bright and Morning Star."

STARLIGHT

The Lord states here that he sent John his angel to give this testimony and these prophecies to the world and to the Christian Church throughout all time.

Christ reconfirms here that he is the Root and Offspring of David. The word *root* could symbolically tie into the tree of life and its root system, and it could also refer to the *grafting* of the Gentile branches into the Olive Tree of the Jewish Jesus Christ. (For related information on the Root of David, refer to Chapter 5:5, under the heading *Root of David;* and Chapter 7:4, under the headings *The Children of Israel* and *Jesus, the Tribe of Judah.*)

What Jesus is doing here, by restating that he is the Root of David, is making it very clear that he is connected to the genetic line of David, the obvious conclusion being that he's Jewish, and thus he is the Old and New Testament messiah, the living conduit between Jew and Gentile. There is no middle ground or condition, no backdoor or forgotten *escape clause* in the fine-print: Jesus, and Jesus alone, is the salvation of the world—*all doors of genuine salvation lead to Christ.*

Lastly, he refers to himself as the Bright and Morning Star, showing us that the Dawn of Christ is fast approaching.[6] (For related information turn to Chapter 2:28, under the heading *The Bright & Morning Star.*)

Revelation 22:17

And the Spirit and the bride say, "Come!" And let him who hears say, "Come!" And let him who thirsts come. Whoever desires let him take the water of life freely.

COME

The Spirit of Jesus who has the Seven Spirits of God and the *bride* of Christ, his glorious Saints, will say, "Come!"

This is an open invitation to all humanity. It is said with passion, an exclamation point, demonstrating the love and urgency in the saying of it. Jesus Christ is passionately calling because he loves you and wants you to come so that he can shower you with blessings.

He also knows time is short in the sense of human death or his imminent return, so thus: *Please, come!*

The original Greek word (*dierchomai*) literally means *come, depart,* or *go,* and *pass, pierce through, travel, walk through.*[7] From this we can gather the meaning behind the word *come* is multilayered and potentially even hyperdimensional:

(1) If you accept the invitation of Christ you will be welcomed into eternity and from there you will have the opportunity to not only literally *come* and *approach* God through Christ, but in relation to exploration you can *travel everywhere* in a hyperdimensional sense. You can *walk through* or *throughout* the Holy Age and all God's Creation!

(2) Interpreting the word *come* as *pierce through* relates to the sacrifice of Jesus Christ on the cross, for his hands, feet, and side were *pierced through.* He's telling us here that because he was *pierced through* for us, we can *pass through* his wounds, or *pass through his sacrifice,* and come home to rest in his eternal love.

(3) In the reading of *And the Spirit and the bride say, "Come!"* the *bride* is a direct reference to believers, thus the word *come* can be interpreted as a duty or command to Christians, compelling them to reach out to and welcome the lost so that you could rephrase it like, *Let believers in Christ witness to the lost and say to them, "Come!"*[8]

In fact, God is calling all the saved in Christ, the Christian Church entire, to reveal to the world the declarations made in the Book of Revelation, the worst-case scenario survival handbook with the best-case survival outcome. He wants everyone, all humanity, to *come and join the family of God* so that they can be a part of his glorious kingdom.

Let those who hear these words say, "Come!"

Whoever is thirsty for the truth in Jesus Christ, let them come!

Whosoever desires it, come and take the free gift of the water of life!

Revelation 22:18

I testify to everyone who hears the words of the prophecy of this book: If anyone adds to these things, God will add to him the plagues that are written in this book.

THE FIRST WARNING

In Chapter 1:3, under the heading *Blessed By These Words*, we learned that this is the only book in the Bible that contains a special promise to obedient readers, (Rev. 1:3) and at the same time curses those who alter its contents (Rev. 22:18–19).

John focuses on the curse by giving a specific warning: to everyone who hears the words of the prophecy of the Book of Revelation, "If anyone dares to add or corrupt or change anything to this book, the Word of God, either by adding to it or taking from it, God will add to them the plagues that are written in this book!"

Revelation 22:19

And if anyone takes away from the words of the book of this prophecy, God shall take away his part from the tree of life, from the holy city, and from the things which are written in this book.

THE SECOND WARNING

The warning continues, with John saying, "If anyone takes away from the words of the book of this prophecy, God will take away his or her part from the tree of life, from the holy city, and from the good things which are written in this book!"

The second warning is aimed at anyone that alters the Book of Revelation, saved or unsaved alike. Anyone who alters the contents of the Book of Revelation will be held accountable.

Revelation 22:20

He [Jesus] who testifies to these things says, "Surely I am coming quickly." Amen. Even so, come, Lord Jesus!

HE COMES QUICKLY

Those who testify to these things, and as well as all humanity, should listen to what Jesus says: "YES, I AM COMING QUICKLY."

Regardless what life throws at us, whatever difficulties, sorrows, or tragedies that may exist and surround us, let us with open hearts and minds listen to the final words spoken by Jesus.

He comes quickly!
He comes suddenly!
He comes unexpectedly!

You are therefore encouraged to prepare your hearts and minds!

Prepare and survive!

This is the last vital warning in the New Testament: Jesus is coming soon, and surely, it is almost the eve of that great day of the Lord. He will come when the prophetic clock strikes the hour, to be sure.

It could be one minute to that hour.

It could be one second.

It could be when your heart stops.

Whatever the case may be, with Jesus as your Survival Plan you will sing his holy name in praise! From the rising of the sun to its going down the Lord's name is to be praised!

The God of Glory comes!

Revelation 22:21

The grace of our Lord Jesus Christ be with you all. Amen.

EVERMORE

With these comforting words, John ends his book with a blessing.

He says, "The grace of the wonderful Lord Jesus Christ, Savior of the world, King of the universe, and Lord of Lords, be with God's people for evermore."

Jesus is coming to put an end to the hard labor, suffering, and tragedy of his servants. His reward is peace and eternal life through his grace, and he will reward every work of faith and labor of love with heavenly treasures. He is coming to receive his faithful people and he will take them to himself to live forever with them in the Second Heaven on the New Earth.

By the grace of Christ we must wait in confident expectance.

Blessed is the one who comes in the name of the Lord! God is the Lord! Christ is the Lord! Give thanks to Christ, for he is good! His mercy endures forever! He has given us light! Praise him, all you stars of light! Praise him, all you hosts and heavenly angels! Praise him for his mighty acts! Praise him with the sound of the trumpet! Praise him heavens of heavens! Praise him for his everlasting love! Let us love one another, for love is of God; and he who loves is born of God and knows God! The God of Glory comes! The grace of Jesus Christ be with God's people forever! Let a stream of Godly prayer flow from your heart to the God of Life!

Let us thirst after greater and deeper enlightenment by the blessed Jesus, Lord of our souls.

Glory be to the Father and to the Son and to the Holy Spirit, as it was in the beginning, is now, and ever shall be, world without end. Amen.

* * * * *

SOURCES:

1. *Tree of Life,* James Josiah Reeve, International Bible Standard Encyclopedia, Online Edition, <http://www.studylight.org>.
   Tree, pg. 1306; *Vegetable Kingdom,* pg. 1340, The New Unger's Bible Dictionary, Moody Press (1988).
   The Garden of Eden; Genesis, Gray's Home Bible Commentary, The Bible Library Delux, version 5.0. suite, CD-ROM, Ellis Enterprises, Inc. (2,000).
2. *Leaf—Phullon/Phule,* #5543 & 5444, pg. 77, Greek Dictionary of the New Testament, Strong's Exhaustive Concordance of the Bible/Dictionary of the Hebrew and Greek Words, Hendrickson Publishers.
3. *The Seven New Things; Revelation,* Gray's Home Bible Commentary, The Bible Library Delux, version 5.0. suite, CD-ROM, Ellis Enterprises, Inc. (2,000).
4. *Dogs—Kuon "wolf" or "wolves",* #2965, pg. 44, Greek Dictionary of the New Testament, Strong's Exhaustive Concordance of the Bible/Dictionary of the Hebrew and Greek Words, Hendrickson Publishers.
5. *Outside—Exo,* #1854, pg. 30, Greek Dictionary of the New Testament, Strong's Exhaustive Concordance of the Bible/Dictionary of the Hebrew and Greek Words, Hendrickson Publishers.
6. *The Seven New Things; Revelation,* Gray's Home Bible Commentary; *Revelation,* Henry's Concise Commentary, The Bible Library Delux, version 5.0. suite, CD-ROM, Ellis Enterprises, Inc. (2,000).
7. *Come—Dierchomai,* #2064, pg. 32, Greek Dictionary of the New Testament, Strong's Exhaustive Concordance of the Bible/Dictionary of the Hebrew and Greek, Hendrickson Publishers.
8. *The Seven New Things; Revelation,* Gray's Home Bible Commentary; *Revelation,* Henry's Concise Commentary, The Bible Library Delux, version 5.0. suite, CD-ROM, Ellis Enterprises, Inc. (2,000).

AFTERWORD: HOPE

Israel has been targeted: Jesus, the Messiah, is coming, and when he comes it will be the end of the world as we know it.

The Book of Revelation makes this very clear. Thus, it is in effect a survival handbook for those in Israel and the world, a worst-case scenario survival handbook with the best-case scenario outcome. It's a survival handbook for those who wish to survive death as well as the frightening, horrific, violent, earth rendering, life altering, but glorious End Time events that are coming.

That's why you have to ask yourself two questions, the two Golden Rules of Survival:

(1) Are you prepared?

(2) What's your survival plan? Or in this case, *Who* is your survival plan?

As Paul says in 2Timothy 4:2 "...be prepared in season and out of season..." Truly, God favors the prepared heart and mind—chance has little to do with it.

Whether or not you agree with the interpretations and conclusions within this manual in regard to how the end of the world as we know it will take place moment to moment is really beside the point—however it pans out, the fact is Jesus is coming. He plainly says so!

What's most important is that you grab hold of this one vital concept: Jesus Christ has an eternal survival plan for you.

He is your survival leader.

He alone can save you, and he wants to and will save you if you just sit down with him and start planning your eternal survival.

You are encouraged to target preparation and seek the truth. Study the Word of God and the Book of Revelation yourself. Do the research so that you can make an informed decision.

It's clear that the world is running toward the cliff-edge and sooner than later it's going to destroy itself. It has been on the path of its own destruction for millennia, and now, for the first time in history humanity has the technology and the potential to blow itself off the face of the planet and exterminate itself, as Christ predicted—if he delayed his return that is exactly what would happen.

There is no perfect *Star Trek* future for humanity because the human heart is broken. Our natures are in a fallen and sinful state, and we will remain in that broken state forever, unchanging without the grace of Jesus Christ—the total destruction of humanity by humanity is our only possible outcome without Christ. This isn't cynicism or bitterness, but a stark and honest realism, and if you are skeptical about this statement just look back through the historical record and it will become very clear: we cannot save or repair ourselves.

There is no survival for humanity without the God of Glory. Only in his glory is there hope. Only in him do we find our value. There is hope for all humanity through the grace of Christ. We can find eternal salvation/repair, truth, beauty, and love, and literal transformation in the heart of our very natures, and we can survive the final devastating years of fallen humanity on earth by simply believing in and living for him.

If you're prepared during these last days, all the better, for you will escape the final three-and-a-half years of the Great and Terrible Tribulation by being raptured—the Fourth Rapture! We can then say with confidence, "Thank you, Lord, that I am divinely led and protected."

This is a comforting prayer for the End Times, but it's also an encouraging prayer through daily life for yourself and for others, especially in times of danger, assuring you of divine protection. In light of the Book of Revelation, the worst-case scenario survival handbook with the best-case scenario outcome, this prayer applies to your future. And what a glorious future awaits you if you allow the Spirit of Glory to lean on you!

Jesus said that his return will happen *quickly!*

He who testifies to these things says, "SURELY, I, JESUS, COME QUICKLY, AND MY REWARD COMES WITH ME. BLESSED ARE THEY WHO KEEP THE WORDS OF THE PROPHECY OF THIS BOOK."

JESUS RAISED FROM THE DEAD

"...knowing that he who raised up the Lord Jesus will also raise us up with Jesus, and will present us with you" (2Cor. 4:14).

THE ETERNAL HUMAN SOUL

"For we know that if our earthly house, this tent (body) is destroyed, we have a building from God, a house not made of clay by hands, (but) eternal in the heavens" (2Cor. 5:1).

LOOK FOR THE THINGS WHICH ARE NOT SEEN

"...while we do not look at the things which are seen, but at the things which are not seen. For the things which are seen are temporary, but the things which are not seen are eternal" (2Cor. 4:18).

BE RECONCILED WITH GOD

"Therefore, if anyone is in Christ, he (or she) is a new creation; old things have passed away; behold, all things have become new" (2Cor. 5:17). "Therefore we are ambassadors for Christ, as though God were pleading through us: We implore you on Christ's behalf, be reconciled to God" (2Cor. 5: 20).

TEMPLES OF THE LIVING GOD

"...you are the temple of the Living God. As God has said, 'I will dwell in them and walk among them. I will be their God, and they shall be my people" (2Cor. 6:16).

HIS LOVE FOR YOU

"...yet for your sakes he became poor, that you through his poverty might become rich" (2Cor. 8:9).

DO NOT DESPISE PROPHECIES & HOLD FAST

"Rejoice always, pray without ceasing; in everything give thanks; for this is the will of God in Christ Jesus for you. Do not quench the Spirit. Do not despise prophecies. Test all things; hold fast (to) what is good. Abstain from every form of evil" (1Thes. 5:16–22).

LET NO ONE DECEIVE YOU

"Let no one deceive you by any means; for that day will not come unless the falling away comes first, and the man of sin (the Antichrist) is revealed, the son of perdition (or ruin), who opposes and exalts himself above all that is called God or that is worshiped, so that he sits as God in the temple of God, showing himself that he is God" (2Thes. 2:3-4).

"And then the lawless one will be revealed, whom the Lord will consume with the breath of his mouth and destroy with the brightness of his coming. The coming of the lawless one is according to the working of Satan, with all power, signs and lying wonders, and with all unrighteous deception among those who perish, because they did not receive the love of the Truth, that they might be saved." (2Thes. 2: 8–10).

GIVE THANKS

"But we are bound to give thanks to God always for you, brethren beloved by the Lord..." (2Thes. 2:13).

SURVIVAL AND SAFETY IS IN THE LORD

"But the Lord is faithful, who will establish you and guard you from the Evil One" (2Thes. 3:3).

It is good to review the rewards given to us by God and to know his wonderful promises to those who believe.

- We are blessed by reading and listening to the words of this prophecy (Rev. 1:3).
- It is revealed that we eat of the Tree of Life, a promise that we live forever (Rev. 2:7).
- It is predicted that we receive the Crown of life, vowing again eternal life for us (Rev. 2:10).
- It is revealed that we are not hurt by the Second Death at the end of the thousand years, pledging that we are transformed into a brand new body (Rev. 2:11).
- We eat of the hidden manna, receiving countless blessings (Rev. 2:17).
- We have a new name written on a white gem stone (Rev. 2:17).
- Jesus gives to everyone according to his or her works (Rev. 2:23).
- It is predicted that we are given power over the nations (Rev. 2:26).
- In Revelation 1:6, we are told that we are made kings and priests.
- It is revealed that we are given the Bright and Morning Star (Rev. 2:28).
- We walk with Jesus, for we are made worthy through him (Rev. 3:4).
- We are clothed in white garments and our names are not removed from the Book of Life (Rev. 3:5).
- Jesus defends us on the Day of Judgment (Rev. 3:5).
- We are made pillars in the temple of God—this confirms we shall be with the Lord forever (Rev. 3:12).
- We have the name of God written on us. We have the name of the new city of Jerusalem written on us. We have the new name of Jesus written on us (Rev. 3:12).
- Jesus is always here, just for the asking (Rev. 3:20).
- It is revealed that we stand with Christ in his glorious throne room (Rev. 3:21).

I AM

Be prepared. Have a Survival Plan.

"God said to Moses, 'I Am who I Am.' And he said, 'Thus, you shall say to the children of Israel, 'I Am has sent me to you" (Ex. 3:14).

Or in other words:

I Am the Seven Spirits of God.

I Am Life.

I Am the Light of the World, the Sun, the Moon, and the Stars.

I Am the Universe.

I Am the Sky and the Heavens.

I Am the Clouds, the Rain, and the Rainbow.

I Am the Breath of Life, the Wind, and the Trees.

I Am the Grass, the Flowers, the Valleys, and the Glens.

I Am the Mountains.

I Am the Rivers and the Oceans.

I Am the Deserts, the Oil and the Wine, the Wheat and the Barley.

I Am the Fish and the Birds of the Air.

I Am the Animals.

I Am Humanity!

I Am You!

I Am Preparation!

I Am your Survival Plan!

I Am Life!

I AM WHO I AM!

"I AM!"

Glory be to the Father and to the Son and to the Holy Spirit, as it was in the beginning, is now, and ever shall be, world without end. Amen and amen.

ABOUT GOD'S SERVANT

I was born in the Republic of South Africa.

These are my hometowns:

In Africa: Durban, Loskop, Draykop, Bergville, Nthabanslope and Pietermaritzburg, Kwazulu/Natal; Pretoria, Transvaal.

In Canada: Calgary and Banff, Alberta; Vernon, Osoyoos, Revelstoke, Victoria, and Whistler, British Columbia.

In the United States of America: San Diego and Lake Tahoe, California; Reno, Nevada; Tucson and Phoenix, Arizona; Honolulu, Hawaii; Kwajalein in the Republic of the Marshall Islands (U.S. Army Headquarters); Provo and Moab, Utah; Breckenridge, Crested Butte, Leadville, Estes Park, Craig, Colorado Springs, Canon City, Westcliffe, Cimarron, and Grand Junction, Colorado; Clayton, Tucumcari, Logan, and Grants, New Mexico; and finally Daytona Beach and Orlando, Florida.

I have studied prophecy and the Book of Revelation over a period of 58+ years. I was drawn into this work through the power of the Holy Spirit and I believe it to be inspired by God. I believe that God's mind was the writer's mind and that God's hand was the writer's hand at the time of writing; I believe God wrote this book through me.

The first draft was written in the states of Colorado and Utah over a four year period. The subsequent draft was complied on the tiny island of Kwajalein in the Republic of the Marshall Islands, 5,000 miles southwest of the California coast. Through God, I believe I was placed in Kwajalein purposely to be alone to receive divine inspiration. Kwajalein gave me the time required to work on the completed manuscript of the Word of God and the Testimony of Jesus Christ. These writings have been edited over a 21 year period in Colorado, New Mexico, and Florida. I love Jesus Christ with all my heart and all my soul and all my mind and all my might, in and in, through and through, and out and out. I'm a person full of energy. I'm ambitious. I continually dwell on God's revelation of prophecy and my hope, preparation, and survival is in Jesus Christ, *the* Survival Plan.

9258350R00302

Made in the USA
San Bernardino, CA
09 March 2014